58

60

64

66

70

76

00

104

106

110

110

110

134

136

142

144

146

154

180

188

190

194

194

194

220

220

222

224

226

226

236

236

238

238

240

242

278

282

284

286

288

298

320

322

324

324

326

1

GRAPHIC INDEX TO
BIRDS OF THE SEASHORE

Birds not to scale   Numbers refer to page and bird number

White-bellied
Sea Eagle
90-2

Brahminy Kite
90-3

Black-headed Gull
134-1

Little Tern
138-5

Gull-billed Tern
138-1

Reef Egret
(Dark morph)
68-2

Reef Egret
(White morph)
68-2

Chinese
Egret
68-1

Great Egret
66-3

Little Egret
66-1

Lesser
Frigate Bird
70-1

German's
Swiftlet
184-4

Peregrine Falcon
96-8

White-breasted
Woodswallow
238-1

Collared
Kingfisher
190-3

Greater Crested Tern
136-1

Buffy Fish Owl
170-2

Common
Sandpiper
122-1

Common
Redshank
120-2

Whimbrel
118-3

Grey-tailed Tattler
122-4

Striated Heron
62-2

Malaysian
Plover
114-1

Kentish
Plover
112-2

Greater Sand
Plover
112-6

Lesser
Sand Plover
112-5

3

GRAPHIC INDEX TO
BIRDS OF COASTAL GARDENS

**Birds not to scale
Numbers refer to page and bird number**

Olive-backed Sunbird
308-3

Glossy Swiftlet
182-2

House Swift
180-3

Glossy Starling
274-8

Brown-throated
Sunbird
310-4

Pied Triller
222-7

Yellow-vented
Bulbul
244-3

Yellow-bellied
Prinia
240-5

Lesser Coucal
164-4

Tree Sparrow
324-1

Bold-striped
Tit-babbler
268-1

Java
Sparrow
316-1

Chestnut Munia
316-4

Spotted-necked Dove
146-5

4

Palm Swift
180-1

Pink-necked
Green Pigeon
146-4

Collared Kingfisher
190-3

Brown-capped
Woodpecker
210-5

Common Iora
220-2

Collared
Scops Owl
174-6

Pied Fantail
298-5

Rufous-tailed Tailorbird
240-2

Scaly-breasted
Munia
316-3

Magpie Robin
284-1

Large-tailed Nightjar
178-5

Zebra Dove
146-4

5

GRAPHIC INDEX TO BIRDS OF PADI FIELDS

Birds not to scale
Numbers refer to page and bird number
✶ Endemic

Pacific
Swallow
238-4

Black-winged
Kite
94-1

White-winged
Black Tern
136-5

Grey Heron
64-1

Purple
Heron
64-2

Great Egret
66-3

Intermediate Egret
66-2

Chinese
Pond Heron
62-1

Cinnamon
Bittern
60-3

Yellow
Bittern
60-2

Yellow
Wagtail
320-1

Eastern
Marsh Harrier
94-2

Barn
Swallow
238-3

Whiskered Tern
136-4

Striated Grassbird
254-5

Common
Moorhen
106-2

Dusky Munia
318-2

Purple
Swamphen
106-3

Little
Egret
66-1

Cattle
Egret
66-4

Red-throated
Pipit
322-2

White-breasted
Waterhen
106-6

Long-toed
Stint
124-4

Wood
Sandpiper
122-2

7

Black-and-
Red Broadbill
212-2

Silver-rumped
Spinetail
186-5

Darter
78-8

Malaysian
Blue Flycatcher
294-7

Chestnut-naped
Forktail
286-7

Brahminy
Kite
90-3

Lesser
Fish Eagle
90-5

White crowned
Forktail
286-6

Common
Sandpiper
122-1

Striated Heron
62-2

Rufous-backed
Kingfisher
192-6

Blue-eared
Kingfisher
192-2

Black-capped
Kingfisher
190-4

GRAPHIC INDEX TO
BIRDS OF RIVERS AND STREAMS

Birds not to scale
Numbers refer to page and bird number

White-crowned
Hornbill
196-1

Wrinkled Hornbill
198-4

Grey-headed
Fish Eagle
90-4

Straw-headed
Bulbul
242-1

Buffy Fish
Owl
170-2

Greater
Coucal
164-2

Great-billed
Heron
64-3

Storm's Stork
56-1

White-chested
Babbler
260-1

Blue-banded
Kingfisher
192-3

Common
Kingfisher
192-1

Stork-billed
Kingfisher
192-4

GRAPHIC INDEX TO BIRDS OF LOWLAND FOREST

Birds not to scale   Numbers refer to page and bird number
★ **Endemic**

Bushy-crested
Hornbill
196-2

Crested Serpent
Eagle
92-2

Wallace's
Hawk-eagle
84-2

Black-headed
Bulbul
240-3

Purple-naped
Sunbird
310-1

Brown
Wood Owl
170-3

Blue-eared
Barbet
204-3

Paradise
Flycatcher
296-1

White-bellied
Woodpecker
206-5

Fairy
Bluebird
228-6

Emerald Dove
144-6

Roulroul
46-2

Great Argus
46-5

10

Bat Hawk
92-4

Echo-locating
Swiftlets
184-1/2/3

Rhinoceros
Hornbill
198-5

Green Imperial
Pigeon
150-1

Bronze
Drongo
232-5

Red-bearded
Bee-eater
194-4

Racquet-tailed
Drongo
232-3

Little
Spiderhunter
308-1

Black-and-
Yellow
Broadbill
212-4

Spotted
Fantail
298-4

Black-headed
Pitta
214-4

Dark-necked
Tailorbird
248-1

White-crowned
Shama
284-5

Maroon
Woodpecker
206-3

11

GRAPHIC INDEX TO
BIRDS OF KINABALU PARK HQ

Birds not to scale
Numbers refer to page and bird number
★ Endemic

Kinabalu Serpent Eagle
92-3 ★

Mountain Imperial Pigeon
150-4

Ashy Drongo
232-2

Sunda Cuckoo-shrike
224-4

Mountain
Barbet
202-2 ★

Bornean
Treepie
236-4 ★

Black-capped
White-eye
272-4

Black-and-Crimson
Oriole
230-5

Mountain
Scops Owl
174-3

White-throated Fantail
298-3

Short-tailed
Green Magpie
236-2

Chestnut-hooded
Laughing Thrush
270-2 ★

Sunda Laughing
Thrush
270-1

Glossy Swiftlet
182-2

Grey-chinned Minivet
222-1

Whitehead's
Spiderhunter
310-2
*

Yellow-breasted
Warbler
252-3

hitehead's
Broadbill
214-2

Ochraceous
Bulbul
248-3

Whitehead's
Trogon
188-4 *

Bornean
Flowerpecker
302-5
*

Chestnut-crested
Yuhina
268-6 *

Temminck's Sunbird
308-5

Bornean
Laughing
Thrush *
270-3

Little
Cuckoo Dove
144-2

Sunda
Bush-Warbler
252-5

13

GRAPHIC INDEX TO
BIRDS OF THE KINABALU SUMMIT TRAIL

Birds not to scale
Numbers refer to page and bird number
★ **Endemic**

Bornean Swif
182-3 *

White-browed
Short-wing
296-6

Blyth's
Shrike-babbler
268-7

Summit Rat
*

Pale-faced
Bulbul
248-5 *

Bornean
Whistler
226-1 *

Little Pied
Flycatcher
292-8

Fruithu
278-

Snowy-browed Flycatcher
292-5

Red-breasted
Hill Partridge
48-5
*

Eyebrowed Jungle Flycatcher
288-1 *

Mountain Tailorbird
240-4

Crimson-headed
Partridge
48-1 *

Bornean Mountain
Ground Squirrel
*

Hylomys

14

Wreathed Hornbill
198-3

Mountain
Black-eye
272-7
*

Island
Thrush
286-2

Mountain
Leaf-Warbler
252-1

Friendly
Bush-Warbler
252-6
*

Tawny-breasted
Parrotfinch
316-4

Golden-naped
Barbet
202-1
*

Bornean
Stubtail
252-7
*

Mountain
Wren Babbler
262-3
*

Bornean
Whistling-
Thrush *
280-7

Grey-throated
Babbler
264-1

Mountain
Treeshew
*

Jentink's Squirrel * 15

THIRD EDITION ACKNOWLEDGEMENTS

The contents of this book are based on the two previous editions, to which a very large number of people made contributions which are hereby recognised. In particular we thank Clive Mann, whose *Checklist to The Birds of Borneo* (2008) provides both the taxonomic and distribution information. Geoff Davison made many helpful suggestions in regard to the first edition. Wong Tsu Shi has been consistently helpful throughout. Professor Fred Sheldon, the foremost taxonomic expert on the birds of Borneo, has provided a constantly updated stream of scientific data. Finally, none of these three books would have been possible without the full support of my family – Honor and Cosmo, and my sister Karen, who once again has risen to the challenge and provided a superb series of additional bird illustrations.

For additional logistical help with this third edition I would like to thank:

UK   Lai, Pool Hai, Louise Chiu, Boyd Chung, John Beaufoy the publisher, Rosemary Wilkinson, John Button of Bookcraft Ltd, and Laurence Logan Lechumanan of Malaysia Tourism.

Sabah   Kah Ho and Pat Wong, Robert Ong, George Hong, Lawrence Chin, Irene Chararuks, Noredah Othman and Dan Darby/Peter Ng of Sabah Tourism, Anthea and Tony Lamb, John and Gina Hamilton.

Brunei   Dr Joe Charles, Anthony Chieng, Hans Dols, Folkert Hindricks, Jenny Maskell, Roger Rajah and Shirley.

For help with content   Jason Anderson, Dave Bakewell, Alim Biun, Andy Boyce, Vivien Chua, Paul (Danum BRL), Chris Hill, Wang Kong Intal, Krys Kamierczak, C.K.Leong, Amrafael Marang, Richard Noske, Hugo Phillipps, Cede Prudente, Jason Azahari Reyes, Ken Searle, Fred Sheldon, Yeo Siew Teck, Amar Singh HSS, Hazwan Suban, Mohammed (Tabin WR), Palin (Tabin WR), Joe Taylor, Ray Tipper, Wong Tsu Shi, Anna Wong, and Yong Ding Li.

All illustrations are by Karen Phillipps apart from Oriental Honey Buzzards (David Mead), Megapodes (Ber van Perlo), Spectacled Flowerpecker (Richard Allen), Kinabalu Honey Buzzard photo (Alim Biun), Graphic Indexes (Alex Lowe), and *Lepeostegeres beccarii* mistletoe (Susan Phillipps). Logan Hamilton provided many excellent maps.

This book is dedicated to the memory of our mother, Susan Mary Phillipps, (18 Jan. 1915–1 Feb. 2013), whose love of Borneo's birds inspired our own.

Front cover illustration   Whitehead's Spiderhunter in territorial display on a *Wightia borneensis* (Foxglove Tree). Both tree and bird are endemic to the Bornean mountains, and can be found in the forest surrounding Kinabalu Park HQ.

Back cover illustration   Bornean Spiderhunter on a *Musa campestris* (Bornean Pink Banana) flower. Both plant and bird are endemic to Borneo's lowland and hill forests, and can be found at Poring in the Kinabalu Park.

Frontispiece (opposite)   Bornean Bristlehead, see page 236.

This edition of *Phillipps' Field Guide to the Birds of Borneo* (3rd Edition) is published by arrangement with John Beaufoy Publishing Ltd.
Published in the United States and Canada in 2014 by
Princeton University Press, 41 William Street, Princeton, New Jersey 08540
nathist.press.princeton.edu
Published in the United Kingdom in 2014 by John Beaufoy Publishing Ltd,
11 Blenheim Court, 316 Woodstock Road, Oxford OX2 7NS, England

10 9 8 7 6 5 4 3 2 1

Library of Congress Control Number 2013948587
ISBN 978-0-691-16167-9

Designed and typeset by Bookcraft Ltd, Stroud, Gloucestershire, UK
Printed and bound in Malaysia by Times Offset (M) Sdn. Bhd.

PHILLIPPS' FIELD GUIDE TO THE
BIRDS OF BORNEO
SABAH, SARAWAK, BRUNEI,
AND KALIMANTAN

QUENTIN PHILLIPPS

ILLUSTRATED BY
KAREN PHILLIPPS

THIRD EDITION

PRINCETON UNIVERSITY PRESS

PRINCETON AND OXFORD

CONTENTS

THE BIRDS OF BORNEO

BIRDING SITES

INTRODUCTION TO THE THIRD EDITION

The cut-off date for this third edition was 31 August 2013. Since the cut-off date for the second edition (1 March 2011) four birds have been added to the Borneo list, see www.borneobirdimages.com. The four new additions to the Borneo Bird List are Willie Wagtail, *Rhipidura leucophrys*, photo Sandakan (Sabah) 26 July 2013 (Hazwan Suban), page 298; Two-barred Warbler, *Phylloscopus trochiloides*, Pulau Tiga (Sabah) 13 Oct. 2011 (Chris Kehoe), page 256; Red-billed Starling, *Sturnus sericeus*, photo Penampang, KK. 7 Dec. 2011 (Sitorus, Leong, Madoya, Pudin), page 276; and Masked Finfoot, *Heliopais personata*, see Davison (2010) and Kukila 17 (2013), page 108.

There are nine additions to the Borneo endemics list, all of which are splits, see full list on page 28; also see page 41.

A definitive 2010 Bird Life International paper by Tobias et al, 'Quantitative Criteria for Species Delimitation: concerning the need to define species limits of tropical forest birds for conservation planning', is likely to result in five splits to be listed in the *Handbook of Birds of the World – Illustrated Checklist of the Birds of the World* (2014):

Bornean Crested Fireback, *Lophura ignita*, is split from *L. rufa* of Sumatra/Malaya, page 44. (HBW)

Bornean Crestless Fireback, *Lophura pyronota*, is split from *L. erythopthalma* of Sumatra/Malaya. (HBW)

Bornean Necklaced Partridge, *Arborophila graydoni*, is split from *A. charltonii* of Sumatra/Malaya, page 48. (HBW)

Bornean Banded Kingfisher, *Lacedo melanops*, is split from *L. pulchella* of Sumatra/Malaya, page 192. (HBW)

Bornean Brown Barbet, *Calorhamphus fulginosus*, is split from *C. hayii* of Sumatra/Malaya, page 204. (HBW)

Bornean Green Magpie, *Cissa jefferyi*, is split by van Balen, Eaton, Rheindt (2011), page 236.

Maratua Bulbul is split from Black-headed Bulbul by Chua & Sheldon (2014), pages 242 and 348.

Maratua Shama is split by Chua & Sheldon (2014), pages 284 and 348.

Bornean Spiderhunter, *Arachnothera everetti*, is split by Moyle et al (2011), page 314.

NEW NAMES FOR BORNEAN BIRDS according to the HBW–Birdlife Checklist (2014).

Philippine Collared Dove, *S. dusumieri*, replaces Island Collared Dove, *Streptopelia bitorquata*, page 146.

Javan Frogmouth, *Batrachostomus javensis*, replaces *B. affinis*, page 176.

Grey Nightjar, *Caprimulgus jotaka*, replaces *C. indicus*, page 178.

Blue-banded Kingfisher, *Alcedo peninsulae*, replaces *A. euryzona*, page 192.

Greater Flameback, *Chrysocolaptes guttacristatus*, replaces *C. lucidus*, page 208.

Checker-throated Woodpecker, *Picus humii*, replaces *P. mentalis*, page 208.

Buff-rumped Woodpecker, *Meiglyptes grammithorax*, replaces *M. tristis*, page 210.

CHANGES TO TEXT AND ILLUSTRATIONS This third edition contains 15 entirely new replacement plates including the Falcons, Doves, Whistlers, Swallows and Martins, Wren Babblers, Warblers, Thrushes, Shamas, Forktails, Sunbirds, and Ground–Cuckoo. In addition another 16 plates have been upgraded with additional or replacement drawings.

How this book is organized

The Borneo Province (The area covered by this *Field Guide* (see map page 23) includes mainland Borneo and the Malaysian islands off the coast of Sabah and Sarawak including Pulau Layang Layang, (hereinafter referred to as P Layang[2], a part of the Spratly Islands group, see page 140 and map page 74). Two birds (Tickell's Blue Flycatcher and White-rumped Munia), listed for the islands of the S China Sea (Natunas, Anambas, Karimatas and Tambelans), are also included. There are a large number of small islands in the Java Sea between SE Borneo and Java. Davison (1999) considers the most appropriate divide between Javan and Bornean birds to be between Matasirih (Borneo) and Masalembu (Java). Therefore we list Orange-footed Megapode for Matasirih, but not the Javan White-shouldered Triller or Pink-headed Imperial Pigeon found on Masalembu.

Visual indexes Eight double pages of illustrations at the front of this book. All the commonest birds of Borneo shown in their typical habitat, enabling quick, easy identification.

Bird breeding, rainfall and climate Typical nesting habits for each bird family are given in the family introductions. Breeding seasons vary dependent on locality and species (see page 34 for a full explanation). Sources which describe breeding months but not the locality can be misleading. Mann (2008) provides a full list including breeding locality.

Vegetation Bird distribution is closely related to both vegetation and altitude. 11 different vegetations types are mapped and described (see pages 30 and 32). Borneo's highest mountains and longest rivers are also shown on the map on inside back cover.

Migration An overview of bird migration to and from Borneo. Other references to migration appear throughout this *Field Guide* and are indexed on page 36.

141 bird plates Each species account has the following information:

The headline gives common English name, Latin/ scientific name, average size in cm, and status.

Bird sizes Sizes given for birds are averages only of a bird skin laid flat measured from tip of beak to tip of tail. Many species can be 5–10% smaller or larger than average size, especially sexually dimorphic birds such as the raptors and owls, where the female is usually larger than the male and the pheasants where the male is often substantially larger than the female. Different sizes are given where they could be significant in identification.

Bird status The headline status description is intended as a general indication only. Note that in this context **Local** means 'locally common' and **Lowland** means 'both lowland and hills'. A full description of status is given in the main text. The status descriptions are self-explanatory.

Malay names The Malay names used in this book are not intended to be comprehensive or definitive. Many Borneans speak Malay/Indonesian as a second language. Local language names are given in Davison (1999). Local Malay geographical terms are explained in the glossary.

Habitat and habits These are described in as much detail as space allows.

Bird descriptions and races No attempt is made to describe each bird in detail as the illustrations opposite the text fulfil this purpose. Only the important features necessary to distinguish one species from another apparently similar species are described. Races are only described where they obviously differ from related Bornean races, and in these cases they are usually illustrated separately and given their own distribution map, such as with the Magpie Robins and Shamas and the Brown Flycatchers. For a full list of all the Borneo bird species see borneobirdimages.com

Bird calls or voice Typical songs are described wherever possible where these would be an aid to identification, as too are distinctive contact calls or alarm calls. The term **Call** is used to cover all types of vocalization. Increasingly birders are using digital recorders to play pre-recorded calls (tape playback) to attract scarce birds known to live in an area. This may be distressing to some birds and responsible birders should keep such activities to a minimum.

Bird distribution maps and distribution descriptions Most bird distribution is dependent on vegetation or tree cover (see page 27). In Borneo original tree cover varies with height above sea level (see 'zonation' page 32) and human activity. Furthermore birds in general but especially frugivorous birds often wander widely. Therefore any source which states that a bird is 'found up to 900 m' is too prescriptive. For this reason typical habitats only, are given for each species, with exceptional records sometimes listed. The distribution maps follow this policy and illustrate original vegetation cover rather than individual records in most cases.

Ecological and text notes This book is a field guide but with a strong emphasis on ecology throughout. Where possible, additional notes on bird ecology and conservation have been included. These notes are not intended to be comprehensive but to highlight interesting aspects of bird behaviour and habitat as it relates to Borneo and the related zoogeographical region known as Sundaland (see page 22).

Birding Borneo Includes 23 pages of maps and text listing the best birding sites in Sabah, Brunei, Sarawak and Kalimantan (see page 328).

Birds illustrated but not yet recorded for Borneo. Borneo is comparatively under bird-watched. There are at least 200 additional species which could turn up as vagrants. 53 of these likely vagrants are illustrated in this *Field Guide*. The best locations to add a new vagrant bird to the Borneo list are the islands off NW Sabah, March–May and September–October.

CONVERSION FACTORS

100 mm	3.93"
1m	3.28'
10 km	6.2 miles

1 ha	10,000 sq m
100 ha	1 sq km
1 ha	2.47 acres

2.59 sq km	1 sq mile
1 sq km	247.1 acres
1 sq mile	259 ha

THE ORIGIN AND EVOLUTION OF BORNEO'S BIRDS

No bird fossils have yet been discovered in Borneo and the bird species resident in Borneo today are probably a small fraction of those that have lived in Borneo during the last 50 million years when modern bird families first developed. Therefore we have to look to the current Borneo bird list for clues as to the origin of Borneo's birds.

The Oriental Region Borneo's birds are a subset of the birds of the Oriental Region (one of 6 bird regions in the world). The Oriental Region includes Sundaland, all of India and most of China. It has only three endemic bird families, the ioras, leafbirds and Fairy Bluebird, and a number of others which probably originated locally later colonized other regions. These families include the pittas, broadbills, swallows, tree swifts, white-eyes and flowerpeckers. A number of tropical bird families such as the trogons and barbets are found in all three major tropical rainforest regions, whilst others such as the hornbills and sunbirds are found in Asia and Africa but are replaced in S. American rainforests by the toucans and hummingbirds. The explanation lies in the distant past when the super-continent of Gondwana linked the landmasses later to become Antartica, S. America, Australia, Africa and India in the S. Hemisphere. Similar pan-tropical distributions apply to many Bornean plants such as the figs. In general plants appear to have older origins and to be more resistant to extinction and better travellers than birds, which explains why Borneo's plants have more relationships with New Guinea than Borneo's birds.

Sundaland In the last 50 million years Borneo has often been connected by 'land bridges' to the Asian continent and to the other islands of the Sunda shelf in a region known as Sundaland, which as a result today shares a closely related avifauna.

The Pleistocene More recently during the million-year Pleistocene epoch which ended some 10,000 years ago, the polar ice caps repeatedly melted, froze and re-melted, resulting in alternately rising and falling sea levels converting dry land to sea during warm periods and turning Borneo into an island. When sea levels were high Borneo birds developed in isolation from their Sundaland relatives. When sea levels fell and Borneo stopped being an island, distinct Sundaland races re-invaded Borneo from Java or Sumatra, either driving out or hybridizing with their relatives in Borneo;

these include the Magpie Robins, Shamas, Forktails, Crimson/Temmincks' Sunbirds and Streaky-breasted/Grey-breasted Spiderhunters. Cave excavations at Niah (Sarawak) and Tapadong (Sabah) indicate that in the past Borneo had a full Sundan fauna including tigers, tapirs and the Javan Rhinoceros, all of which later became extinct (Cranbrook 1988).

'Missing' Sundan Birds The absence in Borneo of many Sundan birds such as Peacocks, Great Hornbill, Button Quail and Sunda Thrush are most likely the result of waves of extinctions during periods of climatic stress, although most bird species did survived by retreating into lowland refugia such as the Riau Pocket during colder periods (Morley 2000).During cold periods montane birds were much more widespread than today as evidenced by relict (remnant) populations of the Whistling Thrush at Bau near Kuching and the Blackeye on Mt Pueh.

Wallace's Line This is the name is given to the marine Makassar trench between Borneo and Sulawesi. Wallace was the first to point out that many Sunda birds such as barbets do not occur in Sulawesi, and many Sulawesi and Australian birds such as honeyeaters do not occur in Borneo. Even when sea levels dropped by 200m during cold periods, the 2,000m deep Makassar Strait prevented most Sundan invaders from moving east into Wallacea, exceptions being the hornbills and sunbirds.

Australian birds Very few Australian birds have managed the reverse journey to reach Borneo by 'island hopping' from New Guinea through Wallacea, one exception being the Megapodes. A possible explanation is that the dominant Sundan birds kept out possible Australian invaders such as cockatoos and honeyeaters by competitive exclusion. See page 318 for a detailed explanation.

Lawas River and Tawau volcanoes Within Borneo, the Lawas River on the west coast and an active volcanic region near Tawau appear to have presented a significant barrier to the movement of birds and mammals between north and south Borneo, along a line which matches the Sabah/Sarawak border. The result is that many Bornean birds have 'species pairs' or separate races which differ north and south of the border, including the two falconets, the White-crowned/White-rumped Shamas and, the Black-headed/Garnet Pittas.

THE BORNEO PROVINCE (the area covered by this field guide) is the area encircled in yellow on the map opposite. Apart from the islands of Layang[2] (page 140) Sipadan (page 332) and Maratua (page 348), it was until *c.*10,0000 years ago entirely one landmass (Sundaland), which explains why the lowland forest birds of Borneo, Java, Sumatra and the Malay Peninsula are so similar. Sundan montane birds are also related but with a much higher level of endemism or uniqueness demonstrating longer periods of climatic and vegetational isolation between the mountains of the different islands.

MALESIA BOTANICAL REGION

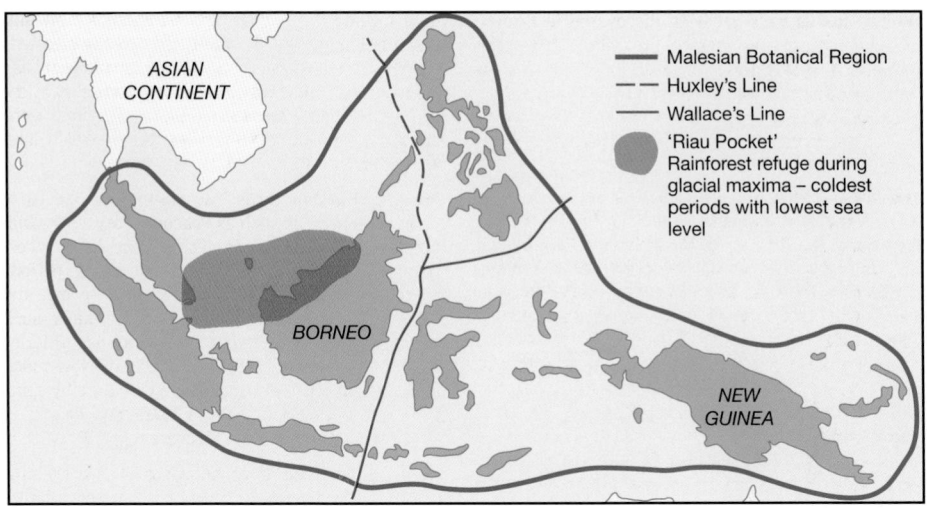

MALAY PENINSULA

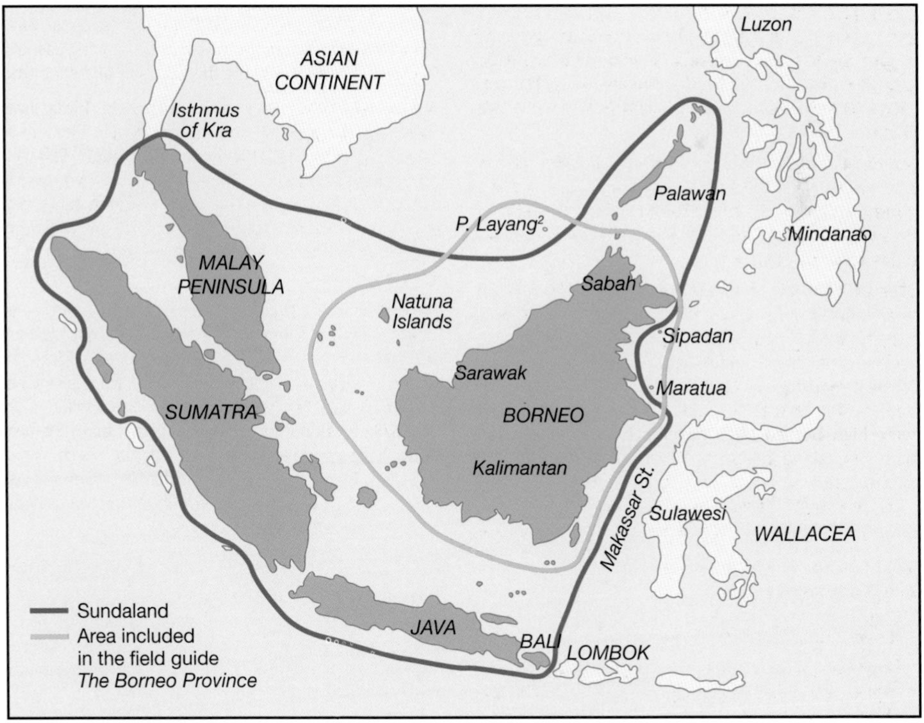

CONSERVATION IN ACTION: SAVING BORNEO'S HORNBILLS

The tide of forest destruction in Borneo has now turned, and local governments are actively planning projects to conserve Borneo's unique wildlife. But how large do national parks and reserves need to be to preserve full biodiversity? Below we use Borneo's hornbills to look at ecological theory as a basis for conservation and land use planning in Borneo. The same approach can also be applied to other fauna. Isolated forest plots are ecologically equivalent to islands, and similar ecological principles apply.

The macro approach In 1967 two American zoologists, MacArthur and Wilson, published a key theory of island biogeography which in simplified terms states that: (a) a species/area relationship exists for different sized islands, larger islands have more species (see opposite), (b) the closer

the island is to the mainland the higher the immigration rate and the more species it will have, and (c) on islands the number of species will eventually reach an equilibrium level where extinction is balanced by immigration. With some modifications their theory of island biogeography is now accepted as a cornerstone of ecological science. A typical example for 7 Sundaland 'land-bridge islands' is shown below. Until around 10,000 years ago all 7 islands were connected by land to the Asian continent (hence the name land-bridge) and therefore would have shared the typical diversity of Sundaland forest bird life at that time. Note that although Sumatra is smaller than Borneo, it is much closer to the Asian continent so that higher extinction rates are exceeded by increased immigration and recolonisation.

Island	Area km²	Hornbill sp	Extinct hornbills	Resident birds	Reference
Sumatra	443,066	10	0	397	McKinnon 1993
Borneo	743,380	8	2	358	McKinnon 1993
Java	53,588	3	7	289	McKinnon 1993
Natuna Besar (Indonesia)	860	2	8	90	Oberholser 1932
Banggi (Sabah)	450	None	10	58	Sodhi et al 2010
Balambangan (Sabah)	113	None	10	37	Sodhi et al 2010
Malawali (Sabah)	38	None	10	13	Sodhi et al 2010

The micro approach The above figures indicate how over long periods of time even large populations inhabiting large areas can become extinct. Therefore when trying to plan reserves to preserve biodiversity this 'macro' approach must be complemented by a more pragmatic

'micro' approach, by selecting a species such as Helmeted Hornbill and multiplying the breeding territory area by a figure for minimum viable population (MVP) here taken as 50 pairs.Below are the figures for some Bornean hornbills based on Leighton 1982.

Hornbill species	Territory	MVP 50 pairs	Suitable reserves
Helmeted Hornbill	7.7 km²	385 km²	Danum 438 km²
Rhinoceros Hornbill	2.30 km²	115 km²	Tawau Hills 280 km²
Black Hornbill	1.10 km²	50.5 km²	Lambir 70 km²

Are Borneo's reserves large enough to preserve full biodiversity?

This 'micro' approach indicates that to preserve all 8 Bornean hornbills, reserves need to be a minimum of 385 km². Many parks and reserves in lowland Borneo are too small to conserve the full biodiversity of Borneo's lowland forest. Most reserves are small 'islands' of forest surrounded by a sea of oil palm. Parks such as Bako (27km²), Kubah (22 km²), Sepilok (60 km²) and Sungai Wain (100 km²) are just not big enough, and will slowly lose their biodiversity as extinction exceeds immigration until they finally reach a species poor equilibrium.

What can be done to preserve hornbill populations (and biodiversity)

1. The larger the reserve the greater the biodiversity. Reserves should always be as large as possible.

2. Logged forest is a valuable reservoir for biodiversity. Studies by Lambert, Johns, Lammertink, Meijaard, Edwards, Sheldon, Styring and others have repeatedly

shown that logged forest acts as a vital refuge for wildlife where it is adjacent to protected forest as at Danum Valley, Maliau Basin and Tawau Hills and enlarges the effective size of the reserve, whilst at other parks the conversion of the neighbourisng forest reserve to oil palm has severely limited the potential to retain biodiversity.

3. Establish protected habitat corridors between smaller reserves as at the Kinabatangan River.

4. Minmise conversion to agriculture and planted forests which have minimal bio-diversity.

5. Purchase agricultural land and re-forest with enrichment planting of fruit trees as at Samboja Lestari.

6. Allocate/lease logged forest to conservation organizations for habitat restoration (many projects in Kalimantan).

7. Where natural populations have been depleted, establish breeding and release centres for hornbills.

8. Where the land area is too small for natural populations to survive, then the only solution may be enrichment planting and supplementary feeding as at Labuk Bay Proboscis Sanctuary and, Tarakan Proboscis Sanctuary.

FIVE KEY CONCEPTS IN CONSERVATION AREA PLANNING

1. Species/area relationships (SAR) Birders know from experience that large areas of forest contain more species of birds than smaller areas, and scientists have repeatedly confirmed the existence of 'species/area relationships' (SAR). In essence larger habitats have more species and greater biodiversity than smaller habitats. SARs apply both to small areas (a garden) up to very large areas (the islands of Java and Borneo). Borneo has more resident birds than Java simply because it is larger, and a large garden will always have more species than a small garden. Diversity varies with area for two main reasons – large areas have more diverse habitats, and different species need different minimum size areas to rear young known as a 'breeding territory', and birds are less likely to become extinct in larger areas because the total population is larger.

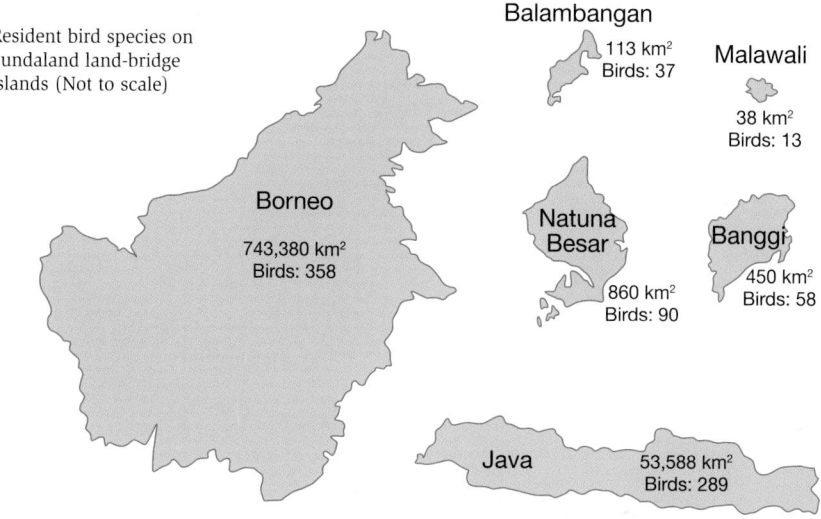

Resident bird species on Sundaland land-bridge islands (Not to scale)

Balambangan
113 km²
Birds: 37

Malawali
38 km²
Birds: 13

Borneo
743,380 km²
Birds: 358

Natuna Besar
860 km²
Birds: 90

Banggi
450 km²
Birds: 58

Java
53,588 km²
Birds: 289

2. Breeding territories of resident birds in virgin rainforest, some local examples (averages).

Species breeding	Territory	MVA 50 prs	Reference	Location
Scaly-crowned Babbler	2 ha	100 ha/1 km²	Fogden 1976	Semengoh
Black-headed Pitta	5 ha	250 ha/2.5 km²	Lambert 1996	Danum
White-rumped Shama	7 ha	350 ha/3.5km²	Fogden 1976	Semengoh
Roulroul	10 ha	500 ha/5.0 km²	Fogden 1976	Semengoh
Argus Pheasant	500 ha	25,000 ha/250 km²	Nijman 2010	Kalimantan
Hawk Eagle	2,500 ha	125,000 ha/1,250 km²	Thiollay 1988	Primary forest

3. Minimum viable population size (MVP) Populations of birds fluctuate over time due to droughts, disease, predation, hunting, competition, genetic problems (in-breeding) and random events such as volcanic explosions. Small populations are much more likely to become extinct than large populations hence the increased rate of extinction on small islands or reserves. The table above uses an MVA of 50 breeding pairs as an illustration. History shows that this is likely to be sufficient only in the short term without additional conservation measures. See Huang (2011) on Pied Hornbills in Singapore for a full discussion.

4. 'Legacy birds' In rapidly changing habitats ornithological survey results are frequently 'distorted' by 'legacy birds' such as hornbills, which can live for 50+ years and may continue to survive in small numbers in plots too small for long term viable populations, e.g. at Lambir (70 km²) and Similajau (90 km²).

5. Cascade effects A large percentage of rainforest plants have mutualistic relationships with birds and mammals as pollinators or seed dispersers. The loss of important seed dispersing hornbills may over time result in dramatic 'secondary' changes to forest diversity known as 'knock on' or 'cascade' effects which can only be ameliorated by expensive enrichment planting of hornbill favoured fruit trees and hornbill reintroduction schemes.

ANATOMY AND PLUMAGE OF A BIRD

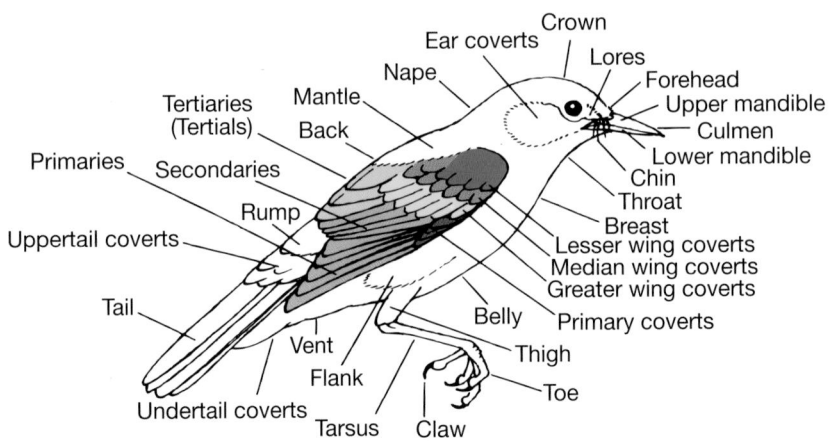

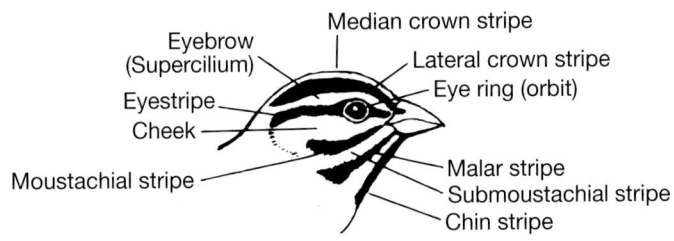

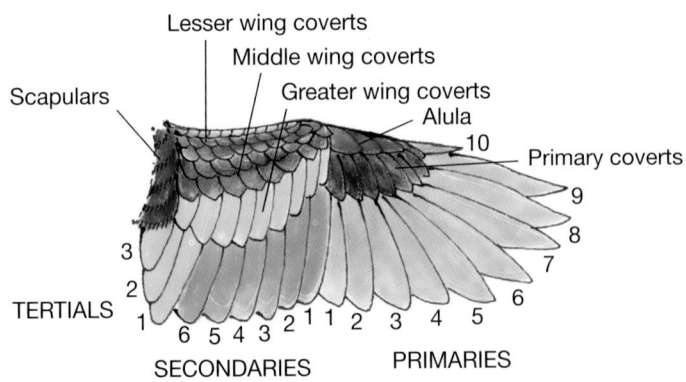

KEY TO DISTRIBUTION MAPS

Coloured maps: Colour key indicating status

| Seabirds | Breeding seabirds | Resident and Resident/migrant | Endemic resident | Migrant only |

Maps indicating extent of distribution

| Throughout Borneo | Offshore island | Coastal | Lowland | Lowland and hills |

| Hills and mountains | Mountains | Hills and slopes | Rivers and alluvial habitat | Local distribution |

The distribution maps These maps are based on a combination of actual records and known habitat. Birds are only likely to occur within their preferred habitat within the distribution shown, e.g. a trogon will only be found in forested areas and a dusky munia in grassland areas within the coloured area. Data is mainly from Mann (2008).

Local nomads The rails and crakes, bulbuls, pigeons and birds such as the Hooded Pitta, are locally nomadic. Unusual records are not shown unless they are of special interest.

Changing distributions Most forest-dwelling specialists, e.g. broadbills, cannot survive forest destruction, therefore distribution is constantly changing as forest is converted to agriculture.

Hills and slopes The hill slope areas on the standard map have been slightly enlarged for clarity.

Migrants Migrants are most common along the NW Bornean coast south to Kuching. The distribution maps mostly do not show irregular records.

Vagrants Vagrants are loosely defined as birds with less than 10 records for Borneo. No maps are given for most vagrants but interesting records are usually listed in the text.

Riverine birds These maps are used both for birds which live along rivers, such as the Fish Eagles, and birds which prefer alluvial or riverine forest, e.g. the Bornean Ground Cuckoo.

Birds which have both resident and migrant races in Borneo In these cases the distribution maps are shown as green (resident) rather than yellow (migrant).

Status descriptions defined. See also Glossary page 38.

Endemic A resident bird species which is only found in Borneo.

Resident At least one breeding record or believed to breed in Borneo.

Migrant A regular visitor from north or south but does not breed in Borneo.

Passage migrant A regular visitor which passes through Borneo to Australia, e.g. waders.

Winter visitor Visits Borneo from north during the northern winter, usually September to April.

Lowland Includes lowland and hills up to around 900m.

Submontane Usually resident from around 600m to around 900m.

Montane Usually resident above around 900m.

Local Locally common, i.e. often common in certain localities but scarce elsewhere.

KINABALU HONEY-BUZZARD photographed by Alim Biun, a wildlife research officer of Sabah Parks, at Mamut, Kinabalu Park on 12 March 2013, one of the most exciting discoveries in Borneo ornithology in the last hundred years. The current taxonomy of Oriental Honey-Buzzard, *Pernis ptilorhynchus*, is unsatisfactory due to lack of ecological data. The resident race of the Oriental Honey Buzzard, *P. p. torquatus*, is found in primary forest throughout Borneo, Sumatra and the Malay Peninsula. In Borneo *P. p. torquatus* plumage normally mimics either Wallace's Hawk-Eagle (more common) or Blythe's Hawk-Eagle – the less common 'Tweedale morph'. See Page 86.

The **Kinabalu Honey-Buzzard** is very different in appearance from both hawk-eagles, and obviously mimics the appearance of the endemic Kinabalu Serpent Eagle found only in the Bornean mountains above 900m. Current taxonomy would place the Kinabalu Honey-Buzzard as a rare melanistic (black) morph of the resident race of the Oriental Honey-Buzzard, *P. p torquatus*; however, honey-buzzard taxonomy is long overdue for a full revision and there is a strong possibility that this magnificent bird will one day be listed as a separate species, endemic to the mountains of Borneo.

Oriental Honey-Buzzard, *Pernis ptilorhynchus*, taxonomy currently recognises three different resident Sundaland races – *P.p. torquatus* (Malay Peninsula, Sumatra, Borneo), *P.p. ptilorhynchus* (Java endemic), and *P.p. palawanensis* (Palawan endemic). DNA studies by Gamauf & Haring (2005) found that these three Sundaland residents were closely related and more distantly related to migrant Oriental Honey-Buzzards. A full taxonomic review would probably split the Oriental Honey-Buzzards into two groups, migrant Oriental Honey-Buzzards and resident Sunda Honey-Buzzards. The Kinabalu Honey-Buzzard would then become a race of the Sunda Honey-Buzzard, *Pernis ptilorhynchus*. A more radical approach would further split the Sunda Honey-Buzzards into five different species including endemic Honey-Buzzards in Palawan, Java and Borneo (Kinabalu Honey-Buzzard) and two additional species now known as *P.p. torquatus*, the mimics of Wallace's and Blythe's Hawk-Eagle.

A new Bornean endemic? So far as is currently known no specimens of the Kinabalu Honey-Buzzard have ever been collected, and this the first time this bird has even been photographed, so it must be extremely rare. Common sense tells us that it is very unlikely that the plumage of the three different Borneo resident morphs of *P.p. torquatus* vary randomly, because the raptors they mimic occupy three different habitats. Thus these three morphs must breed true, in which case each of the three morphs is actually a separate species. Until we have more information about their ecology, however, this cannot be proven. See Ferguson-Lees & Christie (2001) and pages 86 and 88 in this *Field Guide*.

OTHER POSSIBLE FUTURE ADDITIONS TO THE BORNEAN ENDEMICS LIST
(SUBJECT TO FURTHER RESEARCH)

English name	Scientific name	Justification	Page
Collared Owlet	*Galucidium brodiei*	Split based on different call	172
Rajah's Scops Owl	*Otus brookii*	Split based on different call	174
Hair-crested Drongo (Maratua)	*Dicrurus hottentottus*	Split based on appearance	232
Cinereous Bulbul	*Hemixos cinereous*	Split based on appearance	248
Mountain Leaf-warbler	*Phylloscopus trivirgatus*	Split based on appearance	252
Dark Blue Flycatcher	*Cyornis concretus*	Split based on call/appearance	294
Spectacled Flowerpecker	*As yet undescribed*	New species on appearance	306
Purple-throated Sunbird (Maratua)	*Nectarinia sperata*	Split based on appearance	308

FIFTY-NINE ENDEMIC BIRDS OF BORNEO
(SEE PAGE 20 FOR CHANGES SINCE THE SECOND EDITION)

English name	Scientific name	Best location to find	Page
Bornean Crested Fireback	*Lophura ignita*	Danum, Tabin, Sabah	44
Bornean Crestless Fireback	*Lophura pyronota*	Tg Puting, Sabangau	44
Bulwer's Pheasant	*Lophura bulweri*	Maliau Basin, Sabah	44
Bornean Peacock-pheasant	*Polyplectron schleiermacheri*	Sungai Wain, Kalimantan	46
Bornean Necklaced Partridge	*Arborophila graydoni*	Sepilok, Tabin, Tawau Hills	48
Dulit Partridge	*Rhizothera dulitensis*	Pulong Tau; Mulu	48
Red-breasted Hill Partridge	*Arborophila hyperythra*	Kinabalu Park HQ	48
Crimson-headed Partridge	*Haematortyx sanguiniceps*	Kinabalu Park HQ	48
Bornean Falconet	*Microhierax latifrons*	Crocker Range; Danum	80
Bornean Serpent Eagle	*Spilornis kinabaluensis*	Crocker Range	92
Bornean Ground-Cuckoo	*Carpococcyx radiatus*	Kinabatangan	168
Dulit Frogmouth	*Batrachostomus harterti*	Pulong Tau, Sarawak	176
Bornean Frogmouth	*Batrachostomus mixtus*	Kinabalu Park HQ	176
Bornean Swiftlet	*Collocalia dodgei*	Kinabalu Summit Trail	182
Whitehead's Trogon	*Harpactes whiteheadi*	Kinabalu Park HQ	188
Bornean Banded Kingfisher	*Lacedo melanops*	Danum, Maliau Basin	192
Mountain Barbet	*Megalaima monticola*	Crocker Range; Poring; Mulu	202
Golden-naped Barbet	*Megalaima pulcherrima*	Kinabalu Park HQ	202
Bornean Barbet	*Megalaima eximia*	Crocker Range, Poring, Maliau	202
Bornean Brown Barbet	*Calorhamphus fulginosus*	Crocker Range, Sepilok	204
Hose's Broadbill	*Calyptomena hosii*	Mulu; Poring; Pulong Tau	214
Whitehead's Broadbill	*Calyptomena whiteheadi*	Kinabalu Park HQ	214
Blue-banded Pitta	*Pitta arquata*	Poring, Danum, Gng Penrissen	216
Black-headed Pitta	*Pitta ussheri*	Sepilok; Danum; Kinabatangan	216
Blue-headed Pitta	*Pitta baudii*	Danum, Kuala Belalong	216
Bornean Leafbird	*Chloropsis kinabaluensis*	KP HQ, Crocker Rg, Mulu	220
Bornean Whistler	*Pachycephala hypoxantha*	Kinabalu Park HQ	226
Bornean Black Oriole	*Oriolus hosii*	Pulong Tau; Mulu	230
Bornean Black Magpie	*Platysmurus atterimus*	Poring, Sepilok	234
Bristlehead	*Pityriasis gymnocephala*	Sepilok; Danum; Kinabatangan	236
Bornean Treepie	*Dendrocitta cinerascens*	Kinabalu Park HQ	236
Bornean Green Magpie	*Cissa jefferyi*	Kinabalu Park HQ	236
Maratua Bulbul	*Pycnonotus hodiernus*	Maratua, Kakaban	242
Bornean Bulbul	*Pycnonotus montis*	Crocker Range	248
Pale-faced Bulbul	*Pycnonotus leucops*	Kinabalu Summit Trail	248
Bornean Stubtail	*Urosphena whiteheadi*	Kinabalu Park HQ	252
Friendly Bush Warbler	*Bradypterus accentor*	Kinabalu Summit Trail	252
Black-browed Babbler	*Trichastoma perspicillatum*	Bandjarmasin forest	258
Bornean Wren-babbler	*Ptilocichla leucogrammica*	Danum, Sepilok, Semengoh	262
Black-throated Wren-babbler	*Napothera atrigularis*	Danum, Sepilok, Batang Ai	262
Mountain Wren-babbler	*Napothera crassa*	Kinabalu Park HQ	262
Chestnut-crested Yuhina	*Yuhina everetti*	Kinabalu Park HQ	256
Bornean Laughing-thrush	*Melanocichla calva*	Kinabalu Park HQ	270
C-hooded Laughing-thrush	*Garrulax treacheri*	Kinabalu Park HQ	270
Bornean Ibon	*Oculocincla squamifrons*	Poring, Tawau Hills	272
Mountain Black-eye	*Chlorocharis emiliae*	Kinabalu Summit Trail	272
Fruithunter	*Chlamydochaera jefferyi*	Kinabalu Park HQ	278
Bornean Whistling Thrush	*Myophonus borneensis*	Kinabalu Park HQ; Mesilau	280
White-crowned Shama	*Copsychus stricklandii*	Danum; Sepilok; Tabin	284
Maratua Shama	*Copsychus barbouri*	Maratua, E.Kalimantan	284
Everett's Thrush	*Zoothera everetti*	Kinabalu Park HQ	286
Bornean Forktail	*Enicurus borneensis*	KP HQ, Kelabit Highlands	286
Eyebrowed Jungle Flycatcher	*Rhinomyias gularis*	Kinabalu Park HQ	288
Bornean Blue Flycatcher	*Cyornis superbus*	Danum, K Belalong, Mulu	294
Bornean Flowerpecker	*Dicaeum monticolum*	Kinabalu Park HQ	302
Yellow-rumped Flowerpecker	*Prionochilus xanthopygius*	Sepilok; Semengoh, Tg Puting	304
Whitehead's Spiderhunter	*Arachnothera juliae*	Crocker Rng; Mesilau; KNP HQ	314
Bornean Spiderhunter	*Arachnothera everetti*	Poring, Sepilok,Tabin, Danum	314
Dusky Munia	*Lonchura fuscans*	Grassland everywhere	318

VEGETATION AND BIRD LIFE IN BORNEO

Note: maps are distorted in scale. For detailed maps see www.wwf.de

Primary lowland forest (0–300m) 220+ resident birds   The richest ecosystem in Borneo dominated by giant dipterocarp trees, with the greatest diversity of plants, mammals, birds and insects. Lowland specialists include Bornean Ground Cuckoo, Great Slaty Woodpecker, Blue-headed Pitta, Bonaparte's Nightjar and Bristlehead. Only small protected patches remain.

Logged primary lowland forest   Logging affects the structure of the forest and destroys the canopy allowing a thick secondary growth of sun-loving flowering vines and shrubs to thrive. After logging, large woodpeckers decrease whilst small woodpeckers that forage in the undergrowth often increase. Insect-eaters such as pittas, trogons, babblers and flycatchers decline but berry-eating and nectarivorous birds such as bulbuls, leafbirds, flowerpeckers and sunbirds increase.

Hill and submontane forest (300–900m)   As altitude increases, tree height and bird diversity decrease. Many lowland birds are found in the hills but become less common. Characteristic residents include Bulwer's Pheasant, Orange-breasted Trogon, Hose's Broadbill, Banded and Blue-banded Pittas.

Montane forest (900–1,800m)   Around 900m both birds and vegetation change radically. Often enveloped in clouds by the afternoon, the moss forest is dominated by oaks and laurels and covered in epiphytes. Montane birds replace lowland birds.

Upper montane forest (1,800–3,500m)   As altitude increases, the number of bird species decreases but endemism increases. Forest is short and stunted and dominated by berry-bearing bushes. Characteristic birds include Island Thrush, Black-eye, Friendly Warbler, Pale-faced Bulbul and Fruithunter.

Peat swamp forest   Dipterocarp forest of the coastal lowlands growing on a thick layer of swampy peat. Trees often have stilt roots and air-breathing roots. The forest is drained by acidic black water rivers. Many lowland forest birds occur in peat swamp forest but at low densities. Characteristic birds include Wrinkled Hornbill, Hook-billed Bulbul, Grey-chested Jungle Flycatcher, Scarlet-breasted Flowerpecker, Fiery Minivet and Abbott's Babbler.

Kerangas or heath forest   Commonest in S Kalimantan lowlands, scattered patches elsewhere. Kerangas is stunted trees growing on nutrient-poor white sand soils unsuitable for agriculture. Bird life is poor. Characteristic birds include Grey-chested Jungle Flycatcher, White-chested Babbler, Hook-billed Bulbul and Thick-billed Flowerpecker.

Freshwater swamps, rivers and lakes   Large areas along the Mahakam, Kapuas, Barito and Baram rivers and the Kinabatangan River are inhabited by herons, egrets, bitterns, storks, darters and other waterbirds.

Mangrove forest   Coastal forest growing in brackish water in muddy river estuaries. Typical birds include Ruddy Kingfisher, Great Tit, Mangrove Blue Flycatcher, Mangrove Whistler, Lesser Adjutant, herons and migrant waders.

Padi fields   Lack of freshwater habitat has limited waterbird populations in Borneo but the recent expansion of irrigated rice growing in NW Borneo has led to a population explosion of migrant waterbirds such as Common Moorhen, Purple Swamphen, Yellow Bittern and Egrets, which now breed locally.

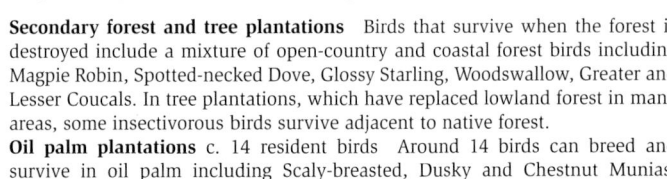

Secondary forest and tree plantations   Birds that survive when the forest is destroyed include a mixture of open-country and coastal forest birds including Magpie Robin, Spotted-necked Dove, Glossy Starling, Woodswallow, Greater and Lesser Coucals. In tree plantations, which have replaced lowland forest in many areas, some insectivorous birds survive adjacent to native forest.

Oil palm plantations c. 14 resident birds   Around 14 birds can breed and survive in oil palm including Scaly-breasted, Dusky and Chestnut Munias, Prinia, Magpie Robin, Spotted-necked Dove, Grass and Barn Owls, Yellow-vented Bulbul, Pied Fantail, White-breasted Waterhen Emerald Dove, Olive-backed and Brown-throated Sunbirds.

The Heart of Borneo Initiative is a multinational project co-ordinated by the WWF to conserve 220,000km² of forested highlands in central Borneo. 'Borneo's forests, water and biological diversity are critical for prosperity of the entire island. The continued maintenance of their natural and cultural wealth is of local, national and global importance. At the very heart of Borneo there lies a uniquely rich, largely forested landscape. It straddles the transboundary highlands of Brunei, Indonesia and Malaysia, and reaches out through the foothills into the adjacent lowlands. Our vision for the heart of Borneo is that partnerships at all levels ensure effective management of a network of protected areas, productive forests and other sustainable land-uses. Borneo's magnificent heritage is thereby sustained forever.' Vision Statement approved by representatives of Brunei, Malaysia and Indonesia at the Heart of Borneo conference in Bali, 12 February 2007. www.panda.org, www.wwf.de (Germany), www.wwf.or.id (Indonesia), www.wwf.org.uk (UK), www.wwf.org.my (Malaysia), www.wwf.nl (Netherlands), www.worldwildlife.org (USA).

CHANGES IN RESIDENT BIRDS

Primary forest to logged forest

| 1,200 tree species 220+ bird species | 1,200 tree species c. 160 bird species | 1,200 tree species 220+ bird species | 1,200 tree species c. 160 bird species |

| Virgin primary forest | Logged forest | Regrowth after 30 years | Logged for second time |

Primary forest to secondary forest

| 1,200 tree species 220+ bird species | | | 80 tree species c.60 bird species |

| Virgin primary forest | Slash and burn | Cultivated hill rice, maize | Fallow 10 years' secondary forest |

Primary forest to plantation

| 1,200 tree species 220+ bird species | | | One tree species c.12 bird species |

| Virgin primary forest | Logged, cleared and burnt | Plant oil palm | After 7 years the world's most productive food crop |

Bare rock	
	4000
SUB-ALPINE VEGETATION	
	2800
UPPER MONTANE FOREST *Rhododendron,* *Leptospermum,* *Schima* Stunted bushes and small trees	
	1800
MONTANE FOREST Chestnuts Conifers *Lithocarpus* (Oaks) *Eugenia, Magnolia* Laurels: *Litsea, Cinna Momum* Ground damp and mossy Vegetation festooned with orchids, ferns and other epiphytes Stunted forest on ridges	
	900
SUBMONTANE and HILL FOREST Predominant vegetation is Hill dipterocarp forest, Laurels increasingly common Figs common	
	300
LOWLAND PRIMARY FOREST Tall dipterocarp forest and figs	
	0

KINABALU PLANT LIFE

ALTITUDINAL ZONATION OF BIRDS AND VEGETATION ON KINABALU

Plant life changes with altitude in Borneo and as vegetation changes so does the birdlife For birds and mammals the main change is at around 900m when mossy cloud forest (montane forest) first appears on ridge tops and again at 1,800m (upper montane forest) when trees become shrunken and covered with moss and epiphytes and berry-bearing bushes become common. (Botanists recognise more altitudinal zones for plants. See Kitayama, 1992.) Most lowland bird families (excluding woodpeckers and kingfishers) develop separate montane species above 900m. Shown on the simplified altitudinal diagram are the barbets, trogons, green broadbills, frogmouths and owls. Laughing-thrushes are exclusively montane in Borneo with no lowland equivalents. Above 1,800m yet another group of birds, the high mountain specialists such as the Island Thrush, appear. Similar species occupy high montane forest throughout SE Asia, a relic of a universally colder climate during the last ice age.

Island Thrush
284-2

Friendly
Bush-Warbler
250-6 *

Whitehead's
Trogon
188-4 *

Mountain
Scops Owl
174-3

Rajah Scops Owl
174-5

...tehead's
...oadbill
...12-2 *

Bornean
Frogmouth
176-5 *

Orange-
breasted
Trogon
188-3

Cinnamon-
rumped
Trogon
188-5

Dulit *
Frogmouth
176-2

...et-rumped
Trogon
188-6

Diard's Trogon
188-1

Red-
naped
Trogon
188-2

Large
Frogmouth
176-1

Collared
Scops Owl
174-6

4095	Kinabalu Summit
4000	
3750	Sayat Sayat rest hut (Kinabalu)
3330	Panar Laban hostel (KNP)
3150	Paka Cave (KNP)
2800	
2643	Gng Trus Madi (Sabah)
2600	Layang Layang shelter (Kinabalu)
2579	Gng Tambayukon (Kinabalu Park)
2423	Gng Murud (Sarawak)
2376	Gng Mulu (Sarawak)
2100	Kamborangoh (Kinabalu)
2000	Mesilau (KNP)
1964	Gng Alab, Crocker Range (Sabah)
1866	Timpohon Gate (Kinabalu)
1800	
1709	Gng Niut (Kalimantan)
1650	Gng Pueh (Sarawak)
1600	Gng Lotong Maliau (Sabah)
1563	Kinabalu Park HQ (KNP)
1369	Gng Dulit (Sarawak)
1350	Rafflesia Centre Crocker Range (Sabah)
1326	Gng Penrissen (Sarawak)
1200	Poring, Langanan (KNP)
1116	Gng Palung
1093	Gng Danum (Sabah)
965	Gng Gading (Sarawak)
913	Bukit Belalong (Brunei)
911	Gng Serapi (Kubah Sarawak)
900	
884	Gng Silam (Sabah)
810	Gng Santubong (Sarawak)
610	Gng Silam restaurant
579	Poring HQ (KNP) (Sabah)
494	Gng Subis, Niah (Sarawak)
465	Lambir Hills (Sarawak)
300	
200	Tabin HQ (Sabah)
100	Signal Hill KK (Sabah)
30	Sepilok (Sabah)
10	Tg Puting (Kalimantan)
0	

THE HEIGHTS OF SOME BORNEAN MOUNTAINS AND BIRDING SITES
In metres (not to scale)

Massenerhebung Effect   Although this plate shows changes of vegetation and birdlife on Kinabalu, changes on other Bornean mountains vary dependent on their size. On small isolated mountains upper montane forest begins at lower altitudes than on larger mountains, known as the 'Massenerhebung Effect'. On Kinabalu upper montane forest begins at around 1,800m but on Gng Palung at 900m and on Gng Mulu at 1,200m (K. McKinnon). Note also that frugivorous birds are often altitudinal migrants during fruiting seasons or droughts and so may be found higher or lower than depicted on occassion. See pages 212 and 276.

Temperature   The daily temperature hardly varies throughout lowland Borneo from around 22°C at night to a maximum of 32°C during the day. Temperature falls approx. 0.55°C for every 100m in altitude. Therefore the Bornean mountains are significantly cooler than the lowlands, e.g. the temperature at KNP HQ (1,563m) averages 9°C lower than at sea level and at Panar Laban on Kinabalu (3,330m), the temperature averages 20°C lower.

CLIMATE, RAINFALL AND BIRD BREEDING SEASONS

Rainfall Wallace described the climate of the region, including Borneo, thus: 'Situated upon the equator, and bathed by the tepid water of the great tropical oceans this region enjoys a climate more uniformly hot and moist than almost any other part of the globe'. Why then do most Bornean birds breed on an annual cycle between January and July each year and why has rice traditionally been grown on an annual cycle in Borneo? The answer relates to rainfall, and the effects of the monsoons.

Bird breeding seasons In most of Borneo rain falls in every month of the year but it is heaviest during the NE monsoon from November to February and at its lightest from March to June. Before the advent of irrigation schemes most farmers planted rice at the beginning of the wettest period (October) and harvested at the beginning of the driest (April). With birds the answer is more complex. Most Bornean birds breed once a year between January and July. Young birds need a diet high in protein to fledge successfully. Therefore even fruit-eating birds such as bulbuls or nectarivorous birds such as spiderhunters switch to an insectivorous diet to feed their young. It has been hypothesised (Fogden, 1972) that the extra rainfall brought by the NE monsoon stimulates plants to new growth. In turn this stimulates a flush of insects feeding on the new leaves. This extra food triggers birds into breeding condition and supplies the additional insects needed to feed their young. The reduced rain early in the year (February onwards) is an additional advantage, allowing birds to spend more of the daylight hours foraging for insects. The benefits of following this seasonal pattern keep most breeding birds on an annual cycle.

Munias breed year round Proof that the above hypothesis was correct would be evidence that birds that do not eat insects are not tied into an annual breeding cycle. This appears to be the case with munias, which are exclusively graminivorous (grain or seed eating) with no insects in their diet. Grains, including grass seed, contain enough protein to fledge young successfully. Munias breed continuously year round in Borneo. See page 316.

Fruiting seasons These normally follow a dry season and there is some evidence of a second peak in frugivorous bird breeding (e.g. by hornbills) around June and July. Pigeons exceptionally feed their young on 'crop milk' not insects and are therefore not affected by insect abundance.

Seabirds breed from March to July This inter-monsoon period is when the seas are calmest and the fishing is easiest. Bornean seas are stormiest during the NE monsoon from October to March, so seabirds also follow an annual cycle. See pages 74, 136, 138, 140.

Herons and egrets breed from April to September In Kalimantan these are the driest months of the year when lakes are shrinking and fish are concentrated in shallow pools. See page 346.

Summary Although rain falls in every month of the year in most parts of Borneo, the seasonality of the monsoons and the variability in the monthly rainfall has the effect of compelling birds to adopt an annual breeding cycle. The climate charts opposite show significant local differences in rainfall patterns and it is likely that the peak breeding season for most birds will vary accordingly.

CLIMATIC SEASONS ON THE NORTH WEST COAST OF BORNEO

January	NE monsoon. Winds blow from the NE. Wet. Many birds singing.
February	NE monsoon. Wet. Many birds singing. Birds start nesting.
March	End of the NE monsoon is followed by drier weather. (Malay: Musim kemarau)
April	Transition period of low winds and calm seas. Most northern migrants depart.
May	Peak bird breeding season for NW Borneo and seabirds. Last of migrants depart.
June	Start of SW monsoon. Light winds, increasing rainfall.
July	Light winds from SW, moderate rainfall. Some early arrival of migrants from N.
August	Summer typhoons bring heavy rain from Philippines. Migrants from N Asia arrive.
September	End of SW monsoon. Light winds, moderate rainfall. Migration increasing.
October	Weather very variable. Peak migration arrival month for most birds from N Asia.
November	Start of the NE monsoon. Often stormy. (Malay: Landas or Musim hujan)
December	NE monsoon, and the wettest period of the year for most of Borneo.

DROUGHTS Every two to seven years (on average every four) Borneo suffers an ENSO (El Nino Southern Oscillation) event where rainfall that normally falls over Borneo moves east into the Pacific. Droughts can last six months and where forest has been damaged by logging or drainage, absence of rain results in catastrophic fires, particularly in the peat swamp forests in the driest areas of S and SE Borneo.

RAINFALL IN DIFFERENT AREAS OF BORNEO
MONTHLY RAINFALL IN MM, JANUARY TO DECEMBER

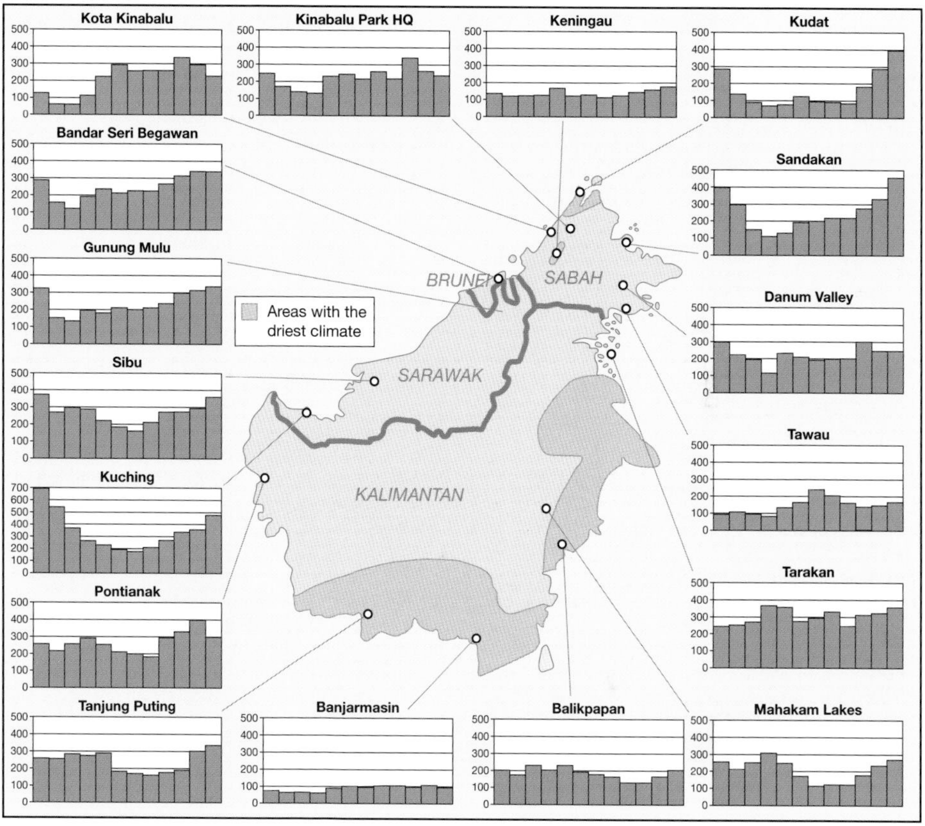

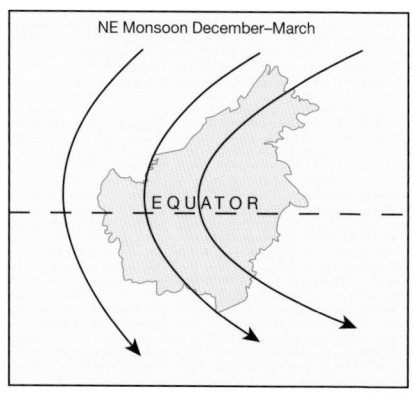

Kota Kinabalu

Kinabalu Park HQ

Keningau

Kudat

Bandar Seri Begawan

Gunung Mulu

BRUNEI   SABAH

Sandakan

Areas with the driest climate

Sibu

SARAWAK

Danum Valley

Kuching

KALIMANTAN

Tawau

Pontianak

Tarakan

Tanjung Puting

Banjarmasin

Balikpapan

Mahakam Lakes

THE MONSOONS

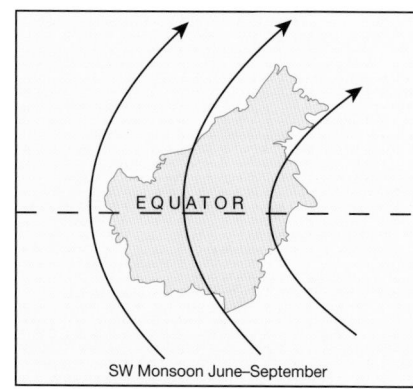

NE Monsoon December–March

EQUATOR

SW Monsoon June–September

35

BIRD MIGRATION

A total of 244 bird species have been recorded as migrants or vagrants to Borneo. At a rough estimate a minimum of 15 million birds reach Borneo each winter from Siberia and NE Asia, with considerably smaller numbers of austral migrants from Australia and Java.

Habitats of migrant birds   Forest migrants include Asian Brown and Mugimaki Flycatchers, Grey Nightjar, Siberian Blue Robin and Hawk-owl, but in Borneo they represent less than 5% of the forest bird population in winter (Fogden, 1976). In the Malay Peninsula the proportion is 10–15% (Wells, 2007). Migrants are most common in coastal habitats and open countryside, and these birds are therefore not seriously affected by forest destruction and agricultural expansion. Some birds, such as egrets and other waterbirds, may even benefit. Records show that N Asia migrants are much more common in Sabah than Kalimantan, indicating no shortage of suitable habitat.

Habits of migrant birds   Tired migrants are often recorded resting on small islands, ships or oil platforms in the South China Sea. Migrant raptors such as Peregrines and Sparrowhawks are regularly recorded hunting birds at these sites especially Brown Shrikes and Barn Swallows.

Migration as a survival strategy   A number of species are present in Borneo as both migrants and residents, e.g. Great Egret, Honey Buzzard, Peregrine Falcon, Ruddy Kingfisher and Brown Flycatcher. Usually the migrant form is more common, indicating that (despite the pitfalls) long distance migration is a highly successful survival strategy.

Navigation and vagrants   Migrant birds use a variety of strategies to navigate and some, at least, are possessed of a magnetic compass, a star chart and an internal clock hard-wired in their brains. Research has shown that some birds navigate by day using the height of the sun above the horizon and at night by using a map of the stars. Thus unless the sky is overcast they know roughly where they are both by day and by night. That these systems occasionally fail is proven by the many vagrants that turn up in Borneo, including 'over-shooters' such as the ducks (which normally winter north of Borneo) and 'reverse migrants' where east and west directions appear to be reversed, e.g. Wheatear and Common Cuckoo.

Night- and day-flying migrants   Most migrants fly by night. Day-flying migrants include the swallows and swifts, all the raptors, and buntings. Bee-eaters and pigeons fly by both day and night. When flying over the sea, land birds have no choice but to continue flying if they have not reached the Borneo coast by dawn. The flight from Vietnam to Borneo is a minimum of 850km (19hr flight at 45km/hr). Look for day arrivals from the west on the NW Borneo coast (Sept.–Oct.).

THE MIGRATION CALENDAR FOR NORTHERN MIGRANTS TO NW BORNEO

January	Look for Brown Shrike, Brown Flycatcher defending winter territories.
February	Check out old sites. Many migrants, e.g. Peregrine, return to the same site each year.
March	Northern migrants start returning north.
April	Most migrants depart. Cattle Egrets in orange breeding plumage before departure.
May	Last migrants depart. Austral migrants, e.g. Sacred Kingfisher, arrive in Kalimantan.
June	Only a few first-year migrants remain including Redshank, Cattle Egret etc.
July	First Yellow Wagtails arrive. First waders arrive at month end.
August	Large numbers of passage waders en route to Australia arrive. First Brown Shrikes.
September	Check coast for waterbirds and raptors. Cattle Egrets arrive in breeding plumage.
October	Peak migration. Check out Layang², Mantanani, Manukan, P Tiga, tip of Borneo.
November	Harriers and Sparrowhawks arrive. Check coast after storms for vagrant seabirds.
December	Most migration complete. Look for Mugimaki Flycatcher in the mountains.

The MAPS Program, Zoonoses and SARS   Between 1963 and 1971 the US Army funded the Migratory Animal Pathological Survey (MAPS) to investigate zoonoses (diseases common to man, birds and other animals) in E Asia. Led by ornithologist H. Elliot McClure, 1,165,000 birds were banded, of which 7,000 recoveries were made. Much of our knowledge of Asian bird migration is based on this work. Most zoonoses are not bird dispersed. Bird host zoonoses include encephalitis, scrub typhus and avian influenza (SARS). SARS usually only poses a threat to man where large numbers of domestic chickens or ducks are kept in crowded conditions, act as a disease reservoir and come into close contact with people. As very few wild birds are handled by very few people, migrant wild birds seldom pose a direct threat to human health.

FURTHER REFERENCES TO BIRD MIGRATION IN THIS FIELD GUIDE

BIRD MIGRATION ROUTES TO BORNEO

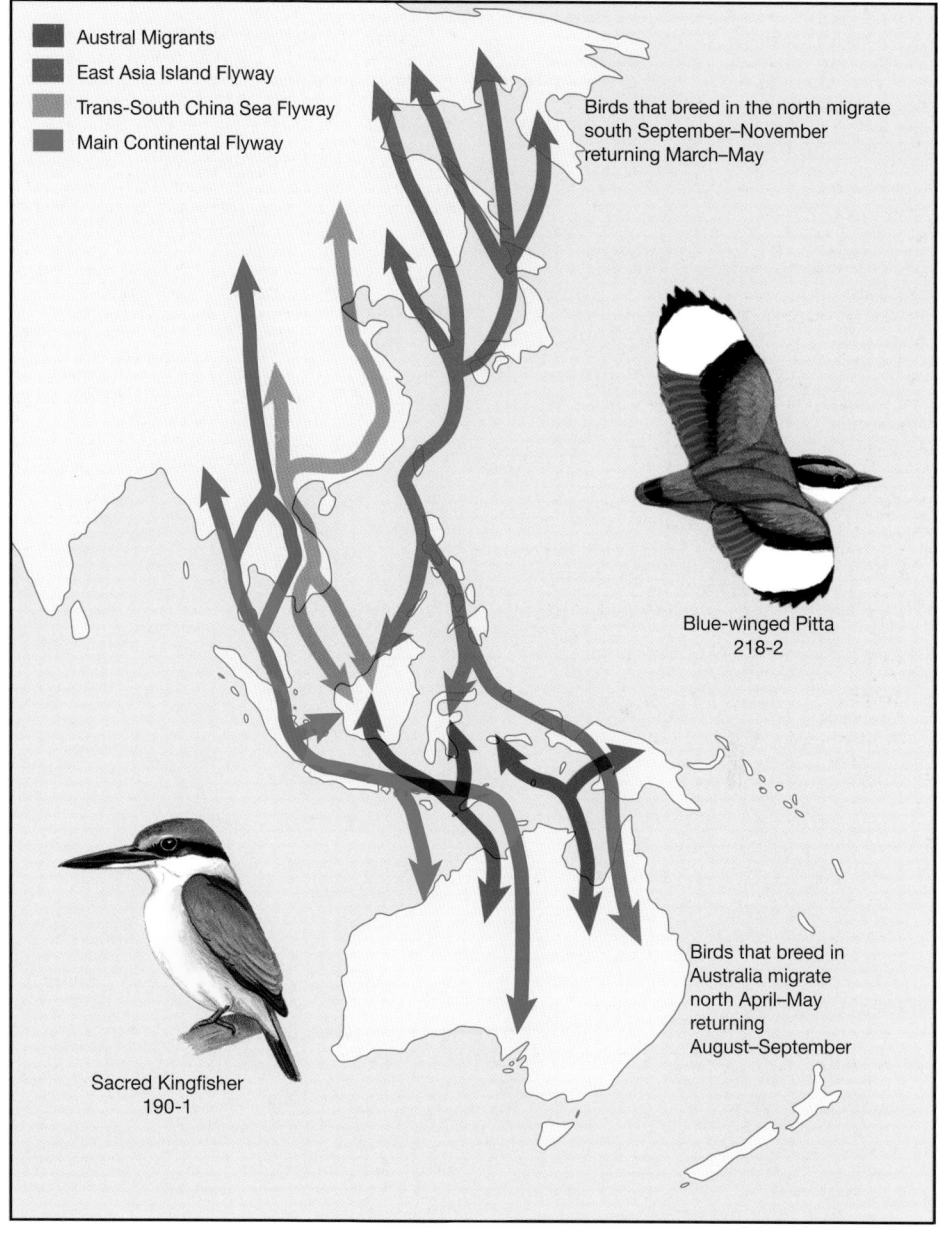

- Austral Migrants
- East Asia Island Flyway
- Trans-South China Sea Flyway
- Main Continental Flyway

Birds that breed in the north migrate south September–November returning March–May

Blue-winged Pitta
218-2

Sacred Kingfisher
190-1

Birds that breed in Australia migrate north April–May returning August–September

GLOSSARY

See also vegetation on page 30, and the anatomy diagram on page 26.

Adult	a bird old enough to breed, and that has acquired definitive plumage. All birds illustrated are adults unless otherwise specified
Allopatric	(of species) similar species occupying habitats which are geographically separated
Arboreal	associated with or living in trees
Aseasonally	not seasonal
Asynchronously	not occurring at the same time
Atoll	a ring-shaped island or reef enclosing a lagoon based on the rim of an extinct submerged volcano e.g. Pulau Layang Layang, Maratua
Austral	from the south; southern
Aviculturist	a person who breeds and rears birds
Batang	river in Sarawak
BSB	Bandar Seri Begawan
Bukit	(Malay) hill
Bund	an earth bank, such as in padi fields or lagoons
Burung	(Malay) bird
Canopy	the upper branches and foliage of trees in a forest forming a layer
Casuarina	(*Casuarina equisetifolia*) (to 20+ m) common tree of sandy seashores with needle-like 'leaves'. Malay: aru, as in Tanjong Aru
Cay	a small, flat, marine island formed from coral-reef material or sand. USA = Key
Cere	bare, fleshy structure containing the nostrils in eagles and parrots
Cline	a gradual change in characteristics in a species across its range
Conspecific	a term applied to individuals that belong to the same species
Corolla	inner whorl of petals of a flower, sometimes tube-shaped
Crèche	family group or flock collectively caring for the young e.g. Chestnut Munia
Crepuscular	active at dusk, or pre-dawn, or both, e.g. nightjars
Danau (D)	(Malay) lake
Dimorphic	occurring in two distinct forms within the same species e.g. Reef Egret. **Sexual dimorphism:** male and female of a species differ in colour or size e.g. Bulwer's Pheasant
Dipterocarp	(a tree belonging to the family *Dipterocarpaceae*) (to 45+ m) large timber trees which dominate the Bornean lowland and hill primary forest; with 2 or more winged seeds which are eaten by rats and squirrels not birds
Disyllabic	having two syllables (e.g. '*cuck-oo*')
Dyak	a people native to parts of interior Borneo
Diurnal	active during the day, the opposite of nocturnal
Eclipse plumage	dull post-breeding adult plumage; typical of ducks and waders
Ecotone	a narrow transition zone between two different habitats, such as forest/oil palm, land/water, often very species-rich in birdlife
Emergent	a very tall tree which projects above the canopy of the rainforest e.g. *Koompassia excelsa* (See below)
Endemic	a species that only occurs in one locality – here referring to Borneo
Epiphyte	a plant that grows upon another plant but is not parasitic (hence epiphytic)
Extirpate	make extinct
Ferruginous	the colour of rust; reddish-brown
Fledge	of a young bird: to have developed feathers ready for flight
Frugivorous	(fructivorous) feeding on fruit
Gecko	a small, insectivorous, nocturnal lizard (Malay name 'cik cak', from its call)

Graminivorous	feeding on grass, cereals etc
Gunung (Gng)	(Malay) mountain
Heliconia	an introduced neotropical plant of the banana family with bright red/yellow flowers much favoured by sunbirds and spiderhunters
Hepatic	the colour of liver; dark reddish-brown as with the hepatic morph of some female cuckoos
Iban	a people of Sarawak (also called Sea Dyaks)
Immature	a young bird not yet old enough to breed: used to denote all plumage phases except the adult and juvenile plumages. With hawk-eagles and gulls this phase can last for several years
Irruptive	birds which breed irregularly in large numbers when conditions are suitable and then disperse widely e.g. the pratincoles and Pin-tailed Parrotfinch
Juvenile	a young bird in its first set of true feathers
Kampung (Kg)	(Malay) village
Kerangas	(Malay) heath forest; forest growing on nutrient-poor, sandy soils; typically stunted but very variable
KK	Kota Kinabalu
KL	Kuala Lumpur
Kleptoparasite	a bird which habitually robs other birds of food e.g. frigatebird
KNP	Kinabalu National Park
KNP HQ	Kinabalu National Park Head Quarters
Koompassia	(*Koompassia excelsa*) (to 75 + m) one of the tallest forest trees, an emergent; often at roadsides. Malay: Tualang or Mengaris. See also illustration page 205
Kota (K.)	(Malay) city or fort
Kuala	(Malay) river mouth
Lalang	(Malay) (*Imperata cylindrica*) 'sword grass'. A sharp-edged grass growing on degraded soils e.g. at Kudat, Sabah and in W Kalimantan
Layang²	Layang Layang. Malay for kite or tern/swift.
Line of gape	in egrets; the line that runs from the beak base to below the eye
Lores	the area between the eye and the side of the beak (hence loral)
Lump	opposite of 'split', the scientific process of reducing the status of species to races or sub-species, thus effectively combining two named species to form one single species, hence lumping them together
Macaranga	(a tree belonging to the genus *Macaranga*, family Euphorbiaceae) large-leaved shrubs typical of logged or secondary forest. The small berries are eaten by doves, bulbuls, leafbirds and spiderhunters. Malay: Mahang
Malay P	Malay Peninsula (this includes part of the isthmus of Kra, which politically is part of Thailand)
Mast	large seeds of forest trees such as the dipterocarps and oaks which flower and fruit en masse (a masting event). Seeds are eaten by squirrels and rats not birds
Melastoma	(*Melastoma malabathricum*) (to 4m, usually less) 'Straits Rhododendron'. Small shrub with pink/purple flowers, common in coastal scrub and along streams, sometimes in forest clearings. The sweet, sticky purple berries are very popular with birds, especially flowerpeckers. Malay: Sendudok
Mimic	an animal or plant which exhibits mimicry (imitation) See page 84
Mist net	a net made of fine threads, used to trap birds for study purposes
Monoculture	the cultivation of a single crop over a large area e.g. oil palm
Morph	a variant form or colour, e.g. Reef Egret.
Moult	to shed feathers in the process of replacing worn plumage
Muara	(Malay) river mouth
Musang	(Malay) civet cat; a common predator of ground birds in forests

Nectarivorous	feeding on nectar e.g. sunbirds, spiderhunters
Neotropics	the biogeographical region comprising Central and South America
Nomenclature	the systematic scientific naming of different bird species
Nocturnal	active at night, the opposite of diurnal
Obligate	a relationship of two species which are reliant on each other for survival. May apply to some flowerpeckers and mistletoes
Outlier	an isolated mountain separated from the main mountain range
Padang	(Malay) an open grassy space, field or clearing
Padi	(Malay) the rice plant– hence padi field or rice field
Palaearctic	of the biogeographical region which includes the cold and temperate zones of Europe, N Africa and Asia north of the Himalayas
Passerine	birds with feet adapted for perching, with three toes forward and one back (includes warblers, thrushes, finches, crows, swallows)
Pelagic	oceanic; inhabiting the open sea returning to shore only to breed e.g. noddies
Pericarp	the wall, pod, husk, shell of a ripened fruit
Pinang palm	a small palm common on farms and in gardens. Produces orange Betel-nut fruits chewed by some local people
Polyandrous	a female having more than one male mate
Polygynous	a male having more than one female mate
Polymorphic	occurring in many different forms e.g. Honey Buzzard plumages
Polysyllabic	consisting of many syllables e.g. woodpecker contact call '*ki ki ki ki*'
Primaries	the larger flight feathers on the outer wing (see anatomy diagram page 26)
Primary forest	original, untouched, virgin forest
Pulau (P)	(Malay) island
Race	the same as subspecies
Raptor	a diurnal bird of prey such as an eagle, falcon, buzzard or hawk
Relict	a species surviving in reduced numbers from a previous era
Riverine	of or relating to a river; living on the banks of a river
Sayat[2]	Sayat Sayat. A mountain hut at 3,750m on Kinabalu
Secondaries	flight feathers on the inner part of the wing (see anatomy diagram page 26)
Secondary forest	degraded forest growing where original/primary forest has been cleared. Can never revert to primary forest unless adjacent to seeding dipterocarp forest
Speculum	a bright patch of plumage on the wings of certain birds, esp. ducks
Stoop	of a bird of prey – to descend swiftly, or swoop on its quarry
Submontane	the foothills or lower slopes of a mountain / mountain range
Subspecies (Race)	a population that differs from other populations of the same species but is not considered genetically different enough to be split into a separate species
Split	the scientific process of describing the differentiating genetic characteristics of a subspecies in order to re-classify it as a separate species e.g. Bornean Swiftlet split from Glossy Swiftlet (see page 182); opposite of 'lump'
Species	a genetically distinct unit that in the wild will usually only breed with its own species
Sungai (Sg)	(Malay) river
Superspecies	a group of closely related subspecies that exist allopatrically but are not distinctive enough to be split into separate species e.g. Yellow Wagtails, Long-tailed Shrikes
Symbiosis	a close relation between two dissimilar organisms living together where each benefits the other e.g. ants and *Macaranga* shrubs
Sympatric	(of species) similar species occurring in the same area; overlapping in distribution
Tanjung (Tg)	(Malay) cape
Tarsus	a long bone in the lower leg of birds (see anatomy diagram)

Taxonomy	the systematic classification of living organisms (see page 92)
Terrestrial	ground living
Thermal	a rising current of relatively warm air, used by birds of prey and storks to gain height during hot days
Tibia	the short bone in the upper leg (see also tarsus)
Trinomial	of scientific names: consisting of three terms – the genus, the species, and the subspecies; see also page 92
Trophic	at the top of the food chain e.g. Serpent Eagle
Ultrabasic	(ultramafic) area of poor soil containing heavy metals where forest is reduced in diversity and height e.g. Marai Parai spur on Kinabalu
Understorey	the relatively open area beneath the main canopy of a forest
Ulu	Up river or remote region of the river headwaters
Upper-storey	the top layer of forest vegetation; see canopy
Vagrant	less than ten records for Borneo

A VERY SHORT HISTORY OF BORNEAN ORNITHOLOGY

Between c.1850 and 1914 a worldwide 'collecting mania' for the skins of newly discovered species of birds developed. London was the centre of this trade. The demand from museums and wealthy private collectors such as Lord Rothschild and the Marquis of Tweedale financed the 6 year travels of Wallace around the Malay Archipelago as well as the collecting expeditions of Everett, Hose and Whitehead in Borneo whose surnames are commemorated in the scientific names of many Bornean birds. Collectors competed to find and describe new species, naming them after their colleagues, a situation which led to many bird races being described as new endemic species a practice known as 'excessive splitting'. Thus Everett's 1889 list contains a remarkable 106 endemics. The lumping (reverse of splitting) started in 1914 when J. C. Moulton Curator of the Sarawak Museum published his *Hand-list of the Birds of Borneo* listing only 72 endemics.

Chasen's *Handlist of Malaysian Birds* (1935) continued this trend with only 31 endemics. Smythies accepted Chasen's list with only a few minor changes and the first edition of the *The Birds of Borneo* listed 28 endemics. Most later ornithologists consider Chasen to be an 'excessive lumper' and since 1981 a reverse trend has developed in favour of 'splitting' so that many endemics listed by Moulton and lumped by Chasen have now been split again.

As a result, although no new Bornean endemics have been discovered in the last 100 years (apart from the Spectacled Flowerpecker in 2009) the list of endemics has risen relentlessly. The figures are slightly distorted by differences of opinion and approach, but the long-term pattern is clear. The Borneo bird list total also continues to increase every year as vagrants and scarce sea birds are added to the list and it is likely that the total will one day exceed 800 (see pages 92 and 240).

Date	Author	Book title	B. Birds	Endemics
1874	Salvadori	*Catalogo sistematico degli Uccelli di Borneo*	392	n/a
1889	Everett	*List of the birds of the Bornean Group of Islands*	536	**106**
1914	Moulton	*Hand-list of the Birds of Borneo*	555	**72**
1935	Chasen	*Handlist of Malaysian Birds*	526	**31**
1960	Smythies	*The Birds of Borneo 1st edition*	554	**28**
1968	Smythies	*The Birds of Borneo 2nd edition*	561	**28**
1981	Cranbrook	*The Birds of Borneo 3rd edition*	582	**32**
1993	McKinnon	*A Field Guide to the Birds of Borneo, Sumatra, Java and Bali*	599	**32**
1999	Davison	*The Birds of Borneo 4th edition*	622	**45**
2001	Sheldon et al	*Ornithology of Sabah*	n/a	**n/a**
2008	Mann	*The Birds of Borneo BOU Checklist*	630	**47**
2009	Myers	*A Field Guide to the Birds of Borneo*	633	**50**
2009	Phillipps	*Phillipps Field Guide to the Birds of Borneo* 1st edn	664	**51**
2011	Phillipps	*Phillipps Field Guide to the Birds of Borneo* 2nd edn	669	**52**
2014	Phillipps	*Phillipps Field Guide to the Birds of Borneo* 3rd edn	673	**59**

MEGAPODES

MEGAPODIIDAE **World 20 species; Borneo 2 species.** The Megapode (large foot) family occurs on forested islands between Borneo and Australia (Wallacea) where there are no ground predators such as civets and wild cats. Apart from an isolated species in the Andamans and Nicobars they are found no further west than Pulau Labuan, NW Borneo. Megapodes use their large feet to create mounds of decaying vegetation in which to lay their eggs. The natural heat of decomposition or warm sand incubates the eggs. Adults frequently attend the mounds to regulate the temperature but when the chicks hatch they dig themselves out and fend for themselves. Megapodes are common on protected islands such as P Gaya, P Manukan and P Tiga but in the past Megapodes were frequently trapped with snares in fences built surrounding their mounds (see below).

1   ORANGE-FOOTED MEGAPODE *Megapodius reinwardt* **37cm   Local resident islands**

[Davison/Mann: Orange-footed Scrubfowl] Common in E Indonesia and found west to islands in the Java Sea off the south east coast of Kalimantan including Kagean, Masalembu, Karamian and also Matasireh,which is considered to have a Bornean avifauna (Davison, 1999) and where it is the only megapode, as Philippine Megapode is not found this far south. Darker than Philippine Megapode with bright orange not dark grey legs and a significant crest. **Call:** Raucous loud double crow (Pizzey). Loud cacklings, gurgles, thuds (Simpson). Often duets. **Range:** Islands of Java Sea and S Sulawesi, to New Guinea and N Australia.

2   PHILIPPINE MEGAPODE *Megapodius cumingii* **35cm   Local resident islands**

[Davison: Philippine Scrubfowl, Mann: Tabon Scrubfowl] Malay: Burung Tambun. Locally common on the forested offshore islands of NW Sabah including Mantanani, Gaya, Manukan, Mengalum and Pulau Tiga. On the east coast found on most islands including the Semporna Islands south to Maratua. Davison found a skeleton on P Layang[2] indicating long distance nomadism. On Pulau Tiga 64 active mounds were found in 1999 compared with 41 in 1986 (Ahmad 1999). The mounds are built in the forest not far from the shore often around a decaying tree stump. Megapodes feed on the ground but roost in trees alone. **Call:** Mournful whistle described as a cat like *miaoow*, often at dusk or in the night. **Range:** Islets off N Borneo, rarely on the mainland. Philippines, Sulawesi and islands.

FIG. 1.—JERAT.

AN HISTORICAL ACCOUNT OF PHEASANT TRAPPING IN N BORNEO (1891)
'A place is sought showing the tracks of the birds and a long pagar (fence) is erected, right across a valley for instance. Openings for jerats (a noose on a sprung sapling) are left every 20 yards or so and jerats are also placed across every bird track. The pagar is so slight that a bird could easily get through it but they don't. When foraging, the birds are not particular where they go, so long as the way is easy, and the food plentiful. Hence the slightest obstacle will turn them. They saunter along the pagar, come to an opening and start through. The moment they step onto the platform, it falls, releases the trigger, up goes the noose and the victim hangs suspended by the legs. It is my favourite trap. Six can be made in an hour at no cost, and it is very effective. I have caught Argus, Fire-back and Bulwer's Pheasants, partridges, porcupine, wild cat, civet cat and even a monkey in them.' Sydney B.J. Skertchly (1891).

adult

chick

2

adult

chick

PHEASANTS AND JUNGLEFOWL

PHASIANIDAE **World 160 species; Borneo 14 species, 2 endemics**. The Bornean pheasant family includes five classic long-tailed pheasants, eight dumpy partridges and one tiny quail. All pheasants are ground birds, eating fallen fruits and seeds and scratching for insects amongst leaves, but they roost in trees at night. Nests are on the ground often hidden at the base of a tree. The male usually has striking colourful display plumage with the female much duller. Often in groups, a male and several females. Calls are often loud and distinctive.

1 BORNEAN CRESTED FIREBACK *Lophura ignita* (M) 60cm, (F) 55cm **Local endemic**

[Malay: Ayam pegar] After Argus, the second commonest Bornean pheasant found in lowland and hill forest throughout Borneo. Enters oil palm where adjacent to forest at Tabin. Previously common in the Kelabit Highlands and Pulong Tau. Frequently seen at Danum. Kalimantan birds are larger than N Borneo birds and in aviculture they are known respectively as Greater and Lesser Bornean Firebacks. Measurements show the size difference is clinal (gradual). **Call:** A variety of croaks and whistles including a loud disyllabic *kiukun* (Delacour). Males often whirr their wings. **Range:** Malay P, Sumatra, Borneo. **Taxonomy:** new split, see page 20.

2 BORNEAN CRESTLESS FIREBACK *Lophura pyronota* (M) 48cm, (F) 43cm **Rare endemic**

[Malay: Mata merah (red eye)] Rare inhabitant of lowland forests. Commonest in the peat swamp forests of S and W Borneo north to Brunei. One record from Kinabalu (1903). Found at Tg Puting and Sabangau (S Kalimantan) but not in NE Kalimantan. In Malaya Davison found the favoured habitat was damp valley bottoms with Bertam palm (*Eugeissona tristis*) undergrowth also favoured by Crested Fireback, but Crested Fireback is dominant and excludes Crestless from such habitat. In the wild both sexes look almost black but with distinctive red facial skin. Borneo race *pyronata* male has distinctive pale silver streaks on neck and chest. **Call:** Less noisy than Crested. Alarm call is a loud *kak* and males advertise with wing whirring (Wells). **Range:** Malay P, Sumatra, Borneo. **BLI:** Vulnerable. **Taxonomy:** new split, see page 20.

3 BULWER'S PHEASANT *Lophura bulweri* (M) 77cm, (F) 50cm **Rare endemic**

[Wattled Pheasant] This magnificent Bornean endemic is locally common in some undisturbed remote hill forests such as the Maliau Basin in Sabah, but generally very scarce. Breeding behaviour is an 'exploded lekking system' where males gather within calling distance (but not within sight) of each other (Rowden). The males call in competition to attract females and, once present, perform a stunning display in which the blue head wattles become massively enlarged and the gleaming white tail is spread wide. Associates with wild pigs (like Ground-Cuckoo) and follows them on their migrations. **Call:** The male breeding call is a shrill two part hoarse hiss *bek-kia* repeated. **Sabah:** Maliau Basin (regular), Tawau Hills. **Brunei:** Labi Hills, Ladan Hills near Mulu. **Sarawak:** Pulong Tau, Lanjak Entimau. **Kalimantan:** Betung Kerihun, Kayan Mentarang, Bukit Raya, Bukit Baka. **BLI:** Vulnerable.

4 RED JUNGLEFOWL *Gallus gallus* (M) 70cm, (F) 42cm **Feral local resident**

The worlds best known gallinaceous bird, the ancestor of the domestic chicken occurs wild in the Malay P, Java, Sumatra and the Philippines but not in Borneo, although handsome fighting cocks with a similar appearance are found in many kampongs. A recently released population derived from wild W Malaysian birds appears to be thriving in oil palm/forest at Tabin, Sabah (Lamb).

BREEDING BULWER'S PHEASANT IN CAPTIVITY Aviculturists are keen to breed Bulwer's Pheasants for re-introduction into areas where they are extinct. However the world's most experienced bird-keepers have been unable to work out what initiates Bulwer's Pheasant mating behaviour. It may be that mating is triggered by the masting or mass fruiting of a forest plant. Many Bornean birds breed when a flush of protein-rich food follows a period of semi-starvation. It may be that these captive pheasants require a more seasonal diet.

The **WILDLIFE CONSERVATION SOCIETY (WCS)**, 'Protecting wildlife and wild places', is an NGO at the forefront of international wildlife conservation. The WCS has been involved in many conservation projects in Borneo, including research on Proboscis Monkeys and Orangutans and surveys of Maludam and Loagan Bunut National Parks. John Rowden of WCS has surveyed Bulwer's Pheasants in Sarawak and Kalimantan and initiated a Bulwer's Pheasant breeding programme at Bronx Zoo, New York. www.wcs.org; www.bronxzoo.com

1

♀

♂

2

♀

♂

male in
display

3

♀

♂

♀

♂

4

PARTRIDGES, QUAIL AND PHEASANTS

1 FERRUGINOUS PARTRIDGE *Caloperdix oculeus* **26cm**   **Scarce resident hills**

Locally common in hills of N Sarawak, e.g. Kelabit Highlands but hardly known in Sabah. Two unconfirmed records from the Tawau area. Two Kalimatan records Gng Latuk and Gng Menyapa. Sexes similar. **Call:** Male calls with a run up the scale, accelerating, repeated eight or nine times breaking into **ee-terang** repeated two to four times. Female replies with a long series of faster notes up the scale (Harrisson). **Range:** Myanmar to Malay P, Sumatra, Borneo.

2 ROULROUL *Rollulus rouloul* **25cm**   **Common resident**

[Davison: Crested Partridge] [Malay: Burung Siul (whistle)] The commonest Bornean partridge found in most types of lowland and hilly primary forest and sometimes in tall secondary forest, usually in small family groups. Feeds in oil palm estates where adjacent to forest (Sheldon re Tawau). Associates with foraging wild pigs. Previously common in the forest at Poring (KNP) around the hot springs. **Call:** Double whistle as in Malay name. **Range:** Malay P, Sumatra, Borneo.

3 BLUE-BREASTED QUAIL *Coturnix chinensis* **15cm**   **Common resident grassland**

[Malay: Burung pikau] [King quail] A tiny round ground bird of wild grassland throughout Borneo including scrub, padi fields, marshy areas and lalang covered hillsides. Bursts from ground, flying low before dropping back into grass. Rapidly colonises new areas of waste grassland and hence believed to be partially nomadic. **Call:** The male has a distinctive three note call in the breeding season variously described as **tok-ta-dau** similar to Malaysian Eared Nightjar (Sheldon) or **pip-it-kan** **pip-it-kan** (Smythies). **Range:** India to Malay P, Sumatra, Borneo, Java, Philippines, Sulawesi to N Guinea, Australia.

4 BORNEAN PEACOCK-PHEASANT *Polyplectron schleiermacheri* **(M) 43cm (F) 33cm**

A rare endemic. Before man arrived this pheasant was probably widespread throughout Bornean lowland and hill forests but appears to be more sensitive to disturbance and hunting pressure than other pheasants. Only one record from Sabah, in recent years (Tongod Forest Reserve in logged forest C Sabah). Never recorded from Brunei. Some possible sight records from remote interior Sarawak. Still widespread in remote hill forests of Kalimantan Ulu. The only place in Borneo where it is encountered regularly is at Sungai Wain near Balikpapan (SE Kalimantan) where Fredriksson and Nijman recorded 19 encounters in a total of 88 field months. **Call:** Contact call is a loud double **cack cack**. Male advertising call is a mournful **wu-wurh** with an emphasis on the second note given at long intervals. Currently being captive bred successfully in Singapore. **BLI:** Endangered.

5 GREAT ARGUS *Argusianus argus* **(M)120cm, (F) 60cm**   **Local resident forest**

[Great Argus Pheasant] [Malay: Kuang raya] The commonest Bornean pheasant, heard regularly in virgin hill forest. Less common in the lowlands and absent from most peatswamp forest. The male clears a display ground of bare earth in the forest from where he calls to attract females to watch him spread his wings in a striking peacock-like show of magnificence. The flesh is not edible and this bird is trapped only for its feathers (Mjoberg). See page 168 re mimicry. **Call:** A characteristic sound of Borneo forests. Two main calls. A repeated slow double note **ku-wow ku-wow** and a series of single hoots **kwow kwow kwow kwow** accelerating and rising in pitch. Typical locations; **Sabah:** Poring (KNP), Sepilok, Gomantong, Danum, Maliau, Tawau Hills. **Brunei:** Tasek Merimbum, Ulu Belait, Ulu Temburong, Kuala Belalong. **Sarawak:** Mulu, Similajau, Samunsam. **Kalimantan:** Barito Ulu, Sungai Wain, Tg Puting, Gng Palung. **Range:** Malay P, Sumatra, Borneo.

WORLD PHEASANT ASSOCIATION For many naturalists Borneo's pheasants symbolise the essence of Borneo itself, stunning, rare, and threatened. Pheasants have always been considered good eating and early explorers as well as indigenous hunters have been keen to catch them. See page 42 for illustration and description of pheasant trapping in Borneo. Pheasant populations are declining everywhere and Borneo is no exception.The World Pheasant Association works for pheasant conservation worldwide. www.pheasant.org.uk

PARTRIDGES

1 CRIMSON-HEADED PARTRIDGE *Haematortyx sanguiniceps* 25cm **Montane endemic**

Locally common in the Bornean mountains, occasionally found in the hills, e.g. recorded from Danum and at low elevations on Mulu. Occurs from Kinabalu south along the mountain chain to the hills of N Kalimantan. Commonest partridge in forest at KNP HQ and recorded in forest along the Summit Trail up to Paka Cave (3,100m). One of the characteristic bird calls of the early morning dawn chorus on Kinabalu. **Call:** Harsh, loud, far carrying double call variously described as ***pom prang pom prang*** or ***took tree took tree***.

2 BLACK PARTRIDGE *Melanoperdix niger* 25cm **Rare lowland forest resident**

A scarce and declining inhabitant of lowland dipterocarp and peatswamp forest formerly most common in SW Borneo. Old records include Kinabalu and Tutong (Brunei). Recent records; **Sabah:** Danum. Tabin (Degullacion). **Sarawak:** Mulu, Semengoh. **Kalimantan:** Gng Palung, Barito Ulu and Tg Puting. In Malaya prefers forest with an undergrowth of stem-less Bertam palms (*Eugeissona tristis*). All black male has been confused with more common Roulroul. **Call:** Double whistle similar to Roulroul. **Range:** Malay P, Sumatra, Borneo. **BLI:** Vulnerable.

3 BORNEAN NECKLACED PARTRIDGE *Arborophila graydoni* 28cm **Endemic**

[Scaly-breasted Partridge] A locally common partridge of the lowland and hill forests of Sabah. Recent records from a seven year old *Acacia mangium* plantation (Sabah Softwoods) near Tawau (Sheldon). **Call:** A two part short liquid warble constantly repeated. Pairs often duet. A three note whistle ***pi pi pi*** from one bird followed by a two note whistle ***pi-u pi-u*** from the other, usually heard in the early morning and late afternoon. Recorded from Crocker Range, Sepilok, Kinabatangan, Danum, Tabin and Tawau Hills. **Range:** Vietnam, Malay P, Sumatra, Borneo. **Taxonomy:** new split, see page 20.

4 RED-BREASTED HILL PARTRIDGE *Arborophila hyperythra hyperythra* 28cm **Endemic**

Race *A. h. hyperythra* is a locally common montane partridge of the Kelabit Highlands and the slopes of Gng Mulu and Gng Murud in N Sarawak found south along the mountain chain to Barito Ulu in Kalimantan. Favours bamboo groves and usually seen in small parties. Usually found lower down on mountains compared with Crimson-headed Partridge and generally less common. **Call:** Similar to the Sabah race described below.

5 RED-BREASTED HILL PARTRIDGE *Arborophila hyperythra erythrophrys* 28cm **Endemic**

Race *A. h. erythrophrys* is a montane endemic recorded from Kinabalu, Gng Trus Madi (Sabah) and surprisingly Gng Dulit, Sarawak (Mann). Calls heard at KNP HQ and in the Crocker Range, but less common than Crimson-headed Partridge. Recorded at Paka Cave 3,100m (Biun). Female has no black marks on throat. **Call:** On Kinabalu it duets in the early morning. A single ringing call repeated 3 times per second is answered by a low double note like ***cuckoo*** once per second (Smythies).

6 LONG-BILLED PARTRIDGE *Rhizothera longirostris* 30cm **Local forest resident**

A scarce resident of lowland primary forest throughout Borneo. Previously locally common near Kuching, e.g. Semengoh, Bako, Gng Penrissen. Scattered recent records from Sabah at Danum (Showler) and in Kalimantan at Barito Ulu (Wilkinson) but obviously in decline. No records from Brunei (Mann). Female is speckled brown above, rufous below. Identify by distinctive call. **Call:** Both male and female call repeatedly ***kan king*** often in duet with calls overlapping, usually at dusk and dawn. **Range:** Malay P, Sumatra, Borneo.

7 DULIT PARTRIDGE *Rhizothera dulitensis* 30cm **Rare montane endemic**

[Long-billed Partridge] [Hose's Partridge]. A rare montane endemic, most records are from the mountains of NE Sarawak. **Sabah:** One collected on Kinabalu (1895). Sight records from the Crocker Range near Tenom (Comber). **Brunei:** No records (Mann). **Sarawak:** Mt. Dulit, Gng Murud. Distinguished from very similar Long-billed Partridge by broader grey breast band and white instead of rufous belly. Female is similar to Long-billed female. **Call:** Not known. **Taxonomy:** Split from lowland Long-billed Partridge by Davison (1999).

Sarawak and
Kalimantan race

Sabah race

RESIDENT DUCKS

ANATIDAE **World 145 species; Borneo 3 residents and 9 migrants.** Ducks are scarce in Borneo apart from the Kapuas Lakes (Danau Sentarum) and the Negara and Mahakam Lakes in Kalimantan. Only three species are resident and are very local in range. This is almost certainly due to a shortage of lakes in northern Borneo. However, with the expansion of irrigation and permanently wet padi fields, the Wandering Whistling Duck appears to be expanding its range north and is now common in Sabah on both coasts. Whistling ducks have distinctive long legs, long necks and upright posture and typical whistling calls in flight. Sexes similar. Usually seen in small flocks, but when breeding these ducks usually nest alone in a quiet backwater. Nine, possibly ten species of migrant ducks are winter visitors to Borneo, all in very small numbers, apart from the Garganey, which has been seen in flocks of thousands at Padas Damit on the Klias Peninsula, W Sabah. These are the same swamps which can be visited on a day trip from Kota Kinabalu to watch Proboscis monkeys during the day and fireflies in the evening. See page 326.

1   LESSER WHISTLING DUCK   *Dendrocygna javanica*   41cm   Scarce resident

Scarce resident in Kalimantan and widespread scarce nomad to all parts of Borneo. Also possible winter migrant to Borneo from continental Asia where it is widespread and common. Inhabits swamps, marshes, jungle pools and mangroves. Easily confused with Wandering Whistling Duck, but the white at the base of the tail is limited to a patch on either side and does not form a band across the full width of the tail. **Call:** 'Utters shrill high-pitched *tsee-tsee, tchee-tchee* while on wing and also when rising from water' (Kear). **Range:** India to S China, Thailand, Malay P, Sumatra, Java, Borneo.

2   WANDERING WHISTLING DUCK   *Dendrocygna arcuata*   45cm   Common resident

Common resident of Kalimantan lakes where it is locally abundant and heavily hunted. Recent breeding records from Miri, Seria, Wasan, Likas, Tempasuk Plain, Sandakan and Tawan. Easily confused with Lesser Whistling Duck. Distinguished in flight by white or fawn U-shaped patch across the rump sometimes broken in the middle, whereas Lesser Whistling Duck has only a small patch of white,or fawn on either side of the tail. When resting distinguished by black speckling at base of neck and clear white scallops on side of body more prominent than Lesser Whistling Duck white markings. **Call:** Shrill polysyllabic twittering *we-wi-wi-wi-wi-wi-whew*, described as 'a rapid descending whistle' (Kear). **Range:** NE Australia, to Java, Sulawesi and Philippines.

3   SUNDA TEAL   *Anas gibberifrons*   42cm   Scarce resident

[Indonesian Teal] Scarce resident of Kalimantan, but no confirmed breeding records. Feeds in both saltwater mangroves and freshwater lakes. Male Sunda Teal is distinguished by prominent bulbous forehead. Otherwise very similar to Australasian Grey Teal, which occurs in Sulawesi and could wander to Borneo, but Sunda Teal is also darker and browner. Both species sometimes have pale or white areas on face and neck, and both look similar in flight with a prominent white speculum, or wing marking. **Call:** 'Male clear *pip* note, female wild laughing cackle especially at night' (McKinnon). **Range:** Java, Bali, SE Sumatra, S Borneo.

ENDANGERED DUCKS AND THE WILDFOWL AND WETLANDS TRUST (WWT)
The White-winged Duck *Asarcornis scutulata* (not illustrated) is a very rare duck which inhabits swamp forest in Sumatra. In Java it has recently become extinct. In Borneo it was probably resident until recently but was never recorded. In 1946 Sir Peter Scott founded the Severn Wildfowl Trust to assist in the captive breeding of rare ducks

Saving wetlands
for wildlife & people

and geese and to establish wet-land refuges where waterbirds could be safe from hunting and habitat destruction. Scott's initiative developed into Wetland Link International (WLI) a grouping of over 100 wetland centres throughout the world. In Asia WLI members include Sungei Buloh (Singapore),Wetland Park (Hong Kong), Kushiro Wetland Centre (Japan). In Sabah the City Bird Sanctuary (Likas) Kota Kinabalu was established to preserve nesting Purple Herons threatened by development. In Sarawak, Loagan Bunut NP preserves peatswamp forest. In Kalimantan, Yayasan Konservasi RASI works to preserve rare aquatic species in the Mahakam River and Lakes. www.wwt.org.uk   www.wli.org.uk

Migrant ducks breed in N Asia and winter north of Borneo in S China, south to the Philippines with a few 'overshooting' each year. After breeding, the majority of male ducks moult into an 'eclipse plumage', similar to the duller female plumage. Ducks usually occur in Borneo in eclipse, in which case the best means of identification is the colour or pattern of the speculum, that part of the wing bar that can be seen when the duck is at rest. Usually seen in small groups. Migrant ducks are most likely to occur between September to April in freshwater marshes and padi fields on the NW coast of Borneo. The best localities to look for these rare vagrants are **Sabah:** Tempasuk swamps, Likas Swamp near KK, Padas Damit on the S coast of the Klias Peninsula, Benoni padi fields near Papar. **Brunei:** Wasan rice scheme. **Sarawak:** Tg Sirik, Loagan Bunut. **Kalimantan:** Kapuas, Negara and Mahakam Lakes.

1   MALLARD   *Anas platyrhynchos*   **58cm**   Vagrant
The commonest duck in Europe is a scarce winter vagrant to Borneo. Look for blue and white speculum. **Call:** Distinctive harsh loud quack or series of half quacks strung together. **Range:** Breeds Europe to E Asia and N America, winters southwards.

2   TUFTED DUCK   *Aythya fuligula*   **42cm**   Vagrant
Winter vagrant. Prefers freshwater but sometimes seen along the coast. Look for crest in both male and female. Recent records from Tawau and Tuaran, Sabah. **Range:** Breeds Europe to E Asia and winters south.

3   GARGANEY   *Anas querquedula*   **40cm**   Scarce migrant
Commonest migrant duck, very rarely occurs in substantial flocks, e.g. hundreds at Wasan Brunei (1989) and thousands at Padas Damit (1984) but generally very scarce. Recorded from interior padi fields, Mahakam Lakes and occasionally rivers. Look for white eyebrow in male. **Call:** Strange crackling sound. **Range:** Breeds Europe to Japan, winters south.

4   NORTHERN SHOVELER   *Anas clypeata*   **50cm**   Vagrant
Scarce winter visitor. Look for extra large bill, flattened at the end. **Call:** Mallard-like quack. **Range:** Breeds Europe to E Asia and N America, winters southwards.

5   EURASIAN WIGEON   *Anas penelope*   **47cm**   Vagrant
Winter vagrant. Look for pale cap in male. **Call:** Descending whistle. **Range:** Breeds Europe to Japan, winters southwards.

6   NORTHERN PINTAIL   *Anas acuta*   **55cm**   Rare migrant
Second commonest migrant duck but very scarce. Look for different shape from other ducks. Long slim tail and long neck. Recent record from Tawau Nov. 2012. Wong T.S. **Range:** Breeds Europe to E Asia and N America, winters south**.**

7   COMMON TEAL   *Anas crecca*   **37cm**   Vagrant
Winter vagrant. Look for small size, dark head and green speculum. Also cream triangle on side of rump of male. **Call:** Short whistle. **Range:** Breeds Europe to Japan, winters southwards.

8   COTTON TEAL   *Nettapus coromandelianus*   **32cm**   Scarce migrant
[Davison: Cotton Pygmy-Goose] A scarce winter visitor to NW Borneo. Possibly also an austral migrant from the south to the lakes of Kalimantan, where it may also breed in small numbers. Very small. Nests in tree holes and sometimes perches in trees. **Call:** Male has loud distinctive rattling call in flight (Kear). **Range:** India to Malay P, Sumatra, Java, Borneo, Sulawesi, Philippines, N Guinea.

9   PACIFIC BLACK DUCK   *Anas superciliosa*   **55cm**   Vagrant from Indonesia
One record of a flock of five from the Mahakam delta in Nov. 1987. Look for striped head pattern of male. **Call:** Similar to Mallard. **Range:** Sumatra, Java, Sulawesi, to Pacific islands.

10   COMMON SHELDUCK   *Tadorna tadorna*   **60cm [Not illustrated]**
No formal record but villagers at Padas Damit (Klias, Sabah) reported that this duck occurred regularly during winter months. Unmistakable. Large upright white duck with green head and bright red bill and forehead. Has a rufous band across chest and a green panel along the trailing edge of the wing.

VAGRANT DUCKS recorded from the Philippines, but not yet from Borneo. Ruddy Shelduck, Spot-billed Duck, Gadwall, Common Pochard, Baer's Pochard, Greater Scaup.

SHEARWATERS AND PETRELS

PROCELLARIDAE/HYDROBATIDAE **World 80 species.** Tubenoses are highly pelagic seabirds, usually frequenting deep ocean waters or the edges of continental shelves. Their tube like nostrils which extend above the beak are an adaptation which allows them to drink saltwater.They only ever come to land, at night, to breed on remote islands, where they nest in large colonies in ground burrows. Islands which seem empty of life during the day can become a hive of activity at dusk. All birds illustrated have been recorded in the S China Sea but not necessarily around Borneo, where they are most likely to be seen after severe storms. Normally silent at sea. Sexes similar. Feed by diving for fish, squid and krill. Usually seen in small groups, occasionally alone. The best regional site for sea-watching is the Sunda Straits, between Java and Sumatra (Sept.–Nov.). See page 72 and 74 (map).

1   STREAKED SHEARWATER   *Calonectris leucomelas*   **48cm**   **Resident S China Sea**
Commonest shearwater in region. Typically seen low over the surface of the sea shearing through the wave tops with typical shearwater flap flap glide, flap flap glide flight on stiff wings. **Range:** Breeds on coastal islands from Hokkaido to S China and winters Sept.–July, in S China Sea, Moluccas, and N Australia.

2   WEDGE-TAILED SHEARWATER   *Puffinus pacificus*   **43cm**   **Oceanic visitor**
Less common than Streaked Shearwater in Borneo waters and most likely to be seen in uniformly dark brown (can appear black) morph as illustrated. A pale morph very similar to Streaked also occurs. **Range:** Breeds tropical Pacific and Indian Ocean islands and wanders after breeding.

3   SOOTY SHEARWATER   *Puffinus griseus*   **43cm**   **Not recorded**
Range: Breeds on islands in S Indian Ocean, SE Australia and New Zealand wandering north after breeding.

4   SHORT-TAILED SHEARWATER   *Puffinus tenuirostris*   **43cm**   **Not recorded**
Occurs in large flocks and often follows fishing trawlers. **Range:** Breeds SE Australia and Tasmania migrating to N Pacific and Japan Sea from June to August.

5   FLESH-FOOTED SHEARWATER   *Puffinus carneipes*   **43cm**   **Not recorded**
Often seen in N Zealand seas and harbours, feeding on fish waste. Flies low over the water with long glide. Distinguished from Wedge-tailed Shearwater by dark tipped, thick, pale bill (and white primary bases). **Range:** Breeds on islands in S Indian Ocean, S Australia, N Zealand migrating north May to August.

6   BULWER'S PETREL   *Bulweria bulwerii*   **27cm**   **Oceanic visitor**
A regular visitor to Borneo waters in small numbers. Less common than Brown Noddy with which it is easily confused. Brown Noddy has a longer bill and no pale band or crescent on the upper wing. Flight is tern like, twisting and erratic flying in wide circles then dropping down to pick food off the surface of the sea. **Range:** Breeds on tropical islands worldwide including islands off Taiwan and S China.

STORM-PETRELS (OCEANITIDAE): **World 20 species.** Small, dark seabirds with typical erratic butterfly or bat-like flight. Storm-petrels feed by picking food from the surface of the sea.

7   SWINHOE'S STORM-PETREL   *Oceanodroma monorhis*   **20cm**   **South China Sea migrant**
The only storm petrel confirmed for Borneo waters, with five records (Mann). All dark petrel with a moderately forked tail. **Range:** Breeds on islands off the coast of Japan and Korea and migrates south through the S China Sea to winter in the Indian Ocean. Migrates south through Sunda Straits in September.

8   MATSUDAIRA'S STORM-PETREL   *Oceanodroma matsudairae*   **20cm**   **Vagrant**
On recent September record in S. China Sea (Martin Wiles). Most likely to be seen in Sulu Sea, Macassar Strait or Java Sea between May to August each year. **Range:** Breeds on S Japan islands and migrates south through the Moluccas and Java Sea to winter in the Indian Ocean.

9   WILSON'S STORM-PETREL   *Oceanites oceanicus*   **20cm**   **Not recorded**
Possibly the commonest bird in the world though little seen because of its pelagic habits. Sometimes follows ships. **Range:** Breeds in huge numbers on the islands of the Antarctic Ocean and crosses the equator to winter in the Atlantic, Indian and Pacific Oceans. Most likely to be seen June to October, during the austral winter.

1

2

Pale
morph

Dark
morph

3

Not to scale

6

5

Not to scale

4

Not to scale

7

8

9

STORKS, IBISES AND SPOONBILLS MALAY: BURUNG UPEH

Storks (CICONIIDAE), ibises and spoonbills (THRESKIORNITHIDAE) are all large waterbirds with distinctive and differently shaped large bills, specialised for different types of aquatic prey. Apart from Storm's Stork and the White-shouldered Ibis, which are birds of riverside forest, the others are birds of coastal marshes and lakes. Sexes similar. Nest in colonies often with other waterbirds. Calls are undistinguished loud grunts. Unlike herons and egrets, which fly with the neck retracted, they fly with the neck fully extended and are capable of soaring on thermals for long periods on hot sunny days. They are generally rare in Borneo due to hunting and have not flourished like the egrets and herons, as the human population expands.

1 STORM'S STORK *Ciconia stormi* **85cm** **Scarce local resident**

An uncommon stork of forested rivers throughout Borneo. Occasionally feeds in padi fields, and marshes. Roosts and nests in tall emergent trees. **Sabah:** Locally common in E Sabah and often seen soaring over the Kinabatangan and Segama riverside forests, when white under tail is obvious. **Brunei:** Regularly seen. **Sarawak:** Rare. **Kalimantan:** Widespread but scarce.Tg Puting suspected breeding. **Range:** Malay P, Sumatra, Borneo. **BLI:** Endangered.

2 LESSER ADJUTANT *Leptoptilos javanicus* **115cm** **Local resident**

[Malay: Burung botak (bald)] Previously a common sight on mangrove mudflats and adjacent swamps throughout Borneo, now scarce as the young were often taken from nesting colonies to fatten for annual feasts. Individuals wander widely and still turn up in coastal marshes. When breeding has orange neck and red face. Breeding reported at Karindingan Island E Sabah, Mahakam Lakes, Tg Puting. **Range:** India to Malay P, Sumatra, Java, Borneo. **BLI:** Vulnerable.

3 WHITE-SHOULDERED IBIS *Pseudibis davisoni* **75cm** **Rare resident**

[Black Ibis P. pappilosa] A small relict population of probably fewer than 50 birds inhabits the riverside forest above Long Iram on the Mahakam river in E Kalimantan. Feeds on the river bank. Occasionally recorded elsewhere, e.g. Tg Puting, Mahakam Lakes. Roosts and nests in tall emergent trees. In flight distinguished by striking white panels on black wings not obvious when at rest: Bright red legs. Bare skin on neck varies in area and colour from blue to pale blue to grey or white in juvenile birds (Sozer). Ibis male is larger and has longer bill than female (Collar/Eames re Cambodia). **Range:** Two populations only, Cambodia and Kalimantan. **BLI:** Critical.

4 BLACK-HEADED IBIS *Threskiornis melanocephalus* **80cm** **Vagrant**

A rare vagrant from the Asian continent with a few winter records from coastal NW Borneo. **Range:** Breeds India to China, winters southwards.

5 GLOSSY IBIS *Plegadis falcinellus* **60cm** **Vagrant**

Several recent June and July records from Likas swamp and Wasan in NW coastal Borneo may be vagrants from a possible (unknown) breeding population in Kalimantan or even austral irruptive migrants. Also recorded as a rare winter visitor to NW Borneo. Recent record one bird Pantai Air Hitam Ketapang, W. Kalimantan, 25 Jan. 2013 (Abdurahman al Qadrie). Worldwide this bird is expanding its range and is resident in surrounding areas. **Range:** S Europe, Africa, SW Asia and India to Java, Sulawesi, Philippines and Australia. Central and South America.

6 ROYAL SPOONBILL *Platalea regia* **80cm** **Not recorded**

Spoonbills seen in Kalimantan are most likely to be this species, a vagrant to Indonesia from Australia. Formerly bred NW Java at Pulau Dua and resident in much of Indonesia. Unlike the Black-faced Spoonbill there are red and yellow markings on the head. Very similar Eurasian Spoonbill *P. leucorodia* could also occur as a vagrant to NW Borneo (Davison). **Range:** Java, Lesser Sundas, Sulawesi, Moluccas, S New Guinea, Australia, to Solomons.

7 BLACK-FACED SPOONBILL *Platalea minor* **75cm** **Vagrant**

One definite Brunei sighting (Mann) and several possible sightings from Sabah and Sarawak. Total world population is c. 700 birds of which up to 170 winter in Hong Kong. Easily confused with Royal Spoonbill but bill is grey rather than black and there are no red or yellow spots on the face. Both species develop crests and yellow breast plumage in the breeding season. Spoonbills on NW Borneo coast are most likely this species but see above. **Range:** Breeds NE China, Korea, winters south to Hong Kong, and rarely Philippines. **BLI:** Endangered.

NIGHT HERONS

GORSACHIUS NIGHT HERONS **World 3 species; Borneo 2 species.** *Gorsachius* night herons are endangered forest herons which build stick nests in trees in their breeding grounds in N Asia. These herons feed on frogs and worms in damp areas of dense forest often along streams. Usually crepuscular or nocturnal. Two species are rare migrants to Borneo, and breeding calls are unlikely to be heard.

1   JAPANESE NIGHT HERON   *Gorsachius goisagi*   49cm   Vagrant

Status uncertain. Wintering individuals recorded annually at the Panaga Club (Seria Brunei) since October 1985 until the present may be Malaysian N. H. See www.borneobirdimages. com and make up your own mind! Unlike Malaysian Night Heron there is no very distinctive immature plumage. More uniform in colour than Malaysian with dark rufous shaggy head feathers rather than a clear black cap. In both species lores (bare skin in front of eye) are normally grey but can vary from bright blue (breeding) to pale yellow in young birds. **Call:** Deep monotonous ***booh-booh*** calls at night in the breeding season (Shimba). **Range:** Breeds Japan, Korea, winters Philippines and Sulawesi. **BLI:** Endangered.

2   MALAYSIAN NIGHT HERON   *Gorsachius melanolophus*   49cm   Rare migrant

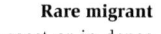

[Tiger Bittern] On migration to Borneo, it can turn up anywhere, on the coast or in dense forest. Although active at night, has often been seen during the day. Has white tips to primary feathers (Japanese has tawny tips) which are only obvious in flight. Often seen in speckled immature plumage in which plumage it may breed (elsewhere). **Call:** Monotonous honk described as ***wu wu wu*** at night in the breeding season. **Range:** There is a famous breeding colony in the Taipei Botanic Gardens. Also breeds Hainan, S China, Thailand, Vietnam, Philippines migrating south to Malay P, Sumatra and Borneo in winter.

NYCTICORAX NIGHT HERONS **World 2 species; Borneo 2 species.** Stocky, short-necked night herons, which leave their day time roosting colonies at dusk to feed in padi fields, swamps and coastal lagoons all night. They often breed in mixed colonies with other herons and egrets, where they eat the eggs and nestlings of other colonists. Elsewhere nesting colonies are often in the centre of busy city parks or zoos. Sexes are similar. Both sexes develop two long white nape plumes when breeding. Juveniles are heavily streaked. Like many herons worldwide, they are increasing in population and range as they benefit from irrigation schemes and the expansion of rice growing. The previously geographically separated populations of Common Night-Herons from the Asian continent and Rufous Night Herons from Australia now have overlapping ranges in Java, Borneo and the Philippines as a result.

3   RUFOUS NIGHT HERON   *Nycticorax caledonicus*   61cm   Locally common resident

[Nankeen Night Heron] Until recently, this bird was almost unknown in Borneo, now it is a scarce but widespread local breeder in small colonies near Kota Kinabalu and has recently been recorded nesting in the centre of Semporna town, E Sabah. Failed breeding attempt at Serasa, Brunei in 1988 (Mann). Immature birds have been mistaken for Malaysian Night Herons which are smaller, with longer necks, smaller heads and much shorter stubby bills. Breeding records: **Sabah:** Semporna, Likas mangroves, Padas River, Papar, Tamparuli. **Brunei:** Serasa. **Sarawak:** Lawas mangroves. (Musa Musba) **Kalimantan:** No breeding records but has been seen at the Kapuas Lakes (NW Kalimantan). **Range:** An Australasian species expanding north to Borneo. Resident in the S Philippines.

4   BLACK-CROWNED NIGHT HERON   *Nycticorax nycticorax*   61cm   Local resident

[Common Night Heron] A widespread and locally common resident in coastal areas and wet padi fields and also a winter visitor from the Asian Continent. Recorded throughout Borneo but commonest in NW Sabah, e.g. 600 roosting at Tempasuk Plain in December 1985 (Lansdowne). Breeding records: **Sabah:** Jalan Jelatik (Likas Swamp), Sungai Darau (UKM Campus KK), Sitompok Lake (Kuala Penyu). **Brunei:** Tasek Merimbun. **Sarawak:** Long Ansok (Sungai Baram). **Kalimantan:** Tg Puting. **Range:** Breeds warm wet areas worldwide apart from E Indonesia and Australia where it is replaced by the Rufous Night Heron. Some northern populations winter south including Borneo.

1

imm.

2

imm.

imm.

3

breeding

4

breeding

BITTERNS

World 12 species; Borneo 5 species. Bitterns are members of the heron family (Ardeidae).Solitary feeders using their camouflage plumage and motionless stance to catch fish and tadpoles by surprise as they swim past in their swampy habitats. Unlike most herons and night herons, bitterns do not normally breed or roost communally. The resident bitterns are not very vocal but like most herons make a harsh **kark** or **kack** alarm call when disturbed. The immature birds are heavily streaked and difficult to distinguish between species. Females are similar to immatures. Both bitterns and night herons have been regularly trapped as night flying migrants in the Philippines and Malaya. Due to cryptic coloration often only seen when flushed from a roadside ditch. Nest alone in marshy areas in a domed nest made of reeds and grasses, on the ground or in low trees. Like other herons the bitterns take off with the neck extended but fly with neck retracted.

1 EURASIAN BITTERN *Botaurus stellaris* **76cm** **Vagrant**

[Davison: Great Bittern] The well known Bittern of Europe and N Asia is a scarce vagrant to Borneo. In Europe inhabits dense reed beds and is usually only detected by loud booming call in spring breeding season, unlikely to be heard in Borneo. Distinguished by large size. **Sabah:** One shot (1985). Photographed 13.12.09 in padi fields at Penampang (Karim Madoya). **Brunei:** Wasan padi fields twice early 1987 (Mann). **Range:** Breeds Europe to Asia, winter vagrant to SE Asia.

2 YELLOW BITTERN *Ixobrychus sinensis* **38cm** **Common resident and migrant**

Thirty years ago the Yellow Bittern was an uncommon winter visitor to Sabah. Nowadays it is a very common resident of padi fields, swamps and drainage ditches in cultivated areas. Increasing in Brunei. Scarce in Sarawak. More common than Cinnamon Bittern in Kalimantan (van Balen, Gonner). Often seen in streaky, immature or female plumage. Look for black shoulder patches in adults and black tips to wings and tail in all plumages. **Call:** Breeding call is a repeated soft **crrrew crrrew**. **Range:** Breeds Asia, winters SE Asia.

3 CINNAMON BITTERN *Ixobrychus cinnamomeus* **40cm** **Common resident and migrant**

Previously the commonest bittern in swamps and padi fields throughout Borneo, but appears to have declined in competition with the less shy and rapidly expanding Yellow Bittern. Prefers thicker vegetation than Yellow Bittern and unlike Yellow Bittern not so often seen in the open. Unlike the Yellow Bittern has no black on wing or tail tips in all plumages. **Call:** Breeding call is a rapid repeated soft **kok kok kok** (Wells). **Range:** Breeds Asia. Some birds move south in winter to India and SE Asia.

4 SCHRENCK'S BITTERN *Ixobrychus eurhythmus* **37cm** **Scarce winter visitor**

[Davison: von Schrenk's Bittern] A small dark bittern with rufous back and pale grey on wings. Females and the similar juveniles are distinguished by the white and buff spots on back and upper wing (Kushlan). Typical bittern habits, a shy migrant to dense swamps, throughout Borneo. Rarely seen, probably due to nocturnal habits, but regularly recorded as a vagrant on migration in NW Borneo. One bird wintered in the lily pond at the Danum Valley Field Centre. **Range:** Breeds N Asia, winters SE Asia.

5 BLACK BITTERN *Dupetor flavicollis* **56cm** **Scarce migrant and local resident**

Locally common in forest ponds and swampy areas at forest edges. Crepuscular and nocturnal. Benefits from logging and forest ponds caused by blocked streams. Very scarce W Sabah but common in E Sabah, and the commonest bittern of the SE Kalimantan Barito and Negara River swamps and lakes and the Mahakam Lakes in E Kalimantan. In Kalimantan it is believed to be both a resident and an austral migrant (Gonner). Possibly the only Bornean bird which is a northern migrant, an austral migrant and a local breeding resident. Back and wing colour varies from dark grey to black. Female is a very dark brown rather than black. Look for distinctive large yellow whiskers on either side of throat. **Call:** Breeding call is a loud repeated **w h o o o** (Pizzey). **Range:** Breeds N Asia winters south. Also resident in Australia and disperses north.

1

2

imm.

♂

3

imm.

♀

♂

4

♀

♂

♀

♂

5

♂

♀

POND HERONS AND STRIATED HERONS MALAY: BURUNG PUCUNG

POND HERONS **World 4 species; Borneo 2 species.** Pond herons are closely related to the Squacco Heron of southern Europe. When flying past, they look like brown cattle egrets with white wings, but on landing they fold their white wings and seem to disappear into the landscape. In winter they occur in a drab eclipse or non-breeding plumage in which is impossible to tell the two species that occur in Borneo apart. The Chinese Pond Heron is only a winter visitor from N Asia so any pond heron seen between June and August is almost certainly a Javan Pond Heron.

1   CHINESE POND HERON   *Ardeola bacchus*   **45cm**   **Scarce migrant to NW Borneo**

Previously a rare winter visitor from Asia but now seen regularly in the padi fields and swamps of NW Borneo south to Kuching. Normally seen in eclipse plumage but can only be reliably distinguished from Javan Pond Heron in breeding plumage, which is usually seen only on arrival in October and before departure in April. It is claimed that non-breeding birds retain dusky wing tips unlike Javan Pond Heron but these markings are not obvious even in photographs. **Range:** Breeds S China, Thailand and winters south to Philippines.

2   STRIATED HERON   *Butorides striata*   **45cm**   **Common resident and migrant**

[Davison: Little Heron] [Little Green Heron] The smallest and commonest heron in Borneo found wherever there are fish and crabs to be caught from the seashore to remote river banks in the interior. Usually seen alone in the open, crouched completely still waiting for prey to swim past. Solitary and very territorial when feeding, driving off other herons. Often crepuscular, and in harbours feeds at night by artificial light. Female has brownish tinge to flanks. When breeding legs turn bright orange. Usually nests in loose colonies, building a stick nest in the mangroves but has been recorded nesting on a steel oil platform 10km off the Brunei coast. **Call:** Like most herons flies off with a loud *kraark* when alarmed. **Range:** Breeds tropical areas worldwide. Migrant race **B. s. amurensis** (larger) is a regular winter visitor to Borneo from the Asian Continent but comparative numbers are not known.

3   JAVAN POND HERON   *Ardeola speciosa*   **45cm**   **Common resident Kalimantan**

Abundant resident of the swamps and lakes of south and E Kalimantan and a locally common winter visitor to Sabah and Sarawak where it was unknown until recently. Normally seen in eclipse (non-breeding) plumage when it is easily confused with Chinese Pond Heron. See above. At height of breeding season develops two white nape plumes and reddish legs. Pond herons in NW Borneo between June and August are likely to be this species. Numerous recent sight records indicate breeding at Tempasuk Plain, Sabah. **Range:** Breeds SE Asia to Malay P, Sumatra, Java, Sulawesi, Mindanao, Lesser Sundas.

BIRDS THAT REACH BORNEO FROM MAINLAND CHINA
Only a small proportion of the birds that breed in mainland China spend the winter in Borneo. Most migrants to Borneo come from further north in E Russia or Japan. The majority of resident breeders that leave China in the autumn follow the Asian coastline southward to Thailand and the Malay Peninsula. Some of these continue on through Sumatra to Java, and further east. However, a variety of birds from mainland China do reach Borneo.
Some examples of Chinese breeding birds that winter in Borneo. Black-capped Kingfisher, Mugimaki Flycatcher, Siberian Blue Robin, Grey Heron, Chinese Pond Heron, Honey Buzzard.
Chinese breeding birds that transit in Borneo. Oriental Plover, Pacific Swift.
Staging posts for passage waders through China that also transit in Borneo. Yalu Jiang on the coast of the Yellow Sea is a major staging post for waders en-route to Borneo and Australia. Other staging posts include Chongming Dao island (Shanghai) and the Mai Po marshes and Deep Bay in Hong Kong. Beijing Bird Watching Society www.cbw.org.cn and www.wwfchina.org/birdgallery/
The most important bird club in China is www.chinabirdnet.org. See also: Wild Bird Society of Shanghai http://shwbs.org
The Hong Kong Bird Watching Society (HKBWS) www.hkbws.org.hk

1

non-breeding

breeding.

2

imm.

adult

3

non-breeding

breeding

LARGE HERONS AND WHITE-FACED HERON   MALAY: BURUNG PUCUNG

ARDEIDAE **World 14 species; Borneo 3 species.** *Ardea* herons are the world's largest herons and include the giant Goliath Heron of Africa. Males and females are similar. Juveniles are streaky and duller than adults. Usually feed alone but roost and breed communally, sometimes in mixed colonies with other herons. Often crepuscular, feeding at dusk. The three Borneo species are found in different habitats, with Grey and Purple Herons showing a preference for freshwater padi fields and irrigation ditches. Most herons can thrive in populated areas as long as they are not persecuted. Unlike storks, ibis, spoonbill and cormorants which fly with the nect extended all herons and egrets fly with the the neck retracted.

1   GREY HERON *Ardea cinerea* **95cm**   Scarce migrant possible resident

The well-known Grey Heron of Europe and N Asia was a rare winter migrant to the whole of Borneo until recently when it has become relatively common in the swamps and padi fields in NW Sabah. Also recorded at Tg Puting where it may breed. Where it is not persecuted it is not shy. Usually fishes by standing motionless at the edge of open freshwater. Has been seen year round, but the summer birds are most likely first year non-breeding migrants. Breeding birds develop bright orange bills and pink legs. **Breeding:** Currently no confirmed records, but increasingly likely. Normally nests in colonies in tall trees close to water. **Call:** Harsh alarm *kraak* as it flies off. **Range:** Breeds Europe to Asia. Northern populations winter south.

2   PURPLE HERON *Ardea purpurea* **85cm**   Local resident and scarce migrant

The Purple Heron is a shy bird of reed and *Acrostichum* swamps (illustrated) and padi fields, often seen in camouflage 'dead stick' pose with neck vertically extended. In winter the population is increased by some migrants from Asia. Nests in small colonies on the ground or in low bushes in the middle of remote swamps. Breeding records: **Sabah:** Likas Bird Sanctuary, KK, Padas Damit, Binsulok. **Brunei:** Wasan, Tasek Merimbun. **Sarawak:** Mukah (old record). **Kalimantan:** Mahakam Lakes, Kuala Mahakam, Tg Puting, Lamandau. **Call:** Harsh croaks. **Range:** Breeds Europe to E Asia. Northern populations winter south.

3   GREAT-BILLED HERON *Ardea sumatrana* **115cm**   Scarce resident

[Dusky-grey Heron] [Giant Heron]. The largest Borneo heron and the only large heron regularly seen along the shore. Normally solitary and very shy. Uncommon but widespread around the Bornean coast. Especially associated with mangroves. Also found along interior rivers often far inland, e.g. at Danum. Underwing is uniform grey in flight unlike underwing pattern of Grey Herons (see illustration). Breeding birds develop long whitish plumes on breast and back. Breeding records from Mahakam Lakes and Kapuas Lakes (NW Kalimantan) Kakaban and Maratua lagoon (E. Kalimantan). **Range:** Coasts of SE Asia south to N Australia.

4   WHITE-FACED HERON *Egretta novaehollandiae* **67cm**   Vagrant

A dispersive Australian species which has been recorded as far north as Taiwan. In Australia common on farms and in urban areas. Distinguished from dark morph of Reef Egret by white face and throat and pale grey body with buffy chest band, not uniform dark grey plumage. Flight pattern is similar to Grey Heron as illustrated with dark primary wing feathers contrasting strongly with pale grey underwing. Two records only, P Mataking E Sabah in March 2004 (Davison 2007) and P Banggi N Sabah (R. Subaraj, 1976).

HERON AND EGRET FEEDING STRATEGIES
Most herons are cryptically coloured 'stand and wait' predators which feed alone. In contrast the white egrets have two entirely different methods of feeding. The first method is to watch where other egrets have found abundant prey such as fish trapped in tidal pools and join in the feeding frenzy. The extra disturbance flushes additional prey so that all individual flock members benefit. Thus all egrets are able to gain from their white 'signal' plumage. Conversely, white plumage may be a disadvantage in standing and waiting for prey, so lone egrets have a second method of feeding. They walk fast along the shore or bank of a ditch, flushing frogs and fish and snatching or stabbing them as they try to escape. Lone egrets normally defend a feeding territory but long-legged Great Egrets that wade in deep water will often associate with a single shorter legged egret such as a Little or Chinese Egret that wades in shallower water, each taking advantage of fish escaping the other.

EGRETS

World 14 species; Borneo 6 species including the aberrant Cattle Egret. Egrets (*Ardeidae*) is a collectiv name for white herons. Egrets both roost and breed in colonies, often in mangroves. Sexes are similar. Whe breeding the legs, bill, iris and lores change colour but with much individual variation. Most egrets, but two i particular, the Intermediate and Chinese Egrets, develop striking fluffy back, breast and nape plumes (aigrettes when breeding. Most of the egrets seen in Borneo are winter visitors (Oct.–April) but there is increasing evidence of a population explosion and local breeding. Many first year migrants also spend the summer i Borneo. When distinguishing egrets the differing habitats and habits of the different species are very useful, bu like most herons, egrets are highly adaptable and are often found behaving untypically when food is available Egrets are usually silent but make harsh calls when startled.

1   LITTLE EGRET   *Egretta garzetta*   **60cm**   **Common migrant and local residen**

Second commonest egret. Normally fishes alone along the seashore, in swamps or wet pad fields. Occasionally in large flocks, e.g. when following a tractor. The only small egret wit all black bill and legs. Two races occur, one *E. g. garzetta* with yellow feet the other *E. g nigripes* (less common) with black feet. *E. g. garzetta* often stirs its yellow foot in water t attract fish as toes look like worms. Breeding records: **Sabah:** None. **Brunei:** Seria. **Sarawak** None. **Kalimantan:** Mahakam Lakes, Sg Negara, Tg Puting. **Range:** Breeds Europe to E Asia Northern populations winter south. Known to be rapidly expanding its range in Europe.

2   INTERMEDIATE EGRET   *Egretta intermedia*   **70cm**   **Common migrant and local residen**

[Plumed Egret]. Less common than Great and Little but not scarce. Feeds in damp grasslan and drainage ditches on frogs and tadpoles, often alone. Intermediate in size between Littl and Great but closer to Little. Like Great has a yellow bill but usually with a blackish tip. Littl has all black bill. Long neck is not as long or as 'kinked' as Great. Line of gape stops below eye, unlike Great where it extends well beyond eye. Breeding records: Likas KK, Mahakan Lakes and Tg Puting. **Range:** Breeds NE Asia, winters south.

3   GREAT EGRET   *Ardea alba*   **95cm**   **Common migrant and local residen**

[Great Egret *Casmerodius albus*] [Great White Heron] [Eastern Great Egret *Ardea modesta* Increasingly common both as a winter visitor and resident breeder in Sabah. Feeds singl along the seashore or river bank, sometimes in flocks in padi fields. In KK, common yea round feeding in lagoons trapped by reclamation bunds. All black legs turn pink when breedin and yellow beak darkens. Breeding records: **Sabah:** Likas, Kinabatangan, Tawau (Wong TS) **Brunei:** Present all year. **Sarawak:** No records. **Kalimantan:** Mahakam Lakes, Tg Puting Lamandau. **Range:** Breeds India, China, Japan to Australia. Northern populations winter south

4   CATTLE EGRET   *Bubulcus ibis*   **50cm**   **Abundant migran**

[Eastern Cattle Egret *Bulbucus coromandus*] Commonest egret. Feeds on grassland insects, n fish. Often feeds on or around grazing cattle or buffaloes, by roadsides and on rubbish dumps Distinguished from Little Egret by yellow bill and short neck. Look for orange breeding patches o arrival from and before departure to northern breeding grounds. Population is increasing but n local breeding records yet. Large winter roosts at Likas (Sabah) and Seria (Brunei) in mangroves Some birds present all year. **Range:** Breeds E Asia. Borneo birds are from Taiwan, Japan.

THE LEGEND OF THE KANAWY PUTIH OR WHITE EGRET

Amongst coastal dwellers on the NW coast of Borneo there are a number of traditional stories or legends associated with white egrets, or Kanawy putih. Because the majority of egrets are migrants and no nests were ever found, egrets were believed to belong to invisible beneficent forest spirits and to provide those spirits with information about events in the human world. From their habit of feeding or roosting by river banks egrets see all the boat traffic that passes by. In olden days rivers were the main highways of Borneo and it was believed that egrets reported to their masters what was happening in the real world. A similar related belief was that white egrets were the spirits of those who had passed away. These traditional beliefs meant that even today egrets are generally safe from being hunted for food in Sabah, unlike other storks and herons. (Adapted from Motley re. Labuan 1855)

1

e.g. nigripes

E.g. garzetta

2

line of gape

br.

non br.

line of gape

br.

3

non br.

4

non br.

br.

CHINESE AND REEF EGRETS

Along Sabah's west coast, the commonest egrets in order of abundance October–May are; Cattle, Little, Great, Intermediate, Reef (dark morph), Chinese, and Reef (white morph). All 6 species are present around Kota Kinabalu and all 7 forms are easily seen in winter months. Chinese and Reef Egret (white morph) are often confused, but can be told apart by differences in bill colour, posture and habitat. In addition, the Chinese Egret is sometimes seen in full breeding plumage on arrival or just before departure north when its long feathery plumes and bright blue lores are distinctive. Little Egret's all black bill and black legs distinguish it from both. Being the scarcest egret in Borneo, reports of white Reef Egrets being seen in large flocks are usually mistaken Chinese Egret flocks.

1 CHINESE EGRET *Egretta eulophotes* 66cm — Scarce winter visitor

[Swinhoe's Egret] A scarce winter migrant to Borneo from N Asia. Usually seen singly, stalking for mudskippers or crabs on mudflats, or fishing along the seashore. Walks upright rapidly along the shore often chasing after small fish with open wings in the shallows. Distinguished from white morph Reef Egret by its less heavy bill, by bill colour (dark with a yellowish tinge to the base of the lower bill), and by extensive nape and back plumes in the breeding plumage. Generally a slimmer, taller more elegant shape, similar to Little Egret. **Sabah:** STAR, Sutera Harbour, Likas Bay. **Brunei:** Brunei Bay, Serasa, Seria, Kuala Tutong. **Sarawak:** Pulau Bruit, Bako, Buntal. **Kalimantan:** Mahakam Delta, Mahakam Lakes, Kutai. **Range:** Breeds in the Yellow Sea between Korea and China and Sea of Japan near Russia on rocky islands, migrating south to the Philippines and Borneo where most of the world population spends the winter months. **BLI:** Vulnerable.

2 PACIFIC REEF EGRET *Egretta sacra* 62cm — Common resident

[Eastern Reef Heron] [Malay: Pucung batu (stone heron)] Both dark and white morphs are locally common and widespread along the Borneo coast. Especially favours rocky sea walls near coastal towns. Usually seen alone feeding from rocks or reef flats at low tide, only occasionally on sandy or muddy shores. Stalks steadily along a rocky coastline in a crouched posture. Stockier and more chunky than Chinese Egret. Has short stout upper leg (tibia) which enables it to hunt easily by crouching forward. Dark and white morphs often associate in small parties with dark morph more common. In W Sabah white morph is usually 10–20% of the population. On coral islands, e.g. Sipadan, Maratua, proportion is usually 50:50. Juvenile white morphs have a distinctive spotted plumage, and a few spots may linger on in white adults. When breeding may have a tuft of head feathers and a few extra plumes on back but not very obvious. Beak colour very variable usually dull grey or yellowish. Breeds on small rocky islands simultaneously with terns April to July so that it can predate the tern chicks to feed its own brood. Breeding records. **Sabah:** Rocky islands off Labuan, Tg Nosong cliffs near Pulau Tiga and recently at Sutera Harbour, K. K. **Brunei:** Pelong Rocks. **Sarawak:** Tukong Ara in Santubong Bay. **Range:** Strictly coastal from E India to Australia and Pacific islands, north to Japan.

CHINESE EGRETS AND THE WORLD'S LARGEST BIRD CONSERVATION ORGANISATION, THE RSPB

At the end of the nineteenth century London was the centre of a massive global trade in bird feathers used as fashion accessories. The feathers most in demand were the decorative egret breeding plumes known as 'aigrettes'. Breeding colonies of Chinese and Intermediate Egrets were being wiped out worldwide as breeding birds were shot at their nests. The result was a population crash from which the Chinese Egret appears never to have fully recovered. The campaign to stop the slaughter resulted in the foundation of the RSPB (The Royal Society for the Protection of Birds) in 1889, now the world's largest bird conservation organisation with over one million members in the UK.

Today the RSPB manages over 200 nature reserves in the UK which attract over 1.5m visitors a year and has many overseas projects. One of the most important of these is the Harapan Rainforest project in Sumatra. By agreement with the Indonesian Government, 100,000ha of logged lowland rainforest are being restored to maximise plant and wildlife diversity. Management is by a partnership of the RSPB, Burung Indonesia, and BirdLife International, with funding provided by partners and external sources. Unlike Borneo, Sumatra has very rich volcanic soils suitable for agriculture and Sumatra's forest birds are under even greater threat than they are in Borneo. The foundation of the RSPB in 1889 probably saved the Chinese Egret from extinction and still today the work of the RSPB is important in preserving the region's birdlife.

www.rspb.org   www.burung.org   www.birdlife.org   www.rainforestsos.org

1

note two-tone bill

non-breeding

breeding

2

breeding
dark morph

breeding
white morph

2

imm.
white morph

non-breeding
white morph

FRIGATEBIRDS

FREGATIDAE **World 5 species; Borneo 3 species, all oceanic visitors.** Each of the three species of frigatebird seen around the Borneo coast has eight different distinguishable plumages, all illustrated here for each species. Frigatebirds do not breed until they are five years old and each year, from the juvenile to the fully adult bird, the plumage changes. In the first two years the young sexes of each species are similar and cannot be distinguished. In the third year males and females begin to develop distinctly different plumages (James).

Habits: Frigatebirds are large seabirds which breed on remote tropical islands and wander long distances to feed. They can be seen along the coast taking advantage of the updrafts over small islands to hang in the air for hours without flapping their wings. Frigatebirds can stay aloft for weeks but more usually are based around small widely scattered roost islands where they spend the night. Most flocks seen in Borneo comprise a majority of Lesser, a few Christmas Island and the occasional Great. At the beginning of November when the strong winds of the NE monsoon hit the west coast of Borneo flocks of frigatebirds can often be seen 'riding the storm' as it tears south down the coast.

Calls: Frigatebirds are not known to make any loud or distinctive calls whilst at sea (Nelson).

Feeding: Frigatebirds are surface feeders picking fish or squid off the surface of the sea. They are known to follow large predatory fish which drive schools of small fish towards the sea surface. In Borneo waters frigatebirds are rarely seen to feed but sometimes follow trawlers. Owing to their minimal energy requirements frigatebirds can go for weeks without food.

Breeding: Although frigatebirds do not breed in Borneo waters, they are often seen along the Borneo coast. All frigatebird males develop an inflated large red throat sac during the breeding season. The sac takes an hour to inflate and is used to show off to females during 'fly past' breeding displays. In Borneo, only a red patch of throat skin can be seen. Frigatebirds begin breeding in their fifth year but even then only produce one young every two years. Therefore population recruitment is very low, and frigatebirds must be very long lived.

Kleptoparasitism: Typically frigatebirds only breed near nesting colonies of boobies. Boobies returning from a successful fishing expedition are assaulted by a frigatebird and forced to drop their fish prey, which is then snatched by the frigatebird and fed to its own young. This feeding strategy is known as kleptoparasitism, a habit shared with skuas. See page 144.

Flight: Frigatebirds are the most aerial of all the world's seabirds with the lowest weight to wing surface ratio. They rarely alight on the surface of the sea but can take off again if necessary. They usually nest in trees, but on some remote Pacific islands they nest on the ground, relying on strong sea winds to provide enough lift for take off.

Predation: Around Borneo frigatebirds roost after dark and leave the roost island just before dawn, it is thought, to avoid predation by locally common White-bellied Sea Eagles.

LESSER FRIGATEBIRD *Fregata ariel* **76cm**   **Common oceanic visitor**

The smallest and commonest frigatebird around the coast of Borneo often seen in small flocks along all coasts. Commonest Sept.–Oct. Least common March to May but seen in every month of the year roosting on P Satang Kechil (Harrison). Occasionally in large flocks, e.g. up to two thousand near Mantanani in March 1982 amongst which were tens of Christmas Island Frigates and less than ten Great (Sheldon). In late October 2005, of a flock of 300 over Mantanani Island around half were Christmas Island Frigates, mixed females and immatures and the other half were Lesser, again mainly females and immatures. There were no Great in the flock. **Range:** The nearest breeding colonies are on islands around the north coasts of Australia from the Lacepede islands off the NW coast to the NE islands of the Great Barrier Reef. Also breeds on oceanic islands in the W Pacific, S Atlantic and Indian Ocean.

FRIGATEBIRD ROOSTING ISLANDS

Frigatebirds are most commonly seen in the vicinity of their roost islands, shared by all three species. Roost islands are very important to frigatebirds, because their feathers are easily waterlogged and they cannot rest on the sea. Favoured roost islands are small dome-shaped islands covered in sticky seeded *Pisonia grandis* trees. The dome shape of favoured roost islands allows frigatebirds to land and take off easily. Pisonia are dispersed by seabirds and usually confined to islands where seabirds breed. **Sabah:** P Maiga (Semporna), P Lungisan (Mantanani), and Kalampunian Damit aka P Ular (P Tiga). **Sarawak:** P Satang Kechil. **Kalimantan:** Pulau Samama (Derawan Islands). The Bajau name for Frigatebirds is Lingisan or Lungisan and this name is often applied to roosting islands. **Regional**: Arua islands (Malacca Straits), Ko Bida stacks (Phi Phi island, Thailand) P Uma (Karimatas), P Rhengis (Tioman) P Ringi (Siantan, Anambas), P Midai (S Natunas), P Rambut (N Java), P Pamalika (Java Sea), P Saboyan (Macassar Strait), Cavili Island and San Miguel Islands (Sulu Sea). See also pages 74, 136.

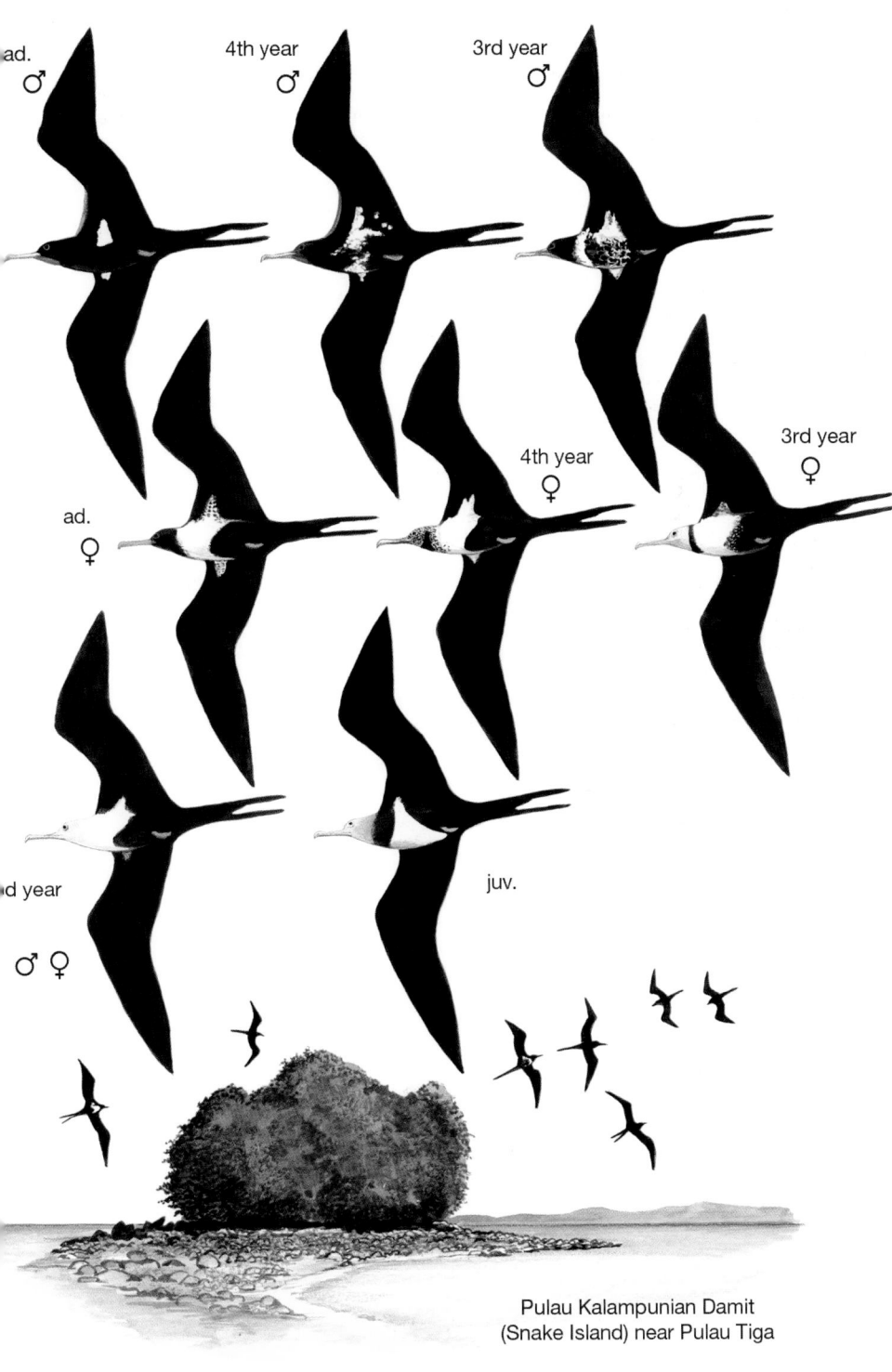

ad.
♂

4th year
♂

3rd year
♂

ad.
♀

4th year
♀

3rd year
♀

d year
♂ ♀

juv.

Pulau Kalampunian Damit
(Snake Island) near Pulau Tiga

CHRISTMAS ISLAND FRIGATEBIRD

CHRISTMAS ISLAND FRIGATEBIRD   *Fregata andrewsi*   **95cm**   **Scarce oceanic visitor**

A globally rare species endemic to Christmas Island (Australia) (Map page 74). The second commonest frigatebird seen around the Borneo coast. Owing to confusion with immature plumages of Lesser Frigatebird, probably under recorded in the past. On Christmas Island, Christmas Island Frigatebirds breed Jan.–Aug. but young birds remain dependent on their parents for at least two years. After breeding a large proportion of the female and immature populations disperse north to the S China Sea where they congregate around roosting islands (see map next page) including Mantanani and Pulau Tiga off the coast of NW Borneo. Satellite tracking has shown that adult birds with dependent young on the nest undertake 28 day, 4,000km trips to find food for their progeny. Satellite tracked birds flew over the mountains of Java at night on their return journeys (James). **Range:** Breeds only on isolated Christmas Island; an estimated 1,600 breeding pairs (4,000–5,000 individuals) in total. **BLI:** Critical.

BIRDING CHRISTMAS ISLAND (AUSTRALIA), 10°30'S, 105°40'E
One of the world's top birding destinations, with nine endemic birds, and numerous seabirds.
Christmas Island endemics: Frigatebird, Abbott's Booby, Imperial Pigeon, White-eye, Emerald Dove, Thrush, Hawk Owl, Goshawk and Glossy Swiftlet. Breeding seabirds include Great Frigatebird, Lesser Frigatebird, Brown Booby, Red-footed Booby, Brown Noddy, Red-tailed Tropicbird, White-tailed Tropicbird. Location: 350km south of W Java. What else to see: Pristine beach and rain forest, 120 million red forest crabs, coconut crabs, endemic fruit bat, good diving and snorkeling for coral fish. Best time to visit: Most birds breed year round. Many forest roads are closed for red crab migration Nov.–Dec. Access: Weekly flights from Bali and Perth. www.christmas.net.au See map next page.

THE SUNDA STRAITS: AN IMPORTANT SEABIRD MIGRATION WATCH SITE
The narrow Sunda Straits (31km wide) between the tip of W Java and the SE tip of Sumatra is a major funnel for regional seabirds moving between the Java Sea/S China Sea and the Indian Ocean. There are likely to be major movements of migrating trans-equatorial terns, skuas, boobies and gulls particularly between Oct.–Nov. and April–May each year. Look also for migrant raptors. See maps pages 74 and 100. Boat trips from Ujung Kulon National Park to volcanic Krakatau Island in the middle of the Straits are likely to be productive. Alternatively try sea watching from the car ferry between Merak (Java) and Bakauheni (Sumatra), before the proposed bridge is built. Merak is two hours' drive west of Jakarta.

BIRDLIFE INTERNATIONAL (BLI), 'Documenting the world's threatened birds and their habitats'.
BLI is a partnership of over 300 conservation NGOs with a special focus on birds, which together, constitute the leading global authority on the status of birds, their habitats and the issues and problems affecting bird life. BLI works in more than 100 countries and promotes sustainable living as a means of conserving birds, and all other forms of bio-diversity. BirdLife International, Wellbrook Court, Girton Road, Cambridge CB3 0NA.
BLI publishes the *Red Data Books* and *Red Lists* which list the current conservation status of all the world's threatened birds. Listings in this Field Guide follow the BLI Red Data Book *Threatened Birds of Asia 2001*, with the following meanings. Note that birds in two categories Near-threatened and Least concern are not listed as such in this Field Guide for lack of space.

BLI: Critically endangered   Faces an extremely high risk of extinction in the wild in the immediate future.
Abbott's Booby, Christmas Island Frigatebird, White-shouldered Ibis, White-rumped Vulture, Chinese Crested Tern, Silvery Wood-pigeon, Yellow-crested Cockatoo (7 sp.).

BLI: Endangered   Faces a very high risk of extinction in the wild in the immediate future.
Japanese Night-heron, Storm's Stork, Black-faced Spoonbill, Bornean Peacock-pheasant, Spotted Greenshank (5 species).

BLI: Vulnerable   Faces a high risk of extinction in the wild in the medium term future.
Chinese Egret, Lesser Adjutant, Mountain Serpent-eagle, Wallace's Hawk-eagle, Black Partridge, Crestless Fireback, Bulwer's Pheasant, Crested Argus, Spoon-billed Sandpiper, Large Green Pigeon, Grey Imperial-pigeon, Short-toed Coucal, Bonaparte's Nightjar, Blue-banded Kingfisher, Blue-headed Pitta, Fairy Pitta, Straw-headed Bulbul, Hook-billed Bulbul, Black-browed Babbler, Bornean Wren-babbler, Brown-chested Jungle Flycatcher, Large-billed Blue Flycatcher, Java Sparrow (23 species).   www.birdlife.org

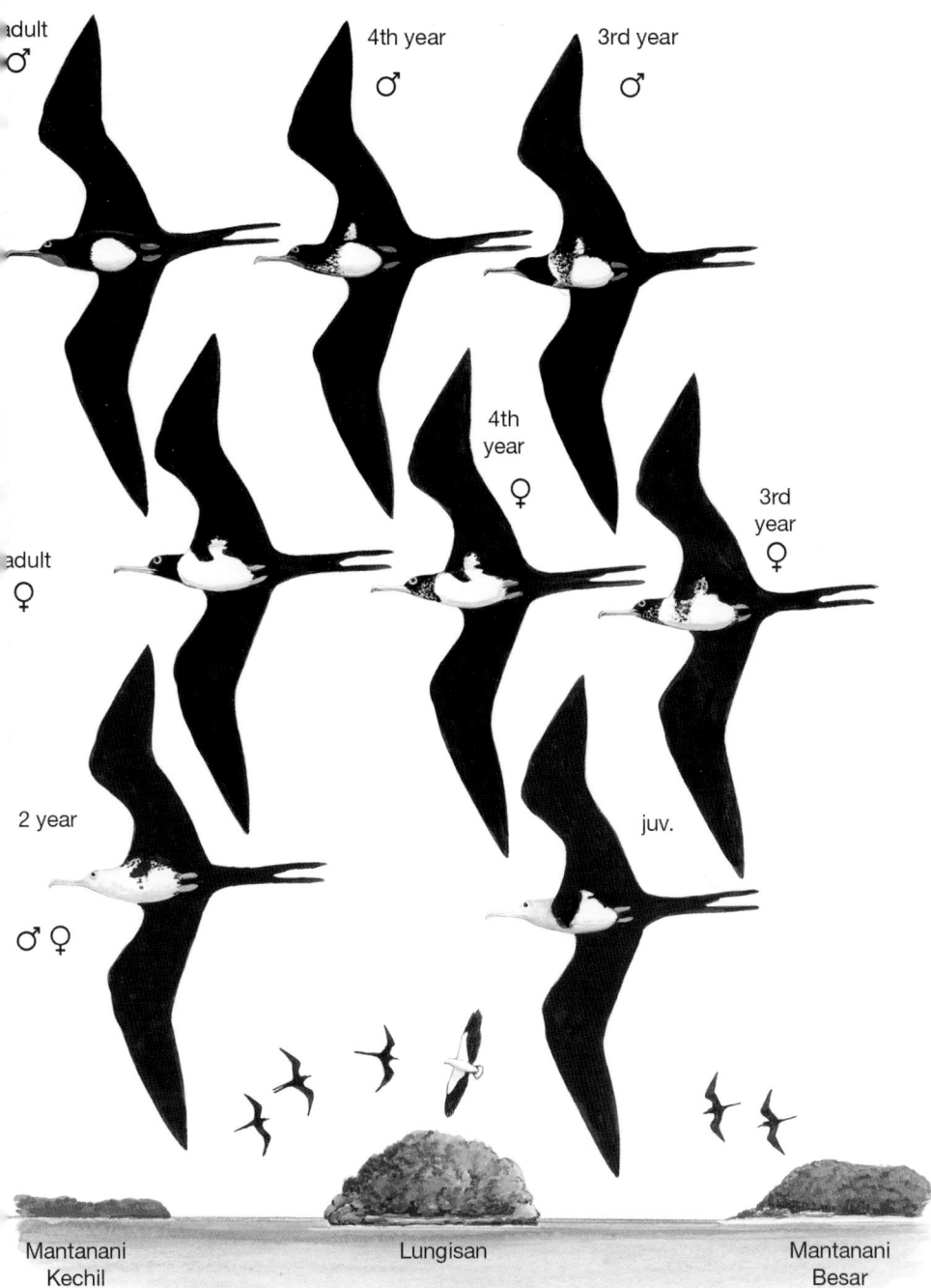

adult ♂

4th year ♂

3rd year ♂

4th year ♀

adult ♀

3rd year ♀

2 year ♂♀

juv.

Mantanani Kechil

Lungisan

Mantanani Besar

All three species of frigatebird can be seen roosting at dusk on Lungisan, one of the three Mantanani Islands 75km north of Kota Kinabalu, Sabah. Lungisan, a dome-shaped island covered in *Pisonia* trees, also has a cave with a large colony of the scarce coastal German's Swiftlet (page 184). During spring and autumn migration rare vagrant birds often occur. Look out also for nesting White-bellied Sea Eagles (page 90), rare island pigeons (page 152) and the globally very rare Mantanani Scops Owl (page 174). See map page 331.

GREAT FRIGATEBIRD *Fregata minor* **95cm** **Scarce oceanic visitor**

The least common of the three frigatebirds found around the coast of Borneo and the only species which has been recorded breeding in adjacent seas. Usually seen out to sea alone but occasionally in mixed flocks with other species. Breeds on Cavili island in small numbers with Red-footed Boobies in N Sulu Sea. Has also been recorded in mixed flocks roosting with Lesser and Christmas Island Frigatebirds on the San Miguel islands in the Sulu Sea just north of Sabah in Philippine waters. See page 136. There are also old records of breeding in the Spermonde Archipelago (Kepulauan Sangkarang) in the Makassar Strait off the SW coast of Sulawesi (Erftemeijer). The scientific and English names are both confusing. In size it is similar to Christmas Island but larger than Lesser. **Range:** Breeds tropical Pacific and Indian Oceans including Christmas Island, Cocos Keeling Islands and islands of the Australian Great Barrier Reef.

SEABIRD BREEDING ISLANDS AROUND BORNEO (see also pages 136, 138, 140)

[Map of the South China Sea region showing seabird breeding islands around Borneo]

Legend:
- ○ Major seabird breeding sites
- ▫ Minor seabird breeding sites
- ● Frigate bird breeding sites
- ▪ Frigate bird roosting sites

Map labels: CHINA; Pratas Islands [Dongsha Islands]; HAINAN; Paracel Islands [Xisha Islands]; CONTINENTAL ASIA; PHILIPPINES; Tubataha Reefs; Spratly Islands [Nan Sha Islands]; Cavili Island; Phi Phi Island; Ko Bida Stacks; MALAY PENINSULA; Layang Layang; Bankoran Reef; Pulau Perak; Mantanani Islands; Sulu Sea; San Miguel Islands; Pulau Rengis (Tioman); Tanjung Nosong; Pulau Tiga; Pelong Rocks; Maiga Island (Semporna); Arua Islands; Pulau Midai; Samama; Popaja; Pulau Ringi (Siantan); Tokong Ara; Pulau Satang Kecil; BORNEO; SULAWESI; Lembeh; Burung; Pulau Uma (Karimata Islands); Pulau Saboyan; SUMATRA; Pulau Pamalika; Spermonde Archipelago; Moromaho; Gunung Api; Bakauheni; Pulau Rambut; Pulau Sangkarang; Karompa Cadi; Manuk; Merak; Sunda Straits; JAVA; Bali & Nusa Penida; TIMOR; Krakatau; Christmas Island; Ashmore Reef; Cocos Keeling Islands; Lacepede Islands; AUSTRALIA

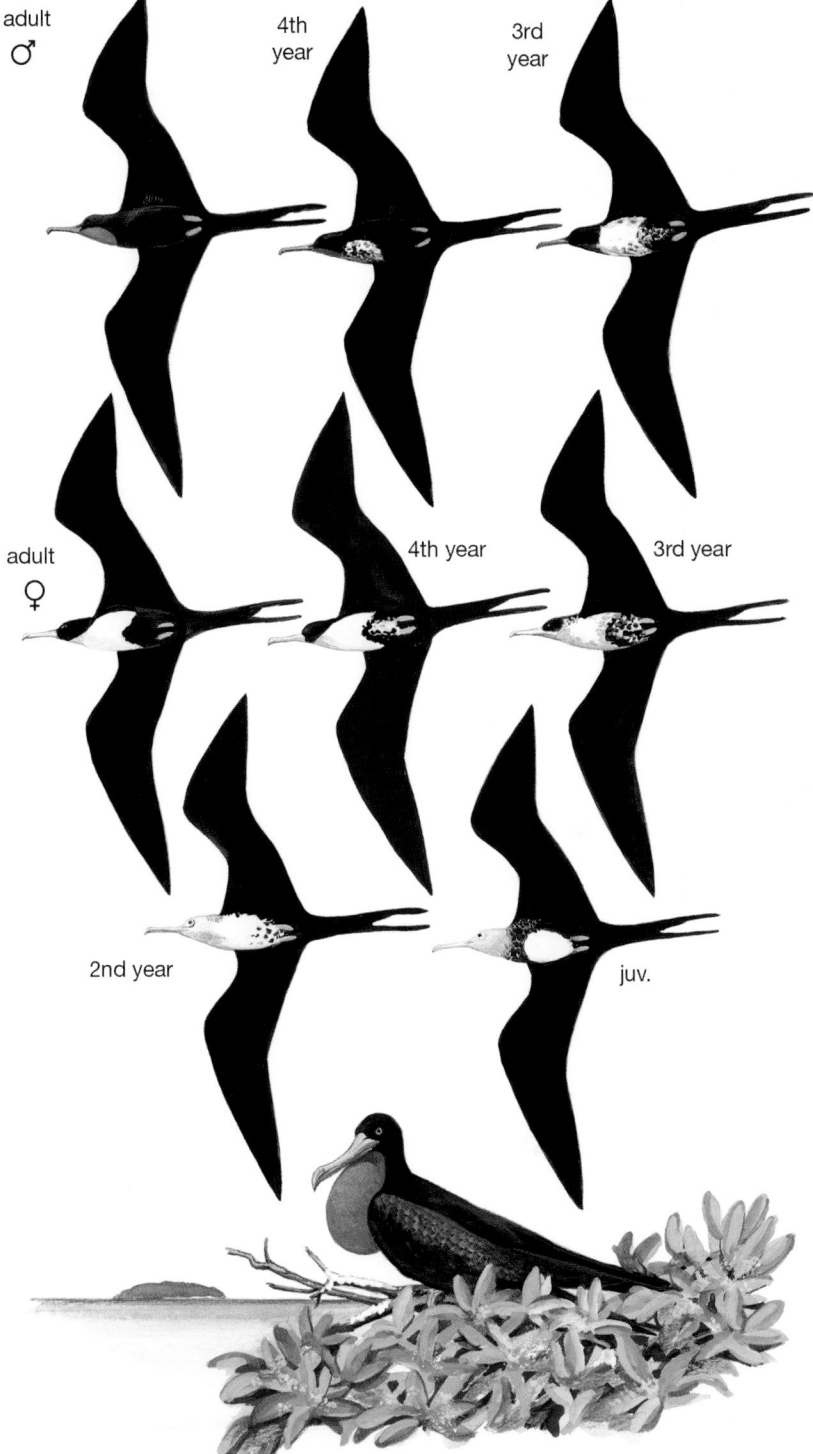

adult
♂

4th
year

3rd
year

adult
♀

4th year

3rd year

2nd year

juv.

TROPICBIRDS AND BOOBIES

TROPIC BIRDS: PHAETHONTIDAE **World 3 species; Borneo 2 species.** Elegant tropical ocean wanderers, which breed colonially in holes in rocky cliff faces. The nearest breeding sites are on Christmas Island (Australia), Bali, and on the isolated volcanic islands of Manuk and Gunong Api in the Banda Sea of E Indonesia. Usually seen alone, far out to sea. Both species have distinctive twin tail feathers, which double the length of the bird. Feed by shallow diving for fish. Generally silent at sea. Males and females similar. Young are heavily scalloped with black markings.

1 RED-TAILED TROPICBIRD *Phaethon rubricauda* **46cm + 40cm tail**   **Not recorded**
No confirmed records for Borneo. One caught off Puerto Princessa, Palawan had been ringed on Johnson Atoll S of Hawaii (Jensen 2005). **Range:** S China Sea, tropical and semi-tropical areas of Pacific and Indian Oceans. Breeding colonies in the Banda Sea (McKinnon). Breeds Christmas Island, Great Barrier Reef and W Australian islands.

2 WHITE-TAILED TROPICBIRD *Phaethon lepturus* **38cm + 40cm tail**   **Vagrant**
The only tropicbird regularly seen in Bornean waters. Records from S China Sea at P Layang[2] (Wiles Oct '06) also Sulu Sea and, Makassar Strait. A golden morph (illustrated) breeds only on Christmas Island where it is common. **Range:** S China Sea, tropical and semi-tropical areas of Atlantic, Pacific and Indian Oceans.

BOOBIES: SULIDAE **World 9 species, Borneo 3 species** [Gannets] Breed colonially on isolated islands, afterwards dispersing. Often seen in small flocks plunge diving for fish. Their breeding grounds are often shared by breeding frigatebirds, which attack the boobies and rob them of fish they have caught. Boobies are normally silent at sea. Males and females distinguished by beak colour. Juveniles take at least two years to reach adult plumage. The three Borneo species have been recorded occasionally inter-breeding at nesting colonies, which may account for difficulties in identification of both juveniles and adults.

3 RED-FOOTED BOOBY *Sula sula* **67cm**   **Vagrant**
Seen in small numbers off the coasts of Borneo. Recorded from P Layang[2], P Manukan and Bako NP. The Manukan bird was washed up on the shore after a storm and kept as a pet by Park staff. Nests in trees on Cavili Island, Bankoran Reef and Tubataha Reef all in the Sulu Sea. (The other two Bornean boobies nest and roost on the ground.) Distinguished by red feet and white tail. Immature is similar to immature Brown Booby, which is much more mottled below. Adult also occurs in a brown morph. **Range:** Breeds on islands in S China Sea, Indian Ocean and Banda Sea. 35,500 nesting pairs recorded from Dong island, Paracels (Xisha Islands) in 2004 (Lei).

4 MASKED BOOBY *Sula dactylatra* **86cm**   **Vagrant**
Less common than Red-footed Booby. Recorded from P Layang[2] and the mouth of Kuching river. Nesting recorded on Spratly Islands, P Layang[2] and islands in the Sulu Sea. Has been reported interbreeding with both Red-footed and Brown Booby. A mainly white booby with grey-blue feet and black tail. Disitnguish from male Abbot's Booby by pointed wings which are mainly white with dark tips and trailing edge. **Range:** Tropical, and subtropical oceans including S China Sea.

5 ABBOTT'S BOOBY *Papasula abbotti* **71cm**   **Not recorded**
A globally rare bird, endemic to Christmas Island, an Australian territory, 350km south of West Java. World population less than 2,500 pairs. Distinguish by long slim blunt ended wings compared with other boobies. Wings are all dark on top unlike Masked Booby. Abbott's Booby also has dark thigh patch on side of body at base of wing, missing in Masked Booby. Dark patch around eye only whereas Masked has dark base to bill. **Range:** Roams Indian Ocean. Recorded in Sunda Straits, off the coast of Sulawesi and in the Banda Sea. Look for in Java Sea off the coast of S Kalimantan. **BLI:** Critical.

6 BROWN BOOBY *Sula leucogaster* **70cm**   **Scarce pelagic visitor and resident**

The only booby commonly seen in the seas around Borneo, but generally scarce. Breeds in large numbers on Spratly islands, P Layang[2] and the islands of the Sulu Sea, where it nests on the ground in dense colonies between March and June. Vagrants are sometimes recorded inland after storms. **Range:** Tropical and semi-tropical oceans. Large numbers breed on the islands around the coast of N Australia.

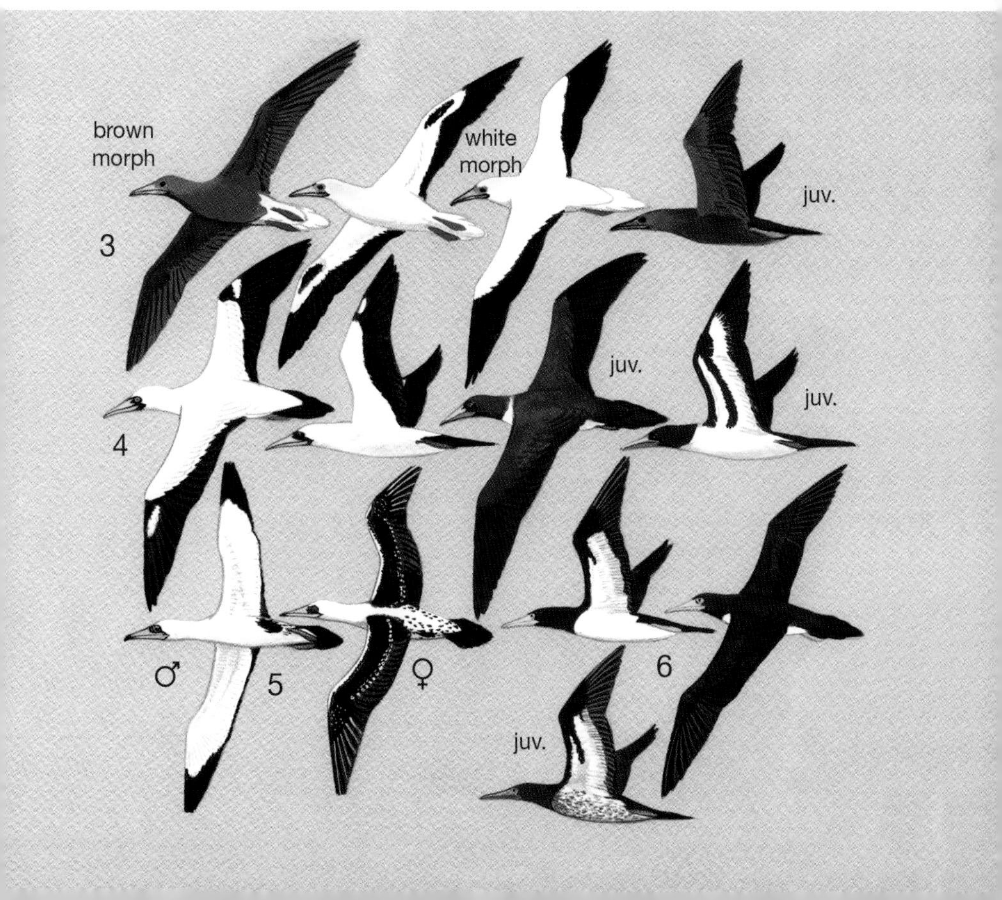

PELICANS, CORMORANTS AND DARTERS

PELICANS: PELICANIDAE   **World 7 species; Borneo 2 species.**

1   GREAT WHITE PELICAN   *Pelecanus onocrotalus*   157cm   **Not recorded**
Formerly common on the Asian continent, the Great White Pelican is a possible vagrant to Borneo. **Range:** Breeds Africa and Asia and winters southwards.

2   SPOT-BILLED PELICAN   *Pelecanus philippensis*   140cm   **No recent records**
Previously a common resident of the Philippines where it is now locally extinct. This species is the most likely source for Spencer St. John's report of 'monstrous pelicans' on Pulau Balambangan, where the Borneo Company had a trading outpost from 1856 to 1872. Distinguished by white spectacle around eye, pink pouch, with grey spots. **Range:** Breeds India, Sri Lanka, Cambodia and Sumatra and disperses widely.

3   AUSTRALIAN PELICAN   *Pelecanus conspicillatus*   150cm   **Not recorded**
Pelicans have been reported from the swamps of S Kalimantan. The most likely candidate is the Australian Pelican, which is a common nomad in N Australia, and in drought years is an irruptive migrant in large numbers, with birds recorded as far north as Java and Sulawesi. **Range:** Breeds in Australia in large colonies.

COMORANTS: PHALACROCORACIDAE   **World 39 species; Borneo 4 species.**   Dark plumaged fish eaters which inhabit both coastal and freshwater lakes. In Borneo they are surprisingly scarce despite being common in surrounding territories. Four species have been recorded, of which two have bred. Vagrants originate from Continental Asia, Java, Sumatra and possibly Australia. Unlike herons, cormorants fly with neck extended. Their feathers absorb water easily to reduce bouyancy so they can chase fish underwater, and after fishing, they need to dry their wings.

4   GREAT CORMORANT   *Phalacrocorax carbo*   88cm   **Vagrant**
This large cormorant, which normally frequents freshwater lakes, has been regularly recorded along the W Borneo coast as a migrant from Asia. Reported nesting on a rocky island off Kg Layang[2], Labuan in 1966. (KV Thompson). **Range:** Africa, Australasia, N America and Eurasia.

5   LITTLE PIED CORMORANT   *Phalacrocorax melanoleucos*   60cm   **Vagrant**
Common resident of E Indonesia, which has been seen once off the coast of the Sangkulirang Peninsula E Kalimantan, 21 September 2001 (Eames). **Range:** Sulawesi, to Australia and New Zealand.

6   LITTLE CORMORANT   *Phalacrocorax niger*   56cm   **Rare resident**
Common resident of Java, where it inhabits both fresh and coastal lagoons in small groups. Recorded breeding on Bangkau Lake, NE of Banjarmasin, by Grabowski in 1851. Recorded nesting in a mixed colony with Darters at Loagan Bunut, Sarawak in 1986 (AC Sebastian). **Range:** Breeds India, SW China, SE Asia, Sumatra, Borneo, Java.

7   LITTLE BLACK CORMORANT   *Phalacrocorax sulcirostris*   61cm   **Vagrant**
[Little Black Shag] Common and increasing in W Java, where it frequents both freshwater pools and the sea coast. Four collected in S Borneo, near Martapura in 1851. Seen at Mahakam Lakes in Sept. 2003 and 2004. Two individuals (Nijman *et al.*). **Range:** Java to Australia.

DARTERS: ANHINGIDAE   **World 2 species; Borneo 1 species.**   Two very similar species are distributed worldwide in tropical forested areas. The Anhinga in S. America and the Darter in the Asia and Africa. Both have long snake-like necks extended in flight and like cormorants need to dry their feathers after chasing fish underwater. Sexes are similar. Breed and roost in colonies.

8   DARTER   *Anhinga melanogaster*   84cm   **Local resident**

[Malay: Burung kosa] A locally common inhabitant of lakes and large rivers in forested areas. Usually seen singly flying overhead. Feeds on fish caught in underwater chases. Along rivers, typically seen in groups drying open wings on an exposed tree. Considered good eating by locals and is generally scarce but recently appears to be making a come-back on the west coast of Borneo e.g. large groups at Tutong sewage ponds, Brunei. **Call:** Generally silent. Breeding records include **Sabah:** Klias Peninsula, Kinabatangan. **Brunei:** Tasek Merimbun, **Sarawak:** Loagan Bunut, **Kalimantan:** Danau Sentarum, Tanjung Puting, Mahakam Lakes. **Range:** Africa, India, SE Asia, Java, Philippines, New Guinea and Australia.

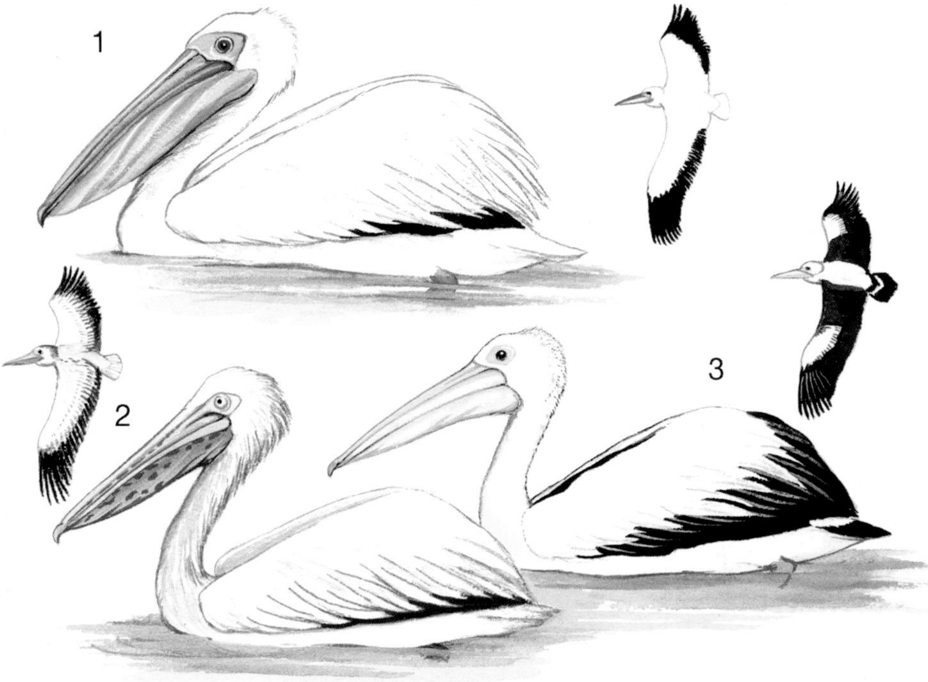
1
2
3

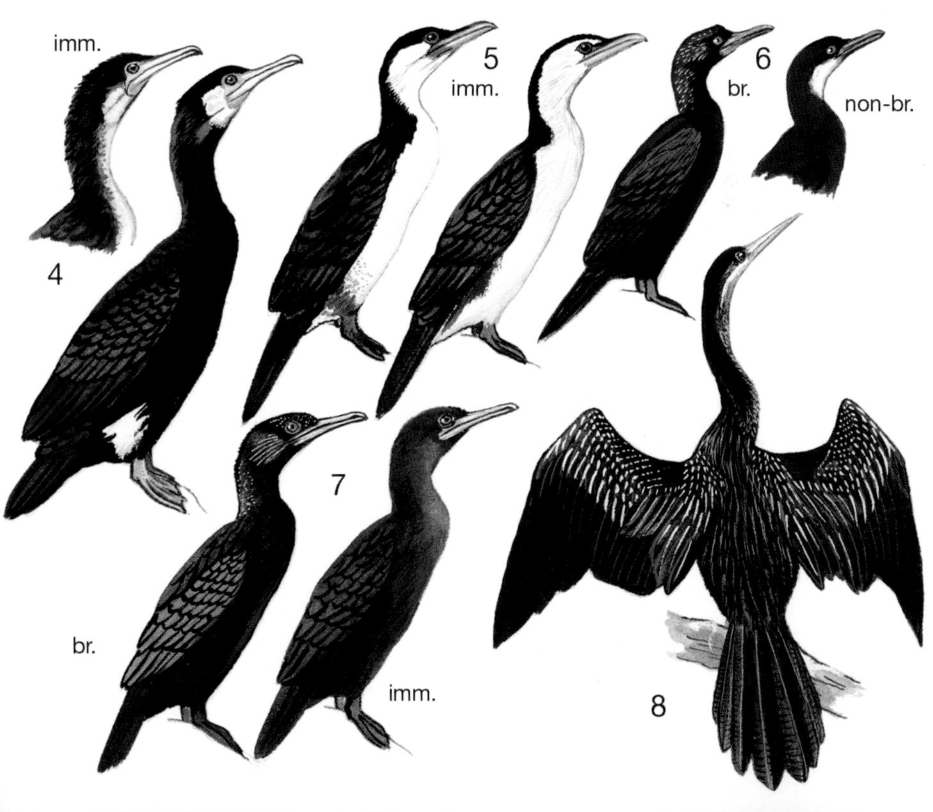
imm.
4
5
imm.
6
br.
non-br.
7
br.
imm.
8

ACCIPTRIDAE: World 237 species; Borneo 39 species.   The diurnal (day flying) birds of prey are collectively known as raptors. Depending on size, Bornean raptors attack and eat prey from large insects up to the size of young monkeys. Females and males are similar with the female usually being substantially larger than the male. It is believed that this is so that she can catch larger prey, thus maximising the potential prey population in their breeding territory. Raptors normally build heavy stick nests in a tree. Nests are often decorated with broken branches of green leaves, believed to be for camouflage. Most breeding raptors are strictly territorial, defending their feeding areas with attacks on similar species passing through. Immature eagles may not develop full adult plumage for several years until they are themselves ready to breed, thus distinguishing themselves from highly territorial adults. When breeding, adults often perform spectacular 'sky dances' in which they swoop on each other and lock talons, tumbling through the air. The secretive Honey-buzzard has a very distinctive sky dance, which is a useful diagnostic feature. See page 86.

Conservation of Forest Raptors: Studies of raptors in Sumatra (Thiollay 1996) found that of the 12 species recorded, 6 species could not survive outside primary forest, including the Rufous-bellied Eagle, Black Eagle, Wallace's and Blythe's Hawk-eagle, Jerdon's Baza and Crested Goshawk.   **Counting Forest Raptors:** Raptors were counted by watching from a convenient vantage point such as a ridge. Between 8.00am and 12.00 'at least one adult of every pair soared, calling or displaying over the forest every day for 5–10 minutes. In SE Asia every forest raptor apart from the falconets exhibits this territorial behaviour.'

THE MISSING MONKEY-EATING EAGLE OF SUNDALAND

It is a curious fact that throughout Sundaland where leaf-eating langurs are the most abundant primate, there is no avian predator large enough to attack and kill an adult langur. This is not the case in Africa and S America, where Hawk Eagles and Harpy Eagles frequently feed on primates. Coincidentally, just north of Borneo lives the enormous Monkey-eating Eagle of the Philippines, *Pithecophaga jefferyi*, which can and does feed on macaque monkeys. However there are no langurs in the Philippines, where they are replaced by abundant leaf-eating colugos (flying lemurs) which provide most of the Philippine Eagle's food. It is possible that there was once a giant monkey-eating eagle in Sundaland which became extinct due to climate change. See page 22.   **Note:** *P. jefferyi* was first collected on Luzon by John Whitehead who named it after his father. See page 214.

VULTURES   **World 13 species; Borneo One vagrant.**   Vultures are very large birds of prey that scavenge dead animals. Vultures are commonest in Africa where the prey is dead wild animals and in India where they feed on dead cows. In India and Tibet 'sky burials' are practised by some communities of Parsees and Buddhists. When people die their bodies are left out on specially constructed towers for vultures to consume. Four vulture species occur in Thailand, Vietnam and N. Malaya, all of which could possibly wander to Borneo across the S China Sea.

INDIAN WHITE-BACKED VULTURE   *Gyps bengalensis*   **88cm; Wingspan 2m**   **Vagrant**

[Davison: White-rumped Vulture] This vulture was previously very common in India extending to Indochina but is now very scarce due to *diclofenac* poisoning, a veterinary drug used to treat cattle. Two vultures seen in the Belait district Brunei on 22 November 1977 by Hilary Fry may have been this species. Juvenile Himalayan Vultures *Gyps himalayensis* were regularly recorded in Singapore between Dec.–Feb. in the past. Ding Li et al (2013)

Indian White-backed Vulture in flight and at rest

♀

Bornean Falconet holding a Letter Butterfly
Idea leuconoe **(Malay: Kupu-kupu surat)**

Letter butterfies flap slowly above forest paths protected from attack by their striking black and white aposematic (warning) markings. Like most members of the *Danainae* (the same sub-family as the Monarch butterflies), their caterpillars feed on poisonous plants and the toxins are passed on to the adults. Occasionally an inexperienced bird will be tempted to try their luck but the nasty taste is usually a deterrent from further action. These 'danger sign' markings are shared by the Falconet and most birds of prey (see page 87), many owls (see page 359), small woodpeckers (see page 211), cuckoos, and by many other Bornean butterflies such as the Glassy Tigers, providing examples of both Batesian and Mullerian mimicry. Collectively the grouping is known as a mimicry ring. See pages 84 and 168.

HAWK-EAGLES

Hawk-eagles are powerful, fierce forest hunters of squirrels, rats, bats, birds and even small monkeys. Sometimes seen circling over the forest, occasionally swooping down to the canopy to attack a squirrel or lizard. More often they perch at the edge of a clearing waiting to swoop on moving prey. Hawk-eagles require very large areas of forest to provide sufficient prey and are often seemingly patchy in distribution. Sexes look similar, and as is the norm with raptors the female is larger than the male. Hawk-eagles make large stick nests generally in tall trees. Their calls are typical far carrying eagle type screams *klip klee, klip klee* which, on present knowledge, are not easily distinguishable between species.

Hawk-eagle Mimicry. Four crested hawk-eagle species occur in Borneo together with the smaller Jerdon's Baza, which mimics adult Wallace's Hawk-eagle. All adult hawk-eagles are also mimicked by the polymorphic races of the Honey Buzzard. Juveniles of all the hawk-eagles have similar pale plumages which are also mimicked by Honey Buzzards. Hawk-eagles may also breed in non adult plumage. These multiple polymorphic plumages confuse birders, taxonomists, museum curators and presumably both the local squirrels and the raptors themselves and therein lies an explanation of why it happens. See following pages for further details of raptor mimicry in Borneo and how to distinguish between mimic and model.

1   RUFOUS-BELLIED HAWK-EAGLE   *Hieraaetus kienerii*   **54cm**   **Scarce resident**

Considered the least common hawk-eagle, widespread in forested areas, throughout Borneo. A specialist feeder on small and medium sized birds such as Green Pigeons. Has been recorded regularly at Gomantong Caves feeding on swiftlets and bats. Harrisson described an attack on a Stork-billed Kingfisher in which both birds died (Smythies 1960). Unlike other hawk-eagles typically stoops or dives on flying birds from high above. **Range:** India to SE Asia to Malay P, Sumatra, Borneo, Java, Philippines and Sulawesi. Recorded as a migrant to Singapore and could also migrate from S Sumatra to SW Borneo.

2   CHANGEABLE HAWK-EAGLE   *Spizaetus cirrhatus*   **70cm**   **Scarce resident**

The largest and commonest hawk-eagle.Widespread in lowland forested areas throughout Borneo. A notorious chicken thief. Survives in forest patches where the other hawk-eagles cannot, e.g. the only hawk-eagle still resident on Singapore.The majority (usually c. 60%) are very dark (almost black) morphs, with smaller numbers of pale and intermediate morphs. The dark morph can be confused with Black Eagle but the Changeable Hawk-eagle is generally more slender with a proportionately longer tail. At close range the beak is entirely black with a black cere unlike the yellow cere and pale beak of Black Eagle. **Range:** India, Myanmar through mainland SE Asia to Malay P, Sumatra, Borneo, Java, Philippines, Sulawesi and the Moluccas

---

OIL PALM, GREEN DESERTS AND HAWK-EAGLES
One early Bornean naturalist (E. Banks of the Sarawak Museum) described Borneo as a 'Green Desert' (1949). At that time Borneo was covered with almost unending virgin tropical forest from north to south. What Banks meant was that the sandstone soils of Borneo were so infertile that staple foods such as rice and maize could not be grown in permanent fields. In contrast the rich volcanic soils of the Philippines, Java and Sumatra allow the same fields to be used year after year. Consequently these fertile islands were deforested and populated first whilst Borneo retained most of its forest. However the development of oil palm clones which can grow in poor soil has totally changed the Bornean landscape. Millions of hectares of oil palm plantations now cover most of the flat land previously occupied by lowland tropical rainforest. Compared with the 200 + resident bird species found in the original habitat an oil palm estate hosts around 9 to 14. Truly large parts of Borneo are now a green desert. Plant mono-cultures usually lead to low diversity of animal life but ecotones where one habitat changes to another are often the richest habitat of all, and this is true of the areas where primary forest still exists next to oil palm. Although most forest animals cannot survive in oil palm plantations alone, in places where they can shelter in the forest and feed in the oil palm, birds such as partridges, hornbills, Fairy Bluebirds, parrots, and bulbuls use oil palm fruit as a back up food supply when forest fruits are scarce. The fallen fruit also attracts rats in large numbers, which in turn attract predators such as giant pythons, cobras, civets, leopard cats and owls at night and hawks and eagles during the day. The forest edge adjoining an oil palm estate such as at Tabin and Sepilok is therefore one of the best habitats in Borneo to search for Hawk-eagles. See also page 340.

1

imm.

adult

imm.

adult

imm.

adult

2

imm.

adult
pale morph

adult
dark morph

HAWK-EAGLES AND JERDON'S BAZA

1   BLYTH'S HAWK-EAGLE   *Spizaetus alboniger*   **52cm**   **Scarce resident**

May be found anywhere in forested areas but prefers the hills. The commonest hawk-eagle in the Crocker Range. The pale juvenile plumage is similar to that of other immature hawk-eagles. The adult is mimicked by the rare Tweeddale morph of the Honey Buzzard. Distinguished by shorter wings which usually only reach the base of the tail and circular nostrils as compared with the slit nostrils of the Honey Buzzard. Has a full crest unlike the stubby crest of Honey Buzzard. **Range:** Myanmar to Malay P, Sumatra, Borneo.

2   WALLACE'S HAWK-EAGLE   *Spizaetus nanus*   **45cm**   **Scarce resident**

Uncommon resident of primary lowland forest throughout Borneo. The smallest hawk-eagle, mimicked both by the much smaller Jerdon's Baza and the similar size resident race of the Honey Buzzard. Juvenile plumage is indistinguishable from juvenile Blythe's. Distinguish from Jerdon's Baza by having feet feathered to base of claws, by shorter wings, so that wings usually do not exceed half tail length and lack of 'notches' on the bill. Distinguished from Honey Buzzard by circular, not slit, nostrils, by full-sized white-tipped crest and by much shorter wings. See page 86. **Range:** Malay P, Sumatra and Borneo. **BLI:** Vulnerable.

3   JERDON'S BAZA   *Aviceda jerdoni*   **35cm**   **Scarce resident**

Widespread but thinly scattered in forest throughout Borneo. Usually quite tame and often seen perched on an open branch along rivers from where it will fly into dense vegetation to seize a lizard or a small snake. Distinguished from Wallace's Hawk-eagle by being smaller with proportionately longer wings and by double notched bill. See also page 80. On the Asian Continent this species flocks with other migrant hawks in small numbers and there is a possibility that some of the birds seen in Borneo are vagrants from mainland Asia. **Range:** India to Malay P, Sumatra, Borneo, Sulawesi, Philippines. In Thailand and Singapore a regular but rare migrant.

MIMICRY AND THE BORNEAN HAWK-EAGLES

When one species (the mimic) adopts the visual appearance of another (the model) it is known as mimicry. Mimicry is common amongst plants (e.g. orchids which mimic insects), snakes, insects and birds, especially the raptors and cuckoos.

Batesian Mimicry is when a weak or edible species adopts the looks of a strong or poisonous species. This is common in butterflies and snakes and it is believed to be the case with Jerdon's Baza, which has adopted almost the exact appearance of the larger more powerful Wallace's Hawk-eagle, presumably to deter other large eagles from attacking it. Predators are reluctant to fight with their own species because even a small injury could result in starvation and death. For Batesian mimicry to work effectively the 'model' must outnumber the mimic. The theory predicts therefore that Jerdon's Baza is likely to be less common than Wallace's Hawk-eagle.

Honey Buzzard Mimicry. An advanced form of Batesian mimicry has developed with the polymorphic honey buzzards, an inoffensive raptor that feeds mainly on bee and wasp larvae. Taken as a whole the population of honey buzzards is quite numerous and is probably equivalent to the total hawk-eagle population of Borneo. If every honey buzzard mimicked the same hawk-eagle species the strategy would not work. Instead, different morphs of honey buzzard, mimic all the different species and plumages of the Bornean hawk-eagles. The rare resident Honey Buzzard (*P. p. torquatus*) mimics the scarce Wallace's and Blythe's Hawk-eagles whilst the commoner migrant Honey Buzzards (*P. p. orientalis*) mimic the other two more widespread hawk-eagles.

Mullerian Mimicry takes place when an unpalatable species adopts similar colours or shapes for a common purpose. For example many venomous insects are banded black and yellow. This then becomes an easy signal for birds to recognise, so it benefits all birds and all black and yellow venomous insects. The Bornean hawk-eagles are very powerful aggressive predators. All young hawk-eagles have very similar juvenile plumages including a prominent crest. These immature eagles are very difficult to distinguish as distinct species. It is suggested here that these juvenile plumages could be regarded as a form of Mullerian mimicry which protect the non-breeding young from being attacked when they wander through an adult hawk-eagle territory. Because hawk-eagles are generally scarce it benefits the young eagles to all look similar so that they are universally recognised and therefore free from speculative attacks by their own or other species. See also page 88.

1

imm.

adult

adult

imm.

2

imm.

adult

adult

imm.

3

imm.

adult

adult

imm.

DISTINGUISHING RAPTOR MIMIC FROM RAPTOR MODEL

HAWK-EAGLE (MODEL)
- Same size as Honey Buzzard.
- Full Hawk-eagle Crest.
- Circular nostril.
- Tarsus feathered to base of toes.
- Short wings to base of tail.
- Distinct ridge above eye.

JERDON'S BAZA (MIMIC)
- 2/3 size of hawk-eagle.
- Full Hawk-eagle type crest.
- Slit nostril.
- Mimics adult Wallace's Hawk-eagle
- Tarsus **not** feathered.
- Two 'notches' on bill.
- Wings to mid-tail.
- Light ridge above eye.

HONEY BUZZARD (MIMIC)
- Same size as Hawk-eagle.
- Small crest or no crest.
- Slit nostril.
- No ridge above eye.

- Tarsus not feathered.
- Long wings to tip of tail.
- Sky dance display flight

flap

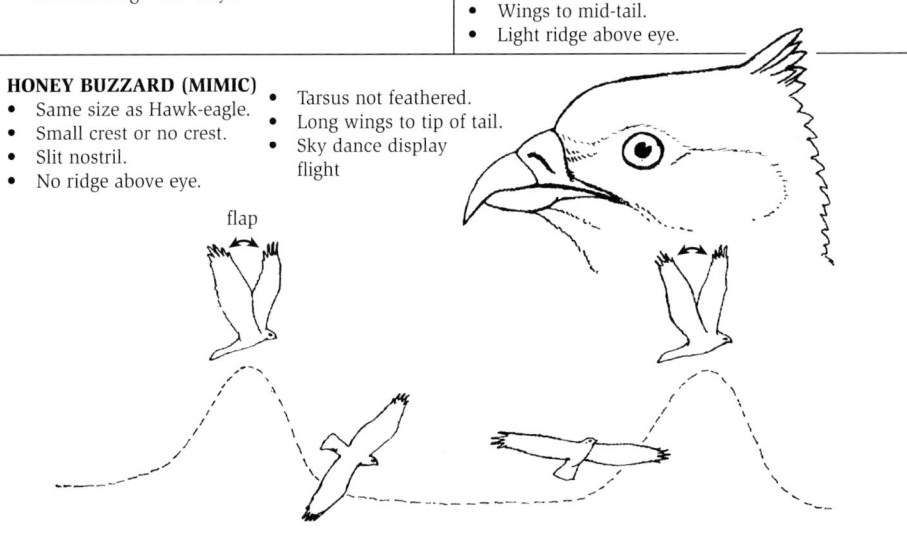

ORIENTAL HONEY BUZZARD   *Pernis ptilorhynchus torquatus*   **50cm   Scarce resident race**

[Crested Honey Buzzard] The resident race *P. p. torquatas* of the Oriental Honey Buzzard mimics both adult Wallace's Hawk-eagle and less commonly Blythe's Hawk-eagle. (Tweeddale morph). There is no immature plumage. Distinguished from Hawk-eagles by different habits which are similar to migrant Honey Buzzards and the distinctive features shown above. Migrant Honey Buzzard males have an orange or brown iris. Females have a yellow iris. Resident Honey Buzzards iris is usually yellow for both sexes, but can be orange. Resident Honey Buzzards are also distinguished by a distinctive breeding display flight or 'sky dance', a repeated upward swoop with wing clapping at the peak followed by a downward stall, illustrated above. **Range:** Race *P. p. torquatus* is confined to Malay P, Sumatra, and Borneo.

♀

♂

A pair of Tweeddale morph Honey Buzzards (mimic of Blythe's Hawk-eagle) attacking Giant Honeybee *Apis dorsata* combs on a *Koompasia excelsia* tree. See full size tree on page 203.

DAVID MEAD

BLACK KITE, BUZZARDS AND BLACK BAZA

1 BLACK KITE *Milvus migrans* **65cm**   **Vagrant**

[Black-eared Kite *Milvus migrans lineatus*] In Hong Kong a very common resident and winter visitor where over 1,000 flock at winter roosts. Often seen circling the harbour. In the Philippines and Borneo a rare vagrant. Distinguished by forked tail. **Call:** Long drawn out half whinnying, half squealing call (Viney). **Range:** Breeds Europe to Japan wintering south.

2 COMMON BUZZARD *Buteo buteo* **54cm**   **Vagrant**

[Myers: Himalayan buzzard] One of the commonest birds of prey in N Europe and N Asia. In winter migrates south in large mixed flocks, including honey buzzards and other raptors. Distinguished from Honey Buzzard by wings held forward not flat. One Borneo record from Brunei Sept. 1987 (Mann). Two races could occur *B. b. japonicus* and *B. b. vulpinous*. **Range:** Breeds Europe to Japan wintering south to Africa, India, SE Asia.

3 ORIENTAL HONEY BUZZARD *Pernis ptilorhynchus orientalis* **50cm Common migrant race**

[Eastern Honey Buzzard] The *orientalis* race of the Honey Buzzard is a common winter visitor found in forested areas where it attacks wasp and bee nests to eat the larvae, wax and honey. Also eats birds, rats, lizards. Occurs in multiple different plumage morphs. Commonest morphs mimic Changeable and Rufous-bellied Hawk-eagles. Most morphs have a distinctive pale throat with broad dark 'necklace'. Usually no or minimal crest, unlike the resident race *P. p. torquatus* which usually has a small crest, and mimics Wallace's and Blyth's Hawk-eagle. Adult males have a grey face covered in smooth dense feathers and brown or orange iris. Females and immatures face is usually blotchy brown to white with yellow iris. In Borneo usually keeps below canopy level, slow flapping from one tree to another. **Range:** Breeds E Siberia to Japan wintering south to India, Malay P, Sumatra, Java, Philippines, Borneo.

Satellite Tracking Migrant Honey Buzzards: Two adults and one juvenile, nesting in Japan, were satellite tracked by Higuchi *et al.* (2005). One adult wintered in Java, another adult travelled through Sumatra to SW Borneo and then on to Mindanao where it wintered. The first year bird stayed on in the Malaya Peninsula and did not return to Japan in the spring.

4 GREY-FACED BUZZARD *Butastur indicus* **45cm**   **Common winter visitor**

The commonest of the migrant raptors that reach N Borneo from N Asia. Perches prominently on tall bare trees in wooded areas and the forest edge. A long slim hawk without the bulk or size of a Honey Buzzard. On migration occurs in large flocks often mixed with other raptors. A Japanese population of around 32,000 birds migrates south through Taiwan and Palawan in October each year to Borneo. See also Crested Goshawk page 98. **Range:** Breeds E. Siberia to Japan. Winters south to Malay P, Sumatra, Java, Philippines, Borneo.

5 BLACK BAZA *Aviceda leuphotes* **33cm**   **Not recorded**

The commonest migrating raptor over the plains of central Thailand with over 100,000 recorded in one day at Chumphon. Crosses to Sumatra at Tg Tuan (Malacca). Most likely to occur as a vagrant in SW Kalimantan. **Range:** Breeds India to S China winters south to Sumatra, Java.

BLUFF AND DOUBLE BLUFF: HONEY BUZZARD AND HAWK-EAGLE PLUMAGES

Wherever they coincide in range honey buzzards mimic the plumage of the local hawk-eagles. This is true of Western Honey Buzzards which winter in Africa. It is also true of the endemic honey buzzards in Java, Sulawesi and the Philippines which mimic the plumage of the resident hawk-eagles. It has been assumed that the purpose is Batesian mimicry, the weaker honey buzzard is protected by mimicking a feared hawk-eagle. It is more likely that both groups benefit from the mimicry. It is suggested here that the hawk-eagles also benefit but in a different way. Squirrels have no idea if the bird they see is a predatory hawk-eagle or merely a harmless honey buzzard. The hawk-eagle has become 'disguised'. The fact that both groups benefit explains their multiple different plumages. Batesian mimicry benefits the mimic most when the mimic is in a minority. Disguise morphs are also of greatest benefit when they are a minority. For example, if a Changeable Hawk-eagle generates a new disguise morph, the Honey Buzzard benefits by copying it. The hawk-eagle does not lose out as a result of the copying, unless the new morph becomes a majority of the population. Hence the development of multiple plumages. The fact that both species benefit gives the arrangement long term genetic stability. See also page 84 and van Balen *et al.* (1999).

1 adult

imm.

adult

2 adult

japonicus

japonicus

japonicus

vulpinus

vulpinus

japonicus

vulpinus

♀

3 ♂

imm.

adult dark ♀

adult ♂

adult ♀

4 adult

adult dark

adult

imm.

5 adult

MARINE AND RIVERINE EAGLES

1   OSPREY   *Pandion haliaetus*   **55cm**   **Scarce migrant**

 A scarce winter visitor, and passage migrant (Sept.–April) from N Asia, a rare resident and a very scarce austral migrant (March–Sept.). Seen all year fishing along the coast but commonest during migration periods. Previously bred on small islets in the Java Sea. Fishes by diving feet first into the water and sometimes submerges unlike White-bellied Sea Eagle which snatches food from the sea surface. The N Australian and Javan race of Osprey is reputed to have a white face with an indistinct pale stripe through the eye not a dark strip which extends down the neck, but plumages vary considerably and distinctions are difficult. **Call:** A shrill whistle. **Range:** Worldwide.

2   WHITE-BELLIED SEA EAGLE   *Haliaeetus leucogaster*   **70cm**   **Common resident**

 [White-breasted Fish-Eagle] A common coastal resident often seen soaring high above its territory. Most small islands have a breeding pair. Feeds by snatching sea-snakes or fish from the surface of the sea and scavenges dead fish. Spectacular 'sky dance' displays when breeding. Nests are a bulky pile of sticks in a tall tree at the highest point of the island. Young birds often wander far inland up large rivers. Note distinctive wedge shaped tail. **Call:** Loud ringing calls when breeding. **Range:** India to SE China, through SE Asia to Australia.

3   BRAHMINY KITE   *Haliastur indus*   **45cm**   **Common resident**

 The commonest bird of prey along the Borneo coast. Also found far inland up rivers and over interior padi fields. In the interior locals regard it as an important omen bird. See page 232. Often seen around busy ports and coastal towns, e.g. Sandakan where a large population scavenges waste from the surface of the sea. Feeds on live fish, dead fish, large insects, lizards and rats. **Call:** A long shrill mewing squeal *chee ee* in flight and when perched (Smythies). **Range:** India to China, throughout SE Asia to Australia and the Soloman Is.

4   GREY-HEADED FISH EAGLE   *Ichthyophaga ichthyaetus*   **70cm**   **Scarce resident**

 A scarce resident of undisturbed coastal areas, estuaries and large rivers, sometimes following the river far inland. Previously resident on P Gaya near KK now locally extinct. Both fish eagle species are seen along the Kinabatangan River, the large rivers of Sarawak and at the Mahakam Lakes. **Call:** Weird loud clanging cries and high-pitched screams (Ferguson-Lees). **Range:** Sri Lanka, India to Malay P, Sumatra, Java, Borneo, Philippines.

5   LESSER FISH EAGLE   *Ichthyophaga humilis*   **60cm**   **Scarce resident**

 Favoured habitat is the headwaters of clear water rivers in the hills but also found near the coast although less commonly than Grey-headed Fish Eagle. **Sabah:** Danum, Kinabatangan. **Brunei:** Seria, Labi, Ulu Temburong. **Sarawak:** Upper reaches of major rivers Mulu, Similajau. **Kalimantan:** Headwaters of major rivers, Tg Puting, Gng Palung. **Call:** Loud repeated *yak yak yak yak*. **Range:** Himalayas to Malay P, Sumatra, Borneo, Sulawesi.

AUSTRAL MIGRANTS   The Osprey is just one of many austral (southern) migrants which visit Borneo each Australian winter March to September. Other austral migrants that reach Borneo include the Sacred Kingfisher, Australian Pratincole, Rainbow Bee-eater, Blue-tailed Bee-eater, Whiskered Tern, Little Grebe and Horsfield's Bronze Cuckoo. Not surprisingly austral migrants are commonest in Kalimantan and are rarely recorded further north. Some birds come from Java, most others from Australia itself. Austral migrants that are likely to occur but have not been recorded yet include Bronze-winged Jacana, page 106, Black-faced Cuckoo Shrike, page 224, Australian Hobby, Australian Kestrel, page 98, and Australian Swamp Harrier. Owing to erratic rainfall patterns in central Australia many Australian waterbirds are irruptive nomads or migrants. They breed in large numbers when temporary lakes become available. Afterwards the young birds disperse widely, often travelling thousands of kilometres, breeding again when they find suitable conditions. Dusky Moorhen and Black-necked Stilt are both irruptive migrants which have bred at least once in Kalimantan and Australian Pratincole is another possibility. Pelicans seen in Kalimantan almost certainly refer to irruptive Australian Pelicans.

1

imm.   adult

2

adult

imm.   adult

nm.

3   imm.

adult

4

5

adult

imm.

4   adult

imm.

5   imm.

adult

BLACK AND SERPENT EAGLES, BAT HAWK

1 BLACK EAGLE *Ictinaetus malayensis* **70cm** Scarce resident

An uncommon large eagle of lowland and hilly forests and wooded grassy hillsides. Typically seen circling low above the forest canopy. Elsewhere in Asia the Black Eagle is a specialist at grabbing prey with its legs in slow flight. Prey is snatched from the canopy (particular young nesting birds), from the ground (rats) and from the walls of caves, including bats and swiftlets in their nests (Ferguson-Lees). Usually seen in pairs. Distinguished from dark phase changeable Hawk-Eagle by yellow cere. **Call:** A single high-pitched descending whistle. Also a plaintive *klee-kee* (Sheldon). **Range:** India, to S. China east to the Moluccas.

2 CRESTED SERPENT EAGLE *Spilornis cheela* **50cm** Common resident

The Serpent Eagle is SE Asia's commonest most widespread forest raptor, and the same is true of Borneo. Perches prominently waiting for a snake or lizard to move in the vicinity, flies to grab it, then takes it back to its perch to eat. Also feeds on birds and rats. Both this and the Kinabalu Serpent Eagle have a similar distinctive underwing pattern and clear yellow facial skin. **Call:** A clear far-carrying repeated two note *klip klee* or *kwee kwee* and single and triple note variations thereof. **Range:** India to S China south to Malay P, Sumatra, Borneo, Java, Palawan.

3 KINABALU SERPENT EAGLE *Spilornis kinabaluensis* **55cm** Montane endemic

[Mountain Serpent Eagle] A locally common endemic serpent eagle found throughout the N Bornean mountains South to Gng Menyopa (E. Kalimantan) above around 900m where the mountain forest becomes stunted on ridges. Hunts by sailing along mountain ridge tops and along dried up riverbeds. Although the range of Crested Serpent Eagle and Kinabalu Serpent Eagle do overlap in height they do not overlap in habitat, and they are found on the same mountains such as Kinabalu, Mulu and Murud in different vegetation zones. Generally darker than Crested Serpent Eagle but very similar. Distinguished by call and habitat. **Call:** 'A diagnostic long thin scream' (Wells). A single drawn out *kiillii* (van Balen). Common in the Crocker Range, Sabah but scarce on Kinabalu. **BLI:** Vulnerable.

4 BAT HAWK *Machaeramphus alcinus* **45cm** Local resident

A locally common resident in the vicinity of bat colonies including large limestone caves and hollow trees in primary forest. Crepuscular. Active mainly at dusk when bats emerge from their sleeping quarters and less often at dawn when the bats return. Will also hunt at night when moon is full. Catches bats and swallows them whole on the wing, immediately looking for the next bat. Catches up to 14 bats per night (Ferguson-Lees). Also eats swiftlets and other birds. Nests and roosts in emergent forest trees with pale trunks typically *Koompasia excelsa* (page 203). During the day snoozes with prominent white eyelids closed giving the false impression of being awake. White on the throat is very variable. Young are blotched white below and on the nape. **Call:** A series of high-pitched *kee* or *kek* calls. **Range:** Africa; Malaya, Sumatra, Borneo.

NAMING THE SERPENT EAGLE: THE DIFFERENCE BETWEEN RACE AND SPECIES

In 1758 the Swedish botanist Linnaeus first proposed a two part (bi-nomial) naming system for all plants and animals, consisting of a genus name and a species name. Linnaean taxonomy and Latin nomenclature (naming) is now used by all the world's scientists to classify all life on earth. With birds a tri-nomial (three part) system including a race or subspecies is now used. In the first edition of Smythies' Birds of Borneo (1960) the Kinabalu Serpent Eagle was listed as *Spilornis* (genus) *cheela* (species) *kinabaluensis* (race) indicating that the Serpent Eagle found on Kinabalu differed only in appearance and size from the lowland Serpent Eagle *Spilornis cheela pallidus*. However, by the third edition (1981) it was listed as Kinabalu Serpent Eagle *Spilornis* (genus) *kinabaluensis* (species) indicating that it was now regarded as a separate (endemic) species. A simple way to define a species is that in the wild one species will only breed with the same species. If two similar looking birds overlap in distribution, or come into regular contact but do not interbreed then they must be separate species. From observations between 1960 and 1981 it appeared that the Serpent Eagle living in the Bornean mountains had a distinctively different call and habits and was not found to breed with the lowland Serpent Eagle, therefore it was 'split' by ornithologists to become a separate (endemic) species (Wells). See also pages 41 and 240.

1

imm.

adult

2

imm.

adult

3

At dusk large numbers of bats emerge from the Gomantong caves whilst swiftlets return to their nests.

HARRIERS AND BLACK-SHOULDERED KITE

HARRIERS [Malay: Lang sawah (swamp) or Lang katak (frog)] are long-winged, long-tailed birds of prey that fly low over marshes and padi fields startling and flushing out rats and waterbirds on which to drop with extended legs. In Borneo they are scarce winter migrants from N Asia. Males and females differ. Young males are very similar to the browner more streaky females. Adult male harriers are rarely seen in Borneo. As usual with raptors females are larger than males. All females and immature males have a white rump patch apart from Western Marsh Harrier. Harriers make a variety of undistinctive whistle calls. See also page 101

1   BLACK-SHOULDERED KITE   *Elanus caeruleus*   **30cm**   **Common resident**

Previously a rare vagrant to the NW coast of Borneo and a scarce resident of Kalimantan but in recent years has become increasingly common over grassland and padi fields often on the edge of towns throughout Borneo. Not shy. Hunts by hovering in one spot looking for prey. Look for distinctive black marks on pale grey wings. **Range:** Breeds throughout much of S Europe, Africa and Asia,.

2   EASTERN MARSH HARRIER   *Circus spilonotus*   **50cm**   **Scarce winter visitor**

[Davison: Eurasian Marsh Harrier] Previously combined with Western Marsh Harrier as one species but now split. The commonest harrier seen in Borneo. Regularly recorded quartering NW coastal padi fields, but quite scarce elsewhere. Harriers roost on the ground at night for mutual protection in small groups of mixed species. One such roost has been reported from the Tempasuk Plain. **Range:** Breeds NE Asia and winters southwards.

3   HEN HARRIER   *Circus cyaneus*   **49cm**   **Rare winter visitor**
A number of scattered sight records from the Tempasuk Plain, Tambunan Plain, Kelabit Highlands and E Kalimantan. Adult male plumage is distinctive but rarely seen. **Range:** Resident worldwide including Americas. In Asia breeds in N China, wintering southwards.

4   WESTERN MARSH HARRIER   *Circus aeruginosus*   **50cm**   **Status unknown**
There are no formal records of this species occurring in Borneo but from sight records may be a regular visitor to the Tempasuk Plain. In recent years has been twice seen in Singapore. Either this bird is undergoing a range expansion or it may have been confused with Eastern Marsh Harrier. Distinguished by lack of bars on tail and by the absence of a white rump in all sexes and plumages. **Range:** Breeds Europe to NW Asia and winters south to Africa, India and rarely, Thailand, Singapore.

5   PIED HARRIER   *Circus melanoleucos*   **45cm**   **Vagrant**
Occurs in the same habitat as Marsh Harrier but much less common. According to Harrison the commonest harrier over the padi fields of the Kelabit Highlands. Elsewhere prefers dryer ground such as young oil palm. **Range:** A globally scarce harrier that breeds in E Siberia, NE China and NE India. A recent aberrant breeding record from Luzon, Philippines.

POTENTIAL MIGRANT RAPTOR WATCH SITES IN BORNEO (see map page 100)
Large migrant raptors such as the Harriers, Honey Buzzard and the Grey-faced Buzzard are probably under-recorded in Borneo because no good migrant raptor watch sites are yet known. Potential hawk watch sites in NW Borneo are (1) Tip of Borneo 30 minutes' drive north of Kudat (3 hours drive north of KK); (2) Northern tip of the Benkoka Peninsula; (3) Telecoms tower in the hills above the old road between KK and Kota Belud; (4) Kokol Ridge above Telipok on the KK to Tuaran road. The best time to look for migrant raptors would be 10.00am–5.00pm in the second half of October for the southward migration and in March for the return journey north to the breeding grounds in N Asia. During the heat of midday these raptors often fly so high they cannot be seen. Satellite tracking of Honey Buzzards by Higuchi prove that some raptors at least arrive in Borneo from the south-west via Sumatra and the Indonesian island of Belitung. Davison and others have seen Japanese Sparrowhawks island-hopping south from Pulau Laut across the Java Sea. Finally, there have been many reports of raptors including Peregrines and Japanese Sparrowhawks arriving on the west coast of Borneo from Vietnam. The shortest distance Vietnam to Borneo is 850 km, so at an estimated speed of 45 km/hour all of these raptors must have flown part of the journey at night.

adult

imm.

1

2

♀

♂

3

♀

♂

4

imm.

♂

5

♀

♂

Tempasuk Plain

FALCONS

FALCONIDAE: **World 58 species; Borneo 7 species, 3 residents, 1 endemic.** Falcons are birds of prey which have frequently been trapped and trained to hunt for their masters (falconry), but there is no falconry tradition in Borneo. Borneo is also the home of the world's smallest falcons, two closely related tiny forest falconets which breed in old barbet or woodpecker holes and feed on Borneo's giant insects. See pages 80 and 213. Falcon females are usually larger than males and some have a streaky plumage similar to juveniles. Calls are not very distinctive – sharp *keks* and screams. Falcons are at the top of the food chain and like many trophic feeders tend to accumulate toxic chemicals in their fat. In Europe and the USA the use of the pesticide DDT on grain crops eaten by pigeons led to the collapse of the peregrine population, which only recovered after DDT was banned.

1   BLACK-THIGHED FALCONET   *Microhierax fringillarius*   **15cm**   **Local resident**

Usually seen perched near the top of a tall dead tree at the edge of primary or mature secondary forest. Often in pairs, sometimes in small family groups. *Microhierax* falconets are believed to be communal hunters and breeders with several adults of both sexes assisting with the feeding of the young (Kemp/Van Zyl re Thailand). In Borneo occurs throughout lowland and hill forests south of the Sabah border. In Sabah replaced by the Bornean Falconet. **Call:** Shrill *kee kee kee*. **Range:** Myanmar to Malay P, Sumatra, Java.

2   BORNEAN FALCONET   *Microhierax latifrons*   **15cm**   **Scarce endemic Sabah**

[White-fronted Falconet] The world's smallest bird of prey. Habits similar to *M. fringillarius* but Bornean Falconet is confined to Sabah. Sexes differ. Male has white forehead, female has orange forehead. Immatures resemble females. Falconets usually feed on large insects but may also catch birds and small lizards. In Sabah, widespread throughout lowland primary forest but scarce. Most common in the hills e.g. Poring, Crocker Range, Danum. Resident at Sepilok. **Call:** Shrill *kee kee kee*.

3   PEREGRINE FALCON   *Falco peregrinus ernesti*   **45cm**   **Scarce resident race**

The uncommon dark resident race *F. p. ernesti* breeds on isolated cliffs in forested areas, but wanders widely and can be seen anywhere in Borneo. Often seen on Kinabalu, but no breeding records. **Breeding records. Sabah:** Segarong Caves (Semporna), Tapadong Caves (Segama River). **Sarawak:** The type specimen was collected nesting on Gng Dulit by Ernest Hose in 1892 (Hose 1929). Also Mulu, Gng Hose, Gng Batu Lawi. **Kalimantan:** Many suitable nesting sites, but no records. **Range:** Resident from Malaya east to N Guinea.

4   PEREGRINE FALCON   *Falco peregrinus calidus*   **45cm**   **Common migrant race**

The pale migrant peregrine *F.p. calidus* is a common winter visitor to NW coastal districts and more rarely occurs throughout Borneo. Flexible in hunting techniques and prey. Often 'stoops' on its victim from a great height. In Borneo recorded feeding on waders, swiftlets and forest birds. For several years a pair wintered in the centre of KK feeding on feral pigeons. Another bird caught bats at dusk as they emerged from their roost in a hollow casuarina tree at Tg Aru beach. **Call:** Sharp *kek kek* calls. **Range:** Breeds arctic tundra winters south.

| Bornean Falconet | Long-tailed Broadbill | Eurasian Hobby | Moustached Hawk-Cuckoo |

Note the similarity of aposematic (danger warning) head patterns, the shape of the black and white markings mimicking a powerful beak. In only 2 of these 4 birds is the threat of potential attack genuine. This is therefore a mimicry ring involving both Batesian and Mullerian mimicry. See page 80.

1

adult

imm

1 adult

2 adult

♂

2

imm

3

adult

imm

juv

adult

juv

4

adult

imm

adult

adult

KESTRELS AND HOBBYS

1 COMMON KESTREL *Falco tinnunculus* **33 cm** **Scarce migrant**

Erratic winter visitor to the NW Borneo coast south to Kuching. In some years common, in others absent. Usually seen perched on a post in open countryside or hovering above grassland with vertical fluttering of wings, a similar habit to Black-shouldered Kite. Sight records from the Mahakam River may refer to vagrant Spotted Kestrels, a common resident of Java and Bali, or vagrant Australian Kestrels which reach Java. **Range:** Breeds Europe to Japan, winters south.

2 SPOTTED KESTREL *Falco moluccensis* **30 cm** **Vagrant**

A resident of the Indonesian islands collected once in Kalimantan *c.* 1850 (See Mann 2008). **Range:** Resident in Java, Bali and the Moluccas.

3 EURASIAN HOBBY *Falco subbuteo* **33cm** **Vagrant**

Two records only. Immature at Wasan Brunei in Oct. (Mann). One on Pulau Layang Layang in late September was hunting small migrant birds (Davison 1999). **Range:** Breeds Europe to Japan, NW China, winters Africa and India.

4 ORIENTAL HOBBY *Falco severus* **25 cm** **Vagrant**

Five definite records (Mann 2008) from forested areas scattered throughout Borneo. Hobbies are small very fast flying falcons, capable of chasing and catching a swifts. In Europe hobbys are typically seen hunting for dragonflies over marshes or chasing swifts . Distinguish from Eurasian Hobby by smaller size and more rufous underparts. **Range:** Breeds India to SW China, east to New Guinea and the Solomon Islands. Some populations winter south. A rare resident of lowland forests in Java and Bali (MacKinnon 1993).

5 AUSTRALIAN HOBBY *Falco longipennis* **33cm** **Not Recorded**

Although never collected in Borneo, this small falcon could easily turn up as a vagrant from Australia. Hobbies are regular recorded in the vicinity of bat caves in Borneo. The problem is distinguishing which species of hobby when in flight at dusk. **Range:** An uncommon resident throughout Australia. Some birds migrate north in the austral winter to N Guinea and E Indonesia.

AUSTRALIAN KESTREL *Falco cenchroides* **33cm**
Not Recorded

[Nankeen Kestrel] Resident in open areas throughout Australia but generally uncommon. Vagrants could easily turn up in south and east Kalimantan. **Range:** An uncommon local nomad throughout Australia and S New Guinea. A regular austral winter migrant to the Lesser Sunda Islands of E Indonesia and an occasional vagrant to Bali and Java.

RODENT PLAGUES AND IRRUPTIVE RAPTORS

Small rodents such as rats and mice breed at a very young age, and produce large numbers of young when food is temporarily abundant. Once the food runs out hordes of starving rodents invade crops and houses looking for food. The story of the Pied Piper of Hamelin is based on such an event. In areas of seasonally dry climates such as N Australia and the steppes of NE Asia rainfall is often erratic. Rainfall results in seeding grasses and an explosion in the populations of both of rodents and their predators, kestrels. In the following drought the rodents die and large numbers of kestrels 'irrupt' or migrate away looking for food. This is why kestrels from the grasslands of NE Asia may be common in NW Borneo in some years and not in others. **Note:** Although fluctuations in rodent populations are often related to food supply, some rodent populations also fluctuate regularly over many years even when food is available. Rodent population cycles were first studied by Elton (1924), and continue to intrigue researchers who are still discovering new twists in the story nearly a hundred years later. See Phillipps & Phillipps (2014) *A Field Guide to the Mammals of Borneo and their Ecology*. See also page 128.

1

♂

♀

♂

♀

2

♀

♂

♀

1 Common
kestrel

3

adult

imm

adult

adult

4

adult
♂

5

imm
♀

imm

Ricefield mouse

GOSHAWK AND SPARROWHAWKS

Sparrowhawks and Goshawks are medium-sized shy birds of prey that normally perch concealed in the top of a leafy tree. They have broad wings that allow them to hunt small birds by surprise as they fly slowly, weaving through the trees of the forest edge. Females are always substantially larger than males and often duller and more streaked. Immature birds resemble females. Calls are harsh shrieks and chatterings. Nests are stick platforms concealed high up in trees. See also flight illustrations page 101

1 CRESTED GOSHAWK *Accipiter trivirgatus* 37–46cm   Local forest resident

A locally common resident of the primary forest edge from the lowlands to the hills. Often perches for long periods at the top of a dead tree overlooking a clearing. Feeds on small birds, nestlings, lizards and snakes. Distinguish from other small hawks by large size and habit of prominent perching. Distinguished from Grey-faced Buzzard by crest and broader wings. **Range:** India to S China south to Malay P, Sumatra, Borneo, Java, Philippines.

2 EURASIAN SPARROWHAWK *Accipiter nisus* 32–39cm   Vagrant

A rare vagrant, most likely to occur on the NW coast. One specimen collected near Kuching and several sight records. **Range:** Breeds Europe to China. Winters south to SE Asia.

3 CHINESE GOSHAWK *Accipiter soloensis* 28cm   Scarce passage migrant

[Davison: Chinese Sparrowhawk] [Frog Hawk] A regular passage migrant through Borneo most likely to occur in NE Borneo. Feeds on frogs and insects in wooded marshland and along forest streams. Raptor watchers on Sangihe Island between Mindanao and Sulawesi estimated that 400,000 raptors (98% Chinese Goshawks) use this route each autumn (www.natural-research.org). **Range:** Breeds E Asia winters east of Borneo in Sulawesi and the Molluccas.

4 BESRA *Accipiter virgatus* 24–36cm   Local submontane resident

A scarce submontane resident found in the forested hills and mountains throughout Borneo. Nesting recorded at KNP HQ and in the Crocker Range. Odd coastal records from Similajau and Lumut, Brunei indicate that migrants from continental Asia might stray to Borneo. Distinguish from other hawks by prominent rufous feathers on breast and thighs distinctive to the Borneo race. **Range:** Breeds India, China, Malay P, Philippines.

5 JAPANESE SPARROWHAWK *Accipiter gularis* 25–30cm   Common winter visitor

The commonest sparrowhawk found in wooded areas throughout Borneo from the lowlands to the hills, but like most sparrowhawks very shy and not often seen. Reaches Borneo both via the Philippines and direct across the S China Sea. Recorded from P Layang[2] and Tembungo Oil Platform (Sabah). Also recorded on migration on islands in the Java Sea en route from Borneo to Java in mid-October (Davison). **Range:** Breeds E Siberia to Japan, wintering south.

EAST ASIAN RAPTOR FLYWAY   Every autumn over a million raptors leave their breeding grounds in NE Asia to winter in SE Asia. Raptors migrate during the day to take advantage of columns of hot air rising off the land (thermals), on which they soar. Thermals are strongest over land, so raptors make sea crossings where the gap is narrowest. As far as possible, raptors follow coastlines, 'island hopping' and roosting on islands overnight. Raptors may fly at night if they have not reached land by nightfall (Bildstein). These habits 'funnel' migrating raptors into 'bottle necks' at sea crossings where large numbers can be watched during peak seasons. East Asian raptor migration routes and watch sites are shown next page. In many countries watch sites are major tourist attractions where thousands of raptors can be seen daily.
Borneo Raptor Watch Sites   The most likely sites and dates are given on page 94.
Commonest Migrant Raptors   At Chumphon in Thailand 21 different raptor species have been recorded on migration (Decandido/Allen). In Borneo the commonest migrating raptors are likely to be Honey Buzzard, Grey-faced Buzzard, Chinese Goshawk and Japanese Sparrowhawk.
www.thairaptorgroup.com, www.bcst.or.th, www.globalraptors.org, www.greenparty.org.tw

1

adult

imm.

adult

2

imm.
♀

♂

imm.
♀

♂

imm.

3

♂

imm.

adult

adult
♂

♂

imm.
♂

4

5

♂

♂

♀

imm.
♂

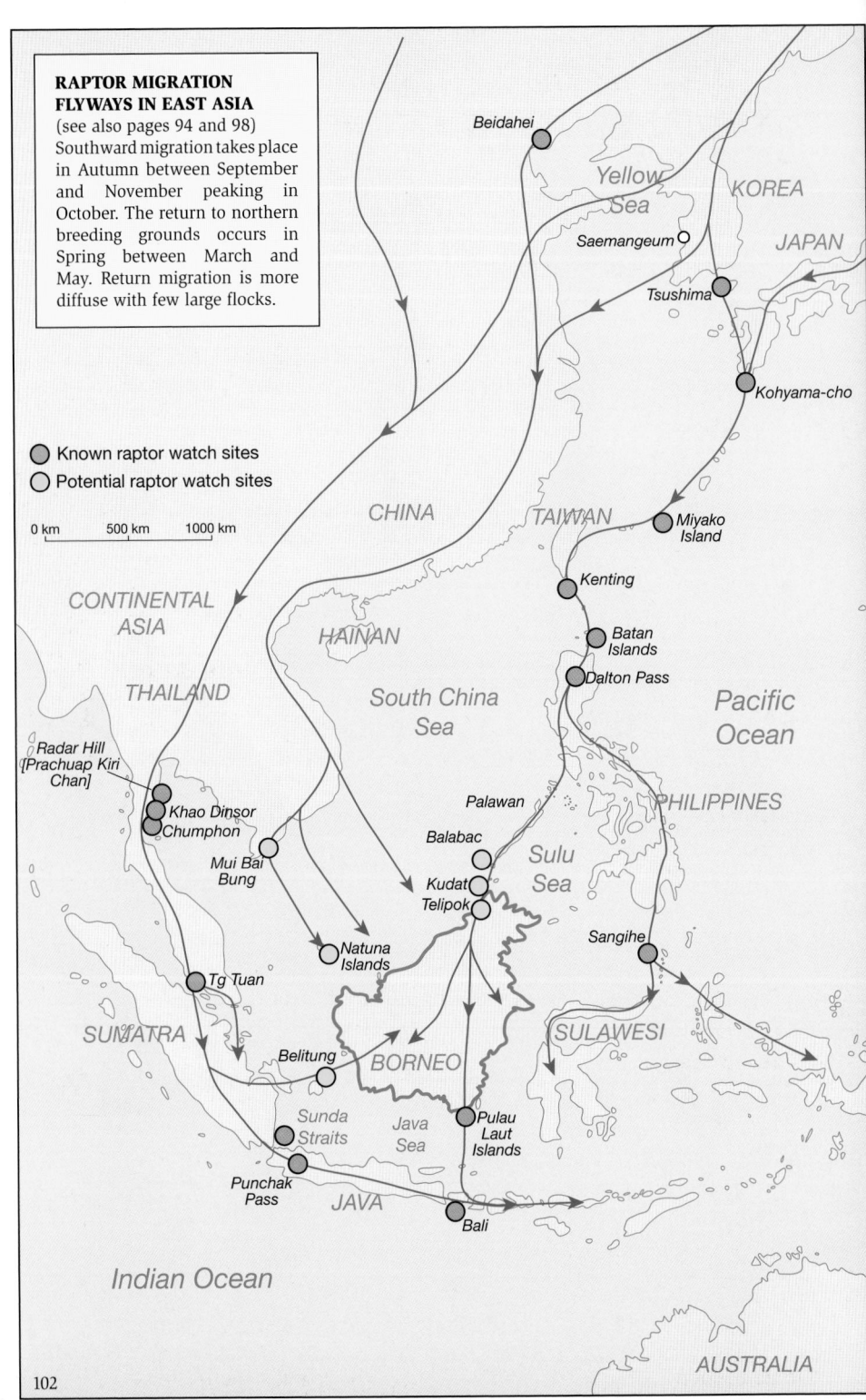

RAPTOR MIGRATION FLYWAYS IN EAST ASIA
(see also pages 94 and 98)
Southward migration takes place in Autumn between September and November peaking in October. The return to northern breeding grounds occurs in Spring between March and May. Return migration is more diffuse with few large flocks.

- ⬤ Known raptor watch sites
- ◯ Potential raptor watch sites

0 km   500 km   1000 km

Yellow Sea
Beidahei
KOREA
JAPAN
Saemangeum
Tsushima
Kohyama-cho
CHINA
TAIWAN
Miyako Island
Kenting
HAINAN
Batan Islands
Dalton Pass
CONTINENTAL ASIA
South China Sea
Pacific Ocean
THAILAND
PHILIPPINES
Radar Hill [Prachuap Kiri Chan]
Khao Dinsor
Chumphon
Palawan
Mui Bai Bung
Balabac
Sulu Sea
Kudat
Telipok
Sangihe
Natuna Islands
Tg Tuan
SUMATRA
Belitung
BORNEO
SULAWESI
Sunda Straits
Java Sea
Pulau Laut Islands
Punchak Pass
JAVA
Bali
Indian Ocean
AUSTRALIA

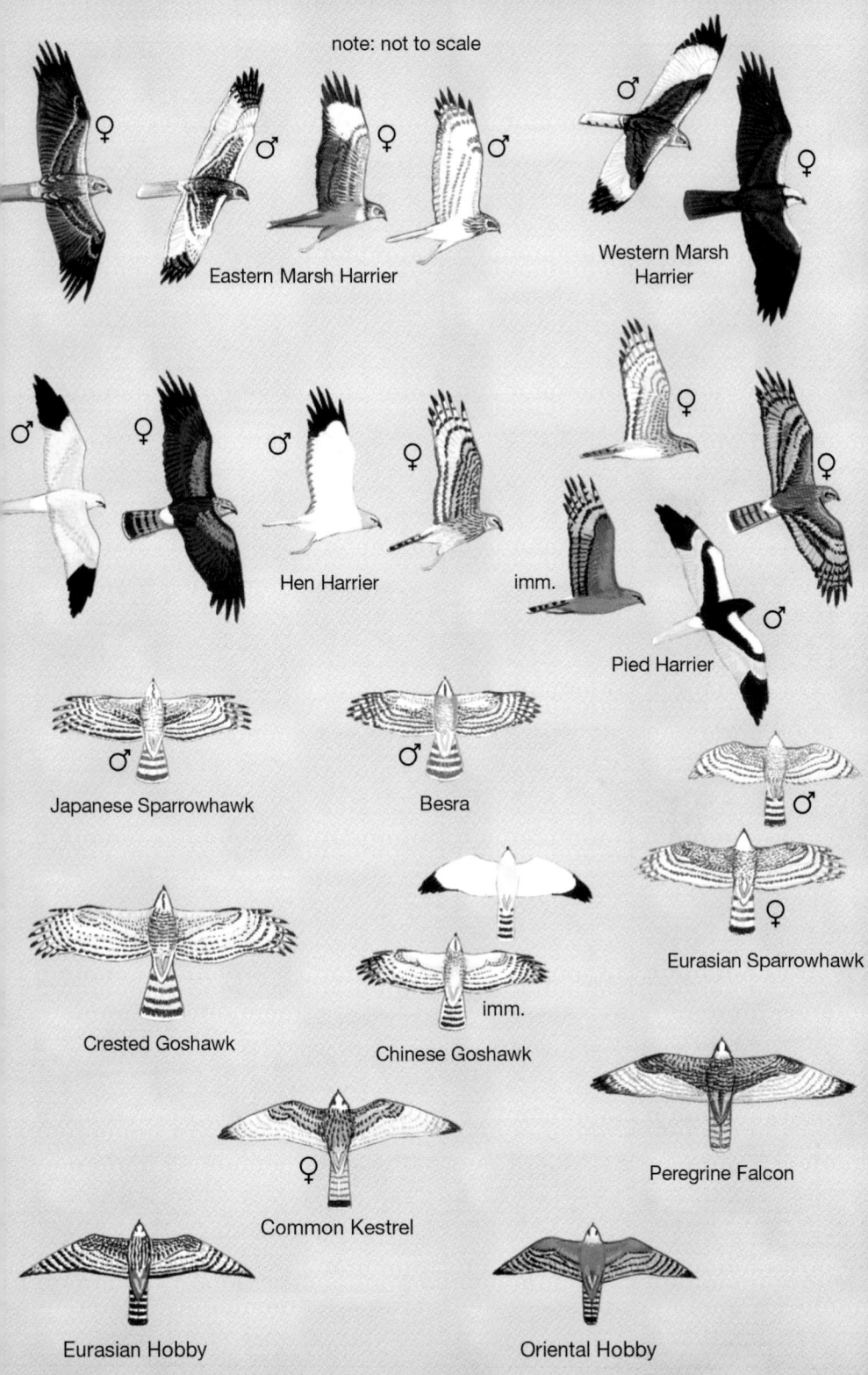

note: not to scale

Eastern Marsh Harrier

Western Marsh Harrier

Hen Harrier

imm.

Pied Harrier

Japanese Sparrowhawk

Besra

Eurasian Sparrowhawk

Crested Goshawk

imm.

Chinese Goshawk

Peregrine Falcon

Common Kestrel

Eurasian Hobby

Oriental Hobby

CRAKES

RALLIDAE **World 150 species; Borneo 15 species.** Shy and secretive birds of freshwater swamps and marshes, often crepuscular. Despite their ungainly looking flight, fast flapping with legs dangling, many local crakes and rails make extensive nomadic movements at night, flying from drying out swamps to wetter areas. Recorded crossing high forested hills such as the Crocker Range in Sabah to get to the interior padi fields of Ranau and Tambunan. Others migrate thousands of kilometres from N Asia to winter in Borneo. Generally monogamous, the males defend breeding territories when nesting making a variety of harsh croaks and wails, often heard at night. Respond well to tape playback. The nests are cup-shaped, usually raised on marshy ground above flood level and concealed in reeds. Young resemble small black domestic chicks. Sexes similar, immatures much duller. Food is a mixture of aquatic insects, worms, snails and grass seeds.

1   RED-LEGGED CRAKE   *Rallina fasciata*   23cm   **Scarce resident and nomad**

Scarce resident of damp grassland and swamps throughout Borneo. Also recorded as a local nomad or migrant at KNP HQ, and Sabah Turtle Islands. In the Philippines inhabits lalang grass covered hillsides as well as swamps. **Call:** The territorial call is a loud series of nasal **pek** calls, repeated every half second at dawn and dusk in the breeding season (Robson). A series of loud **ehh** calls followed by an ascending trill most frequent at dawn and dusk (Jeyarajasingam). **Range:** India to Philippines, Sumatra, Borneo, Java, Bali, Sulawesi.

2   SLATY-LEGGED CRAKE   *Rallina eurizonides*   25cm   **Not recorded**

Resident in the Philippines and Sulawesi. A migrant from Continental Asia to the Malay Peninsula, Singapore, Sumatra and W Java but no records yet for Borneo. Most likely to be found along the banks of forest streams or rivers in NW Borneo. Very similar to Red-legged Crake but has grey legs. **Call:** Loud **kek-kek** and croaking **kraah** calls, often at night (Shimba).

3   BAILLON'S CRAKE   *Porzana pusilla*   18cm   **Rare migrant possible resident**

Widespread in seasonally flooded lakes and swamps in Asia and Australia. Recorded rarely as a winter migrant on the west coast of Borneo. A record from E Kalimantan may be a local breeder or an austral migrant. A small crake with green legs. Look for distinctive black and white barred underparts. Face is grey with a buffy stripe through eye. **Call:** 'The males advertising call is a hard, dry rattle lasting 1–3 seconds, repeated every 1–2 seconds' (Taylor). **Range:** Europe to Asia, Borneo, New Guinea, Australia.

4   RUDDY-BREASTED CRAKE   *Porzana fusca*   21cm   **Rare migrant possible resident**

A scarce resident in Kalimantan swamps including the Mahakam Lakes and a rare vagrant to the coastal districts of W Borneo. Recent record Penampang Oct 2011 (Lai Jiun Loong). **Call:** Less vocal than other crakes (Taylor). Harsh **tewk** or **kyot** notes like knocking on a door (Robson). A soft **kek** uttered infrequently and a sharp whinnying trill with a slightly descending pitch (Jeyarajasingam). **Range:** South and E Asia to Malay P, Philippines, Sulawesi.

5   BAND-BELLIED CRAKE   *Porzana paykulli*   22cm   **Rare migrant**

Little known migrant to swamps, padi fields throughout Borneo. Has been collected in the Kelabit Highlands. Scarce throughout its global range with habits little known. **Call:** The advertising call is distinctive, a loud metallic clangour tailing into brief trills like the sound of a wooden rattle mainly uttered at dusk and dawn or at night (Taylor). **Range:** Breeds N Asia winters SE Asia.

6   WHITE-BROWED CRAKE   *Porzana cinerea*   20cm   **Local winter visitor**

Locally common resident of lowland swamps and padi fields but rarely seen. Similar in size to Baillon's Crake but has plain not striped underparts and a distinct white stripe in front of the eye. **Call:** Repeated two note contact call given by pairs or members of a group variously described as **cutchi cutchi cutchi** (McKinnon), **ee-ah, ee-ah, ee-ah** (Sheldon), **chika chika chika** (Taylor). **Range:** Malay P, Borneo, Sumatra, Java, Bali, Sulawesi, Philippines to Polynesia.

RAILS AND JACANAS MALAY: SINTAR OR AYAM SAWAH (SWAMP HEN)

1 WATER RAIL *Rallus aquaticus* **31 cm**   **Vagrant**
[Eastern Water Rail *Rallus indicus*] Rare vagrant to W Borneo, 7 records only. Not recorded in Sabah or Philippines, therefore must cross the S China sea direct from Vietnam. **Call:** Grunting notes rising in the middle of the call to high pitched, trilling whistles, likened to piglets squealing, and usually dying away into more grunts (Taylor). **Range:** Europe, Africa, Asia.

2 SLATY-BREASTED RAIL *Gallirallus striatus* **24 cm**   **Common resident**

Second commonest rail, widespread in padi fields, swamps and mangroves. Illustration shows *G. s. gularis* the S Borneo race. N Borneo race *G. s. striatus* is darker above and below and without white throat. **Call:** A buzzing **kech**, repeated 10 to 15 times, starting weakly, becoming stronger and then fading (McKinnon). **Range:** SE Asia, Philippines, Sumatra, Java, Sulawesi.

3 BARRED RAIL *Galliralllus torquatus* **34 cm**   **New immigrant from Phillppines**
First recorded on Pom Pom Island, Semporna in Dec 2010 (Sally Usher/M&M Burge). Recently recorded P Seligan, Sabah (Hamit Suban/Adrian Migiu). Sabah is only 50 km from Tawi Tawi which has a Philippine avifauna and future range expansion of this and other Philippine birds to the Bornean mainland is likely. Distinguish by head marking with white stripe below eye. Sexes similar. Immature has pale brown instead of rufous breast band. **Call:** Harsh croaks and screams given by more than one bird at a time from dense cover (Taylor). **Range:** Philippines, Sulawesi, New Guinea.

4 BUFF-BANDED RAIL *Gallirallus philippensis* **30 cm**   **Rapidly expanding population**
A common resident of the Philippines and Australia. First recorded Sabah at Tempasuk Plain Oct. 2007 (Madoya). Now widespread. Recent records from Kota Kinabalu; Wasan, Brunei; Miri, Kuching. First recorded Borneo 2004 (Myers). Breeding Ketapang, W. Kalimantan 2009 (Udin, Abdurrahman al Qadrie), Penampang 2013 (Cheah). **Call:** Territorial call *coo-aw-ooo-aw-ooo-aw* like braying donkey. (Pizzey). **Range:** Africa, Asia, Philippines, Sulawesi, New Guinea, Australia and New Zealand.

JACANAS: WORLD: 7 species. **BORNEO**: 2 species, 1 possible vagrant. Long legged freshwater birds with very long toes which allow them to walk on top of lilies and other floating plants. All species are believed to have the sex roles reversed and are polyandrous the female mating with multiple different males, who incubate the eggs and rear the young.

5 PHEASANT-TAILED JACANA *Hydrophasianus chirurgus* **33 cm**   **Vagrant**
Most birds are seen in the eclipse (non breeding) plumage which includes non breeding female, male and immature. Sexes are reverse sexually di-morphic, the female being brighter and larger than the male when breeding. Has distinctive white wings tipped black and white underwing in flight. Resident at Bangkau Lake, SE Kalimantan in 1882 but no longer present. Two recent records: Tempasuk (Lansdown Feb. 1986) and Tawau (Wong T.S Nov. 2007). **Range:** Breeds Pakistan to China, south to SE Asia. Some northern populations winter south.

6 BRONZE-WINGED JACANA *Metopidius indicus* **29cm**   **Not recorded**
A common resident of wetlands in S Sumatra and Java. This bird could easily turn up in Kalimantan. **Range:** India to Malay P, Sumatra, Java

7 COMB-CRESTED JACANA *Irediparra gallinacea* **23 cm**   **Local Kalimantan resident**
A locally common resident of the swamps of the Barito River and Negara Lakes in SE Kalimantan. Also recorded from the Mahakam Lakes in E Kalimantan. Adults have bright red chicken like combs on the head. Females are polyandrous soliciting many different males to mate. The male constructs the nest and after egg laying takes over parental responsibility. Unlike the Pheasant-tailed Jacana both sexes have similar plumages. Call: Thin piping (Slater). **Range:** Borneo, Mindanao to S Moluccas, Lesser Sundas to NE Australia.

NOMADIC CRAKES AND RAILS Some of the most obvious recent bird immigrants to Borneo have been rails and water hens including Moorhen, Purple Swamphen, Buff-banded Rail and more recently the Barred Rail. One explanation for their range expansion is the large increase in irrigated ricefields in Borneo. Rails are often trapped as night flying migrants in Asia. To survive the drying out of their favoured swampy habitat rails have developed a nomadic lifestyle which enables them to rapidly colonise new areas once suitable habitat becomes available.

breeding

non-breeding

WATERCOCK, MOORHENS, COOT AND WATERHEN

1 WATERCOCK   *Gallicrex cinerea*   **40cm**   **Scarce resident and migrant**

Crepuscular inhabitant of swamps and padi fields. Occurs in mangroves on migration. Sexually dimorphic, unusual in rails. Normally seen in dull streaky brown plumage which could be female or male eclipse (non-breeding) plumage. Only very rarely seen in male breeding plumage when it can be distinguished from Moorhen by larger size and lack of white markings on side. A scarce migrant from Continental Asia to NW Borneo and a possible resident of the Kalimantan lakes. One breeding record from the Tempasuk Plain (Harrap). **Call:** A noisy bird in the breeding season with a call of three components 10–12 *kok* notes then 10–12 more rapid booming *utumb* notes and finally 5–6 *kluck* notes (Neelakantan). **Range:** Breeds Asia, northern populations winter south. Very large numbers trapped for food on the coast of NW Java during migration seasons may be of Bornean origin.

2 COMMON MOORHEN   *Gallinula chloropus*   **31cm**   **Common resident and migrant**

Previously a common resident of the Kalimantan lakes and a scarce winter visitor to NW Borneo. Now an increasingly common resident of swampy areas throughout Borneo. Not common in Sarawak but recent breeding records from Kelabit Highlands (Gregory-Smith). Comes out to feed in small groups on open areas of swamp and marsh, running back to hide in dense vegetation when disturbed. **Call:** Loud *prunk*. **Range:** Africa, Europe to Asia, Borneo, Sumatra, Java, Sulawesi. Also Americas.

3 PURPLE SWAMPHEN   *Porphyrio porphyrio*   **42cm**   **Local resident**

[Purple Gallinule] [Black-backed Swamphen]. Common resident at the Kalimantan lakes. An increasingly common resident in W Sabah in padi fields and freshwater swamps. Often feeds in loose groups with Common Moorhen but larger, more brightly coloured and shyer. **Call:** Very vocal. The song is a long powerful series of plaintive nasal rattles (Taylor). **Range:** Africa, Europe, SE Asia, Australia. **Taxonomy:** Look out for very pale Philippine race *P.p. pulverulentus* which could occur.

4 DUSKY MOORHEN   *Gallinula tenebrous*   **30cm**   **Status unknown**

An Australian species, previously recorded nesting on Bangkau Lake in SE Kalimantan (Negara Lakes) by Grabowsky in 1882. No records in recent years. Many Australian waterbirds, e.g. pelicans, stilts, moorhen are irruptive in drought years and may temporarily occupy new territory before disappearing. In Australia prefers open water and avoids areas of water hyacinth. Distinguish from Common Moorhen by red not green legs and no white on flanks. **Call:** Rapidly repeated, resonant *koks*, strident *kerk*, repeated shrieks (Pizzey). **Range:** Sulawesi, Lesser Sundas and S Moluccas to Australia.

5 COMMON COOT   *Fulica atra*   **40cm**   **Vagrant**

Scarce vagrant. Five records from NW Borneo including one present at Panampang for a month in January 2010 (C.K. Leong and Roger Rajah). Prefers open freshwater lakes where it dives to feed on water plants. Has distinctive white bill and knob above beak. **Call:** Sharp repeated *kik kik kik*. **Range:** Europe and Africa to Japan, India, Java, Bali, New Guinea to New Zealand.

6 WHITE-BREASTED WATERHEN   *Amaurornis phoenicurus*   **30cm**   **Common resident**

[Malay: Burung ruak ruak] The most common and least shy Bornean rail, found in swamps, grasslands and mangrove swamps throughout Borneo, including swamps in open country in the mountains. Feeds on grass seeds, fallen padi, insects and tadpoles. Frequently seen crossing roads, often with fatal results to the waterhen. **Call:** Extremely vocal loud gurgles and croaks followed by a steady *kru ark, kru ark, kru ark* heard from swamps at night. **Range:** India to SE Asia, Philippines, Borneo, Java, Sulawesi.

7 MASKED FINFOOT   *Heliopais personata*   **52cm**   **Vagrant**

A globally rare vagrant to Borneo with two records from the N.W. coast. One from Sabah and the other from Maludam in Sarawak in 2004. See Davison (2010), Beintema (2007), Kukila 17 (2013). **Habits:** A large shy waterbird which prefers shady jungle rivers and dense mangrove swamps. **Range:** Breeds Bangladesh, Myanmar, Cambodia, Thailand. Winters south to Malaya and Sumatra.

1

+ non-breeding ♂

breeding ♂

2

4

5

6

juv

7

♂

♀

OYSTERCATCHER, AVOCET, STILTS AND LAPWINGS

1   EURASIAN OYSTERCATCHER   *Haematopus ostralegus*   **45cm**   **Vagrant**
One record only of a bird that spent the winter of 2005–2006 on the mudflats at Bako and Buntal near Kuching. Unmistakable and can only be confused with the very similar Australian Pied Oystercatcher which could possibly stray to the coast of S Kalimantan. However, Pied Oystercatcher has a much reduced white panel on the wing that cannot be seen when the bird is at rest. **Call:** A clear *kleet* or *kleep*. Breeds Europe to E Asia, dispersing south in winter.

RECURVIROSTRIDAE   **World 12 species; Borneo 3 species.**   The Recurvirostridae includes the Pied Avocet, a large black and white wader similar to a stilt but with a long upcurved bill, which it sweeps from side to side in shallow water, a recent vagrant to Borneo.

2   PIED AVOCET   *Recurvirostra avosetta*   **44cm**   **Vagrant**
Two recent records: Buntal Bay nr Kuching (Kong/Bakewell), and Tuaran padi fields nr KK Dec. 2011 (Lai, J.L.). This long-legged elegant black and white wader with black legs and an upcurved bill is unmistakable. In Hong Kong it is an abundant winter visitor to the Deep Bay Wetland Centre with over 5,000 recorded on 23 Feb. 2003. **Range:** Breeds temperate Europe to Asia moving south in winter.

3   BLACK-WINGED STILT   *Himantopus himantopus*   **32cm**   **Scarce winter visitor**

A bird of the Asian Continent which is an increasingly common, regular migrant to NW Borneo in winter months, and has been recorded on migration at P Layang[2]. Feeds in freshwater marshes and wet padi fields, usually in small groups. Distinguished from next species by clear white neck of adults although immature often has a variable amount of dark grey on hind neck. **Call:** Variety of sharp *kik kik kik* calls. **Range:** Europe to Asia, Africa, India, Americas.

4   BLACK-NECKED STILT   *Himantopus leucocephalus*   **37cm**   **Scarce austral migrant**

[White-headed Stilt] An Australian bird which disperses N in the austral winter (May–Sept.) as far as Taiwan and Japan (See also page 90). Recorded in the swamps of NW Borneo May to June in similar habitat to Black-winged Stilt. Distinguished from Black-winged by very variable black hind neck in adults. One breeding record from the Mahakam Lakes in 2000 (Gonner). **Call:** Variety of sharp *kik kik kik* calls. **Range:** Australia, N Zealand, Java, Philippines.

5   GREY-HEADED LAPWING   *Vanellus cinereus*   **36cm**   **Scarce migrant**
Ten + winter records from coastal districts of NW Borneo. Occurs on the coast and on dry or wet grassland, padi fields and stony riverbeds. In flight shows striking pattern of white underbody and under wing contrasting with black wing tips. **Call:** Sharp and loud *kirritt kiritt* (Bhushan *et al.*). **Range:** Breeds S Russia to Japan, and N China migrating south in winter.

6   NORTHERN LAPWING   *Vanellus vanellus*   **32cm**   **Vagrant**
This common very distinctive European bird is a scarce vagrant to Borneo. Two winter records from Brunei only. Preferred habitat is open grazing grounds and damp marshes. **Call:** High-pitched mewing. **Range:** Europe to China and Japan dispersing south in winter. [Note: Both Lapwings are members of the Plover family CHARADRIIDAE. See next page.]4

WETLANDS INTERNATIONAL (WI)   Long before the advent of the nation state, migrant waterbirds were flying unhindered from one country to another. With no ownership of their waterbird populations, nations had no motivation for their conservation. Recognition of these problems led to the international Convention on Wetlands (Ramsar, 1971) and the foundation of WI.
A WATERBIRD CENSUS is organised annually in January to count waterbirds in each Asian nation simultaneously. Local volunteers are always welcome. Data analysis is used to provide early warnings of problems such as pollution. The annual census is organised by WI (previously AWB) a global charity and NGO based in the Netherlands, dedicated to wetland conservation and sustainable management worldwide. WI has carried out work in Kalimantan on the ecological restoration of damaged peatswamp forests at Sabangau. WI also holds the database for world Ramsar Sites (Wetlands of Global Importance). In Borneo, Ramsar Sites include Danau Sentarum (Kalimantan, Lower Kinabatangan-Segama Wetlands (Sabah) and the Kuching Wetlands National Park (Sarawak).   www.wetlands.org   See also page 124.

1

Eurasian   Australian

2

3

4

5

6

SAND PLOVERS AND SMALL PLOVERS

PLOVERS: *CHARADRIIDAE*. WORLD: 65 species. **BORNEO:** 13 species including the Lapwings (see previous page) The 8 very similar small plovers with short necks can be confused with each other. All are migrant apart from the Malaysian Plover, and are usually seen in non-breeding plumage. The 4 commonest are easily distinguished. The two Sand Plovers can be told from the others by the lack of a white hind collar. Kentish Plover is also very common on beaches but has a clear white hind collar. Little Ringed Plover is most common in wet grassland and has a continuous dark breast band. All small plovers flock together on the coast and roost together on coastal grassland. They feed with a characteristic stop-run-stop-run habit.

1 LITTLE RINGED PLOVER *Charadrius dubius curonicus* **16cm**   **Common migrant**

Common Oct–April on the coast often mixing with other plovers, but prefers damp grassland throughout Borneo. Recorded in all months of the year except June. Distinguished by yellow eye ring, pale yellow or flesh coloured legs, and white rear hind collar. A resident race *Charadrius dubius dubius* occurs in the Phillipines and Sulawesi but not yet Borneo. It should be looked for along stony river banks in the lowlands of N Borneo. **Call:** Often calls *pew* in flight. **Range:** Europe to Asia, India to Philippines, Indonesia.

2 KENTISH PLOVER *Charadrius alexandrinus* **17cm**   **Common migrant**

Common Oct–April on the coast with a preference for sandy beaches. Often mixes with other small plovers. Has grey or blackish legs and prominent white hind collar. Distinguished by different habits from the resident Malaysian Plover which is usually seen in pairs on white coral sand beaches or on offshore islands and rarely mixes with other plovers. Kentish Plovers in Borneo with pale pinkish legs are the large-billed E.Asian race *C.a.nihonensis* which may have a complete breast band (Bakewell). **Call:** Soft *hwick* (Viney). **Range:** Europe to China and Japan wintering south to India, S E Asia.

WHITE FACED PLOVER *Charadrius dealbatus*   (illustrated next page)   **Vagrant**
Previously considered a race of Kentish Plover. Believed to breed along the S China coast and winter south to Thailand and the Malay Peninsula. Upper parts paler brown than Kentish, with more extensive white on the forehead and much reduced brown breast tabs (see Kennerley et al 2008). One recent record from Buntal (Bakewell).

3 COMMON RINGED PLOVER *Charadrius hiaticula* **19cm**   **Vagrant**
Similar habits to Little-ringed Plover but much rarer. Has yellow orange legs like Little-ringed but no yellow eye ring, and a more prominent white eyebrow. Unlike Little-ringed has clear white wing bar in flight. In breeding plumage has distinctive black tipped orange bill. **Call:** Soft distinctive *coo-eep*. **Range:** Europe to E Asia wintering S to Africa and SE Asia.

4 LONG-BILLED PLOVER *Charadrius placidus* **21cm**   **Vagrant**
Scarce vagrant to the beaches of NW Borneo. A recent record from Lok Kawi beach KK wintered 2009–10. (A. Reyes) Has continuous thin black breast band even in non breeding plumage. Note that Kentish Plover very rarely has a continuous dark breast band. Generally has longer legs, longer wings and longer bill compared with other small plovers. **Call:** Distinctive *pi wi* . **Range:** Breeds Russia to Japan, wintering southwards.

5 LESSER SAND PLOVER *Charadrius mongolus* **20cm**   **Common migrant**

Slightly less common than Greater. Feeds on coastal mudflats and beaches but at high tide often roosts in mixed flocks on nearby grassland e.g. airports. Difficult to distinguished from Greater except by smaller size when seen together, unless in breeding plumage. Unlike Greater and Kentish which dash after crabs, Lesser prefers to hunt for marine worms and is far less active. (Bakewell). Race *C. m atrifons* could occur with all dark forehead. **Call:** Distinct double or triple note call (Viney). **Range:** Breeds E Siberia tundra. Winters SE Asia, Australia.

6 GREATER SAND PLOVER *Charadrius leschenaultii* **22cm**   **Common migrant**

Common passage migrant and winter visitor. Slightly more common than Lesser. Occurs in similar habitat. Like Kentish actively hunts for small crabs by waiting and then chasing over the sand, in a stop-start-stop sequence. Distinguish from Lesser by heavier bill, bigger size and different call. A good distinguishing feature is that Lesser's bill is blunt-ended and bulbous for the final third of its length. Greater's bill is sharp/taper-ended, and is bulbous for the terminal half of its length (David Bakewell). **Call:** A soft trill *chirrr*. **Range:** Breeds central Asia from Turkey to Mongolia, migrating south in winter to Africa, India, China, Philippines, Australia.

1

juv

non-br

br

2

juv

non-br

br ♂

3

non-br

br

br

4

non-br

frons

br

non-br

5

mongolus

6

juv

non-br

br

MALAYSIAN PLOVER, LARGE PLOVERS AND TURNSTONE

1 MALAYSIAN PLOVER *Charadrius peronii* **15cm** **Local resident**

The only resident wader in Borneo, apart from Beach Stone Curlew which is both very large and very scarce. Usually seen in pairs, on white coral sand beaches. Many island beaches have a resident pair. Rarely associates with flocks of migrant waders seen along the coast. Adult male is similar to adult male Kentish Plover to which it is closely related but black hind collar extends around back of neck. Plumage on back is more mottled compared with Kentish Plover's plain back. **Call:** Undistinctive *chip*. **Range:** Thailand. Malay P, Sumatra, Java, Bali, Sulawesi, Philippines.

2 ORIENTAL PLOVER *Charadrius veredus* **23cm** **Scarce passage migrant**

[Eastern Sand Plover] Scarce passage migrant found on dry grassland. Distinctive upright posture and combination of long legs, long neck and small head distinguish this bird in winter. In breeding plumage male has very distinctive white head contrasting with orange breast. Female (not illustrated) has orange head and breast with white throat. **Call:** In flight a sharp whistling *chip-chip-chip* (Bushan *et al.*). **Range:** Breeds in the dry grassland of W China and Mongolia wintering south to the arid plains of N and Central Australia.

3 PACIFIC GOLDEN PLOVER *Pluvialis fulva* **24cm** **Common migrant**

One of the commonest Bornean waders found in flocks both on mudflats along the coast and on wet and dry short grassland inland (Sept.–Feb.) but recorded year round. Smaller and browner than Grey Plover which is less common and prefers sandy beaches. Very distinctive breeding plumage often seen on arrival and just before departure. **Call:** Plaintive whistles **Range:** Breeds Siberia to Alaska. Winters south to Africa, India, Australia.

4 GREY PLOVER *Pluvialis squatarola* **30cm** **Common migrant**

Less common than Golden Plover and normally confined to coastal mudflats and beaches. Seen mainly on passage but does overwinter. Larger and greyer than Golden Plover. In flight has distinctive black patches where body meets under wing (axillaries). Normally seen in ones or twos. **Call:** Slurred whistle *tlee-oo-ee* the second syllable lower in pitch (Geering *et al.*). **Range:** Breeds N Europe, to Alaska wintering south to Africa, India, SE Asia, Australia.

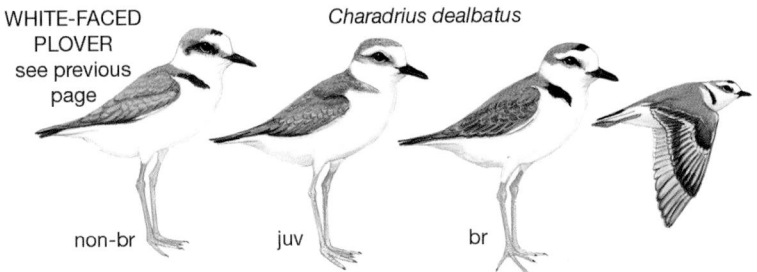

WHITE-FACED PLOVER see previous page

Charadrius dealbatus

non-br   juv   br

SANDPIPERS, SNIPE, CURLEWS AND ALLIES: SCOLIPACIDAE **World 86 species; Borneo 40 species.** Usually birds of muddy beaches or marshes which wade in shallow water probing for clams and worms. The Scolopacidae have very varied and distinctive beaks, the many odd shapes specialised for extracting different types of prey from the mud.

5 RUDDY TURNSTONE *Arenaria interpres* **22cm** **Scarce passage migrant**

Scarce but regular passage migrant seen along the coast during peak migration periods. Often in small groups usually turning over beach flotsam and jetsam in search for insects. Migrant birds have been recorded feeding on noddy eggs on Tubataha Reef in the Sulu Sea. Asian turnstone breed in E Siberia and Alaska with the majority spending the winter months along the coast of Australia. **Call:** Clear, rapid, rolled, staccato *trik tuk-tuk-tuk* or shorter *tuk-e-tuk* (Geering). **Range:** Breeds N Europe to Canada wintering south to Mexico, Africa, SE Asia and Australia.

1 non-br ♂ ♀ ♂

2 juv non-br br ♂

3 juv non-br br

4 non-br br

5 juv non-br br non-br

SNIPE AND WOODCOCK

Woodcock and snipe are long-billed, cryptically coloured birds, active mainly at night probing for worms in soft damp ground. Woodcock inhabit damp forests and snipe are birds of marshes and damp grasslands. Typically they crouch low concealed in damp grass until disturbed when they rise at the last minute with an abrupt zig zag flight and a characteristic alarm call. Snipe species are easily confused in the field. In the hand specimens of the three commonest snipe can be distinguished by the number of needle-like pin feathers in the tail.

1   EURASIAN WOODCOCK   *Scolopax rusticola*   **34cm**   **Vagrant**

A rare migrant with records from Danum and Panaga (Brunei). Breeding Woodcock have a crepuscular display flight known as 'roding' in which they perform a slow flight with rapid wing beats over a forest clearing. In Mindanao, Sulawesi and Java/Sumatra there are three rare endemic woodcocks which inhabit mossy mountain forest. The possibility remains of a very rare relict resident species in the Borneo mountains. Distinguish from snipes by habitat. Also by habits and by bars on head instead of longitudinal stripes. **Call:** Grunts or growling notes in roding flight. **Range:** Breeds Europe to N Asia wintering S to Africa and SE Asia.

2   JACK SNIPE   *Lymnocryptes minimus*   **18cm**   **Not recorded**

A scarce winter migrant to Taiwan and the Philippines from N Asia. A possible record from Brunei (Mann) but no definite Borneo records. Smallest snipe. No coloured feathers in tail. Very reluctant to flush (can sometimes be picked up by hand), and flies off straight, a short distance only, with no call. **Range:** Europe to Siberia wintering south to Africa, Indochina.

3   COMMON SNIPE   *Gallinago gallinago*   **27cm**   **Scarce winter visitor**

The common snipe of Europe. In Borneo is probably the least common of the three commonest snipe. In flight distinguish by white trailing edge to secondary feathers and in the hand 12 to 18 tail feathers, 14 broad feathers and 4 pins. **Call:** On flushing a distinct *sniiipe* and rapid zig zag flight in large circle. **Range:** Breeds Europe to Japan wintering south to SE Asia. Also occurs in the Americas.

4   PINTAIL SNIPE   *Gallinago stenura*   **27cm**   **Common winter visitor**

Commonest snipe in Sarawak including padi fields of the Kelabit Highlands. Distinguish in the hand by 26 to 28 tail feathers of which 6 to 8 are pins. **Call:** *quack* or *squek* when flushed and short zig zag flight. All Borneo snipes are spasmodically common in marshy areas from time to time, indicating that they are locally nomadic as well as migratory winter visitors. **Range:** Europe to China wintering south to Africa, SE Asia, Australia.

5   SWINHOE'S SNIPE   *Gallinago megala*   **28cm**   **Common winter visitor**

Commonest snipe in Sabah. Generally found in wetter areas than Pintail Snipe (Sheldon). Distinguish in the hand by 20 or 22 tail feathers. No wire-like pin tail feathers. In Europe snipe are often hunted for food and sport and Borneo records are mainly derived from the hunting records of early European residents. **Call:** Usually silent when flushed, flight straight. **Range:** Breeds Siberia wintering south to India, SE Asia.

6   JAPANESE SNIPE   *Gallinago hardwickii*   **30cm**   **Not recorded**

[Latham's Snipe] An estimated world population of 36,000 birds breeds in N Japan and adjacent Russia and winters in marshes along the east coast of Australia. There are no records from the Philippines, Borneo or even Wallacea and only a few records from Taiwan and New Guinea. **Call:** Loud *chak* when flushed (Geering *et al.*). **Range:** Breeds N Japan wintering in Australia.

7   GREATER PAINTED SNIPE   *Rostratula benghalensis*   **24cm**   **Scarce resident**

Scattered records from padi fields throughout Borneo indicate an expanding range. Recent breeding records west coast Sabah (Sheldon). Crepuscular and nocturnal. Female is larger and brighter than male and polyandrous. See page 106. **Call:** Breeding female calls long drawn out *koh koh koh* at night. **Range:** Africa to Asia inc. Japan, Philippines, Malay P, Sumatra, Borneo and Java. Another closely related species is an uncommon endemic in Australia.

CURLEW, WHIMBREL, GODWIT AND DOWITCHER   MALAY: B. KEDIDI

1   EURASIAN CURLEW   *Numenius arquata*   **60cm**   **Rare passage migrant**

 This curlew and the next are the largest waders seen on the Borneo coast. They are often hunted and are usually very shy. A scarce passage migrant usually less common than Far-eastern Curlew. Distinguished by slightly smaller size, white under wing and white rump patch seen in flight. Hunts for small crabs and worms on mudflats often in small parties. **Call:** Loud melancholy *curlew*. **Range:** Breeds Europe to N China wintering S to Africa, SE Asia.

2   FAR EASTERN CURLEW   *Numenius madagascariensis*   **62cm**   **Scarce passage migrant**

 A scarce migrant that stops over on passage to and from Australia. More common than Eurasian Curlew, and distinguished by uniform brown rump and uniformly dark underwing. Female bill is up to 3cm longer than male bill. **Call:** Loud melancholy *curlew* but said to be less musical than Eurasian curlew (Viney). Most likely to be seen on extensive mudflats backed by mangroves. **Range:** Breeds E Siberia migrating south to Indonesia, Australia, New Zealand.

3   WHIMBREL   *Numenius phaeopus*   **43cm**   **Common passage migrant and winter visitor**

 The commonest of the curlew tribe in Borneo. Most common on passage but present throughout the winter. Often in small flocks but may feed alone along the edge of the tide or along the banks of muddy rivers. Much smaller than curlew and has distinct head markings of dark and light stripes. Usually roosts in small groups on mangrove roots with other waders. May also roost on short coastal grasslands at high tide but does not feed on grass, unlike Little Curlew. **Call:** Rapid series of seven to nine notes *ti ti ti ti ti ti ti*. **Range:** Circumpolar tundra breeder wintering south to Africa, Arabia, India, Australia and South America.

4   LITTLE CURLEW   *Numenius minutus*   **31cm**   **Very scarce passage migrant**

 A scarce passage migrant with a preference for areas of short dry grass, such as airports, padangs and coastal grazing grounds. Small curlew, with distinctively shaped head and beak. Almost the entire world population c. 180,000 birds winters in Australia flying to the east of Borneo. Recent record Penampang 9 Oct 2011 (C.K. Leong). **Call:** 'In flight, soft whistle *te-te-te*, rising slightly in pitch with each note' (Geering *et al.*). **Range:** Breeds in grassy clearings in Siberian forests wintering in grassy areas of N Australia.

5   BLACK-TAILED GODWIT   *Limosa limosa*   **39cm**   **Scarce passage migrant**

 Uncommon passage migrant to coasts. Distinguished from Bar-tailed Godwit by straight not upturned bill and clear white wing bar in flight. Could be confused with Asian Dowitcher with which it frequently associates but feeds by probing from side to side and picking for food in shallow water not rapid vertical probing in mud. **Call:** Short quiet *took* or *keiki*, often repeated (Geering *et al.*). **Range:** N Europe to E Asia wintering S to Africa, India, Australia.

6   BAR-TAILED GODWIT   *Limosa lapponica*   **41cm**   **Common passage and winter visitor**

 Less scarce than Black-tailed Godwit from which it is distinguished by slightly upturned bill and no white on wing. Recent satellite tracking studies have shown that the Alaskan population flies over 11,000km non stop to winter in New Zealand and along the E coast of Australia. In Borneo commonest during migration and these passage birds probably winter on the W coast of Australia. **Call:** 'Barking *kak-kak*, deep *kirruc*' (Geering *et al.*). **Range:** Breeds N Europe to E Asia and Alaska wintering south to Africa, India, Australia and N Zealand.

7   ASIAN DOWITCHER   *Limnodromus semipalmatus*   **33cm**   **Scarce winter visitor**

 Global population estimated at 24,000. An uncommon winter visitor to coastal mudflats particularly the seaward side of mangroves. Looks superficially like a small Black-tailed Godwit with long straight bill but feeds in typical dowitcher or knot style, rapid probing of the mud with a sewing machine action. Larger than Long-billed Dowitcher and has black not yellow legs. In flight has no white on back or rump. Bill is all black unlike Godwit bills which have a pink base. **Call:** A soft *eeahh* sometimes repeated up to ten or more times. **Range:** Breeds E Siberia wintering in SE Asia. Up to 8,000 winter on the NE coast of Sumatra.

1

non-br

2

non-br ♀

br ♂

juv

3

variegatus

juv

adult

4

5

juv

br

non-br

6

juv

br ♂

non-br

baueri

7

juv

br

non-br

REDSHANK, GREENSHANK AND SANDPIPERS

1 TEREK SANDPIPER *Xenus cinerea* **23cm** Common passage migrant

Commonly seen in small flocks along the coast during peak migration periods and some birds stay to over winter. Very active when feeding at the edge of the tide. Often mixes with other waders. Distinguished by upturned bill with yellow base and yellowish legs. **Call:** 'Sharp, fluty **twit-wit-wit-wit** rising in pitch with each syllable' (Geering *et al.*). **Range:** Breeds temperate Europe to Asia and winters southwards to Africa, India and Australia.

2 COMMON REDSHANK *Tringa totanus* **29cm** Common winter visitor

A common wader of extensive mudflats and mangrove estuaries, occasionally seen in freshwater habitats inland. Some birds are present in every month. Shy and easily spooked, taking off with a loud **teuhuhu** when alarmed. Has distinctive red legs in breeding season becoming more orange in winter. **Call:** A musical, whistling **teu-hu-hu** with a pitch drop after the first note. **Range:** Breeds temperate Eurasia in open marshland, winters S to coastal areas.

3 SPOTTED REDSHANK *Tringa erythropus* **32cm** Scarce passage migrant

A scarce passage migrant to coastal areas often mixed in flocks with other waders. Can be found both on freshwater ponds and along the shore. Distinguished from Redshank by longer bill, by having no white on the wings in flight and by call. **Call:** Sharp, loud **te-wit**, both at rest and on the wing. **Range:** Breeds in tundra from Europe to NE Siberia and winters south to Africa, India and SE Asia.

4 COMMON GREENSHANK *Tringa nebularia* **35cm** Scarce winter visitor

Locally common. Usually feeds alone in rice fields or ponds in mangroves. Distinguish by large size, heavy, slightly upturned bill and green legs. Tail is barred unlike plain tail of Nordmann's Greenshank. Also has longer legs which project beyond the tail in flight, unlike short legs of Nordmann's which do not project beyond the tail. **Call:** Very loud **chew-chew-chew** when startled. **Range:** Breeds N Eurasia and winters southwards.

NORDMANN'S GREENSHANK	COMMON GREENSHANK
Both inner and outer toes are webbed	Web on outer toe only

5 NORDMANN'S GREENSHANK *Tringa guttifer* **32cm** Rare passage migrant

[Spotted Greenshank] Global population est. at under 1,000. Scattered records from NW Borneo and Tawau. Easily confused with Common Greenshank with which it often associates. Prefers mudflats but can occur anywhere along the coast. Distinguished from Greenshank by thicker bill with greenish yellow base, by plain white not barred under wing, plain white tail with no barring and shorter legs. Overall much whiter than Common with less streaking on breastsides and paler grey on upperparts and head (Bakewell). In the hand check the toe webbing. Legs greenish yellow. **Call:** Lekagul and Round report a 'piercing and oft repeated **keyew**'. **Range:** Breeds on Sakhalin Island and in coastal forest along the Sea of Okhotsk in E Russia. Winters along the coasts of NE Sumatra, W Malaya P and S Bangladesh. **BLI:** Endangered.

6 MARSH SANDPIPER *Tringa stagnatilis* **26cm** Scarce winter visitor

Locally common in wet padi fields and freshwater marshes during the winter months in north west Borneo. Rarely seen in saltwater habitats. Relatively tame, a slim elegant bird distinguished by its thin needle bill and very long legs, often in small groups wading in shallow pools. **Call:** Feeble **chiu chiu**. **Range:** Breeds temperate Eurasia and winters southwards.

1

non-br   br

juv

juv

on-br

2   br

juv

br

3

juv

non-br

non-br

br

4

non-br

br

5

non-br

non-br

br

juv

non-br

br

6

juv

SANDPIPERS, TATTLER AND RUFF

1 COMMON SANDPIPER *Actitis hypoleucos* **20cm**   **Common winter visitor**

The commonest wader in Borneo, found near water everywhere except the mountains. Recognised by plain grey back, with white shoulder patch and habit of bobbing as it walks. Characteristic flight is very low over the water, a flicker of wing beats interspersed with glides. Usually seen singly walking the shore or a river bank, but roosts communally in small groups. **Call:** Rapid series of musical whistles, *twi wi wi wi wi*. **Range:** Breeds Siberia, winters S to SE Asia.

2 WOOD SANDPIPER *Tringa glareola* **22cm**   **Common winter visitor**

The commonest wader of the padi fields and freshwater marshes, abundant in areas such as the Tempasuk Plain in winter. In the Mahakam Lakes (Kalimantan) recorded from July through to March with up to 10,000 birds present. **Call:** In flight rapidly repeated *hwit hwit hwit*. **Range:** Breeds in open areas of N pine forests, wintering south to SE Asia and Australia. A bird ringed by the MAPS programme (W coast Sabah) was recovered in the Amur River valley of E Siberia.

3 GREEN SANDPIPER *Tringa ochropus* **23cm**   **Scarce winter visitor**

Like Wood Sandpiper prefers freshwater swamps and padi fields but much less common. Distinguished from Wood Sandpiper by dark under wing as it flies up with whiter rump and darker tail bars. Call is also distinctively different. **Call:** 'Rises with a shrill *weet a weet* zigzags at first, then climbs high, circles, and finally drops to the ground some distance away' (Viney). **Range:** Breeds N Europe to N Asia, winters SE Asia.

4 GREY-TAILED TATTLER *Heteroscelis brevipes* **25cm**   **Common winter visitor**

Widespread along the coast in winter months preferring muddier habitat compared with Common Sandpiper. Also found along rocky shores and reefs. Like all sandpipers walks steadily searching for food but the Tattler moves very rapidly with head down and tail up bobbing like a Common Sandpiper but not so markedly. Often roosts in small flocks with other waders. **Call:** Distinctive two note whistle. **Range:** Breeds NE Siberia winters SE Asia south to Australia.

5 WANDERING TATTLER *Heteroscelus incana* **28cm**   **Not recorded**

An American relative of the Grey-tailed Tattler which occurs in Japan, Taiwan, and Australia as a regular vagrant but not so far recorded from Borneo. **Call:** 'Distinguished from Grey-tailed Tattler by flight call, a plaintive rippling trill' (Geering *et al.*). In habits restricted to rocky coasts and never found on mudflats. **Range:** Breeds in NE Siberia and Alaska migrating south to western coast of N America and N South America.

6 RUFF *Philomachus pugnax* **Male 29cm Female 22cm**   **Scarce passage migrant**

A scarce passage migrant usually only seen during peak migration and rarely with spectacular male breeding neck feathers. Prefers freshwater or brackish ponds along the coast, often in mixed flocks with other waders. Distinguished from other waders, by small head, long neck, heavy body and upright posture. Also has unique white 'V' on rump. **Call:** Very quiet. **Range:** Breeds Europe to E Siberia and most winter in Africa and India, scarce in SE Asia, Australia.

THE COMMONEST WADERS THAT OVERWINTER IN BORNEO

Although large numbers and varieties of waders can be seen along the Borneo coast during peak migration periods in Sept.–Oct. and March–April, the majority of these birds are passage migrants on their way to or from Australia. See page 106 and 116. The waders that remain after November are winter visitors, that spend the majority of their year in Borneo but breed in the forests and tundra of Siberia and NE Asia. The best known of the winter visitors is the Common Sandpiper found from the coast to far up the rocky rivers of the interior. Also common but much shyer are the Wood Sandpiper and Long-toed Stint which can be found in padi fields. Usually solitary and less common in the same habitat are Green Sandpiper and Greenshank. Along sandy coasts look for Greater and Lesser Sand Plover, Kentish Plover, Grey-tailed Tattler, Whimbrel and Terek Sandpiper. In damp grassland, look for Golden Plover and Little Ringed Plover. Redshank is commonest on muddy coasts near mangrove estuaries.

1   br   juv

2   br   non-br

3   br   non-br

4

5   br   br   non-br

6   juv

non-br   ♀   ♂   ♂

STINTS AND SANDPIPERS

1   RED-NECKED STINT   *Calidris ruficollis*   **14cm**   **Passage migrant and winter visitor**

Common passage migrant. Usually seen in large flocks along the coast, occasionally around freshwater ponds. Recorded in every month of the year. A very small, active wader usually seen in pale non-breeding plumage. A bird ringed in Victoria, Australia on 4 December 1982 was collected on W coast Sabah, 25 April 1983 (Sheldon). **Call:** High-pitched, rough *kreet* in flight. **Range:** Breeds NE Siberia and Alaska, wintering S to Australia and New Zealand.

2   LITTLE STINT   *Calidris minuta*   **14cm**   **Vagrant**

A few records from the NW coast indicate that this bird which normally winters further west may stray off course. May be under recorded due to similarity with Red-necked Stint. In breeding plumage has white throat not red as with Red-necked Stint. Juvenile birds have a prominent white 'V' on the back. **Call:** Single or repeated, sharp, high-pitched *stet* in flight, very different from Red-necked Stint. **Range:** Breeds N Eurasia, and winters S to India, Africa.

3   TEMMINCK'S STINT   *Calidris temminckii*   **15cm**   **Scarce passage migrant**

Regularly recorded along the coast but like Long-toed Stint prefers freshwater ponds and padi fields, but much scarcer. Looks like a miniature Common Sandpiper with very plain upperparts in non-breeding plumage. Distinctive flight, fluttering and jinking like a bat or butterfly. **Call:** When flushed utters a continuous ringing *tirr* very different to Little Stint (Viney). **Range:** Breeds N Eurasia and winters south.

4   LONG-TOED STINT   *Calidris subminuta*   **16cm**   **Common passage migrant**

Common passage migrant and winter visitor to freshwater habitats such as ponds and padi fields, often with much larger Wood Sandpipers. More upright stance than other stints. Looks like smaller version of Sharp-tailed Sandpiper (Viney). Has pale yellow legs similar to Temminck's Stint and unlike the dark legs of the other stints. **Call:** Flock rises with 'concerted' calls of *soo-soo-soo'*. (Smythies). **Range:** Breeds Central N Asia and winters S to Australia.

5   SPOON-BILLED SANDPIPER   *Eurynorhynchus pygmaeus*   **16cm**   **Vagrant**

A globally scarce wader with a total population estimated at under 2,000 pairs. One record from the Philippines and one possible record from NW Borneo. Normally seen mixed up in flocks of Red-necked Stints where it can be distinguished by its very active feeding behaviour as it rushes around sweeping its bill from side to side to suck up its tiny prey. **Call:** Flight call said to be a quiet, rolled *preep* or a shrill *whee* (O'Brien). Note: Flight illustration of the tail pattern of the Spoon-billed Sandpiper is common to all the stints illustrated here. **Range:** Breeds NE Siberia, migrates south through Kamchatka, Japan, Korea, E China and Hong Kong to winter along the coasts of Vietnam, Thailand, Myanmar and in particular Bangladesh. **BLI:** Vulnerable

---

BANDING WADERS AND THE AUSTRALASIAN WADER STUDY GROUP (AWSG)

Scientists are keen to discover more about the long distance migratory routes of the waders that breed in Russian E. Siberia, N Asia and American Alaska but migrate south to Australia each autumn. These waders pass through many different countries on their twice yearly journey, principally Japan, Taiwan, Korea, China, Philippines, Thailand, Vietnam, Malaysia, Singapore, Brunei and Indonesia. In many of these countries there are active wader study groups that trap waders with nets and mark them with flags (flagging) or coded rings (banding) placed around their legs. Many countries including Russia, USA, Japan, China, Taiwan, Korea and New Zealand have groups involved in Asian wader banding but the Australasian Wader Studies Group (AWSG) is the most active. This is appropriate as Australia hosts approximately half of the wintering population of the Asian waders, out of an estimated total population of around five million birds.

It is important to find out both the origin and destination of each population of waders as well as the most important 'staging posts' or feeding stops used en route. The destruction of one breeding area or an important staging post could seriously affect the global population of a bird that is not resident in just one country but a visitor to many. See also pages 110 and 126.

To help with this research, if you see a wader with a coloured flag on its leg, please note the colour (red, yellow etc), which leg (left or right) and placement on the leg (above knee or below knee) and send details to www.environment.gov.au/biodiversity/science/abbbs/ or www.shorebird-network.net

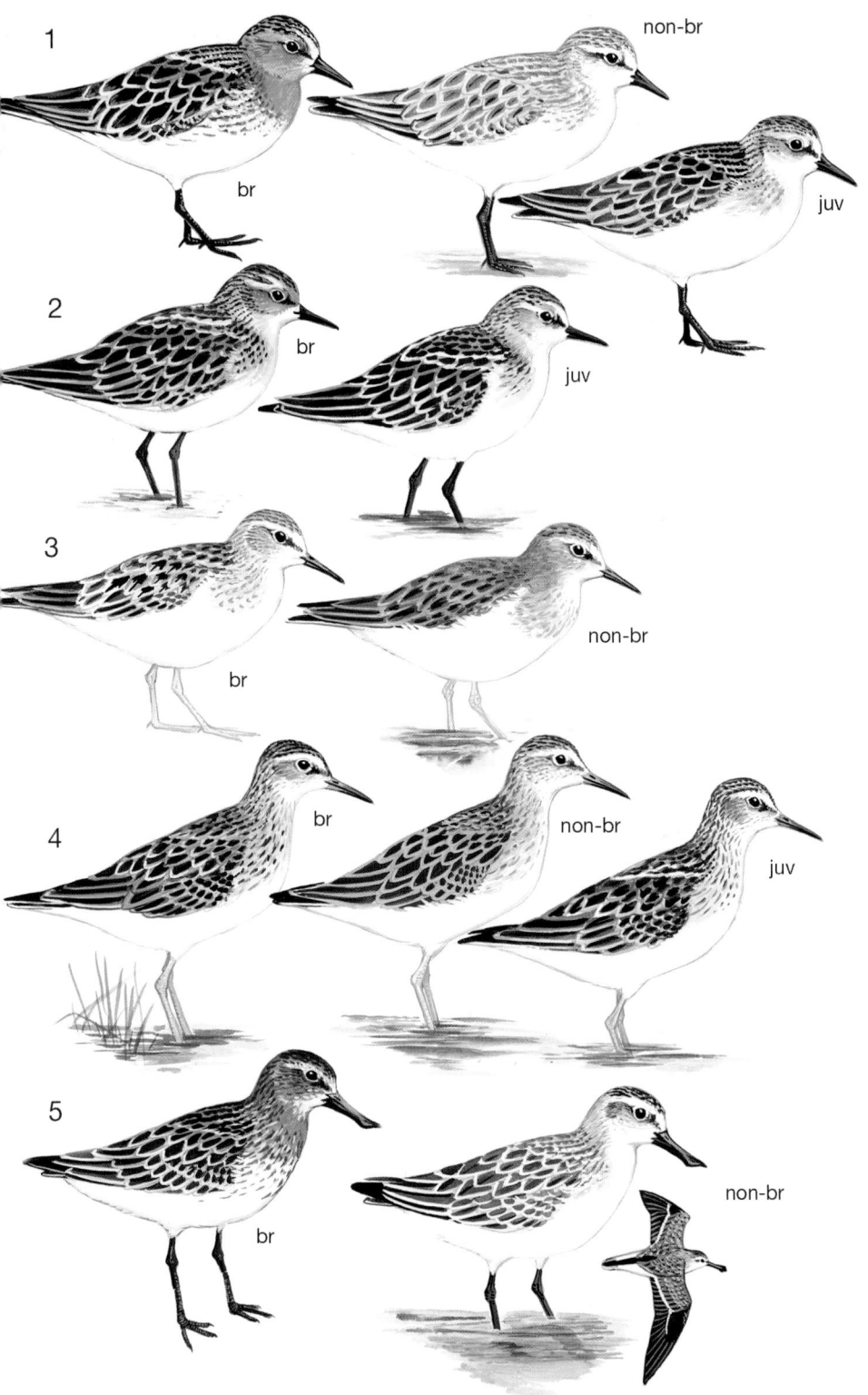

1   br   non-br   juv

2   br   juv

3   br   non-br

4   br   non-br   juv

5   br   non-br

DOWITCHERS AND SANDPIPERS

1   LONG-BILLED DOWITCHER *Limnodromus scolopaceus*   28cm   **Vagrant**

Although this bird breeds in NE Siberia and Alaska, the majority winter along the west and south east coasts of N America. Sometimes feeds at inland pools as well as the coast. Feeds with a 'sewing machine' action in shallow water. Occasional visitor to Hong Kong and at least one record for Borneo at Tempasuk swamps. When feeding, the body has a very rounded appearance described as 'having swallowed a grapefruit' (O'Brien 2007). **Call:** Single, short, sharp *keek* sometimes repeated. **Range:** Breeds NE Siberia, Alaska, wintering S along USA W coast.

2   SHORT-BILLED DOWITCHER *Limnodromus griseus*   23cm   **Not recorded**

Smaller than Long-billed Dowitcher and with similar habits, this is an American bird which has been recorded in Japan and could possibly occur in Borneo. 'Best separated from Long-billed Dowitcher by call, a mellow *chu-du-du*' (Viney). Both Short and Long-billed Dowitcher have yellow legs unlike black legs of Asian Dowitcher. **Range:** Breeds Alaska and Canada wintering south along the North American coast.

3   BROAD-BILLED SANDPIPER *Limicola falcinellus*   18cm   **Scarce passage migrant**

A scarce migrant found along the coast on mudflats in small numbers often in mixed flocks with Curlew Sandpipers and Red-necked Stints. Distinguished from Curlew Sandpiper by heavier bill which is distinctively down-turned at the end only, not throughout its length. Distinguished from Dunlin (page 126) by dark and pale stripes on head. **Call:** High-pitched buzzing trill. **Range:** Breeds N Eurasia and winters southwards to Australia.

4   SHARP-TAILED SANDPIPER *Calidris acuminata*   22cm   **Scarce passage migrant**

A scarce migrant which can occur on the coast in mixed flocks but which prefers wet grassland or freshwater marshes. Has a distinctive rufous crown in all plumages. Can only be confused with Pectoral Sandpiper in which crown is much duller. World population is approx 160,000 the majority of which winter in Australia. **Call:** Distinctive plaintive *wheep* in flight often repeated. **Range:** Breeds NE Siberia and winters south to Australia and New Zealand.

5   PECTORAL SANDPIPER *Calidris melanotus*   23cm   **Not recorded**

A scarce passage migrant through Hong Kong, not yet recorded from Borneo. Like Sharp-tailed Sandpiper prefers freshwater marshes and ponds. Has less streaking on vent and sides (almost plain white) than Sharp-tailed Sandpiper. Although it mainly winters in S America, small numbers regularly winter in both West and E Australia and New Zealand and therefore some of this population is likely to passage through Borneo. **Call:** Flight call is a short, trilled *churrk*. **Range:** Breeds Siberia to Canada and winters in Australasia and S America.

BIRDS THAT REACH BORNEO FROM KOREA

Despite its small size Korea is an important staging post for many birds that migrate to Borneo. Large numbers of raptors including Chinese Goshawks, Honey Buzzards, and Japanese Sparrowhawks funnel through Korea on their migrations to and from Borneo. See page 102. Very large numbers of waders that breed in the forests and tundra of E Siberia use the coastal mudflats of the Yellow Sea as a re-fuelling stop on their migrations to and from Australia. It is believed that most of the Chinese Egrets that winter in Borneo breed on islands in the Yellow Sea off the coast of Korea. One of the most important wader staging sites in Asia used to be the Saemangeum estuary which borders the Yellow Sea. The mudflats of Saemungeum previously hosted globally important populations of Spoon-billed Sandpiper, Great Knot and Red Knot as well as 17 other shorebird species, including Sharp-tailed Sandpiper, Broad-billed Sandpiper, Asian Dowitcher and Spotted Greenshank. The Saemungeum estuary was reclaimed from the sea by the Korean Government between 2006 and 2008 and converted for use as golf courses and agricultural land. This destruction of a globally important bird habitat took place despite very strong opposition from local NGO's such as Birds Korea and other national and international environmental groups.

Birds have been global travellers since long before the start of recorded human history, passing through many different countries. Unless there is full co-operation between different nations to preserve the staging posts used by these birds, the unco-ordinated, unilateral, actions of a single country can seriously affect the population of many migrant birds. For further information: www.birdskorea.org and www. eaaflyway.net. See also page 110 and page 124.

KNOTS, SANDPIPERS AND PHALAROPES

1 GREAT KNOT   *Calidris tenuirostris*   **28cm**   Scarce passage migrant

Scarce passage migrant through Borneo en route to Australia, with a few first year birds staying over. Has been seen in every month of the year. Prefers large areas of soft coastal mud on which it walks steadily probing with its beak in a sewing machine action. Feeds on small clams which it swallows whole. **Call:** Double note whistle *knot knot*. **Range:** An estimated global population of 375,000 breed on the tundra of E Siberia, and winter around the coast of Australia.

2 RED KNOT   *Calidris canutus*   **25cm**   Scarce passage migrant

Similar habits to Great Knot but less common. Usually seen in small tightly knit flocks probing for small clams along the edge of the sea. Knots can be distinguished from other waders by their sewing machine feeding methods, and from each other by call, size and by rump and tail markings. **Call:** Single note *knot*. **Range:** Circumpolar breeding on far northern tundra and winters coastally southwards to Australia.

3 CURLEW SANDPIPER   *Calidris ferruginea*   **23cm**   Scarce passage migrant and visitor

Uncommon passage migrant, with some birds staying throughout the winter. Occurs every month except July. Prefers soft coastal mud often wading at the edge of the sea. Occasionally feeds around freshwater ponds. Distinguished from other waders by small size and relatively long down-curved bill. Distinguished from Dunlin by white rump. **Call:** Flight call a low, trilled, *chrreep* (O'Brien). **Range:** Breeds Arctic and winters S to Africa, Australia. Very common HK.

4 SANDERLING   *Calidris alba*   **21cm**   Scarce passage migrant and winter visitor

Scattered records from all coasts. Generally prefers wave battered beaches where it runs rapidly along the tide line. Sometimes seen in small flocks. Palest and whitest of all the small waders in winter plumage. Has distinctive dark band to shoulder of closed wing. In the hand has no hind claw unlike other waders. **Call:** Squeaking note *pweet*. **Range:** Circumpolar tundra breeder, winters south along coasts reaching Australia and S America.

5 DUNLIN   *Calidris alpina*   **22cm**   Vagrant

A few scattered records from the NW coast. Normally winters north of Borneo but may overshoot. Note bill shape. **Call:** Harsh *triii*. **Range:** Circumpolar tundra breeder, winters south along coasts. Recorded Penampang November 2009 (Madoya).

6 RED-NECKED PHALAROPE   *Phalaropus lobatus*   **19cm**   Passage migrant

Scarce passage migrant usually seen at sea in small flocks. Sometimes on coastal pools, inland rivers or padi fields in the interior. Feeds by spinning on the water and uses bill to suck up insects drawn in by the vortex. Distinguished from Grey Phalarope by very thin needle-like bill. **Call:** Flight call: hard, squeaky *pwit* or *kit* – lower and huskier than Grey Phalarope (O'Brien). **Range:** Tundra breeder, winters E of Borneo in Sulawesi and Moluccan seas.

7 GREY PHALAROPE   *Phalaropus fulicarius*   **22cm**   Vagrant

[Red Phalarope] One record of two, in a large flock of Red-Necked Phalarope off the coast of Sarawak. Note larger size. **Call:** Sharp-whistled *psip* or *pseet*, often in rapid succession, higher, clearer and more metallic than Red-necked Phalarope (O'Brien). **Range:** Tundra breeder, winters at sea south.

BORNEAN WADERS THAT BREED ON THE RUSSIAN ARCTIC TUNDRA

Most of the waders that passage through Borneo and winter in Australia breed in the far north close to the Arctic Circle. Here summer lasts less than four months from mid-May to mid-August. The treeless tundra is covered in marshy ponds providing rich breeding sites for billions of mosquitoes and midges, sometimes so dense that it is impossible to see more than a few metres. With an abundance of insect food, factors that prevent waders breeding successfully are poor weather (late spring or early autumn snow) and predation by Arctic Foxes, skuas, Snowy Owls and Peregrine and Gyr Falcons. These predators preferentially feed on lemmings whose population fluctuates each year. In years with few lemmings, the predators feed on young waders instead and as a result hardly any young waders survive. In years when lemmings are abundant the majority of young waders survive to migrate south to their wintering grounds.

non-br

br

juv

non-br

br

juv

non-br

br

juv

non-br

br

juv

non-br

br

juv

non-br

♀

♂

1st winter

non-br

♀

♂

1st winter

GREBES, PRATINCOLES AND STONE CURLEW

PODICIPEDIDAE **World 21 species; Borneo 2 species.** Grebes are surprisingly scarce in Borneo probably due to the absence of grebe-favoured habitat, open freshwater lakes. Little Grebes easily form 'superspecies' where birds from different islands could be either very distinct races, or poorly differentiated species. Little Grebes are resident in the Philippines, Sulawesi, Java, and Sumatra. Migrant birds from the north have recently colonised the Malay P. Grebes swim on lakes and dive frequently to catch fish and invertebrates.

1 LITTLE GREBE *Tachybaptus ruficollis poggei* 25cm Vagrant
[Dabchick] An old record from Labuan and more recent records from Sandakan, Sukau, Gomantong and Brunei of vagrant birds from the Asian continent. Probably under recorded due to small size and habit of diving for long periods. A very likely future colonist of Borneo. **Call:** High-pitched whinnying trill. **Range:** Resident from India to Japan with some birds moving south in winter.

2 AUSTRALASIAN GREBE *Tachybaptus novaehollandiae javanicus* 24cm Vagrant
An old sight record of a Little Grebe from Banjarmasin is most likely the Indonesian race of Australasian Grebe, which breeds in Java. Previously considered a race of Little Grebe. Distinguished from Little Grebe by being darker below with a black throat and much reduced area of rufous on side of neck. **Call:** Similar to Little Grebe. **Range:** Breeds Australia and Indonesia, nomadic and dispersive. Has recently colonised New Zealand.

GLAREOLIDAE **World 14 species; Asia 4 species; Borneo 2 species.** Graceful long-winged waders which hunt for insects like swallows over open grassland, rivers or marshes. Sometimes chase insects on the ground. Nomadic and migratory often in large flocks. Tend to breed opportunistically and colonially on open land such as dry fields whenever conditions are suitable.

3 AUSTRALIAN PRATINCOLE *Stiltia isabella* 24cm Scarce migrant from south

[Long-legged Pratincole] The population fluctuates widely depending on conditions in central Australia. In good years after a successful breeding season large numbers irrupt northwards to the Indonesian islands. Irregularly recorded from Kalimantan, Kuching, and as far N as the Tempasuk Plain in August. **Call:** Shrill sweet *hoo wee too* or *hoo wee* (Geering *et al.*). **Range:** Breeds on dry plains of inland Australia (Sept.–Oct.), afterwards moving north.

4 ORIENTAL PRATINCOLE *Glareola maldivarum* 24cm Resident and passage migrant

[Eastern Collared Pratincole] A scarce but regular passage migrant through Borneo from Asia to Australia. Occasional birds seen year round. Large numbers bred Tempasuk Plain in April 1981, and at Wasan Rice Scheme (Brunei) in March 1987 (4 pairs). **Call:** Sharp *chek chek* calls. **Range:** Breeds from Pakistan to China and Philippines. Some populations are resident and locally nomadic. Others winter S to Australia. Geering *et al.* report a flock of 2.88 million birds seen on NW Australian coast in February 2004.

BURHINIDAE **World 9 species; Borneo 1 species.** Most stone curlew species inhabit dry plains, hunting for insects, lizards and small mammals. Typically most active at night when they utter loud wailing alarm calls. In Mexico the Double-striped Stone Curlew is kept as 'guard bird' for this reason, and warns ranch owners of strangers approaching at night, with noisy mournful calls.

5 BEACH THICK-KNEE *Esacus magnirostris* 53cm Rare resident

[Beach Stone Curlew] In Borneo a rare inhabitant of coral sand beaches on remote islands occasionally seen elsewhere when caught up in passing flocks of migrant waders, e.g. Tg Aru beach, Sibu town, Kuching airport. Usually crepuscular or nocturnal but has been seen during the day at low tide, chasing crabs along the shore or on reef flats. In Australia has been recorded feeding on mudflats and roosting in mangroves. Nest is a shallow hollow at the top of the beach amongst beach debris. **Call:** The territorial call is an unmistakable harsh *wee loo*, usually at night. **Range:** Resident along undisturbed tropical beaches from N Australia, N to the Philippines, W to the Andaman islands and E to the Solomon islands in the Pacific.

LARGER GULLS

LARIDAE   **World 156 species; Borneo 1 species.**   Gull Habits: In northern climates gulls are the commonest seabirds scavenging at rubbish dumps and often seen around fishing ports where their harsh raucous screaming calls are a characteristic sound. Gulls are less pelagic than terns generally keeping to the coast and unlike terns' bouncing, twisting flight they fly steadily and direct, occasionally soaring, and often settle on the water. Gulls generally breed colonially on the ground near inland freshwater lakes. Different gull species often associate in mixed flocks. Sexes are similar. Gulls take two to four years to reach adult plumage, with young gulls streaked and speckled brown. Young gulls wander very widely for their first two years before breeding. Vagrant gulls are therefore most likely to be seen in sub-adult plumages. Gulls prefer colder seas than terns and are scarce near the equator. However, they frequently follow ships to feed on their waste and therefore travel very widely. Sixteen different species of gulls have been recorded for Hong Kong at the northern end of the South China Sea, nine species in the Gulf of Thailand, four species in the Philippines, three on the east coast of Malaya at the southern end of the S China Sea and so far only one species (Black-headed) has been recorded for Borneo. On the assumption that gulls have been underecorded we illustrate in this Guide the five additional gulls most likely to be found off the Borneo coast as strays or vagrants, especially during and after the strong typhoons that develop in the northern S China Sea every summer.

1   HEUGLIN'S GULL   *Larus heuglini*   **60cm**   **Not recorded**
Commonest large gull along the S China coast between November to April. Smaller and darker than Yellow-legged Gull. Considered by some (American Ornithologists Union) to be race of the Lesser Black-backed Gull. **Range:** Breeds Eastern and Central Asia wintering south to South and East Asia. Has been recorded from both the E and W coasts of Malaya and Singapore.

2   YELLOW-LEGGED GULL   *Larus cachinnans*   **66cm**   **Not recorded**
A very large heavy gull, significantly larger and paler than Heuglin's Gull. Confusingly the local race of the Yellow-legged Gull (*L. c. mongolicus*) has pink or greyish legs unlike Heuglin's Gull which does have yellow legs. **Range:** Breeds South and Central Asia wintering south to South and East Asia.

3   BLACK-TAILED GULL   *Larus crassirostris*   **47cm**   **Vagrant**
Commonest gull around Hong Kong from November to March. Most immature gulls have a black tail band but lose this in their adult plumage, however, the Black-tailed Gull retains the band even as an adult. One unconfirmed record from KK harbour (Mann). **Range:** Breeds N and E China coast and in winter moves south. Recorded from Olango Island, Cebu, Philippines. Vagrants have been recorded off all coasts of Australia.

SIGNAL PLUMAGES AND CAMOUFLAGE PLUMAGES   Seabirds are generally white, but are sometimes dark, and sometimes speckled. See also pages 64 and 144.
Camouflage plumages   Most bird plumages are cryptic, designed to blend into the background or camouflage the bird against predators. The speckled brown plumages of waders which helps to camouflage them against a beach background are a good example. In contrast seabirds and many flocking waterbirds such as egrets, storks or pelicans have bright white feathers seemingly designed to make them as obvious as possible. Firstly unlike (small) waders, (large) seabirds are not at risk from most predators. Secondly they feed mainly at sea, and their plumage is normally white below and darker above like a fish, known as counter shading.
Counter shading   Seen from below against the sky a white belly is an optimum camouflage. Why then are some seabirds dark below, for example the Noddies? It has been suggested that Noddies sometimes feed at night, and the main reason could again be camouflage.
Signal plumages   Whilst gulls and terns are camouflaged against fish, their main prey, they are easily visible to other seabirds against a dark sea. The white feathers of seabirds can be read as a signal by other seabirds. Often fish occur in isolated schools and it benefits all seabirds to be able to recognise immediately if another seabird has discovered such a shoal, enabling it to join in the feeding frenzy (Furness). White egrets have similar signal plumages for the same reason.
Juvenile plumages of gulls and terns   Both young terns and gulls hatch with brown speckled plumage but terns adopt an adult plumage within six months, whilst gulls take up to four years to reach adult plumage. Gulls are specialists in scavenging (but also fish) whereas terns specialise in catching live fish (but also scavenge). It is likely that young inexperienced gulls spend most of their time scavenging rather than fishing and the protective effects of their speckled camouflage plumage are more important than the counter shading plumage required for fishing.

adult
non-br

1st winter

2nd winter

1st winter

adult br

adult
non-br

1st winter

2

1st winter

adult br

2nd winter

adult br

adult br

adult
winter

adult summer

1st winter

2nd winter

SMALLER GULLS

1 BLACK-HEADED GULL *Larus ridibundus* **40cm** Common winter visitor

The only gull so far definitely recorded for Borneo. Previously considered scarce. Recently increasingly common especially around ports such as Sandakan and KK in N Borneo in winter. Usually in small flocks, often roosts with terns on sandbanks. In winter adult loses black head which is replaced by a dark spot behind the eye. **Range:** Breeds across N Europe to Asia wintering southwards. Large flocks up to 12,000 occur in Hong Kong in winter.

2 SAUNDERS' GULL *Larus saundersi* **32cm** Not recorded

Global population estimated at maximum 7,000 and decreasing. Flies more like a tern than a gull with bouncing flight. In winter adult looks very similar to Black-headed Gull. Distinguished by short black stubby bill, and smaller size. **Range:** Breeds along the coast of E China. Winters to Japan, S China coast south to the coast of Vietnam. **BLI:** Vulnerable.

3 BROWN-HEADED GULL *Larus brunnicephalus* **46cm** Not recorded

The commonest gull in the Gulf of Thailand where it is a very common winter visitor. Largest of the small gulls. Separated in flight from other gulls by large white patch at base of primaries known as 'headlights' (Viney). In winter adult loses brown head which is replaced by a dark spot behind the eye. Distinguish from Black-headed Gull in winter by larger size, pale not dark eyes and wing pattern. **Range:** Breeds around lakes in Tibet and Mongolia wintering on the coasts of Hong Kong, Thailand, and the west coast of the Malay Peninsula.

OTHER GULLS THAT COULD OCCUR OFF THE BORNEO COAST (Not illustrated)

HERRING GULL *Larus argentatus*. Two records from the Philippines.
Note: **VEGA GULL** *Larus vegae* is considered a race of Herring Gull by many.
SLATY-BACKED GULL *Larus schistisagus*. One record from Mindanao, Philippines.
SABINE'S GULL *Xema sabini*. Breeds in Arctic and crosses equator to winter in the southern oceans. Often scavenges around boats. One record off W Sumatra 1984 (McKinnon).

USEFUL BOOKS FOR DISTINGUISHING DIFFICULT SEABIRDS

Because of their varied age-related plumage and very similar races gulls, terns and skuas are often extremely difficult to distinguish in the field, or even from photographs. For birders interested in sea watching we highly recommend the following guides by Olsen and Larsson: *Skuas and Jaegers* (1997), *Terns of Europe and N. America* (1995), *Gulls of Europe, Asia and N America* (2005). Also *Seabirds of the World* by Harrison (1987) and *Albatrosses, Petrels and Shearwaters* by Olney and Scofield (2007).

WHY SEABIRDS ARE SO SCARCE IN BORNEAN WATERS

Many birders have commented upon the scarcity of seabirds around Borneo compared with the colder seas in the north and south of the globe. There are three major reasons for this.

Worldwide the best places to see seabirds are the fish-rich edges of the continental shelves, where deep ocean currents cause upwellings of nutrients and minerals which feed the tiny algae (plants) on which the fish feed. Borneo's Sunda shelf seas are just too shallow. Secondly, cold stormy seas in the northern and southern hemispheres are particularly rich in fish because cold stormy water has a much higher oxygen content than calm tropical waters, and storms also create upwellings of plant nutrients. Borneo's warm relatively calm seas are not as fish-rich as colder waters north and south. Finally, there are no secure nesting sites for seabirds around the coast of Borneo. For centuries local fishermen have collected seabird eggs from the few rocky islets where seabirds breed limiting population growth (see pages 22, 74, 138 and 140).

Thus the population of seabirds around Borneo is limited both by lack of food and human predation. The seabird populations of Sandakan and Kota Kinabalu harbours, where sewage dumping has increased the fish population, is proof that local seabird populations are food-limited elsewhere around Borneo. The fact that seabirds started nesting on Pulau Layang Layang as soon as it was built is proof of a lack of secure nesting throughout Malaysian and Indonesian seas. See page 142.

adult non-br

1st winter

adult br

adult non-br

1st winter

adult br

1st winter

adult non-br

adult br

CRESTED AND MARSH TERNS MALAY: BURUNG TARA TARA OR CAMAR

LARIDAE **World 45 species; Borneo 15 species including 4 residents.** Elegant, mainly white seabirds, usually seen in small flocks along the coast or out at sea. Flocks often comprise more than one species. Roost on sandbanks or fishing stakes. Unlike gulls, do not usually alight on the water. Nest in colonies on the ground on isloated small rocky islands. The two migrant *Chlidonias* Marsh Terns are often seen inland over swamps, padi fields and large rivers, surface fishing with twisting acrobatic flight for small fish and insects. The breeding plumages of terns are usually distinctive but in Borneo terns on winter migration are mainly seen in non-breeding plumage or juvenile plumages which can be easily confused. Calls are usually a series of sharp **kek** calls or **chirrups** which are not distinctive between species.

1 GREATER CRESTED TERN *Sterna bergii* **48cm** Common visitor

[Swift Tern] Seen year round but commonest in winter. Usually in small flocks but sometimes seen individually perched on a floating log out to sea. Plunge dives for fish. Nests in Tubbataha Marine Park, Sulu Sea (Philippines) and on Layang[2] (March–July) in small numbers. **Range:** Breeds India to SE Asia wintering S. Also breeds around Australia sometimes in huge colonies moving N (May–Sept.). Borneo birds probably come from both north and south.

2 LESSER CRESTED TERN *Sterna bengalensis* **40cm** Scarce winter visitor

Less common than Greater Crested Tern but similar habits. Distinguished from Greater Crested Tern by smaller size and orange rather than yellow bill. In breeding plumage black on forehead extends to the base of the beak. Amount of black on head in non-breeding plumage is variable but generally less than with Greater, leaving eye surrounded by white in winter. **Range:** Breeds India to SE Asia wintering southwards.

3 CHINESE CRESTED TERN *Sterna bernsteini* **40cm** Rare winter visitor

Three records from the coast of Sarawak, the last collected from Buntal in February 1913. This tern was believed to be extinct until four pairs were discovered breeding on Matsu Dao island between the Chinese Fujian coast and Taiwan. The terns were breeding on a rocky islet surrounded by low vegetation amongst a much larger colony of Greater Crested Terns. Subsequently another small breeding colony was discovered on the Qingdao Islands. Distinguished from other Crested Terns by dark tip to yellow-orange bill. Amount of black on head in non-breeding plumage is variable but similar to Lesser rather than Greater, leaving eye surrounded by white in winter. **Range:** Historically always very scarce, breeding along the China coast and wintering S. Currently on the verge of extinction. **BLI:** Critical.

4 WHISKERED TERN *Chlidonias hybridus* **26cm** Common visitor from north and south

Marsh tern found on the coast, and over coastal swamps and padi fields. Often mixes with White-winged Tern but less common in N Borneo. On the Mahakam Lakes (Kalimantan) it is by far the commonest tern, both as a winter migrant from the north (Sept.–May) and as an austral migrant (Feb.–Oct.). Flocks of 2,000 + terns regularly recorded (Gonner). Distinguish from White-winged Tern by head pattern. **Range:** Breeds Europe, Asia, Africa and Australia.

5 WHITE-WINGED BLACK TERN *Chlidonias leucopterus* **25cm** Common winter visitor

Commonest marsh tern in N Borneo. Found along the coast and river estuaries, e.g. Brunei and Kuching Rivers. Feeds on insects over flooded padi fields including the Kelabit Highlands during passage Oct.–Dec. Often in mixed flocks with Whiskered Tern. On the Mahakam Lakes (Aug.–May), less common than Whiskered. (Gonner). In winter plumage distinguished by head pattern of distinct dark spot behind the eye and reduced black cap. **Range:** Europe to Asia.

BLACK TERN *Chlidonias nigra* **25cm [Not illustrated]** Not recorded

A third marsh tern is a potential vagrant to Borneo from breeding grounds in central European and Asian lakes. In breeding plumage (unlikely) all black body and wings are distinctive. In winter has very distinct dark side panels (saddle bars) on white breast. Both White-winged and Whiskered immatures sometimes show side panels but they are smaller and paler compared with those of Black Tern.

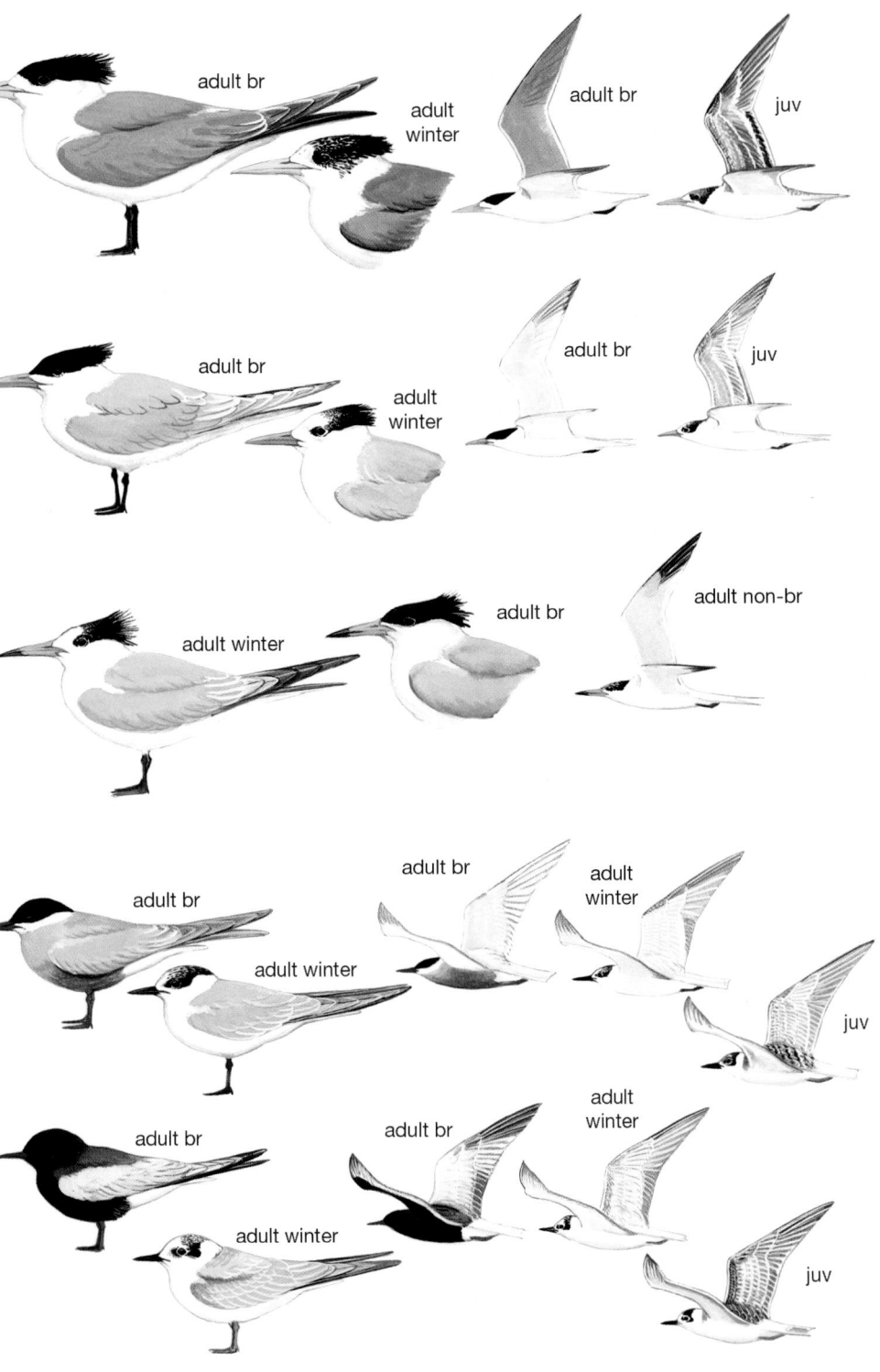

adult br

adult winter

adult br

juv

adult br

adult winter

adult br

juv

adult winter

adult br

adult non-br

adult br

adult winter

adult br

adult winter

juv

adult br

adult winter

adult br

adult winter

adult br

adult winter

juv

GULL-BILLED, CASPIAN, SOOTY, BRIDLED AND LITTLE TERNS

1   GULL-BILLED TERN   *Sterna nilotica*   **39cm**   **Common winter visitor**

A visitor from the north (and possibly the south) to river estuaries and the coast of Borneo.
Commonest in winter months but seen in every month of the year. Birds present from May
to August are most likely austral migrants. Large heavy appearance resembles a gull as much
as a tern. Distinguished by black bill and legs from Common Tern and by shape of cap from
Black-naped Tern. Fishes the surface of the sea, does not dive. **Range:** Worldwide.

2   CASPIAN TERN   *Sterna caspia*   **49cm**   **Vagrant**
A few scattered winter records from the northern coasts of Borneo. Giant size and bright red bill make this
tern unmistakable. Dives almost vertically for fish. Often roosts in flocks with other terns. Breeds China coast
and after a successful breeding season populations irrupt south and birds are seen all around the S China Sea.
Range: E Europe to N Asia wintering S to Australia.

3   SOOTY TERN   *Sterna fuscata*   **35cm**   **Local island resident**

Breeds in large colonies on Layang² and Tubbataha Reef (Sulu Sea), but fishes out to sea and
only seen occasionally along the Borneo coast. On Layang² breeds April to June when seas
are calm. Flocks follow large predatory fish and snatch fish from the surface. Has no oil gland
and so cannot get wet. Does not settle on water. Distinguished by white forehead with no
white eyebrow. **Range:** The world's commonest tropical tern, breeds in all the warm oceans.

4   BRIDLED TERN   *Sterna anaethetus*   **31cm**   **Local island resident**

Fishes out at sea, not along the coast but seen regularly on blue water boat trips and
occasionally on the coast after storms. Breeds on rocky islands off the north west coast
of Borneo in small colonies with other terns during the calm sea period April to June, inc.
Tokong Ara, Pelong Rocks and Tg Nosong. Distinguished from Sooty by white eyebrow. Unlike
Sooty does settle on sea surface. **Range:** Found throughout the tropical oceans of the world.

5   LITTLE TERN   *Sterna albifrons*   **23cm**   **Common resident and visitor**

Borneo's smallest tern. An increasingly common winter visitor to the Borneo coast and the only
tern that breeds on the mainland. Nests on sandy beaches in small colonies. Scattered breeding
records from the north west coast include Sejingkat (Sarawak) in August 2006, Belait (Brunei)
and Likas Sept 2012 (Eugene Cheah). Regularly nests at BSB airport Nests on mudflats exposed
in the dry season at the Mahakam Lakes (Gonner). **Range:** Coasts and coastal lakes worldwide

---

SEABIRDS OF THE SULU SEA   The Sulu Sea which separates N Borneo from the S Philippines is scattered
with small islands, some densely populated, but most uninhabited. Nearly everyone who lives on these islands
makes their living from the sea in some way, catching fish, collecting sea-cucumbers (trepang), farming
seaweed, or collecting shells and corals. Dugongs occur, dolphins are common and Byrde's Whale and Whale
Sharks visit often. These remote islands are best visited by 'sleep on board' dive boats out of Palawan. Visit
Mar.–June when calm seas allow seabirds to breed. See map page 74 and pages 70, 72, 76, 136, 140, 142.
TUBBATAHA REEFS, 08°57'N, 119°48'E
160km south of Puerto Princessa (Palawan). Large numbers of seabirds breed on two uninhabited coral
atolls known as North and South Reefs. A marine National Park since 1988. Breeding birds include Brown,
and Masked Boobies, Greater Crested Tern, Sooty Tern, Black Noddy (nests in low trees), Brown Noddy
(nests on the ground), Little Tern and Reef Egret.
CAGAYANCILLO, 9°34'N, 121°12'E
31 small islands 320km east of Puerto Princessa with a human population of c. 8,000. There are small
breeding colonies of Sooty Tern and Black-naped Terns on isolated rocky islets in the area.
CAVILI ISLAND, 9°16'N, 120°49'E
A small 150ha island with a population of around 300 people. 40km SW of Caganyancillo.
This island contains a small 'sacred grove' of protected *Pisonia alba* trees with breeding Red-footed
Booby, Great Frigatebird and Black Noddy. Lesser Frigatebird roosts.
Seabirds are also found breeding or roosting in lesser numbers on Bankoran Island, Bancauan Island,
Maeander (Bastera) Reef, Manuk Manukan and on the small wooded San Miguel Islands in the south of
the Sulu Sea (near Borneo) where all three frigatebirds roost.   www.wwf.org.ph

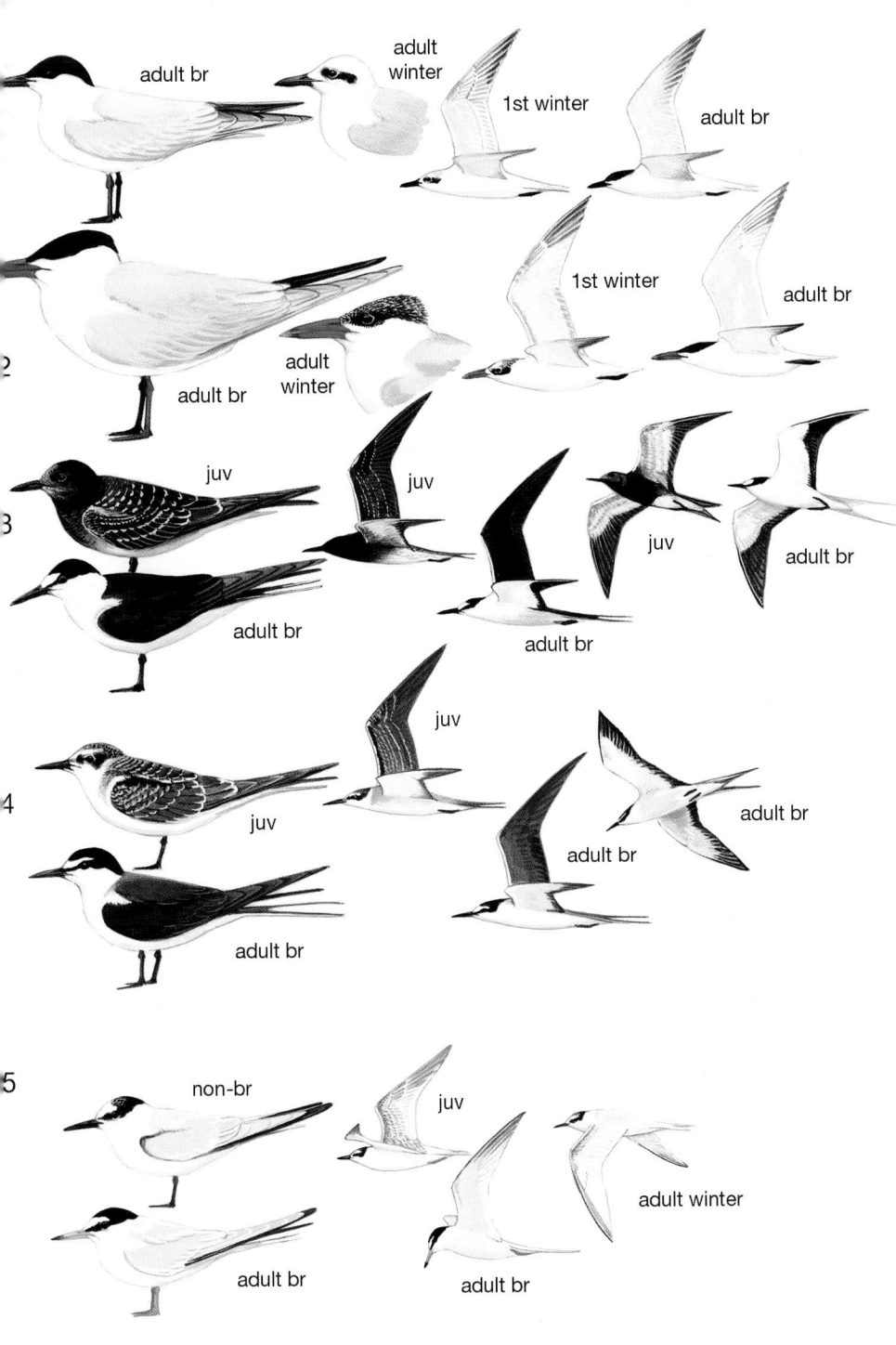

adult br

adult winter

1st winter

adult br

2

adult br

adult winter

1st winter

adult br

3

juv

juv

juv

adult br

adult br

adult br

4

juv

juv

juv

adult br

adult br

adult br

5

non-br

juv

adult winter

adult br

adult br

COMMON, ROSEATE, ALEUTIAN AND BLACK-NAPED TERNS

1 COMMON TERN *Sterna hirundo longipennis* **36cm** **Scarce passage migrant rac**

The Common Tern of Europe is a scarce visitor to Borneo seas on its passage from China *
Australia and back. Often in small flocks with other terns. Large flocks may occur during pea
migration Sept.–Dec. and April–May, e.g. 3,900 along the Sarawak coast April 1986. Commone
on the west coast but also seen east coast. All records refer to race *S. h. longipennis* which has
black bill year round. **Range:** Breeds Europe to Asia wintering south to Africa, Australia.

2 COMMON TERN *Sterna hirundo tibetana* **36cm** **Not recorded rac**

Common Tern race *S. h. tibetana* with a red bill when breeding could also occur around Borneo as it is a regula
passage migrant through Hong Kong. Otherwise similar to *S. h. longipennis.*

3 ROSEATE TERN *Sterna dougallii* **39cm** **Scarce resident**

Scattered records from around the Borneo coast and a regular breeder in small numbers on th
Pelong Rocks at the mouth of the Brunei River. Very similar to Common Tern but has some re
on the bill even in non-breeding plumage. Generally whiter above than Common Tern and als
has long white outer tail feathers. In breeding plumage has faint tinge of pink on underpart
Range: Worldwide. Breeds on small islands in Sulu Sea, S China and Sulawesi Sea.

4 ALEUTIAN TERN *Sterna aleutica* **34cm** **Vagran**

First recorded off the Sarawak coast April 2005. Several recent winter records from KK waterfront and Semporn
(Wong Tsu Sui). **Range:** Breeds May to September along the coast of Alaska and Siberia dispersing south to th
Pacific Ocean and South China Seas.

5 BLACK-NAPED TERN *Sterna sumatrana* **34cm** **Common resider**

The commonest resident tern. A regular annual breeder April–June on Tukong Ara, Pelon
Rocks and Tg Nosong. Occasionally breeds on other small rocky islands along the coas
which are usually abandoned the following year. After the young have become independen
disperses out to sea during the NE Monsoon and usually not seen again along the coast unt
the following April. **Range:** Tropical Indian and Pacific Oceans.

ARCTIC TERN *Sterna paradisaea* **36cm [Not illustrated]** **Not recorde**

The Arctic Tern has a circumpolar breeding range in the far north of the globe. In winter it migrates south usuall
crossing the equator and is found in all oceans of the world. Probably under recorded in the South China Sea du
to similarity in appearance with Common and Roseate Terns and is listed here for reference only.

TERN BREEDING ROCKS OFF THE COAST OF NW BORNEO
Between the north west tip of Borneo and Tg Datu at the southern tip of Sarawak there are hundreds of
small rocky islets along the coast of Borneo. Three of these in particular are occupied by breeding seabirds
each year during the calm sea period April to June. The eggs and young are often taken by passing
fishermen and predated by sea snakes and Reef Egrets that breed in the same locations to coincide with
the breeding terns. See map page 74, also pages 68, 136.

TANJONG NOSONG STACKS, SABAH (05°38'N, 115°36'E)
A group of isolated rocky cliffs at the north west tip of the Klias peninsula on the mainland opposite Pulau
Tiga. (Ideally these cliffs should be incorporated into the adjacent Pulau Tiga National Park.) Breeding
Bridled and Black-naped Terns and Reef Egrets.

PELONG ROCKS, BRUNEI DARUSSALAM (05°05'N, 115°03'E)
A group of small rocky islands with a few trees, off shore Muara near the entrance to the Brunei River. No
access without the previous approval of the Brunei Museum. Breeding Bridled, Black-naped and Roseate
Terns, Reef Egrets and Pied Imperial Pigeons.

TUKONG ARA-BANUN, SARAWAK (01°47'N, 110°09'E)
Two small rocky islands in Santubong Bay, opposite Damai Beach which is 30 minutes' drive from
Kuching. Now protected as part of the Talang Satang Islands National Park. No public access. Breeding
Bridled, Black-naped Terns and Reef Egrets, which predate the young terns.

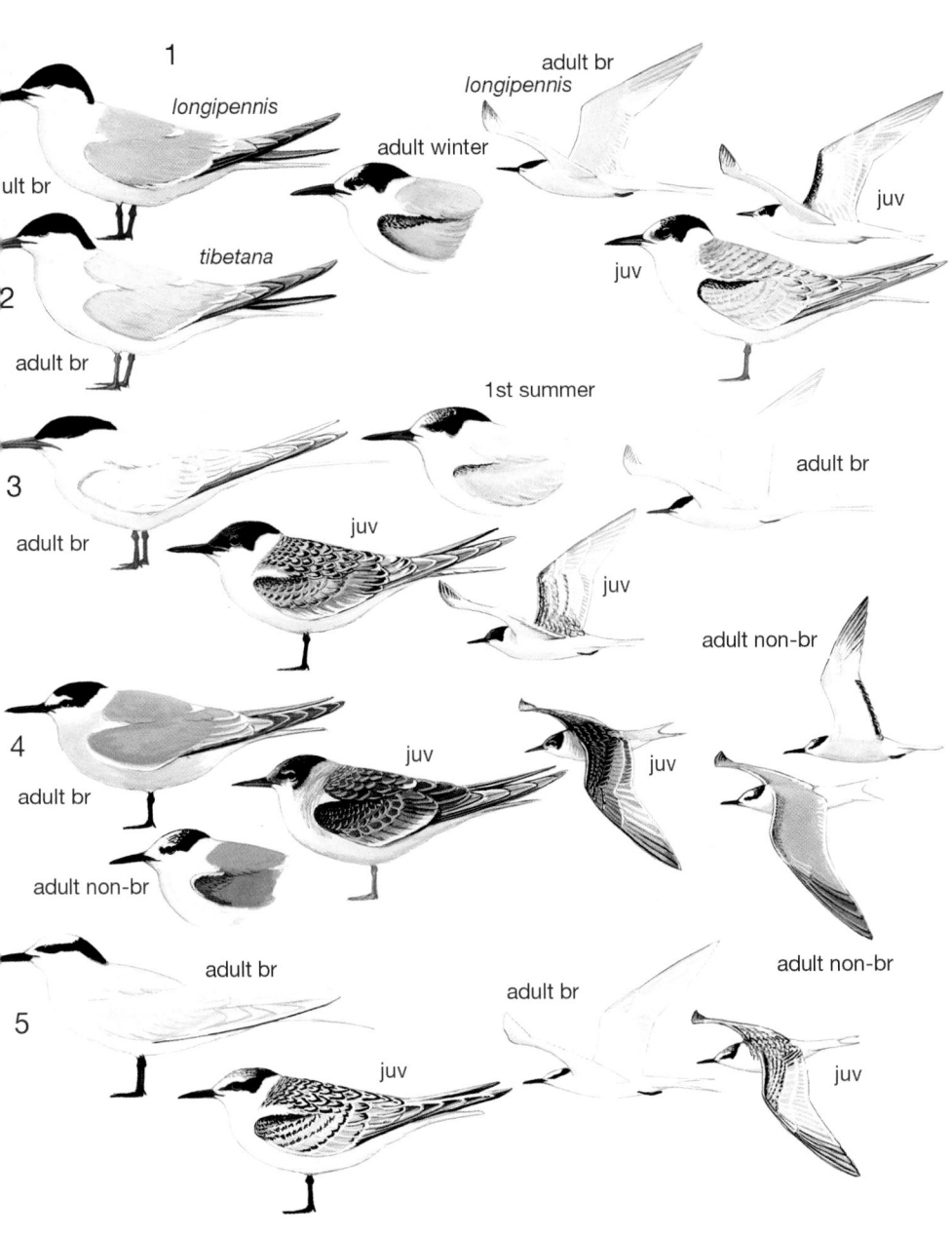

1 *longipennis*

ult br

adult br
longipennis

adult winter

juv

juv

2 *tibetana*

adult br

3

adult br

1st summer

adult br

juv

juv

juv

adult non-br

4

adult br

juv

adult br

juv

adult non-br

adult non-br

5

adult br

juv

adult br

juv

NODDIES

1   WHITE NODDY   *Gygis alba*   **28cm**   **Not recorded**

[Fairy Tern or White Tern] Reputed to breed on the disputed Xi Sha islands (Paracel Islands) administered b
China, in the centre of the S China Sea approx. 200km off the coast of Hainan Island. Has been recorded o
Sumatra, and more recently from the Sulu Sea (Jensen 2005). The only completely white tern. Unusually fo
terns lays a single egg on the bare branch of a tree. Usually non-migratory. Very rarely seen along mainlan
coasts. **Range:** Breeds only on remote undisturbed tree-covered oceanic tropical islands worldwide.

2   BLACK NODDY   *Anous minutus*   **36cm**   **Rare oceanic visito**

[White-capped Noddy] The two dark noddies are tropical seabirds that breed on isolate
oceanic islands in large colonies. Usually only seen near mainland coasts after severe storms
Significantly smaller (slightly darker) and less common than the Brown Noddy. Always nest
in trees, whereas the Brown Noddy nests on the ground. The noddies are believed to feed o
small squid and fish that come to the surface of the sea at night hence their dark plumage
Breeding colonies close to Borneo Cavilli Island, Sulu Sea, Pulau Kebatu, 50km south o
Belitung and probably one of the Tambelan Islands. **Range:** Tropical areas of Pacific an
Atlantic Oceans. Huge colonies nest on the islands of the Australian Great Barrier Reef.

3   BROWN NODDY   *Anous stolidus*   **42cm**   **Locally common residen**

[Common Noddy] The second commonest nesting bird on P Layang[2] where several hundred
nest March–Aug. Young disperse after breeding and can be seen occasionally along th
Borneo coast after storms Oct. to March. Can only be distinguished reliably from Black Nodd
by larger size and ground nesting habits. Underwing has two tone appearance in compariso
to plain underwing of Black Noddy. **Breeding colonies close to Borneo** Paracel Islands an
P Layang[2] (S China Sea), Tubbataha Reef and Bankoran island (Sulu Sea), P Kayu Ara,
Damar (Anambas), P Mandariki (Tambelan islands), P Lari Larian (Makassar Strait). **Range**
Tropical Oceans worldwide. Breeds in large colonies on remote islands dispersing widely afte
breeding. Colonies nest all around the north coasts of Australia-.

PULAU LAYANG LAYANG, 07°22'N, 113°50'E (ISLAND OF SEA SWALLOWS)

P. Layang[2], 300km north west of Kota Kinabalu, is by far the most important site for breeding seabirds
in both Bornean and Malaysian waters. It is possibly one of the most important sites in the S China Sea.
Previously a flat coral island on the rim of a large sunken volcano (atoll), it has been developed primarily
as a Malaysian naval air base and secondarily as one of Asia's top deep water dive destinations, renowned
for Hammerhead Sharks and large coral fish such as groupers and wrasses. See map page 74. Also pages
76, 136, 138, 140.

The Malay name Layang Layang means 'swallows or swifts' reflecting the large numbers of swallow-like
seabirds (noddies and terns) present. The name is shared with the first stop on the Kinabalu Summit Trail
(due to the many swiftlets present) and a coastal village on P Labuan.

Pulau Layang[2] is part of the Spratly Group (Nansha islands in Chinese) about 150 low sandy islets and
scattered cays towards the southern end of the S China sea. Politically these islands are divided between
Malaysia, the Philippines, Vietnam and China and ownership disputes remain to be resolved. Therefore
other islands in the Spratlys and Paracels (Xisha islands) which are known to host large numbers of
breeding seabirds are off limits to visitors, e.g. Dong Island (Paracels) which had 35,500 breeding pairs of
Red-footed Booby in 2004 (Lei).

Breeding seabirds (in order of abundance)   Sooty Terns, Brown Noddy, Greater Crested Tern, Brown
Booby, Black-naped Tern, Little Tern, Pacific Reef Egret.

Migrant land birds   This is probably the best place anywhere in Borneo to add rare vagrants to the
Borneo bird list. Small isolated islands on key migration routes act as a magnet for tired migrants. Birds
recorded: Black-winged Stilt, Hoopoe, Forest Wagtail, Common Kingfisher, Japanese Sparrowhawk, Grey-
faced Buzzard, Megapode, White-tailed Tropicbird, Peregrine Falcon, Eurasion Hobby, Northern Boobook.

When to visit   Most seabirds breed on Layang Layang between March and August. The dive resort (and
therefore public access) is closed from September to February. For migrating land birds the best months
to visit would be March–April and September–October Access: Layang[2] is about one hour's flight north
west of KK. Nearly all visitors are divers on three to seven day package deals.

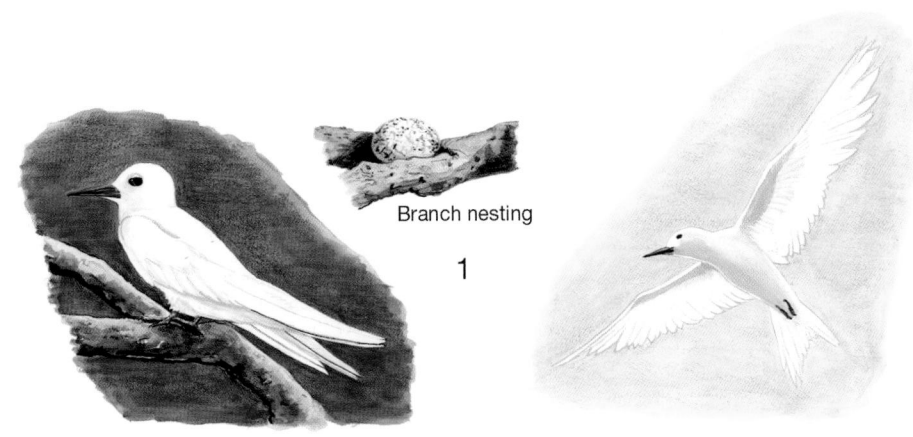

Branch nesting

1

2

Tree nesting

3

Ground nesting

SKUAS (JAEGERS)

STERCORARIIDAE   **World 7 species; Borneo waters 5 species.** Heavily built aggressive seabirds, whic[h] feed by scavenging, stealing from other seabirds (kleptoparasitism) and hunting birds and lemmings. Fo[ur] species breed on remote islands near the Arctic and migrate south in the winter. The other three species bree[d] on Antarctic islands and migrate north in the austral winter. Skuas prefer cold seas but are great wandere[rs] and vagrants can appear in marine habitats anywhere in the world. Skuas seen in Borneo waters are usual[ly] trans-equatorial migrants, crossing the equator on their annual migrations from the Arctic to the Antarctic an[d] back. As they rapidly pass through the S China Sea they are not often seen. However, where other seabirds a[re] abundant, for example Kota Kinabalu harbour, an individual skua can hang around for months persecuting th[e] local terns. Sexes are similar but females are approximately 15% larger than males. Skuas can occur in bo[th] light and dark (less common) morphs. The variable juvenile and immature plumages of the first two years ca[n] confuse. Only the differing shapes of the adult tail extensions are truly distinctive but note that these may b[e] missing in young or moulting birds.

1   LONG-TAILED SKUA (JAEGER)   *Stercorarius longicaudus*   **32cm + 22cm tail**   **Vagra[nt]**
The least common of the northern skuas. Only two possible records from coastal Borneo. Small light dainty skua wit[h] extra long tail extensions in breeding plumage. Distinguished from Arctic Skua by size and by long tail extension[s]. Normally migrates well out to sea. **Range:** Breeds in Arctic region, wintering in S Atlantic and S Pacific.

2   POMARINE SKUA (JAEGER)   *Stercorarius pomarinus*   **54cm + 19cm tail**   **Rare migra[nt]**

The largest and heaviest skua, and the commonest skua in Bornean waters, seen regular[ly] but in very small numbers. Distinguished by spoon-shaped tail extensions present year roun[d] in adult birds. When breeding, the Pomarine Skua is a specialist predator on Arctic lemming[s] which vary greatly in abundance each year. In a good lemming year the skuas will have hig[h] breeding success leading to irruptive movements of birds southwards, with many sighting[s]. **Range:** Breeds Arctic tundra, wintering in Atlantic, Pacific, SE Asian, Australasian waters.

3   ARCTIC SKUA   *Stercorarius parasiticus*   **43cm + 13cm tail extension**   **Vagra[nt]**
[Davison: Parasitic Jaeger]. Very scarce migrant with only two definite records. **Range:** Breeds Arctic, winterin[g] at sea in Atlantic, Pacific and Australasian waters. Seen off KK Oct 2010 (A. Reyes).

4   SOUTH POLAR SKUA   *Catharacta maccormicki*   **53cm**   **Vagra[nt]**
Several records from off shore W Sabah. Most likely to be seen on migration at beginning or end of Austr[al] summer September to February. **Range:** Breeds on Antarctic islands wintering north of the equator in Atlanti[c] Pacific and Indian Oceans.

5   BROWN SKUA   *Catharacta antarctica*   **63cm**   **Not recorde[d]**
Range: Breeds on Antarctic Islands normally wintering below the equator in S hemisphere but immature bird[s] may occasionally cross the equator.

WHY SKUAS AND OTHER BORNEAN BIRDS HAVE DIFFERENT COLOUR MORPHS
There are three main reasons for birds of the same sex and species to appear in different plumages or morphs: disguise, mimicry, and camouflage. Worldwide, these morphs are commonest amongst the raptors and other predatory birds. See also pages 64, 84, 88, 104, 130, 162.
Disguise morphs include the Changeable Hawk-eagle and Long-tailed Shrike. These different plumages may be disguises to fool potential prey into thinking that the bird they see is harmless.
Mimicry is most common with the polymorphic plumages of the Honey Buzzard designed to fool the more powerful Hawk-eagles that they could also be Hawk-eagles. The hepatic phase of female cuckoos appears to mimic Kestrel plumage. One likely reason is to frighten away the host bird, whilst the female cuckoo exchanges its own egg with that of the host.
Camouflage is common with scops owls and frogmouths, which often occur in at least three plumage variations, dark, pale and rufous. Over time the colour morph that most matches the background colours of the habitat is likely to predominate. The predominance of dark morph Reef Egrets also appears to be for camouflage because it varies between rocky shores where dark is more common, to white sand beaches where both white and dark are equally common. With skuas, studies have shown that the skuas that live near colonies of seabirds and hunt mainly by kleptoparasitism tend to be dark for camouflage against the surface of the sea, whereas those that hunt on the tundra are pale so that they are camouflaged against the sky.

1

br

moulting

juv
*pale
morph*

dark morph

juv

*intermediate
morph*

br
*dark
morph*

br
*pale
morph*

non-br

juv
pale morph

2

br
pale morph

non-br
pale morph

juv
intermediate

*breeding
morph*

3

adult intermediate

adult

pale morph

juv
*pale
morph*

4

adult

juv

5

DOVES AND PIGEONS

COLUMBIDAE   **World 310 species; Borneo 21 species.**   Although there is no scientific distinction between pigeons and doves, 'dove' usually refers to ground feeding, seed eating, pigeons with long tails. Sexes generally similar. Pigeons build flimsy stick nests, laying one or two white eggs. The male broods during the day, the female at night. The young are fed on tofu-like 'pigeon's milk' which the parent manufactures in its own crop. Seed eating pigeons obtain their protein from grains and seeds but how Imperial Pigeons survive on a purely fruit diet is a mystery. Perhaps protein is obtained by ingesting fig wasp larvae in unripe figs. Known for their soft, peaceful cooing calls and often kept as pets. Also considered to be good eating and either domesticated for that purpose (Feral Pigeon) or heavily hunted.

1   RUDDY CUCKOO-DOVE   *Macropygia emiliana*   **30cm**   **Submontane resident**

Locally common in hilly country and the lower levels of mountains up to around 1,500m. Overlaps in range with Little Cuckoo-Dove which is more of a mountain bird. Both species feed on the berries of secondary growth found in old clearings or forest edge. **Call:** A loud repeated **wa-oo**. 'It is noticeably less disyllabic and repeated less often than the call of the Little Cuckoo Dove' (Sheldon). **Range:** Sumatra to Java, east to N Guinea.

2   LITTLE CUCKOO-DOVE   *Macropygia ruficeps*   **28cm**   **Montane resident**

Montane resident throughout the mountains of Borneo, generally common e.g. at KNP HQ but nomadic. Occasionally seen in the foothills of mountainous areas, at other times found high on Kinabalu feeding on seasonal berries. **Call:** '**croo-wuck, croo-wuck** repeated very rapidly. The **croo** is only audible at close quarters and all that can be heard from a distance is **wuck wuck wuck**' (Smythies). **Range:** Vietnam to Malay P, Sumatra, Borneo, Java.

3   PHILIPPINE COLLARED-DOVE   *Streptopelia dusumieri*   **30cm**   **Escape**

[Island Collared-Dove, *Streptopelia bitorquota*; Javanese Turtle Dove] Common throughout the Philippines in open country and mangroves. Often kept as a pet. There are two records from E coast Sabah at Sandakan and Si Amil island, and one from Kuching; probably escaped birds which have not become established. Distinguished from Spotted Dove by plain dark (not spotted) collar. Young Spotted Dove looks similar. **Call:** 'A mournful **tuk-mm-mm** or harsher **ker-r-r-r, krr-rr** repeated several times' (Kennedy *et al.*). **Range:** Philippines, Java to Timor.

4   ZEBRA DOVE   *Geopelia striata*   **21cm**   **Common resident**

[Davison: Peaceful Dove] [Malay: Merbuk] Believed to have originated from escapes in Kalimantan and Kota Kinabalu (first recorded 1965). Now abundant on grassy wasteland close to human habitation throughout most of Borneo. Smaller and less shy than Spotted Dove. Commonly caged for its soothing call and popular in Java for singing contests. **Call:** Soft **kur kurr kurr kurr** repeated. **Range:** Myanmar to Malay P, Sumatra, Borneo, Philippines, Java.

5   SPOTTED DOVE   *Streptopelia chinensis*   **30cm**   **Common resident**

[Spotted-necked Dove]. Abundant resident of padi fields, and grassland throughout Borneo including cleared and cultivated areas in the hills and mountains. Shyer than Zebra Dove which has ousted it from areas close to dwellings. **Call:** The Malay name **tekukor** describes the call. There is a stress on the last note. **Range:** India, China, to Malaya P, Sumatra, Borneo, Java, Philippines.

6   EMERALD DOVE   *Chalcophaps indica*   **25cm**   **Common nomadic resident**

[Malay: Punai tanah (ground)] A common ground dove of islands, coastal, secondary and primary forest in the lowlands and hills. Flies rapidly through the forest understorey and is often trapped in mist nets. Look for distinctive white bars on lower back as it flies off. A common night-flying nomad. Feeds on fallen *Macaranga* seeds, a shrub of disturbed forest. The Danum population increased seven fold after logging (Lambert). **Call:** A fast repeated mournful **tik hoo**, the first part inaudible from a distance. Locals call in males with a bamboo flute and trap with a hand net. **Range:** SE Asia to Australia where it is known as the Green-winged Pigeon.

Around 54 species of small *Macaranga* trees with large leaves invade recently-logged forest and the sides of new forest roads. Nomadic Emerald Doves predate the small hard seeds. The illustration shows fallen flowers and seeds of *Macaranga tanarius*, a common species. See page 365.

GREEN PIGEONS

The *Treron* green pigeons [Malay: Punai] are fig eating specialists and Borneo is a centre of diversity for both fruit eating pigeons and fig trees, with 138 + species of fig tree recorded. Figs are high in calcium and sugars but very low in protein. Other birds that eat figs such as hornbills also eat insects and small animals to obtain their protein. However, like doves, green pigeons have strong muscular gizzards containing swallowed grit which they use to grind up the tiny fig seeds. It must be these minute seeds which provide the protein in their diet. Like other pigeons, green pigeons are very fond of salt and are frequent visitors to the natural salt springs scattered throughout Borneo. Locals exploit this habit by placing nets or traps over the springs to catch the green pigeons for food, e.g. at Pa Main, Pa Umor and Pa Bangar, in the Kelabit Highlands. Sexes differ. Usually in small flocks. Both Pink-necked and Little Green Pigeons develop thin red eye rings when breeding.

1 THICK-BILLED GREEN PIGEON *Treron curvirostra* **27cm** **Local nomadic resident**

Locally common in lowland primary and submontane forest. All the green pigeons are nomadic night-flying migrants, with the Thick-billed probably the most nomadic. Locally abundant when fig trees are fruiting and then completely disappears from an area. Distinguished by red bill base of both sexes. **Call:** Similar to that of Pink-necked (see below) but not as loud or clear. **Range:** India to Malay P, Sumatra, Philippines.

2 CINNAMON-HEADED GREEN PIGEON *Treron fulvicollis* **27cm** **Scarce resident**

Locally common in undisturbed coastal swamp and mangrove forests, rarely seen elsewhere, but has been recorded inland as far as Mulu and Gng Dulit in Sarawak (Mann). In S Kalimantan one of the commonest green pigeons in the swamps of the Barito and Negara Rivers and at Tg Puting and Sabangau. Like all the green pigeons locally nomadic. **Call:** A reeling *coo* rising and falling (Goodwin). **Range:** Malay P, Sumatra, Borneo.

3 LITTLE GREEN PIGEON *Treron olax* **22cm** **Common nomadic resident**

Locally common in coastal, secondary, primary and submontane forest throughout Borneo. Locally nomadic, stray birds have been recorded from the Tembungo Oil Platform off NW Sabah and the Sabah Turtle Islands. Note distinctive white iris. **Call:** 'The chuckling call typical of *Treron* species is in this bird preceded by a nasal winding up whine' (Holmes). 'Its call resembles that of a crying child' (Thompson). Utters a coucal like call for long periods (Batchelor). **Range:** Malay P, Sumatra, Java, Borneo.

4 PINK-NECKED GREEN PIGEON *Treron vernans* **29cm** **Common resident**

The most common green pigeon, abundant on islands, and in coastal and secondary forest where populations have not been depleted by shooting or trapping. Often seen in fig trees but not a fig specialist like other green pigeons. Often feeds in towns and gardens on Malay Cherry *Muntingia* an introduced shrub from Central America with small red berries now very common thanks to this pigeon. Roosts communally, when it is trapped by locals with sticky latex and sold for food. **Call:** A very odd call, a prolonged chuckling gurgle. **Range:** Thailand, Malay P, Sumatra, Java, Sulawesi, Philippines.

5 LARGE GREEN PIGEON *Treron capellei* **36cm** **Scarce resident**

The least common green pigeon. Unlike other green pigeons, which typically occur in flocks, usually seen singly or in pairs. Specialises in feeding on large figs only. Confined to lowland primary forest with numbers reduced significantly after logging. Not as flexible in diet or habitat as Green Imperial Pigeon, which thrives in logged forest. Edge of tail is dark with a pale terminal band like other green pigeons, but not like Green Imperial which has an all dark tail and a grey not green head. Female (not illustrated) is similar to male but orange breast band is less obvious. Distinguish by size and much heavier bill from other green pigeons. Also note yellow feet. All other Green and most Imperial Pigeons have red feet. **Call:** A deep gurgling, not a boom like the Imperial Pigeons (Davison). **Range:** Malay P, Sumatra, Borneo, Java. **BLI:** Vulnerable.

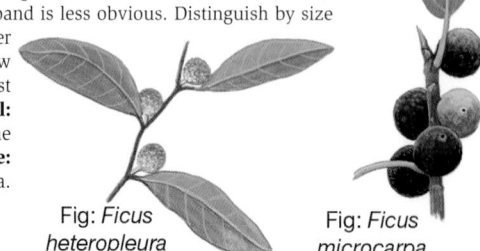

Fig: *Ficus heteropleura*

Fig: *Ficus microcarpa*

FRUIT DOVES AND PIGEONS

PTILINOPUS **World 14 species; Borneo 2 species.** The *Ptilinopus* fruit doves are commonest and most diverse on the thousands of small forested islands between Borneo and the Pacific Islands where they appear to thrive in the absence of monkeys. Like green pigeons, fruit doves swallow fruit whole but unlike them they void the seeds intact thus assisting seed dispersal for their fruit tree hosts. Both Borneo species appear to be highly nomadic, the Black-naped Fruit Dove moving between small islands at night, whilst the Jambu Fruit Dove is probably the most nomadic of all the Bornean pigeons. Despite their colourful plumage they are surprisingly difficult to see when feeding in the top of a fruiting tree.

1 JAMBU FRUIT DOVE *Ptilinopus jambu* **28cm**   Scarce nomadic resident

Widespread but very scarce nomad in primary and submontane forest. Usually seen alone. One of the commonest forest birds trapped on night-flying migration studies in the Malay Peninsula. Recorded nesting in forest in the Kelabit Highlands and in montane forest at KNP HQ. In Kalimantan recorded from Tg Puting, Banjarmasin and the Sangkulirang Peninsula. Both sexes have distinctive white eye-ring. **Call:** 'A low soft *coo*, seldom uttered' (Robinson). **Range:** Malay P, Sumatra, Borneo, Java.

2 BLACK-NAPED FRUIT DOVE *Ptilinopus melanospila* **27cm**   Scarce island resident

A common fruit dove of open wooded areas in Mindanao, Sulawesi and Java but in Borneo, a scarce island specialist found on large islands such as Banggi and Balambangan (occassionally on mainland. Wiles) but commonest on the small islands of E Borneo e.g. Semporna Islands and Maratua. Usually solitary. Locally common, e.g. three nests found on Sipadan, E Sabah in Oct. 1989 (Lambert). **Call:** A double *hoo hoo* repeated in every 7 to 10 seconds often for several minutes. **Range:** Sumatra, Java, Borneo, Philippines, Sulawesi, Moluccas.

3 FERAL PIGEON *Columba livia* **32cm**   Common resident

[Davison: Rock Pigeon] (Malay: Burung acang) Originally domesticated, now feral in many Bornean towns, living on man-made structures. In Kota Kinabalu they provide the major part of the diet for a pair of migrant Peregrine Falcons each winter. **Range:** Wild birds live on cliffs from the deserts of the Middle East to the coastal cliffs of W Europe. Feral birds in cities world wide, often regarded as pests.

4 NICOBAR PIGEON *Caloenas nicobarica* **40cm**   Rare island nomad

Found on most of the small forested islands around Borneo feeding on fallen fruits on the forest floor, but irregular and scarce. Unlike the Imperial Pigeons which are seed dispersers a seed predator with a muscular gizzard. Regular on Pulau Tiga, Mantanani, Maratua and Sipadan. Appears almost black, with distinctive short white tail as it takes off in the forest gloom. Roosts in trees but never seen feeding in the canopy. Nests communally on small islands. Crepuscular and often active at night. **Call:** Harsh growl *growoo* repeated slowly. **Range:** From Nicobar Islands (Bay of Bengal) along coasts and on islets to the Pacific.

ISLANDS AND RATS Whitehead suggested that pigeons like nesting on islands because there are no monkeys to rob their nests. The major threat nowadays is the ubiquitous, tree climbing, Black Rat *Rattus rattus*, spread inadvertently by man. Rats are serious predators of island birds worldwide but on many islands rats have been successfully eliminated by systematically poison baiting the whole island. In Borneo, Sangkalaki (Derawan islands) was cleared of rats to protect baby turtles, but the island birds should also benefit in the long run. See page 348.

NIGHT-FLYING FRUGIVOROUS NOMADS Birds that specialise in eating small berries are often highly nomadic. Patches of fruiting shrubs in secondary forest are widely scattered and fruit intermittently. Nomadic frugivores include Jambu Fruit Dove, Emerald Dove, Black and White Bulbul and Black-headed Bulbul. Like the migrants from the north that reach Borneo each winter most local nomads fly at night, often over high mountain ridges. Studies at Dalton Pass in the Philippines and at Frazer's Hill in the Malay Peninsula have found that on dark moonless nights, migrant birds are confused by bright lights on ridge tops and can be easily trapped. In The Malay Peninsula the commonest local nomads are Hooded Pitta, Emerald Dove and Jambu Fruit Dove. More limited studies in the Crocker Range particularly those by Sheldon at Rinangisan prove that night-flying local nomads are equally common in Borneo. See also pages 36 and 218.

1

♂

♀

2

♂

♀

3

Nutmeg
Myristica fragrans

4

juv

Large imperial pigeons and small fruit doves are important dispersers of forest fruit seeds. The seeds are swallowed whole and later defecated or regurgitated. In contrast the Nicobar Pigeon feeds on the dropped seeds using a grit-filled muscular gizzard to grind them up. Nutmeg trees are very common on small islands around Borneo, where the seeds are dispersed by Grey and Pied Imperial Pigeons and predated by Nicobar Pigeons.

IMPERIAL PIGEONS AND WOOD PIGEONS

Imperial Pigeons [Malay: Pergam] are very large fruit pigeons which have evolved to swallow large fruits whole and regurgitate the seeds intact, thus perpetuating their own ideal habitat. Many small islands around the coast of Borneo are covered in fig and nutmeg trees as a result of this. Three out of the four Bornean Imperial Pigeons are associated with small islands, as well as both the rare *Columba* wood pigeons. Sexes similar. Usually seen in flocks.

1   GREEN IMPERIAL PIGEON   *Ducula aenea*   45 cm   **Common lowland resident**

Common in lowland forested areas throughout Borneo from the coast to the hills. Heavily shot, now making a comeback where guns are banned. Every fruiting fig tree attracts these birds. Also fond of laurels and oil palm. At Tg Aru, Kota Kinabalu, small flocks roost on the islands of the Tunku Abdul Rahman Park but feed on the mainland. They fly in from the islands an hour after dawn and start drifting back from 4.30pm onwards. An occasional Pied Imperial may join the flock. **Call:** A lovely deep *coo, click hroooo* (Smithies). **Range:** India to S.China, Philippines, Malay P, Sumatra, Borneo to N Guinea.

2   GREY IMPERIAL PIGEON   *Ducula pickeringii*   40 cm   **Rare island resident**

Rare nomadic visitor to islands of N Borneo including Tiga, Manukan, Mantanani, Semporna Islands, Sipadan. Green I.P. may also roost and feed on these islands and can be confused. Green I.P has diagnostic rufous vent unlike pale vent of Grey. Green I.P. back is iridescent greenish bronze whilst Grey's back is iridescent greyish mauve, i.e. more reddish purple than Green. The commonest large pigeon on Maratua, Kakaban and Sangkalaki islands (E Kalimantan) where Green does not occur. **Call:** A deep *whrrooh* repeated intermittently. **Range:** N Bornean islets to Sulu Islands. Islands off Palawan and Talaud Islands. **BLI:** Vulnerable.

3   MOUNTAIN IMPERIAL PIGEON   *Ducula badia*   45cm   **Common montane resident**

Nests in the Bornean mountains but wanders widely to the lowlands for seasonal fruits and possibly also sea salt as they often visit the mangroves. In the Kimanis area flocks were seen in the mangroves from Oct. to Feb. but spent the rest of the year in the mountains (Batchelor). In Sabah common at KNP HQ and in the Crocker Range. **Call:** *whroom, whroom,* or *whroom whroom whroom* (Sheldon). Range: India to Malay P, Sumatra, Java.

4   PIED IMPERIAL PIGEON   *Ducula bicolour*   42 cm   **Scarce island resident**

[Malay: Burung Rawa]. Occurs sporadically on most of the small islands around Borneo coast but often absent. Like all island pigeons flies nomadically from one island to another depending on seasonal fruiting, probably at night. Sometimes seen far out to sea during the day. May fly to the mainland to feed. but returns to roost on the island e.g Satang and Talang Islands (Sarawak). Recorded breeding Pelong Rocks, Brunei, **Call:** 'A chuckling *hu hu hu*' (Robinson and Chasen). **Range:** Islands from the Andamans to Australia.

5   WHITE-THROATED PIGEON   *Columba vitiensis*   42 cm   **Rare island resident**

[Davison: Metallic Pigeon] Rare nomadic resident of small islands. Two mainland records Tawau coast and Mahakam River. Two races illustrated. (**5a**): *C. v. griseogularis* is found on islands off E. Borneo south to the Mahakam River. (**5b**): *C. v. anthracina* has been recorded on islands off N W Borneo e.g. Mantanani, Manukan etc. south to Pulau Tiga. Looks black in flight. Flushes with loud wing clapping. **Call:** A deep base *wuuuu woooo*, the first note rising, the second level, often repeated a second time (Kennedy). Usually in small flocks. **Range:** A small island specialist from the Philippines to the Pacific.

6   SILVERY PIGEON   *Columba argentina*   40 cm   **Very rare island resident**

Until 100 years ago locally common on small islands off SW Borneo. Only two recent global records. A photograph from the Mentawi Islands. W. Sumatra. (Lee et al 2009) and two captives photographed in Hong Kong (Crimson Lam 1 July 2000) Very similar to Pied Imperial with which it flocks but white of Pied is replaced with silvery grey. Look for distinctive red eye ring, red bill base and red feet and distinctive under-tail and under-wing markings. See Yong (2009) and Sarawak Museum skins on www.borneobirdimages.com. **BLI:** Critical.

Pigeon Plum
*Elaeocarpus
sphaericus*

5a

5b

1 2 3

4 6

PARROTS

PSITTACIDAE: World: 315 species. Borneo: 5 resident species. Elsewhere parrots are often kept as pets, bu in Borneo only the tiny Blue-Crowned Hanging Parrot may be seen in small, rattan cages hanging from the verandah of kampong houses. The other Borneo parrots do not survive well in captivity and are rarely trapped Parrots nest in holes in rotten trees which they enlarge from an old barbet or woodpecker hole. Often very raucous with loud screeching calls as flocks fly overhead to evening roosts. Parrots are serious seed predator like doves, but also feed on fruits, young leaves and opportunistically on insects.

1 RING NECKED PARAKEET *Psittacula krameri* **40cm**   **Escape**

The commonest parrot in India and parts of Africa, and very commonly kept as a pet worldwide. In London UK an expanding feral population now exceeds 25,000 birds. Escaped birds regularly seen at Tg Aru beach (Kota Kinabalu) where it has inter-bred at least twice with Blue-naped Parrots. Note that the native forest-dwelling Long-tailed Parakeet which has distinctive pink cheeks has also been seen as an escaped bird at Tg Aru beach

2 RED-BREASTED PARAKEET *Psittacula alexandri* **34cm**   **Scarce local residen**

Large flocks recorded around Banjarmasin in 1855 (Motley). Now very scarce with scattered records from SE Kalimantan (Barito River) west to Kendawangan. Elsewhere raids orchards padi fields and maize crops. Female is similar to but has duller head markings than male with deeper red on breast. **Call:** Raucous loud trumpeting scream, shrill whistles and nasal honking (Juniper). **Range:** India to Malay P, Sumatra, Java, Borneo. Feral in Singapore.

3 LONG-TAILED PARAKEET *Psittacula longicauda* **40cm**   **Local residen**

A locally common resident of coastal forests, travelling widely to feed including cultivated areas and oil palm estates where it is considered a pest. At Gng Palung (Kalimantan) and Loagan Bunut (Sarawak) occurs in large roosting flocks of several thousand. Common at Tg Puting. In the Malay P, often nests communally in dead trees (Wells). **Call:** High pitched screeching typical of parrots. **Range:** Malay P, Borneo, Sumatra.

4 BLUE-NAPED PARROT *Tanygnathus lucionensis* **30cm**   **Local residen**

Previously common in the Philippines, but now extinct most areas. A population of *c.*10C birds on P. Mantanani was trapped out in the 1970s. May still occur on small Si Amil Is., E Sabah. Still common on P Maratua, E. Kalimantan. See page 348. A small population on P Tiga is believed to result from Typhoon Greg, 26 Dec 1996, which blew parrots south down the coast from Tg Aru (A. Reyes). Around 30–50 birds breed in the old casurina trees at Tg Aru beach, Kota Kinabalu. A shortage of nesting holes limits the population. Sexes similar. **Call:** Harsh squawks and donkey like braying. **Range:** Philippines, Talaud Is.

5 BLUE-RUMPED PARROT *Psittinus cyanurus* **18cm**   **Local residen**

Locally common in lowland primary and logged forest throughout Borneo, e.g. at Sepilok, but often absent. Look for red underwing of both sexes. Female has a brownish not a blue head and no red beak like the male. Does not survive in captivity and so rarely trapped. **Call:** A shrill, sharp, whistled note or series of notes, surprisingly musical for a parrot, most often heard from birds in swift flight at canopy level (Holmes). Shrill sharp chittering *chi, chi chi* or *chew-ee* (Juniper). **Range:** Myanmar to Malay P, Sumatra, Borneo.

6 BLUE-CROWNED HANGING PARROT *Loriculus galgulus* **12cm**   **Common residen**

[Malay Lorikeet] [Malay: Serindit, from call] Common resident of primary and secondary forest throughout Borneo. A nomadic visitor to cultivated and montane areas. Feeds on soft fruits, nectar and oil palm near forested areas. Rests and sleeps hanging upside down like a bat. Nests in old barbet or woodpecker holes. **Call:** Flies swiftly and directly high up uttering a distinctive shrill very rapid rattle. Birds are very sociable, so that birds flying overhead can be called down by captive birds and get stuck to latex prepared by the trapper. In the wild often seen in pairs but in captivity adult males are rare. **Range:** Malay P, Borneo, Sumatra.

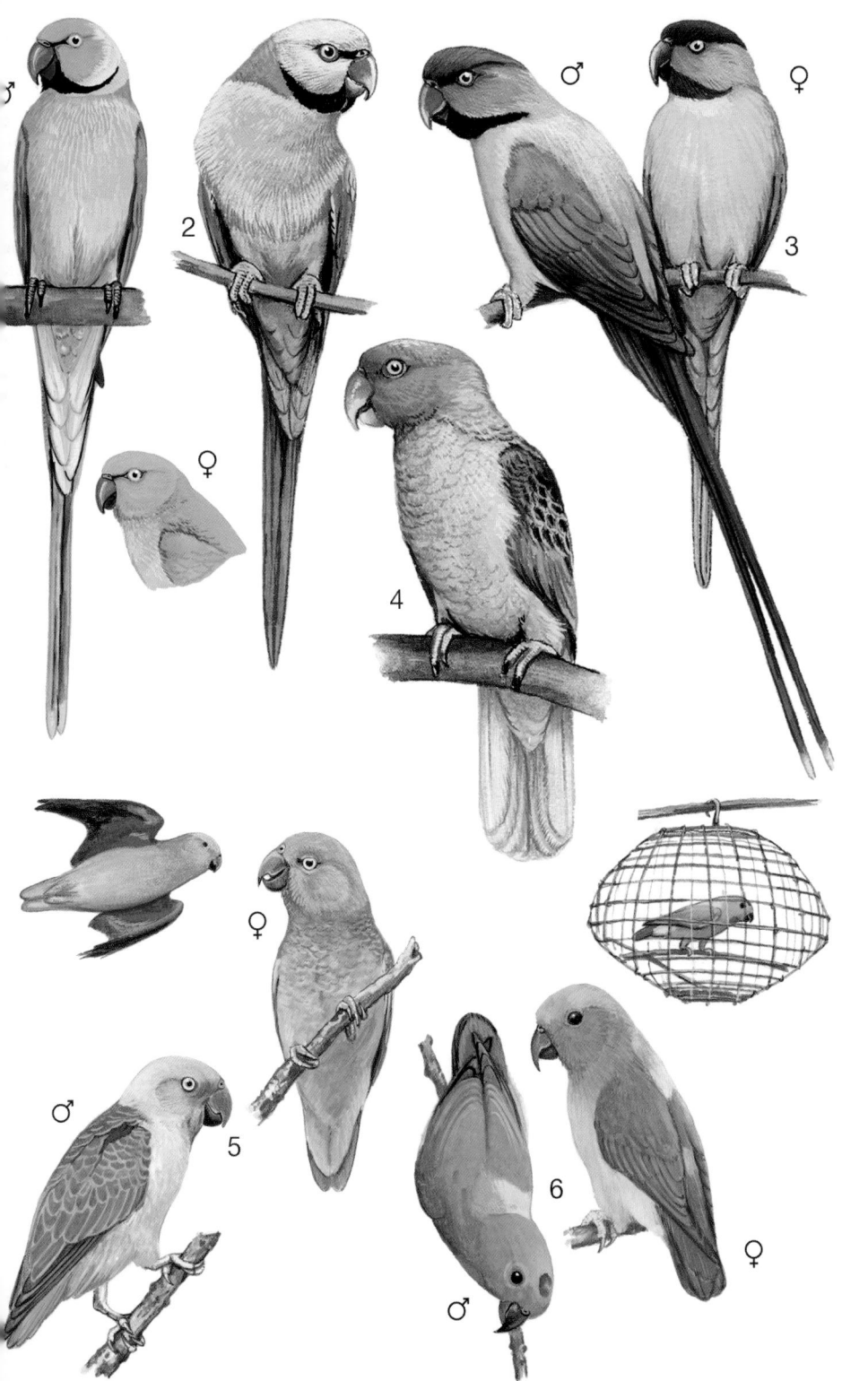

HAWK-CUCKOOS

HIEROCOCCYX CUCKOOS **East Asia 8 species; Borneo 6 species including 3 residents and 3 migrants.** Hawk-cuckoos are so named because they closely resemble sparrowhawks in appearance but the flight is shallower with the wings not raised above the horizontal. In behaviour they are typical cuckoos placing their eggs in the nests of host birds to hatch and rear. The males of the three resident species have distinctive loud, manic double calls which echo through the forest, often at night. The three winter visitors call rarely in Borneo and are considered scarce. Hawk-cuckoos are commonest in the mountains due to a preferred diet of hairy caterpillars (moth larvae) which are abundant in mountain forests. Hawk-cuckoos are the only cuckoos with a very distinctive very common streaky sub-adult plumage, in which they may breed. Apart from Large and Dark Hawk-cuckoos all Bornean species may have a pale patch of feathers on the wing as well as a pale or white bar on the nape. The young are streaked on the front, not barred like young *Cuculus* cuckoos.

1 LARGE HAWK-CUCKOO *Hierococcyx sparverioides* 40cm — Vagrant

Five records only from NW Borneo including Mesilau (Hutchinson) and Brunei (Moore). **Call:** *pi-peeah pi peeah pi-peeah* (brain fe-ver) up to six times increasing in pitch and intensity before starting again at the beginning. **Range:** Breeds from the Himalayas to Taiwan migrating south to Philippines, Borneo, Sulawesi and Java.

2 WHISTLING HAWK-CUCKOO *Hierococcyx nisicolor* 29cm — Scarce migrant

A scarce winter visitor which prefers montane forest. Both adult and immature have rufous on the belly unlike Javan Hawk-Cuckoo. Immatures of both are heavily streaked and easily confused. **Call:** A shrill thin piping whistle *gee-whiz gee-whiz gee-whiz* each note rising in pitch, the first note lower in pitch then the second, the phrase repeated about 20 times sharp and crisp (Payne). **Range:** Breeds Himalayas to S China migrating south in winter.

3 DARK HAWK-CUCKOO *Hierococcyx bocki* 31cm — Local resident

A scarce but locally common (e.g. KNP HQ) resident of hill and montane forests. **Breeding:** In Borneo host unknown. In Malay P, Chestnut-capped Laughing-thrush and spiderhunters (Davison). **Call:** A two note whistle variously described as *pee-ha pee-ha* (Wells) or *pi-phu pi-phu* (Robson). **Range:** Mountains of Malay P, Sumatra, Borneo. **Taxonomy:** Previously considered a race of Large Hawk-cuckoo.

4 MOUSTACHED HAWK-CUCKOO *Hierococcyx vagans* 26cm — Common resident

Locally common resident in lowland and hills, inhabiting the forest understorey. **Call:** A two syllable phrase *chu-chu chu-chu chu-chu* repeated every two seconds. Also a mellow whistle *peu peu peu* the first notes given singly, then in hurried couplets ascending in scale in a crescendo, then a sudden stop *hee hee hee hi-hi hi-hi, hi-hi HI-HI* (Payne). Breeding: In Borneo one host is the Rufous-winged Philentoma. In S Thailand, Abbott's Babbler. **Range:** Thailand, Malay P, Sumatra, Borneo, Java.

5 RUFOUS HAWK-CUCKOO *Hierococcyx hyperythrus* 29cm — Scarce migrant

[Northern Hawk-cuckoo] [Horsfield's Hawk-cuckoo] A scarce winter visitor to N and E Borneo. Recent records from P. Maratna E. Kalimantan. **Call:** Two part buzzy whistle *ju-ichi ju-ichi* similar to the double call of Whistling Hawk-cuckoo but harsher and longer (Payne). **Range:** Breeds Japan to NE China migrating in winter to Borneo, Philippines and Sulawesi. In Japan Rufous Hawk-cuckoo young has yellow patch on inner wing elbow to trick foster parents into giving more food. See illustration. **Taxonomy:** Previously considered a migrant race of Javan Hawk-cuckoo.

6 JAVAN HAWK-CUCKOO *Hierococcyx fugax* 29cm — Local resident

[Davison: Hodgson's Hawk-cuckoo] [Malaysian Hawk-cuckoo] Inhabits forest throughout Borneo. Lacks rufous underparts in all plumages. **Breeding:** Hosts recorded as Grey-headed Flycatcher, Black-throated Babbler. **Call:** A series of shrill, slurred doublets or triplets *pi-kwik pi-kwik pi-kwik* each note rising in pitch. Another call is a long rapid sequence of shrill buzzy whistles *pee pee pee* that rise up the scale in crescendo, then drop at the end *trrrrtitititititirrrrrrrrrr* (Payne). **Range:** Malay P, Sumatra, Borneo. **Taxonomy:** Previously considered the resident race of Rufous Hawk-cuckoo.

imm

adult

2

adult

imm

3

ult

imm

5

4

adult

adult

imm

6

imm

Note extra
false mouth
on wing of
baby Rufous
Hawk-cuckoo

CUCULUS CUCKOOS

Africa and Asia 11 species; Borneo 5 species. The well-known Common Cuckoo of Europe, is a vagrant to Borneo. Four similar *Cuculus* cuckoos also occur, both as residents and migrants. Young *Cuculus* cuckoos are heavily barred not streaked like young Hawk-cuckoos. Cuckoo young are usually much larger than the host bird. The large, barred baby cuckoos seen in the forest at KNP HQ are the progeny of the Sunda Lesser Cuckoo. These cuckoos lay their eggs in the nest of a 'host' species that rears the chick until it fledges. Cuckoo groups (gens) specialise in specific hosts and their eggs resemble the eggs of the host species. Common Cuckoo females lay 8–25 eggs each year, swallowing a host egg before depositing her own. The young cuckoo later ejects any eggs or fledglings from the host nest to die below. *Cuculus* cuckoos are best distinguished by the different male calls. Female *Cuculus* cuckoos have a distinctive bubbling call: *kwik kwik kwik kwik*. Females resemble males but with buffy tinge to upper breast. Females commonly occur in a brown barred 'hepatic' morph.

1 COMMON CUCKOO *Cuculus canorus* 32cm   Vagrant

One possible record from Labuan and another from Kinabalu (Mann). In flight shape resembles pointed-winged hawks, e.g. Kestrel, Peregrine, but unlike them when flying keeps wings below body level. When perched often sits with dropped wings. Has grey back, narrow belly bars and no dark band on tail. **Call:** Male: *cuck-oo cuck-oo*. Female: Bubble call. Hepatic female is not barred on rump. **Range:** Breeds Europe to Japan. Migrates from N Asia SW to Africa.

2 INDIAN CUCKOO *Cuculus micropterus* 32cm   Resident and winter visitor

Common resident in and scarce migrant to lowland and hill forests. Male and female similar, no hepatic phase. Unlike other *Cuculus* has a brownish not grey back and a dark band near end of tail. Commonest near rivers. **Call:** Male: Four whistled notes, *hoo hoo hoo uhoo* the first three the same pitch, the last lower or alternating high and low pitch. In Sabah calls Oct.–April (Sheldon). Female has bubble call. **Range:** Resident SE Asia. A northern race breeds China and winters south to Australia, passing through Borneo on passage.

3 HIMALAYAN CUCKOO *Cuculus saturatus* 32cm   Scarce winter visitor

Locally common winter visitor and passage migrant to lowland and submontane forest throughout Borneo. Very similar to Oriental. Distinguished by call. **Call:** Male, usally four notes, sometimes three: *hop hoo hoo hoop*   *hop hoo hoo hoop* or *hop hoo hoop*   *hop hoo hoop* and so on. **Range:** Breeds Himalayas to S China wintering south to Philippines, Malay P, Sumatra, Borneo, Java to New Guinea and Australia where it is a scarce winter visitor to Cape York and the N Territory.

4 ORIENTAL CUCKOO *Cuculus optatus* 32cm   Scarce winter visitor

Locally common winter visitor and passage migrant to lowland forest throughout Borneo. Has broader belly bars than Common Cuckoo and grey back and no black bar near end of tail like Indian Cuckoo. Female hepatic is heavily barred on rump. Cannot be distinguished from Himalayan by sight but skins have longer wings. **Call:** Male: A series of double notes *hoop hoop*   *hoop hoop* etc. Female has bubble call. **Range:** Breeds N Palearctic wintering S to SE Asia, Borneo, Australia. **Taxonomy:** Erritzoe et al (2012) consider *C. optatus* to be the northern race of *C. saturatus*.

5 SUNDA CUCKOO *Cuculus lepidus* 29cm   Montane resident

[Oriental Cuckoo] [Sunda Lesser Cuckoo] Common resident of mountain forest in Borneo south to N Kalimantan. Possibly also Muratus Mts (Davison). **Breeding:** On Kinabalu the hosts are Mountain Leaf Warbler and Yellow-breasted Warbler. April, May, August records. **Call:** Male: A series of triple notes with a slight pause after the first note, e.g. *hop hoo hoop*   *hop hoo hoop* etc. Commonly heard at KNP HQ Feb.–March. Calls have been described as very similar to both Hoopoe and Golden-naped Barbet. The call is higher-pitched than Himalayan Cuckoo. Female has bubbling call. **Range:** Malay P, Sumatra, Borneo.

6 ASIAN LESSER CUCKOO *Cuculus poliocephalus* 25cm   Not recorded

[Little Cuckoo] No confirmed records for Borneo, however, it is a likely vagrant. The smallest *Cuculus* cuckoo. Underparts less heavily barred than other *Cuculus*. **Call:** Male has six note whistle *tep-pen-kaketaka* rising on the first four notes and falling on the last two (Brazil 2009). Female has bubble call. **Range:** Breeds S Japan, Korea, China, winters south west to India and Africa.

1 ♀

♂

2

♀

♂

4 ♀

♂

adult

imm

6

Mountain
Leaf-warbler

juv

GLOSSY AND BRONZE CUCKOOS

CHRYSOCOCCYX CUCKOOS **Africa to Australia 14 species; Borneo 4 species and 1 possible migrant.** Small, heavily marked, secretive little cuckoos with shimmering gold, green, bronze and violet plumage. In Borneo these cuckoos are a mixture of resident, migrants from the north and migrants from the south, causing much confusion amongst birders. Australia is a stronghold with five resident species which live in semi-arid areas subject to variable rainfall causing irruptive movements if food is short after a good breeding season. Young birds may then expand their range north to the Indonesian islands in the austral winter April to September. At least one and possibly all the Australian species reach Borneo. These small cuckoos creep about in dense shrubbery looking for insects, then fly fast through forest gaps to next shrub. Found in primary, secondary, and scrub forests and plantations. Some fruit in diet. Calls are not as loud or as distinctive as other cuckoos. Typical brood parasites, laying their eggs in the nest of host birds.

1 ASIAN EMERALD CUCKOO *Chrysococcyx maculatus* 17cm **Not recorded**
Not yet recorded for Borneo but is a likely vagrant from continental Asia as this migrant species occurs in neighbouring countries. **Call:** A loud whistle of three notes *kee-kee-kee* (Payne). **Range:** Breeds N India, to S China migrating S in winter to Thailand, Malay P, Sumatra.

2 VIOLET CUCKOO *Chrysococcyx xanthorhynchus* 16cm **Common resident**
 Inhabits lowland and hill forest and forest edge, mangroves, plantations and secondary forest. Records of night-flying migrants indicate either local nomadic movements or migrants from Asia. Male has bright red eye ring. Juvenile has rufous head and back, otherwise similar to female. Typically flies fast and straight above canopy. **Breeding:** Host in Borneo Brown-throated Sunbird (Sepilok). In Asia Scarlet Sunbird, Little Spiderhunter and Yellow-bellied Prinia. **Call:** 'The flight is dipping, the dips synchronised with a rather shrill *kie-vik*, one of the characteristic sounds of the forest, although easily overlooked by someone not familiar with it' (Holmes). Also a shrill descending trill (Payne). **Range:** Malay P, Sumatra, Borneo.

3 HORSFIELD'S BRONZE CUCKOO *Chrysococcyx basalis* 17cm **Scarce austral migrant**
 Rare irruptive migrant from Australia, most likely to be found in coastal scrub. Sometimes in small parties, e.g. five at Jerudong June–July 1985 (Mann). Five at Pulau Layang[2] May 2002 (Moller). In Australia inhabits desert edge scrub. Note that the barring on underparts is not complete. The centre of the belly remains white unlike Little and Gould's. May occur in juvenile plumage in which underparts are less distinctly marked. **Call:** 'A series of whistles with a downward inflection' (Slater). **Range:** Rare austral migrant from Australia April to Sept.

4 LITTLE BRONZE CUCKOO *Chrysococcyx minutillus* 15cm **Rare resident**
 Widespread resident of dense lowland scrub and forest but very scarce. Sheldon reports three collected in E Sabah. Male has red eye ring and red iris. Female has green or grey eye ring and brown iris. White barred black below with no buffy tinge like the next species. **Breeding:** Birds collected in breeding condition in February and April (NE Borneo). Elsewhere hosts are Gerygones and Sunbirds. **Call:** A distinctive extended downward trill, four notes descending, *tew, tew, tew, teweew* (Slater). Six clear notes falling fast in a long trill (Simpson). **Range:** Malay P, Philippines, Borneo, Sulawesi, Lesser Sundas, New Guinea, Australia. In NE Australia this species is resident and does not migrate. Easily confused with the next species.

5 GOULD'S BRONZE CUCKOO *Chrysococcyx poecilurus* 15cm **Local resident**
 Inhabits coastal forests, swamp forests and mangroves in N and E Borneo. Sheldon reports 19 collected in Sabah. Reportedly very common in S and SE Kalimantan (Holmes). Very similar to Little Bronze Cuckoo in appearance but has a variable amount of buff on the side of the breast and buff edging to the underside of the outer tail feathers. **Call:** No difference reported to Little Bronze call. **Range:** In Australia this cuckoo is considered to be conspecific with Little Bronze Cuckoo as they breed when territories overlap (Payne 2005). However the Australian population are known migrants, heading north in the austral winter April to Oct. There is a strong possibility that some at least of the Borneo birds are austral migrants.

1

♂   ♀

2

♀

♂

2
juv.

♀
Scarlet
Sunbird

3

4

5

DRONGO AND BRUSH CUCKOOS

MALAY: BURUNG SEWAH (TENANT

The cuckoos described on this page are all typical cuckoos, laying their eggs in the nest of a host bird. Despit the fact that some of them are very common, the breeding habits are still little known. They are best located b their calls as these cuckoos are often heard but not often seen.

1 BANDED BAY CUCKOO *Cacomantis sonneratii* **22cm** Common resident

Commonly heard calling from secondary forest, but rarely seen. Juvenile is similar to adult Note grey eyering. **Breeding:** No records for Borneo. Elsewhere host is Common Iora Erpornis and Minivet. **Call:** A shrill rhythmic four note call *smoke-yer-pepper* distinguishe from four note call of Indian Cuckoo (page 158) by being quicker, more plaintive and les deliberately enunciated (Holmes). Also in the breeding season, a rising call of four slow notes followed by three to six faster notes of two to three syllables, rising in pitch to a sudden stop (McKinnon). **Range:** India to Malay P, Sumatra, Borneo, Java.

2 PLAINTIVE CUCKOO *Cacomantis merulinus* **21cm** Common resident

Most commonly heard cuckoo especially in coastal and secondary forest, and gardens. Also in primary and logged forest. Juvenile is very similar to adult Banded Bay Cuckoo but does not have a white eyebrow and underparts are more buffy as illustrated. Note black eyering **Breeding:** Host is Common Iora, Streaky-breasted Spiderhunter, Yellow-bellied Prinia Tailorbirds. **Call:** Mournful whistle *tay-ta-tee, tay ta tee*, increasing in speed and rising in pitch. Sometimes heard at night. A second call is a descending series *pwee, pwee, pee-pee pee-pee*, similar to Scarlet-rumped Trogon but louder and more persistent (Sheldon). **Range:** Malay P, Sumatra, Borneo.

3 BRUSH CUCKOO *Cacomantis variolosus* **23cm** Scarce resident

[Davison: Rusty-breasted Cuckoo *Cacomantis sepulcralis*] Scarce resident of lowland forest and forest edge,. Note yellow eyering. Female has hepatic phase. **Breeding:** Host in Borneo Chestnut-naped Forktail, elsewhere usually Flycatchers. **Call:** 'The diagnostic song is a long series of at least 10 plaintive high whistles, *heet, heet, heet* at a constant speed falling slightly in pitch. Also a *tay-ta-wi* call repeated about four times up the scale almost identical to one of the songs of the Plaintive Cuckoo' (Holmes). **Range:** Malay P, Sumatra, Borneo, Java, Philippines, Sulawesi, Australia.

4 FORK-TAILED DRONGO-CUCKOO *Surniculus dicruroides* **24cm** Vagrant

Common on the Asian Continent and in Palawan. A rare vagrant to Borneo with only three records, one from Natunas. Previously considered conspecific with Square-tailed Drongo-cuckoo but raised by Payne (2005) to a full species. Very similar in appearance but differs in shape of tail. **Call:** A series of piping whistles rising up the scale the second note lower than the first (Payne). **Range:** Breeds India, S China, wintering to Thailand, Malay P, Sumatra, Java.

5 SQUARE-TAILED DRONGO-CUCKOO *Surniculus lugubris* **24cm** Common resident

The most commonly heard cuckoo in primary forest throughout Borneo. Mimics appearance of drongos but differs in having white 'socks', white markings on underside of tail and small beak without hooked end. Some have white nape patch. **Breeding:** Sings Dec. to March in Sabah (Sheldon). Host in Asia, babblers. In Borneo Chestnut-winged Babbler. **Call:** 'Loud clear mellow whistles rising evenly up the scale one two three four five six as if one were practising a musical scale in the wilds of the jungle' (Payne). **Range:** Malay P, Sumatra.

WHY SOME CUCKOOS MIMIC BIRDS OF PREY Both the hawk-cuckoos and the *Cuculus* cuckoos bear a remarkable similarity to sparrowhawks, in flight and appearance. In addition the white nape patch on many hawk-cuckoos matches the white nape feathers seen when a sparowhawk bends its head to tear at its prey and the hepatic phase of female cuckoos appears to mimic kestrel plumage. The likely reason for female mimicry is to frighten away host birds whilst the female cuckoo exchanges its own egg with that of the host, so that this parasitic behaviour is not observed. The likely reason for male mimicry is that male cuckoos call loudly from prominent perches for long periods. Sparrowhawks could easily home in on these calls but would be reluctant to attack another hawk for fear of injury. See also page 142.

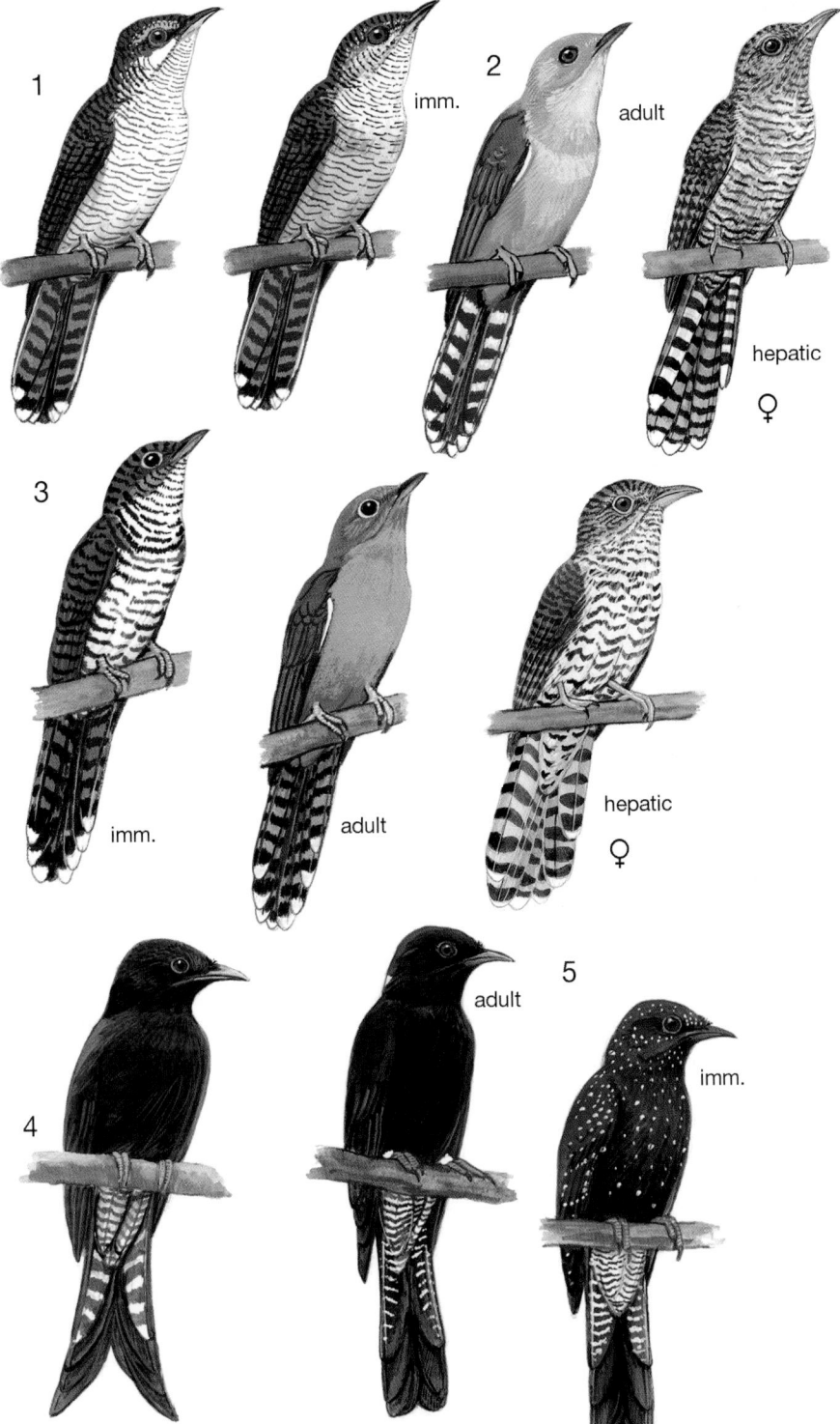

1

imm.

2

adult

hepatic ♀

3

imm.

adult

hepatic ♀

4

adult

5

imm.

COUCALS, KOEL AND CHESTNUT-WINGED CUCKOO

CUCULIDAE Coucals [Malay: Bubut] are nest building cuckoos, which construct untidy round football siz
nests low down in dense vegetation. Two species are very common birds of scrub and open countryside. Th
third (Short-toed Coucal) favours primary forest. Coucals are primarily insect and small animal eaters huntin
low down and on the ground. They also eat fruit and are very fond of snails. Males and females are alik
Coucals are often seen after rain drying their open wings at the top of a bush. Coucals are usually seen singl
and are probably strictly territorial. They have very deep far-carrying calls, one of the commonest bird sound
in secondary forest and farms. Some Bornean locals attribute magical health giving properties to young coucal
and their nests, which are used in local ubat (medicines) by being pickled in brandy, which is then drunk c
used as a rub on arthritic joints.

1 SHORT-TOED COUCAL *Centropus rectunguis* 30cm **Scarce residen**

A little known inhabitant of the understorey of lowland primary forest, particularly riverin
scrub. Often confused with Lesser Coucal but less streaky and has different call. Rare i
Kalimantan. **Call:** Like Greater Coucal but slower, more hoarse and resonant (Fogden). *
series of faster ascending ***boop*** notes heard at dusk (Wells re Malaya). **Sabah:** Danum, Sepilok
Brunei: Kota Batu, Bangar, Seria, Kuala Belait. **Sarawak:** Mulu, Niah, Similajau, Semengoh
Kalimantan: Kutai, Gng Palung. **Range:** Malay P, Sumatra, Borneo. **BLI:** Vulnerable.

2 GREATER COUCAL *Centropus sinensis* 53cm **Common residen**

Common in secondary and degraded forest, mangroves and cultivated areas throughout Borneo
Feeds on insects, small animals. Agricultural areas of Borneo were attacked by a plague o
introduced Giant African Snails *Achatina fulica* in the 1950s but they almost vanished after the
Greater Coucal started eating them. **Call:** A series of far-carrying low notes descending in pitch
booh booh booh booh booh booh booh booh. May also have a second call similar to the ***kok
ok kok ok*** call of the Lesser Coucal. **Range:** Malay P, Sumatra, Borneo.

3 BORNEAN GROUND-CUCKOO *Carpococcyx radiatus* 60cm **Rare endemic**

Included here for size reference. See page 168.

4 LESSER COUCAL *Centropus bengalensis* 33cm **Common resident**

The commonest coucal. Seen in swamps, grasslands, scrub and the forest edge from off
shore islands up to the mountains, throughout Borneo. Moults into a streaky eclipse plumage
similar to immature when not breeding. See illustration. **Call:** Three or four ***booh*** notes
similar to Greater Coucal but faster. Also a second call, a sharp distinctive ***kok ok kok ok, kok
ok kok ok***. These calls may be dueted. **Range:** Malay P, Sumatra, Borneo.

5 CHESTNUT-WINGED CUCKOO *Clamator coromandus* 45cm **Scarce winter visitor**

Scarce but widespread in most habitats in winter months Oct.–March but most often seen in
NW Borneo. One record for Kalimantan (Mann). Hunts for insects like a malkoha. Raises crest
when alarmed. **Call:** Harsh chatter ***chee-ke-kek*** similar to Brown Shrike (Batchelor). Distinct
monotone whistle ***bee bee*** given every few seconds (Kennedy *et al.*). **Range:** Breeds Himalayas
to S China wintering in India, Thailand, Malay P, Sumatra, Borneo, Java and Philippines.

6 ASIAN KOEL *Eudynamys scolopacea* 42cm **Common winter visitor**

A large, fruit-eating, parasitic cuckoo. Common in winter months (Oct.–April) on small islands
and in the coastal forests of NW Borneo. Joins imperial and green pigeons in fruiting fig trees.
When a bird is present the call can be heard frequently throughout the day. **Breeding:** No
breeding records yet for Borneo but Koels are increasingly common year round in the vicinity of
towns such as Kuching and Kota Kinabalu where introduced mynas are common. **Call:** Male:
A three part rising whistle ***ka-wao*** repeated 8–10 times at a louder and higher pitch. Female:
A rising gobble (Harrisson). **Range:** Breeds Asian mainland including Singapore where the
population is expanding and the host is the House Crow. Resident in Philippines where mynas
are the host. According to Whitehead (1893) young koels in Palawan are glossy black like their
fathers to deceive their black myna hosts.

imm

imm

adult

adult
breeding

4

2

non-br

5

♀ 6

♂

MALKOHAS

CUCULIDAE **World 14 species; Borneo 5 species.** Malkohas are common birds of the forest and th forest edge. Although they enter tree plantations and orchards to hunt for insects, malkohas are birds c lowland forests and do not survive in cultivated areas. Malkohas are not common in the hills and only ver rarely wander to the mountains. Unlike most Bornean bird families which have montane representatives ther are no montane malkohas. Malkohas are nest building cuckoos which build stick nests in trees. They fee primarily on insects and small animals but also take some fruit. In four out of five Borneo Malkohas the sexe are alike. Malkoha plumages are dull browns, greens and greys but they have brightly coloured patches c bare skin around the eyes (orbital) and colourful red or green beaks. All the Bornean malkohas apart fro Chestnut-breasted have distinctive white spots at the end of the tail feathers. Their loose plumage wets easil and malkohas can be seen drying their open wings after rain. Malkohas utter a large variety of soft not ver distinctive calls, often described as similar to the calls of frogs or squirrels. Only the most memorable are give here. Malkohas hunt like squirrels or tree shrews for insects in family parties through the canopy and lowe storey of forest trees before gliding a short distance to the next tree on broad wings with long white tipped tail Malkohas often join mixed species hunting parties, although not usually as core members.

1 BLACK-BELLIED MALKOHA *Phaenicophaeus diardi* **34cm** Local resider

A small dark malkoha with bright red orbital skin. Note absence of brown on underparts Generally scarce but locally common in lowland and hill forest throughout Borneo. Usuall seen in family parties. **Sabah:** Poring, Danum, Kinabatangan, Sepilok, Tabin. **Brune** Widespread in the lowlands (Mann). **Sarawak:** Similajau, Semengoh. **Kalimantan:** Tg Puting Gng Palung. **Call:** A sharp *pwew-pwew* (Norman). **Range:** Malay P, Sumatra, Borneo.

2 CHESTNUT-BELLIED MALKOHA *Phaenicophaeus sumatranus* **40cm** Local resider

Locally common in lowland primary and secondary forest throughout Borneo. Onl occasionally found in the hills. Favours coastal, peatswamp, and mangroves more than othe malkohas, e.g. the only Bornean malkoha species which still survives in Singapore. **Sabah** Klias, Danum, Tg Aru. **Brunei:** BSB, Tasek Merimbun, Seria (Mann). **Sarawak:** Lambir Hills Similajau, Bako, Santubong. **Kalimantan:** Tg Puting, Barito Swamps, **Call:** A rapid *tok-tok tok-tok-tok-tok-tok*. **Range:** Malay P, Sumatra, Borneo.

3 RED-BILLED MALKOHA *Phaenicophaeus javanicus* **46cm** Scarce resider

The rarest of the malkohas in Borneo. Inhabits lowland and hill forest. More likely to be foun in submontane areas than other Malkohas. **Call:** A clear whistled *who-oo* repeated every 1 seconds (Sheldon). Also a variety of frog- and squirrel-like calls. **Sabah:** Poring, Danum Crocker Range, Sepilok. **Brunei:** Jerudong, Seria, Bukit Teraja, Kuala Belalong (Mann) **Sarawak:** Mulu, Kelabit Highlands, Lambir Hills, Similajau. **Kalimantan:** Kayan Mentarang Tg Puting, Gng Palung. **Range:** Malay P, Sumatra, Borneo, Java.

4 CHESTNUT-BREASTED MALKOHA *Phaenicophaeus curvirostris* **49cm** Commo

Along with Raffles's, one of the two commonest malkohas. Found in primary, secondar forest and orchards from the lowlands to the hills throughout Borneo. Often joins in mixe hunting parties. Male has chin rufous and iris light blue, female chin grey and iris yellov (Payne). The only malkoha with no white tips to tail feathers. Vowles reported *lutino* bird from Brunei in which the green plumage on the back was replaced by turquoise blue. **Call:** loud *wee-oo*, lower on the second note (Sheldon). Also a variety of chicken-like clucking call (Payne). **Range:** Malay P, Sumatra, Borneo, Java, Palawan.

5 RAFFLES'S MALKOHA *Phaenicophaeus chlorophaeus* **30cm** Common resider

The smallest and one of the commonest malkohas of primary and secondary lowland forest Usually seen in active family parties, gleaning for caterpillars in the dense vegetation of th forest edge. The only malkoha with both blue beak and blue orbital skin. The only malkoh in which sexes differ greatly in plumage. Male has brown/rufous head, female has a grey head. The area of grey on breast and throat of females varies, possibly related to age (Payne) Common in swamp forest including Tg Puting. **Call:** A plaintive series of descending whistle *whiow, whiow, whiow, whiow*. **Range:** Malay P, Sumatra, Borneo.

GROUND-CUCKOO

CUCULIDAE   **World 3 species. Borneo 1 endemic.**   Only three species of ground-cuckoos exist. The Coral billed Ground-cuckoo is a scarce resident of Thailand, Cambodia, Laos and Vietnam. The Sumatran Ground cuckoo is extremely rare and was recently rediscovered after being trapped in a pheasant snare in the Barisan Mountains. In Borneo the Ground-cuckoo is thinly scattered throughout lowland forest, only absent from densely populated SE Kalimantan. It is both very shy and either very scarce or rare apart from a few protected areas of untouched forest where it is heard regularly and seen occasionally.

BORNEAN GROUND-CUCKOO   *Carpococcyx radiatus*   **60cm**   **Rare endemic**

Early European explorers of Borneo became familiar with the Ground-cuckoo as they surveyed virgin primary forest. Short of food and living off the land, their local assistants would build fences set with pheasant snares each time they moved camp. See illustration page 42. Often a Ground-cuckoo was an unwelcome catch. Unwelcome, because the bird has an unpleasant smell and is considered inedible, probably due to a diet of nasty-smelling millipedes and noxious beetles.

Habits: As with Bulwer's Pheasant, Ground-cuckoos are known to follow Bearded Pigs and Sun Bears as they forage in the forest and expose grubs and worms which the waiting birds then snatch. They appear to be fairly resilient birds because there is a record of a female that survived the long boat trip to Europe in the 1880s and lived happily at London Zoo for 18 years, regularly laying eggs. In Borneo the nest has never been found.

Habitat: Research carried out by Fredriksson and Nijman at Sungei Wain near Balikpapan found that Ground cuckoos showed a clear preference for alluvial and swamp forest over high flat, slope and ridge forest. Other reports confirm that the preferred habitat appears to be undisturbed lowland riverine forests.

Description: Birds have been recorded with both bright green and bright blue facial skin. The significance of the colour difference is unknown. The original type specimen of the Ground-cuckoo was described as having bright red facial skin but this has never been seen in live birds. The immature has a rufous-brown wash to the chest fading into white on the belly.

Similarity to Pheasants: A number of observers, including Wallace, have commented on the similarity in appearance, gait and habits of the Ground-cuckoo to the local pheasants. Three Bornean pheasants have bright blue facial skin, Bulwer's, Great Argus and the Crested Fireback. Great Argus is reputed to have inedible flesh so this is probably a case of both Mullerian mimicry (Argus + G. Cuckoo) combined with Batesian mimicry (Bulwer's + Fireback) a relationship known as a 'mimicry ring'. See page 84.

Call: A deep far-carrying repeated double call *whoo hooh whoo hooh whoo hooh*. Also has a single hoarse note repeated every 1.5 seconds by the male. The female responding with a soft clucking (Hill). A harsh alarm call has also been recorded. Ground-cuckoos respond well to tape playback which indicates that they are strictly territorial.

Sabah: At Danum heard and seen regularly. A resident pair in the forest at the Mennagol river, Kinabatangan frequently respond to tape playback. Recorded in hilly forest at Maliau Basin.

Brunei: Two old records from Sungai Tutong. Not recorded from Batu Apoi forest reserve (Ulu Temburong) despite intensive research in recent years. Two recent records from Ulu Belait and Sungai Semaba.

Sarawak: Recent records for Mulu, Similajau and Samunsam but nowhere easy to see.

Kalimantan: Sight records by researchers in Kalimantan indicate how difficult it is to see a Ground-cuckoo. At Gng Palung sightings were six in seven field years (Laman). At Sg Wain sightings numbered 32 in seven field years (Fredriksson and Nijman). **BLI:** Near threatened.

MUTUALISTIC ASSOCIATIONS BETWEEN BIRDS AND MAMMALS IN BORNEO

Mutualism is an association of two entirely different species that co-operate together for their mutual benefit. In Borneo it is extremely common between birds and plants e.g. pollination and seed dispersal and much less common between mammals and birds. In his book *Field Book of a Jungle Wallah* (1929), Hose describes how drongos associate with troops of macaque monkeys. Elsewhere in this Field Guide mutualistic associations are described for Gibbons and Black Hornbills, Tree Shrews and Grey-bellied Bulbuls, Bulwer's Pheasant and Bearded Pigs, Roulroul and Bearded Pigs, Cattle Egrets and buffaloes, Black Drongos and cattle, and above for Ground-cuckoos and Bearded Pigs or Sun Bears. It is suspected to occur between Sun Bears and Honeyguides but has yet to be recorded. It is likely that the birds' warning calls help alert the mammals of impending danger. In Europe the well-known Robin also closely associates with foraging wild boar, a habit with has been transferred to a close association between Robins and people working on their gardens.

Pheasants, partridges and ground-cuckoos have often been recorded following bearded pigs and sun bears as they forage the forest floor breaking open rotten wood to look for grubs and turning over soil and leaf litter in search of worms, snails and millipedes. Both parties benefit as the birds act as security guards for the mammals, providing additional eyes and ears alert to potential danger.

OWLS

STRIGIDAE **World 161 species; Borneo 15 species.** The Malay name for owl translates as Ghost Bird. A belief in ghosts is common in the culture of many Borneans. Perhaps because of this association many locals are genuinely frightened of owls. Owls are nocturnal birds of prey feeding on large insects, birds, rats, flying squirrels, bats and especially rats. Borneo hosts 24 different species of rats and mice and they form a signficant proportion of the diet of the larger owls. Owls nest in tree holes, which holes are often used as daytime roosts, the same roost being used every day. Sometimes a concealed perch is used for roosting. Owls regurgitate the bones and feathers of their prey in pellets which accumulate below their roosts. These pellets can be dissected to discover the owl's diet. If you hear persistent alarm calls from birds surrounding a hidden object in a tree, it is nearly always a snake or an owl being 'mobbed' by the local birds. Males and female owls are similar but females are usually larger. Owls use their excellent hearing to hunt for prey in the dark. Many owls have ear tufts which are erected when they are excited. The actual ear hole is hidden behind the feathers of the facial disc. Owls defend their territories with distinctive mournful hoots made by both male and female often in duet. The female call is usually similar to, but recognisably different from the male. Owls respond well to tape playback and a digital recorder is essential if you are interested in surveying the local owl population.

1 BARRED EAGLE-OWL *Bubo sumatranus* 45cm   Scarce resident

The least common of the three large Borneo owls. A scarce resident in lowland forest. Has been recorded from the Kelabit Highlands and at 1,600m on Gng Menyapa E. Kalimantan (Brickle et al.) but the Brown Wood Owl is usually more common in the hills. Has been recorded (rarely) breeding in trees in the centre of towns, e.g. Kuching and BSB (Brunei). Feeds on birds, snakes and particularly rats. Like the other large owls, found around the mouths of swiftlet and bat inhabited caves, such as Gomantong, Mulu and Niah. **Call:** Very varied. Commonest call is a pair of distinctly spaced notes *huh huh* repeated (Wells re Malaya). A low pitched *who-who* (Sheldon). **Range:** Malay P, Sumatra, Borneo, Java.

2 BUFFY FISH OWL *Ketupa ketupu* 45cm   Common resident

By far the most common of the three large owls. Found on islands, e.g. P Gaya, P Tiga (Sabah), in coastal forest, along rivers in primary forest (Danum) and around rice fields in the hills (Kelabit Highlands). Normally found near water including coastal Casuarina forest, swamps, padi fields, streams and rivers. Usually feeds on fish and frogs but has also been recorded feeding on insects and rats. Like Wood Owl also often seen near bat caves where it feeds on bats and swiftlets. Has been recorded feeding on insects attracted by lighted buildings at night (Mann). **Call:** A wide variety of wails, drumming notes and ringing calls have been described by different observers. **Range:** India, to Malay P, Sumatra, Borneo, Java.

3 BROWN WOOD OWL *Strix leptogrammica* 47cm   Local resident

The second commonest of the three large owls. Locally common but often scarce or absent. Found in all types of forest from the coast to the mountains. Especially common at the edge of oil palm and primary forest, e.g. Tabin, Sepilok. The owls live in the forest but feed on rats in the oil palms at night. One of the best places to find large owls is behind the kitchen of forest lodges. Rats feed on the waste food and owls feed on the rats. **Call:** A hoarse *whoh-whoh* with both notes on the same pitch (Sheldon). A rich tremulous *huhuhuhoo* (Wells re *Malaya)*. A single hoot followed by a vibrating note *who whowwwwooh*. Also a single loud *whooh*. Common at Danum, Panaga, Similajau, Tg Puting. Recorded from forest at KNP HQ **Range:** India to Malay P, Sumatra, Java.

LARGE OWLS ON KINABALU A number of observers have reported the presence of a large wood owl on Kinabalu in the montane forest between Park HQ and the Kamborangoh Power Station, including evidence of breeding. The call of this owl is a single loud *whooh*. In Java the montane race of the Brown Wood Owl was split by Konig/Becking 1999 and described as a new wood owl species Bartel's Wood Owl *Strix bartelsi* based on a distinctive call 'A single very powerful drawn out *whooh*'

There has been speculation that the wood owl on Kinabalu might be Bartel's Wood Owl, however it is now known that the Brown Wood Owl found in the Borneo lowlands also often calls with a single loud *whooh*. This evidence throws into doubt the original validity of Bartel's Wood Owl description as a separate species and identifies the Kinabalu owl as (almost certainly) a Brown Wood Owl.

1

2

3

Grey Tree Rat

Long-tailed
Giant Rat

RATS, OWLS AND FOREST DIVERSITY

Bornean forests are the most diverse in the world, with some 3,000 + tree species. This diversity is largely the result of two factors – competition between tree species to disperse their seeds, and strategies used by trees to avoid seed predation, which is most intense where seed supply is clumped.

Borneo hosts 27 species of rats and mice which both consume (predate) and disperse the seeds of forest trees by scatter hoarding and larder hoarding. Research has shown that different rat species have preferences for different tree seeds and therefore positively influence tree species diversity in Borneo. Owls which predate rats therefore may have the opposite effect.

See Phillipps (2014), *Phillipps' Field Guide to the Mammals of Borneo and their Ecology*.

BAY OWLS, BARN OWLS AND TYPICAL OWLS

1 ORIENTAL BAY OWL *Phodilus badius* **27cm**   **Scarce resident**

An uncommon inhabitant of lowland and hill primary forest throughout Borneo. Typically seen perching sideways on vertical saplings near the forest floor presumably in order to hunt forest rats. Recently recorded in overgrown oil palm next to the forest at Sepilok (Ong), and from montane forest at Kinabalu Park HQ (Andy Boyce). **Call:** A soft frogmouth-like ***hu-li***. Also a striking musical sequence of three notes in rising tremulous phrases starting successively lower down the scale (Wells re Malay P). **Range:** India to S China south to the Malay P, Sumatra, Borneo, Java and Philippines.

2 BARN OWL *Tyto alba* **38cm**   **Local resident**

[Eastern Barn Owl *Tyto javanica*] In Sabah and Sarawak captive birds from W Malaysia have been released on oil palm estates to control rat pests, but these introductions have not been successful (Siburat). Not seen away from oil palm estates. The name derives from its habit in Europe of nesting in barns and old buildings. Compared with Grass Owl, has paler back, and more heart-shaped facial disc. **Call:** A bone chilling scream. **Range:** Worldwide.

3 EASTERN GRASS OWL *Tyto longimembris* **38cm**   **Scarce but increasing resident**

Common resident of SE Asian grassland first recorded Borneo at Ranau, Sabah (1,000m) in 1999 (Biun). In 2003 found ground-nesting on an oil palm estate at Lahad Datu (Noor). Recent sight records from the Tempasuk Plain, Tuaran (A. Reyes), Papar (Wiles) and breeding West Kalimantan (van Balen). Facial disc has darker rim, and flatter top than Barn Owl. Male facial disc is white, female disc is pale speckled brown. In flight look for distinctively dark wing tips. **Call:** Hissing scream louder than Barn Owl (Pizzey). **Range:** India to SE Asia, Philippines to Sulawesi, to Australia.

4 NORTHERN BOOBOOK *Ninox scutulata japonica* **30cm**   **Scarce migrant race**

[Brown Hawk-Owl] The migrant race *N. s. japonica* is occasionally encountered along the NW coast on oil rigs and small islands during migration. Birds later move inland but only one record from Kalimantan. Similar habits to the resident race (see below). **Call:** Monotonous and hollow double note ***whoop whoop*** with an audible gap between the two notes but rarely calls in winter quarters (King). **Range:** Breeds China to Japan. Winters south to SE Asia.

5 BOOBOOK *Ninox scutulata borneensis* **25cm**   **Local resident race**

[Malay: Pungkok]. Widespread, local resident of forest edge habitat from lowlands to the hills. Feeds on large insects such as beetles and dragonflies. Distinguished from the larger migrant race (see above) by being 20% smaller and considerably darker. Note: Female owls including this species are usually 10–15% larger than males. **Call:** A hollow mellow double note ***whoo-wup*** with an accent on the second syllable and no gap between the two notes (King). **Range:** Resident India to SE Asia, Malay P, Sumatra, Borneo, Java. **Taxonomy:** See King (2002) re distinguishing the two races found in Borneo.

6 COLLARED OWLET *Glaucidium brodiei* **16cm**   **Scarce resident**

Locally common in montane forest, e.g. at KNP HQ, sometimes found in submontane areas south to N Kalimantan. The only Bornean owl which calls and is active in daytime. Feeds on birds, e.g. Ashy Drongo, Temminck's Babbler and large beetles. Has distinctive buff hind collar with two dark patches giving the appearance of eyes on the back of the head. **Call:** Monotonous ***poop te poop poop*** followed by a ***poop te poop*** repeated, concealed in the top of a tree (Sheldon). **Range:** Himalayas to S China, Taiwan, Vietnam, Thailand, Malay P, Sumatra, Borneo. **Taxonomy:** A potential future split to be known as *G. borneense* as the call is distinctly different from the continental race.

7 SHORT-EARED OWL *Asio flammeus* **37cm**   **Vagrant**

A rare winter vagrant from continental Asia. Two records for Borneo, Kuching and Bandar Seri Begawan Airfield where one was killed by a plane. Seven records from the Philippines. Elsewhere typically seen late during the day flying low over marshes and grassland like a short-winged harrier. A pale owl but heavily streaked above and below unlike plainer Grass and Barn owls. Look for dark patch on under wing near shoulder. **Call:** Usually silent. **Range:** Worldwide but not Wallacea, Australia.

Face   Back of head   6

SCOPS OWLS

1 ORIENTAL SCOPS OWL *Otus sunia* 18cm **Not recorded**

A scarce winter visitor to Malaya and Sumatra, and a possible vagrant to the coast of W Borneo. Migrants have been recorded from a boat between Vietnam and Borneo in the S China Sea (Ellis and Kepler). Distinguished from Collared Scops Owl by lack of a white hind collar, more prominent white V on back and by yellow not red eyes. Occurs in grey and rufous morphs, also some intermediates. **Call:** Repetitive loud tonk *tiok clock clock* – sounds like a nocturnal barbet (Viney). Does not call in winter quarters in the Malay Peninsula (Wells). **Range:** India to Japan. Some northern populations winter south to Malay P and Sumatra. In Malaya found in open country not primary forest.

2 MANTANANI SCOPS OWL *Otus mantananensis* 18cm **Local resident**

The only owl found on the Mantanani Islands where it is very common. A small island specialist, confined to a few islands off the coast of Palawan and in the Sulu Sea. It is suspected but not proven that these owls may time their breeding to coincide with the influx of small birds from Asia during peak migration periods as these islands are stepping stones on the most important flyway from the Philippines to Borneo. A rufous morph reported. **Call:** A simple *waa* followed by a descending series of short *waas*. The female has a lower harsher call than the male (Sheldon). **Range:** In Borneo only known from the Mantanani Islands (Sabah). Also Sulu Archipelago and islands off Palawan, e.g. Rasa island, Ursula Island.

3 MOUNTAIN SCOPS OWL *Otus spilocephalus* 18cm **Common montane resident**

A common resident of the higher mountains throughout Borneo, south to N Kalimantan. On Kinabalu common in the forest around KNP HQ. A mist netting survey found that these owls were common from Park HQ up to Paka Cave at 3,100m (Biun). **Call:** Distinctive double hoot *hoo hoo* and a soft whistle similar to the call of the Bornean Frogmouth (Biun). **Range:** Mountains of India to SE China, Taiwan, SE Asia, Malay P, Sumatra, Borneo, Java.

4 REDDISH SCOPS OWL *Otus rufescens* 19cm **Scarce resident**

An uncommon small owl of the interior of primary forest where it hunts in the understorey low down. Found throughout Borneo from the swamp forest of Tg Puting in Kalimantan to the hills of Sabah, but nowhere common. Only a rufous morph is known. **Call:** 'The distinctive call is a single, rather high- pitched, drawn out note *hew*, repeated at 7–10 second intervals' (Davison). **Range:** Malaya, Sumatra, Java, Borneo.

5 RAJAH SCOPS OWL *Otus brookii* 23cm **Rare resident**

An extremely rare montane scops owl that looks like a large Collared Scops Owl. Only four specimens for Borneo. Two records from KNP. One picked up dead on the Summit Trail at 1,900m (1986). A male bird found dead at 1,650m on 8 August 1998. Both specimens had disappeared from the Kinabalu Park HQ museum in Oct 2011. Despite intensive mist netting on Kinabalu at all levels which trapped 20 Mountain Scops Owl this bird was not found (Biun). The other two Bornean records are from the top of Mt Dulit (Sarawak) at 2,000m and Mulu 915m. It is likely that this is one of Borneo's scarce submontane specialists and should be looked for in forest lower down than the Mountain Scops Owl. Sumatran birds have orange yellow iris. Bornean birds not known. **Call:** 'A series of *whaooo* notes, followed by a string of single or double *whaoo* notes for up to a minute' (Holmes re Sumatra). A double hoot uttered rather explosively (Konig re Sumatra). **Range:** Mountains of Sumatra locally common. Borneo (three skins) and Java (one skin). **Taxonomy:** A likely future split to become a new Borneo endemic.

6 COLLARED SCOPS OWL *Otus bakkamoena* 20cm **Common resident**

[Sunda Scops Owl *Otus lempiji*] The commonest small Bornean owl. Found in cultivated areas and the forest edge from the coastal lowlands to the hills. Feeds mainly on large insects, e.g. beetles, cicadas, leaf hoppers but also eats small birds and mammals. Both sexes also occur in a rufous morph (Whitehead). **Call:** Soft *pwok* repeated intermittently in breeding season. **Range:** India to China, Korea, Taiwan, SE Asia, Malay P, Sumatra, Borneo, Java, Philippines.

1

Grey
Morph

Grey
Morph

ufous
Morph

Grey
Morph

2

3

4

5

6

Brown
Morph

FROGMOUTHS

PODARGARIDAE   **World 14 species. Borneo 6 species including 2 endemics.**   Frogmouths are strictly nocturnal inhabitants of forest and forest edge. Their wide beaks allow frogmouths to swallow large prey such as big insects, and small lizards whole. All frogmouths have extensive bristles and feathers around their beaks, extending back over their ears. They hunt by sitting and waiting for an insect to move on the ground and flying to snatch it, but they may also sally after insects in flight. In Borneo frogmouths build tiny cup-shaped pad nests on a thin branch often low down and often near a clearing in which one white egg is laid, It is believed that only the male incubates during the day and only the female at night. On the nest, the male enters a 'brooding trance' in which he makes no response to possible threats. The night brooding female does not enter a trance and fluffs up her feathers when alarmed (Kaplan re Australia). With some species, up to three colour morphs are found, dark brown, grey or rufous and these morphs may or may not be sex specific in different species. Calls are either whistles or hoarse *gwaa* notes which may be heard in duet and which may be sex specific.

1   LARGE FROGMOUTH   *Batrachostomus auritus*   **40 to 43cm**   **Rare resident**

Rare, but widespread in lowland primary forest throughout Borneo. In the Malay P, also occurs in disturbed forest (Wells). Distinguished by very large size. **Sabah:** Kinabalu, Danum, Tabin. **Brunei:** Ulu Temburong, Tasek Merimbun. **Sarawak:** Mulu, Similajau. **Kalimantan:** Kayan Mentarang, Kutai, Tg Puting, Gng Palung. **Call:** 'A powerful throbbing rattle' (A.B van den Berg in Wells re Malaya). **Range:** Malay P, Sumatra, Borneo.

2   DULIT FROGMOUTH   *Batrachostomus harterti*   **34 to 37cm**   **Endemic**

A rare submontane resident found on Mt Dulit and in the Kelabit Highlands in N Sarawak south to Mt Liang Kubung in NW Kalimantan. Skins have been collected from 305m to 1,220m in altitude. There are no confirmed records from Brunei or Sabah. Distinguished by large size and location. Usually darker and always smaller than Large Frogmouth which is a lowland bird in Sarawak. **Call:** Single clear whistle (King/Yong) (John Arifin).

3   SUNDAN FROGMOUTH   *Batrachostomus cornutus*   **23 to 28cm**   **Scarce resident**

[Sunda Frogmouth] The least rare frogmouth being found in secondary lowland forest throughout Borneo and also the Kelabit Highlands. Male is usually dark brown and female rufous but plumage is very variable and both sexes can appear grey, brown or rufous. Distinguished from Blyth's Frogmouth by slightly larger size, and a preference for disturbed secondary forest habitat. **Call:** 'A descending series of *gwaa* notes, all starting on the same pitch like the caw of a crow' (Marshall). **Range:** Sumatra, Java, Borneo.

4   GOULD'S FROGMOUTH   *Batrachostomus stellatus*   **21 to 25cm**   **Rare resident**

Rare but widespread in lowland and hill primary forest throughout Borneo. Sexes similar. Both sexes occur in a brown morph as well as the normal rufous morph. Distinguished from Sundan and Blyth's Frogmouths by plain breast with indistinct pale scallop pattern and no dark chest band or distinct heavy white spotting. **Call:** A four syllabel slurred whistle (Harrap). **Range:** Malay P, Sumatra, Borneo.

5   BORNEAN FROGMOUTH   *Batrachostomus mixtus*   **20 to 22cm**   **Endemic**

[Davison: Short-tailed Frogmouth *Batrachostomus poliolophus*] A rare endemic submontane and montane resident throughout the Bornean mountains. At KNP HQ a rufous bird on a nest was seen in daytime on 19 April at the far end of the Silau Silau trail at Kiau View Corner (Ebenhard). A year later mist netting at this site caught a Mountain Scops Owl but not the frogmouth. One recently netted on Trus Madi (1,450m) had eaten beetles (Sheldon). **Call:** A pure, whistled *pwau* repeated every two to three seconds (Myers).

6   JAVAN FROGMOUTH   *Batrachostomus javensis*   **19 to 25cm**   **Rare resident**

[Blyth's Frogmouth *B. affinis*] [Horsfield's Frogmouth *Batrachstomus javensis*] Thinly scattered inhabitant of primary forest thoughout Borneo. Male is usually dark brown and female rufous. Distinguished from Sundan by smaller size, and preference for undisturbed forest. A rufous bird on a nest photographed by Hitoshi Nakayasu at Poring during the day poses questions about male incubation and dimorphism within sexes. **Call:** 'A frenzied descending series *gwaa gwaa gwaa gwaa gwaa*' (Marshall). **Range:** SE Asia to Malay P, Sumatra, Java, Borneo, Palawan.

1

♀

2

♀

3

grey
morph

rufous
morph

4

♂

5

♀

♀

6

♂

NIGHTJARS

MALAY: BURUNG TUKANG (WORKMAN

CAPRIMULGIDAE **World 67 species; Borneo 5 species.** Early European planters spending hot still night in the lowlands of Borneo often blamed the endless *tok tok tok* calls of the Large-tailed Nightjars for their insomnia. In cultivated areas the *tok tok* call remains one of the characteristic sounds of the NW Bornean night. In SE Kalimantan the common nightjar is the Savanna Nightjar which has a sharp *chweep* call made by the bird in flight.

Nightjars are cryptically coloured night birds which roost and nest on the ground, and feed on insects, swooping on them in the air or hawking them from a prominent perch. The nest is usually a simple scrape amongst dead leaves with two camouflaged eggs. In other areas nightjars time their nesting so that chicks hatch during periods of full moon when it is easier for their parents to hunt for insect food.

Nesting birds will often feign a broken wing to distract a potential predator. The open country species often settle on roads at night where they are frequently killed by motor vehicles. Nightjars are best distinguished by their very different habitats and their distinctive calls. Males and females are similar, but the female's pale markings are much fainter, often with buff replacing the male white markings.

Nightjars have a light reflecting layer of cells or *tapidum lucidum* at the back of their eyes. This causes their eyes to reflect red or silver at night like many mammals, and provides extra vision in dim conditions.

1 MALAYSIAN EARED NIGHTJAR *Eurostopodus temminckii* **28cm** Local resident

[*Lycornis temminckii*] A bird of forest clearings and the forest edge found throughout Borneo and locally common. Much more of a forest bird than Large-tailed Nightjar and generally feeds higher up, often over the forest canopy. **Call:** A three note call described as *what to do* or *tok-tadow* heard at dawn and dusk (Sheldon). **Sabah:** Poring, Sepilok, Danum. **Brunei:** Ulu Temburong, Ulu Belait, Kuala Balai Rd. **Sarawak:** Kelabit Highlands, Bako, Similajau. **Kalimantan:** Kayan Mentarang, Kutai, Sg Wain, Tg Puting, Muratus Mts. **Range:** Malay P, Sumatra, Borneo.

2 BONAPARTE'S NIGHTJAR *Caprimulgus concretus* **20cm** Rare resident

[Sunda Nightjar] A rare, thinly scattered resident of lowland primary forest with a supposed preference for forested river banks. A small dark nightjar with a prominent white throat, no white on the wing but with white tips to the two outermost tail feathers. **Sabah:** Danum **Brunei:** Kuala Belalong. Recent records from peat swamp forest at Panaga and Belait by Hindricks and Bakewell. **Sarawak:** Common at Semengoh (Fogden). **Kalimantan:** Gng Niut, Kutai. Commonest nightjar at Sabangau but not recorded from similar habitat at nearby Tg Puting. **Call:** A most unexpected sound. A low mournful, double noted *waouuuu*, the second note descending in pitch, sings only once or twice per minute (Cleere). **Range:** Sumatra Borneo. **BLI:** Vulnerable.

3 GREY NIGHTJAR *Caprimulgus jotaka* **28cm** Scarce winter visitor

Scarce migrant from Japan and Eastern Siberia which spends the winter months in Borneo. On migration can turn up anywhere including small islands but prefers clearings in mountain forest. A typical location would be the Kamborangoh Road at KNP HQ where it appears at dusk to catch moths along the forest edge. **Call:** A rapidly repeated *tuck tuck tuck*, or *chunk chunk chunk*. **Range:** Breeds N Asia winters south to SE Asia.

4 SAVANNA NIGHTJAR *Caprimulgus affinis* **22cm** Local resident

The commonest nightjar in SE Kalimantan, often seen around the towns of Balikpapan and Banjarmasin. May also occur sporadically elsewhere. In Singapore has recently colonised open land reclaimed from the sea and is spreading north up the Malay P. (Davison). The smallest and palest nightjar, with a penchant for very flat open land. **Call:** A distinctive high-pitched *chweep* whilst in flight (Viney). **Range:** India, to SE Asia, Sumatra, Java, Borneo, Philippines.

5 LARGE-TAILED NIGHTJAR *Caprimulgus macrurus* **28cm** Common resident

Commonest nightjar in open grassy and cultivated areas throughout most of Borneo. In SE Kalimantan much less common than Savanna Nightjar. Also occurs in open grassy areas in hills and mountains where forest has been destroyed. **Call:** *tok tok tok* continuously, sometimes exceeding 100 *toks* or even more according to insomniacs. **Range:** India, to SW China, SE Asia, Malay P, Sumatra, Borneo to New Guinea and N Australia.

178

SWIFTS AND TREESWIFTS

SWIFTS   APODIDAE **World 99 species; Borneo 16 species.** Swifts are probably the world's mos
competent fliers, but, if by mischance they end up on the ground they cannot take off again and will soon
die. Swifts spend most of their lives on the wing, feeding on insects, and in some species both copulating and
sleeping. Despite a similar appearance they are unrelated to swallows, flying higher and faster often gliding
on sickle-shaped wings. In stormy weather they fly low in front of the storm. Swifts have small, weak, legs
which prevent them from normal perching. Instead they cling to vertical surfaces such as cliffs and tree trunks
Their calls are generally undistinctive squeaks or screeches. Originally most swifts built their nests in caves or
under cliff overhangs. These swifts often now prefer to build their nests on buildings or under bridges. Swift
greatly benefit humans, by feeding on and reducing the mosquito population. Many building owners in Bornee
recognise this, and welcome the swifts that colonise their property.

1   ASIAN PALM SWIFT   *Cypsiurus balasiensis*   10cm   Local residen

Locally common throughout Borneo. Associates with wide leaved palms, e.g. Pinang Palm
(*Areca*) and ornamental fan palms in towns and gardens. Only occasionally associates with
Coconut Palms. The nest is a small cup of fibres built on the underside of a palm leaf. A small
pale swift best identified from habitat. Very similar in appearance to Grey-rumped Treeswift
but only half the size and never perches upright on branches. **Call:** A very high-pitched *teu
tew tew tew* (Sheldon). **Range:** India to Malay P, Sumatra, Borneo, Java, Philippines.

2   PACIFIC SWIFT   *Apus pacificus*   19cm   Scarce passage migran

[Fork-tailed Swift] An uncommon passage migrant often in mixed flocks with other swifts and
swallows in all areas, throughout Borneo. Commonest in September or April on migration
through Borneo to or from Australia. Clean white rump is similar to House Swift but pale grey
throat is less obvious than white throat of House Swift, and tail is more forked. **Call:** Long
high-pitched *dzee dzee* (Pizzey). **Range:** Breeds N Asia, winters Australia.

3   HOUSE SWIFT   *Apus nipalensis*   14cm   Common residen

[Little Swift] Common inhabitant of open countryside throughout Borneo. Commonest in
towns where it breeds in conglomerations of nests clumped together in colonies under the
eaves of old shop houses, e.g. Gaya St., Kota Kinabalu. Shop keepers consider the nests good
luck. Also nests under bridges and below cliffs, e.g. on Berhala Island (Sandakan) and Telok
Asam at Bako NP and Satang Islands. Sheldon found up to three eggs in a nest but only
ever one fledgling. Young swifts are known to 'nest hop' to avoid nest parasites. Nests are
frequently occupied by Glossy Starlings. **Call:** A shrill rattle. **Range:** Africa to Asia. Malay P,
Sumatra, Borneo, Philippines, Sulawesi.

TREESWIFTS HEMIPROCNIDAE   **World 4 species; Borneo 2 species.**   Unlike true swifts, the treeswifts have
strong legs and can perch normally. Usually seen perched on a dead branch at the top of a tree from which they
glide forth on stiff wings to catch insects. Most active at dawn and dusk in small flocks circling together over a
clearing. Sexes differ. Build tiny cup-shaped nests on a bare branch high up in the open in which one white egg
is laid. The brooding bird often appears just to be sitting normally. The young bird is heavily barred.

4   GREY-RUMPED TREESWIFT   *Hemiprocne longipennis*   20cm   Common resident

Widespread and common in coastal, secondary and primary forest throughout Borneo. In
flight look for large size, long tail and slower more gliding flight compared with other swifts.
Perches very upright on a bare twig at the top of tall trees, e.g. on the tops of Casuarinas at Tg
Aru beach, Kota Kinabalu. **Call:** A series of high-pitched squeaks. **Range:** Myanmar, Thailand
to Malay P, Sumatra, Borneo, Java, Philippines, Sulawesi.

5   WHISKERED TREESWIFT   *Hemiprocne comata*   15cm   Local resident

A common inhabitant of open areas and clearings in forested areas throughout Borneo. Usually
seen perched on a bare branch at the forest edge. The distinctive white whiskers are very
noticeable. **Call:** 'Their squeaky calls can be heard along roadsides, even at mid-day when
most other species are quiet' (Sheldon). **Range:** Malay P, Sumatra, Borneo, Philippines.

1

2

3

4

imm

5

♂

♀

♂

♀

Colony of
House Swift
nests

NON-ECHO-LOCATING SWIFTLETS

Swiftlets are a subgroup of the swift family with short tails and active fluttering flight, some of the commonest birds of the Bornean skies. The Bornean swiftlets can be split into two groups, the four echo-locating swiftlets which breed in perpetually dark caves (described next page) and the three non-echo-locators, one of which, the Glossy Swiftlet is probably the commonest Bornean bird. The remaining two non-echo-locating swiftlets are very rare and little known.

1 WATERFALL SWIFT *Hydrochous gigas* **16cm** **Status unknown**

[Giant Swiftlet *Aerodramus gigas*] A globally scarce large mystery swiftlet probably both resident and migrant. Breeding pairs build perpetually damp mossy nests behind mountain waterfalls. The largest all dark swiftlet. Usually seen in tightly knit large roving flocks of 20–50 birds (Eaton). Recorded as a night flying migrant in the Malay P. **Call:** Trilling flight calls, usually in chorus (Becking). Regularly recorded Poring and Maliau Basin. No Kalimantan records. **Range:** Hills of Malay P, Sumatra, Java.

2 GLOSSY SWIFTLET *Collocalia esculenta* **9cm** **Common resident**

[Davison: White-bellied Swiftlet *Aerodramus esculenta*] One of the commonest birds of Borneo. Seen everywhere in the sky, from the coast to lowland oil palm to montane forests, always active, feeding on mosquitoes and other small insects. In towns, breeds in small colonies in shady buildings such as multi-level car parks where it is considered a nuisance. In the forest builds nests under small rocky overhangs. Nests in the same large caves as echo-locating swiftlets but only where there is enough light to see. The nest is made from grass glued to a wall with saliva and is of minimal value, but this bird is often used by swiftlet farmers as a foster parent of Edible-nest Swiftlets. **Call:** A high-pitched trill. **Range:** Malay P, to N.Guinea.

3 BORNEAN SWIFTLET *Collocalia dodgei* **9cm** **Montane endemic**

[Mann: Linchi Swiftlet *Collocalia linchi*] A recent split by Moyle (2007). A very rare swiftlet known only from the Borneo mountains. Recently found nesting on a Kinabalu Summit Trail hut at 2,370m. Very similar to Glossy Swiftlet but has a greenish gloss to the feathers not a bluish gloss. In size slightly smaller and more white below with no whitish tail spots. This species probably occurs round KNP Park HQ but the birds nesting at the Park HQ office are Glossy not Bornean. In the hand has no feather on hind toe unlike Glossy Swiftlet (Moyle 2007). Another recent record from Ulu Lauhon, Maligan Range in S Central Sabah (Sheldon).

4 HIMALAYAN SWIFTLET *Collocalia brevirostris* **13cm** **Not recorded**

A large migrant swiftlet that could occur as a vagrant in Borneo. Any migrating swiftlet seen out at sea or over remote islands may be this species. Distinguished by large size and pale rump and underparts. Birds from the W Himalayas are paler than those from the east. Both forms are illustrated. **Range:** Breeds Himalayas to C China wintering south to Malay P, Sumatra.

GLOSSY SWIFT FOSTERING AS A STRATEGY FOR EDIBLE NEST SWIFTLET FARMING
Swiftlet farming for edible nests began in Java and has since expanded rapidly with an estimated 200,000 + occupied swiftlet houses in Java, Sumatra, Borneo, Malay P, Thailand and Vietnam. Farming started by chance when Edible-nest Swiftlets (ENS) began nesting in empty houses. Farmers expanded their ENS colonies by switching ENS eggs into the active nests of the very common Glossy Swiftlet so that the Glossy could foster the young ENS. As an adult bird the ENS returns to its 'home colony' to build a white nest. In the jungle both ENS and Glossy nest in the same caves but Glossy always nests in daylight whilst ENS always nests in darkness. To be successful at fostering, these differences in nesting habitat must be replicated by the farmer by building open but sheltered areas for Glossy next to dark chambers for ENS. See next page.

SWIFTLET FARMING GOES HIGH TECH The fostering strategy was too slow for some farmers who wanted instant colonies of ENS in their empty properties. Once a building has been converted into a suitable cave-like space the farmers play DVDs pre-recorded with the sounds of an active ENS colony, to attract passing ENS to nest in their building. In Indonesia, P Malaysia and Thailand tens of thousands of shop houses have been converted into potential ENS farms. Many towns in Borneo now have novice farmers attempting to enter this potentially highly profitable industry but the reported success rate of new conversions is less than 15%.

ECHO-LOCATING SWIFTLETS

The four echo-locating swiftlets (ELS) nest in perpetual darkness in the most remote areas of limestone caves using the sound of their reflected calls to navigate. ELS can be told apart only by their different nests, three of which are valuable edible nests. Limestone caves occur in many areas of Borneo, apart from Brunei. The largest caves such as Mulu and Niah in Sarawak and Gomantong in Sabah may host hundreds of thousands of swiftlets together with millions of bats. The echo-location abilities of ELS are not accurate enough to catch insects so these swiftlets feed during the day and roost next to their nests at night. Some large caves contain nests of all three common species, usually in small separate colonies. Glossy Swiftlets also nest in the same caves but only where they can navigate by daylight. Predators of bats and swiftlets such as snakes, owls, eagles and civets are often seen around the cave mouth and inside the caves. These caves are best visited at dusk and dawn to watch the spectacular changeover of bat and swiftlet populations. See also pages 182 and 186 for further information on the edible nest industry.

1 WHITE-NEST SWIFTLET *Aerodramus fuciphagus* **12cm** **Common resident**

[Mann: Edible-nest Swiftlet] The second commonest ELS. Builds the most valuable 'white' nest from saliva. A single nest weighs c. 8.3 grams and is currently worth c. US$25 at wholesale and c. US$50 at retail. The nest is harvested from the cave walls by climbers, and sold for consumption as 'bird's-nest-soup'. A pair will re-build up to five times a year. Normally two eggs. Borneo population is estimated at 300,000 birds (Lim/Cranbrook). **Call:** A series of double clicks used in an echo location rattle. **Range:** Malay P, Sumatra, Borneo, Java.

2 BLACK-NEST SWIFTLET *Aerodramus maximus* **13cm** **Common resident**

[*Aerodramus maxima*] The commonest ELS. Based on current nest production the estimated Borneo population is around 2.65 million birds (Lim/Cranbrook), a very substantial decline from estimates based on recorded harvests in the 1930s. See following page. Builds a dark nest made of saliva mixed with feathers and plant material, worth about 20% of the value of a white nest. Normally one egg. Nests in joined up colonies. **Call:** A series of single clicks used in an echo-location rattle. **Range:** Myanmar, Malay P, Vietnam, Sumatra, Borneo, Java.

3 MOSSY-NEST SWIFTLET *Aerodramus salanganus* **14cm** **Scarce resident**

[*Aerodramus vulcanorum*] The third commonest ELS. Builds a small mossy nest which is of no commercial value, on a ledge. Normally two eggs. Nests in loose colonies. Widespread in Sarawak caves including Niah and Mulu. In Sabah, breeds at Gomantong. In Kalimantan, on Maratua Island. **Call:** A series of double clicks used in an echo-location rattle. **Range:** Sumatra, Borneo, Natuna Is, Basilan (SW Philippines), Java.

4 GERMAN'S SWIFTLET *Aerodramus germani* **12cm** **Local resident**

[*Aerodramus fuciphagus germani*] The least common of the ELS, previously considered a race of Edible-nest Swiftlet. Resembles the Edible-nest Swiftlet apart from a paler rump. Produces a valuable white nest. Replaces the Edible-nest Swiftlet in coastal areas where it nests in small colonies in crevices in sea cliffs or small caves. **Sabah:** P Gaya, Lungisan Island (illustrated) next to Mantanani Island with approx 1,200 birds, Berhala Island nr. Sandakan. **Sarawak:** Both Satang Islands, P Lakei at Bako NP. **Kalimantan:** Maratua Island. **Call:** A series of double clicks used in an echo-location rattle. **Range:** Rocky cliffs and caves along coasts and small islands from Hainan and Myanmar S to the Malaya P., Borneo, Palawan and Sulu Sea.

RESOURCE PARTITIONING BY THE SWIFTLETS OF BORNEO
Four different swiftlets with similar lifestyles co-exist in lowland Borneo. How do these abundant aerial insectivores manage to survive inter-specific competition. (Lourie and Tompkins 2000) (Harrisson 1974)
GLOSSY SWIFLET: (8 grams) The smallest and most agile swiftlet. Forages low, weaving close to vegetation. Diet contains a high proportion of beetles and aphids.
BLACK-NEST SWIFTLET: (17 grams). Largest and least agile of the four. Majority of diet is large flying ants and termites which swarm in forested areas and are adversely affected by forest destruction.
WHITE-NEST SWIFTLET: (13 grams) Specialises in tiny flying insects such as fig-wasps and insects with aquatic larvae eg mosquitoes, gnats and mayflies found near fresh water ponds and rivers.
MOSSY NEST SWIFTLET: (13 grams) Similar varied diet as White-nest but takes larger prey. Population is limited by the need to find suitable nesting ledges in caves.

1

2

3

Gomantong Caves
Sabah

4

Lungisan, showing nesting
cave of German's Swiftlet

Mantanani Besar

NEEDLETAIL SWIFTS

APODIDAE **World 4 species. Borneo 3 species.** Large powerful swifts with distinctive cigar-shaped bodies. They have a series of spines projecting from their tail hence their name.

1 WHITE-THROATED NEEDLETAIL *Hirundapus caudacutus* **19cm** Passage migrant

 A scarce passage migrant through Borneo on its way to and from Australia regularly reported from the west coast of Borneo in both September/October and in April on the return journey. Distinguished by very distinctive contrasting plumage. As with all needletails the white belly looks U-shaped from below. Swifts migrate both by night and day, and migrant swifts are often seen in mixed flocks. **Range:** Breeds E Siberia to Japan, China, winters E Australia.

2 SILVER-BACKED NEEDLETAIL *Hirundapus cochinchinensis* **19cm** Not recorded

[White-vented Needletail]. Not so far reported from Borneo but a likely vagrant to the west coast. Distinguished from White-throated by darker throat, and absence of white loral spot. **Range:** Breeds Himalayas to S China, Taiwan, winters mainland SE Asia, S to Malay P, Sumatra, Java.

3 BROWN NEEDLETAIL *Hirundapus giganteus indica* **21cm** Not recorded

[Davison: Brown-backed Needletail] The migrant form *H. g. indicus* is a very likely migrant to Borneo in winter. Unlike the resident race *H. g. giganteus* (see below) has pale loral patch at base of beak but brown back, unlike White-throated. **Range:** India to China. Some birds winter south.

4 BROWN NEEDLETAIL *Hirundapus giganteus giganteus* **21cm** Scarce resident

 The resident race of the Brown Needletail is only locally common, typically seen in small parties hawking for insects over forest or marsh. Likes feeding over ridge tops, e.g. at KNP HQ. Wings drum as they swoop low to drink from rivers. Breeds and roosts in hollow forest trees. 'Daily movements of these birds are remarkably predictable. For example, flocks going to roost will often travel along a road or river at exactly the same time each evening' (Sheldon). **Call:** High-pitched squeak. **Range:** Malay P, Sumatra, Borneo, Java, Palawan.

5 SILVER-RUMPED SPINETAIL *Rhaphidura leucopygialis* **11cm** Common resident

 [Davison: Silver-rumped Needletail] There are 12 species of spinetail swifts in the world (mainly African) but only one in Borneo. A common swift of the forest and forest edge frequently seen in the afternoon swooping low to drink from forest rivers. Distinguished by distinctive wing shape, silver-white rump and square tail. Breeds in small colonies in tree hollows. **Call:** High-pitched chatter. **Range:** Myanmar to Malay P, Sumatra, Java, Borneo.

EDIBLE-NEST SWIFTLETS: HARVESTING OF CAVE NESTS IN BORNEO (see previous page)
The edible nests of cave swiftlets are harvested commercially three to five times a year, the parent birds rebuilding a new nest in the same location each time. The nesting season begins in August in Sarawak and March in E Sabah. Harvesting begins as soon as the first nests of the season have been constructed. Some of the early chicks and eggs of White-nest Swiftlets are taken for fostering by Glossy Swifts in swiftlet farms, but inevitably, many early eggs and young are lost. In well managed caves one would expect that the eggs and young of White-nest Swiftlets would be switched into Black-nest Swiftlet nests but this does not happen. All available nests are harvested and in late harvests thousands of eggs and young are abandoned on the cave floor to be eaten by rats, snakes and civets. In the better regulated caves such as Gomantong and Niah the swiftlets are allowed one successful breeding session after the first nest has been taken (Lim/Cranbrook).

FALLING PRODUCTION OF NESTS FROM SWIFTLET CAVES IN BORNEO
Not surprisingly edible nest production from the wild (caves) appears to be falling year by year. At Niah, a population of three million Black-nest Swiftlets has been reduced to 300,000 birds in 50 years. Some basic research on swiftlets has been carried out but much remains unknown. For example why are Black-nest Swiftlets much commoner than Edible-nest Swiftlets? Do they feed on different insects, or over different habitats? What is the foraging space and range? How does forest destruction affect the swiftlets' food supply? In the long run production from caves is likely to be superseded by 'farmed' production. As yet no proper scientific principles have been applied to swiftlet nest farming either and many farmers fail to succeed. Once science replaces trial and error perhaps cave swiftlets will be allowed to nest in peace.

TROGONS

TROGONIDAE   **World 39 species including the quetzal of Central America; Borneo 6 species including one endemic, the magnificent Whitehead's Trogon, one of 'Whitehead's Trio'.** Trogons are stunningly attired unobtrusive birds of primary forest. Usually seen sitting quietly upright on a shaded forest branch for long periods. Trogons feed on insects and occasionally fruit by hunting through leaves or flying from a perch to snatch an insect in mid-air. Davison (1999) points out that the two large lowland trogons, Diard's and Red-naped, are sympatric but avoid competition by foraging at different levels in the forest. The two small submontane trogons, Orange-breasted and Cinnamon-rumped are also sympatric and partition resources in a similar manner. Sexes differ. Often seen in pairs and respond well to tape playback. Nest in holes excavated in rotten tree stumps. Contact calls are a plaintive series of soft notes, and harsh chattering when alarmed. Trogons are rarely found in secondary forest, and they struggle to survive in logged forest. Males are brighter than females and wing bars are black and white, not black and buff. All trogons have bright blue or purple orbital skin.

1   DIARD'S TROGON *Harpactes diardii*   **30cm**   **Lowland resident**

Locally common in lowland and hill forest throughout Borneo including peatswamp and kerangas forest. At Danum in a study comparing bird populations in logged and unlogged forest Lambert found that of all the trogons only Diard's survived in logged forest with numbers much reduced. Note: Underside of tail is speckled white, not plain white as with other trogons. **Call:** A series of 8–10 notes, faster than Red-naped and falling in pitch towards the end. **Range:** Malay P, Sumatra, Borneo.

2   RED-NAPED TROGON *Harpactes kasumba*   **33cm**   **Lowland resident**

Generally scarce but locally common throughout the lowlands and hills. Only found in undisturbed primary forest. Unlike Diard's, which prefers the understorey, hunts for insects in the upperstorey of the forest. Underside of tail is plain white unlike Diard's Trogon. **Call:** A series of six or seven slow notes on the same pitch *hau hau hau hau hau hau hau*. **Range:** Malay P, Sumatra, Borneo.

3   ORANGE-BREASTED TROGON *Harpactes oreskios*   **25cm**   **Sub montane resident**

Scarce inhabitant of hilly and submontane forest. Hunts in the upperstorey of the forest and often joins mixed feeding flocks. Widespread in N Borneo, e.g. Poring (KNP), Danum, Mulu and Gng Penrissen but absent from Brunei and S Kalimantan. The only male trogon with no red in plumage. **Call:** 'A repeated *pew   pew   pew   pew   pew* of three to five notes all on the same pitch or slightly descending at the end. Also a series of harsh grunts' (Sheldon). **Range:** Myanmar to Malay P, Sumatra, Borneo, Java.

4   WHITEHEAD'S TROGON *Harpactes whiteheadi*   **33cm**   **Scarce montane endemic**

The only truly montane trogon, confined to undisturbed mountain forest above 900m especially favouring the understorey in damp gloomy valleys. Uncommon from Kinabalu south to Kayan Mentarang. **Call:** A series of harsh notes on an even scale *wark   wark   wark   wark*. **Sabah:** KNP HQ, Mesilau, Crocker Range. **Sarawak:** Mulu, Gng Dulit, Kelabit Highlands/ Pulong Tau, Usun Apau Plateau. **Kalimantan:** Kayan Mentarang.

5   CINNAMON-RUMPED TROGON *Harpactes orrophaeus*   **25cm**   **Submontane resident**

Widespread but scarce throughout Borneo in undisturbed primary forest with a preference for hilly or submontane localities, where it hunts in the understorey of the forest. **Sabah:** Poring, Sepilok, Danum, Tabin. **Brunei:** Seria, Anduki, Andulau (Mann). **Sarawak:** Gng Penrissen, Similajau. **Kalimantan:** Sg Wain, Barito Ulu, Gng Palung. **Call:** Three or four descending notes *pew   pew   pew   pew* fading away at the end. **Range:** Malay P, Sumatra, Borneo.

6   SCARLET-RUMPED TROGON *Harpactes duvaucelii*   **23cm**   **Lowland resident**

The smallest and commonest of the Bornean trogons. Widespread in primary forest and occasionally disturbed forest throughout Borneo. Perhaps more frugivorous than other trogons. Locally nomadic. Distinguish from Cinnamon-rumped by red rumps of both sexes. Both sexes of both species have blue eyebrows. **Call:** Commonly heard. A soft series of notes falling in pitch, and speeding up towards the end. **Range:** Malay P, Sumatra, Borneo.

KINGFISHERS

ALCEDINIDAE **World 84 species; Borneo 12 species.** Kingfishers are colourful 'sit and wait' predators. Locally common, they are found in most Borneo habitats apart from the mountains. The riverine species plunge-dive for fish but most Borneo kingfishers attack insects, crabs or lizards on the ground. The prey is brought back to the perch, whacked until dead and swallowed whole, head first. Kingfishers are monogamous with pairs holding territories which are strictly defended. At least four species are migrants, three from N Asia and the Sacred Kingfisher from Australia but kingfishers are never seen to flock or in family parties. Sexes usually similar. Juvenile kingfishers often have faint chest bars. The larger kingfishers make distinctive loud harsh calls. The small kingfishers utter a piercing whistle as they zip past. Nests are usually tunnels excavated in an earth bank but they may be adapted from tree holes. Youngsters shoot their droppings out backward towards the entrance hole which is often stained white just before the young fledge.

1 SACRED KINGFISHER *Todiramphus sanctus* **22cm** Scarce migrant

A very scarce migrant from Australia May to September. Feeds on insects over dry ground. Most likely to be seen in Kalimantan coastal districts. A recent record from Kinabatangan (Daisy O'Neil). **Field notes:** Significantly smaller than Collared Kingfisher. Young Collared Kingfishers can show slightly buffy underparts in first year but no buffy mark in front of eye. **Call:** 'Loud four or five notes, slightly descending *kik-kik-kik-kik*' (Slater). **Range:** Breeds Australia, migrating north in the austral winter, to Java, Sumatra, Singapore and Borneo.

2 CHESTNUT-COLLARED KINGFISHER *Actenoides concretus* **23cm** Scarce resident

[Davison: Rufous-collared Kingfisher] Quiet forest kingfisher. Commonest in the hills and submontane areas. Absent from peatswamp forest. Usually seen perched immobile and silent low down in dense understorey vegetation of primary forest. Feeds on insects taken from the ground. Described as a 'ghost bird' for its shy habits and ventriloquial call (Dennis Yong). Sexes differ. **Call:** 'An often repeated *wee-it*, rising on the second part, often given just before dawn' (Sheldon). **Range:** Malay P, Sumatra, Borneo.

3 COLLARED KINGFISHER *Todiramphus chloris* **24cm** Common resident

[White-collared Kingfisher] [Malay: Raja Udang (King of the Prawns)] Common in coastal forest parks and gardens throughout Borneo. Also found in padi fields in remote interior valleys, e.g. Tambunan to Tenom valley (Sabah) and Kelabit Highlands (Sarawak) (Gregory-Smith). Migrant race *T. c. collaris* has been recorded from Brunei and Tembungo Oil Platform NW Sabah. Feeds on large insects, geckos and beach crabs, not fish. Can only be confused with much rarer Sacred Kingfisher, which has buffy markings in front of eye. **Call:** Harsh *chek chek chek* commonly heard at dawn in coastal districts. **Range:** Resident Middle East to Australia and Pacific Islands.

4 BLACK-CAPPED KINGFISHER *Halcyon pileata* **30cm** Scarce winter visitor

Formerly a very common winter visitor to Bornean rivers, Sept. to April. Now increasingly scarce. A common night-flying migrant in Malay P. Perches on branches along rivers and occasionally dives for fish but feeds mainly on large insects such as dragonflies. Has contrasting white panels on wings only obvious in flight. **Call:** A short *ki ki* (Brazil). **Range:** Breeds China, Taiwan, Korea, migrates south to Malay P, Sumatra, Borneo, Java, Philippines.

5 RUDDY KINGFISHER *Halcyon coromanda* **25cm** Scarce winter visitor and resident

The resident race, *H. c. minor*, is locally common in the understorey of mangrove and nipah palm forest, around the coast of Borneo. More rarely found along large rivers and forest streams, e.g. at the Rainforest Discovery Centre, Sepilok. Feeds on fish, crabs and insects. The migrant race, *H. c. major*, is even rarer than the resident, with a few records from coastal W Sabah. Like many kingfishers has a bright silver blue panel along centre of back when flying off. **Call:** A repeated series of whistles, each whistle consisting of a rapid series of descending notes. Calls mainly in early morning and late afternoon. The call is easily imitated and the bird can be called in. **Range:** Breeds China, Korea, Japan, winters SE Asia.

6 WHITE-THROATED KINGFISHER *Halcyon smyrnensis* **27cm** Vagrant

The commonest kingfisher of lowland Sumatra and the Malay Peninsula where it inhabits cultivated areas and gardens. One record (Nov. 2008) of a vagrant to West Kalimantan (van Balen).

H. c. minor

H. c. major

imm

KINGFISHERS

1 COMMON KINGFISHER *Alcedo atthis* **15cm** **Common winter visitor**

[River Kingfisher] Commonest in NW coastal districts Sept.–April but found throughout lowland Borneo with a preference for coastal swamps, rivers, and wet padi fields. Often perches on a small twig overhanging the water. Male has all black bill. Female has mainly orange lower bill. **Call:** A shrill whistle as it shoots along a river, the silver blue back irridescent in the sunlight. **Range:** Breeds Europe to Asia. N Asian populations winter south to SE Asia

2 BLUE-EARED KINGFISHER *Alcedo meninting* **15cm** **Common resident**

[Deep Blue Kingfisher] More of a forest bird than the Common Kingfisher and more likely to occur along inland rivers and streams in lowland primary forest but also found in coastal swamps and mangroves. Male has orange at base of lower bill. Female lower bill is all orange. Juvenile has rufous instead of blue ear coverts. **Call:** A high-pitched whistle shorter than the Common Kingfisher. **Range:** India to Malay P, Sumatra, Borneo, Java, Sulawesi.

3 BLUE-BANDED KINGFISHER *Alcedo peninsulae* **18cm** **Scarce resident**

[*Alcedo euryzona*] The least common of the Bornean kingfishers. Found along clear rocky rivers and streams in the lowlands and hills with a preference for submontane localities. Occasionally in coastal swamps. Sexes differ. Looks like a large dark Blue-eared Kingfisher with contrasting sky-blue back. Distinguish by blue breast-band of male. **Call:** A loud whistle less shrill than Common Kingfisher (Fry). **Range:** Myanmar to Malay P, Sumatra, Borneo, Java. **BLI:** Vulnerable.

4 STORK-BILLED KINGFISHER *Pelargopsis capensis* **35cm** **Locally common resident**

[Malay: Burung buaya (crocodile)] Inhabits the forested edge of coastal swamps, mangroves and rivers up into the hills but generally scarce. Most Sabah/Brunei birds have pale orange head as illustrated. **Call:** Alarm call is an explosive wail sometimes followed by a weird loud laughing *cack, cack, cack, cack.* Territorial call is a series of screaming double notes – *wiok wiok*, repeated (King). **Range:** India to Malay P, Sumatra, Borneo, Java, Philippines **Taxonomy:** Sabah race appears to be undescribed. Sumatra and Borneo race (*P. c. cyanopteryx*) has a buff cap (Fry). This may apply to some birds from SW Borneo.

5 BORNEAN BANDED KINGFISHER *Lacedo melanops* **20cm** **Uncommon endemic**

Locally common inhabitant of the understorey of primary forest. Favours hilly and submontane localities and occasionally wanders to the mountains, e.g. KNP HQ, but not regular at this level. Feeds in forest on insects. Not associated with streams or rivers. Sexes differ. Often raises and lowers crest. **Call:** A series of high-pitched, two-tone mournful whistles – *pee-yoo, pee-yoo*. Responds well to tape playback. **Range:** Myanmar, Malay P, Sumatra, Borneo, Java **Taxonomy:** new split, see page 20.

6 RUFOUS-BACKED KINGFISHER *Ceyx rufidorsa motleyi* **14 cm** **Sabah race**

[Oriental Dwarf Kingfisher] A common inhabitant of the understorey of lowland primary forest in Sabah especially near streams and small pools. Usually seen as shrill peeping red flash as it zips past. Feeds on small lizards, insects, spiders, fish and tadpoles and nests in earth banks and termite nests. Frequently caught in mist nets set at ground level in primary forest. **Call:** Shrill *peep* in flight. **Range:** C.f. *motleyi* is confined to Sabah with some intermediates in Brunei and Labuan.

7 RUFOUS BACKED KINGFISHER *Ceyx rufidorsa rufidorsa* **14 cm** **Sarawak/Kalimantan**

[Oriental Dwarf Kingfisher] Habits as above. The common race in Sarawak and Kalimantan but not found in Sabah. The wings are rufous/mauve with only the primary feathers dark blue/black. Note that both races have an all-mauve back. **Range:** Malay Peninsula, Palawan, Sumatra, Borneo, Java.

8 BLACK-BACKED KINGFISHER *Ceyx erithaca* **14 cm** **Possible vagrant**

This is the continental form of Oriental Dwarf Kingfisher resident north of the Malay Peninsula. It is a common winter migrant to the Malay Peninsula and Singapore and a possible vagrant to the islands and coast of NW Borneo. No confirmed Borneo records. Note distinctive blue/black mantle at the top of the mauve back: **Range:** Resident from India to Hainan south to Thailand. Winter migrants are common in the Malay Peninsula south to Singapore. **Taxonomy:** See Lim, Sheldon, Moyle (2010).

BEE-EATERS, ROLLER AND HOOPOE

BEE-EATERS: MEROPIDAE **World 24 species; Borneo 3 species.** [Malay: Burung berek-berek] Bee eaters are colourful specialist predators on venomous flying insects such as bees and wasps. Both wild and domesticated honey bees are a favourite food and in Europe the Bee-eater is regarded as a serious pest by honey farmers. Bee eaters normally perch on a branch near a bee hive flying out to snatch individuals from below as they pass. They return to the branch to kill the bee by banging it on the wood. The venom sac and sting are removed before swallowing. Bee-eater sexes are similar. Two Borneo species possess central tail streamers to aid in acrobatic flight. For nesting, long tunnels are excavated in soft ground in which the white eggs are laid. The two open country bee-eaters are gregarious, breeding together in colonies, flocking together at evening roosts and undertaking local migrations in small chirruping flocks flying both by night and day.

1 BLUE-THROATED BEE-EATER *Merops viridis* **28cm**   **Common nomadic resident**

The commonest bee-eater in Borneo. Breeds in small colonies in sandy coastal areas (Jan.-July) before dispersing to forested areas where it is usually seen alone hawking insects from the tops of forest trees. In Sabah most birds breed on the west coast before leaving for the forested interior. Frequently recorded flying at night over BSB, Brunei (Mann). At Tenom (Sabah) this species hunted Giant Bees *Apis dorsata* from a branch near the colony. The bee sting was rubbed on the branch to release a bee alarm pheromone. This scent attracted guard bees which were snatched by the bee-eater (Koeniger). **Call:** Flocking birds call constantly with musical *chirrups*. **Range:** Breeds S China, S to Malay P, Sumatra, Borneo, Java, Philippines, Sulawesi. Northern populations are migratory and might occur in Borneo.

2 RAINBOW BEE-EATER *Merops ornatus* **25cm**   **Vagrant**

One record only, a small flock on Pulau Maratua (East Kalimantan) in Aug. 2010. This bee-eater is an austral migrant breeding in Australia and wintering (May to Sept) in Sulawesi and the islands east to New Guinea. Distinguished from Blue-tailed Bee-eater by chestnut on head and black throat patch. Similar Chestnut-headed Bee-eater of Sumatra and Java could also occur, but has chestnut on head extending to cover the back as well and a chestnut band above the black band on the throat.

3 BLUE-TAILED BEE-EATER *Merops philippinus* **30cm**   **Common migrant from south**

Locally common in open country in Kalimantan with flocks of hundreds regularly recorded but no breeding records. Most likely these birds are seasonal migrants from Java or Sumatra. In N Borneo a scarce vagrant. Both this and Blue-throated have a blue tail. Yellow throat with green head is distinctive. **Call:** Plaintive trill *kwink kwink, kwink kwink, kwink* given in flight (McKinnon). **Range:** India to Malay P, Sumatra, Java, Philippines, Sulawesi.

4 RED-BEARDED BEE-EATER *Nyctyornis amictus* **30cm**   **Common resident**

A locally common resident of primary and old secondary forest throughout lowland Borneo. Normally perches concealed, flying out to snatch insects. The male forehead is lilac, the female red, juvenile green. The red beard may deceive passing bees into approaching a supposed flower. Nests alone excavating a tunnel in an earth bank. **Call:** A growling alarm call and a series of deep hoarse descending call notes *ha-ha-ha-ha-ha*. **Range:** Myanmar to Malay P, Sumatra, Borneo.

ROLLERS: CORACIDAE **World 12 species; Borneo 1 species.**

5 DOLLARBIRD *Eurystomus orientalis* **30cm**   **Common resident and winter visitor**

[Malay: Tiong batu] A common resident of lowland forests throughout Borneo, the population increased by migrants from the Asian continent during winter months. Residents nest high up in tree holes and attack other birds. Rollers are famous for their flight skills. The name derives from the large transparent circular panels on the wing which resemble silver dollars. **Call:** Harsh *shack*. **Range:** Breeds India to Japan winters south in SE Asia.

6 COMMON HOOPOE (UPUPIDAE) *Upupa epops* **30cm**   **Vagrant**

One species worldwide, with eight records from NW Borneo south to Kuching. Feeds on the ground in grassy areas. **Call:** A soft far carrying *hoop hoop hoop*. **Range:** Breeds Africa, Europe, Asia. Some N Asian populations winter south to SE Asia.

1 adult

imm

3

2

imm

♂

♀

4

imm

5

6

SMALL HORNBILLS: BUCEROTIDAE

WORLD: 45 species. **SE Asia**: 13 species. **BORNEO:** 8 species. Hornbills pair for life. Hornbills nest in large tree holes where the female is sealed in for protection against predators. (See illus page 200) Two species, Bushy-crested and White-crowned, are co-operative breeders, in which the family group all help to feed the helpless female and young. The other hornbills are pair breeders where only the male feeds the female. Hornbills always lay 2 to 5 eggs but pair breeders usually only produce one young. The weakest young is often eaten either by the strongest young or by the female. Young birds are fed initially on small animals and insects, and later on fruit, there is some evidence that abundant fruiting leads to nesting and in years of poor fruiting hornbills may not breed. The smaller hornbills have a varied diet, feeding on fruit, insects and animals including lizards, birds, rats and bats whilst the larger hornbills are mainly frugivorous. Sexes differ. The male is usually larger than the female with a larger brighter casque. Juvenile casques are significantly smaller. For the first year young birds resemble either male or female dependent on species (see below) apart from White-crowned, Rhinoceros and Helmeted which have distinctively different juvenile plumages. All hornbills can be very noisy especially when defending their territories, only the most distinctive calls are described here.

1 WHITE-CROWNED HORNBILL *Aceros comatus* **85 cm** Scarce resident

[*Berenicornis comatus*] The rarerest and most carnivorous of the hornbills. Prefers dense shrubby vegetation next to rivers in lowland and hill forest where it hunts in family parties of 4 to 6 for insects and small animals. A co-operative breeder. Adult white crest distinctive. Juvenile is all dark with white tip to tail and grey flecked crest. **Sabah:** Sepilok, Tabin, Danum, Kinabatangan, Tawau Hills. **Brunei:** Ulu Temburong, K. Belalong. **Sarawak:** Mulu, Lambir Hills, Similajau, Samunsam. **Kalimantan:** Very scarce. Gng Palung, Muratus Mts. Barito Ulu, Sangkulirang Peninsula. **Call:** The quietest hornbill. Lively, hollow, pigeon-like – *kuk kuk, kuk kuk kuk* (McKinnon). **Range:** Myanmar to Malay P, Sumatra, Borneo.

2 BUSHY-CRESTED HORNBILL *Anorrhinus galeritus* **70 cm** Common resident

The commonest hornbill of inland logged and virgin forests from the lowlands to the hills, throughout Borneo. No white in plumage. Occurs in small, noisy flocks of 8 to 12 hunting in the canopy. A co-operative breeder. Juveniles resemble males. **Call:** A shrill yelping, like young puppies. Similar to that of the Pied Hornbill, but the notes are mostly disyllabic (Holmes). The group territorial call given sitting shoulder to shoulder is rising and falling gobbles followed by a short series of sharp cries that rise in pitch and finally end in loud high pitched screams (Leighton) **Range:** Malay P, Sumatra, Borneo.

3 ORIENTAL PIED HORNBILL *Anthracoceros albirostris* **75 cm** Common resident

More common on islands and in coastal and secondary forests than other hornbills and often found inland along rivers. Usually seen in noisy flocks but pairs separate from the flock to breed alone. Distinguish from Black by black marks on white bill of both sexes and white belly. Tail colours can confuse, see below. Juveniles resemble females. **Call:** Strident cackling and yacking. **Sabah:** Islands of the TARP from where it sometimes flies to the mainland to feed, Nexus, Pulau Tiga, Sepilok, where often in gardens. **Brunei:** Panaga. **Sarawak:** Talang and Satang Islands. **Kalimantan:** Common throughout the lowland forests (Holmes). **Range:** India to Malay P, Sumatra, Borneo, Java, Sulawesi.

4 ASIAN BLACK HORNBILL *Anthracoceros Malay Pnus* **75 cm** Common resident

A common inhabitant of primary lowland, peat swamp and tall mangrove forest. More often found inland and in hill forest than Pied Hornbill. Has been recorded following gibbons at Barito Ulu, Kalimantan, to feed on insects disturbed by the gibbons (Galleti and McConkey 1998). A territorial pair breeder but sometimes seen in flocks. Has the most variable plumage of all the Bornean hornbills. Around half of both sexes have a grey or white stripe over the eye. As with Pied, tail usually looks black above and part white below but tail can look all black or all white depending on feather growth and tail spread. Distinguish by all white bill of male, dark bill and red facial skin of female and all black belly of both sexes. Juveniles resemble females. **Call:** A coarse, rasping note that recalls the squealing of a nervous pig (Holmes). **Range:** Malay P, Sumatra, Borneo.

hanamixis polystachya (Amoora)
Meliaceae

LARGE HORNBILLS: BUCEROTIDAE

1 WRINKLED HORNBILL *Aceros corrugatus* **75 cm** **Scarce resident**

Generally scarce but locally common. The commonest hornbill of the peat swamp forests o
Brunei and Sarawak. Like Wreathed non-territorial, pair breeding and semi-nomadic moving from
area to area dependent on local fruiting. Smaller than Wreathed Hornbill. Only last two thirds o
tail is white, whereas Wreathed has all-white tail. Juvenile resembles male. **Call:** 'Deep, echoing
calls – *rowwow* or *wakowwakowkow*' (McKinnon). **Range:** Thailand, Malay P, Sumatra, Borneo

2 WREATHED HORNBILL *Rhyticeros undulatus* **100 cm** **Scarce resident**

Widespread throughout Borneo but only locally common. Prefers hill forest but is also
common in the peat swamp forests of SE Kalimantan, e.g. Sabangau and Tg Puting. Semi-
nomadic, wide ranging and non-territorial. When not breeding usually in flocks which often
roost communally. The only hornbill found at higher levels on Mount Kinabalu up to 3,300m
Has very distinctive coloured throat pouches: male – yellow, female – blue, immature – green
Juvenile resembles male. **Call:** A loud harsh, dog-like bark used to maintain flock coherence
Range: India to Malay P, Sumatra, Borneo, Java.

3 RHINOCEROS HORNBILL *Buceros rhinoceros* **110 cm** **Locally common resident**

[Malay: Burung torak] Found in primary forest throughout Borneo. Heavily hunted fo
feathers used in traditional ceremonies. The only hornbill with a black band on a white tail
Bill and white plumage is often stained orange with oil from gland at base of tail. Male has
red iris, female white iris. Juvenile lacks casque. Usually in pairs often with a juvenile but
juveniles and non breeders often form large nomadic flocks. **Call:** A series of loud honks
breaking into raucous cackles as the bird flies off. **Range:** Malay P, Sumatra, Java, Borneo.

4 HELMETED HORNBILL *Buceros vigil* **120 cm + 25cm tail extn.** **Scarce resident**

[Malay: Burung tebang mentua (chop down mother-in-law's house)] The rarest hornbill
Uncommon in lowland and hill forest. Has heavy solid ivory bill used in aerial clashes ir
territorial and feeding disputes. Look for long tail feathers, grey with white tip. Juvenile is al
brown including beak and lacks casque. **Call:** The most distinctive bird call in Borneo. 'A series
of identical, loud, hollow ***took*** notes, gaining in speed before drawing to an amazing climax o
maniacal laughter and ***tee poop*** notes' (McKinnon). **Range:** Malay P, Sumatra, Borneo.

RESOURCE PARTITIONING BY THE HORNBILLS OF KUTAI, E. KALIMANTAN

A two year study of hornbill ecology in virgin lowland forest at Kutai showed how 7 different Bornean
species (all except Pied) exploited different rainforest niches and were thus able to exist sympatrically.
(Leighton and Leighton 1983). Hornbills generally preferred energy rich oily fruits such as such as aglaias
(*Meliaceae*), nutmegs (*Myrsticaceae*), laurels (*Lauraceae*), durians (*Durionaceae*), macarangas and
baccaureas (*Euphorbiaceae*) but these trees were thinly spread and fruited only intermittently.

Wreathed and Wrinkled were non-territorial, and flocks flew long distances to exploit the scattered
fruiting of trees with oily fruits. Juvenile and sub-adult Rhinoceros Hornbills adopted the same tactic,
whilst established pairs of Rhinoceros remained faithful to their breeding territory. As oily fruit were often
locally scarce the frugivorous territorial hornbills, Rhinoceros, Helmeted, Black and Bushy-crested – used
commonly available sugar-rich figs as a staple food supply. When figs were scarce an increasing proportion
of time was spent hunting for insects and small animals. Within this overall framework different hornbill
species had different hunting strategies and concentrated their efforts on different levels in the forest.

SPECIES	TERRITORY	PREFERRED DIET	% FIGS IN DIET
White-crowned	1.0 km²	Carnivorous	low
Black	1.1 km²	Small figs	40%
Bushy-crested	1.3 km²	Oily fruits	variable
Rhinoceros	2.3 km²	Medium figs	50%
Helemted	7.7 km²	Large figs	100%
Wreathed	Non territorial	Oily fruits	variable
Wrinkled	Non territorial	Oily fruits	variable

1

♀

♂

2

♂

♀

3

♂

♀

4

♂

Dysoxylum angustifolia
Meliaceae

Knema furfuracea
Myrsticaceae

Nothaphoebe umbelliflora
Lauraceae

phanamixis polystachya
Meliaceae

HORNBILL ECOLOGY

HORNBILL ECOLOGY Hornbills are both 'trophy' species (everyone knows them and wants to see them) and 'indicator' species for the ecological wellbeing of an area. Bornean lowland forest should host all 8 species but often does not, due to logging which destroys the forest fruit trees, hunting, or forest fragmentation into small 'islands' not large enough to sustain a breeding population (see page 24). Just as the health of the hornbill population depends on the forest, the health of the forest depends on the hornbills. Hornbills are major consumers and dispersers of forest fruits, mainly figs. Figs are a substantial part of the diet of many forest birds and animals. If the fig tree population crashes due to a lack of hornbills this will eventually reduce the populations of barbets, binturongs, gibbons, orangutans and other forest frugivores.

THE FUTURE FOR HORNBILLS IN BORNEO: SEPILOK AS AN EXAMPLE Many protected areas in Borneo are too small to sustain viable populations of all the Bornean hornbills. Currently all 8 species of Bornean hornbills survive at Sepilok. Most ecologists would agree that the minimum viable breeding population for any species is around 50 pairs. Sepilok is approx. 60 km² in area. This is just large enough to sustain breeding populations of the smaller hornbills, but inevitably the populations of the nomadic and larger hornbills will eventually die out at Sepilok. From Leighton's studies of hornbill territories at Kutai it is predictable that the larger hornbills will become extinct at Sepilok in the following order – Wreathed, Wrinkled, Helmeted and finally Rhinoceros – unless substantial areas of the surrounding oil palm are converted back into forest.

FIG TREE FRUITING IN BORNEO Borneo hosts over 138 different species of figs of which around 27 canopy species provide the major part of the diet of the larger hornbills, in particular the Rhinoceros and Helmeted. Most Bornean fruit trees do not follow a clear seasonal pattern and fruit erratically. Research has shown that the fig species consumed by birds, including figs of the same species, are genetically programmed to fruit asynchronously, i.e. at random intervals and different times. Other Bornean trees, e.g. dipterocarps and oaks, are programmed to fruit simultaneously in massive 'masts' so that individual seeds have a better chance to survive seed predators, such as rats and porcupines. Figs behave in the opposite way because their seeds pass straight through most birds' digestive systems unharmed. The fig tree benefits if its seeds are eaten and fruits erratically to maximize the chances of seed dispersal away from the mother tree. The fact that each individual fig tree competes to produce fruit when other figs are not fruiting is of enormous benefit to the forest birds and animals as it means that a constant food supply is ensured.

HORNBILL REINTRODUCTION: In many parts of the world hornbill populations have been reduced and re-introduction programmes are in place or planned for the Philippines, Thailand, S Africa and Singapore. However successful re-introduction requires suitable habitat. Studies in Borneo, Sumatra and Sulawesi have found that the hornbill population is strongly co-related with the density of forest fruit tree especially fig trees. The Panaga Club used by Shell employees at Seria (Brunei) is an example of what is possible. A thriving population of nearly 80 Pied Hornbills survives in a patch of remnant coastal forest. There are many similar coastal resorts along the Bornean coast where Pied Hornbills could be successfully re-introduced provided enough fruit trees are planted, and nest boxes provided.

MALE HORNBILLS IN FLIGHT

1	WHITE-CROWNED HORNBILL	*Aceros comatus*	85 cm	Scarce resident
2	BUSHY-CRESTED HORNBILL	*Anorrhinus galeritus*	70 cm	Common resident
3	WRINKLED HORNBILL	*Aceros corrugatus*	75 cm	Scarce resident
4	WREATHED HORNBILL	*Rhyticeros undulatus*	100 cm	Scarce resident
5	ASIAN BLACK HORNBILL	*Anthracoceros malayanus*	75 cm	Common resident
6	ORIENTAL PIED HORNBILL	*Anthracoceros albirostris*	75 cm	Common resident
7	RHINOCEROS HORNBILL	*Buceros rhinoceros*	110 cm	Locally common resident
8	HELMETED HORNBILL	*Buceros vigil*	120 cm + 25cm tail extension	Scarce resident

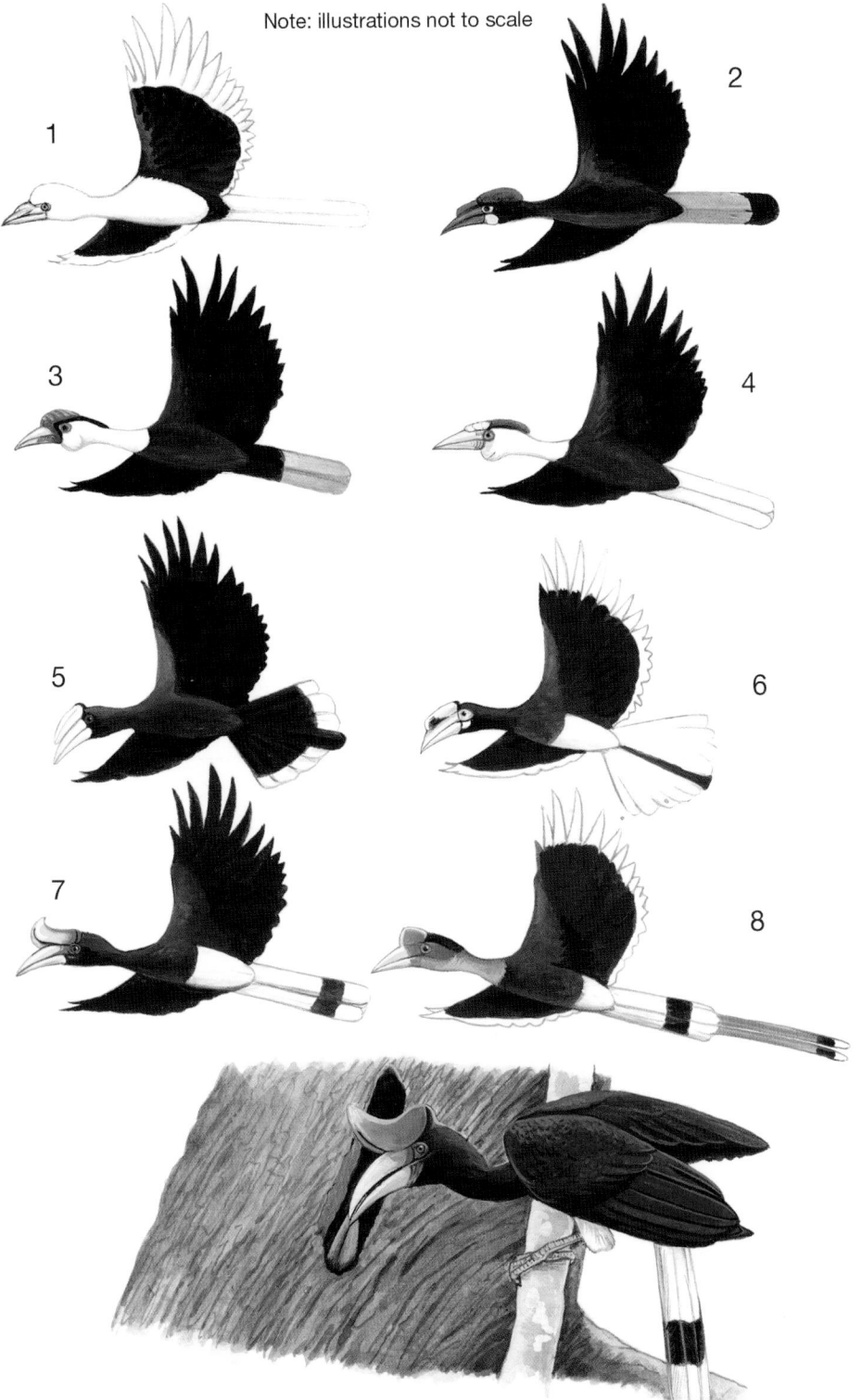

Note: illustrations not to scale

RAMPHASTIDAE   **World 82 species; Borneo 9 species including 3 endemics and 1 aberrant.**   Borneo is the world centre of barbet distribution. Monotonous barbet calls that continue all day are the characteristic sound of the Bornean forest. These territorial calls are the best means of barbet identification, as the green musician is usually camouflaged at the top of a tall forest tree. Barbets call by pumping and vibrating two large bare-skin sacs on either side of the throat with the beak closed. They periodically turn their head to widen the broadcast range, which gives the call its ventriloquial quality. Barbets are named for the large whiskers or bristles (barbs) at the base of the bill. Like woodpeckers, barbets are zygodactylous with two toes pointing forward and two back, which enables them to perch upright on tree trunks. Barbets roost individually in holes which they excavate themselves in rotten tree trunks with their large bills. These roost holes may later be enlarged for use as nests. Numerous blind starter-holes may be a strategy to deceive snakes which systematically investigate such holes. Barbets feed mainly on fruit as well as some insects and small lizards and whilst usually solitary and territorial are often seen feeding together in fruiting fig trees. The illustration opposite shows the relative altitude range of barbets on Kinabalu. Altitude ranges listed in the text follow Mann (2009).

1   GOLDEN-NAPED BARBET   *Megalaima pulcherrima*   20cm   **Montane endemic**

A common montane resident of primary and secondary forest (600–3,200m). Usually found higher up than Mountain and Bornean Barbets. Forms a superspecies with Yellow-crowned Barbet, which replaces it at lower levels (Mann). **Call:** *took-took-trrrrook, took-took-trrrook* etc. Always two *tooks* but these are poorly audible at a distance. Also a winding up call consisting of a series of rolling notes with pauses in between, becoming shorter and shorter until finishing on three or four notes' (Smythies). **Sabah:** KNP HQ, Poring, Crocker Range. **Brunei:** No records. **Sarawak:** Mulu, Kelabit Highlands. **Kalimantan:** Kayan Mentarang.

2   MOUNTAIN BARBET   *Megalaima monticola*   20cm   **Montane endemic**

Common inhabitant of mountain forest (750–2,200m). Usually found lower down than Golden-naped Barbet but ranges overlap. Forms a superspecies with Red-throated Barbet which replaces it at lower levels (Mann). Facial markings similar to female Red-Throated Barbet but has no red spot at base of bill. **Call:** A very fast series of notes about four per second *tuk tuk tuk tuk* with a *tu-ruk* hiccup after about twenty notes before continuing *tuk tuk tuk tuk tu-ruk*. **Sabah:** Crocker Range (common), KNP HQ (scarce), Poring. **Brunei:** No records. **Sarawak:** Mulu and central mountain chain, Kelabit Highlands. **Kalimantan:** Kayan Mentarang, Muratus Mts, Gng Niut.

3   BORNEAN BARBET   *Megalaima eximia*   15cm   **Montane endemic**

[Black-throated Barbet] Smallest Borneo barbet. Uncommon inhabitant of mountain forest (425–2,140m). Usually found at same level as Mountain Barbet but lower than Golden-naped. Forms a superspecies with Blue-eared Barbet which replaces it in the lowlands (Mann). Immature (illustrated) with bluish forehead and throat was previously believed to be an adult race found only on Kinabalu (Short). **Call:** *took-took took* repeated *took-took took* and so on (Moyle). Also a series of very fast notes very similar to the call of the Mountain Barbet but with no hiccups. **Sabah:** Poring, Mesilau, Crocker Range. **Brunei:** No records. **Sarawak:** Mulu, Gng Penrissen. **Kalimantan:** Kayan Mentarang, Ulu Barito, Gng Niut.

4   YELLOW-CROWNED BARBET   *Megalaima henricii*   21cm   **Submontane resident**

Common inhabitant of submontane forest throughout Borneo (0–1,220m). On higher mountains replaced by Golden-naped Barbet at the montane forest ecotone at around 900m. **Call:** A very distinctive call, *trrroook-took-took-took-took*, repeated. A rolling note followed by four *tooks*, repeated without a break for 10 or 20 seconds, each individual phrase lasting just over one second. An interesting recording by Scharringa has three different barbets calling simultaneously at Poring, Yellow-crowned, Gold-whiskered and Blue-eared. **Range:** Malay P, Sumatra, Borneo.

5   GOLD-WHISKERED BARBET   *Megalaima chrysopogon*   30cm   **Common resident**

Borneo's largest barbet. Inhabits forests throughout Borneo with a preference for hill forest (0–1,525m). **Call:** 'A loud quick double note *tagu tagu tagu tagu tagu* some 25 per 10 seconds in a series of 30 to 50 double notes. Also a winding up call of seven to eight notes repeated, the number of notes decreasing gradually until only two or three are given at each repeat' (Davison). **Range:** S Thailand, Malay P, Sumatra, Borneo.

3

imm

2

4

5

Yellow-crowned
Barbet at
fig tree

LOWLAND BARBETS AND HONEYGUIDE

1 RED-CROWNED BARBET *Megalaima rafflesii* **25cm** Common residen

[Many-coloured Barbet] Locally common and widespread in lowland forests throughou
Borneo including kerangas and degraded forests. Not usually found with Red-throated Barbe
and less sensitive to disturbance (Mann). Commonest barbet at Bako and Santubong. **Call**
A deep-toned resonant call, **took-took** (slight pause) **took-took-took** to 10–15 notes at the
rate of three per second. The pause after the first two notes is invariable and most distinctive
(Smythies). **Range:** Malay P, Sumatra, Borneo.

2 RED-THROATED BARBET *Megalaima mystacophanos* **23cm** Common residen

[Gaudy Barbet] Common in lowland forests throughout Borneo, including secondary
peatswamp and kerangas forests. The only Bornean barbet where the sexes differ significantly
in plumage. Forms a superspecies with Mountain Barbet which replaces it in the mountains
(Mann). **Call:** Irregular series of **tok** notes uttered in phrases of one to four notes, at a rate o
one per second (McKinnon), i.e. slower and more hesitant than other barbet calls. Whitehead
described a common call as **pooh pooh lentogok lentogok**. **Range:** Malay P, Sumatra, Borneo.

3 BLUE-EARED BARBET *Megalaima australis* **16cm** Common residen

[Little Barbet] The commonest Bornean barbet found in primary and secondary forest and
cultivated areas. Forms a superspecies with Bornean Barbet which replaces it in the mountains
where ranges coincide, e.g. on Kinabalu and Trus Madi in Sabah and at Gng Penrissen near
Kuching (Mann). Male has black 'ear', female 'blue' ear. Immature has all blue throat. **Call:**
A repeated double note **tu-rook tu-rook tu-rook**. Another call is **prrk, prrk, prrk**, etc which is
dueted with the normal call. **Range:** India to SW China, south to Malay P, Sumatra, Borneo, Java.

4 BORNEAN BROWN BARBET *Calorhamphus fuliginosus* **17cm** Common endemic

A common resident of primary and secondary forest most common in the hills. Does not behave
like a barbet. Often seen in family groups hunting amongst tree trunks for insects, constantly
whistling to each other. Possibly a social and colony nester and a brood host to the honeyguide.
Usually bores a nest hole in an active *Cremorogaster* ant or termite nest. Has bright red or orange
feet. Male has black bill. Female, pink or greyish bill. Plumage very variable. **Call:** Very high-
pitched, whistle-like squeak. **Taxonomy:** new split, see page 20. Borneo has two endemic races,
C. f. tertius (Sabah/Brunei) and *C. f. fuliginosus* (rest of Borneo), which has a rufous head and a
rufous wash on belly as well as a rufous throat.

HONEYGUIDES: INDICATORIDAE **World 15 species; Borneo 1 species.** In Africa, honeyguides lead humans
and Honey Badgers to bees' nests so that they can share the bounty when the nest is raided, a habit not recorded
in Asia. Honeyguides eat all parts of the comb including the wax. In Nepal honeyguides defend territories based
on the location of Giant Rock Bee colonies. In Peninsula Malaysia males have been recorded calling endlessly from
prominent calling posts, often the same site for many years. When one male was shot he was soon replaced by
another male using the same calling post (Wells). Honey Bee nests in Borneo are usually either very prominent
hanging from giant *Koompassia* trees (illustrated) or concealed (often low down) in tree holes. The prominent
nests are well defended by highly venomous migratory Giant Honey Bees *Apis dorsata*. They are predated by
wandering Honey Buzzards (see page 86), whereas the tree hole nests are occupied by small stingless bees,
predated by wandering Sun Bears. Honeyguides would need assistance to access either type of nest but no form
of co-operation has yet been recorded in Borneo. Like cuckoos, honeyguides are brood parasites. In Borneo one
host is believed to be the Brown Barbet which often nests in holes in ant and termite nests.

5 MALAYSIAN HONEYGUIDE *Indicator archipelagicus* **16cm** Scarce resident

Scarce, but widespread inhabitant of lowland primary forest throughout Borneo. In Nepal
the closely related Orange-rumped Honeyguide *Indicator xanthonotus* is highly territorial and
polygonous, chasing off other males from bee colonies and mating with numerous visiting
females, which are allowed to eat the waxy bee combs (Cronin/Sherman). Male Honeyguide
has red eyes and yellow shoulder patches (often obscured). **Call:** 'Male gives harsh, cat-like
cry followed by a churring **miaow-krrruuu**. The second syllable is a reviving rattle that rises
in pitch like a toy aeroplane' (McKinnon). **Sabah:** Poring, Danum, Sepilok, Crocker Range.
Brunei: Kuala Belalong, Tasek Merimbum, Jerudong, Badas. **Sarawak:** Mulu, Similajau,
Bako, Semengoh – seven individuals mist-netted in one year (Fogden). **Kalimantan:** K
Mentarang, Sungai Wain, Barito Ulu, Danau Sentarum. **Range:** Malay P, Sumatra, Borneo.

1

2 ♀ ♂

3 ♂

♀ imm

Koompassia excelsa
on the road to Tabin
December 2004
with Giant Honey Bee
nests hanging from
the branches.

4 ♂

♀

5 ♂

imm

Sarawak/
Kalimantan

C. f. fuliginosus

Sabah/Brunei

C. f. tertius

WOODPECKERS

PICIDAE **World 210 species; SE Asia 42 species; Borneo 18 species.** Woodpeckers are noisy colourful bird with distinctive harsh *kek kek kek* calls and shrill *ki ki ki* trills. When breeding, woodpeckers advertise by 'drumming' their heavy bill on a hollow branch like a pneumatic drill. The powerful bill is also used to excavate nest holes in tree trunks. All woodpeckers have a distinctive straight but dipping flight. The larger woodpeckers have a habit of flying down to the base of a tree and hopping up the trunk before flying to the base of the next tree. For this they prefer either tree plantations or the interior of tall primary forest unimpeded by the thick vegetation that occurs in logged forest. Many forest woodpeckers commonly join other birds in mixed insect-hunting flocks when their loud calls act as a rallying cry. See page 270. Different woodpecker species avoid competition by foraging on different surfaces and at different levels (Meijaard). Most woodpeckers are surface gleaners of ants that trail up and down tree trunks, but the White-bellied and Orange-backed are specialist feeders on beetle larvae in dead wood and the Maroon and Crimson-winged Woodpeckers hammer on branches to expose termites and ants to peck (Lammertink).

1   COMMON FLAMEBACK   *Dinopium javanense*   30cm   **Local resident**

[Common Goldenback] Locally common in coastal forests especially mangroves throughout Borneo. Occasionally found inland, e.g. at Danum. Often nests in dead coconut palms like Banded. Could only be confused with Greater Goldenback which occurs in similar habitat in SE Borneo only. Distinguished by head pattern. **Call:** A trill, softer and less staccato than other woodpeckers (Sheldon). **Range:** India to Malay P, Sumatra, Borneo, Philippines.

2   OLIVE-BACKED WOODPECKER   *Dinopium rafflesii*   25cm   **Scarce resident**

Widespread in primary and secondary forest throughout the lowlands and mountains but very scarce. One of the least common of the Bornean woodpeckers, but one of the commonest woodpeckers in the Kelabit Highlands. Like other woodpeckers, feeds mainly on ants and often joins mixed species feeding flocks. **Call:** Loud single *chak* calls and a fast staccato laugh lasting two to four seconds (Short). **Range:** Malay P, Sumatra, Borneo.

3   MAROON WOODPECKER   *Blythipicus rubiginosus*   23cm   **Common resident**

Found in primary and logged forest throughout Borneo from the lowlands to the mountains. Usually forages low down in the forest undergrowth investigating fallen logs. Often joins mixed species insect-hunting parties. **Call:** Very noisy and calls constantly. A constant harsh *tsik, tsik, tsik* contact call as it forages. A loud ringing *keeah* repeated – an omen call of the Dayaks. See page 234. A machine-gun like chatter when it flies (Sheldon). **Range:** Malay P, Sumatra, Borneo.

4   RUFOUS WOODPECKER   *Celeus brachyurus*   21cm   **Common resident**

Common in primary and secondary forest and cultivated areas. Feeds mainly on ants and usually bores its nest hole in occupied carton ants (*Crematogaster*) nests as with Brown Barbet. Also recorded feeding on nectar, figs and banana stem sap. Often seen in family groups. Feeds actively from the ground up to the canopy of tall trees. **Call:** Three to five typical woodpecker shrieks, all on the same pitch *kee-kee-kee-kee-kiu-kiu* (Batchelor). **Range:** India to Malay P, Sumatra, Borneo, Java.

5   WHITE-BELLIED WOODPECKER   *Dryocopus javensis*   42cm   **Local resident**

[Great Black Woodpecker] Locally common in primary and occasionally in secondary forest throughout the Borneo lowlands and hills.Usually in family parties, which call to each other constantly as they move through the forest. **Call:** Very noisy. Typically a loud *keow* or *keow keow keow*. Often seen flying great distances high up and thus seems to have substantial dispersal ability (Sheldon). **Range:** Resident Japan S to Malay P, Sumatra, Borneo, Philippines.

THE IMPORTANCE OF UNLOGGED AREAS IN LOGGED FORESTS   At Danum in a comparative study of logged and unlogged forest Lammertink found that Great Slaty populations declined by 85% and Checker-throated by 83% after logging. As the Great Slaty Woodpecker is strictly a lowland forest bird, there is no 'reserve' population in mountain forests which could re-populate logged lowland forest, once it has regenerated back. This research emphasises the importance of maintaining unlogged lowland reserves such as Danum to preserve a representative cross-section of the bird fauna whilst the surrounding forest is logged.

Note
three
toes

WOODPECKERS

1 BANDED WOODPECKER *Picus miniaceus* **23cm** Common resident

The commonest of the mid-sized woodpeckers and like most of them has a very wide altitud range from the coastal forests of Tg Puting and Bako to the mountain forests of Kinabalu Frequently recorded at KNP HQ. Like other mid-sized woodpeckers prefers tall trunk unimpeded by thick vegetation, e.g. virgin primary forest and coconut plantations but no logged forest. Often excavates nests in dead coconut palms. **Call:** Loud woodpecker-like *ke* or series *kee kee kee kee kee*. **Range:** Myanmar, Thailand, Malay P, Sumatra, Borneo.

2 CRIMSON-WINGED WOODPECKER *Picus puniceus* **25cm** Scarce resident

Widespread in primary, logged and secondary forest throughout Borneo from the lowland to the mountains but scarce. Often in mixed feeding flocks. Forages by hammering to expos ants and termites. **Call:** A distinctive two note call unlike other woodpeckers *kee kyu* wit an emphasis on the first note and a series of descending notes *kui kui kui kui kui*. **Range** Myanmar, Thailand, Malay P, Sumatra, Borneo, Java.

3 CHECKER-THROATED WOODPECKER *Picus humii* **27cm** Scarce resident

[*P. mentalis*] Locally common in undisturbed primary forest in lowlands, hills an mountains. Like the other mid-sized woodpeckers. Checker-throated prefers forest with a open understorey and is therefore rarely found in logged forest but is widespread where th forest is undisturbed (Lammertink). Commonest mid-sized woodpecker at KNP HQ. **Call** Has a very quiet, un-woodpecker-like call (Norman). **Range:** Myanmar, to Malay P, Sumatr Borneo, Java.

4 ORANGE-BACKED WOODPECKER *Reinwardtipicus validus* **30cm** Scarce resident

Scarce but locally common inhabitant of all types of forests throughout Borneo from coast forest in the lowlands, e.g. Tg Puting (Kalimantan) to the mountains, e.g. KNP HQ. where has been recorded nesting. Prefers forest with an open understorey. Often in family partie Hammers on dead wood like White-bellied. **Call:** Very vocal with a variety of calls. Typical ca is *kee wheet* or a series *wheet wheet wheet wheet*. **Range:** Malay P, Sumatra, Borneo, Java.

5 GREATER FLAMEBACK *Chrysocolaptes guttacristatus* **31cm** Rare local residen

[*C. lucidus*] [Greater Goldenback] A scarce inhabitant of coastal forest on the E and S coast c Borneo only. Closely associated with mangroves. Known from only three localities. (1) Coasta forest from Sandakan south to Tawau in Sabah. (2) Mahakam River delta. (3) Tg Puting. Ver similar Common Goldenback (See page 206) occurs in the same area. Distinguished by hea pattern and by different eye colour (Noske). **Call:** Varies from loud sharp *kik kik kik* t stuttering staccato *kik ki-ki-ki-ki-ki* (Kennedy re Philippines). **Range:** Borneo, Philippines.

Greater Flameback ♂   Common Flameback ♂

6 GREAT SLATY WOODPECKER *Mulleripicus pulverulentus* **50cm** Scarce residen

World's largest woodpecker. Confined to undisturbed lowland primary forest but sometime wanders into nearby logged forest and plantations. Usually very scarce but common i Brunei. Feeds on ant and termite nests in large trees. A cooperative breeder usually seen i family groups. Up to 11 birds recorded. Female lacks red cheek patch of male. **Call:** It utter a peculiar but quite distinctive whinnying note (Smythies). A loud double call note, also bubbling scream (Sheldon). A loud laughing call *rout-a-rout-a-rout-rout-rout* (Batchelor) **Range:** India to Vietnam south to Malay P, Sumatra, Borneo, Java, Palawan.

1 ♀ ♂

2 ♀ ♂

3 ♀ ♂

4 ♀ ♂

5 ♂

Note
four
toes

♀

6 ♂

WOODPECKERS AND PICULETS

PICUMINAE **World 31 species (mainly S American); Borneo 2 species.** Piculets are tiny members of th[e] woodpecker family with large feet and soft tails which hunt low down in thick tangled vegetation on smal[l] dead twigs and branches.

1 SPECKLED PICULET *Picumnus innominatus* **10cm** **Rare residen[t]**

Scarce but widespread in Sabah only in primary forest. Locations include Tawau Hills, Gomantong, Sepilok, Danum, Tabin and Maliau Basin. Unconfirmed sight records from BS[B] (Brunei), Mulu, Semengoh and Sungai Wain may be mistakes. Often confused with Yellow[-] vented Flowerpecker page 304 and small green *Chrysococcyx* cuckoos page 160 but ha[s] distinctive spotted front. In Malaya most common in submontane forest and joins mixed feedin[g] flocks (Wells). **Call:** A thin sharp *tsik* (Short). **Range:** India to Malay P, Sumatra, Borneo.

2 RUFOUS PICULET *Sasia abnormis* **10cm** **Common residen[t]**

Found in primary and secondary lowland and hill forest but prefers the thick tangle[d] vegetation of disturbed or logged forest where it is very common. One of the forest bird[s] that benefits from logging. A quiet tapping low down from the centre of a thicket of vine[s] and rattans is usually the bird. Female lacks the yellow forehead of the male. **Call:** A lou[d] *tseet* or *tseet tseet* (Sheldon). An Iban omen bird. See page 234. **Range:** Myanmar to Mala[y] P, Sumatra, Borneo, Java.

3 BUFF-RUMPED WOODPECKER *Meiglyptes grammithorax* **15cm** **Common residen[t]**

[*M. tristis*] Inhabits lowland and hill forest including logged forest. Often feeds on ant[s] colonies hosted by hollow stemmed *Macaranga* trees most common in logged forest or fores[t] edge. See page 365.Also targets ants nests in leaf bundles. Usually in family groups, often i[n] mixed feeding flocks. Fast moving and usually high up. **Call:** Typical of the woodpeckers drumming, chittering and churring. **Range:** Malay P, Sumatra, Borneo.

4 BUFF-NECKED WOODPECKER *Meiglyptes tukki* **21cm** **Common residen[t]**

Common in lowland and hill forests feeding on ant and termite nests and investigatin[g] epiphytes in the dense forest understory. Often hunts low down investigating tree stump[s] and fallen logs. Often in family parties and associates with other woodpeckers, drongos fantails and malkohas in mixed feeding flocks. Equally common in logged and unlogged fores[t] (Lammertink). **Call:** Typical drumming and *chittering*. **Range:** Malay P, Sumatra, Borneo.

5 BROWN-CAPPED WOODPECKER *Dendrocopus moluccensis* **13cm** **Local residen[t]**

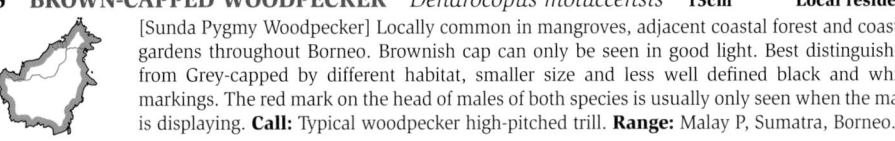

[Sunda Pygmy Woodpecker] Locally common in mangroves, adjacent coastal forest and coasta[l] gardens throughout Borneo. Brownish cap can only be seen in good light. Best distinguishe[d] from Grey-capped by different habitat, smaller size and less well defined black and whit[e] markings. The red mark on the head of males of both species is usually only seen when the mal[e] is displaying. **Call:** Typical woodpecker high-pitched trill. **Range:** Malay P, Sumatra, Borneo.

6 GREY-CAPPED WOODPECKER *Dendrocopus canicapillus* **15cm** **Residen[t]**

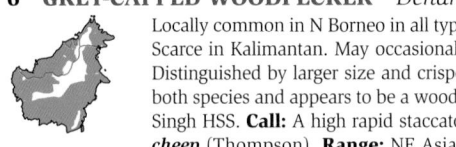

Locally common in N Borneo in all types of inland forest including primary forest and plantations Scarce in Kalimantan. May occasionally overlap with Brown-capped Woodpecker in mangrove[s] Distinguished by larger size and crisper markings. A buff wash on the underparts may occur o[n] both species and appears to be a wood stain. See www.borneobirdimages.com, photos by Amma[r] Singh HSS. **Call:** A high rapid staccato *kik kik*. Also drumming, rattling calls and a softer *chee[p] cheep* (Thompson). **Range:** NE Asia south to India, China, Malay P, Sumatra, Borneo.

7 GREY-AND-BUFF WOODPECKER *Hemicircus concretus* **14cm** **Local residen[t]**

Locally common in lowland and hilly primary and secondary forest and plantation[s] throughout Borneo. Occasionally found in forest gardens. A tiny, highly active woodpecker The male has a bright orange crest that glows in the sunlight. Usually in pairs gleaning insect[s] from leaves as well as tree trunks and branches. At dusk roosts in groups of multiple shallow cavities drilled towards the top of tall dead trees (Lammertink 2011), presumably a strateg[y] to defeat nocturnal predatory snakes. **Call:** Typical woodpecker trills and *kik kik kik* contac[t] calls. **Range:** Malay P, Sumatra, Borneo, Java.

'Small but dangerous!' is the message given by the red, white and black aposematic (danger) markings decorating these small woodpeckers. As anyone who has untangled one of these woodpeckers from a mist net knows, it is a message that should be taken seriously. See page 81.

BROADBILLS

EURYLAIMIDAE   **World 15 species; Borneo is a hot-spot with 8 species, including 2 endemics.** The three green *Calyptomena* broadbills (illustrated next page) are almost exclusively fruit eaters. The remaining five broadbills (illustrated opposite) are primarily insect-eaters with varied habits. Borneo hosts many of the world's largest insects including giant leaf eating stick insects. The insectivorous broadbills use their wide beaks to grip, break up and swallow their giant prey. Sexes are similar. All broadbills build round pendulous nests usually overhanging a ravine or gully, easily mistaken for a dangling epiphyte and difficult for a predator to access. Dusky and Long-tailed Broadbills are co-operative breeders and are nearly always seen in groups. The remaining three insectivorous broadbills are believed to be pair breeders, with both sexes co-operating in nest building. They are only occasionally seen in groups. Broadbill calls are worth learning. The Black-and-Yellow and the closely related Banded Broadbill have very distinctive and unusual calls which are a characteristic sound of the Bornean forest. All the broadbills species need primary forest to survive, for example, there are no broadbills left in Singapore.

1   DUSKY BROADBILL   *Corydon sumatranus*   **27cm**   Scarce resident

The least common of the insect-eating lowland broadbills. Found in primary forest of the lowlands and hills where it hunts in family groups for large insects and lizards in the top of the tree canopy. Often crepuscular (Bruce in del Hoyo). Look for distinctive large pink bill and pink skin round eye. Has conspicuous white spots on tail and white wing bar in flight. Orange streak on back is often concealed. **Sabah:** Poring, Kinabatangan, Tabin, Danum. **Brunei:** Extremely uncommon (Mann) but widespread including records from Kuala Belalong. **Sarawak:** Mulu, Similajau, Semengoh. **Kalimantan:** Kayan Mentarang, Kutai, Gng Palung. **Call:** A series of six to eight screaming notes, rising up the scale *hi-ky-ui   ky-ui   ky-ui* (Lambert). **Range:** Vietnam to Malay P, Sumatra, Borneo.

2   BLACK-AND-RED BROADBILL   *Cymbirhynchus macrorhynchos*   **23cm**   Common resident

Often seen in pairs along forested river banks from the coast to the interior. The nest is suspended from a branch over the water with the appearance of detritus trapped by a dangling liana in a flood. Sometimes flies down to pick up food such as freshwater crabs or fish from the water's edge. **Call:** Not very vocal. 'The typical call is a monotonous *tyook, tyook, tyook, tyook*' (Batchelor). 'Monotonous rasping *wiark wiark* and rising trill, softer and briefer than Black-and-Yellow Broadbill' (McKinnon). **Range:** Myanmar, Thailand, Malay P, Sumatra, Borneo.

3   BANDED BROADBILL   *Eurylaimus javanicus*   **21cm**   Common resident

Much larger and less common than the Black and Yellow Broadbill, but with similar habits, a similar call and a similar distribution in forest areas throughout Borneo. Distinguished by lack of a white collar. Male has distinctive ruff on chest. **Call:** 'A buzzing trill similar to the call of the Black-and-Yellow Broadbill but starts with an introductory whistled *wheoo*, accelerates more rapidly and cuts off more abruptly' (Lambert). **Range:** Malay P, Sumatra, Borneo, Java.

4   BLACK-AND-YELLOW BROADBILL   *Eurylaimus ochromalus*   **15cm**   Common resident

Commonest broadbill, found in all types of forest from lowland to hills throughout Borneo. Hunts for insects in small parties in the middle canopy of the forest. A loose flock of 10 to 15 birds seen, in which they bowed their heads sharply whilst calling (Thompson). Often joins mixed species hunting parties. Distinctive bright plumage includes yellow eye ring and white collar. **Call:** Very distinctive accelerating buzzing trill heard throughout the day. Once learnt never forgotten. **Range:** Myanmar, Thailand, Malay P, Sumatra, Borneo.

5   LONG-TAILED BROADBILL   *Psarisomus dalhousiae*   **25cm**   Local submontane resident

Inhabits submontane forest from Kinabalu south along the central mountains of Borneo where it is locally common. Usually seen in active, small parties hunting for insects. Look for very distinctive head pattern. Male has yellow spot on nape (Lean Y.L.). In flight has prominent white panel on underside of wings. **Call:** 'Each call is a series of five to eight sharp whistles *piu piu piu piu* all on the same pitch and falling in tone' (Davison). **Sabah:** Seen regularly in the Crocker Range. **Brunei:** No records. **Sarawak:** Mulu, Kelabit Highlands. **Kalimantan:** Recorded from 1,700m on Gng Lunjut, Kayan Mentarang (van Balen.) **Range:** From the Himalayas to mountains of Malay P, Sumatra, Borneo.

Phobaeticus chani
"Chan's megastick"
(56 cm)

GREEN BROADBILLS

The three green *Calyptomena* broadbills specialise in eating large fruits, particularly figs which they can swallow whole with their wide gape. Usually seen singly, they gather to feed in fruiting fig trees. Like most frugivorous birds it is probable that they feed their young largely on insects. Sexes differ, female plumage is duller with fewer black markings. Male Green and Whitehead's Broadbill have been seen to perform show off acrobatics including flights in the presence of females. Only females have been recorded building nests and incubating eggs (Lambert) which is further evidence of male polygyny or promiscuity. Many frugivorous forest birds wander widely in search of food and the broadbills are no exception. For example, all three *Calyptomena* broadbills have been recorded from around the hot-spring clearing at Poring in the hills at the base of Kinabalu. However, only the Green Broadbill is a full time resident. See Zonation Plate page 32 for normal altitudinal distribution on Bornean mountains.

1   GREEN BROADBILL   *Calyptomena viridis*   **18cm**   **Common resident**

[Malay: Burung seluwit] Commonest of the all green broadbills. Found in lowland primary forest throughout Borneo (0–1,300m). Like all broadbills the population declines in logged forest. **Call:** A soft bubbling trill that increases in tempo and has an upward inflection, *toi toi oi oi oi oick* (Lambert). Also a contact call, a froglike bubbling rattle *oo-turr* (King). **Range:** Myanmar, to Malay P, Sumatra, Borneo.

2   HOSE'S BROADBILL   *Calyptomena hosei*   **20cm**   **Scarce submontane endemic**

The rarest and least known broadbill. Found throughout the hills and lower slopes of mountains from Kinabalu (Poring) to NE Kalimantan (0–1,680m). Generally scarce but locally common in the mountains of north and central Sarawak. **Sabah:** Poring, Maliau Basin. **Brunei:** No records. **Sarawak:** Mulu, Kelabit Highlands, Usun Apau Plateau and Lanjak Entimau. **Kalimantan:** Kayan Mentarang, Gng Liang Kubong. **Call:** Soft dove-like cooing with neck bobbing (Harrisson).

3   WHITEHEAD'S BROADBILL   *Calyptomena whiteheadi*   **25cm**   **Montane endemic**

Found in pristine montane forest throughout Borneo, occasionally wandering lower to surrounding hills when fruit is scarce in the mountains (600–1,850m). Has been seen feeding (rarely) on moths around lights at KNP HQ and occasionally joins in mixed insect-hunting parties common in mountain forest. **Call:** Males in particular are very vocal, including a loud screeching *eek eek eek*, harsh woodpecker-like rattles and a series of *wark wark wark* calls.

ALTITUDINAL MIGRATION OF FRUIT-EATING BIRDS ON KINABALU
A one year study (Kimura *et al.*) found that berry-bearing, bird-dispersed plants fruited throughout the year at higher levels (Summit Trail 1,863–3,300m) on Kinabalu but lower down, at Park HQ (1,560m) and Poring (600m), fruiting was seasonal. Kimura hypothesised that the continuous (non seasonal) fruiting in higher montane forests acts as a refuge for lowland frugivores during lean seasons at lower altitudes. Most Bornean fruit eating birds are notably nomadic in habit. Most bird-dispersed plants (such as figs) benefit from fruiting aseasonally and asynchronously so that they maximise their chances of getting eaten and thereby dispersed. Inevitably this chaotic timing of fruiting leads to local fruit scarcity, forcing frugivorous birds to wander widely, to the benefit of the fruiting plants. (See also *Fig Tree Fruiting in Borneo,* page 200.)
On Kinabalu, altitudinal migration of frugivores is two way. Birds normally seen around Park HQ, (Whitehead's Broadbill) are seen irregularly at Poring and vice versa. For example lowland bulbuls (Black-headed) are seen occasionally at Park HQ. During severe droughts higher montane birds such as Island Thrush and Black-eye are often seen around Park HQ. Likewise birds normally seen round Park HQ such as pigeons, doves and bulbuls are irregularly seen feeding higher up Kinabalu on seasonal berries. Kimura's hypothesis is almost certainly correct. See also *Zonation of Birds on Borneo Mountains* page 32 and pages 148 and 278.

JOHN WHITEHEAD 1860–1899   One European bird (Corsican Nuthatch, *Sitta whiteheadi*) and many rare Bornean and Philippine birds are named in honour of John Whitehead who grew up in London but spent most of his adult life collecting birds in remote parts of Asia. Most famous are the three endemics that make up Whitehead's Trio: Whitehead's Broadbill, Trogon and Spiderhunter. Whitehead's magnificent book *The Exploration of Mount Kina-Balu* (1893) describes his struggles. John Whitehead died of malaria on Hainan Island (South China Sea) at age 38, still searching for rare birds.

RESIDENT PITTAS

PITTIDAE   **World 31 species; Borneo 10 species including 4 endemics, 2 international migrants, 1 local migrant and 1 status unknown.**   Borneo is the world focus of pitta distribution and a magnet for pitta lovers. Pittas are elusive rainbow-coloured short-tailed ground-thrushes of the primary forest floor. They build globular nests of leaves low down in thick undergrowth. Pittas feed in damp forest gullies on worms and snails found by flicking over the leaf litter. They often hop away from danger rather than flying. Pittas are notoriously shy and best located by their whistle calls, most common at dawn and dusk in the breeding season December to June. Breeding birds are strongly territorial and respond well to call playback. Pittas roost alone at night on a thin twig 1–2m off the ground and can be picked out by torchlight on night walks. Note that all four migrant/ nomadic pittas illustrated on next page have white wing patches which are variable in both shape and size and which are not distinctive between species.

1   GIANT PITTA   *Pitta caerulea*   28cm   Rare resident

The largest, shyest and rarest of the Bornean pittas. Inhabits lowland and hill primary forest. Very fond of snails which it breaks open by smashing on a stone anvil. **Call:** Easy to imitate long mournful whistle with a slight downward inflection at the end. At Danum, Lambert reported calling Oct.–March at dawn and dusk. **Sabah:** Sepilok, Danum. **Sarawak:** Mulu, Pulong Tau, **Brunei:** Ulu Temburong. **Kalimantan:** Gng Palung, Gng Lumut (Wielstra/ Pieterse). **Range:** Malay P, Sumatra, Borneo.

2   BLUE-BANDED PITTA   *Pitta arquata*   17cm   Rare endemic

A rare and elusive inhabitant of submontane and hill forest slopes with a supposed preference for bamboo groves characteristic of disturbed forest. **Call:** A soft mournful whistle confusingly similar to the calls of Garnet Pitta and Rail Babbler but longer, flatter and slightly higher pitched. **Sabah:** Poring, Crocker Range, Danum, Tawau Hills. **Brunei:** Ulu Temburong. **Sarawak:** Mulu, Pulong Tau, Lambir Hills, Gng Penrissen. **Kalimantan:** Gng Palung, Barito Ulu, Kayan Mentarang, Gng Lumut.

3   GARNET PITTA   *Pitta granatina*   15cm   Local resident

A locally common inhabitant of lowland primary and logged forest from the Sabah border southwards. **Call:** A prolonged whistle rising in power with a sudden cut off. This call is similar to, and has been confused with, the calls of Blue-banded Pitta and Rail Babbler. **Brunei:** Ulu Temburong, **Sarawak:** Mulu, **Kalimantan:** Tg Puting. **Range:** Malay P, Sumatra, S Borneo.

4   BLACK-CROWNED PITTA   *Pitta ussheri*   15cm   Local endemic

[Davison: Black and Crimson Pitta] A locally common inhabitant of lowland primary and logged forest in Sabah only. Recently 'split' (Lambert, 1996) from Garnet Pitta which replaces it in lowland primary forest in the rest of Borneo. These two pittas are believed to be strictly lowland birds replaced on slopes and in submontane localities by the much rarer Blue-banded Pitta. Both Black-headed and Blue-banded are present at Danum but with different habitat preferences (Lambert). **Call:** Similar to Garnet Pitta but slightly more prolonged. **Sabah:** Danum, Tabin, Sepilok.

5   BORNEAN BANDED PITTA   *Pitta schwaneri*   22cm   Scarce endemic

A scarce endemic resident of forested slopes and hills where it is locally common. Rarely recorded in the lowlands apart from limestone hills e.g. Gomantong, Kinabatangan and Mulu Caves where snails are abundant. **Call:** A regular repeated *pow pow, pow* also *whrr whrr whrr.* **Sabah:** Poring, Danum, Kinabatangan, Gomantong. **Brunei:** Bukit Teraja, Bukit Belalong (Mann). **Sarawak:** Mulu, Kelabit Highlands, **Kalimantan:** K Mentarang, Muratus Mts. **Taxonomy:** Split by Rheindt and Eaton 2010 from Javan and Malayan forms.

6   BLUE-HEADED PITTA   *Pitta baudii*   17cm   Local endemic

A locally common inhabitant of lowland primary and logged forest. **Call:** A soft descending tri- syllabic whistle. The female alarm note is a nasal drawn out *hwee ouu.* Most calling is heard Feb.–March at Danum (Lambert). **Sabah:** Danum, Gomantong, Kinabatangan, Maliau, Tabin, Tawau Hills. **Brunei:** Sungai Tutong, Kuala Belalong (Mann). **Sarawak:** Mulu, Samunsam. **Kalimantan:** Kutai, K Mentarang, Sungai Wain, Tg Puting, Gng Palung. **BLI:** Vulnerable.

MIGRANT AND NOMADIC PITTAS

1 FAIRY PITTA *Pitta nympha* 20cm — Rare winter visitor

A rare winter visitor recorded from Oct. to March in forested areas. Only nine museum specimens known for Borneo. Two recent photographs (www.borneobirdimages.com) and recent sightings from Danum (Sabah) and Kubah (Sarawak) indicate that this Pitta is a scarce but regular visitor to west and central Borneo. Very similar to Blue-Winged Pitta but with a clear white stripe just above the eye. **Call:** Clear *kwah-he kwa-wu* (Lambert), *phureu werp weurgh* (Gooddie). **Range:** Small numbers breed in Japan, Korea and mainland China with a stronghold in Taiwan. In winter migrates south to Vietnam and Borneo. The Borneo specimens probably originated in S China (Erritzoe). **BLI:** Vulnerable.

THE BIRDS OF TAIWAN Taiwan is the world stronghold for the Fairy Pitta with an estimated 1,750 pairs breeding in the forested central mountains. In Mandarin Chinese the Fairy Pitta is called *ba-se-niao* or eight colours bird. Fairy Pittas leave Taiwan in Oct. for their wintering grounds in Borneo returning in May to start nesting. The migration path remains a mystery as there are no records of Fairy Pitta from the Philippines. However, many N Asian birds do passage through Taiwan en route to Borneo including Japanese Sparrowhawk, Chinese Goshawk, Honey Buzzard, Grey-faced Buzzard and Brown Shrike. See maps page 36 and 100. Fortunately there are many active conservationist bird groups in Taiwan under the umbrella of the Chinese Wild Bird Association (previously- Wild Bird Federation Taiwan) www.bird.org.tw

---

2 BLUE-WINGED PITTA *Pitta moluccensis* 18cm — Common migrant

Regular migrant to NW coastal Borneo from Oct. onwards when it can be found in gardens scrub and frequently in mangroves. Later moves inland. In Oct. often crashes into lighted windows at night. A few June to August records indicate possible local breeding. **Call:** A repeated double whistle *yeeow yeeow yeeow yeeow*. **Sabah:** STAR, Nexus (See page 324) and also as a night-flying migrant in the Crocker Range. **Brunei:** Panaga. **Sarawak:** Many coastal records. **Kalimantan:** Kayan Mentarang. **Range:** Breeds S China south to Thailand, migrates across the S China Sea to Borneo during Asian dry season. Only two records from the S Philippines.

3 MANGROVE PITTA *Pitta megarhyncha* 20cm — Vagrant

One Borneo record only from the Baram River in Sarawak, possibly a post-breeding disperser from the east coast of Malaya. Similar to Blue-winged Pitta, but head is generally darker brown. Distinguished by very large heavy bill used to feed on molluscs and crabs on mangrove mudflats. **Call:** Similar to Blue-winged Pitta. **Range:** Mangrove forests from Myanmar to the Malay Peninsula. Does not normally migrate but young birds may disperse.

4 HOODED PITTA *Pitta sordida muelleri* 18cm — Locally common nomadic resident race

Resident in both primary and secondary forest. Feeds on worms in damp forest. A locally nomadic night-flying migrant. May be common in some areas at times and absent at other times. All 4 migrant pittas have variably sized clear white wing panels, only seen in flight. **Call:** A double or triple repeated *whi whi whi whi whi whi*. Also a repeated *skyew skyew skyew*. **Sabah:** KNP, Sepilok, Danum, P Tiga, Kinabatangan. **Brunei:** Not recorded. **Sarawak:** Niah, Mulu. **Kalimantan:** Danau Sentarum, Sungai Wain.

5 HOODED PITTA *Pitta sordida cucullata* 18cm — Continental race (not recorded)

A migrant race *P. sordida cucullata* breeds in Vietnam and Thailand. In winter it migrates south to Malaya and Sumatra but has not been recorded in Borneo. Has a chocolate-brown instead of all black head. **Range:** India to S China, Thailand, Malay P, Sumatra, Borneo, Java to New Guinea.

A flock of nomadic Hooded Pittas crossing the Crocker Range at night.

IORAS AND LEAFBIRDS

IORAS: *AEGITHINIDAE.* **WORLD:** 4 species. **BORNEO:** 2 species. The two Borneo ioras are similar lookin small yellow green birds which glean insects in the canopy. The sexes differ with the male being bright than the female. Ioras build small cup shaped nests high in the canopy and are frequent unknowing hosts t *Cacomantis* cuckoos.

1 GREEN IORA *Aegithina viridissima* **13 cm** Locally common resider

A locally common resident of forest canopy and forest edge throughout Borneo. Favours ta forest whilst the Common Iora prefers more open areas such as secondary forest and garden At the ecotone and in mangroves the two species often overlap. Often in small parties an joins mixed species insect hunting flocks. **Call:** Typically a steady *tzee tzee tzee tzee*, or *wit.-dit-dit* with the first note slurred upwards (Sheldon). **Range:** Malay P, Sumatra, Borne

2 COMMON IORA *Aegithina tiphia* **14 cm** Common resider

A common inhabitant of islands, coastal and secondary forest and gardens throughout Borne When breeding the head of the male Common Iora is dark, changing to bright yellow i eclipse. Long white feathers on the rump are obvious in display flights. Strictly territoria and usually in pairs never seen in parties **Call:** The male call is a distinct *wheeeeeeee-chu* also described as *whee-ee-ee-ee-ee-ee-ee-ee pyorr-rr-rr* (Wells), a characteristic sound c coastal forests and gardens. **Range:** India to Malay P, Sumatra, Borneo, Java.

LEAFBIRDS: *IRENIDAE.* **WORLD:** 11 species. **BORNEO:** Four species inc. one endemic. All leafbirds hav brush-tipped tongues for nectar feeding but are primarily berry feeders. They swallow small fruits who but spear large fruits with their lower bill to help remove the skin before swallowing. Leafbirds are commo in both primary and tall secondary forest, often in small family parties, and frequently join mixed-specie insect hunting parties. All Borneo species apart from Blue-winged have hook-tipped bills to help captur insects (Wells). All adult males have a prominent blue malar stripe which is subdued in females and absent i juveniles and the female Bornean. Leafbirds are expert songsters and use mimicry of aggressive spiderhunter and drongos to help defend fruit and nectar sources. Male leafbirds are often kept for singing. See page 242.

3 LESSER GREEN LEAFBIRD *Chloropsis cyanopogon* **17 cm** Common resider

A common inhabitant of lowland forest throughout Borneo. Lesser and Greater males can onl be distinguished by size. Females are distinguished by differing throat and eye ring colours Both Greater and Lesser males have small concealed blue patch on wing only revealed i flight. **Call:** Similar to Oriental Magpie Robin but richer (Batchelor). **Range:** Thailand t Sumatra and Borneo.

4 GREATER GREEN LEAFBIRD *Chloropsis sonnerati* **22 cm** Common resider

A common inhabitant of lowland and hill forest throughout Borneo, but less common tha Lesser. Female yellow throat and eye ring distinctive. Due to their diet of small fruits suc as the *Macarangas* which flourish in disturbed forests, leafbirds benefit from logging. **Cal** Song is rich and varied, louder than White-rumped Shama and Magpie Robin but without th continuity (Batchelor). **Range:** Thailand, Malay P, Sumatra, Borneo, Java.

5 BORNEAN LEAFBIRD *Chloropsis kinabaluensis* **17 cm** Endemi

[Mann: Montane Blue-winged Leafbird] Montane endemic found from Kinabalu soutl to Kayan Mentarang. Notably nomadic and often locally abundant following seasona fruiting. The only leafbird where both sexes have a black throat. Female lacks blue mala stripe. Split by Wells 2003. **Call:** A high pitched twittering and a rapidly repeated *chit chit, chit* (Myers).

6 BLUE-WINGED LEAFBIRD *Chloropsis cochinchinensis* **17 cm** Local resider

Locally common in the lowland forests south of the Sabah border. Recent photos from Maliau Basin by Khairul Ikhwan Matnin are the first confirmed Sabah records, See www borneobirdimages.com. Less common than Greater and Lesser. Distinguish by prominen yellow on crown of both sexes. **Call:** Two note contact call is *kwip-kweep*. The male i considered to be the best songster of all the Bornean leafbirds. See page 242. **Range:** India t Malay P, Sumatra, Borneo, Java.

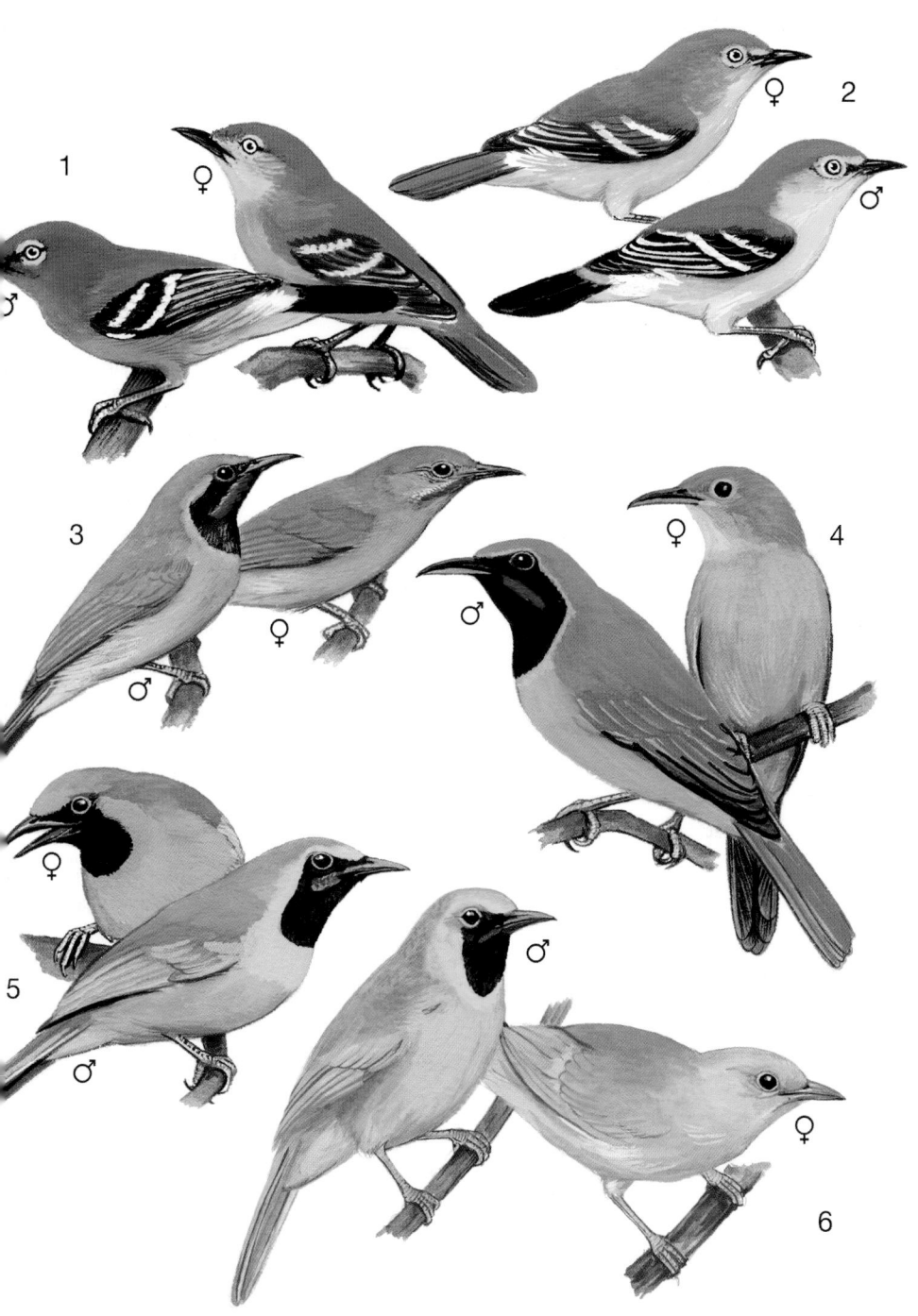

MINIVETS

CAMPEPHAGIDAE **World 12 species; Borneo 5 species, 1 migrant, 3 residents and 1 statu unknown.** The Malay name meaning 'eye of the day' or 'dawn bird' alludes both to the fiery colours minivets and their propensity to be most active early in the day. These small, brightly coloured members the Cuckoo-Shrike family are most obvious in mountain forests at sunrise. Typically they are seen perched bare twigs in the canopy of forest trees in pairs or small family groups following each other one by one they flutter from the top of one tree to another in bouncing flight. Calls are twitterings distinctive to minive but not distinctive enough to distinguish different species. As minivets are so similar in looks but general prefer different habitats, habitat is a good guide to species identification. Minivets build small cup-shaped nes concealed in foliage high in the canopy. They are believed to feed almost exclusively on insects gleaned fro the top layer of the canopy. Minivets have been reported flocking to fruiting fig trees to feed on the insec attracted by the fruit, not the fruit itself. Sexes have a distinctively different plumage with the red of the ma being replaced by orange or yellow in the female. Immatures usually resemble females.

1 GREY-CHINNED MINIVET *Pericrocotus solaris* **17cm** Common montane reside

[Mountain Minivet] Common in the forest of the Bornean mountains but scarce or absent fro S Sarawak and Kalimantan. Frequently seen in the forest around KNP HQ and at Mesilau. Th only other minivet with which it might be confused is the Scarlet Minivet as ranges overla from around 650m to around 1,200m on forested mountains. However, female Grey-chinne has no yellow on the side of the face and both male and female Scarlet Minivet have a sma secondary, brightly coloured wing patch compared with the single wing patch of the Gre chinned. **Range:** Himalayas to Malay P, Sumatra, Borneo.

2 FIERY MINIVET *Pericrocotus igneus* **15cm** Local reside

A locally common resident of open lowland forest in N Borneo, coastal Casuarina forest particular and swamp woodland in Kalimantan. In many areas such as at Danum, Sepilok an Tg Puting it overlaps with Scarlet Minivet. However, Fiery is smaller and female Fiery h an orange-yellow rump compared with the green rump of the Scarlet. (See below re. wi pattern) Typical localities; **Sabah:** Klias, P Tiga, Nexus. **Brunei:** Seria, Badas. **Sarawa** Similajau, Bako. **Kalimantan:** Sungai Wain, Gng Palung, Kendawangan. **Range:** Malay Sumatra, Borneo, Palawan.

3 SCARLET MINIVET *Pericrocotus flammeus* **19cm** Common lowland reside

A common resident of lowland primary and secondary forest not typically found along th coast where Fiery Minivet is most common. Distinguished from all other similar Bornea minivets by having a second, smaller, coloured wing panel in addition to the main pane Whitehead recorded that they overlapped with Grey-chinned Minivet at Melangkap on th western slopes of Kinabalu, and could sometimes be found in mixed flocks at that leve **Range:** India to S China, Thailand, Malay P, Sumatra, Borneo, Java, Philippines.

4 SMALL MINIVET *Pericrocotus cinnamomeus* **15cm** Status unknow

The Small Minivet is a common inhabitant of India, Thailand and Java, where it prefers coast or dry open countryside. There is only one record for Borneo, an individual collected in Kalimantan. This bird could be a vagrant from Java, or evidence of a small, undiscovered reli population in S Borneo left over from the last ice age (10,000 years ago) when Borneo w joined to Java by dry land. See pages 154 and 320. **Range:** India to Vietnam, Thailand, Mala P, Sumatra, Borneo, Java. **Taxonomy:** According to Mann (2008) the single specimen close resembles the Indochinese race *P.c. sarcedas* which is not found in Java and may be an error.

5 ASHY MINIVET *Pericrocotus divaricatus* **20cm** Scarce migra

A scarce migrant from Asia, most common in NW Borneo and typically preferring coast Casuarinas or similar open forests for its winter sojourn. The most likely origin of the Bornea Ashy Minivets is Japan where they breed in broadleaved forests in Honshu and Kyushu fro mid-April to September and have been seen in flocks of up to 100 on migration. **Call:** distinctive high trilling *hir r r r* usually from a high perch and in flight' (Yamashina). **Rang** Breeds Japan to China, wintering south to Malay P, Sumatra, Borneo, Philippines.

CAMPEPHAGIDAE World 86 species; Borneo 6 species. Cuckoo-shrike plumages standardise on greys blacks and whites. Females are duller or paler than the males. Feed almost exclusively on insects. The Cuckoo shrikes were previously known as Caterpillar Shrikes for their habit of gleaning foliage for caterpillars.

1 LARGE WOOD SHRIKE *Tephrodornis gularis* **18cm** Scarce resident

[*Tephrodornis virgatus*] Now considered by taxonomists to be a Monarch. See page 300 Scarce resident of lowland and hills in primary, secondary and plantation forests. Hawks for insects from an exposed canopy perch. Often in small parties and joins mixed species hunting flocks. Note heavy bill, black eye stripe and no white on tail. **Call:** A variety of harsh contact calls. **Range:** India to S China, Thailand, Malay P, Sumatra, Borneo, Java.

2 BLACK-WINGED FLYCATCHER-SHRIKE *Hemipus hirundinaceus* **15cm** Resident

Common resident of all types of lowland forest including secondary growth and coastal forest throughout Borneo. Usually seen in pairs hawking insects from the tree tops. Overlaps with Bar-winged Flycatcher Shrike in the hills. **Call:** A variety of distinct calls. One is a three syllable buzzing ***dee-dit-do***. Another is a high-pitched buzz consisting of three descending notes endlessly repeated (Sheldon). **Range:** Malay P, Sumatra, Java.

3 BAR-WINGED FLYCATCHER-SHRIKE *Hemipus picatus* **15cm** Resident

Inhabits secondary and plantation forest occasionally primary forest from the lowlands to the mountains but commonest in submontane areas. Like the Black-winged Flycatcher Shrike hunts for insects by hawking around a clearing or foraging in small parties through the canopy. Both species build a very small cup-shaped nest on an open branch high up in a tree and are therefore easy targets for parasitic cuckoos. **Call:** A high pitched staccato *sittitititi* (Myers). **Range:** India and Himalayas to Malay P, Sumatra, Borneo.

4 SUNDA CUCKOO-SHRIKE *Coracina larvata* **23cm** Common montane resident

Common inhabitant of montane forest from Kinabalu south to the Muratus Mts. Often in mixed hunting parties. **Call:** A low pitched whistle ***pit-teeoh*** descending on the ***oh***. They also shriek like raptors and make loud squeaking noises (Sheldon). **Range:** Sumatra, Java Borneo. [Very similar, but paler Black-faced Cuckoo-shrike *C. novaehollandiae* migrates from Australia north to Indonesia (April–Sept). Could occur in SE Kalimantan.]

5 BAR-BELLIED CUCKOO-SHRIKE *Coracina striata* **28cm** Scarce resident

Scarce but widespread resident of lowland forests especially peatswamp forest, in small noisy flocks keeping to the top of the canopy, and flying high up. Occasionally found in the hills, e.g Danum. **Call:** Sharp whistles and calls when flocking (Sheldon). A loud ***cree-ack*** (Batchelor) **Sabah:** Klias, Kinabatangan, Tabin. **Brunei:** Wasan, Ulu Temburong. **Sarawak:** Bako Semengoh. **Kalimantan:** Kutai, Tg Puting. **Range:** Malay P, Sumatra, Borneo, Philippines.

6 LESSER CUCKOO-SHRIKE *Coracina fimbriata* **20cm** Common resident

Widespread throughout Borneo from the lowlands to the hills in all types of forest and locally common. Usually seen hunting for caterpillars in the canopy. Also recorded eating small quantities of fruit. Female is heavily barred on the front and rump. Undertail of both sexes marked with black and white bars. **Call:** A fairly rapid ***sweet-sweet-sweet-sweet*** all on the same pitch (Sheldon). **Range:** Myanmar, Thailand, Malay P, Sumatra, Borneo, Java.

7 PIED TRILLER *Lalage nigra* **16cm** Common resident

A common resident of small islands, coastal and secondary forest, parks and gardens throughout Borneo. Often seen foraging for insects on golf courses and in coastal Casuarina and in mangroves. Roosts communally in post-breeding flocks. The nests are often parasitised by *Cacomantis* and *Chrysococcyx* cuckoos. **Call:** A variety of calls including a distinctive double syllable ***chwee whuk*** also described as a 'frog like double croak' (Ong). **Range:** Malay P, Sumatra, Borneo, Java, Philippines.

WHISTLERS, GREAT TIT AND NUTHATCH

WHISTLERS: PACHCEPHALIDAE   World 51 species; Borneo 3 species, 1 endemic.   The whistlers originate in Australia, and Borneo is towards the western end of their range. Whistlers are sedentary birds of the forest understorey which behave both like babblers and flycatchers, sometimes gleaning foliage for caterpillars, at other times sallying for mosquitoes. In Borneo males and females are similar. The nest is cup-shaped hidden in foliage. The young are plain not spotted. Whistlers are named for their very varied whistled calls.

1   BORNEAN WHISTLER *Pachycephala hypoxantha*   16cm   Local montane endemic

Inhabits the Borneo mountains where it is locally common, gleaning for insects in the middle to upper canopy often in mixed species flocks. Legs vary from pink to grey (Jason Anderson). **Call:** Song is a series of easily whistled notes ***dee-dee-dee-dee-dit*** with the last note higher. Also variations thereof with some notes higher, others lower (Sheldon). Common at KNP HQ and up to Paka Cave (3,100) on the Summit Trail. Also found high up on Mulu and Gng Murud. Occurs south to Gng Niut and Gng Pueh in SW Sarawak.

2   WHITE-VENTED WHISTLER *Pachycephala homeyeri*   14cm   Local resident

[Whitehead's Thick-head] A common Philippine resident found on a few islands off the E coast of Sabah including Si-Amil and Pandanan islands off Semporna and at Sipadan SE Sabah where there were between 50 and 100 individuals in the remnant 3ha forest in 1985. A bird of the understorey, tame and easily approached. **Call:** A loud whistled song of short phrases repeated. Contact call is a distinctive soft whistle (Francis/Andau). **Range:** Borneo, Philippines.

3   MANGROVE WHISTLER *Pachycephala grisola*   14cm   Common resident

A common inhabitant of coastal forest and offshore islands where it fills the ecological niche normally occupied by babblers and flycatchers (Sheldon). **Call:** Several loud, easily copied whistles, e.g. ***oo-oo-oo-oo chew-it***, the last note of which is slurred up to a higher pitch (Sheldon). Common on P Gaya, P Manukan (Sabah), Bako, Similajau (Sarawak). The commonest bird in forest on P, Maratua. Common in peat swamp forest at Sabangau and dipterocarp forest further inland (Dragiewicz). **Range:** Bangladesh to Malay P, Sumatra, Borneo, Java, Palawan.

TITS: PARIDAE   World 53 species; Borneo 1 species.   The tits are familiar birds in the gardens of Europe across N Asia to Japan. Also common in N America where they are known as chickadees. In Borneo only one species, obviously a relic of colder periods during the Pleistocene, see page 22. They hunt for insects amongst leaves and in crevices on the trunks and branches of trees. Originally most tits nested in old woodpecker holes but in Europe and N America they often occupy man-made nest boxes.

4   GREAT TIT *Parus major*   13cm   Rare resident

[Myers: Grey Tit *Parus cinereus*] Common in the forests of Europe to Japan but in Borneo a rare to locally common resident of mangroves occasionally found in adjacent coastal or riverine forest. The race found in Borneo is greyer and plainer than birds seen in Europe. **Sabah:** Kuala Penyu (Klias), Kuala Kinabatangan. **Brunei:** No records (Mann). **Sarawak:** Lawas, Buntal, Santubong. **Kalimantan:** Banjarmasin (locally common), Kuala Kapuas. **Call:** Typical call ***chee chee***. **Range:** Europe to Japan south to Malay P, Sumatra, Borneo, Java and the Lesser Sunda Islands.

NUTHATCHES: SITTIDAE   World 24 species; Borneo 1 species.   The curious nuthatch has probably one of the widest altitudinal distributions of any forest bird in Borneo, similar only to the Erpornis and Gerygone. All these birds are found in forest from wooded coastal islands to high up in the mountain forests of Kinabalu.

5   VELVET-FRONTED NUTHATCH *Sitta frontalis*   12cm   Locally common resident

Occurs throughout the coastal and primary forests of Borneo. Generally scarce and probably most common in the hills and mountains, e.g. at KNP HQ. Distinctive red beak and legs. The female lacks the black eyebrows of the male. Juvenile has black bill. Searches trunks and bark for insects, often upside down. Nests in old woodpecker or barbet holes. **Call:** A loud disyllabic ***click chwit*** note followed by an insistent ***chit, chit, chit, chit*** repeated (Wells re Malay P). **Range:** Himalayas to Malay P, Sumatra, Borneo, Java, Palawan.

SHRIKES

LANIIDAE **World 72 species; Borneo 4 species, 1 resident**. Shrikes are small predators with characteristic plumages, posture and habits. They are usually seen perched upright on roadside telephone wires or bare branches overlooking a field from where they fly down to snatch a large insect, lizard or small mammal from the grass. They fly low over the ground swooping upwards to their next perch. Shrikes build small cup-shaped nests often in the centre of a thorny bush. Sexes are similar but juveniles are heavily barred, which is seen more faintly in first year birds.

1 LONG-TAILED SHRIKE *Lanius schach schach* 25cm   Scarce migrant race from Asia

L. s. schach is an uncommon winter visitor to the north west coastal districts of Borneo. All races of the Long-tailed Shrike have distinctive white wing panels seen in flight. A very dark morph occurs elsewhere. **Call:** All shrikes have a distinctive harsh rattling chatter when alarmed which often discloses their presence in dense vegetation. **Range:** Breeds S China to Vietnam, some winter south.

2 LONG-TAILED SHRIKE *Lanius schach nasutus* 25cm   Vagrant race from the Philippines

L. s. nasutus is the race of Long-tailed Shrike that is a common resident of, and confined to the Philippines. There are two records from Sandakan, most likely vagrants from the Philippines but possibly escapes.

3 LONG-TAILED SHRIKE *Lanius schach bentet* 25cm   Local resident race in Kalimantan

Locally very common in parts of S Kalimantan where it is seen along roadsides in cultivated areas. Recent records indicate range expansion to cultivated areas of W. Kalimantan, and E. Sabah. This race has a variable amount of black on the forehead, sometimes claimed to be distinctive from Malayan and Javan forms which are also very variable. **Call:** Males have a very attractive soft warbling song usually incorporating passages mimicking the songs of other birds, and for this reason they have been frequently trapped and entered into singing contests in Java (Jepson). See page 242. It has been suggested that shrikes use vocal mimicry to attract and kill small song birds, Harris and Franklin (2000). **Range:** Malay P, Sumatra, Borneo, Java, Bali, Lesser Sundas.

4 BROWN SHRIKE *Lanius cristatus lucionensis* 20cm   Scarce winter visitor race

This race of the Brown Shrike with a grey head and back is said to be commonest in the Kelabit Highlands of NE Sarawak. It has been recorded throughout Borneo. It is occasionally seen on passage in the coastal districts of NW Borneo where it is considerably less common that *L. c. cristatus*. **Range:** Breeds China, Korea, Japan and winters southwards.

5 BROWN SHRIKE *Lanius cristatus cristatus* 20cm   Common winter visitor race

Very common visitor to coastal districts of NW Borneo in winter months. Once settled in birds occupy the same area of ground throughout the winter months and are often quite agressive chasing other shrikes away from their chosen winter territory. **Range:** Breeds Central Russia to NE Asia, winters southwards. A passage migrant through Taiwan en route to the Philippines and Borneo.

6 TIGER SHRIKE *Lanius tigrinus* 19cm   Scarce winter visitor

[Thick-billed Shrike] A regular winter visitor to the north west coast of Borneo. Much less common than the Brown Shrike in Sabah but equally common in Brunei and more skulking, often keeping to the centre of dense vegetation. Shrikes are known as 'Butcher Birds' because of their habit of storing excess prey in a 'larder'. The larder can be a thorny bush or a spiky barbed-wire fence. Dead insects and small mammals are impaled on the spikes for later retrieval, when prey is scarce. This habit is known in breeding quarters in Japan and winter quarters in the Malay Peninsula but has yet to be recorded for Borneo. **Range:** Breeds China, Korea, Japan, winters southwards.

7 SOUTHERN GREY SHRIKE *Lanius meridionalis pallidirostris* 25cm   Vagrant

One bird at Wasan, Brunei in October 1990 (Mann). This shrike forms a 'super species' with Great Grey Shrike *Lanius excubitor* (not illustrated) which differs in that the black eye stripe runs through to the base of the all black bill. Both species or intermediates are equally likely to occur in Borneo as vagrants. **Range:** Breeds central Asia, winters Africa and India.

Dark
Morph

1

adult   imm

2

♀ imm

4

adult

5

3

imm

6

♀

♂

7

ORIOLES AND FAIRY BLUEBIRD

ORIOLIDAE **World 34 species; Borneo 5 species.** Spectacularly coloured birds with fluty whistles, orioles have often been trapped and caged both for their beauty and their voice. In Borneo they are little known forest birds and are not usually kept as pets. Females are usually much plainer than males. Juveniles are usually streaked. The flight is typically undulating. Nests are skilfully woven hammocks slung from branches in the tree canopy. Usually monogamous and not known to flock, unlike other fruit eating birds. Feed on a varied diet of fruit and insects.

1 DARK-THROATED ORIOLE *Oriolus xanthonotus* 18cm **Common resident**

Common in primary and tall secondary forest throughout Borneo, from the lowlands to the hills. The lowland oriole most likely to be seen by birders. Note that the common forest dwelling Black-headed Bulbul, page 243, which can appear brilliant yellow with a black head in bright sunlight, is often mistaken for an oriole. **Call:** A loud, mournful, *see-saw* whistle higher pitched on the first note (Sheldon). A musical double note *oo-up*. **Range:** Malay P, Sumatra, Borneo, Java, Palawan.

2 BLACK-NAPED ORIOLE *Oriolus chinensis* 26cm **Vagrant**

Resident in all surrounding areas but in Borneo known only from scattered skins and a few sight records assumed to be escapes. It is more likely that they are vagrants from Continental Asia as this is a known migrant to the Malay Peninsula. In Singapore it is one of the 10 commonest birds, having become established in the 1920s. **Call:** A loud, usually three part liquid whistle, *ku-i-oo*, with much variation (Davison). **Range:** Breeds N Asia, Philippines. Some birds winter south.

3 BORNEAN BLACK ORIOLE *Oriolus hosii* 21cm **Very local submontane endemic**

[Black Oriole] Apart from recent records from Paya Maga on the Sarawak/Sabah border this bird is unknown in Sabah and Brunei. In Sarawak it is a scarce resident of submontane forests of central Sarawak north to Gng Mulu where it is very scarce. In Sarawak it is replaced above 1,000m by the Black and Crimson Oriole where it occurs. In Kalimantan recorded from Kayan Mentarang and Mt Batu Tiban. **Call:** Three part fluty whistle *hi-hawa-huwit* rising at the final syllable, repeated (Ch'ien C. Lee).

4 BLACK-HOODED ORIOLE *Oriolus xanthornus* 20cm **Scarce local resident**

A scarce local resident of mangrove, riverine and coastal forest on the east coast of Sabah and in E and SE Kalimantan. Recorded in Sabah from Kinabatangan, Gomantong, Lahad Datu, Tawau and in Kalimantan, Sangkulirang Pensinsula, and Sungai Wain near Balikpapan. **Call:** Similar to Black-naped Oriole, liquid, whistled call of four notes *yiu-hu-a-yu* with middle notes stressed answered by three note *tu hue* or *tee-heh* (Smythies). **Range:** India to Vietnam, Malay P, Borneo.

5 BLACK-AND-CRIMSON ORIOLE *Oriolus cruentus* 22cm **Local montane resident**

A montane resident from Kinabalu south to Kalimantan. Commonest in the north, especially on Kinabalu in forest around KNP HQ, feeding on fruits or in mixed species hunting parties. Has been confused with Island Thrush (page 284) but has a grey bill as opposed to the blackbird's yellow bill and the blackbird is not normally found as low as KNP HQ. **Call:** A loud *ee-oo* descending in pitch on the *oo* (Sheldon). **Range:** Malay P, Sumatra, Java.

FAIRY BLUEBIRDS: IRENIDAE
Only two species of Fairy Bluebirds exist, one is a Palawan endemic. The other is widespread in tropical Asian forests. The closest relatives are the leafbirds.

6 ASIAN FAIRY-BLUEBIRD *Irena puella* 25cm **Common resident**

A common inhabitant of lowland and hill primary and tall secondary forest. Feeds primarily on fruit, which is snatched in sallying flight. The same technique is also used to feed on flying termites. Flocks to feed in fruiting fig trees, along with hornbills, barbets and pigeons. Generally a bird of the canopy, but nests low down in the dark understorey of the forest building a flimsy platform of sticks in a shrub in which it lays two eggs. Sexes differ. Immatures resemble females. **Call:** The contact call heard constantly when birds are present is a distinctive sharp *whit whit* or *whit whet* and variations thereof. **Range:** India to Malay P, Sumatra, Borneo, Java, Palawan.

DRONGOS

DICRURIDAE   **World 24 species; Borneo 6 species.**   Common, conspicuous, noisy birds of forest clearings which hawk insects from a prominent perch. Sexes alike. Drongos construct a very small nest on an open branch which they defend aggressively. Drongos have a large variety of loud raucous calls which ring through the forest. They often mimic other forest birds. Drongos are generally insectivorous but may take fruit. Drongos are active members of mixed species insect-hunting parties where they appear to act as 'leader species'. See page 268.

1   BLACK DRONGO   *Dicrurus macrocercus*   29cm   Scarce winter visitor

A lowland open country bird resident in continental Asia, which moves south in winter. As most Borneo drongos are strictly forest birds, the Black Drongo can be distinguished by habitat and extra long forked tail. In Asia this Drongo has been known to attack and eat small birds. Seen occasionally at Tempasuk Plain (Oct.–April), perching in the open, sometimes on buffaloes in order to feed on disturbed insects. **Range:** Iran to S China, winters S to SE Asia.

2   ASHY DRONGO   *Dicrurus leucophaeus*   29cm   Common montane resident

In Borneo a prominent bird of the forest edge of submontane and montane forests found south to Gng Penrissen. Conspicuous at KNP HQ and Mesilau, where it perches on telephone wires. **Call:** A variety of chirps and whistles. **Range:** China to Malay P, Sumatra, Borneo, Java. [In Continental Asia the Ashy Drongo is a lowland bird which moves south in winter months. Any open country lowland record of a Ashy Drongo is likely to be a continental vagrant.]

3   GREATER RACQUET-TAILED DRONGO   *Dicrurus paradiseus*   Common resident

Length: 30cm + 30cm tail racquets. The most conspicuous of the drongos found in lowland primary and tall secondary forest throughout Borneo. Distinguished by long prominent tail streamers or racquets. 40% of birds have no racquets and can be confused with Crow-billed Drongo (Smythies). Often joins insect-hunting parties. *'Birds of two species that are regularly found in mixed species flocks, Yellow-bellied Bulbuls and Racquet-tailed Drongos, seek out a foraging Lesser Treeshrew and perch about 1.5–2m below it, intently watching the treeshrew. The birds allow the treeshrew to advance ahead, then fly to the next perch below. The rummaging tupai flushes hidden insects, which the birds sally to catch. Many insects have an escape behaviour of dropping down when disturbed from foliage and these two follower bird species profit from the disruptive foraging of the treeshrew by simply waiting, flying from one perch to the next, keeping below the mammal'* (Emmons re. Danum). **Range:** India to Malay P, Sumatra, Java.

4   CROW-BILLED DRONGO   *Dicrurus annectans*   26cm   Scarce winter visitor

A scarce migrant drongo which can be found anywhere on migration, e.g. oil rigs, small islands, but prefers forested habitats particularly in north west coastal Borneo. Easily confused with Racquet-tailed Drongo that is missing its racquets. Distinguished by habitat, and wide twisted ends to forked tail feathers. Has much heavier bill than Black Drongo. **Range:** Himalayas to S China, winters south to Thailand, Malay P, Sumatra, Borneo, Java.

5   BRONZED DRONGO   *Dicrurus aeneus*   23cm   Common resident

Smallest drongo common in primary and secondary forests throughout the lowlands and hills. Like the Racquet-tailed often perches prominently over forest clearings noisily hawking insects but is less affected by logging than Racquet-tailed and is often found in disturbed forest. Distinguished from other drongos by its smaller size. **Range:** India to S China, Thailand, Malay P, Sumatra, Borneo.

6   HAIR-CRESTED DRONGO   *Dicrurus hottentottus*   32cm   Common submontane resident

[Spangled Drongo] Common resident of submontane areas throughout Borneo, occasionally in the mountains, e.g. at KNP HQ. Unusually also resident on small islands off NE Kalimantan (P Maratua, and P. Matasirih). The race on Maratua has a white iris similar to the Sulawesi race. Distinguished from other drongos by long hairs emanating from forehead and twisted tail feathers. **Call:** It is both shy and very noisy, often making an extraordinary racket from the centre of dense vegetation. **Range:** Breeds S China to Malay P, Sumatra, Java, Philippines.

2

3

4

6

Mainland

Maratua

CROWS, BLACK MAGPIE AND TREEPIE

CORVIDAE **World 22 species; Borneo 9 species.** Crows are prominent flocking scavengers in many citie around the world but in Borneo members of the crow family including jays, magpies and treepies are usual scarce forest birds with a generalist diet including fruit, large insects, small mammals, reptiles, birds' egg and fledglings. Sexes are similar. The calls are loud and harsh, a distinctive component of the sound-scape lowland and mountain forest.

1 RACQUET-TAILED TREEPIE *Crypsirina temia* **35cm** Status unknow
In Java and Bali an increasingly scarce inhabitant of secondary and scrub forest. Only one record from Borne two specimens collected in SE Kalimantan in 1851 possibly from a now extinct relict population which lingere on after rising sea levels cut the land bridge between Java and Borneo around 15,000 years ago. See pages 1! and 320. **Range:** Myanmar, Thailand, Indochina, Java, Bali.

2 BORNEAN BLACK MAGPIE *Platysmurus atterimus* **36cm** Common endemic rac

Common resident of lowland primary forest, usually in family parties, with up to 20 bir present (Thompson). Flies with very shallow wing beats producing a distinctive *whoo* nois **Call:** A very vocal mimic with a variety of whistles and chatters. One call is a *creak* like rusty hinge. 'The typical song is four notes, the first and last on the same pitch, the middle tw higher and faster in beat' (Sheldon). **Taxonomy:** Split by Myers (2009). Unlike the Malaya and Sumatran races the Borneo bird has no white on the wing and has a distinctive call.

3 SLENDER-BILLED CROW *Corvus enca* **48cm** Local reside

[Malay: Gagak] Locally common in lowland and hill primary forest and plantations throughou Borneo. Usually in shy small groups. Often absent from apparently suitable habita Distinguished by shallow wing beats (always below horizontal) compared with deep wing bea of Large-billed Crow. **Call:** A high-pitched *caw* different from deep caw of the Large-bille Crow (Davison). Also a distinctive three note call *squack squack squack* or *whack whac whack* described as 'banjo-like' given in display flight. **Range:** Malay P, Sumatra, Borneo, Jav Philippines, Sulawesi.

4 LARGE-BILLED CROW *Corvus macrorhynchos* **51cm** Status unknow
[Myers: Southern Jungle Crow] A common bird of cultivated areas in Asia, often in association with ma and not usually shy. In Borneo a few scattered records from Labuan, Niah, Miri, Sandakan and Kalimanta Some records may arise from confusion with Slender-billed Crow, others may be either wind or ship-assiste vagrants. There is no evidence yet of a sustained breeding population in Borneo. Distinguished by muc heavier bill, by green not grey gloss to plumage, by deeper call, different habits and by wing beats abov horizontal. **Range:** N Asia south to Malay P, Sumatra, Borneo, Java, Philippines.

5 HOUSE CROW *Corvus splendens* **43cm** Resident Kota Kinabalu onl
First recorded Papar (Sabah) 1983 (Sheldon). A small breeding population has been resident in Kota Kinaba town centre since 1997. A small flock hangs around the fish market on the waterfront. Distinguished fror Large-billed Crow by grey collar on a black background. **Range:** India to Malay P. Large populations exist i many Asian cities including Kuala Lumpur and Singapore by scavenging on rubbish and road kills.

THE CRESTED JAY – A DAYAK OMEN BIRD (see next page) Until recently (and even today in some remote areas) many of the interior tribes of Borneo held traditional beliefs that certain birds brought important messages from their gods. When these gods saw humans undertaking a new project such as a hunting expedition or building a new longhouse they appeared as messengers in the form of birds to warn humans if the project was likely to be successful. With the Ibans the senior god (Singalang Burong) appeared as a Brahminy Kite and other related gods took the form of other 'omen birds'. Omen birds were usually common birds with distinctive calls in particular the Rufous Piculet, Maroon Woodpecker, Scarlet-rumped Trogon, Diard's Trogon, Banded Woodpecker, White-rumped Shama and Crested Jay.
To continue with a project after a negative warning was considered seriously risky. Omen bird species and the exact interpretation of omen events varied from area to area but for many tribes most daily activities were ruled by these beliefs. Summarised from '*Iban Augury*' by J.D. Freeman in *The Birds of Borneo* by B.E. Smythies (1960).

JAY, GREEN MAGPIES, TREEPIE AND BRISTLEHEAD

1 CRESTED JAY *Platylophus galericulatus* 28cm

Common resident

[Malay: Burung hujan (rain)] A common resident of lowland and hill forest throughout Borneo. The prominent crest is erected when excited. **Call:** The loud and harsh rattling call precedes family hunting parties as they work their way around their territory, re-appearing in the same area at regular intervals of a few days. An important omen bird of the Ibans, the very distinctive call indicating likely success in a farming project or an expedition. See also page 234. The call is also believed by some to predict rain, hence the Malay name. **Range:** Malay P, Sumatra, Borneo, Java.

2 BORNEAN GREEN MAGPIE *Cissa jefferyi* 32cm

Local resident

Locally common resident of montane forest. Common at KNP HQ. where it often appears in the early morning to feed on moths attracted overnight to the roadside lights. Often joins mixed species hunting parties. Not found south of the Usun Apau plateau in C Sarawak (Mann). A recent record from Gng Manyapa E. Kalimantan (Brickle et al 2010). Note no black marks on wing tips unlike *C. chinensis.* **Call:** A variety of harsh whistles and chatterings. **Range:** Java, Borneo. **Taxonomy:** Split by van Balen, Eaton, Rheindt (2011).

3 COMMON GREEN MAGPIE *Cissa chinensis* 34cm

Scarce resident

In Borneo the less common of the two green magpies, a scarce inhabitant of submontane primary and secondary forest from Kinabalu south to N Sarawak. Not found south of Pulong Tau (Mann). Generally found lower down than Short-tailed Green Magpie. At KNP this bird has been recorded both from Poring (600m) and at Kambarangoh on the Summit Trail at 2,100m (Biun) but is not seen regularly at either location. Whitehead, who climbed Kinabalu from the west (Kota Belud and Kiau), found this bird common in secondary forest on the lower slopes. **Call:** A three syllable whistle from which it gets its local name of *ton-ka-ka* (Whitehead). A loud shrill *nee-new* in which the *nee* is higher pitched usually repeated twice (Sheldon). **Range:** Himalayas to Malay P, Sumatra, Borneo.

4 BORNEAN TREEPIE *Dendrocitta cinerascens* 40cm

Locally common endemic

A large, noisy, common and bold member of the bird community of the Bornean mountains from Kinabalu south to the headwaters of the Mahakam River in Kalimantan. Not found at Gng Penrissen near Kuching or in the Muratus Mts, SE Kalimantan. In mountainous areas often found at low elevations, e.g. Kelabit Highlands. Prominent and active in the forest around KNP HQ. Feeds on insects and berries and presumably small animals, birds' eggs and fledglings. **Call:** One of the commonest sounds of mountain forests, very varied but typically a bell-like *choing* and a harsh *shraank.*

BRISTLEHEADS: PITYRIASEIDAE **WORLD: One species unique to Borneo**, the sole member of the Pityriaseidae, most closely related to the shrikes of Africa. In Borneo the closest relatives are the wood-shrikes philentomas and the ioras but the split was probably as long as 20 million years ago. (Sheldon/Moyle 2009).

5 (BORNEAN) BRISTLEHEAD *Pityriasis gymnocephala* 26cm

Scarce endemic

[Bald-headed Wood-shrike] A generally scarce but locally common resident of lowland and hill primary forest throughout Borneo. Widely distributed but absent from many areas. Usually most common in peatswamp forest. Nearly always found in family parties of 5–12 birds gleaning insects in the middle canopy. Sexes differ. Male has red thighs but no red on flanks. Female has red thighs and red patch on flanks. Juvenile has black thighs, patches of red on flanks and underparts and no yellow on head. Black ear patch is absent in juvenile. Both sexes have white wing flash in flight. **Call:** Very vocal. A common call has been described as a series of extraordinary nasal wheezes. Also a variety of peculiar whistles. **Sabah:** Sepilok (common), Danum, Tabin. **Brunei:** Kuala Belalong, Ulu Belait. Anduki Forest Reserve. **Sarawak:** Mulu, Lambir Hills, Samunsam, Similajau, Batang Ai. **Kalimantan:** Kutai, Tg Puting, Barito Ulu, Gng Palung.

WOODSWALLOW, SWALLOWS AND MARTINS

SWALLOWS and MARTINS: HIRUNDINIDAE **World 87 species; Borneo 6 species, 1 resident.** Li
swifts, swallows catch insects on the wing, but unlike swifts they have normal feet and can perch on twi
or telephone wires where winter migrants often line up in rows. Sexes are similar. All species occur in mix
flocks especially during migration.

1 BARN SWALLOW *Hirundo rustica* **20cm** **Common winter visit**

Abundant (Aug.–April) throughout the lowlands and hills especially in open countrysid
Large flocks (250,000 +) roost in the centre of Tenom in central Sabah where they ha
become a tourist spectacle. Birds arrive just after sunset and settle on telephone wires
facing the same direction (Lamb). Large winter roosts also at Beaufort (W Sabah), Pontian
and Banjarmasin (Kalimantan). Migrants fly by day crossing the S China Sea. Distinguish
from resident Pacific Swallow by dark band below the pink or rufous throat. Immature bir
often lack adult tail streamers. **Call:** Short hard twittering *veet veet* (Brazil). **Range:** Bre
Europe to Japan wintering south.

2 RED-RUMPED SWALLOW *Cecropsis daurica* **18cm** **Scarce migra**

A scarce migrant usually mixed in with flocks of swallows. Very similar to Striated Swallo
but smaller and with no streaks on the red rump. Brazil suggests distinguishing by ca
See above. **Call:** A complex series of twittering notes, slower, lower and harsher than Ba
Swallow (Brazil). **Range:** Breeds Europe to Japan wintering south.

3 STRIATED SWALLOW *Cecropsis striolata* **20cm** **Scarce migra**

A scarce winter visitor very similar to and closely related to Red-Rumped, but larger a
more heavily streaked. Resident on the Asian continent and in the Philippines where
builds bottle-shaped mud nests under river bridges which should be looked for in Borne
Vowles recorded family parties at Tutong, Brunei in June 1980. **Call:** A harsh *pin* and *quits*
or a gravelly *kvertch* (Brazil). **Range:** Breeds Myanmar to S China, Taiwan, Philippine
throughout SE Asia except Borneo.

4 PACIFIC SWALLOW *Hirundo tahitica* **14cm** **Common reside**

Common resident in open countryside throughout Borneo, often seen around hum
settlements. Usually associates in pairs which perch together but post breeding often mix
with other migrant swallows. Builds a half cup-shaped nest out of mud pellets attached to t
wall of a building protected by the roof overhang. **Call:** Similar to Barn Swallow but shril
(Brazil). **Range:** India to Malay P, Sumatra, Borneo, Java, Philippines.

5 ASIAN HOUSE-MARTIN *Delichon dasypus* **13cm** **Vagra**

A regular visitor in very small numbers to the west coast south to Pontianak. Note white rump. **Range:** Bree
N Asia inc. Japan, NE China, wintering south to Malay P, Philippines, Borneo. Recently recorded Gng Menya
E. Kalimantan (Brickle et al). Darker Northern House-martin, *Delichon urbica*, may also occur.

6 SAND MARTIN *Riparia riparia* **13cm** **Vagra**

Rare winter visitor with most records from NW coastal districts. Often mixed in with flocks of swallows. Lo
for distinctive brown breast band. **Range:** Breeds Europe to Japan wintering south. Note: Very similar Pa
Martin *R. paludicola* (Resident Luzon) with pale brown throat and upper breast could also occur.

WOODSWALLOWS: ARTAMIDAE **World 10 species; Borneo 1 species.** The woodswallows originate
Australia. Sexes similar. The only passerine with powder downs hence their silky smooth appearance. T
closest relative in Borneo is the Bristlehead.

7 WHITE-BREASTED WOODSWALLOW *Artamus leucorhynchus* **18cm** **Reside**

A very common resident of open countryside throughout the lowlands and hills. Often on sm
islands. Perches high up on bare branches or telephone wires, gliding out on stiff triangu
wings to snatch at insects with their feet. Often in noisy parties, sitting in rows. Breeds in loc
colonies, a small cup nest high up, when pairs are very aggressive, harassing other birds. **Ca**
A wheezy chatter. **Range:** Sumatra, Borneo, Java, Philippines, Sulawesi to Australia.

H. r. gutteralis

1

H. r. saturata

2

3

4

Asian

Northern

5

6

7

Asian

Northern

TAILORBIRDS AND PRINIA

TAILORBIRDS **World 13 species; Philippines 9 species; Borneo 4 species.** Tailorbirds are a subgroup
the insectivorous warblers. Like most warblers they have loud distinctive territorial songs and a varied repertoi
of other calls. Only the most typical calls are described here. All the Bornean tailorbirds are common. Tailorbird
are named for their ability to 'sew' large leaves together to make a nest pocket. Pockets are constructed fro
one or two large leaves and lined with soft materials. The thread is spider silk teased out to make a knot. Mal
and females sometimes differ and in these cases juveniles resemble females.

1 DARK-NECKED TAILORBIRD *Orthotomus atrogularis* **10cm** **Local resider**

The least common tailorbird. Searches for insects in the canopy of primary and seconda
forest, forest gaps and the forest edge throughout Borneo. The three lowland tailorbird
species can be easily distinguished by their different tail colours, which in the case of th
Dark-necked is greenish. **Call:** A high clear urgent double note call *dweet dweet, dweet dwe*
uttered repeatedly. **Range:** India to Malay P, Sumatra, Borneo.

2 RUFOUS-TAILED TAILORBIRD *Orthotomus sericeus* **11cm** **Common resider**

The commonest tailorbird. Inhabits small islands, coastal gardens, cultivated areas and fore
edge throughout Borneo. Red-headed occurs in same habitat but has a preference for dens
scrub and mangroves. Sexes similar. Distinguish by rufous tail. All tailorbird species frequent
act as hosts to the *Cacomantis* cuckoos. **Call:** Lively rapid two note *wu-chi wu-chi wu-c*
repeated continuously. **Range:** Malay P, Sumatra, Borneo, Philippines.

3 RED-HEADED TAILORBIRD *Orthotomus ruficeps* **11cm** **Common resider**

[Ashy Tailorbird] Often overlaps in distribution with Rufous-tailed but more of a forest bi
with a preference for mangroves. Commonest tailorbird in Brunei (Vowles). Also found at th
edge of primary forest up to and including the hills. Distinguished by 'bald-headed look' an
grey tail tipped white. **Call:** A vast variety of calls, typically two well defined short notes *t*
preet, ta-preet repeated continuously. **Range:** Malay P, Sumatra, Borneo, Java.

4 MOUNTAIN TAILORBIRD *Orthotomus cucullatus* **12cm** **Common resider**

[Myers *Phyllergates cucullatus*] A common resident of the mountains throughout Borne
Searches for insects in the forest and forest edge. Sexes similar. Juveniles have all greenis
head. The tinkling disjointed song is a characteristic sound of the forest at KNP HQ. **Call:**
thin, high-pitched whistle *dee dee dee di-dee*, five notes, last note either rising or falling
pitch, repeated continuously. **Range:** Mountains of India to Malay P, Sumatra, Borneo, Jav
Philippines, Sulawesi, Moluccas.

5 YELLOW-BELLIED PRINIA *Prinia flaviventris* **13cm** **Common reside**

A common resident of marshes and long grass throughout Borneo found from coastal garde
to roadside scrub in the hills and mountains. Usually shy and skulking, making short fligh
above the grass, to view intruders. The nest is an oval ball with a side entrance built out
grass stems low down. The plumage is highly variable and does not relate to either age
sex. The head can be any shade of grey. The underparts range from no yellow to bright yello
(Vowles). **Call:** The song is a very fast melodic rippling phrase repeated continuously. Th
contact call is a nasal *mew*. When flying the wings often make a *snap*. **Range:** India to Mal
P, Sumatra, Borneo, Java.

TO SPLIT OR NOT TO SPLIT? A DILEMMA FOR SCIENTISTS Birds are regarded as separate species
if they do not breed when they overlap in distribution (sympatric). Related species often do not overlap
in range because they are isolated on islands, by high mountains or by wide rivers (allopatric). These
allopatric birds often differ significantly in appearance, call or habits. It is then debateable as to whether
they are a separate species (to be split) i.e. which would not breed even if they overlapped in distribution
or a just a different race or subspecies (to be lumped). Allopatric island races are often split into different
species, which is why the Philippines with so many islands is considered to possess nine species of
tailorbirds compared with only four in Borneo. See also pages 41, 92 and 348.

240

Tailorbird nest
with young
Banded Bay Cuckoo
(not to scale)

BULBULS

PYCNONOTIDAE **World 138 species; SE Asia 39 species; Borneo 25 species including 2 endemics.** Wherever you are in Borneo there is likely to be a cheerful bulbul close by. In gardens and cultivated areas the Yellow-vented Bulbul is ubiquitous. In secondary scrub the shyer, drab Olive-winged Bulbul is commonest and in forested areas the strikingly coloured Black-headed Bulbul is often seen. Bulbuls feed mainly on berries and like most fruit-eaters range widely depending on fruiting seasons. Black-and-White bulbuls and Black-headed Bulbuls are notably nomadic. Breeding bulbuls build untidy cup-shaped nests and feed their young on insects, sallying for prey. Sexes are similar. Apart from the wonderful rich song of the Straw-headed Bulbul most bulbul calls are undistinguished.

1 STRAW-HEADED BULBUL *Pycnonotus zeylanicus* 22cm Local resident

[Golden-capped Bulbul] [Malay: Empuluh buaya (crocodile)] The largest bulbul, previously very common in forested areas along streams and rivers throughout Borneo. In Borneo, rivers are often the main highways and this bird is now very scarce due to trapping for the Javan bird trade. Still common in protected areas such as Danum and Kinabatangan (Sabah). **Call:** The song is a rich, prolonged chuckling warble, often in continuous duet, more powerful but less varied than the Shamas. **Range:** Malay P, Sumatra, Java. **BLI:** Vulnerable.

2 MARATUA BULBUL *Pycnonotus hodiernus* 16.5cm Endemic confined to Maratua

A common bird on Maratua found both in the forest and in village gardens. Silvery grey with a dark almost black head and a pale rump. **Taxonomy:** Split from the Black-headed Bulbul by Chua, Sheldon et al (2014) See page 348

3 BLACK-HEADED BULBUL *Pycnonotus atriceps atriceps* 15cm Common resident

A common forest bulbul found in lowland primary and secondary forest throughout Borneo. Distinguished by black band on yellow tail and striking blue eye with a bluish sheen to feathering around eye. Often mistaken for an oriole. Nomadic, e.g. a dead bird found on top of Gng Tambayukon, KNP at 2,580m. In Brunei arrives to breed in the Anduki FR in March/April then disappears (Vowles). **Call:** A *chinky* contact note like two pebbles knocked together, also a five note song *doo da dit dit do* followed by a series of *chuk* sounds (Sheldon). **Range:** India to Malay P, Sumatra, Borneo, Java, Bali and Palawan.

4 BLACK-AND-WHITE BULBUL *Pycnonotus melanoleucos* 16cm Nomadic resident

Widespread but uncommon and nomadic. One found dead at 3,050m on Mt Kinabalu. Can be confused with N and E Borneo race of black-bellied Magpie Robin but white shoulder patch is more ragged and habits are of a forest bulbul whereas Magpie Robin hunts insects low down or on the ground. This curious coincidence of aposematic markings is as yet unexplained pages 81 and 211. **Call:** A constantly repeated *ee o lay*, the first note is highest, the second is lowest and slides into a third (Sheldon). **Range:** Malay P, Sumatra.

5 GREY-BELLIED BULBUL *Pycnonotus cyaniventris* 15cm Scarce resident

Very scarce but widespread in both primary and secondary forest, with a preference for riverine forest. Often feeds with other bulbuls and leafbirds in fruiting shrubs. **Call:** A high-pitched series of five notes, the last four of which climb a scale (Sheldon). **Sabah:** Poring, Danum, Sepilok. **Brunei:** Labi, Kuala Belalong (Mann). **Sarawak:** Mulu, Similajau, Semengoh. **Kalimantan:** Kutai, Sg Wain, Tg Puting. **Range:** Malay P, Sumatra, Borneo.

BORNEO'S SINGING BIRDS Borneo is home to some of the world's finest singing birds. In N Borneo the closely related White-rumped and White-crowned Shamas and often the Straw-headed Bulbul are kept for their melodious songs. In Java where bird keeping is an ancient tradition bird singing competitions have developed as a major industry (Jepson). Birds are graded for the variety and power of their songs with mimicry being an important part of the repertoire. In order of perceived singing skills the most valued Borneo species are: 1. Orange-headed Thrush. 2. Long-tailed Shrike, 3. White-rumped Shama, 4. Oriental Magpie Robin, 5. Chestnut-capped Thrush, 6. Straw-headed Bulbul, 7. Greater Green Leafbird, 8. Blue-winged Leafbird, and 9. Hill Blue Flycatcher. Only Straw-headed Bulbuls and Chestnut-capped Thrushes are bred in captivity; the remainder are trapped in the wild, many of them in Borneo. Populations of the Straw-headed Bulbul have been decimated by this trade. The other species are probably more seriously affected by forest conversion to agriculture.

BULBULS

1 PUFF-BACKED BULBUL *Pycnonotus eutilotus* 20cm   Local resident

A locally common bulbul of the understorey of lowland primary and hill forest throughout Borneo. Common in peat swamp forest at Tg Puting (Kalimantan) and recorded in hill forest at Gng Penrissen (Sarawak). Joins mixed species insect hunting parties and flocks with other frugivores at fruiting trees. May be a specialist feeder on forest understorey figs. Distinguished from other brown bulbuls by small crest, white tips to tail feathers and contrast between partly white underparts and plain brown back. **Call:** A tuneful series of four notes first rising and then falling, more musical than most bulbuls. **Range:** Malay P., Sumatra, Borneo. **BLI:** Vulnerable

2 OLIVE-WINGED BULBUL *Pycnonotus plumosus* 18.5cm   Common resident

The second commonest bulbul in coastal areas, but much shyer than Yellow-vented and keeps to degraded scrub and the edges of secondary forest. Found also in inland and hill forest where it is less common. Usually the commonest bulbul on small islands where it is a bird of the forest edge, e.g. P Gaya, P Tiga. Sometimes it is the only bulbul, e.g. Semporna Islands (Yong). **Call:** Similar to Yellow-vented Bulbul. **Range:** Malay P, Sumatra, Borneo, Java, Palawan.

3 YELLOW-VENTED BULBUL *Pycnonotus goiavier* 17.5cm   Common resident

Commonest bulbul in town gardens and cultivated areas throughout Borneo where it is a bold, successful opportunist, feeding on grassy lawns, attacking ripe fruit and chasing insects in flight. In open countryside found in the hills and mountains. **Call:** Cheerful loud warbled chuckles. Commonly seen in post breeding flocks of over 100 at evening roosts. **Range:** Thailand, Malay P, Sumatra, Borneo, Java, Sulawesi, Philippines.

4 CREAM-VENTED BULBUL *Pycnonotus simplex* 17cm   Common resident

[White-eyed Bulbul] Both this and the Red-eyed Bulbul are small, common, brown bulbuls of the forest and forest edge, very similar and often confused. The adults of both species have red or orange red eyes, the immatures have whitish or greyish eyes (Wells). The underparts are a contrasting pale cream unlike the brownish underparts of Red-eyed Bulbul. The commonest bird of the inland forest on P Gaya (Wells). **Call:** 'A simple *prrrt   prrrt* on one pitch' (Sheldon). 'Short emphatic song phrases *quick chop* and *quick plick chop*' (Wells re Malaya). **Range:** Malay P, Sumatra, Borneo.

5 RED-EYED BULBUL *Pycnonotus brunneus* 17.5cm   Common resident

Both Cream-vented Bulbul and Red-eyed Bulbul live in the same area of forest (sympatric) and it has been suggested that Red-eyed Bulbuls prefer logged or secondary forest whereas Cream-vented prefer undisturbed primary forest. Historical records appear to show that Red-eyed is increasing in comparison with Cream-vented. Red-eyed has uniform pale brown underparts. Cream-vented underparts are paler and contrast more strongly with the upperparts. **Call:** Series of high-pitched bubbling notes, the last ones rising sharply: *pri-pri-pri-pri-pri-pit-pit* (Robson). **Range:** Malay P, Sumatra, Borneo.

6 BLUE-WATTLED BULBUL *Pycnonotus nieuwenhuisii* 18cm   Status unknown

[Nieuwenhui's Bulbul] Only three birds have ever been recorded, a skin from the upper Kayan river in Kalimantan, a skin from Lesten, Sumatra, and sightings at riverside fruiting *Macaranga* trees near the Belalong Field Centre in Brunei by RSR Williams. Possibly an extremely rare resident, most likely a rare hybrid between Black-headed Bulbul and Grey-bellied Bulbul (Williams). Proposed DNA studies by R Jan den Tex may prove definitive.

7 SPECTACLED BULBUL *Pycnonotus erythrophthalmos* 17cm   Common resident

Common throughout the lowlands of Borneo in primary and mature secondary forest where it is the commonest bulbul of the forest understorey, whereas most bulbuls prefer the forest edge. Similar to Cream-vented and Red-eyed Bulbuls but distinguished by orange-yellow eye ring and paler throat. After logging at Danum the population of this bulbul tripled making it by far the commonest bulbul (Lambert). **Call:** 'A sweet prolonged, light *tweedle tweedle tweet tweet dit dit dit*, the *dits* going down the scale' (Sheldon). **Range:** Malay P, Sumatra, Borneo.

1

in display

2

3

imm

4

5

imm

6

7

imm

BULBULS

1 RED-WHISKERED BULBUL *Pycnonotus jocosus* **20cm** **Escape**
A common bird of the Asian Continent often kept as a pet bird. Feral populations have become established in Singapore and Sumatra. Recorded as an occasional escape in Borneo, but not established. A bird of cultivated areas and open countryside. **Call:** A melodious song usually issued from a prominent perch on the top of a small tree. **Range:** India to SE Asia.

2 SOOTY-HEADED BULBUL *Pycnonotus aurigaster* **20cm** **Feral Kalimantan resident**
A bird of cultivated areas and plantations. One of the commonest bulbuls in Java and Bali now expanding its range in Singapore, Sumatra and Borneo where there are scattered widespread records from Kalimantan presumably resulting from escaped pet birds. First recorded Palangkaraya 1984. (McKinnon). More recently recorded Tarakan, Samarinda, Banjarmasin and Pontianak. Often in small noisy flocks. Often kept as a pet in Java. **Range:** S China to SE Asia.

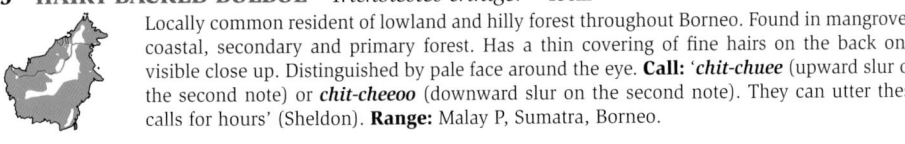

3 HAIRY-BACKED BULBUL *Tricholestes criniger* **15cm** **Common resident**
Locally common resident of lowland and hilly forest throughout Borneo. Found in mangroves, coastal, secondary and primary forest. Has a thin covering of fine hairs on the back only visible close up. Distinguished by pale face around the eye. **Call:** '*chit-chuee* (upward slur on the second note) or *chit-cheeoo* (downward slur on the second note). They can utter these calls for hours' (Sheldon). **Range:** Malay P, Sumatra, Borneo.

4 HOOK-BILLED BULBUL *Setornis criniger* **18cm** **Local resident**
A scarce local resident of lowland primary forest found throughout Borneo. Closely associated with nutrient-deficient soil forest such as kerangas, peatswamp, and ultrabasic. Rare elsewhere. Possibly mainly insectivorous. Their large size and white tail spots make them easy to identify (Sheldon). **Sabah:** Klias. **Brunei:** Widespread. **Sarawak:** Bako, Similajau. **Kalimantan:** Tg Puting. **Call:** 'This species travels in noisy flocks and utters a harsh *currrk* among other noises' (Batchelor). **Range:** Sumatra, Borneo. **BLI:** Vulnerable.

5 STREAKED BULBUL *Ixos malaccensis* **20cm** **Scarce resident**
Resident in primary and secondary forest of the lowland and hills throughout Borneo. Flock to fruiting trees with other birds. One mist-net record from Paka Cave 3,100m (Biun). Has rough feathers on head and a white front with contrasting streaks. 'Distinguished from other bulbuls by long bill and wings which are especially noticeable in its flight silhouette' (Sheldon). **Call:** A creaking gate contact call, unlike most bulbuls (Sheldon). **Range:** Malay P, Sumatra, Borneo.

6 YELLOW-BELLIED BULBUL *Criniger phaeocephalus* **20cm** **Local resident**
[*Alophoixus phaeocephalus*] A locally common inhabitant of primary and logged forest from the coast to the hills. At Danum whilst studying treeshrews Emmons found that it was a forest understorey specialist following insect-gleaning Lesser Treeshrews *Tupaia minor* whilst they foraged through dense tangles of vines. The bulbul would wait below the treeshrew until it flushed an insect which would be snatched by the bulbul. Racquet-tailed Drongos were often in close attendance. See page 232. Also recorded feeding on oil palm fruit. **Call:** 'A loud *chac* at intervals, in rapid flight through the understorey' (Davison). **Range:** Malay P, Sumatra, Borneo.

7 BUFF-VENTED BULBUL *Iole olivacea* **17.5cm** **Scarce resident**
[*Ioie olivacea*] Uncommon resident of lowland and hill forest throughout Borneo with a preference for secondary and logged forest. Easily distinguished by prominent white eye and head pattern of rough rufous feathers on crown with a pale eyebrow and a dark streak through the eye. **Sabah:** Poring, Sepilok, Kinabatangan, Danum. **Brunei:** Tasek Merimbun, Bukit Teraja, Labi, Ulu Temburong, Kuala Belalong. **Sarawak:** Similajau, Mulu. **Kalimantan:** Kutai, Sungai Wain, Tg Puting. **Range:** Malay P, Sumatra, Borneo.

Yellow-bellied
Bulbul
following
Lesser
Treeshrew

BULBULS OF THE HILLS AND MOUNTAINS

1 FINSCH'S BULBUL *Criniger finschii* 16cm **Scarce resident**

A scarce to locally common resident of lowland and secondary forest throughout Borneo with a preference for hilly or submontane areas. Does not flock like other bulbuls. Possibly more insectivorous than other bulbuls. Recorded as having a preference for roadside scrub rather than primary forest (Sheldon). Yellow throat feathers often slightly puffed out. Has dirty yellow underparts like Hairy-backed Bulbul, but unlike that bulbul no pale face. **Range:** Malay P, Sumatra, Borneo.

2 GREY-CHEEKED BULBUL *Criniger bres* 20cm **Common resident**

[*Alophoixus bres*] One of the commonest bulbuls of lowland primary forest throughout Borneo. Also common in the hills and wanders into the mountains, occasionally overlapping with Ochraceous Bulbul. This is the lowland equivalent of the montane Ochraceous, and like Ochraceous has a puffed-out white throat and a permanently erect crest. Distinguished by yellow belly and grey cheeks. **Call:** 'A throaty, rasping upward slur, followed by sweeter, clear descending notes' (Sheldon). **Range:** Malay P, Sumatra, Borneo, Java, Palawan.

3 OCHRACEOUS BULBUL *Criniger ochraceus* 22cm **Common montane resident**

[*Alophoixus ochraceus*] Common throughout the mountains of Borneo. One of three common mountain bulbuls including Pale-faced and Cinereous which also puff up white throat but has white belly not brown, and a feeble crest unlike the erect crest of Ochraceous. Often participates in mixed species insect-hunting parties. **Call:** A metallic *creek* followed by a series of quick musical *pew* notes (Sheldon). **Range:** Myanmar to Malay P, Sumatra, Borneo.

4 CINEREOUS BULBUL *Hemixos cinereous* 20cm **Common submontane resident**

[Ashy Bulbul *Hemixos flavala*] Common resident of the Borneo hills and mountains including outliers, e.g. Gng Niut and the Muratus Mts in Kalimantan. Occasionally in the lowlands, e.g. Sepilok (Sabah) Niah Caves (Sarawak). Puffs out white throat like the montane Ochraceous Bulbul but distinguished by white belly. Also no crest, only a patch of rough feathers on the head. A noisy bulbul often in family parties. **Call:** The call note sounds like the mew of a cat (Thompson). **Range:** Malay P, Sumatra, Borneo. **Taxonomy:** Split by Fishpool and Tobias in del Hoyo 2005 from Ashy Bulbul. However the Borneo race is quite unlike the dull grey Cinereous Bulbul of Sumatra and Malay P. (see Plate 60 in Mckinnon 1993) and is a potential Bornean endemic with the scientific name *Hemixos connectens* and a proposed common name of Sociable Bulbul.

5 PALE-FACED BULBUL *Pycnonotus leucops* 17.5cm **Higher montane endemic**

[Davison/Mann: Flavescent Bulbul *Pycnonotus flavescens*] Locally common bulbul of the higher mountains of Borneo generally found in upper montane forest. For example commoner on the Kinabalu Summit Trail than at KNP HQ and occurs to the limit of vegetation. Very common on the summits of Gng Tambayukon, Gng Trus Madi (Sabah) and Gng Mulu in Sarawak. **Range:** Himalayas to Thailand and Borneo. Not found Malay Peninsula. **Taxonomy:** Split by Fishpool (2005) as listed here. Not accepted by Mann (2008).

6 SCALY-BREASTED BULBUL *Pycnonotus squamatus* 15.5cm **Rare submontane resident**

A rare but widespread locally nomadic bulbul of submontane primary and secondary forest throughout Borneo. This beautiful bulbul is unmistakable. **Call:** 'An abrupt descending metallic *prrt prrt*' (Sheldon). **Sabah:** Crocker Range, Poring, Danum. **Brunei:** Ulu Temburong, Kuala Belalong. **Sarawak:** Gng Mulu, Matang, Gng Penrissen. **Kalimantan:** Kayan Mentarang, Muratus Mts, Gng Palung. **Range:** Malay P, Sumatra, Borneo, Java.

7 BORNEAN BULBUL *Pycnonotus montis* 17.5cm **Montane endemic**

[Davison/Mann: Black-crested Bulbul *Pycnonotus melanicterus*] This bulbul is confined to secondary growth and forest edge in the mountains (600–1,550m) where it is generally scarce. Occurs south to Barito Ulu in Kalimantan but not found on Gng Penrissen and Gng Pueh (Sarawak). Locally common, e.g. Crocker Range, Rafflesia Centre. Scarce on Kinabalu. **Call:** Very vocal. 'A whistled *grrrt grrrt*' (Sheldon). **Taxonomy:** Split by Fishpool (2005). See Mann (2008).

GERYGONE, LEAF AND REED-WARBLERS

1 GOLDEN-BELLIED GERYGONE *Gerygone sulphurea* 9cm **Common resident**

[Flyeater] Found in all types of lowland and hill forest throughout Borneo but commonest i mangrove and coastal forest. Often common on islands, e.g. Sipadan. Up to 1,800m on Tru Madi, Sabah (Sheldon). More often heard than seen. Feeds high up in the canopy gleanir for insects in small active family parties. **Call:** Best identified by very high-pitched son which rises and falls. In the Malay Peninsula the song varies in different areas (Wells) an this may be true of Borneo also (Davison). **Range:** Vietnam to Malay P, Borneo, Sumatra Java, Philippines.

2 INORNATE WARBLER *Phylloscopus inornatus* 11cm **Vagran**

[Yellow-browed Warbler] One confirmed sight record from Damai Beach nr Kuching, 3 Jan. 199 (Hale) and another at KNP Kamborangoh 24 Oct 2008 (Bakewell). Distinguished from Arcti Warbler by double wing bar on boldly marked wings. Distinguished from Greenish Warble (page 254) by white tips to tertiaries. **Call:** Plaintive high-pitched *tsee-weest* and a thin sprin, song (Viney). **Range:** Breeds Siberia, Mongolia, China, Korea, winters south to SE Asia.

3 ARCTIC WARBLER *Phylloscopus borealis* 12cm **Common winter visitor**

Commonest migrant warbler to overwinter in Borneo. Found in any type of lowland or hil forest. On migration during Sept./Oct. often on small islands or along the coast. A large plai warbler with a single clear wing bar (sometimes a faint second bar). Bolder and more activ than other warblers as it gleans for insects in wooded areas. Two races occur: *P. b. boreali* from Siberia and *P. b. xanthodryas* from Kamchatka and Japan. Distinguished by song. **Call** The contact call, common to both races is a unique metallic *dzik* or *chik* and a disyllabi *zirik* or *tset tset*. **Song:** *P. b. xanthodryas*: A simple but distinctive shivering trill of up to 1! notes which lasts four or five seconds. **Song:** *P. b. borealis*: Similar to but shorter than *P. b xanthodryas* and interspersed with the contact call (Baker). **Range:** Breeds N Europe, Siberia winters SE Asia. **Taxonomy:** Recent DNA and vocal analysis indicates that the Arctic Warble should be split into three cryptic species, all of which are likely to occur in Borneo. Se Hoefferle, A. et al (2013), Alstrom, P. et al (2011) and Saitoh, T. et al (2010).

4 EASTERN CROWNED WARBLER *Phylloscopus coronatus* 13cm **Not recorded**

Common winter visitor to Malay P, but not yet Borneo. Distinguished from Arctic Warbler by brighter greer upperparts with a single yellow wing bar, and different contact call. **Contact call:** a soft *phit-phit* (Baker). **Range:** Breeds Siberia, to Japan, winters S to SE Asia.

5 BLACK-BROWED REED WARBLER *Acrocephalus bistrigiceps* 14cm **Not recorded**

Common winter visitor to Malay P but no records for Borneo. **Range:** Breeds NE Asia, winters SE Asia.

6 CLAMOROUS REED WARBLER *Acrocephalus stentoreus* 17cm **Rare resident**

[Australian Reed-warbler *A. australis*] Locally common resident of Kalimantan swamps with one possible record from Brunei (Mann). Occurs in similar habitat to the migrant Oriental Reed-Warbler. Very difficult to distinguish from Oriental Reed Warbler except by time of year. **Call:** 'A series of raspy staccato *chi-wes chi wes* or *chi wi chi wi*. Also a harsh *chip ut chip ut* often preceded by a soft *che che che*' (Fisher re Philippines). **Range:** Resident Middle East to China, S to Australia.

7 ORIENTAL REED WARBLER *Acrocephalus orientalis* 19cm **Common winter visitor**

[Eastern Reed Warbler] In winter months (Sept.–April) often heard calling from dense marshes and swamps throughout Borneo. Usually skulking but less shy than Clamorous Reed-Warbler. Has very pale greyish streaks on breast unlike plain white breast of Clamorous and has pink gape (mouth) compared with yellow gape of Clamorous (van Balen/Prentice). **Call:** Loud harsh *chark* or *tchak* alarm call. Song is harsher, faster and lower than Clamorous (Simpson/ Day).**Range:** Breeds NE Asia, wintering south to SE Asia and Australia.

P. b. borealis

P. b. xanthodryas

1 MOUNTAIN LEAF-WARBLER *Phylloscopus trivirgatus kinabaluensis* 11cm Resident

Race *P. t. kinabaluensis* is found on Kinabalu only from Park HQ to scrub-filled gullies on the bare summit. The commonest bird observed along the Summit Trail (Biun). Distinguished by distinctive crown pattern and pale grey-green underparts and head. Very active hunting for insects and often found in mixed species flocks. A brood host to Sunda Lesser Cuckoo. See page 158. **Call:** The most melodius of the Bornean warblers with a high-pitched thrush-like quality (Sheldon). **Range:** Kinabalu only. A possible endemic species.

2 MOUNTAIN LEAF-WARBLER *Phylloscopus trivirgatus sarawacensis* 11cm Resident

Race *P. t. sarawacensis* is common on mountains throughout Borneo including Trus Madi in Sabah where Sheldon found it from 1,450m to 2,600m. Occurs south to Gng Penrissen and Pueh in SW Sarawak. This race is bright yellow instead of greenish-grey both below and on the head. Yellow birds have also been recorded on Kinabalu in the same habitat as *P. t. kinabaluensi* although less common. There are two possibilities: (a) birds of the Kinabalu race have a yellowish juvenile plumage (Davison) or (b) *P. t. kinabaluensis* is a separate species endemic to higher levels on Kinabalu. **Range:** Mountains of Sumatra, Borneo, Java, Philippines.

3 YELLOW-BREASTED WARBLER *Seicercus montis* 10cm Common resident

A common warbler of mountain forest throughout Borneo, found south to Gng Pueh in SW Sarawak and the Muratus Mts in SE Kalimantan. Very active gleaning for insects in both primary and secondary forest. Often joins mixed hunting parties. Brood host to Sunda Lesser Cuckoo, *C. lepidus.* **Call:** A high-pitched seesaw buzz, *di-da-di-da-di-da,* lasting about a second. Contact call is a regular high-pitched *gee* (Sheldon). **Range:** Malay P, Sumatra, Borneo.

4 YELLOW-BELLIED WARBLER *Abroscopus superciliaris* 11cm Local resident

A locally common resident of submontane primary and secondary forest throughout Borneo. Common at Poring (KNP). Occurs patchily in the lowlands, e.g. Tabin and Danum (Sabah), Semengoh (Kuching). Especially associates with bamboos. **Call:** A descending series of around eight notes at a steady pace (Sheldon). **Range:** Himalayas to Vietnam south to Malay P, Sumatra, Borneo, Java.

5 SUNDA BUSH-WARBLER *Cettia vulcania* 13cm Local montane resident

Montane resident of the forest edge from Kinabalu (up to 3,700m) south to Gng Lunjut, K Mentarang. Common Kinabalu and Crocker Range in roadside scrub. In Sarawak common higher up on Gng Mulu and Gng Murud but absent elsewhere. Very skulking but responds well to tape playback. Often half cocks tail. Has a clear pale eyebrow unlike Friendly Bush Warbler. **Call:** A distinctive long note *wheeoooh* which rises then falls. A pleasantly undulating whistled *chee-hu-weoo* quite different from the repetitive nasal buzzing of the Friendly Bush-Warbler (Kennerley). **Range:** Sumatra, Java, Borneo, Palawan. **Taxonomy:** A young bird on Trus Madi (2,350m) had buffy yellow not greyish white underparts (Sheldon). (Note: this is similar to the Javan race.)

6 FRIENDLY BUSH-WARBLER *Bradypterus accentor* 15cm Montane endemic

[Kinabalu Friendly Warbler] Found only at higher levels on Sabah's three highest mountains, Kinabalu, Tambayukon and Trus Madi. On Kinabalu occurs from Timpohon Gate (1,866m) up. Most common from Layang² (2,100m) to Panar Laban (Biun) at 3,330m. Hops low down in the undergrowth. Often very tame. Distinguished by dark spots on white throat and breast. **Call:** Not vocal. 'The song is a rather loud and far-carrying high-pitched reeling or buzzing' (Harrap).

7 BORNEAN STUBTAIL *Urosphena whiteheadi* 10cm Montane endemic

Scarce endemic resident of the undergrowth and forest floor of montane forest from Kinabalu (up to 3,100m) south to K Mentarang, Barito Ulu and Gng Liang Kubung in Kalimantan. Not found Gng Penrissen and Gng Pueh (Mann). Locally common in the forest around KNP HQ, Crocker Range, and higher up on Mulu and Gng Murud. Identify by very short tail and feeble song. **Call:** A soft very high-pitched single tremulous note repeated every few seconds.

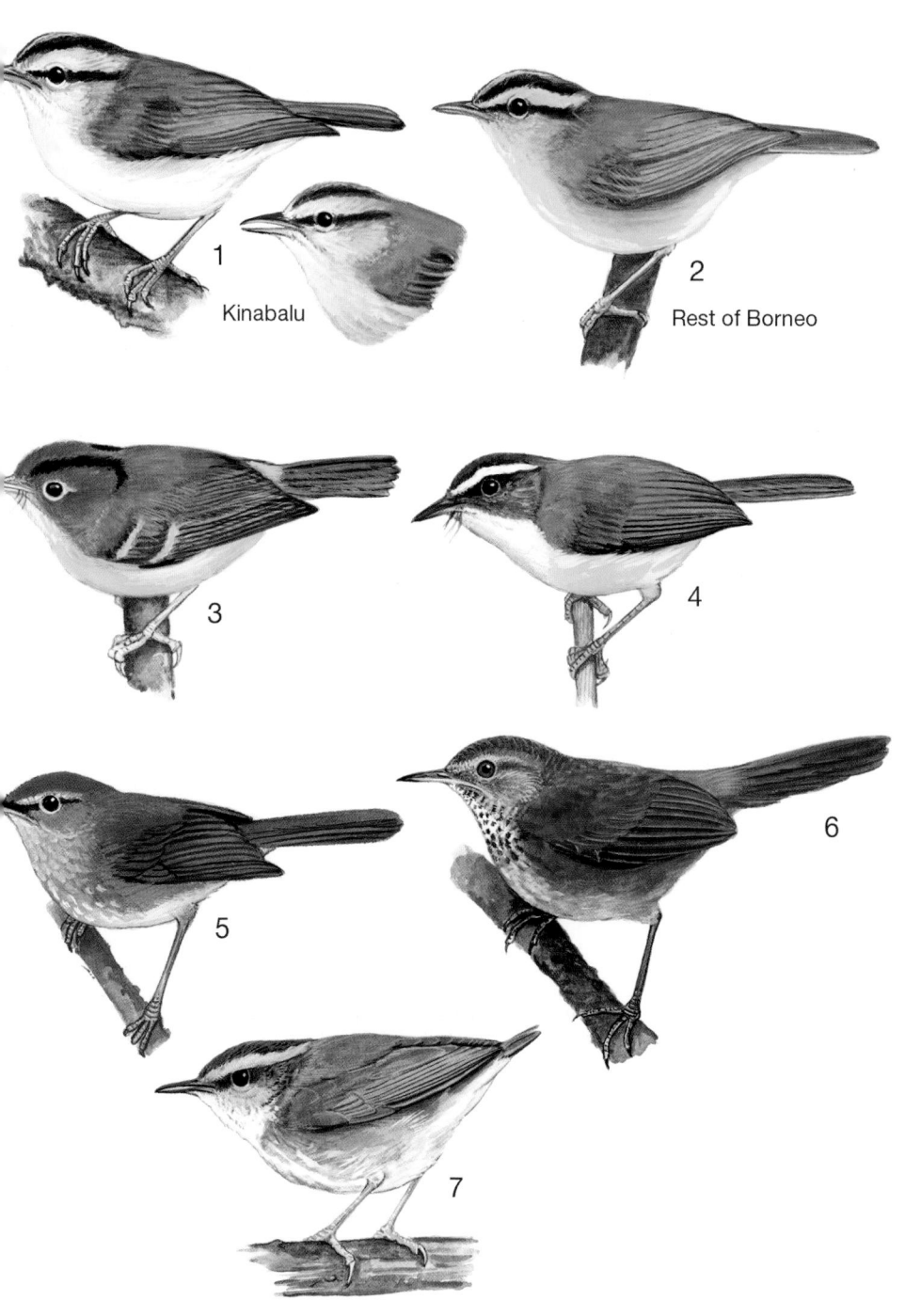

1

Kinabalu

2

Rest of Borneo

3

4

5

6

7

CISTICOLAS AND GRASSHOPPER WARBLERS

1 RUSTY-RUMPED WARBLER *Locustella certhiola* 15cm Scarce winter visit<

[Pallas's Grasshopper Warbler] Secretive migrant to swamps and padi fields. Most records a<
from NW Borneo. Very similar to Lanceolated Warbler but paler and larger with white tips <
tail feathers. **Call:** *Locustella* (Grasshopper) warblers are often very vocal, making a series <
loud *chacks* and *churrs* from the centre of dense vegetation. Song is similar to Middendorff<
but more complex (Brazil). **Range:** Breeds C Asia to N China, winters south to India and S
Asia.

2 MIDDENDORFF'S WARBLER *Locustella ochotensis* 16cm Rare winter visit<

Larger and plainer than the other *Locustella* warblers. Forms a superspecies with Rust<
rumped Warbler. Like Rusty-rumped often fans tail in flight showing white terminals spc<
but these are less contrasting than Rusty-rumped. A rare migrant to swamps and dam<
grasslands of NW Borneo. **Call:** Song consists of rather jarring short warbles a shrill grindir<
viche viche viche (Baker). **Range:** Breeds E Siberia, Japan, N China, winters south to S
Asia.

3 LANCEOLATED WARBLER *Locustella lanceolata* 12cm Rare winter visit<

Smallest and scarcest Grasshopper Warbler, with no white tips to tail. Thirteen records fro<
NW Borneo not yet including Brunei. Inhabits wet marshes and dense damp vegetation. **Ca**<
Distinguished from other *Locustella* warblers by very distinctive reeling song similar to tl<
stridulations of a locust or grasshopper (Baker). Often sings at night. **Range:** Breeds Euroj<
to Siberia and Japan, winters south to SE Asia.

4 ZITTING CISTICOLA *Cisticola juncidis* 11cm Not record<

This bird is a common resident of grassland and swamps in all surrounding areas but surprisingly no recor<
yet for Borneo. Distinguished by small size and short tail with black band followed by white tips. **Call:** Male
breeding season makes a distinctive high aerial flight song, an insistent *chip chip chip chip* (Viney). **Rang**
Europe, Africa, India to Malay Peninsula, Sumatra, Java, Philippines, Sulawesi to Australia.

5 STRIATED GRASSBIRD *Megalurus palustris* 26cm Common reside<

[Striated Warbler] First recorded Lahad Datu (Francis, 1982).This immigrant from tl
Philippines has spread rapidly in grassland, and cultivated areas. Common in Sabah, Brun<
and expanding in E Kalimantan and Sarawak. Often sings from telephone wires. Distinguish<
from other warblers by bold habits and much larger size. **Call:** Loud reeling chirrups. Alarm c<
is constant loud *ticks*. The smaller (22cm) very similar Tawny Grassbird *M. timoriensis* is al<
common throughout the Philippines and could well occur in Borneo. Has a plain buffy head a<
unstreaked breast. **Range:** India to China, S to Thailand, Java, Philippines.

6 GOLDEN-HEADED CISTICOLA *Cisticola exilis* 11cm Local reside<

[Bright-headed Cisticola] [Bright-capped Cisticola] Two records only. Pontianak Airport (197<
and Kendawangan (1994) both sites in W Kalimantan**.** Presumably an overlooked resident
dense swamps and rough grassland. Crown feathers often raised. Male head becomes brig<
golden when breeding. **Call:** Distinctive unusual monosyllabic nasal call 'bleating' (Viney
Range: India to China, Vietnam, Thailand, Malay Peninsula, Java to Australia, Philippines

---

POTENTIAL FUTURE BIRD COLONISTS FROM THE PHILIPPINES

With the rapid conversion of forest to grassland and plantation in Sabah, a number of Philippine
birds have colonised NW Borneo recently including Striated Grassbird and Grass Owl. There are other
Philippine species which are also likely to colonise Borneo through range expansion. They may already
be present in the lalang-covered hillsides of the Kudat Peninsula and the swamps of Tempasuk. These
potential residents include Striated Swallow, Little Ringed Plover, Philippine Mallard, Zitting Cisticola,
Oriental Skylark, Tawny Grassbird, Barred Button Quail and Horsfield's Bush Lark (already resident in S
Kalimantan). See also pages 318.

MIGRANT WARBLERS

Most Asian warblers are small plain skulking birds of thick vegetation and dense swamps. Males and females a᷈
similar. Even taxonomists working with skins find them difficult to tell apart. For these reasons, and the fact th
early collectors concentrated on the forest birds, warblers are probably the group most under recorded in Borneo ar
therefore most likely to generate new species records once mist netting studies in areas such as the Tempasuk Pla
are undertaken. We list here some of the unrecorded warblers most likely to be discovered in Borneo. In the breedi᷈
season warblers have very distinctive songs, and sometimes also sing and respond to tape playback in winter quarte᷈
To find new warblers in Borneo a mist net, a digital recorder and a digital camera would be essential tools.

1 STREAKED REED WARBLER *Acrocephalus sorghophilus* **13cm** **Not record᷈**
Recorded in fairly large numbers as a night-flying migrant at Dalton pass in N Luzon, Philippines (Kenne᷈
et al.). **Call:** 'Typical series of raspy churring notes but much quieter than Oriental Reed Warbler' (Fishe᷈
Distinguished from similar warblers by lack of white tip to tail and unstreaked underparts. **Range:** Breeds N
China. Winters Philippines. **BLI:** Vulnerable.

2 DUSKY WARBLER *Phylloscopus fuscatus* **12cm** **Not record᷈**
An abundant winter visitor to Deep Bay in Hong Kong. One Philippine record. **Call:** 'Continually repeated har᷈
tschack tschack as it moves methodically through bushes, reeds and mangroves in open country' (Viney᷈
Range: Breeds E Asia winters southwards.

3 GRAY'S WARBLER *Locustella fasciolata* **15cm** **Not record᷈**
An uncommon but regular migrant throughout the Philippine Islands recorded from 28 Aug. to 29 May. Extreme᷈
skulking but stands like a chat upright on the ground. Keeps to dry undergrowth (Viney). **Call:** 'A pleasa᷈
musical *twit-twop twit-twat tit-tet-tat-tot-twop*. The first two phrases alternating back and forth, the final seri᷈
dropping downwards as if counting 1,2,3,4,5' (Kennedy/Robson). Distinguished from Oriental Reed Warbler ᷈
smaller size and darker plumage. **Range:** Breeds Russia to Japan. Winters Philippines, Sulawesi, Moluccas. Mo᷈
likely to be found along Borneo's east coast.

4 RADDE'S WARBLER *Phylloscopus schwarzi* **14cm** **Not record᷈**
Largest leaf warbler. A scarce passage migrant through Hong Kong. Two records from the Philippines. Common win᷈
visitor Thailand. Distinguished from Dusky Warbler by eyebrow turned up at the end. One record only, 13 Oct. 20᷈
Pulau Tiga (Chris Kehoe). **Call:** Contact call is a soft almost hesitant *chek chek* or *qurrt qurrt* (Baker). **Rang᷈**
Breeds E Siberia, N China, Korea, winters SE Asia.

5 TWO-BARRED WARBLER *Phylloscopus trochiloides* **12cm** **Vagra᷈**
[Greenish Warbler *Phylloscopus plumbeitarsus*] A scarce passage migrant through Hong Kong. Common wint᷈
visitor Thailand. Distinguished from Arctic Warbler by double wing bar and different call. **Call:** Distinctive lou᷈
di-syllabic *chi-wee* (Viney). **Range:** Breeds Europe to E Asia, winters south to India and SE Asia.

6 BLUNT-WINGED WARBLER *Acrocephalus concinens* **14cm** **Not record᷈**
Scarce passage migrant through Hong Kong. No records from Philippines. A regular but uncommon wint᷈
visitor to Thailand. Distinguished by rufous rump and short eyebrow. One record only 13 Oct. 2011 Pulau Ti᷈
(Chris Kehoe). **Call:** A short quiet *tcheck*, also a soft drawn out *churr*. Sometimes gives scratchy warbli᷈
subsong before spring departure (Lekagul/Round). **Range:** Breeds Afghanistan to S China winters SE Asia.

7 PALE-LEGGED LEAF WARBLER *Phylloscopus tenellipes* **13cm** **Not record᷈**
Regular passage migrant through Hong Kong in small numbers. No records from Philippines. Common wint᷈
visitor to Thailand, regular but uncommon Malay Peninsula. **Call:** Distinctive loud metallic *chink* accompani᷈
by tail pumping (Viney). **Range:** Breeds NE Asia winters SE Asia.

8 THICK-BILLED WARBLER *Acrocephalus aedon* **20cm** **Not record᷈**
Regular passage migrant through Hong Kong in small numbers. No records from Philippines. Common wint᷈
visitor to Thailand, regular but uncommon Malay Peninsula. Behaves and looks like a bulbul. Distinguishe᷈
from warblers by short primaries and lack of eyebrows. **Call:** Insistent *chack chack* and a harsh chatte᷈
(Viney). **Range:** Breeds N Asia winters south to India and SE Asia.

WARBLER PLUMAGES With warbler plumages so similar, classification of species is now based on
DNA and song studies. Note that plumages differ significantly between newly moulted 'fresh' (bright)
plumage just after birds arrive and 'worn' (dull) plumage just before departure.

Fourteen jungle babblers (Timaliidae) occur in Borneo. They hunt insects on the ground or low down in dens tangles of vines in the forest understorey. They are best identified by their distinctive calls. Like most babbler they are very shy. However, they respond well to tape playback. Jungle Babblers build round leafy nests lov down near the ground. Sexes are similar. Young are plain not spotted.

1 BLACK-CAPPED BABBLER *Pellorneum capistratum*   **17cm**   **Common residen**

One of the commonest babblers, found in all types of primary and secondary forest from the coast to the hills. Similar habits to pittas, but walks not hops along the ground. **Call:** In Sabah calls differ E and W of the Crocker Range. On W coast a three note call is common, long shor long (the last two notes slurred and rising). East of the C Range the call is usually two notes the first rising, the second falling (Sheldon). **Range:** Malay P, Sumatra, Borneo, Java.

2 TEMMINCK'S BABBLER *Trichastoma pyrrogenys*   **15cm**   **Local submontane residen**

[*Pellorneum pyrrogenys*] Scarce inhabitant of lower montane and montane primary and secondary forest throughout Borneo. Found south from Kinabalu to Gng Penrissen and Pue near Kuching and the Muratus Mts in SE Kalimantan. Locally common in the forest at KN HQ. Recorded from Rhino Ridge, Danum. Often joins mixed species hunting flocks. **Call:** *A* two note whistle *wi-chu wi-chu* usually repeated twice. **Range:** Borneo, Java.

3 SHORT-TAILED BABBLER *Trichastoma malaccense*   **14cm**   **Common residen**

[*Malacocincla malaccense*] Common resident throughout the lowland and hilly forests of Borneo Typical locations, Danum, Tabin, Mulu, Similajau, Semengoh, Tg Puting. Common throughou Brunei (Mann). Hunts close to the ground. Distinguished by short tail and distinctive call. **Call** A series of five to seven loud whistles, each whistle descending in pitch often anticipated b a short *tu tu tu*. Also *fit-zweet* or *fit fit zweet* (Sheldon). **Range:** Malay P, Sumatra, Borneo.

4 MULU SHORT-TAILED BABBLER *Trichastoma malaccense feriatum*   **14cm**   **Mystery**

[*Malacocincla malaccense feriatum*] One specimen collected on Gunung Mulu in 1898, bu this species was not found again by the Royal Geographical Society Expedition in 1977–78 Possibly a scarce montane relative of the Short-tailed Babbler or a new endemic for Borneo Has rufous crown and uniform ochraceous underparts apart from central underbelly, unlike Short-tailed Babbler, which does occur in the lowland forest at Mulu.

5 HORSFIELD'S BABBLER *Trichastoma sepiarium*   **14cm**   **Local residen**

[*Trichastoma sepiarium*] Locally common throughout Borneo in all types of forest from the lowlands to the hills. Prefers thick undergrowth near streams in primary forest. Common a Sepilok, Bako. **Call:** One to three short whistles followed by single longer and slurred whistle Three spaced whistles, the middle note lower than the others, *tip top tiu*, very recognisable once learnt (Smithies). Inhabits the same forest as Short-tailed Babbler. **Range:** Malay P Sumatra, Java, Borneo.

6 ABBOTT'S BABBLER *Trichastoma abbotti*   **16cm**   **Local residen**

Scarce in Sabah where it has been reported from Klias. Inhabits mangrove and nipah fores and kerangas forest on poor sandy soils. Also found in secondary forest along river bank but absent from primary forest. Locally common in Sarawak, e.g. Similajau, Bako an in Kalimantan at Tg Puting. Distinguished from White-chested Babbler by rufous orange undertail coverts and vent. **Call:** A short series of fluty whistles, typically a series of three notes which dips on the middle note or four notes which dip on the first note (Nash). The call in Lower Belait, Brunei, matches Kalimantan calls, but differs significantly from birds in Peninsula Malaysia (David Bakewell). **Range:** Myanmar to Malay P, Sumatra, Borneo.

7 BLACK-BROWED BABBLER *Trichastoma perspicillata*   **16cm**   **Endemi**

Previously considered a race of Horsfield's Babbler, but now split. See Mann (2009). Only on record, a skin collected near Banjarmasin c. 1845. SE Borneo has a dryer and more seasona climate than the rest of Borneo with some relict birds of Javan origin. It is the most heavil populated and de-forested part of the island, so this bird could well be extinct. See also pag 154. **BLI:** Vulnerable.

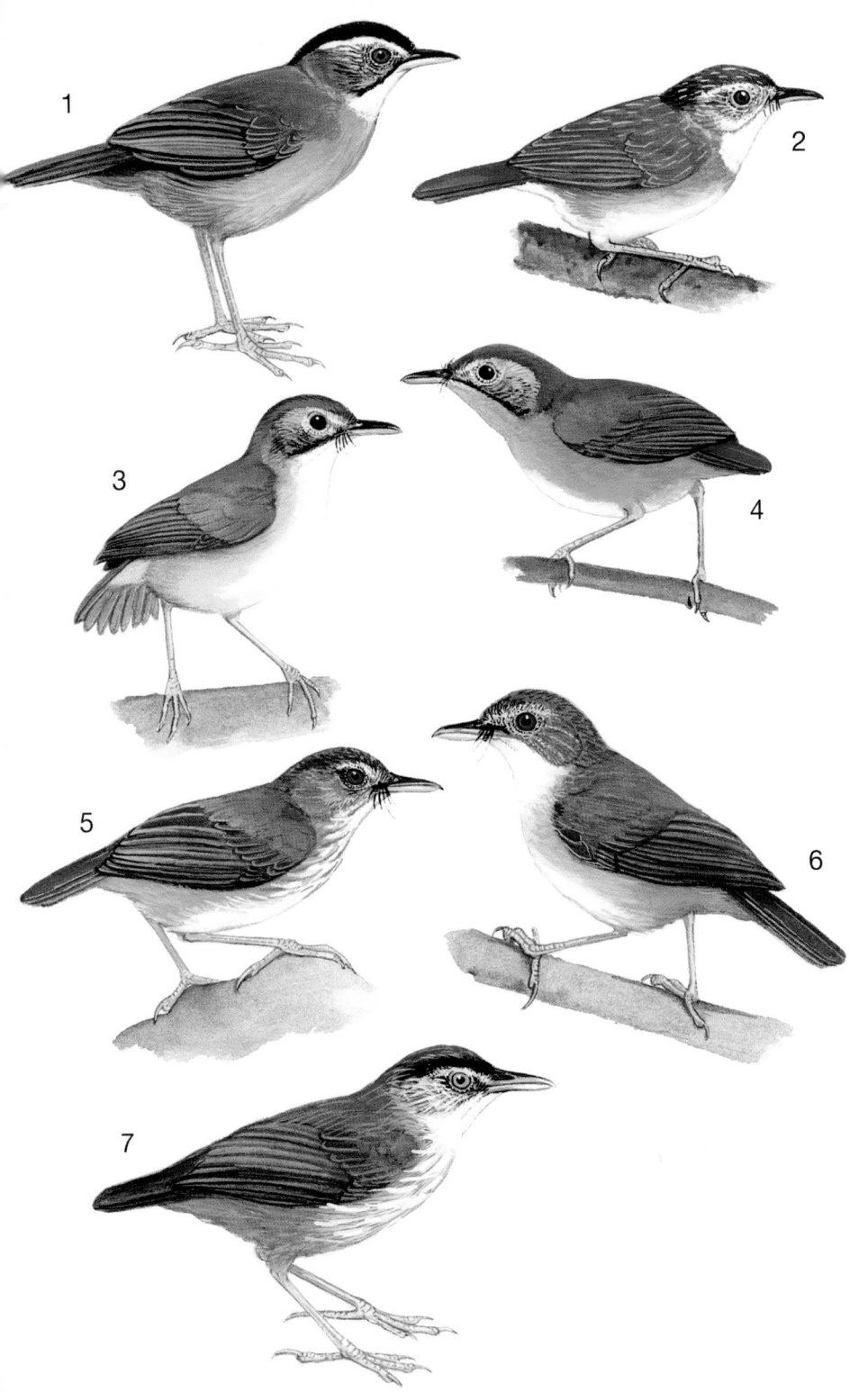

JUNGLE BABBLERS

1 WHITE-CHESTED BABBLER *Trichastoma rostratum* 15cm **Common resident**

Common in lowland and hill forest throughout Borneo. Prefers coastal and secondary forest and primary forest along rivers and streams. Has slight rufous tint on tail, primaries and crown. Very similar to Sooty-capped but no dark cap. Typical locations, **Sabah:** P Gaya Kinabatangan. **Brunei:** Throughout the lowlands (Mann). **Sarawak:** Bako. **Kalimantan:** Tg Puting. **Call:** A very noisy bird. Smythies described one characteristic call as *min-ta duit min ta duit min-ta duit* [Malay: Ask for money]. **Range:** Thailand, Malay P, Sumatra, Borneo.

2 FERRUGINOUS BABBLER *Trichastoma bicolor* 17cm **Local resident**

A locally common resident of primary and logged forest throughout Borneo from the lowlands to the hills. Typical locations, Danum, Kuala Belalong, Semengoh, Tg Puting. Distinguished by bright rufous upper parts and clean white underparts. Often joins mixed hunting parties. **Call:** A noisy bird. A characteristic call is a series of simple loud whistles rising in pitch *wee-eet* or *hweet*. **Range:** Thailand, Malay P, Sumatra, Borneo.

3 MOUSTACHED BABBLER *Malacopteron magnirostre* 16cm **Common resident**

A common resident of primary forest throughout Borneo. Declines in population after logging (Lambert). Distinguished from similar Sooty-capped by distinct moustache separating white throat from cheek and indistinct pale eye ring. **Call:** A two phrase melody *doo-da-doo* (on one pitch) followed by four notes descending. As with other *Malacopteran* species, the mate chimes in with counterpoint notes (Sheldon). **Range:** Thailand, Malay P, Sumatra, Borneo.

4 SOOTY-CAPPED BABBLER *Malacopteron affine* 16cm **Common resident**

Common resident throughout Borneo in all types of lowland forest but with a preference for secondary forest or forest edge and gaps in primary forest. Slightly smaller and browner with a hint of chestnut in the crown as compared with Moustached Babbler (Sheldon). **Call:** Two songs. One is a slow, plaintive song consisting of two descending notes, followed by two phrases of three descending notes. The second song follows the same theme, but is clearer and more cheerful. It is simply two phrases of three descending notes sung rapidly and with an accent on the first (and highest) note in each trio (Smythies). **Range:** Malay P, Sumatra, Borneo.

5 RUFOUS-CROWNED BABBLER *Malacopteron magnum* 17cm **Common resident**

A common resident throughout the forests of Borneo from the lowlands to the hills, in all types of forest. Population declined after logging at Danum. (Lambert). Common at Sepilok, Bako, Tg Puting. Usually seen investigating tangled vines in the understorey in small family parties. Note grey streaks on throat and chest and grey not pink legs. **Call:** A cheerful, descending scale of rapidly repeated notes (Sheldon). **Range:** Malay P, Sumatra, Borneo, Palawan.

6 GREY-BREASTED BABBLER *Malacopteron albogulare* 15cm **Scarce local resident**

[White-throated Babbler *Ophrydornis albogularis*] Similar habitat to Hook-billed Bulbul. Prefers forest on poor soils, e.g. peatswamp, kerangas and ultrabasic where it is locally common, throughout Borneo, e.g. **Sabah:** Klias. Danum (Edwards). **Brunei:** Labi area, Kuala Belalong, Badas. **Sarawak:** Similajau, Niah, Semengoh. **Kalimantan:** Barito Ulu, Tg Puting. Sabangau. Note very clear white eyebrow and yellow lores. **Call:** A song of five slow, pure whistles, *whet whet WEET whiet whiet* with a heavy emphasis on the third note (Davison re Danum). **Range:** Malay P, Sumatra, Borneo.

7 SCALY-CROWNED BABBLER *Malacopteron cinereum* 15cm **Common resident**

A common resident throughout the lowlands of Borneo with a preference for undisturbed lowland primary forest. At Danum, the commonest babbler in primary forest but the population crashed 90% in logged forest (Lambert). Common at Bako and P. Gaya K.K. Investigates the undersides of terminal leaves and leaf tips for insects (Emmons). Often in family parties. Distinguished from Rufous-crowned by plain throat and black scaly markings on rufous crown and pink not grey legs. **Call:** Four wheezy rising and one dropping note, with repeated delivery of the four wheezy rising notes beginning at different pitches (Sheldon). **Range:** Vietnam, Thailand, Malay P, Sumatra, Borneo, Java.

grey

pink

WREN-BABBLERS

With five species and three endemics, Borneo is a world centre of wren-babbler distribution. Like the pittas wren-babblers are specialist ground birds of undisturbed primary forest, turning over dead leaves to find insects such as dung beetles. Like the pittas they suffer a population decline after logging. Unlike pittas, wren-babblers are often found in small family parties which appear to travel and hunt together. Owing to their camouflage plumage and secretive habits they are little known and most are considered scarce or rare.

1 BORNEAN WREN-BABBLER *Ptilocichla leucogrammica* **17cm** **Rare endemic**

[Myers: Bornean Ground-babbler] A rare shy resident of lowland primary forest throughout Borneo, apart from S Kalimantan. Mist netting at Danum by Lambert showed that this locally common bird was severely reduced by logging. Hunts for insects and grubs in fallen wood. **Call:** 'A two or three note whistle, ***doo dee*** or ***doo doo dee*** in which the last note is higher than the first. If two ***doo*** notes are sounded they are on the same pitch' (Sheldon). **Sabah:** Danum, Tabin, Sepilok. **Brunei:** Ulu Temburong. **Sarawak:** Mulu, Similajau, Gng Penrissen, Semengoh, Batang Ai. **Kalimantan:** K Mentarang, Gng Palung, Kutai.

2 STRIPED WREN-BABBLER *Kenopia striata* **14cm** **Scarce resident**

A scarce resident of lowland and hill forest throughout Borneo. Note distinctive white streaks on back. **Call:** A soft plaintive hoarse whistle followed by an abrupt ***pitchu*** like a creaking hinge. The ***pitchu*** is often absent and may originate from the female in duet. **Sabah:** Sepilok, Danum, Tabin, Kinabatangan, Maliau. **Brunei:** Ulu Temburong. **Sarawak:** Mulu, Similajau, Samunsam, Batang Ai. **Kalimantan:** Kayan Mentarang, Gng Palung, Kutai. **Range:** Malay P, Sumatra, Borneo.

3 MOUNTAIN WREN-BABBLER *Napothera crassa* **15cm** **Montane endemic**

Locally common resident of submontane to montane forest throughout Borneo. Common in the forest around KNP HQ, high up on Mulu, and on the summit of Trus Madi at 2,600m (Sheldon). Common on Gng Penrissen near Kuching. Usually in shy skulking family parties in the forest underbrush. May overlap with Eye browed Wren-babbler. Distinguished by lack of white spots on back and larger size. **Call:** 3 descending notes ***chee, chee chiyoo***. **Contact call:** a soft ***churr***.

4 EYEBROWED WREN-BABBLER *Napothera epilepidota* **11cm** **Scarce resident**

A scarce resident of primary submontane and montane forest from Kinabalu south to Kalimantan. Overlaps in altitude with Mountain Wren Babbler but usually found at lower elevations. Occupies the forest floor of primary hill forest, rather than montane forest. Like Mountain Wren-Babbler has buffy longitudinal streaks on the wing coverts but in addition has a scattering of small white spots. **Call:** 'A thin clear sad falling whistle ***cheeeoo, chheeeeeu*** or ***piiiiiu*** repeated at intervals of 2–5 seconds' (Robson in del Hoyo). **Range:** Himalayas, SW China, Vietnam, Thailand, Malay P, Sumatra, Borneo, Java.

5 BLACK-THROATED WREN-BABBLER *Napothera atrigularis* **18cm** **Rare endemic**

A rare resident of lowland primary forest throughout Borneo. Mist netting at Danum by Lambert showed that this bird was locally common but numbers were severely reduced in logged forest. **Call:** (1) Trysyllabic monotone whistle ***piupiupou***. (2) A series of six notes, three up, one even, next descending, then last one up again. Very distinctive. **Sabah:** Danum, Tabin, Sepilok. **Brunei:** Ulu Temburong. **Sarawak:** Mulu, Pulong Tau, Niah, Similajau, Samunsam, Batang Ai. **Kalimantan:** Kayan Mentarang, Gng Palung, Kutai.

BABBLER POPULATIONS AND LOGGING   Most babblers are insect eaters that eat some fruit, whilst most bulbuls are fruit eaters that eat some insects. After forest is logged, the plant composition and forest structure changes, with an overall loss of diversity. The total number of birds remains unchanged or even increases, but the diversity, i.e. number of different species declines. Many frugivores (such as bulbuls) and nectarivores (such as sunbirds) benefit from logging because the extra sunlight stimulates the growth of flowering plants and berry fruiting secondary shrubs. Most insect-eating birds, however, do suffer from logging. Studies by Johns, Lambert and Mead at Danum comparing bird populations of logged and unlogged forest found population declines in all three species of locally resident wren-babblers after logging.

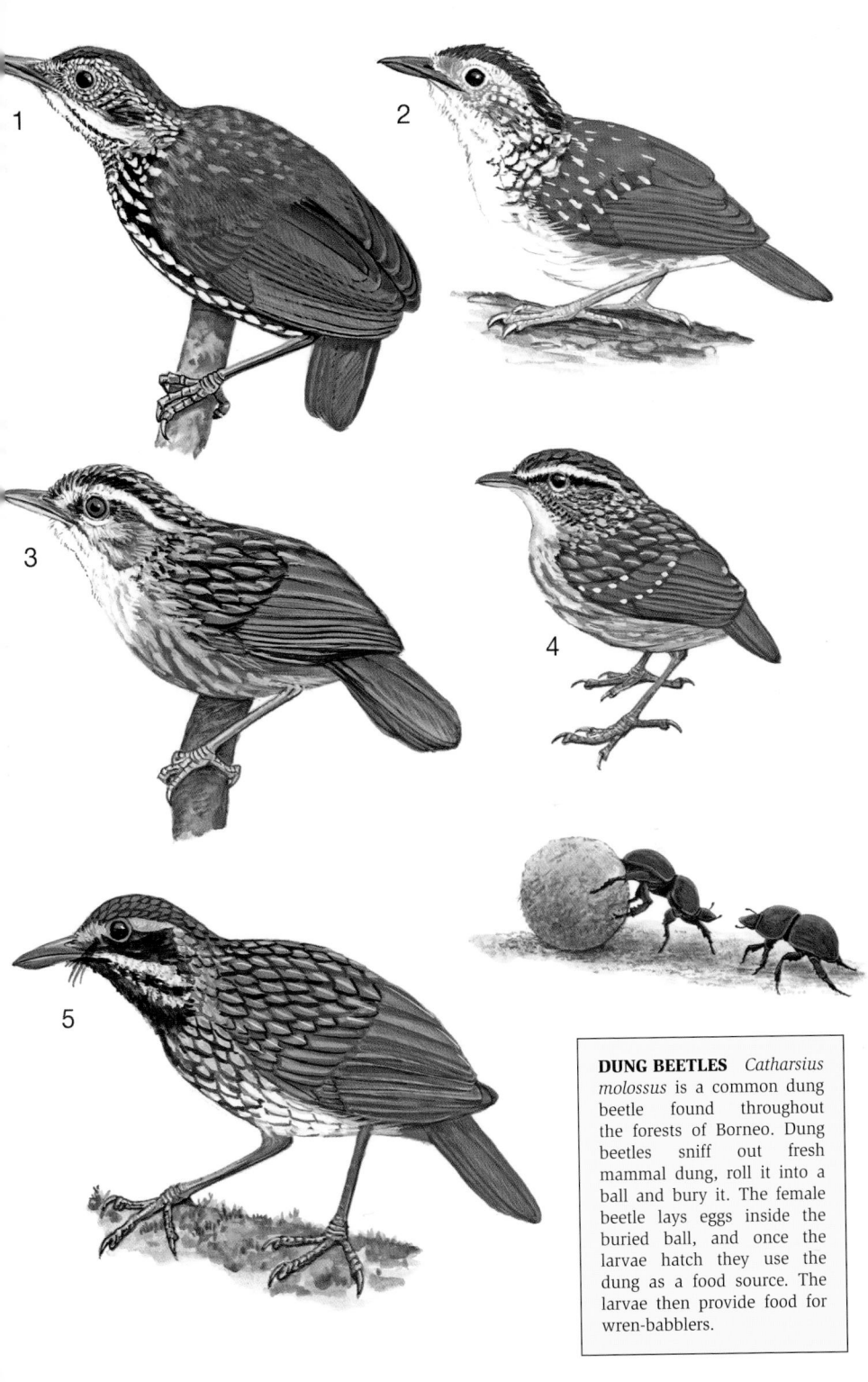

DUNG BEETLES *Catharsius molossus* is a common dung beetle found throughout the forests of Borneo. Dung beetles sniff out fresh mammal dung, roll it into a ball and bury it. The female beetle lays eggs inside the buried ball, and once the larvae hatch they use the dung as a food source. The larvae then provide food for wren-babblers.

STACHYRIS TREE-BABBLERS

Nearly always in noisy groups and believed to be co-operative breeders.

1 GREY-THROATED BABBLER *Stachyris nigriceps* 13cm Local montane resident

Locally common submontane and montane resident. The commonest babbler in forest and roadside scrub at KNP HQ and up the Summit Trail, usually found in small parties. Often joins mixed species hunting flocks. **Call:** The most common call is a descending trill. It also gives a *zee zee zee zee* contact call and also a high-pitched rapid trill which sounds like a high thin whistle from a distance (Sheldon). **Range:** Himalayas, to Thailand, Malay P, Sumatra, Borneo.

2 RUFOUS-FRONTED BABBLER *Stachyris rufifrons* 12cm Scarce resident

A scarce resident of hill and submontane forest. In Sabah, and some other areas, e.g. Similajau, widespread in lowland secondary forest. 'A warbler-like babbler that that flits from leaf to leaf and stays higher in the trees than other *Stachyris* species, often in mixed flocks' (Sheldon). Danum population increased 2.5 times after logging (Johns). **Call:** Similar to Chestnut-winged Babbler but higher pitched. The typical cadence is a long *poop* followed by a rapid succession of short *poops* on the same pitch (Sheldon). **Range:** Myanmar to Malay P, Sumatra, Borneo.

3 GREY-HEADED BABBLER *Stachyris poliocephala* 15cm Local resident

A local resident of lowland primary and hill forest throughout Borneo with a preference for steep slopes and submontane localities. Forages in small parties. Shy and often found to be commoner in mist nets than by observation. At Danum population declined after logging (Johns). **Call:** Less noisy than most babblers. 'Calls include quiet descending *dji dji dji du* and a more even *dji dji dji dji dji'* (Robson in del Hoyo). **Range:** Malay P, Sumatra, Borneo.

4 WHITE-NECKED BABBLER *Stachyris leucotis* 15cm Scarce resident

A scarce resident of lowland and hill forest throughout Borneo, with a preference for hill slopes and submontane localities. Typical sites; **Sabah:** Crocker Range, Sepilok, Danum, Maliau. **Brunei:** Kuala Belalong. **Sarawak:** Mulu, Pulong Tau, Gng Penrissen. **Call:** 'The quite loud and carrying song is an isolated phrase of usually four resonant whistles *heuw* or *feuw'* (Wells re Malaya). **Range:** Malay P, Sumatra, Borneo.

5 CHESTNUT-RUMPED BABBLER *Stachyris maculata* 17cm Common resident

A common resident of lowland forests throughout Borneo. After logging at Danum the population declined. (Johns, Lambert). The babbler most likely to join in mixed species hunting parties. **Call:** On Pulau Sibatik (SE Sabah) the forest is filled with their clear cheerful persistent calls, a loud *whop, whop, whop a whop* and *wallap, wallop, wallop* (Norman). **Range:** Malay P, Sumatra, Borneo.

6 BLACK-THROATED BABBLER *Stachyris nigricollis* 16cm Common resident

A common resident throughout the lowlands of Borneo with a preference for disturbed primary forest and poor soil kerangas forest. Typical localities; **Sabah:** Poring, Sepilok, Kinabatangan, Tabin. **Brunei:** Seria, Tasek Merimbun, Sg Tutong. **Sarawak:** Similajau, Semengoh, Niah, Matang. **Kalimantan:** Kutai, Sg Wain, Tg Puting, Gng Palung. **Call:** A series of clear, deliberate, monotone whistles, a dozen or more notes of which the first one or two are emphasised, frequently accompanied by low churring notes from the mate (Holmes). Similar to call of Fluffy-backed Tit-Babbler (Harrap). **Range:** Malay P, Sumatra, Borneo.

7 CHESTNUT-WINGED BABBLER *Stachyris erythroptera* 12cm Common resident

A common resident of lowland forest throughout Borneo. Prior to logging was the second commonest babbler in primary forest at Danum. After logging the population doubled to make it the most common babbler in logged forest (Lambert). **Call:** 'They utter a soft rolling *huh huh huh huh huh* on a high note followed by *ho ho ho ho ho* on a lower note, made by vibrating their throats like barbets, fully revealing the blue patches of skin on either side of their throats' (Norman) which appear to be more obvious in males than females. **Range:** Vietnam, Thailand, Malay P, Sumatra, Borneo.

male in display

♂

♀

7

SCIMITAR AND RAIL-BABBLER

SCIMITAR BABBLERS: Thirteen species of scimitar babblers are found from the Himalayas through SE Asia to the mountains of Java. Only one species occurs in Borneo. They are known for their loud calls, in which pair duet with each other.

1 CHESTNUT-BACKED SCIMITAR-BABBLER *Pomatorhinus montanus* **20 cm**

Scarce resident

Resident in lowland forest throughout Borneo. Locally common in hills and submontane areas. Peers into crevices and holes in trunks and branches in a search for insects – the same foraging niche as Lesser Treeshrew and Slender Treeshrew (Emmons). Often joins mixed hunting parties. **Call:** A quickish *wu-pwi wu-pwi wu-pwi* given three to five times with an immediate response from the second bird *wu-pu pu pu pu pu*. Also a throaty husky *whor-wup* (Robson). **Sabah:** KNP HQ, Poring, Sepilok, Danum, Gomantong, Tabin, Tawau Hills. **Brunei:** Ulu Temburong, Kuala Belalong. **Sarawak:** Mulu, Kelabit Highlands, Similajau, Gng Penrissen, Semengoh, Samunsam. **Kalimantan:** Kayan Mentarang, Sungai Wain, Tg. Puting, Barito Ulu, Muratus Mountains, Gng Palung, Gng Niut. **Range:** Malay P, Sumatra, Borneo.

RAIL-BABBLERS: EUPETIDAE **World 18 species; Borneo 1 species.** The Rail-babblers or Jewel-babblers are centred in New Guinea but recent DNA studies have shown that the Rail Babbler is more closely related to the strange *Picatharthes* or Rockfowl of W Africa than any other Asian or Australian bird. The nest is a shallow cup hidden low down in thick vegetation.

2 RAIL-BABBLER *Eupetes macrocerus* **29 cm**

Rare resident

A scarce, very shy mystery bird throughout its range. A widespread ground bird of lowland and hill forest with a preference for submontane localities. Walks like a rail, taking slow deliberate steps, jerking its head forward at each step. When hunting for invertebrate prey runs fast through the forest. When disturbed, runs away rather than flies. Look for blue skin on neck which is often inflated when calling. **Call:** A monotone whistle very similar to and often confused with the calls of Garnet and Blue-banded Pitta, but shorter, thinner, given more often and no inflection (Yeo S. T.) **Sabah:** Poring, Danum, Tabin, Tawau Hills. **Brunei:** No records. **Sarawak:** Mulu, Pulong Tau, Niah, Gng Penrissen. **Kalimantan:** Sungai Wain, Tg Puting, Barito Ulu, Gng Palung. **Range:** Malay P, Sumatra, Borneo.

BABBLER FORAGING STRATEGIES AND GUILDS Despite the common impression that the babblers are all LBJs (little brown jobs) and too difficult to identify, forest ecologists find them to be some of Borneo's most fascinating birds. It is very easy to observe that an egret has different habits from a hornbill but not so obvious that each babbler species occupies a different ecological niche, forages in a different manner and specialises in hunting different prey. Coincidentally some of these foraging or hunting niches are shared with other birds or mammals. These similar foraging strategies have been described as 'guilds', after the Old English word for profession. For example a wren-babbler may be described as a member of the same guild as a pitta because both are 'terrestrial, litter gleaning insectivores' or ground dwelling birds that hunt for food by turning over leaves. Many tree-babblers, cuckoos, malkohas and treeshrews similarly are all members of the same guild of arboreal, foliage gleaning insectivores because they all hunt for insects through bunches of leaves in trees. See Mead (2008).

SPECIALIST BABBLERS OF DISTURBED FOREST: BOLD-STRIPED TIT-BABBLER AND FLUFFY-BACKED TIT-BABBLER (page 268) Before man arrived in Borneo most of the land was covered in unchanging primary forest. Tree falls and landslides would temporarily open forest gaps allowing sunlight through, which in turn stimulated a flush of secondary growth before the giant dipterocarps slowly asserted their dominance and closed the canopy again. Apart from these temporary gaps, the only open areas were along the banks of rivers and at ecotones. Despite the scarcity of secondary growth, certain birds such as Striped Tit-babblers and Fluffy-backed Tit-babblers exploited these areas as a specialist niche. With the coming of man and the felling of the forests, these relatively scarce areas of 'secondary forest' are now, in the lowlands at least, more extensive than the primary forest itself and the scarce birds that exploited a locally limited niche are now some of the commonest birds in Borneo. See next page.

imm

male in display

TIT-BABBLERS, FULVETTA, ERPORNIS AND YUHINA

1 BOLD-STRIPED TIT-BABBLER *Macronous bornensis montanus* 13cm Saba

[Mann: Striped Tit-babbler *Macronous gularis*] Race *M. b. montanus* is very common
Sabah and E Kalimantan in secondary forest and scrub jungle. Labuan birds are intermedia
(Mann). Usually in small parties, but like most babblers skulks in the undergrowth makin
a lot of noise. Has a strong preference for disturbed/secondary forest and after logging
Danum the population increased eight fold (Johns). See page 266. **Call:** Contact call is
continuous ***chrr chrr.*** Males and females often duet ***uchup uchup uchup.*** Also a series
intermittent barbet-like ***chonk chonk chonk*** calls. **Range:** Borneo, Java.

2 BOLD-STRIPED TIT-BABBLER *Macronous bornensis bornensis* 13cm Resider

[Mann: Striped Tit-babbler *Macronous gularis*] Common resident of secondary forest, riv
banks and coastal scrub in SW Borneo from the lowlands to open areas in the hills. Paler o
head, less heavily striped below and more yellow below than the Sabah race. **Call:** Simil
to Sabah race. **Range:** Borneo, Java. **Taxonomy:** The Borneo/Java Tit-Babblers were split b
Collar/Robson (2007) from the Striped Tit-babbler of Continental Asia. See Mann (2009).

3 FLUFFY-BACKED TIT-BABBLER *Macronous ptilosus* 15cm Common resider

Common resident of secondary, disturbed, logged forest and mangrove edge throughou
lowland Borneo. After logging at Danum the population of this babbler increased four fol
(Johns). See page 266. **Call:** Very noisy. Typical call is a series of hoots ***tonk, tonk-ton***
(Smythies), or ***pong, pong*** (Madoc). Male Raises the loose hair-like feathers on its back whe
calling and puffs out blue-skin cheek pouches. both sexes have distinctive blue skin aroun
eye. **Range:** Malay P, Sumatra, Borneo.

4 BROWN FULVETTA *Alcippe brunneicauda* 14cm Local lowland resider

[Brown Quaker Babbler] [Common Nun-babbler]. A locally common resident of primar
and secondary forest throughout Borneo from the lowlands to the hills including the Kelab
Highlands and Gng Penrissen. Usually found in small family parties and often joins mixe
species hunting parties in the canopy. See page 270. Listen for the call. Feeds on insects an
small berries. **Call:** Its song is one of the commonest sounds of Sabah's forests. It is an up an
down series of notes, ***do-di-do-di-do-dee-do*** (Sheldon). **Range:** Malay P, Sumatra, Borneo.

5 ERPORNIS *Erpornis zantholeuca* 12cm Scarce lowland resider

[White-bellied Yuhina *Yuhina zantholeuca*] A scarce resident of forest throughout Borneo fron
the lowlands to the hills. Locally common in submontane areas, e.g. Crocker Range, Poring, Mulu
and also on Pulau Laut, SE Kalimantan (Davison). Usually solitary, sometimes in small parties
Often joins mixed-species insect-hunting parties. **Call:** A soft rapid series of four rising notes, ***che***
che-che-che, and nasal buzzing, churring and beeping calls (Sheldon). **Range:** Himalayas to
China south to Malay P, Sumatra, Borneo. **Taxonomy:** Related to S. American Vireonidae

6 CHESTNUT-CRESTED YUHINA *Yuhina everetti* 14cm Common montane endemi

Common in mountain forests and submontane areas throughout Borneo south to Gn
Penrissen (Sarawak) and Gng Palung (Kalimantan). Very common at KNP HQ in small famil
groups that come into the open and feed on insects and small berries. Often joins mixe
species insect-hunting parties. Builds small cup-shaped nests in overhangs or holes in banks
Believed to be a co-operative breeder where the whole family rear young. **Call:** High-pitche
twittering.

7 BLYTH'S SHRIKE-BABBLER *Pteruthius aeralatus* 13cm Montane residen

[White-browed Shrike-babbler *P. flavicapis*] Common inhabitant of montane forest throughou
Borneo. Common on Kinabalu in forest at KNP HQ. Found south to Gng Pueh (Sarawak) an
Muratus Mts (SE Kalimantan). Actively gleans insects, often in mixed species flocks in the
middle to upper canopy. Males and females differ. **Call:** ***doo-du-dit-du-dit*** or ***doo-du-dit-dit***
du. The ***dit-du*** sequence might be interpreted as ***teacher.*** The song is repeated over and ove
(Sheldon). **Range:** Himalayas to Malay P, Sumatra, Borneo. **Taxonomy:** Related to S. Americar
Vireonidae. For name change from White-browed Shrike-babbler see Rheindt and Eaton (2009)

male in display

LAUGHING-THRUSHES

The Laughing-thrushes form a subgroup of the babblers, known for their loud 'laughing calls'. (The be
known songster is the Hwamei, popular in China for singing contests. It does not occur in Borneo except as
commonly imported cagebird). The three Borneo species have very loud distinctive calls. All three species a
confined to the Bornean mountain forests and all three are common in the forest around KNP HQ, the Chestnu
hooded Laughing-thrush in particular being so bold that it is hard to miss when climbing Kinabalu. Sexes a
similar. The young are plain like babblers, not spotted like flycatchers and thrushes. Laughing-thrushes buil
messy cup-shaped nests, well hidden in vegetation. All three species are seen in family groups and may bree
co-operatively. Food is a mixture of insects and fruit and they often join the mixed species insect-huntin
parties characteristic of the Borneo mountain forests.

1 SUNDA LAUGHING-THRUSH *Garrulax palliatus* **25cm**   **Local montane reside**

[Grey-and-Brown Laughing-thrush] Locally common in mountain forest throughout th
central mountain chain from Kinabalu south to Kalimantan Ulu. Also found on Gng Palun,
Kalimantan. Shyer and more skulking compared with Chestnut-hooded Laughing-thrush
Nearly always seen in family parties often making up the core component of mixed specie
hunting parties. Look for very distinctive blue skin round eye. **Call:** Has a very distinctiv
group call, starting with descending whistles exchanged between group members then risin
to a group crescendo of chuckles, fading quickly away. **Range:** Sumatra, Borneo.

2 CHESTNUT-HOODED LAUGHING-THRUSH *Rhinocichla treacheri* **25cm** **Montane endemi**

[Smythies/Mann: Chestnut-capped Laughing-thrush *Garrulax mitratus*] One of the mo
noticeable birds of the forest and forest edge in the Borneo mountains. Also found in lo
valleys in mountainous areas. Occurs throughout the central mountains from Kinabalu sout
including Ulu Temburong (Brunei) and Gng Niut and the Muratus Mountains in Kalimanta
At KNP HQ often seen in the open feeding on insects on lawns and fruits and berries in th
gardens. **Call:** Very noisy, heard most often during the dawn chorus, but common througho
the day, a series of loud descending plaintive whistles. Typically seven notes but ofte
shorter. According to Sheldon 'Bornean and Sunda Laughing-thrushes responded as groups t
recordings but Chestnut-hooded responded singly or in pairs. This suggests the possibility c
group territories for the other two laughing-thrushes and pair territories for Chestnut-hooded
Taxonomy: A recent split by Collar and Robson (2007). See Mann, 2008.

3 BORNEAN BALD LAUGHING-THRUSH *Melanocichla calva* **25cm** **Montane endemi**

[Bald-headed Laughing Thrush] [Smythies/Mann: Black Laughing-thrush *Garrulax lugubri.*
Previously regarded as con-specific with the similar bird with a feathered head found in th
Sumatran and Malayan mountains. In Borneo the immature has a feathered head whilst adu
is bald. Less common than the other two laughing-thrushes, it is also more strictly confine
to pristine montane forest from Kinabalu south along the mountain chain to Mulu and Pulor
Tau. Not so far recorded from Kalimantan. **Call:** A variety of loud hoots and ringing whistle
(Sheldon). **Taxonomy:** A recent split by Collar and Robson in del Hoyo (2007) who name
Bare-headed Laughing-thrush. See Mann, 2008.

MIXED SPECIES INSECT-HUNTING PARTIES (bird waves) are common in both lowland and mountain
forests. Often the forest may appear empty of birdlife but moments later a hunting party will pass by
in a wave of activity. By hunting together, at all levels of vegetation, bird flocks both flush and catch
more insects. The range of different bird sizes and abilities maximises catching success. Flocking is most
common when birds are not breeding. Parties appear to focus around noisy 'leader species'. In the lowlands
these leaders are typically noisy drongos and *Malcopteron* babblers (Laman re. Gng Palung). In the Malay
Peninsula McClure (1967) found that canopy flocks often appeared to focus around noisy Brown Fulvettas.
At Danum, Mead (2008) found that Chestnut-rumped Babbler was the key species around which flocks
developed, and their calls kept the group together. In the Borneo mountains the leaders are usually laughing-
thrushes. Standing on a ridge in mountain forest the group call of the Sunda Laughing-thrush can be heard
moving along the valley below and appears to act as a rallying call to all nearby birds to join the group
hunting party. Wren-babblers, squirrels and treeshrews often join in when a bird flock moves through their
territory but they usually cannot keep up with a fast moving bird flock, so the composition of these flocks
is constantly changing.

1

2

adult

3

adult in display

imm

ZOSTEROPIDAE   **World 96 species; Borneo 7 species.**   White-eyes are one of the commonest oriental p
birds, kept for their twittering songs. They are erratically distributed and only locally common in Borneo. Like th
sunbirds most white-eyes have brush-tipped tongues for sipping nectar from flowers. They also eat insects and a
often seen feeding on small berries. White-eyes are usually seen in family parties or small twittering flocks flyi
above the canopy. The nest is a small pocket hung from a twig. Males, females and immatures have matchi
plumage. Due to similarity of appearance the different species are best separated by habitat and location. Whit
eyes seen in the vicinity of towns may well be exotic escapes not illustrated in this Field Guide.

1   ORIENTAL WHITE-EYE   *Zosterops palpebrosus*   **11cm**   **Scarce coastal forest reside**

A scarce resident of mangrove forests, coastal riverine forest and coastal swamp forest along th
coast of W Borneo. Usually in small active flocks which make a constant twittering. Similar
Everett's White-eye, with which it may occasionally overlap in coastal forest. Distinguished
habitat, by pale yellow streak running from the beak to the eye above the black lores and by yellow
plumage on back. **Range:** Afghanistan to Malay P, Sumatra, Borneo, Java, Lesser Sundas.

2   LEMON-BELLIED WHITE-EYE   *Zosterops chloris*   **11cm**   **Kalimantan island reside**

Found only on small islands in the Java Sea off the coast of S Kalimantan including th
Karimatas, Pulau Matasirih and Pulau Marabatuan. One possible record from mangroves
Serasa, Brunei in 1987 (Mann). Similar to Javan with no grey on flanks but has black lor
with just a touch of yellow above and no yellow forehead. **Range:** Moluccas, Sulawesi ar
adjacent small islands.

3   JAVAN WHITE-EYE   *Zosterops flavus*   **9.5cm**   **Scarce Kalimantan reside**

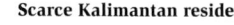

[Mangrove White-eye] An uncommon resident of mangrove and adjacent coastal forest along th
coast of S Kalimantan Common in riverside forest at Tg Puting, and Sabangau, S Kalimantan.
is believed that the coastal White-eyes may be semi-nomadic local migrants due to their erra
occurrence and their known habit of colonising small islands in the Moluccas and the Pacific. Simil
to Lemon-bellied but lacks black lores and has distinctive yellow forehead. **Range:** Borneo, Java.

4   BLACK-CAPPED WHITE-EYE   *Zosterops atricapilla*   **11cm**   **Local montane reside**

A locally common inhabitant of montane forest and occasionally submontane forest patchi
throughout Borneo. Common in the forest around KNP HQ and in the Crocker Range. May overla
with Everett's in submontane areas. Distinguish by dark head and white (not brown) iris givi
the impression of a double white eye-ring. **Brunei:** Gunung Pagon. **Sarawak:** Gunung Mul
Kalimantan: Gng Lunjut (Kayan Mentarang) Muratus Mountains. **Range:** Sumatra, Borneo.

5   EVERETT'S WHITE-EYE   *Zosterops everetti*   **11cm**   **Local lowland reside**

The only white-eye likely to be seen in inland lowland forest where it is scarce. Prefers submonta
localities where it overlaps with Black-capped White-eye which is normally found in montar
forest. Very similar to Oriental White-eye but has no pale yellow streak above black lores. H
brown iris unlike white iris of Black-capped. Overall darker than Oriental. Large flocks seen in tre
plantations near Tawau, Sabah (Sheldon). **Range:** Thailand, Malay P, Philippines, Borneo.

6   BORNEAN IBON   *Oculocincta squamifrons*   **9cm**   **Submontane endem**

[Smythies/Mann: Pygmy White-eye] Generally very scarce but locally common througho
Borneo in the hills and lower mountains. A tiny warbler-like bird that feeds on insects, nect
and small berries in small family parties. **Sabah:** Crocker Range, Gng Magdalena (Tawa
Hills), Gng Trus Madi. **Brunei:** Not recorded. **Sarawak:** Gng Mulu, Kelabit Highlands, Gr
Penrissen. **Kalimantan:** Barito Ulu, Gng Niut.

7   MOUNTAIN BLACK-EYE   *Chlorocharis emiliae*   **14cm**   **High mountain endem**

[*Zosterops emiliae*] The commonest bird at higher levels on Gng Kinabalu, Gng Tambayukon an
Gng Trus Madi in Sabah. Often in small parties feeding on raspberries and rhododendron necta
as well as insects and small berries. See page 371. The wings make a distinct ***trrt trrt*** as the
fly past in the mist when all else is silent. Occasionally seen around KNP HQ, especially durir
droughts. **Brunei:** Not recorded. **Sarawak:** Mulu, Pulong Tau, Gng Pueh. **Kalimantan:** Gng Niu

MYNAS AND STARLINGS

STURNIDAE   **World 114 species; Borneo 11 species.**   The intelligence, adaptability, and scavenging habit* of starlings and mynas have led to a close association with humans. As humans and cultivation increase s* have the populations of starlings and mynas. Both mynas and starlings are often kept as pets for their 'talking abilities and frequently occur as feral species outside their normal range. Often seen in large flocks especiall* at roosts, sometimes in the centre of towns. Calls are a varied range of harsh cackles, keks and whistles, ofte* combined with mimicry of other bird calls. Males and females are usually similar but juveniles are often muc* duller and sometimes streaked. Nests are usually a hollow or hole of some sort, including hollow trees, an* buildings. Many of the N Asian species move southwards in winter months. Borneo is south of their norm* winter range but overshooting vagrants of several species have been recorded. The increasingly common broo* parasitic Koel lays its eggs in the nests of host mynas but this has not yet been recorded for Borneo.

1   JAVAN MYNA   *Acridotheres javanicus*   **25cm**   **Fer***
[Pale-bellied Myna] [White-vented Myna] An expanding feral population in Kuching, first recorded in th* 1980s. Several records from Banjarmasin 1978 to 1989 (Mann). Since 2004 established at Sepilok and expandin* locally in oil palm and along roads (Davison). Established in Tawau since 2007. **Call:** A variety of harsh cal* and loud fluty whistles. **Range:** Originally Java. Feral populations widespread in Asia.

2   CRESTED MYNA   *Acridotheres cristatellus*   **25cm**   **Fer***
[Chinese Crested Myna] Originally from China and commonly kept as a pet for its 'talking' skills, this is a successfu* feral species in many parts of Asia. First recorded Tg Aru KK in 1978, and common there today. Nests in holes in beac* Casuarinas, for which it competes with Blue-naped Parrots and Collared Kingfishers. Widespread records from othe* towns, e.g. BSB, Brunei but no established populations. **Call:** A triple musical whistle. **Range:** Resident China, Vietnam*

3   COMMON MYNA   *Acridotheres tristis*   **25cm**   **Fer***
Small feral breeding populations have been recorded round KK, BSB and Kuching with scattered records fro* elsewhere but nowhere have populations become fully established. Around Kuching less successful tha* Javan Myna. Several recent records Kalimantan (Iqbal et al 2013). **Range:** Africa, Kazakhstan, Iran to Chin* Indochina, S to Malay P. Introduced Australia.

4   SULAWESI MYNA   *Acridotheres cinereus*   **25cm**   **Fer***
[White-vented Myna] This striking pale grey myna from South Sulawesi is often kept as a pet. A small fer* flock has recently become established in the Tawau area E.Sabah. (Wong Tsu Shi). **Range:** Endemic to * Sulawesi. Feral populations also occur on Flores and Sumba in the Lesser Sunda islands of Indonesia.

5   ROSY STARLING   *Sturnus roseus*   **21cm**   **Vagra***
First recorded at Tg Aru beach (Davison 1999), but several recent winter records of juveniles mixed in wit* flocks of Glossy Starlings from Pulau Tiga (Chris Kehoe) and Pulau Mantanani (Dave Bakewell) indicate that * has been overlooked in the past. **Range:** Breeds in Central Asia wintering S to India and SE Europe. Vagran* regularly turn up in the Malay Peninsula.

6   EUROPEAN STARLING   *Sturnus vulgaris*   **21cm**   **Vagra***
One of the commonest birds in Europe and introduced worldwide. A vagrant to Borneo. 3 records, Tempasu* Nov. 1986 (Robson), Pulau Tiga 17 Oct. 2007 (Kehoe), and Penampang K.K. 7 Dec. 2011 (C.K.Leong/Johnatha* Soon). May occur in a uniform pale brown juvenile plumage with a dark bill. **Call:** Sharp *keks* and *wheezes*. Ofte* imitates other birds. **Range:** Europe, Africa, Asia.

7   HILL MYNA   *Gracula religiosa*   **28cm**   **Common reside***

[Grackle] [Malay: Burung Tiong] A common resident of tall forest throughout Borneo. Ofte* kept as a pet for its ability to mimic humans. In captivity very fond of very hot chilli pepper* Now scarce close to inhabited areas due to robbing of tree hole nests. In Assam the loca* erect nest boxes in the forest and sell the young. Usually in pairs. **Call:** A loud distinctiv* descending whistle, *whee ooo*. **Range:** India to Malay P, Sumatra, Borneo, Java.

8   ASIAN GLOSSY STARLING   *Aplonis panayensis*   **20cm**   **Abundant reside***

Very common, very noisy, inhabitant of towns, cultivated areas, coastal forest, islands an* primary forest edge throughout Borneo. Roosts in large flocks, often in towns. Young bird* are heavily streaked. Flocks feed on the nectar of flowering trees. Raids fruit orchards an* scavenges around picnic areas and outdoor restaurants for scraps. Often nests in the crow* of palm trees. **Call:** Harsh chatterings and high-pitched metallic chanks. **Range:** India t* Malay P, Sumatra, Java, Borneo, Sulawesi, Philippines.

MIGRANT AND VAGRANT STARLINGS

1 PURPLE-BACKED STARLING *Sturnus sturninus* **17cm** **Vagrant**
[Daurian Starling] Purple back usually not obvious. Has a double white wing bar compared with single wing bar of Chestnut-cheeked Starling. A scarce passage migrant through Hong Kong. One collected Baram River Sarawak (Nov. 1892). An immature on P. Tiga on 17 Oct. 2007 and 10 the following morning (Chris Kehoe). Recent record Brunei 7 Sept. 2013 (Schiolberg). **Range:** Breeds Mongolia to Korea, winters south to SE Asia Malay P, Sumatra, Borneo.

2 RED-BILLED STARLING *Sturnus sericeus* **22cm** **Not recorded**
[Silky Starling] An abundant winter visitor to Hong Kong and N Vietnam. First record for Borneo at Penampang Dec 2011 (Jordan Sitorus, C.K. Leong, Karim Madoya). **Range:** Breeds Central and S China wintering southwards

3 CHESTNUT-TAILED STARLING *Sturnus malabaricus* **19cm** **Not recorded**
Resident in continental Asia with some populations wintering south to N Malay Peninsula. Inhabits open countryside with trees. A possible vagrant or escape. **Range:** Breeds China, India to Thailand and Indochina, wintering south.

4 CHESTNUT-CHEEKED STARLING *Sturnus philippensis* **17cm** **Scarce migrant**
[Violet-cheeked Starling] [Violet-backed Starling] An uncommon but regular migrant to the Philippines in winter, usually in flocks. In Borneo a very irregular winter visitor, in some years not seen. In other years large flocks feed in cultivated areas and roost in towns (Mann). Recent records from Sepilok and Tabin. Flocks of up to 5,000 have been recorded at Danau Jempang, Mahakam Lakes (Gonner). Often in flocks and roosts with Glossy Starling. **Call:** Harsh *kek kek* calls. Often imitates other birds in breeding season in Japan. **Range** Breeds Sakhalin Island, Russia and Japan, winters in Philippines, Borneo, Sulawesi.

5 WHITE-SHOULDERED STARLING *Sturnus sinensis* **18cm** **Vagrant**
A regular vagrant to the Philippines and at least two records from the W coast of Borneo. **Range:** Breeds China, Hong Kong and winters south to Malay Peninsula.

6 WHITE-CHEEKED STARLING *Sturnus cineraceus* **21cm** **Not recorded**
A common winter visitor to Hong Kong which could occur as a vagrant in Borneo. **Range:** Breeds N China Mongolia, Korea, Japan winters southwards.

7 ASIAN PIED STARLING *Sturnus contra* **22cm** **Not recorded**
[Asian Pied Myna *Gracupica contra*] This starling is often kept as a cagebird in the region and could easily turn up as an escape, particularly in Kalimantan. One record for Palangkarya Kalimantan in Aug. 1984 (Holmes) **Range:** India to Myanmar, Cambodia, Sumatra, Java.

8 BLACK-COLLARED STARLING *Sturnus nigricollis* **28cm** **Vagrant**
[Black-collared Myna *Gracupica nigricollis*] Abundant and increasing in Hong Kong, this bird regularly turns u both as a vagrant and an escape in the Malay P. Recorded Wasan, Brunei, Oct. 1991 (Mann); Penampang (Sabah) Oct. 2008 (Degullacion); Oct. 2011 (Ng, Cheah, Madoya). Note: juvenile plumage is very dull with no black colla **Call:** Nicknamed 'hurdy gurdy' bird due to its loud cheerful piping cry *chee we chee, chee we chee* (Viney). **Range** Breeds S China, S to Thailand.

9 COLETO *Sarcops calvus* **29cm** **Status unknown**
An unusual looking starling with bare pink head skin. Common and widespread in the Philippines including the islands of the Sulu Sea. Often kept as a pet, for its ability to mimic human speech. In Borneo there are four specimen collected on Banggi Island off the north tip of Borneo. These skins in the Sabah Museum are probably escapes, a the skins show cage wear. **Call:** A delightful combination of tinkling, chime-like notes, mixed with mechanical hars gurgles and splutters. Rather like the warming up of an orchestra (Kennedy *et al.*). **Range:** Philippines endemic.

THE HARIBON FOUNDATION AND THE BIRDS OF THE PHILIPPINES

Possessing much richer volcanic soils then Borneo and consequently being far more heavily populated, the Philippine Islands are now largely deforested with many endemic forest birds such as the Philippine Eagle struggling on the brink of extinction. See also pages 136, 252, 314, 320. For further information on the Philippines avifauna see: www.haribon.org.ph. We highly recommend the excellent book, *A Guide to the Birds of the Philippines* (2000) by Kennedy, Gonzales, Dickinson and Fisher for research on Philippine birds.

1

♀ imm

♂

2

♂

♀

3

4

♀

♂

5

♀

♂

6

♂

♀ imm

7

juv

adult

8

imm

adult

9

MIGRANT THRUSHES AND FRUITHUNTER MALAY: MURA

TURDIDAE **World 336 species; Borneo 23 species.** The thrushes are one of the world's greatest bird families. Originating in the Himalayas they have spread to remote islands of the Pacific and Atlantic and are found almost everywhere except Antarctica. In Borneo the thrushes include migrant robins from Asia, the resident forktails and shamas and the odd endemic Fruithunter. Thrushes are flexible in habit, feeding on fruit and insects both on the ground and in trees. Sexes normally differ with the female being much duller than the male. The young are distinctively spotted like young flycatchers, but unlike young bulbuls or babblers. Nests are usually neat cup shapes concealed in a leafy branch or tree hollow. Many thrushes are renowned for their melodious songs and are popular cagebirds. The songs are used for territorial defence and thrushes respond readily to tape playback.

1 SIBERIAN THRUSH *Zoothera sibirica* **22cm** Vagrant

Three vagrant records Gng Matang (Kuching), Oil Rig (Bintulu) and P Selingaan (E Sabah). No records from Philippines. In Hong Kong a scarce passage migrant and winter visitor Nov.– April. Elsewhere usually skulks low down in forest undergrowth but may join flocks of other migrant thrushes in fruiting trees. Male appearance distinctive. Female distinguished by white eyebrow combined with spotted breast. **Range:** Breeds Siberia, winters SE Asia.

2 WHITE'S THRUSH *Zoothera aurea* **30cm** Vagrant

[Eurasian Scaly Thrush] [Davison: Scaly Thrush *Zoothera dauma*] Vagrant to the north west coast of Borneo. Records from P Mantanani and P Manukan indicate that it crosses the S China Sea directly from Vietnam and Thailand. On the continent inhabits the understorey of damp forests. An uncommon winter visitor to the Philippines. **Call:** The song is an eerie loud ringing whistle, the last part slowing as if an echo. (Kennedy *et al.*). **Range:** Breeds Russia to Japan south to SE Asia dispersing south in winter.

3 EYEBROWED THRUSH *Turdus obscurus* **23cm** Local winter visitor

Locally common in large flocks feeding on secondary forest berries in the N Bornean hills and mountains Oct.–March. A flock of c.20 feeding on snails and berries present on Maratua E Kalimantan, January 2011. In cold northern climates most plants fruit in autumn coinciding with movements of migrant thrushes who eat the fruit and disperse the seeds. A similar relationship may exist between this thrush and montane forest in Borneo. See below. **Call:** Thin *tsee* or *zee*. **Range:** Breeds Siberia, winters S India, SE Asia.

4 JAPANESE THRUSH *Turdus cardis* **21cm** Vagrant

[Grey Thrush] One record of an adult male outside the entrance to KNP HQ 5 March 2006 (Bowley). Male breast plumage is distinctive but female can easily be confused with other migrant thrushes. **Range:** Breeds Korea, Japan, China, dispersing southwards in winter.

5 FRUITHUNTER *Chlamydochaera jefferyi* **21cm** Montane endemic

[Black-breasted Fruit-Hunter] Widespread but scarce in mountain forests from the KNP along the mountain chain to Gng Penrissen, Gng Niut and Bukit Baka (Kalimantan). At KNP wanders widely in small groups in search of fruit up to Panar Laban. During a severe drought Fruithunters hunted for snails in the KNP HQ mountain garden, smashing their shells on rocks (Biun). Often joins mixed insect-hunting parties. A nest found along the Silau Silau trail in March was a deep mossy cup in a tall sapling c. 10m off the ground. The female incubated and was fed with a fig and other fruits by the male. **Call:** 'A quiet high pitched *seep*' (Parr).

MIGRANT THRUSHES AND FRUITING SEASONS ON KINABALU A one-year study (Kimura *et al.*) found that berry-bearing, bird-dispersed plants fruited throughout the year at higher levels (Summit Trail) on Kinabalu. Lower down at Park HQ, there were two peaks in fruiting Oct.–Dec. and April. At Poring Kimura found a major peak in Oct.–Nov and a small peak in May. Kimura hypothesised that peak fruiting seasons on Kinabalu were timed to coincide with the arrival and departure of the migrant Eyebrowed Thrush. This theory is interesting but unproven. A one year study is not long enough to define definite fruiting seasons which are known to be affected by irregular climatic factors, such as droughts. More long term data are required. See also pages 32–37, 148 and 214

CHATS, ROCK-THRUSH AND WHISTLING THRUSH

1 WHEATEAR *Oenanthe oenanthe* **14cm**   **Vagran**
[Davison: Northern Wheatear] Five winter records from NW Borneo, one from the Philippines. Perches on low rock or bush in open country, flying low to the next perch. **Range:** Breeds N Europe to N Asia winterin south to Africa, Middle East and India.

2 SIBERIAN STONECHAT *Saxicola maurus* **14cm**   **Vagran**
[Davison: Common Stonechat] Ten winter records from NW Borneo. No records from the Philippines. Simila habits to Wheatear and Pied Bushchat. **Range:** Breeds Europe, N Asia wintering south to Africa, India, SE Asia

3 PIED BUSHCHAT *Saxicola caprata* **13cm**   **Vagran**
One seen 2 May 1998 at KNP HQ, most likely a post breeding juvenile disperser from the Philippines where this is common resident in open country, breeding March to June. Like other chats frequently flicks wings and spreads tail **Call:** Song is a delightful clear whistle comprising six notes. It sounds like a cheery 'It's a wonderful day' repeated a 5–10 second intervals (Kennedy *et al.*). **Range:** Breeds Iran to Indochina, Philippines, Java, Sulawesi.

4 BLUE ROCK-THRUSH *Monticola solitarius pandoo* **23cm**   **Not recorded (race**
Blue Rock-thrush males vary greatly in the proportion of red and blue on their breast. Race *pandoo*, whic breeds in S China, has an all blue breast and may possibly turn up in Borneo.

5 BLUE ROCK-THRUSH *Monticola solitarius philippensis* **23cm**   **Scarce winter visitor rac**

Race *philippensis* is seen in winter months on rocky roadsides, coastal cliffs and larg buildings. Usually solitary, occasionally in pairs. Commonest in coastal W Sabah, muc scarcer further south. Recent winter records Maratua, E. Kalimantan. Breeds in Philippines Malay P and Sumatra on limestone cliffs so it would not be surprising to find it breeding i Borneo. **Call:** The call note is a grating ***tchak*** which is sometimes repeated to form a doubl call (Sheldon). **Range:** Breeds Europe to SE Asia. Northern birds winter southwards.

6 WHITE-THROATED ROCK-THRUSH *Monticola gularis* **19cm**   **Not recorde**
A scarce winter visitor to Malay P from the north which could easily turn up in Borneo. Both male and femal have narrow but clear white throat patch. Typical thrush habits. Inhabits the forest understorey and feeds o the ground. **Range:** Breeds NE Asia winters SE Asia.

7 BORNEAN WHISTLING THRUSH *Myophonus borneensis* **25cm**   **Endemi**
[Davison/Mann: Sunda Whistling Thrush *Myophonus glaucinus*] Only locally common in hil and montane forest in the vicinity of rocky cliffs and rocky streams. Common in the fores from KNP HQ up the Summit Trail to Paka Cave at 3,100m. Common at Mesilau where tam birds feed on moths around the road lights often commencing well before dawn. Small lowlan populations around limestone caves at Mulu and at Bau Caves near Kuching are most likel a relic of colder climates during the last ice age (see below). Frequently raises tail and rapidl flicks it open like a fan. Immature has pale streaks. Female is duller and browner than male **Call:** A clear loud single whistle. **Sabah:** Kinabalu from Poring to Paka Cave, Crocker Range Gng Trus Madi. **Brunei:** Kuala Belalong probable (Biun). **Sarawak:** Mulu from sea level t 1,750m, Bau, Gng Penrissen, Gng Pueh. **Kalimantan:** Ulu Kapuas and Gng Liang Kubung **Taxonomy:** Split by Collar (2005). See Mann, 2008.

THE ORIGIN OF BORNEO'S MONTANE BIRDS   Of the 52 endemic Bornean birds listed in this *Field Guide* (see page 29), 37 are restricted to the mountains and hills with the remaining 15 found in the lowlands. In addition the Bornean mountains host many distinctive Bornean races of Sundaland birds, e.g. Temminck's Babbler and Ochraceous Bulbul. In ecological terms mountains are 'islands' surrounded by a 'sea' of much hotter lowland forest. During cooler periods in the earth's geological history Sundaland's mountains were more or less connected by similar forest and the mountain birds we see today would have been common lowland birds. As global temperatures rose these birds retreated to the mountains. For example Sunda Bush-warbler and Island Thrush are common in the Sundaland mountains but are not found in the intervening lowlands. Endemism is highest on mountains and on small isolated islands because the small population leads to increased inbreeding. See also page 22 and 348).

MIGRANT ROBINS

1 JAPANESE ROBIN *Luscinia akahige* **14cm**   **Vagran**
[*Erithacus akahige*] One record only of a bird found on a ship off the north west coast of Sabah on 25 Nov. 197
(Casement). A scarce winter visitor to Hong Kong. Not yet recorded from the Philippines. **Call:** Distinctive tri
(Viney). **Range:** Breeds Japan and winters S and E China.

2 SIBERIAN RUBYTHROAT *Luscinia calliope* **15cm**   **Vagran**
Two records from Panaga (Brunei) in March and Oct. 1980 (Eden) and a singing male on Kinabalu 27 Jan
1992. A common passage migrant and winter visitor to Hong Kong. An uncommon but regular winter visit
to the Philippines. Probably under recorded in Borneo. Normally skulks in the undergrowth of thick bushes c
reed beds. More often heard then seen. **Call:** Contact call is a plaintive whistle and a variety of *whist* note
In winter quarters utters 'a loud plaintive territorial song' (Viney). **Range:** Breeds E Siberia to Japan. Winter
south to Thailand and Philippines.

3 RUFOUS-TAILED ROBIN *Luscinia sibilans* **14cm**   **Not recorde**
An uncommon passage migrant through Hong Kong. Winters Hong Kong, Vietnam, Thailand so vagrants coul
easily turn up in Borneo. Distinctive habit of standing with cocked tail which it pumps constantly. **Call:** Contac
call is a quiet rattle (Viney). Song is a repeated silvery trill falling slightly in pitch towards the end (Robson
Range: Breeds NE Asia and winters south to Thailand.

4 BLUETHROAT *Luscinia svecica* **15cm**   **Not recorde**
A locally common passage migrant through Hong Kong which winters in N Thailand and Vietnam. Coul
occur as a vagrant in Borneo. Both male and female have distinctive rufous panels on either side of the tail an
prominent white eyebrow. **Call:** Repeated *cheech* (Viney). **Range:** Breeds N Europe to Alaska wintering sout
to India and SE Asia.

5 SIBERIAN BLUE ROBIN *Luscinia cyane* **15cm**   **Scarce winter visit**

A common winter visitor to NW Borneo, much scarcer further south. Feeds on the forest floo
and along the banks of forest streams. Has a distinctive habit of vibrating its tail up and dow
as it walks along the ground. Frequently caught in mist nets during faunal surveys. Ofte
recorded as a night-flying migrant in Malaya, Philippines and Borneo during migration (Oc
and April). One of a few migrants adversely affected by oil palm expansion. **Call:** The alarn
call is a low *chuck chuck chuck* (Viney) repeated rapidly. Note pink legs. **Range:** Breed
Siberia to Japan, wintering south to SE Asia.

6 ORANGE-FLANKED BUSH ROBIN *Tarsiger cyanurus* **15cm**   **Vagran**
[Red-flanked Blue-tail *Luscinia cyanurus*] Two winter records Danum and Klias (Sabah). **Call:** A strider
wheest and a quiet **chack chack** (Viney). Note black legs. **Range:** Breeds N Asia winters SE Asia.

AMBASSADORS FROM JAPAN: JAPANESE BIRDS THAT WINTER IN BORNEO
A large number of birds that breed in Japan May–August spend the winter months in Borneo. Amongst
others these birds include the Siberian Blue Robin and also the Great, Intermediate, Little and Cattle Egrets,
Grey-faced Buzzards, Honey Buzzards, Sparrowhawks and Peregrine Falcons, Ashy Minivets, Brown and
Tiger Shrikes, Paradise, Blue-and-White and Mugimaki Flycatchers, Common, Pacific and Striated Swallows,
and Yellow and Grey Wagtails. The list almost certainly includes the rare and endanged Fairy Pitta and
the Japanese Night Heron, as well as most of the birds listed above on this page. In recent years Japanese
scientists and researchers have become increasingly active in zoological and ecological research in Borneo
and produced much valuable data on Borneo's birdlife including studies of migrant Honey Buzzards
(Higuchi *et al.*), fruiting seasons and birds on Kinabalu (Kimura *et al.*), *Photo Guide to the Birds of Kinabalu*
(Nakayasu, Asama), Bird-pollinated plants at Lambir Hills (Yumoto) and *Pollination Ecology of the Rainforest
at Lambir Hills* (Roubik, Sakai *et al.*). In addition the Government of Japan was the major sponsor of the
BirdLife International Red Data Book *Threatened Birds of Asia* (2002) which lists many threatened Bornean
birds. The major bird conservation group in Japan with 50,000 + members is the Wild Bird Society of Japan
(WBSJ). It has helped organise a number of highly effective campaigns to save migrant birds from hunting
in Japan and Taiwan en route to Borneo. www.wbsj.org. See also page 36.

MAGPIE ROBINS AND SHAMAS

1 ORIENTAL MAGPIE ROBIN *Copsychus saularis adamsi* **20cm**   **Common Sabah ra‹**

Male has black belly and black tail. Female is dark grey above and light grey below fadi›
to white on lower belly. Inhabits mangroves and open countryside including gardens but n
forest where it is replaced by the shamas. Hunts for insects on the ground in typical thrus‹
fashion but also eats berries in trees. In E Sabah expanding its range as forest is converted ‹
oil palm. Found south to the E Kalimantan border where it is replaced by similar but whit
tailed race *C. s. pluto*. **Call:** Often trapped for its fine song which is, however, considere‹
inferior to the song of the shamas. See also page 242. **Range:** See below.

2 ORIENTAL MAGPIE ROBIN *Copsychus saularis pluto* **20cm**   **Common Kalimantan ra‹**

Race *C. s. pluto* is similar to *adamsi* with black belly but has white on tail edge of both ma›
and female. Found throughout SE and E Borneo north to the Sabah border. Appears to ‹
expanding range north of the border where it interbreeds with *C.s adamsi*. **Range:** Magp
Robins are found from Pakistan to the Philippines and Java. Also on Madagascar and t‹
Seychelles Islands where DNA studies show that these populations are related to Asian bir‹
(Sheldon).

3 ORIENTAL MAGPIE ROBIN *Copsychus saularis musicus* **20cm**   **Common Sarawak ra‹**

Common in SW Kalimantan and throughout Sarawak. Has white belly and black an‹
white tail. Unlike the other two Borneo races the female has light grey instead of dark gre›
upperparts. At the Sarawak-Sabah border north to Kota Kinabalu there is a wide region ‹
overlap where the two races vary gradually from south to north (clinal). According to DN‹
studies by Sheldon *et al.* (2009), *C. s. musicus* is probably a recent invader from Sumat‹
gradually hybridising with and swamping the other two Borneo races.

4 WHITE-RUMPED SHAMA *Copsychus malabaricus* **27cm**   **Common reside›**

[Malay: Murai rimba] Occupies the understorey and forest edge of lowland and hill prima›
and secondary forest in most of Borneo south of the Sabah border. Female shamas are simil‹
to but duller than males. **Call:** Both *Copsychus* shamas are fine songsters and males a‹
frequently trapped for their rich chuckling songs. Shamas are expert mimics, often imitati›
other bird calls. See also page 242. **Range:** India to Malay P, Sumatra, Borneo, Java.

5 WHITE-CROWNED SHAMA *Copsychus stricklandi* **25cm**   **Common endem‹**

Similar in habits and habitat to White-rumped Shama but confined to Sabah and N
Kalimantan, south to the Sangkulirang Peninsula. Common on P Gaya but on P Tiga it ‹
replaced by the Magpie Robin which has occupied its ecological niche. **Call:** Similar to Whit‹
rumped Shama. Local aviculturalists frequently breed shamas, but believe that young bir‹
from the wild are stronger birds and better songsters so trapping continues. **Taxonomy:** ‹
Malbaricus and *C. stricklandi* hybridise over a wide area with *C.malaricus* being found as f‹
north as Danum (Sheldon et al).

6 MARATUA SHAMA *Copsychus barbouri* **30cm**   **Endemic to Pulau Maratu‹**

Similar to the White-crowned Shama but about 20 per cent larger. In most birds white ‹
completely absent from the tail, but a minority have a variable amount of white in the side ta›
feathers. One of the commonest birds on Maratua Island in East Kalimantan, where it forage‹
for insects in the forest understorey, coming out to feed on paths in the early morning and la‹
afternoon. There are no Magpie Robins on Maratua, and the Shama is unusually commo›
with territorial males singing at 50-metre intervals along forest paths.

7 RUFOUS-TAILED SHAMA *Trichixos pyrropygus* **21cm**   **Scarce reside›**

[Malay: Murai api (fire)] A scarce resident of lowland forest throughout Borneo, much le‹
common than the other shamas and strictly confined to primary forest. In the Malay Peninsu‹
inhabits peatswamp forest to the exclusion of other shamas (Wells). Common Danum, ‹
Puting and Sabangau. Like the other shamas, it nests in a concealed tree hollow. **Call:** Th‹
song is a series of loud mournful whistles quite unlike the rich chuckles and varied song ‹
the other shamas. **Range:** Malay P, Sumatra, Borneo.

RESIDENT THRUSHES AND FORKTAILS

1 CHESTNUT-CAPPED THRUSH *Zoothera interpres* **16cm** Scarce reside

An extremely shy and wary inhabitant of the primary forest understorey throughout Borne Previously believed to be very rare. However, mist netting has revealed that it is local common at Poring and Serinsim in the KNP and at Danum, Mulu and Semengoh. Night-flyin records indicate nomadic movements. A mist netting record from 2,100m on the Kinaba Summit Trail (Biun). **Call:** In Java a popular songbird which is now being bred in captivi for this purpose (Jepson). **Range:** Thailand, Malay P, Sumatra, Borneo.

2 ISLAND THRUSH *Turdus poliocephalus* **20cm** Local montane reside

[Mountain Blackbird] A locally common inhabitant of the stunted rhododendron an *Leptospermum* forest of the Sabah mountain tops, including Kinabalu, Tambayukon and Tru Madi. Occurs around KNP HQ during droughts but normally lives much higher up. Ofte confused with Maroon Oriole ,very common around KNP HQ, which has a grey not yello bill. Female is similar to but duller than male. **Call:** Harsh warning chatter similar to Europea Blackbird. **Range:** Taiwan, Philippines, Sumatra, Borneo, Java, Sulawesi to Pacific Islands.

3 ORANGE-HEADED THRUSH *Zoothera citrina* **21cm** Scarce resident possible migra

A very local resident of montane and submontane primary forest in Sabah and also a possib winter visitor from Asia. Regularly seen in the forest around KNP HQ. Also recorded from Tru Madi and the Crocker Range. One record from Gng Palung, Kalimantan (Mann). **Call:** In Jav this bird is a star performer in popular bird singing contests and large numbers are harveste from wild nests owned by local farmers to train as songsters (Jepson). See page 240. **Rang** China, India to Malay P, Java.

4 EVERETT'S THRUSH *Zoothera everetti* **23cm** Montane endem

A scarce inhabitant of montane forest from Kinabalu south to the mountains of N Sarawa including Mulu and Pulong Tau. Not recorded Kalimantan. Resident at Bukit Ular near th start of the Kinabalu Summit Trail and at Mesilau. A bird of the forest floor, very secretiv and shy. In flight it makes a quiet clicking or muttering noise and its underwing is distinctiv for its wide white stripe (Sheldon). The pale area on the face is very variable, sometimes completely encircles the eye. **Call:** Soft musical song.

5 BORNEAN FORKTAIL *Enicurus borneensis* **28cm** Montane endem

Found along rocky streams in montane primary forest where it replaces very similar lowlan forktail *E. leschenaulti*, in which tail of male is shorter. Distinguished by location. Population of the two White-crowned Forktails may overlap in submontane areas, e.g. lower slopes c Gng Dulit (Sarawak). Typical locations are KNP HQ, Trus Madi, Kelabit Highlands, Kalimanta mountains. **Call:** A shrill double whistle. **Range:** Himalayas to S China. **Taxonomy:** Split b Moyle *et al.* (2005).

6 WHITE-CROWNED FORKTAIL *Enicurus leschenaulti* **25cm** Local residen

A scarce resident of forested swampy areas and streams throughout the lowlands and hills c Borneo. Typical locations; **Sabah:** Poring, Sepilok, Gomantong, Danum, Tawau Hills. **Brunei** Ulu Temburong, Kuala Belalong. **Sarawak:** Gng Penrissen, Semengoh. Distinguished from E *borneensis* by shorter tail of male and location. **Call:** Similar to *E. borneensis*. **Range:** Mala P, Sumatra, Borneo, Java. **Taxonomy:** See Wells (2002) and Moyle *et al.* (2005).

7 CHESTNUT-NAPED FORKTAIL *Enicurus ruficapillus* **20cm** Local residen

Found throughout forested Borneo along small streams but commonest in the hills an submontane areas. Like the other two forktails, very wary of disturbance, flying off wit a shrill whistle along the stream. **Sabah:** Poring, Sepilok, Danum, Tabin. **Brunei:** Ul Temburong, Kuala Belalong. **Sarawak:** Mulu, Similajau, Gng Penrissen. **Kalimantan:** Kutai Sg Wain, Barito Ulu. **Call:** Loud three notes higher on the second note (Sheldon). **Range** Malay P, Sumatra.

FLYCATCHERS

MUSCICAPIDAE **World 328 species; Borneo 38 species.** The Flycatchers are one of the world's large bird families with their highest diversity in tropical forests. They include the Jungle Flycatchers, the Typic Flycatchers (including the Brown and the Blue Flycatchers), the Fantails and the Paradise Flycatchers an Monarchs.

JUNGLE FLYCATCHERS **World 11 species; Borneo with 5 species including 1 migrant and 1 endemic i the world centre of distribution.** Jungle flycatchers inhabit the understorey of primary forest gleaning insect from low vegetation like babblers or sometimes from the ground like thrushes. They occasionally sally fo insects like typical flycatchers and join mixed feeding flocks that pass through their territory. Males and female are similar. Young are heavily spotted like all flycatchers. With their quiet unobtrusive habits and similar brow plumages they are best distinguished by locality. The nests are globes suspended from a twig.

1 EYEBROWED JUNGLE FLYCATCHER *Rhinomyias gularis* 15cm **Montane endemi**

Found throughout the Borneo mountains including the Muratus Mountains in SE Kalimantan b generally very scarce. Locally common and tame in the forest understorey on Kinabalu at KN HQ and Mesilau. **Call:** Very quiet. Repeated alarm call *prrrt* (van Balen). **Taxonomy:** Previousl regarded as part of a superspecies with three other races confined to different islands in th Philippines. Now classified as a Borneo endemic. Split by Wolters (1980). See Mann 2008.

2 RUFOUS-TAILED JUNGLE FLYCATCHER *Rhinomyias ruficauda* 15cm **Residen**

A very scarce submontane resident recorded from Kinabalu south to Mulu and throughou the Sarawak mountains to Gng Penrissen near Kuching. No Kalimantan records. **Call:** A rapi series of 1, 2 or 3 high-pitched notes *chirr chirr chirr* or a pleasant *cheep cheep chirr* followe by a high-pitched buzz or trill (Kennedy re Philippines). **Range:** Borneo, Philippines.

3 FULVOUS-CHESTED JUNGLE FLYCATCHER *Rhinomyias olivacea* 15cm **Residen**

A scarce resident of the lowland forests of Sabah and Brunei including the islands of Bangg and Balambangan but not Gaya or Manukan Islands (TARP). Not known from Sarawak c Kalimantan. Netted in scrub at Serinsim (northern slopes of Kinabalu) where one woul normally expect Grey-chested Jungle Flycatcher (Sheldon). Possibly under recorded. **Call** 'A fine tinkling song of 6–8 notes on a descending scale, frequent low *churr* notes' (Wells) **Range:** Malay P, Sumatra, Borneo, Java.

4 GREY-CHESTED JUNGLE FLYCATCHER *Rhinomyias umbratilis* 15cm **Residen**

A locally common resident of lowland and hill forest throughout Borneo. Common on P Gay (Sabah), Bako (Sarawak) and at Tg Puting (Kalimantan). In Borneo and the Malay Peninsul the only jungle flycatcher found in peatswamp forest where it is common and where othe jungle flycatchers do not occur (Wells). **Call:** 'Its five note song is like a squeaky door. Th first note is lowest (although very high pitched) and is followed by four higher, descending notes' (Sheldon). **Range:** Malay P, Sumatra, Borneo.

5 BROWN-CHESTED JUNGLE FLYCATCHER *Rhinomyias brunneatus* 15cm **Vagran**
One mist netted BSB (Brunei) by Mann Oct. 1982 is the only record for Borneo. Distinguished from other Jungle Flycatchers by yellow lower mandible and faint grey/brown scallops on white throat. The main wintering are is the Malay Peninsula where it is regular but uncommon in the understorey of lowland primary forest an where it has been recorded as a night-flying migrant (Wells). **Call:** Haunting ventriloquial song with a doubl high inflection followed by three whistles. Has a human quality (Viney). **Range:** Breeds SE China, winte visitor to Malay P, Singapore. A relict population is resident in the Nicobar Islands. **BLI:** Vulnerable.

BROWN FLYCATCHERS

Of the 10 migrant flycatchers that occur in Borneo, four are small, mainly plain, greyish brown birds that breed in N Asia but winter in Borneo. One might ask why any flycatcher bothers to leave in the spring, with so many mosquitoes in Borneo and this is exactly the case with one race of the Asian Brown Flycatcher. Two races are migrants, but a third race *M. d. umbrosa* is a scarce local breeder. Borneo flycatchers are usually unobtrusive birds of the forest understorey, but the Brown Flycatchers are birds of the forest edge. They sally for insects from a prominent perch overlooking a forest clearing, usually returning back to the same perch. Migrant Brown Flycatchers defend winter feeding territories by chasing away other flycatchers in Borneo. Unlike most other flycatchers, males and females are similar. Juveniles are spotted. First year birds often occur in Borneo and some still retain vestiges of spotting on the back. Calls are sharp chits and indistinct soft songs.

1 FERRUGINOUS FLYCATCHER *Muscicapa ferruginea* **12cm** **Scarce winter visitor**

Scarce to rare migrant with scattered records from NW Borneo with an apparent preference for the hills. Also one record from P Sipadan (E Sabah). Only one record from Sarawak (Gng Murud) and no Kalimantan records. Easily distinguished from the other brown flycatchers by brighter colours especially the bright rufous rump and flanks and the prominent white eye ring. **Range:** Breeds Himalayas to S China and winters in SE Asia.

2 DARK-SIDED FLYCATCHER *Muscicapa sibirica* **13cm** **Scarce winter visitor**

Scarce migrant to the whole of Borneo but most common in NW Borneo. Inhabits forest from the coast to the mountains. Plumage is variable and this bird is easily confused with Grey-streaked Flycatcher. The extent and density of streaking varies from almost none to quite heavy. Breast is generally darker with streaks less contrasting than in Grey-streaked. **Range:** Breeds NE Asia and winters in SE Asia.

3 GREY-STREAKED FLYCATCHER *Muscicapa griseisticta* **15cm** **Rare winter visitor**

Scarce to rare migrant with scattered records, mainly from the edges of coastal forest on both the NW and NE coasts of Borneo. Usually more heavily streaked than Dark-sided Flycatcher with streaks more contrasting against a whiter background. Also white streak in front of the eye is more prominent than in Dark-sided Flycatcher, and tip of primary feathers is the same length as the tail, unlike the shorter wings of the other brown flycatchers. **Range:** Breeds NE Asia and winters east of Borneo in Wallacea.

4 ASIAN BROWN FLYCATCHER *Muscicapa dauurica dauurica* **12cm** **Commonest race**

The nominate race of the Brown Flycatcher *M. d. dauurica* is a common migrant, widespread in winter months, found in all areas but with a preference for clearings in the forest in the hills where it sallies for insects from a prominent perch. Because at least three races of Brown flycatcher occur in Borneo, *M. d. dauurica* has probably been over recorded in the past and the other two races listed below under recorded. **Range:** Breeds Central Siberia, N China to Japan wintering SE Asia.

5 ASIAN BROWN FLYCATCHER *Muscicapa dauurica williamsoni* **12cm** **Scarce race**

[Considered by some taxonomists to be a separate species, Brown-streaked Flycatcher *Muscicapa williamsoni*] This migrant race is much less common than *M. d. dauurica* in Borneo. Scattered records include September migrants on Pulau Layang[2]. Distinguish from *M. d. dauurica* by indistinct broad brown streaks on the buffy to brownish buff breast and flanks (Davison). Lower bill pale yellow, except dark tip. **Range:** Breeds Myanmar to N Malaya. Winters south to Malay Peninsula.

6 ASIAN BROWN FLYCATCHER *Muscicapa dauurica umbrosa* **12cm** **Scarce resident race**

A scarce resident of lowland forest with a few scattered breeding records from Sabah (Sepilok), and Brunei at Lamunin and Labi (Mann 2008) and E Kalimantan (van Balen). Darker all over than the migrant species and with shorter wings. Evidence of breeding Brown Flycatchers would be diagnostic. Typically flycatchers build their nests in a tree hollow but the Brown Flycatcher is reputed to build a small cup-shaped nest on an open branch.

1

imm

imm var.

2

adult

3

imm

adult

juv

6

adult

m

4

5

dult

SMALL FLYCATCHERS

1 YELLOW-RUMPED FLYCATCHER *Ficedula zanthopygia* 13cm Vagrant

Five sight records including Pulau Layang[2], Tawau Hills, Brunei and Tg Puting indicate that this is a very scarce but regular winter visitor. Male has distinctive white eyebrow. First winter males resemble females but have a black tail. **Range:** Breeds N Asia, winters south to SE Asia.

2 NARCISSUS FLYCATCHER *Ficedula narcissina* 13cm Scarce winter visitor

An uncommon winter visitor to all parts of Borneo, most common in NW Borneo. 'During 12–14 April 1983 dozens of night migrating individuals were attracted to a light set on a helicopter platform at 1,300m at Rinangisan in the Crocker Range near the Beaufort to Tenom road' (Sheldon). First winter males resemble females. Look for prominent yellow eyebrow on male. Two males feeding on berries at Gng Penrissen 4 March 2009 Bakewell. **Range:** Breeds Sakhalin Island, Japan, winters south to Hainan, Philippines, Borneo.

3 GREEN-BACKED FLYCATCHER *Ficedula elisae* 13cm Not recorded

Previously considered a race of the Narcissus Flycatcher. Distinguished from Yellow-rumped Flycatcher by green not black back. This close relative of the Narcissus Flycatcher is a regular winter visitor to the Malay P. in small numbers. **Range:** Breeds E China, NE Hebei, Shanxi, winters south to S Thailand, Malay P, Singapore.

4 MUGIMAKI FLYCATCHER *Ficedula mugimaki* 13cm Locally common winter visitor

Scarce winter visitor throughout Borneo with a preference for submontane and montane areas. Locally common at KNP HQ in winter months. First winter males similar to females. Distinguished from Rufous-chested Flycatcher by the smaller eyebrow of the male, by different localities (islands on migration or mountain forest) and by preferred habitat – forest edge not forest understorey. **Range:** Siberia, China, Korea, winters south to SE Asia.

5 SNOWY-BROWED FLYCATCHER *Ficedula hyperythra* 11cm Montane resident

A very common resident of the understorey of mountain forests, including Kinabalu, Crocker Range and Mulu. Hunts for insects low down amongst shrubs and fallen logs. Often tame and curious about passing strangers. Both males illustrated are of Kinabalu birds race *F.h. sumatrana*. See page 296 re plumages. The males of a relict population on Gng Penrissen, Gng Niut and Gng Pueh in SW Sarawak have black sides to face and have been described as *F.h. mjobergi*. **Call:** A high-pitched squeaking song, *zu zee zu zu*, with the *zee* note being higher in pitch (Sheldon). **Range:** Himalayas to China, south to Malay P, Sumatra, Borneo, Java, Philippines.

6 TAIGA FLYCATCHER *Ficedula albicilla* 13cm Scarce winter visitor

[Red-breasted Flycatcher *Ficedula parva*] [Red-throated Flycatcher] Previously considered a race of Red-throated Flycatcher. A regular winter visitor in small numbers mainly to NW Borneo coastal districts. Adult male has distinctive red throat bordered with grey. Most birds seen are females or the similar first winter males. Both sexes have distinctive white panels on either side of the tail and a habit of cocking the tail and quivering the wings at the same time. **Call:** A harsh chatter. **Range:** Breeds N Siberia, winters southwards.

7 RUFOUS-CHESTED FLYCATCHER *Ficedula dumetoria* 11cm Lowland resident

A scarce resident of the understorey of lowland and hill forest throughout Borneo with a preference for submontane localities. **Sabah:** Poring, Danum. **Brunei:** Ulu Temburong, **Sarawak:** Semengoh, Gng Penrissen, Gng Gading. **Kalimantan:** Kutai, Sungai Wain, Gng Palung. Similar to Mugimaki but smaller. Mugimaki is more likely to be seen at the forest edge, not in the understorey. The eyelids are a distinctive bright blue. **Call:** *sst sst* (Harrisson). **Range:** Malay P, Sumatra, Borneo, Java.

8 LITTLE PIED FLYCATCHER *Ficedula westermanni* 11cm Common resident

One of the commonest most easily seen flycatchers of the Borneo mountains. Forages through the canopy often perching prominently on bare branches. **Call:** A distinctive repeated *pi pi pi churrr churrr* and variations thereof, often heard in the forest around KNP HQ and along the Crocker Range. Common Gng Penrissen, Muratus Mts. **Range:** Himalayas to Malay P, Sumatra, Borneo, Philippines, Sulawesi.

BLUE FLYCATCHERS

1 BLUE-AND-WHITE FLYCATCHER *Cyanoptila cyanomelana* **17cm** **Winter visito**

Scarce winter visitor found throughout Borneo but commonest in NW Borneo in mountain forest, e.g. KNP HQ. First year males are similar to females but with some blue on the wings. As with other migrant flycatchers often seen on the NW Borneo islands, e.g. P Layang[2], P Mantanani, P Manukan and P Tiga during peak migration periods in October. Frequently feed on berries, as well as insects. **Range:** Breeds Siberia, China, Korea, Japan, winters in SE Asia.

2 DARK BLUE FLYCATCHER *Cyornis concretus* **19cm** **Scarce resident**

[White-tailed Blue Flycaycher] An uncommon resident of primary forest from the lowland to the mountains with a preference for submontane slope forest e.g. Poring where it is locally common. Unlike the Continental race *C.c.concretus* which has white tail panels these are absen in Bornean males but present in females. **Call:** A soft, slightly upslurred drawn out *pwee* (Myers 2009). **Range:** India to Vietnam south to Malay P., Sumatra, Borneo. **Taxonomy:** Differences in plumage, habits and call indicate that *C.c.everetti* the Bornean endemic race should probably be split as a new Bornean endemic species *Cyornis everetti* pending further research.

3 HILL BLUE FLYCATCHER *Cyornis banyumas* **15cm** **Scarce resident**

Found in submontane forest throughout Borneo. Scarce in Sabah. Recorded from Crocke Range and Sayap (KNP). On Gng Mulu it replaces the Bornean Blue Flycatcher at 450m (Wells). In SE Kalimantan abundant in the Muratus Mts (Davison). **Call:** Male has a very fine song and is trapped from the wild for the Javan bird trade. See page 240. **Range:** Himalaya to S China south to Malay P, Borneo, Java. In the Malay Peninsula both resident and migran races occur.

4 BORNEAN BLUE FLYCATCHER *Cyornis superbus* **15cm** **Endemic**

An uncommon endemic resident of the understorey of primary forest with a preference for the hills. Overlaps with Large-billed Blue in lowland primary forest but is less common. It replaces the Malaysian Blue in tall forest inland of riverine forest and scrub (Wells). **Call:** A quick series of five notes (Sheldon). **Sabah:** Poring, Kinabatangan, Danum, Sepilok, Tabin, Tawau Hills. **Brunei:** Andulau, Kuala Belalong, Sungai Rampayoh. **Sarawak:** Mulu, Gng Penrissen. **Kalimantan:** Kutai, Wain, Mentarang, Barito Ulu, Gng Palung, Gng Lumut.

5 PALE BLUE FLYCATCHER *Cyornis unicolor* **16cm** **Scarce resident**

A scarce resident of submontane primary forest throughout Borneo. Also found in the lowlands, e.g. at Danum, Kinabatangan. Unlike the other blue flycatchers which frequent the forest understorey keeps to the canopy of tall forest and therefore is rarely seen. The light blue plumage of the male could be confused with male Verditer Flycatcher but look for pale forehead, grey belly and white under tail coverts, absent in Verditer. **Range:** Himalayas to S China, south to Malay P, Sumatra, Borneo, Java.

6 LARGE-BILLED BLUE FLYCATCHER *Cyornis caerulatus* **14cm** **Scarce resident**

The characteristic blue flycatcher of inland lowland forest, where it replaces the Mangrove Blue typical of coastal forests (Smythies). This habitat is the most threatened by agriculture hence its listing as vulnerable. On Mulu, found in forest away from the riverside habitat of the Malaysian Blue (Wells). Rare in Kalimantan. Note distinctive black chin of male. **Call:** 'A soft hissing buzz followed by a higher clear, descending note' (Sheldon). 'A typical flycatcher song of two or three thin metallic notes climbing up and down the scale' (Gonner). **Range** Sumatra, Borneo. **BLI:** Vulnerable.

7 MALAYSIAN BLUE FLYCATCHER *Cyornis turcosus* **13cm** **Common resident**

The commonest blue-and-orange flycatcher in inland primary and tall secondary forest throughout Borneo, from the lowlands to the hills. In coastal forest and mangroves replaced by Mangrove Blue Flycatcher. Usually found close to rivers and streams in flat alluvial flood plain forest where it sallys for insects in the forest understorey. **Call:** Contact call *tik tik* **Song:** Sweet but almost inaudible ditty (Batchelor). **Range:** Malay P, Sumatra, Borneo.

C.c. caerulatus

6

C.c. rufifrons
(S.W. Borneo only)

BLUE FLYCATCHERS AND SHORTWING

1 INDIGO FLYCATCHER *Eumyias indigo* **14cm**   Common montane resident

A common resident of the mountain forests of Sabah but very local further south. A very obvious and tame resident of the forest edge at KNP HQ, sallying for insects from roadside bushes and trees. Male and female similar. The amount of white in the tail is very variable. **Brunei:** The only record is from Gng Pagon, Ulu Temburong. **Sarawak:** Recorded Gng Murud and Gng Mulu only. **Kalimantan:** Recorded only from Gng Lunjut, Kayan Mentarang. **Call:** A high-pitched sequence of soft whistles. **Range:** Sumatra, Borneo, Java.

2 VERDITER FLYCATCHER *Eumyias thalassina* **14cm**   Scarce resident

A widespread but thinly scattered, resident of submontane forests. Less commonly also in the lowlands, e.g. Gomantong. Plumages are very variable from dark blue to pale greenish blue, the female always being duller and paler than the male. **Call:** A high-pitched random warble lasting five or six seconds and repeated fairly frequently (Sheldon). **Range:** Breeds Himalayas to Malay P, Sumatra, Borneo. A possible migrant from Continental Asia to Borneo.

3 PYGMY BLUE FLYCATCHER *Muscicapella hodgsoni* **10cm**   Rare montane resident

[*Ficedula hodgsoni*] A rare resident of submontane and montane forest, from Kinabalu south to Barito Ulu in Kalimantan. Locally common in the Crocker Range and on Mt Trus Madi (Sabah). A tiny flycatcher which behaves like a warbler. Actively gleans for insects through leaf bunches and hanging vines. Constantly cocks tail and flicks its wings at the same time. **Call:** A high-pitched *tsee-oo*, with an accompanying staccato churred trill. Also a high-pitched *pink* (Sheldon). **Range:** Himalayas to Malay P, Sumatra, Borneo.

4 MANGROVE BLUE FLYCATCHER *Cyornis rufigastra* **14cm**   Common resident

The commonest blue and orange flycatcher in coastal forest and mangroves throughout Borneo. Sometimes found inland when its range can overlap with Malaysian Blue Flycatcher, e.g. at Tasek Merimbun (Brunei) and Tg Puting (Kalimantan). The only blue flycatcher found on both small and large islands around Sabah including Banggi and Pulau Tiga and all the islands of TARP near KK. **Call:** Four descending notes followed by a slurred, abruptly ending, rising note, *do do do do deet* (Sheldon). **Range:** Malay P, Sumatra, Borneo, Java, Philippines.

5 TICKELL'S BLUE FLYCATCHER *Cyornis tickelliae* **14cm**   Local resident

A Sumatran species which has been recorded on the Anamba Islands (normally considered to have a Bornean avifauna) between Sumatra and Borneo. It does not occur on the Bornean mainland. **Range:** India to Indochina south to Malay P, Sumatra.

6 WHITE-BROWED SHORTWING *Brachypteryx montana* **15cm**   Montane resident

A scarce bird of densely vegetated gullies often near mountain streams. Regularly visits the bare rocks of the Kinabalu summit area and in Kelabit Highlands seen at edge of rice fields. Found in the mountains south from Kinabalu to Mulu and Kayan Mentarang. Feeds on insects, snails. **Call:** The song is frequently heard but the bird is not often seen. One of the most beautiful sounds of the Bornean mountains, a long drawn out fluting song, with an eerie or melancholy quality. It is often uttered in ravines for (apparent) maximum acoustic effect (Sheldon). **Range:** Myanmar to Malay P, Sumatra, Borneo, Java, Philippines.
Note: The Shortwing is considered to be a small thrush but is included on this plate because of a superficial similarity to the blue flycatchers.

PLUMAGE OF THE BLUE CYORNIS FLYCATCHERS The plumage of first year males of some of the migrant flycatchers which visit Borneo e.g. Mugimaki and Blue and White is similar to that of the female. In contrast young males of the blue *Cyornis* flycatchers appear to progress straight from spotted juvenile to adult blue plumage without going through an immature phase. Adult *Cyornis* plumage however does vary considerably in appearance firstly because the brighter blues (which are used for display) are derived from structural colours which act like a mirror and will vary in intensity dependent on the viewing angle. Secondly both male and female *Cyornis* plumage colour appears to deepen and intensify with age.

PARADISE FLYCATCHERS AND FANTAILS

PARADISE FLYCATCHERS: MONARCHIDAE **World 13 species; Borneo 3 species.** Like the other monarc flycatchers, paradise flycatchers are polymorphic. Males can occur rarely as short-tailed brown morphs and eve rarer white females have been recorded. 'The phases appear to be age related, white birds being older, males may t in breeding condition in brown short-tailed plumage, and females rarely attain long white-tailed plumage' (Mann,

1 ASIAN PARADISE-FLYCATCHER *Terpsiphone paradisi* **22cm and 45cm Common resident**

A common, distinctive inhabitant of lowland forests throughout Borneo. Sexes differ in plumag and in form with the male possessing tail feathers up to 45cm. Hawks insects in the understorey primary forest. Male often seen flying across a river or path with white tail streamers trailing. Nes are neat cups built in the fork of a sapling. May be polygynous, see below. However, male doe incubate (Davison). **Call:** A rapid loud sequence of whistles variously described as *auk auk au* or *twit twit twit* or *kick kek ke*. **Range:** Breeds India to China south to Malay P, Sumatra, Borne Northern populations are migratory and could occur as vagrants.

2 JAPANESE-PARADISE FLYCATCHER *Terpsiphone atrocaudata* **Vagran**

One record of a vagrant at KNP HQ 23 Jan. 1992. Call: A strident tri-syllabic *gih gih gih* (Yamashina). **Rang** Breeds Japan south to Batan Islands (N Philippines) wintering south.

FANTAIL FLYCATCHERS: RHIPIDURIDAE **World 44 species; Borneo 3 species.** In Malay the fantail flycatche are known as Murai Gila or Mad Thrush for their ceaseless activity. They flit from one branch to another constant fanning their tails. All three species have prominent white tail tips and their constant tail flicking is probably strategy to startle and flush insects. The three Borneo species occupy very different habitats. Males and females a similar. Fantails build small neat cup-shaped nests. They are highly territorial when nesting.

3 WHITE-THROATED FANTAIL *Rhipidura albicollis* **18cm Local resident**

The common fantail of mountain forests and their edge. Often joins in mixed species huntir flocks. At KNP HQ. it frequents the roadside lights at dawn searching for moths. **Call:** distinctive series of high-pitched descending notes often followed by a series of ascendir notes. Illustrated is N Borneo race *R. a. kinabalu*. Race *R. a. sarawacensis* found at Gr Penrissen and in Kalimantan has only faint narrow throat stripe. **Range:** India to Malay Sumatra, Borneo.

4 SPOTTED FANTAIL *Rhipidura perlata* **18cm Local resident**

The common fantail of lowland and submontane primary forest. Hunts for insects in the canop often in mixed species hunting parties. Whitehead considered it rare but it is likely there w little virgin forest left on his route from Kota Belud to Kinabalu even in 1887. Overlaps with bo Pied Fantail and White-throated at the ecotone. **Call:** A series of six or seven melodious not and a variety of cheerful whistles. **Range:** Malay P, Sumatra, Borneo, Java.

5 PIED FANTAIL *Rhipidura javanica* **17cm Local resident**

The common fantail of open countryside, gardens, small islands, mangroves and secondar forest throughout Borneo. Sometimes found in oil palm plantations. Common in cultivate areas in the hills, e.g. Kelabit Highlands. **Call: *swit-sweet*** or **swit swit swit** **sweet swe** **sweet** the sweet note slurring upwards. (Sheldon). **Range:** Myanmar to Vietnam south Malay P, Sumatra, Borneo, Java, Philippines.

6 WILLIE WAGTAIL *Rhipidura leucophrys* **21cm Vagran**

A common garden bird throughout Australia. One record from Sandakan (Sabah). Photographed by Hazwa Suban at Kg. Istemewa, Batu Sapi, 18 July 2013, after it had been in the area for 3 months. Probably a austral migrant which overshot. Slightly larger than Pied Fantail. No white tips to the tail feathers. Instead fanning the tail it wags the tail from side to side whilst walking on the ground hunting for insects. The whi eyebrow is very variable, and changes with the bird's sex and emotional condition from near invisible conspicuous (Pizzey). **Range:** Resident Australia to New Guinea and Seram in the Moluccas. Locally migrator and dispersive. A vagrant has been recorded from the Chatham Islands, New Zealand.

CANARY FLYCATCHERS AND MONARCHS

CANARY FLYCATCHERS: CULCICAPA **World 2 species; Borneo 1 species.** The Canary flycatchers a considered most unusual by taxonomists because they are the only flycatchers where the young are not spotte and they may not be flycatchers at all.

1 GREY-HEADED CANARY FLYCATCHER *Culicicapa ceylonensis* **11.5cm**   **Reside**

[Grey-headed Flycatcher] A locally common resident of primary forest throughout Born with a wide altitude range from the lowlands to the mountains up to around 1,600m. Mc commonly found in the primary forest understorey, where it perches alone or in pairs, haw insects and calls for long periods of time (Sheldon). Also hawks for insects at the forest ed and in tree plantations. Very active and often flicks its tail. Whitehead recorded this bi acting as a host to Javan Hawk Cuckoo *H. fugax* on 29 April. **Call:** Five note *saw-see-saw-se saw* (Sheldon). **Range:** Himalayas to Vietnam, south to Malay P, Sumatra, Borneo, Java.

MONARCH FLYCATCHERS: MONARCHIDAE **World 97 species; Borneo 3 species.** Monarchs are bo forest insectivores which glean insects from leaves and branches and hawk insects in flight. Previously regarde as flycatchers, DNA studies show they are related to wood shrikes. Most birds bathe regularly to keep the feathers in good condition. Usually this just means preening their feathers after the daily afternoon rain showe The monarchs (including the paradise flycatchers) are particularly known for plunging into rivers or pools t bathe on sunny days. The blue plumage of both the philentomas can appear grey or blue depending on th light. They build small cup-shaped nests on small branches. Sexes differ in plumage and the male Rufou winged Philentoma appears in three different morphs.

2 BLACK-NAPED MONARCH *Hypothymis azurea* **12.5cm**   **Common reside**

[Malay: Burung kangan] Common resident throughout Borneo in all types of primary fore from the lowlands to the hills. Often occurs on islands, e.g. P Gaya, P Tiga, P Maratua an in peatswamp and secondary forests. Very common in N Borneo, less common further sout but occurs south to Tg Puting. On P Maratua endemic race *H. a. aeria* male has no blac nape and the female has blue not brown back, a possible split. See page 344. **Call:** A lou series of notes on the same pitch *sweet-sweet-sweet*. On P Tiga the birds called *chi-choy-cho choy* with the *chi* note on a higher pitch than the *choy* (Sheldon). **Range:** India to Malay Sumatra, Borneo, Java, Philippines.

3 MAROON-BREASTED PHILENTOMA *Philentoma velatum* **17.5cm**   **Scarce reside**

An uncommon resident of forest throughout Borneo with a wide altitude range from se level up to c. 1,650m. Found in both primary and logged forest and adjacent tree plantatior where it hunts for insects at all levels from the canopy to the ground. Often conspicuous du to noisy active behaviour and often seen near streams. **Call:** Crys *chazz, chazz, chazz* as flies, and a sharp *chup chup*, followed by *chazz, chazz* with the head turning side to sid when perched (Norman). **Sabah:** Crocker Range, Poring, Sepilok, Gomantong, Kinabatanga Danum, Tabin. **Brunei:** Labi, Kuala Belalong. **Sarawak:** Mulu, Kelabit Highlands, Similajau Gng Penrissen, Niah, Semengoh. **Kalimantan:** Kayan Mentarang, Kutai, Barito Ulu, Gn Palung. **Range:** Malay P, Sumatra, Borneo, Java.

4 RUFOUS-WINGED PHILENTOMA *Philentoma pyrhopterum* **15cm**   **Local resider**

A locally common resident in forests throughout Borneo with a wide altitude range up t around 1,500m. More flexible in habitat than Maroon-breasted Philentoma and more ofte occurs in secondary and peatswamp forest. A rare entirely rufous morph has been recorde and under 5% of males occur in a pure blue morph (illustrated) which appears to mimi the female Maroon-breasted Philentoma. **Call:** A loud double whistle with the first not higher than the second *wee tooooo*. **Sabah:** Poring, Sepilok, Kinabatangan, Danum, Tabir **Brunei:** Ulu Temburong, Kuala Belalong, Tasek Merimbun, Seria, Badas. **Sarawak:** Mulu Kelabit Highlands, Similajau, Semengoh, Gng Penrissen. **Kalimantan:** Kayan Mentarang Kutai, Sungai Wain, Barito Ulu, Tg Puting, Gng Palung. **Range:** Vietnam, Thailand, Malay Sumatra, Borneo.

DICAEIDAE   **World 58 species; Borneo 12 species including 2 endemics.**   Flowerpeckers are found only
the Oriental Region south to Australia with Borneo at the centre of their world distribution. Only the Philippin
with 14 species has more than Borneo. In Australia the single flowerpecker is known as the Mistletoe Bird a
throughout their global range flowerpeckers are very closely associated with epiphytic mistletoe plants. T
characteristic contact call of all flowerpeckers is a steady *chit chit chit chit* as it zips overhead. In half the Borne
flowerpeckers sexes are similar, in the others the female is duller than the male. Immatures resemble femal
but have pale or orange beaks. Young males rapidly develop scarlet patches like their fathers. Flowerpeck
nests are simple open topped pockets normally hung under a roof of large leaves. Flowerpeckers favour
food is undoubtedly ripe mistletoe berries but they feed widely on the small berries of secondary scrub plar
especially *Melastoma.* They also attack large ripe fruits, eat insects and pollen and sip nectar. Like the sunbir
and spiderhunters some flowerpecker possess white pectoral tufts on either side of the breast. These tufts are se
on young birds and both sexes although often concealed when the wing is closed. Unlike sunbirds, flowerpecke
do not host young cuckoos presumably because they feed their young on a diet of mistletoe berries.

1 PLAIN FLOWERPECKER   *Dicaeum concolor*   8cm   Scarce submontane reside

[*D. minullum*] Common on the Asian continent this is an uncommon but widespre
bird of secondary forest in the Bornean hills and submontane localities. Harrison fou
it to be abundant in the Kelabit Highlands in NE Sarawak. Regularly seen Crocker Ran
(Sabah). Occasionally found in the lowlands, e.g. Tg Puting and Sungai Wain (Kalimantar
Distinguished from Thick-billed and Brown-backed Flowerpeckers by its clearly smaller a
thinner bill and lack of any streaking underneath. **Range:** Himalayas to S China, south
Malay P, Sumatra, Borneo, Java.

2 SCARLET-BACKED FLOWERPECKER   *Dicaeum cruentatum*   9cm   Common reside

The second commonest flowerpecker (after Orange-bellied) in coastal and secondary scrub a
the forest edge throughout Borneo. A variety of different colour morphs have been report
including a singing male with a black back at Tawau (Gretton) and another male with oliv
grey wings. Also one record of a hybrid with Scarlet-headed Flowerpecker. See Mann 2008. T
white on the belly of the male may only be a narrow streak. Closely associated with mistletoe
Range: Himalayas to China, south to Malay P, Sumatra, Borneo.

3 SCARLET-HEADED FLOWERPECKER   *Dicaeum trochileum*   8cm   Local reside

The commonest flowerpecker in Java, but in Borneo confined to degraded forest and op
cultivated areas of SE Kalimantan from Samarinda in the east, south and west to Mua
Kendawangan on the south coast. Common in the countryside around Banjarmasin and
Tg Puting. This is one of a few relict Javan birds such as Savanna Nightjar and Red-breast
Parakeet remaining from the period when Java was connected to Borneo by land 10,000 yea
ago (see page 154). **Range:** S Sumatra, Borneo, Java.

4 ORANGE-BELLIED FLOWERPECKER   *Dicaeum trigonostigma*   8cm   Common reside

The commonest flowerpecker of coastal and secondary forest, throughout Borneo from t
lowlands to the hills. Often in town gardens. More nectarivorous than other flowerpecke
At Sepilok near the Orangutan Centre there is an avenue of purple flowered *Lagerstroem*
trees covered in mistletoes, one of the best localities in Borneo to easily view a large varie
of flowerpeckers. **Range:** Bangladesh to Malay P, Sumatra, Borneo, Philippines.

5 BORNEAN FLOWERPECKER   *Dicaeum monticolum*   8cm   Montane enden

[Black-sided Flowerpecker Davison/Mann] A common inhabitant of montane forests
throughout Borneo including the Muratus Mts in SE Kalimantan,
and Gng Penrissen near Kuching. At KNP HQ often seen
feeding on the berries of the pink-flowered *Medinella* bushes
which have been planted everywhere. Also feeds on mistletoe
berries. **Range:** Endemic, most closely related to the endemic
Grey-sided Flowerpecker of Sulawesi, an unusual relationship for a
Bornean bird. See page 320.

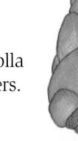

Flower of Loranthaceae misletoe

Lepeostegeres beccarii

The bracts at the base of the flower stop nectar thieves and the long corolla
tubes mean the flower can only be pollinated by Long-billed Spiderhunters.
The fruit are eaten by flowerpeckers. See pages 306 and 314.

Medinella berries

FLOWERPECKERS

1 SCARLET-BREASTED FLOWERPECKER *Prionochilus thoracicus* **10cm** **Reside**

Widespread throughout the lowlands and hills. Generally scarce, but locally common in are of poor soils, e.g. Casuarina and coastal forests, peatswamp and kerangas forest and fore on ultrabasic soils. **Sabah:** Klias, Sepilok. **Brunei:** Kuala Belait, Tutong. **Sarawak:** Mul Similajau, Semengoh. **Kalimantan:** Tg Puting, Barito Ulu, Gng Palung. **Range:** Malay Borneo.

2 CRIMSON-BREASTED FLOWERPECKER *Prionochilus percussus* **10cm** **Rare reside**

A rare mystery flowerpecker found throughout the lowlands and hills of Borneo in all types forest but very scarce. Very similar to Yellow-rumped but both male and female have distincti white moustache and no yellow rump. **Sabah:** Crocker Range, Poring, Danum. **Brune** Kuala Belalong where much less common than Yellow-rumped (Mann). **Sarawak:** Similaja Semengoh. **Kalimantan:** Tg Puting, Barito Ulu. **Range:** Malay P, Sumatra, Borneo, Java.

3 THICK-BILLED FLOWERPECKER *Dicaeum agile* **10cm** **Scarce reside**

Very common on the Asian continent, in Borneo it is very scarce found in a few scatter localities including primary forest at Danum and Tabin. Strongly associated with mistleto but also feeds on insects. At Sabah Softwoods near Tawau mixed species bird flocks includi up to 30 Thick-billed Flowerpeckers fed on *Pierid* butterfly larvae infestations in Albiz plantations (Sheldon). An individual fed on figs at Sepilok (Bakewell). Usually in fami parties or small flocks. Has a very distinctive habit of wagging and fanning tail which marked with faint white spots at the tip. Note orange red iris. Sexes similar. **Range:** India Vietnam, south to Malay P, Sumatra, Borneo, Java, Philippines.

4 YELLOW-RUMPED FLOWERPECKER *Prionochilus xanthopygius* **9cm** **Endem**

Common in all types of forest throughout Borneo from the lowland to the hills. Record feeding on a wide variety of small berries, nectar and insects. Easily confused with Crimso breasted Flowerpecker which is much rarer. Female is similar to female Crimson-breasted b both male and female have distinctive yellow rumps and no white malar stripe on side of fac At Danum ten times more common in logged than in unlogged forest (Lambert).

5 BROWN-BACKED FLOWERPECKER *Dicaeum everetti* **10cm** **Rare reside**

A globally rare flowerpecker (closely related to Thick-billed) found in coastal kerang secondary forests and forest edge in the lowlands and the hills. Rare in Sabah except at Kli and in Kalimantan except at Gng Palung. In Sarawak found Kubah NP, Lanjak Entimau a Pulong Tau. Recent record from peat swamp forest, Lower Belait, Brunei (Bakewell). Sheld (1985) suggests that this flowerpecker may be a poor soil i.e. Kerangas and Peat swar specialist the same habitat preferred by Hook-billed Bulbul and White-throated Babbl Distinguished from Plain Flowerpecker by large size and from Thick-billed by white ir Sexes similar. **Range:** Malay P, Borneo.

6 YELLOW-BREASTED FLOWERPECKER *Prionochilus maculatus* **10cm** **Reside**

The commonest flowerpecker of the understorey of lowland forests throughout Borneo a also found in the hills. Commonly trapped in forest understorey mist netting surveys. Joi mixed species insect-hunting parties. Also feeds on fruiting trees in the canopy and alo the forest edge. Sexes similar. Note orange crown patch. Common in peatswamp forest at ' Puting. **Range:** Malay P, Sumatra, Borneo.

7 YELLOW-VENTED FLOWERPECKER *Dicaeum chrysorrheum* **9cm** **Scarce reside**

Generally scarce in lowland forest throughout Borneo and most common in the hills. Sex similar. Has been misidentified as Speckled Piculet (Mann). Note yellow vent and rum **Sabah:** Crocker Range, Danum, Kinabatangan. **Brunei:** Seria, Labi, Badas, Kuala Belalon **Sarawak:** Mulu, Pulong Tau, Semengoh, Samunsam. **Kalimantan:** Tg Puting, Barito U Gng Palung. **Range:** Himalayas to Malay P, Sumatra, Borneo, Java.

SPECTACLED FLOWERPECKER   *Species novum*   **Possible Endemi**

If confirmed this flowerpecker will be the first entirely new endemic bird species to be recorded for Borne in over 100 years. Extensively photographed from the canopy walkway at Danum Valley on 18 June 2009 b an American bird guide Richard E. Webster. Further visits to the walkway by Webster, Rose Ann Rowlett an David P. Edwards confirmed that there were at least 2 adult birds feeding on a fruiting *Viscum* mistletoe. worldwide search of museum specimens by Edwards appears to confirm that that this flowerpecker is new science. A very similar flowerpecker was photographed at Mesilau on Kinabalu by Yeo Siew Teck on 21 De 2008. **Description**: Presumed male is dark slaty grey on the back, paler grey on the belly with a prominer broad white streak running from throat to lower belly. There is a slight buffy tinge to the white patch on th lower belly and under tail coverts. Distinguish by prominent white eye-ring broken in the middle and tw white streaks (super loral) running from the top and bottom of the eye to the top and bottom of the base c the beak. Presumed female is similar but duller and the buffy tinge extends from the lower belly to the throa Both birds had prominent white pectoral tufts. **Call**: Typical flowerpecker sharp flight notes. **Song**: A serie of high pitched *see see see* notes rising and then falling in pitch. **Habits**: Two different adults were seen a different times visiting a fruiting mistletoe growing on a *Koompasia* tree 35m above ground level. Four othe species of flowerpeckers – Yellow-breasted, Yellow-rumped, Yellow-vented and Orange-bellied – fed on th same mistletoe but at different times. **Habitat**: Edwards notes that the bill looks similar to the bill of Orange bellied Flowerpecker which has a varied diet taking a mixture of nectar, insects and berries as well as mistlet fruit. However the undoubted rarity of the Spectacled Flowerpecker indicates a specialised diet, see belov **References**: Edwards, D.P., Webster, R.E., Rowlett, R.A., (2009) 'Spectacled Flowerpecker': a species new t science discovered in Borneo? in BirdingASIA 12: 38–41.
www.borneobirdimages.com

FLOWERPECKERS AND MISTLETOES IN BORNEO   Mistletoes are epiphytic parasites which grow on the branches of a 'host' tree. Nearly all Bornean mistletoes belong to two related botanical families , the *Viscaceae* (c.90 spp in Borneo) and the *Loranthaceae* (c.180 spp in Borneo). These two mistletoe families are distinguished by their differing flowers. Loranthus flowers are usually conspicuously coloured red, orange or yellow and designed for bird pollination. Some Loranthus genera such as *Macrosolen, Lepeostegeres* and *Dendrophthoe* have bundles of long corolla tubes perfectly designed for a spiderhunters long bill (see page 314). Others have shorter tubes, but nearly all have a brightly coloured bulbous tip which explodes when touched for the first time by a foraging white-eye or sunbird showering pollen over the forehead of the bird. *Viscum* flowers on the other hand are usually small and inconspicuously coloured greenish or white, designed for insect pollination. Both mistletoe families are common throughout Bornean forests, but the *Viscaceae* are common also in gardens and seashore trees whilst the *Loranthaceae* are commonest in hill and mountain forests.

In Borneo all the mistletoes produce small berries designed to be eaten by and dispersed by flowerpeckers. All flowerpeckers have digestive systems specialised for eating mistletoes. The mistletoe berry is swallowed whole and the skin (pericarp) enters the stomach where it is digested. The single sticky seed is shaped like a tadpole with a trailing white sticky tail. The seed by-passes the stomach and sticks to the flowerpecker's vent as it emerges. To get rid of the seed the flowerpecker 'wipes its bottom' on the branch on which it is sitting. The seed gets glued to the branch by the sticky tail and soon germinates a root like hastorium which enters the host tree to steal water and nutrients. Some species of mistletoe have sticky seeds but with no tails and in these cases the bird strips the skin and swallows the seed which is regurgitated after a few minutes. The bird then wipes its bill on a branch which glues the seed to the branch.

The relationship between flowerpeckers and mistletoes in Borneo is very close. Other frugivorous birds rarely eat mistletoe berries, and flowerpeckers often feed the berries to their young as well as insects. Unlike the similar sized ioras, sunbirds and tailorbirds there are no Borneo records of flowerpeckers acting as deluded hosts to cuckoos, presumably because of this specialised diet. It is believed that some Bornean flowerpeckers, e.g. Orange-bellied, are generalist feeders whilst others such as the Plain Flowerpecker are mistletoe specialists. It is possible but unproven that certain Bornean flowerpeckers may have an obligate (exclusively dependent on each other) relationship with certain species of mistletoes, and the distribution of both species would then coincide.

Richard

SUNBIRDS

NECTARINIIDAE   **World 119 species; Borneo 10 species.**   Sunbirds are most diverse in Africa, 11 species reac the Malay Peninsula, 10 occur in Borneo and only one reaches Australia. Sunbirds are specialist nectar feeders whic also feed on insects and small berries. They can hover for short periods to feed but are unable to do so continuousl like the South American hummingbirds. Two species, Olive-backed and Brown-throated, are found in gardens an cultivated areas, the others are birds of the forest edge. Sunbirds build hanging pockets with porch roofs for nest sometimes in surprisingly exposed situations and perhaps as a result they often act as hosts to cuckoos. Males an females are usually dissimilar, the male being much brighter than the female. In some species the male has an eclips plumage after breeding in which the underparts resemble the female. As with flowerpeckers and spiderhunter some species develop bright yellow pectoral tufts, patches of brightly coloured feathers on either side of the breas These feathers are often concealed when the bird is resting. Their high-pitched *cheep   cheep   cheep* calls are hear all day in gardens and along the forest edge. The calls are usually distinctive enough to recognise as coming fror a sunbird but not different enough to distinguish between species. Both males and females are frequently foun attacking their own image in a wing mirror or reflective window pane. Sunbirds are highly territorial, rarely seem t wander and are never seen in flocks apart from the Rubycheek which does occur in family parties.

1   PURPLE-THROATED SUNBIRD   *Nectarinia sperata*   **9cm**   **Scarce residen**

[van Hasselt's Sunbird] The smallest sunbird. Widespread in forest throughout Borneo fron the coast to the hills. Highly active, feeding on canopy flowers in tall forest. The male is tiny jewel, like a large iridescent bee. Males of both this and Copper-Throated can appea almost black in shade. Distinguished by size and the yellow pectoral tufts of Copper-throated Female has thin white eye ring. **Range:** India to Malay P, Sumatra, Borneo, Java, Philippines **Taxonomy:** Philippine and Borneo birds are potential future splits. The race on Maratua 1 *N.s. trochilus* is closer to the Philippine race than the Borneo mainland race (Mann).

2   COPPER-THROATED SUNBIRD   *Nectarinia calcostetha*   **13cm**   **Local residen**

[Macklot's Sunbird] The largest sunbird. Locally common in mangroves and adjacent coasta forest and gardens, but otherwise scarce. Male looks almost uniform black in shade apar from yellow pectoral tufts (often concealed) but glitters iridescent purple and red in sunlight Common on the islands and mangroves around Kota Kinabalu, e.g. Likas Swamp, P Gaya an P Manukan at Sepilok and at Bako near Kuching. Common at Tg Puting. **Range:** Myanmar t Malay P, Sumatra, Borneo, Java.

3   OLIVE-BACKED SUNBIRD   *Nectarinia jugularis*   **10cm**   **Common residen**

[Yellow-breasted Sunbird] The commonest sunbird, found in gardens and cultivated areas, o islands, in coastal scrub and along the forest edge inland to the hills. Often builds its hangin pocket nest in the open from the eaves of houses, telephone wires and prominent twigs i gardens. Young male has thin black stripe on throat. Female has white side tail feathers, useful distinction from female Brown-throated. **Range:** S China to Malay P, Sumatra, Borneo Philippines, Java to Australia.

4   EASTERN CRIMSON SUNBIRD   *Aethopyga siparaja*   **11cm**   **Common lowland residen**

[Yellow-backed Sunbird] [Crimson Sunbird]. Common inhabitant of cultivation, secondar forest and forest edge throughout the lowlands of Borneo. Easily confused with Temminck' which also occurs locally in the lowlands. Male has blue forehead and dark blue not red tai Underparts are a darker grey not pale grey with yellowish tinge. Both the red sunbird male have yellow rumps. Red sunbirds with grey rumps are believed to be males in eclipse (non breeding) plumage. Breeding male has short tail extension. **Range:** India to Malay P, Sumatra Borneo, Java, Philippines, Sulawesi.

5   TEMMINCK'S SUNBIRD   *Aethopyga temminckii*   **11cm**   **Common montane residen**

[Scarlet Sunbird] The common sunbird of the Bornean mountains and submontane forest At KNP HQ often feeds on cultivated flowers in the Mountain Garden. Also occurs in sma populations in the lowlands throughout Borneo, e.g. **Sabah:** Danum, Tabin, Maliau. **Sarawak** Similajau, Semengoh, Samunsam. **Kalimantan:** Muara Kendawang, Danau Sentarum, Sunga Wain. Breeding male has 3cm tail extension. Male has red forehead and red tail. **Range** Malay P, Sumatra, Borneo.

♀ 1

♂

♂ 1a

Maratua race

♀ 2

♂

♀ 3

♂

male in eclipse

♂ 4

imm

♀

♀ 5

♂

imm

SUNBIRDS

1 PURPLE-NAPED SUNBIRD *Hypogramma hypogrammicum* **15cm** **Common resident**

Common throughout the lowlands and hills, in both primary and secondary forest. Uses similar habitat to Little Spiderhunter, the understorey of forest or scrub jungle but feeds on small berries and insects and the pollen of banana and ginger flowers rather than nectar. Less visible but more commonly trapped in forest mist-nets than other sunbirds. The commonest sunbird in both logged and unlogged forest at Danum (Lambert). A brood host to the Violet Cuckoo. Female lacks the purple nape and rump of the male but has similar streaking below. **Range:** Myanmar to Malay P, Sumatra, Borneo.

2 PLAIN SUNBIRD *Anthreptes simplex* **12cm** **Common resident**

Inhabits coastal forest but also found in lowland and hill forest edge throughout Borneo. Perhaps more insectivorous than most sunbirds but often feeds on flowering coconuts. Common in ultrabasic forest on Gng Meliau in central Sabah (Sheldon). 'A plain chunky sunbird with a grey throat. Male has iridescent blue forehead. Extremely warbler-like in their leaf gleaning behaviour in the *Albizia* plantation canopy' (Sheldon). **Range:** Malay P, Sumatra, Borneo.

3 RED-THROATED SUNBIRD *Anthreptes rhodolaema* **12cm** **Local resident**

[Rufous-throated Sunbird] An uncommon sunbird, but widespread in primary forest and forest edge. Similar to the much more common Brown-throated Sunbird which is normally found in open countryside and coastal forest only. 'Distinguished from male Brown-throated by a greenish belly, reddish cheeks and more red on the wing coverts' (Sheldon). Recorded in Casuarinas at Bako (Hall). **Range:** Malay P, Sumatra, Borneo.

4 BROWN-THROATED SUNBIRD *Anthreptes malacensis* **13cm** **Common resident**

[Plain-throated Sunbird] The second commonest sunbird in gardens and cultivated areas but scarce in inland forests where it is replaced by Red-throated although distribution of the two species does overlap along the forest edge. Strongly associated with flowering coconut and usually the commonest sunbird on islands and in coastal coconut plantations. **Range:** Myanmar to Malay P, Sumatra, Borneo, Java, Philippines.

5 RUBYCHEEK *Chalcoparia singalensis* **10cm** **Local resident**

[Ruby-cheeked Sunbird] A locally common sunbird of all types of lowland forest from the coast to the hills. Recorded hunting for insects and pollen in beach Casuarinas. Has an unusual non-tubular tongue unlike the tubular tongues of other sunbirds and is considered to be a primitive ancestor of the other sunbirds (Mann). Exclusively insectivorous and not known to feed on nectar (Ammar Singh). The only sunbird found in small family parties. Unlike other sunbirds the nest is concealed under an overhanging bank. **Range:** Bangladesh to Malay P, Sumatra, Borneo, Java.

THE RED BEAN CREEPER AND THE *CAESALPINIAS*

One of the most popular sunbird-pollinated flowers in Bornean gardens is the Pride of Barbados *Caesalpinia pulcherrima*, a thorny bush from C America with multiple heads of yellow or orange flowers. Coincidentally the yellow flowers of *Caesalpinia bonduc*, a thorny climber of Bornean beach forest, is also popular with sunbirds. It is found along tropical coasts worldwide including the Caribbean where its hard grey pearl-like seeds are known as 'knicker nuts'. Yet another *Caesalpinia*, the thorny Red Bean Climber *C. latisiliqua* is found scattered through tall forest from the coast to the mountains. The flowers are small dull greenish yellow panicles on long stalks but the stalks themselves and the large seed pods are bright scarlet. Usually the flowering heads only appear in full sunlight above the canopy of tall forest but if you are lucky enough to find this creeper flowering low down on a roadside cutting it is a worth a wait as the red beans flag up the copious nectar awaiting the local population of sunbirds, spiderhunters, flowerpeckers, white-eyes and leafbirds. Often even bulbuls arrive to feast on the abundant nectar. Thus the tropical *Caesalpinia* family has evolved in a mutually beneficial way to benefit the local nectar-feeding birds in S America, SE Asia and throughout the Pacific.

Olive-backed Sunbird
feeding on *Caesalpinia latisiliqua*

NECTARINIIDAE   **World 9 species. Borneo 8 species.**   Spiderhunters are named for their habit of hovering in front of spider webs to snatch the owner and his larder, but they are primarily solitary nectar feeders or forest flowers. They also feed on small berries. All spiderhunters have similar distinctive flight calls a rapid *chk chk chk* given in dipping flight, with the speed and tone varying greatly between species. On landing a flower spiderhunters announce their arrival with a single loud *chk*. Breeding males have a wheezy song Spiderhunter nests are elongated hammocks attached to the underside of banana or other large leaves by sewing with spider-silk thread. Sexes are similar. Some males have orange pectoral tufts on either side of the breast used in breeding displays. The understorey trap-lining Spiderhunters fly very fast low down through gaps in the forest. They often mistake windows in a building for forest gaps and can be found stunned on dead below the glass.

1   LITTLE SPIDERHUNTER   *Arachnothera longirostra*   16cm   **Common resident**

Very common in lowland primary and secondary forest throughout Borneo and wanders to banana groves in cultivated areas. One of the trap-lining spiderhunters, a specialist feeder on the nectar of banana and ginger flowers in the understorey of the forest. In forest mist-netting surveys usually the most commonly trapped bird. In the Malay Peninsula 12 Little, plus 4 Grey-breasted and a Spectacled Spiderhunter were all netted at one banana clump in one morning (Wells). Has distinctive white eye markings on face similar to Thick-billed but easily distinguished by white not green throat and white tips to tail lacking in Thick-billed. **Range:** India to S China, Malay P, Sumatra, Java, Borneo, Philippines.

2   THICK-BILLED SPIDERHUNTER   *Arachnothera crassirostris*   16cm   **Scarce resident**

A scarce resident of lowland and hill forest throughout Borneo. Often confused with Little Spiderhunter, but much less common. The eye markings are similar to Little Spiderhunter but less distinct. Easily distinguished by a plain olive green throat and breast compared with the white throat and yellow breast of Little Spiderhunter. Common in gardens at Sepilok where it specialises in feeding on *Bauhinia* flowers. **Range:** Malay P, Sumatra. Borneo.

3   SPECTACLED SPIDERHUNTER   *Arachnothera flavigaster*   22cm   **Scarce resident**

[Greater Yellow-eared Spiderhunter]. The largest spiderhunter. A widespread but scarce resident of lowland and hill forest throughout Borneo. Also found in plantations. Often confused with Yellow-eared Spiderhunter because of similar yellow cheek patches. This bird has a distinctive fully complete yellow eye ring in comparison with the Yellow-eared Spiderhunter which is missing the bottom section of the eye ring. **Range:** Malay P, Sumatra, Borneo.

4   YELLOW-EARED SPIDERHUNTER   *Arachnothera chrysogenys*   18cm   **Scarce resident**

A scarce resident of lowland forest throughout Borneo. Feeds on canopy flowers but will also fly down to feed on banana flowers. Very fond of small *Macaranga* berries in common with bulbuls, leafbirds, flowerpeckers and sunbirds. Both Yellow-eared and Spectacled have similar yellow cheek patches but Yellow-eared only has the upper half of a yellow eye ring not a full yellow eye ring. These two large spiderhunters often aggressively defend favoured bunches of flowers from other spiderhunters. **Range:** Malay P, Sumatra, Java, Borneo.

BIRD-POLLINATED FLOWERS IN BORNEO

In Borneo the majority of native forest plants have small inconspicuous flowers pollinated by bees and other insects. The remaining flowers are pollinated by wind, by birds, by bats and even squirrels, e.g. *Madhuca* (Yumoto). Bird-pollinated flowers are a minority reproductive method for Bornean plants but there are enough of these flowers to support eight different spiderhunters, ten sunbirds and seven white-eyes. Bird-pollinated flowers divide into two types. Firstly, there are those with long flower tubes or corollas, such as the rhododendrons, bananas, mistletoes and gingers, which provide a specialised niche for birds with very long tongues (specifically spiderhunters) as well as long tongued nectivorous bats and hawk moths. Secondly, there are flowers with short corollas, which provide nectar for insects such as bees and butterflies as well as birds with short bills specifically sunbirds and white-eyes, e.g. *Syzygium*, *Caesalpinia* and *Bauhinia*.

Orchid Tree, *Bauhinia blakeana*, is a small sterile hybrid ornamental flowering tree which produces no seeds. It originated in Hong Kong where it is the national flower. Introduced Orchid Trees are planted in many Bornean gardens, including Sepilok where the flowers attract Thick-billed Spiderhunters, usually very difficult to find elsewhere.

1

Musa beccarii
Beccari's banana flower

2

Syzygium malaccensis
Malay apple flower

4

Alocasia macrorrhiza
Elephant-ear aroid fruit

STREAKED SPIDERHUNTERS

1 LONG-BILLED SPIDERHUNTER *Arachnothera robusta* 22cm   **Scarce resident**

An uncommon resident of lowland and hill forest throughout Borneo. Recorded occasional at KNP HQ. A specialist feeder on Loranthaceae mistletoe flowers, which have very lor corollas perfectly designed for this spiderhunter's bill. Distinguished from the heavi streaked Streaky-breasted and Grey-breasted Spiderhunters by light streaks on an olive-gree (not grey) breast and black not pink or reddish legs. **Range:** Malay P, Sumatra, Java, Borne

2 WHITEHEAD'S SPIDERHUNTER *Arachnothera juliae* 18cm   **Montane endem**

Locally common in montane forest throughout Borneo. A canopy bird, which feeds on epiphyt rhododendrons and red *Aeschenanthus* flowers growing high up on the trunks of forest tree Commonly seen feeding in the tops of pink-flowering *Wightia* (foxglove) trees in the dry seasc (see cover). Often seen in dipping flight high above the forest at KNP HQ. Common Sinsuro Rd. and Rafflesia Centre (Crocker Range, Sabah) and in montane forest at Mulu, Pulong Tau ar Kayan Mentarang. **Call:** Song 'a buzzing insect-like *erz, dee erz*' (Buckton).

3 BORNEAN SPIDERHUNTER *Arachnothera everetti* 18cm   **Local resident**

[Streaky-breasted Spiderhunter *Arachnothera affinis*]. A common inhabitant of submontane ar lower montane forests throughout Borneo and also in lowland forest throughout Sabah. Recorde from Sepilok, Danum and Tabin. In the KNP common from Poring up to the level of KNP H(One of the trap-lining spiderhunters, a specialist feeder on the nectar of banana and ging(flowers in the understorey of the forest. Distinguished from *A. modesta* by larger size and heavi(streaking from throat to lower belly. Both this and *A. modesta* have pink/reddish legs, a usef distinguishing mark from the black legs of the Long-billed Spiderhunter. Males are substantial larger and heavier, c. 25%, than females (Sheldon). **Taxonomy:** split by Moyle et al (2011).

4 GREY-BREASTED SPIDERHUNTER *Arachnothera modesta* 16cm   **Scarce resident**

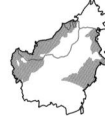

A scarce resident of lowland forest in Kalimantan, Sarawak and Brunei. Not found in Sabah. Bo(*A. modesta* and *A. affinis* have been recorded from Ulu Temburong, possibly in confusion. A excellent photograph in Hessels (2008) shows *A. affinis* (labelled as *A. modesta*) at Temburon There are no definite areas in Borneo where the two species are known to overlap in distributio Both are trap-lining spiderhunters with very similar habits and are probably unable to co-exi in the same area. Distinguished by smaller size and less heavy streaking which is usually abse from the throat and lower belly. Has pink/reddish legs similar to Streaky-breasted and unli the black legs of the Long-billed Spiderhunter. **Range:** Malay P, Borneo, Sumatra.

NECTAR ROBBING Many of the common flowers in Borneo gardens, such as bright red, orange or yellow cannas and hibiscus, originated in S or Central America and are adapted to be pollinated by long-billed hummingbirds. Nevertheless sunbirds have taken to these foreign flowers with gusto. Where flowers such as cannas are adapted for different sized beaks, the sunbird gains access by piercing a hole at the base of the corolla, thereby 'nectar robbing' without providing a pollination service. Nectar robbing has also been reported for native flowers such as the durians designed for bat pollination but robbed by spiderhunters (Yumoto).

BANANAS, GINGERS AND TRAP-LINING SPIDERHUNTERS Spiderhunters divide into two groups by habits. The first group are canopy and forest-edge birds, which feed on the nectar of seasonally flowering trees such durians and climbers such as the red bean *Caesalpinia*, page 311. The second group flies very fast in the forest understorey and feeds on wild banana and ginger flowers. This group includes Little, Grey-breasted and Streaked. Banana clumps flower continuously so these birds visit all the local banana groves at least once a day, a habit known as 'trap lining'. Borneo is a centre of diversity for both spiderhunters and wild bananas. Most wild bananas (*Musa* species) are pollinated by nectar feeding bats at night. Each evening a new red cream or purple bract opens exposing the white banana flowers for visiting bats, but unusually for bat-pollinated flowers the nectar flow continues the following day, providing food for spiderhunters as well, thus maximising the chances of successful pollination. Day-flowering wild bananas with upright buds also occur, see page 313 and front cover. Upright banana flowers are primarily pollinated by spiderhunters and sunbirds not bats (Itino). Ground-flowering gingers *Etlingera* and *Hornstedia* are also specialist spiderhunter flowers (Lamb).

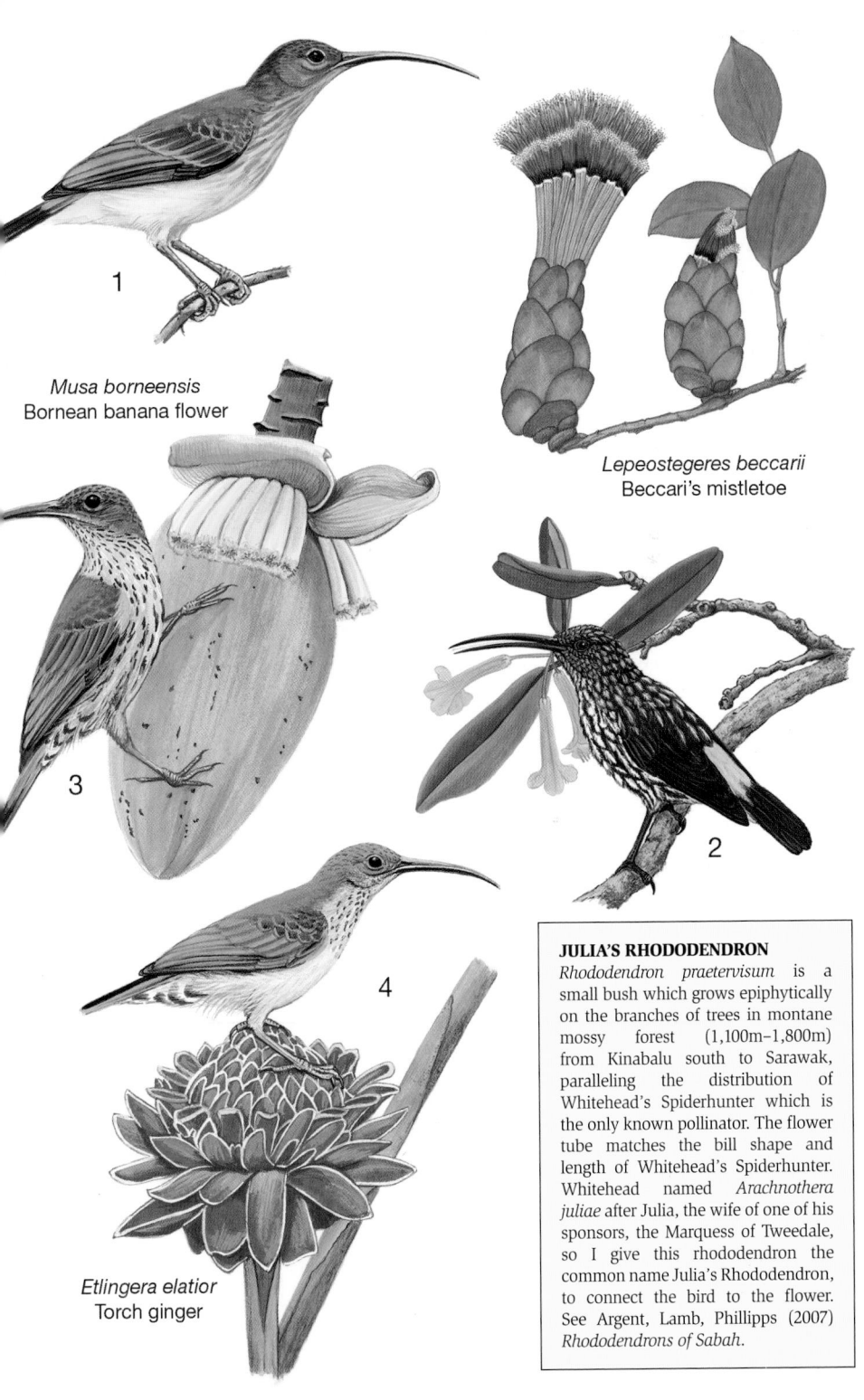

1

Musa borneensis
Bornean banana flower

Lepeostegeres beccarii
Beccari's mistletoe

3

2

4

Etlingera elatior
Torch ginger

JULIA'S RHODODENDRON

Rhododendron praetervisum is a small bush which grows epiphytically on the branches of trees in montane mossy forest (1,100m–1,800m) from Kinabalu south to Sarawak, paralleling the distribution of Whitehead's Spiderhunter which is the only known pollinator. The flower tube matches the bill shape and length of Whitehead's Spiderhunter. Whitehead named *Arachnothera juliae* after Julia, the wife of one of his sponsors, the Marquess of Tweedale, so I give this rhododendron the common name Julia's Rhododendron, to connect the bird to the flower. See Argent, Lamb, Phillipps (2007) *Rhododendrons of Sabah*.

AVADAVAT AND MUNIAS

ESTRILDIDAE **World 41 species; Borneo 12 species including 3 endemics.** Munias are small finch with heavy bills that feed almost exclusively on grass and bamboo seed. Munias are extremely sociable, near always seen in small flocks and some species are communal breeders. Munias nest and roost in untidy globes grass and leaves, often several nests in the same tree. Unlike most other Bornean birds munia nests are found every month of the year apart from the White-bellied Munia where breeding appears to be seasonal indicatin a partially insectivorous diet. See page 34. Calls are usually soft twitterings and a sharper contact call. Youn munias are a uniform pale buff with a dark bill, until their second moult when the dark lower mandible become pale, like the upper mandible. Munias are popular cagebirds and as a result, escapes of alien species may occu

1 JAVA SPARROW *Padda oryzivora* **16cm** Locally common reside

A feral population has become established in various parts of Borneo including Kota Kinabal Kuching and Jerudong in Brunei, but after many years numbers remain small and localise In the 1880s Motley reported large numbers around Banjarmasin, but they are not seen toda In 1893 Whitehead predicted that the expanding Labuan population would drive out the oth munias but this has not happened. In Java and Bali it was at one time a serious pest of the ric fields but due to extensive trapping for the cagebird trade it is now considered scarce. **Cal** 'The contact call is a kind of **tchuk** which is used between male and female and flocks in fligh (Restall). **Range:** Native to Java and Bali. Many feral populations worldwide. **BLI:** Vulnerable

2 RED AVADAVAT *Amandava amandava* **10cm** Escap

First noted in 1969 in Kota Kinabalu, small feral populations may have become establishe in Kota Kinabalu, in Brunei at the Wasan Rice Scheme and possibly in S Kalimantan Alabio. Bright red beak and red plumage with white spots of the male is distinctive. This a commonly kept cagebird in SE Asia, the Philippines and Java. **Range:** India to Vietnam Java, Bali.

3 SCALY-BREASTED MUNIA *Lonchura punctulata* **11cm** Increasingly common reside

First recorded from Banjarmasin by Holmes in 1974 and from Likas, Sabah in 1993 (Heath Now widespread throughout Borneo in cultivated country following an extremely rapid rang expansion. **Call:** 'A loud contact call when the bird is separated from others **kit-tee kit-te** with the second syllable higher than the first. Also a sharp alarm note **tchep**' (Restall). **Rang** India to China, south to Malaya, Sumatra, Borneo, Java, Philippines, Sulawesi.

4 CHESTNUT MUNIA *Lonchura atricapilla* **11cm** Common resider

[Black-headed Munia] The commonest Bornean munia, often seen in small flocks on lawn padangs, airfields, grassy swamps and ripening padi fields. Feeding flocks on lawns progres steadily as individuals at the rear fly to land just ahead of the front row and continue to feed. crèche feeder where the whole flock feed all the new youngsters (Restall). **Call:** Shrill **peet pe** and harsher **tink tink**. **Range:** India to Malay P, Sumatra, Borneo, Java, Philippines, Sulawesi

5 WHITE-HEADED MUNIA *Lonchura maja* **11cm** Escap

A pair seen in Papar in 1962 by Batchelor. **Range:** Malaya, Sumatra, Java, Bali.

6 WHITE-RUMPED MUNIA *Lonchura striata* **11cm** Status unknow

Common resident of the Malay P, this munia was seen in the Anamba Islands in Aug. 1899 by Kloss, possibl an escape. The current situation is unknown. **Range:** India to Malay P, Sumatra.

7 WHITE-BELLIED MUNIA *Lonchura leucogastra* **11cm** Scarce nomadic resider

An uncommon bird of the forest edge throughout Borneo, not normally seen in flocks an obviously nomadic. Described by Restall as a 'woodland munia'. Three races occur, whic vary in the amount of streaking on the head and rufous coloration on the back. Illustrate is *L. l. smythiesi* found in W Borneo. **Call:** 'The male's contact call is a strong **twyrt** and th female responds with a **tee tee tee**' (Restall). Common at Tabin (Sabah) both in roadside gras and along the forest edge. **Range:** Malay P, Sumatra, Borneo, Philippines.

RARE AND ENDEMIC MUNIAS

1   CREAM-BELLIED MUNIA   *Lonchura pallidventer*   **12cm**   **Status unknow**

 Described by Robin Restall (1996) as a new Bornean endemic munia based on 9 individua purchased from the Jakarta bird market between 1990–1991 with an origin described by th vendor as the hinterland of Bandjarmasin in SE Kalimantan. These birds are most like hybrids between the Kalimantan races of White-bellied and Scaly-breasted Munias whic both occur in the area. (van Balen 1998).

2   DUSKY MUNIA   *Lonchura fuscans*   **10cm**   **Common lowland endem**

 The second commonest munia and the most ubiquitous of all Borneo's endemic birds. Muc shyer and more skulking than the more common Chestnut Munia. Found everywhere there grass, including gardens, town padangs and golf courses. Often seen along grassy river ban and around interior padi fields, where it is a serious pest of ripening padi (rice crop), muc hated by local farmers. **Call:** 'A shrill *pee pee*' (Williams in Smythies).

3   SPOT-SIDED MUNIA   *Lonchura* species   **10cm**   **Status unknow**

A possible new endemic munia for Borneo illustrated from a single live female obtained by Robin Restall fro the Jakarta bird market in 1990 and said to be from the Banjarmasin area. Not yet seen in the wild. **Call:** buzzing *tzit*' (Restall).

4   TAWNY-BREASTED PARROTFINCH   *Erythrura hyperythra*   **10cm**   **Rare reside**

 [Bamboo Munia] A rare montane resident of the climbing bamboo belt in the Borne mountains. On Kinabalu found at 2,500–3,000m (Biun). On Trus Madi found at 1,700–2,350 (Sheldon). On Mulu 1,520–1,800m (Mann). Feeds on bamboo seed but known to attack h padi, e.g. at 400m in Kayan Mentarang (van Balen). Female has no blue on head. **Call:** 'C the wing the bird continually utters its call-note, which is a hissing sound like *tzit tzit*, b when settled it is silent' (Whitehead). **Range:** Borneo, Java, Philippines, Sulawesi.

5   PIN-TAILED PARROTFINCH   *Erythrura prasina*   **15cm**   **Scarce nomadic reside**

 A scarce, irregular irruptive migrant, seen mainly around ripening hill padi in the interior a occasionally elsewhere. Highly mobile flocks which seemingly appear out of nowhere can devasta a rice harvest. Before rice grew in Borneo this bird probably fed entirely on bamboo seed. Climbi *Racemobambos* bamboos are most common in the hills and mountains. Groves with the san genetic origin flower, seed and then die en-masse, forcing this bird into a nomadic existence. As b padi is also seasonal this restricts the overall population. **Call:** 'Flies fast and direct with shrill *ta tzit tzit* calls' (McKinnon). **Range:** Vietnam south to Malay P, Sumatra, Borneo, Java.

HONEYEATERS AND INVASIVE SPECIES: MUNIAS, MYNAS AND TREE SPARROWS

The Scaly-breasted Munia was first recorded in Borneo in 1974 since when the population has exceeded the populations of Dusky and Chestnut Munias. In the last 30 years at least four different species of Mynas have established breeding populations in Borneo for the first time. The Tree Sparrow first recorded in 1964 is now one of Borneo's commonest birds. Other more recent 'invaders' which have established large breeding populations include the Zebra Dove, the Buff-banded Rail and the Grass Owl. Obviously none of these birds could have 'invaded' without the recent dramatic increase in man's activities in Borneo. The expansion of agriculture and roads including irrigated rice fields and plantations has provided abundant food resources (vacant niches) for the invaders. There are 3 lessons that can learnt from this. (1) Without vacant ecological niches no new species would have invaded. (2) Once vacant niches became available they were rapidly filled by a variety of different bird species. (3) No new birds have been able to invade Borneo's virgin primary rain forest. The most likely explanation is that the core of Borneo's rain forests have been relatively stable in terms of structure and diversity for the last 50 million years allowing time for evolution to populate every exploitable food niche with specialist birds. The result is that there is no surplus food for new invaders to exploit. This explanation solves a number of bio-geographic puzzles. For example honeyeaters are the most diverse bird family in Australia and have managed to invade both New Zealand and distant (4,000km) Hawaii. There are 3 species of honeyeaters in Sulawesi yet none managed to cross the 100km Makassar Strait to Borneo. The most likely explanation is honeyeaters did arrive in Borneo but that they were unable to survive competition from established birds. See Ford, H.A. (2000).

Munia scaring devices
Tempasuk Plain

MOTACILLIDAE   **World 9 species; Borneo 5 species, all migrants.**   Like the Shrikes, the Wagtails have
tendency to form superspecies. The taxonomic result is a few species with each species having a large numbe
of races or subspecies. Both wagtails and pipits constantly wag their tails and bob their heads as they search fo
insects, possibly to startle their prey into flight. Wagtails fly with a dipping motion uttering a distinctive sharp ca
as they fly. Breeding plumage males have the brightest most distinct colours but these plumages are only likely t
be seen in September on arrival and in March before departure. In winter females and males look very similar.

1–3   YELLOW WAGTAILS   *Motacilla flava*   18cm

Common winter visito

The commonest wagtail. Abundant in grassy areas, coastal plains and cultivated countrysid
in winter months throughout Borneo. The local Malay name is beras beras (rice) becaus
they are commonly found in dry rice fields. Usually roost in flocks in reed beds or long gras
25,000 recorded at a roost at Tempasuk in Dec. 1984 (Sheldon).

1. Race: *M. f. taivana*   Breeds Sakhalin, adjacent Siberia, and Hokkaido.   **Commo**
2. Race: *M. f. macronyx*   Breeds SE Siberia and N China.   **Ra**
3. Race: *M. f. tsuchutschensis.*(Smythies lists as *M. f. simillima*)   Breeds NE Siberia.   **Commone**

4   CITRINE WAGTAIL   *Motacilla citreola*   20cm

Not recorde

A scarce winter visitor to Hong Kong and N Thailand. Several records for Singapore but not yet recorded f
Borneo. **Range:** Breeds Russia, Central Asia wintering south to India, Thailand.

5   GREY WAGTAIL   *Motacilla cinerea*   19cm

Common winter visito

Very common in winter months throughout Borneo along rocky streams, roadsides and rock
slopes. Flocks along the coast on passage but usually alone. Often confused with Yellow Wagta
but white throat and yellow belly are much brighter than Yellow Wagtail. White bars on wing
are much plainer than pattern on Yellow (see illustration). Also distinguished by very differe
habitat. **Range:** Breeds N Europe to China, Japan, winters south to Africa, SE Asia.

6–10   WHITE WAGTAILS   *Motacilla alba*   20cm

Scarce winter visito

[Pied Wagtail] An uncommon winter visitor to the coastal districts of NW Borneo with tw
records from east coast Sabah. No records from Kalimantan. Birds have been recorded yea
round, presumably first year birds. Only race *M. a. ocularis* has definitely been recorded bu
other races are likely.

6. Race: *M. a. leucopsis*   Breeds E China, Korea.
7. Race: *M. a. alboides*   Breeds Himalayas west to SW China.
8. Race: *M. a. ocularis*   Breeds the eastern half of Siberia south to N China.
9. Race: *M. a. baicalensis*   Breeds Central Asia.
10. Race: *M. a. lugens*   Breeds Kamchatka, Sakhalin and adjacent mainland coast. Also Japan.

11   FOREST WAGTAIL   *Dendronanthus indicus*   17cm

Rare winter visito

The scarcest wagtail with scattered records from coastal areas of NW Borneo. Rare furthe
south. Wags whole body including tail from side to side, not up and down, and unlike othe
wagtails often perches in trees. Normally seen feeding on the ground in wooded areas but o
passage can be found anywhere, e.g. 3 on Pulau Layang[2] on 26 Sept. 1998 (Davison). **Rang**
Breeds China to Japan, winters south to SE Asia.

THE KELABIT NEW YEAR AND THE ARRIVAL OF THE YELLOW WAGTAIL

The Kelabits are rice farmers occupying a remote upland plain in the NE corner of Sarawak. During
World War II Tom Harrisson, later a famous curator of the Sarawak Museum, spent four years living in
the Kelabit Highlands, recording the habits of birds and man. The first lunar month of the Kelabit year
(Aug.–Sept.) is named *Yellow Wagtail Arrives* (Sensulit mad'ting). The second month is *Yellow Wagtail
Stays* (Sensulit pererang). The following lunar months are named successively after the Brown Shrike, the
Japanese Sparrowhawk and the Eyebrowed Thrush. The arrival of the wagtail precedes the arrival of the
NE Monsoon bringing the wettest months of the year and the best time to plant the rice. The Kelabits use
the arrival as an important indicator of when to prepare the ground for rice planting. (Summarised from
Birds and Man by T. Harrisson in *The Birds of Borneo* by B.E. Smythies, 1960.)

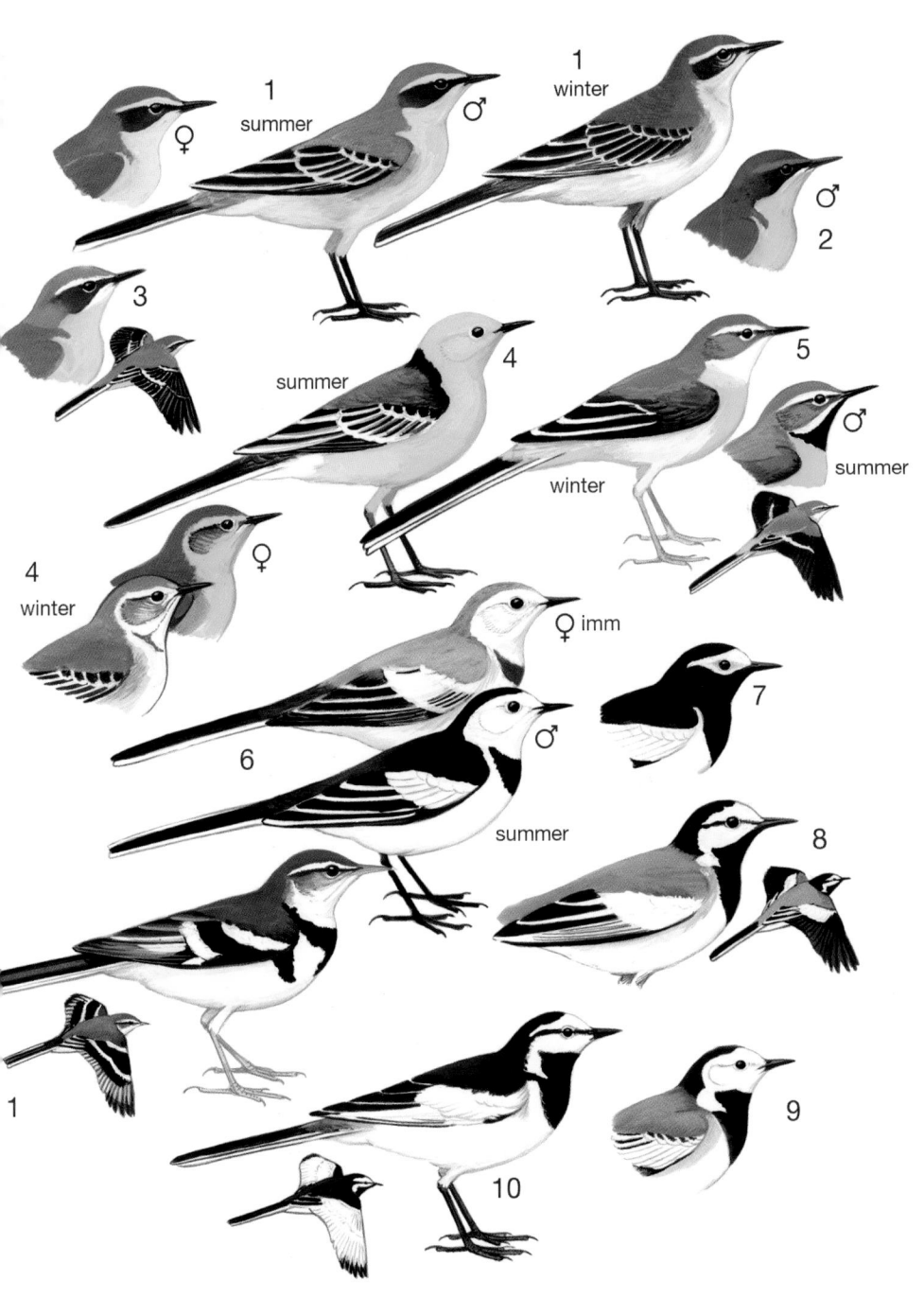

PIPITS

MOTACILLIDAE   **World 18 species; Borneo 5 species including 4 migrants and 1 resident.** Pipits a
streaked brown and buff birds with long tails found on grazing land, roadsides, lawns and coastal grasslar
and mudflats. Like the closely related wagtails, pipits constantly wag their tails up and down as they walk. Lil
the wagtails they also have white outer tail feathers which can be seen as they fly off in strongly dipping fligh
As with other open country birds, pipits have benefited from agricultural expansion in Borneo, especially th
Paddyfield Pipit.

1   RICHARD'S PIPIT   *Anthus richardi*   18cm   Locally common winter visit

Largest Bornean pipit with long legs and distinctive upright stance. Previously considered th
migrant form of the resident Paddyfield Pipit. Frequently hovers before landing in long gras
In Sabah a common winter visitor to coastal grassland often in small flocks, less commo
further south. Distinguished from Paddyfield Pipit by larger size, habits and call and from th
other pipits by large size and upright stance. **Call:** 'A loud explosive harsh **shreep, pschree**
or **dscheep** usually given singly and somewhat reminiscent of the sound made when a piec
of cloth is very quickly torn. Very different from the call of the Paddyfield Pipit' (Alstrom
Range: Breeds Siberia, China, Mongolia, Taiwan, Korea, winters SE Asia.

2   RED-THROATED PIPIT   *Anthus cervinus*   16cm   Common winter visitc

The commonest migrant pipit throughout Borneo. Seen on passage on the coast befo
moving on to winter in wet grassy areas in the interior. A common visitor to the Kelab
Highlands. On arrival in September often retains vestiges of breeding plumage, a distinctiv
reddish throat and breast. This fades soon after arrival in September and reappears just befo
departure in April. Heavily streaked on back and rump. **Call:** 'A thin high pitched crystal-clea
drawn out usually single **peeez**, or differently transcribed **pssih**, almost explosive' (Alstrom
Range: Breeds Siberian tundra and winters SE Asia and Africa.

3   PADDYFIELD PIPIT   *Anthus rufulus*   16cm   Locally common resider

The only pipit that breeds in Borneo. Locally common, nesting in short grassland in Sabah o
both east and west coasts. Common in Brunei but scarce further south. A common resider
of both Balikpapan and Berau airfields (E Kalimantan). Previously considered to be a race o
Richard's Pipit. Distinguished from Richard's by smaller size, different call and by distinctiv
breeding habits. Distinguished from other pipits by upright posture and breeding behaviou
Around Kota Kinabalu breeds Dec. to June, when pairs nest on uncut lawns. When breedin
male has low fluttering display flight above grassland. Builds small cup-shaped nest on th
ground. **Call:** 'A short rather harsh **chep**, often repeated, sometimes very quickly, e.g. **che**
chep very different from Richard's Pipit' (Alstrom). **Range:** Breeds India to Malay P.

4   PECHORA PIPIT   *Anthus gustavi*   16cm   Scarce winter visitc

An uncommon visitor to NW Borneo coastal districts. No records from Kalimantan. A dar
heavily streaked pipit most likely to be confused with Red-throated Pipit when that bird i
not in breeding plumage. Unlike other pipits, skulking and shy with a preference for path
or tracks in wooded areas. When disturbed flies up and then drops down into cover withou
calling, unlike Red-throated Pipit, which usually calls when flushed. In hand distinguishe
from other pipits by the exposed tips of the primary feathers not being covered by terti
feathers. See page 41. **Range:** Breeds N Siberia, winters Philippines, Borneo, Sulawesi.

5   OLIVE-BACKED PIPIT   *Anthus hodgsoni*   16cm   Rare winter visitc

[Indian Tree Pipit] A rare winter visitor with several records from NW coastal districts. Recer
record from Gng Menyapa E Kalimantan on a forest track (Brickle et al. Nov. 2007). The Asia
counterpart of the European Tree Pipit which it closely resembles. Feeds on the ground b
prefers bushy, wooded areas in comparison with other pipits. When disturbed flies up 1
perch on branches or telephone wires. Distinguished from other pipits by plain olive-gree
back with slight streaks and by distinctive face pattern. The broad supercillium (eyebrow) i
buffy in front of the eye and white or cream above the eye, bordered above by a thin blac
streak. Also has a distinctive whitish ear spot. **Call:** 'A short high pitched **beez** or **bizz** whic
is usually uttered singly' (Alstrom). **Range:** Breeds Central Asia, China, winters south t
India, Thailand, Philippines and Borneo.

LARKS: ALAUDIDAE

LARKS: WORLD: 91 species. **BORNEO** 2 species. Like pipits, larks have white outer tail feathers and brown streaky plumage, and like pipits they feed and run on the ground. However their bills are thicker, used for eating seeds as well as insects. They have rounded wings and fluttery flight and often a short crest can be seen. Females and males are similar. When breeding larks have a distinctive display flight where they rise in the air on round fluttering wings singing melodiously. Nests are small scrapes on the ground.

1 HORSFIELD'S BUSH LARK *Mirafra javanica* 14 cm Scarce resident

[Davison: Australasian Bush-lark] [Singing Bushlark] [Eastern Bushlark]. In Borneo a scarce resident of Kalimantan recorded from Bandjarmasin and Pontianak. They sit close to the ground on short legs. When flushed has very distinctive fluttering hovering flight with drooping short white edged tail. **Call:** Melodius song in display flight or from perch. **Range:** Dry areas of Asia, from India to S China, Thailand, Borneo, Java to Australia. An uncommon resident of open grassland and dry padi fields in the Philippines which could easily expand to Sabah.

2 ORIENTAL SKYLARK *Alauda gulgula* 16 cm Not recorded

Breeds Philippines and could easily turn up in Borneo as a migrant or by range expansion. **Call:** A dry buzzing *drzz* (Viney). **Range:** Breeds Iran to S China. Northern populations winter south.

3 EURASIAN SKYLARK *Alauda arvensis* 17cm Vagrant

Two records, a small flock on Kuching golf course Nov/Dec 1950 (skins) and 3 at Tawau 14 Feb 1962 (sight record-Norman). Similar to Oriental Skylark but larger and with a white trailing edge to the wing and rufous shoulder patch. Both Skylarks occur in many varying races and only photographs and or skins can provide definite identification. **Call:** Distinctive *chirrup* (Viney).

SPARROWS: *PASSERIDAE.* **WORLD** 36 species. **BORNEO:** One recent immigrant. The House Sparrow *Passer domesticus*) and it's close relative the Eurasian Tree Sparrow are often described as 'invasive species' having spread to urban areas throughout the world. In truth it is man that it is the 'invasive species' and it is the ability of these two species to survive on the waste generated by man that has allowed these birds to thrive in towns and cities. The House Sparrow does not occur in Borneo instead the vacant ecological niche has been occupied by the Tree Sparrow a scarce resident of farmland in Europe.

4 EURASIAN TREE SPARROW *Passer montanus* 14 cm Common resident

First recorded breeding in various port towns from the 1964 onwards, now established in open countryside and on small islands throughout Borneo always living in close proximity to man. Feeds on lawns and scavenges waste food in towns. Builds messy nests of grass stalks in roofs or in dense clumps of vegetation. Often in flocks. Sexes similar. Juveniles much plainer. **Call**: Cheerful chirps and chirrups. **Range:** Breeds Europe to E and SE Asia.

THE SPECIALIST BIRDS OF SE BORNEO AND HORSFIELD'S BUSHLARK

In geologic time Borneo has several times been connected to Java by dry land for long periods, the last time during the Pleistocene ice ages around 10,000 years ago, when sea levels were much lower (see page 22). The climate of SE Kalimantan is similar to that of Java – dryer and more seasonal than the rest of Borneo. The result is that SE Borneo has a specialist bird fauna with Javan affinities including Horsfield's Bushlark, Red-breasted Parakeet, Savanna Nightjar, Javan White-eye, Long-tailed Shrike and Scarlet-headed Flowerpecker. Relict populations of Small Minivet, Racquet-tailed Treepie and Black-browed Babbler may still exist, as well as rare endemic munias. In the mid 1800s the Bandjarmasin area was the most heavily collected area of Borneo by early naturalists such as Motley, Grabowski, Bock and Lumholtz. Possible future vagrants include austral/indonesian nomads such as Black-faced Cuckoo Shrike, Australian Kestrel and Spotted Harrier *Circus assimilis* of Sulawesi/Australia.

WEAVERS AND BUNTINGS

WEAVERS: *PLOCEIDAE.* **WORLD** 95 species. **ASIA** 5 species

1 BAYA WEAVER *Ploceus philippinus*   **15 cm   Escape**
Weavers are mainly of African distribution. They flock in grassland, building elaborate woven nests hung in tree colonies. The entrance hole is a downward facing shaft to deter access by predatory tree snakes. Three species are resident in Java and Sumatra. A feral breeding colony has been established on the outskirts of Sandakan since at least 2008. A new colony reported from Tenom (Sabah) at Kg Baab by Ken TJ Lee and S.K.Chee in June 2012. More recently (June 2013) Jason Anderson recorded breeding 10km north of Keningau, so presumably Baya Weaver has colonised most of the Tenom-Keningau valley. **Range:** India to Vietnam, south to Malay P.

Baya Weavers *Ploceus philippinus*
at a nesting colony

BUNTINGS: *EMBERIZIDAE.* **WORLD** 156 species. **BORNEO:** 4 species, all vagrants. Buntings are streaked brown, seed eating finches of grassland and grassy swamps. Males and females differ. Most have white side panels on tails. Males have distinctive head pattern when breeding but otherwise resemble the dull very variable females and juveniles. Buntings breed in N and NE Asia moving south in winter. Borneo is beyond their normal migratory range but some vagrants overshoot. 20 species are recorded for Hong Kong, three for the Philippines, five for the Malay P, and five for Borneo. Simple chip type calls are not distinctive.

2 LITTLE BUNTING *Emberiza pusilla*   **13 cm**   **Vagrant**
Three records for Borneo. Bau (Sarawak); Tempasuk Plain (Sabah); P. Tiga 14 Oct. 2009 (Kehoe). Distinguished by small size and pale eye ring. **Call:** *tsew* and *pwick* (Viney).**Range:** Breeds Siberia, winters India, SE Asia.

3 YELLOW-BREASTED BUNTING *Emberiza aureola*   **15 cm**   **Vagrant**
Vagrants recorded Kuching, Wasan in Brunei (several times), Papar (Sabah). Vast numbers are trapped in China each Autumn and sold tinned as 'rice birds'. **Range:** Breeds Europe to Siberia and N Japan, winters south.

4 COMMON REED BUNTING   **Vagrant**
One possible sight record from the Tempasuk Plain. Usually in reed beds. **Call:** A falling *chrr* followed by a rising plaintive *chween*. **Range:** Breeds Europe to E Asia wintering south.

5 BLACK-HEADED BUNTING *Emberiza melanocephala*   **18 cm**   **Vagrant**
Two single records from Brunei (Mann) and several Oct. records in different years from the grassy lawn at the N. Park HQ on Pulau Tiga, are presumed to be this species (Dymond). Two females on P. Manukan, Nov. 2009. (P. Olsson). Distinguish by large size and heavy bill. Unlike most buntings has no white on side of tail. **Range:** Breeds Europe, C Asia, winters south.

6 RED-HEADED BUNTING *Emberiza melanocephala*   **18 cm**   **Not recorded**
Both this and the Black-headed bunting breed in Central Asia in Kazhakstan and surrounding areas and winter in NW India. Therefore the birds that turn up in Borneo are seriously off course. Black and Red Headed Buntings hybridise on their breeding grounds where their populations overlap, and only males in breeding plumage are properly distinguishable.

BIRDING THE KOTA KINABALU (KK) AREA

1 **Dalit Beach and Rasa Ria Resort, Tuaran** (6°09'N, 116°08'E) 1hr by car north of KK. Public beach next to luxury beach resort surrounded by *Casuarina* forest, buffalo grazing land, riverine lagoons and mangroves. Purple Heron, White-breasted Waterhen, Pink-necked Green Pigeon, Blue-throated Bee-eater, Crimson Sunbird, Large-tailed Nightjar, Collared Kingfisher, Brahminy Kite, Cinnamon Bittern, Honey Buzzard, Frigatebirds, Ashy Minivet, Fiery Minivet.

2 **Nexus Karambunai Resort** (6°06'N, 116°06'E) 30min drive north of KK. Luxury beach resort with golf course; backed by a hill with regenerating secondary forest. Herons and egrets roost on trees on the golf course. Typical birds include Woodswallow, Pacific Swallow, Plain Sunbird, Brown-throated and Olive-backed Sunbird, Striated Heron, Pied Triller, Common Iora, Collared and Stork-billed Kingfishers, Cattle Egret.

3 **Kota Kinabalu: City of Egrets** (5°59'N, 116°04'E) Surprisingly good for birds. Migrant Peregrines in winter on office buildings, breeding Java and Tree Sparrows, House Swift colony in Gaya Street, Glossy Swiftlets nesting in multi-level car parks.
KK Waterfront: Good for Whiskered and White-winged Terns, Black-headed Gulls, Reef Egrets and Great Egrets. Reclamation lagoons attract all species of egret except Cattle Egret.

4 **Likas Bay and Likas Swamp** (5°59'N, 116°06'E) 10min by car north of KK. A busy main road separates the beach and coastal park from a freshwater lagoon, covered in water hyacinth. Little, Great and Chinese Egrets and waders. Whimbrel, Greater and Lesser Sand Plover and Little Ringed Plover are common on the coast in winter. **Likas Swamp** The lagoon has regular Grey and Purple Herons, Moorhens, Purple Gallinules, Wandering Whistling Ducks.

5 **KK City Bird Sanctuary, Likas** (5°59'37'N, 116°06'18'E) 10min by car north of KK. On the far side of Signal Hill behind KK, 100ha of remnant mangrove and brackish pools with an information centre and boardwalk. Intermediate and Little Egrets feed amongst the mangroves. A small nesting colony of Purple Herons can be seen from a hide. Look for Striated Heron, Greenshank, Blue-eared and Common Kingfishers, Blue-throated Bee-eaters.

6 **Signal Hill Lookout Platform** (5°59'N, 116°04'E) 20min walk from central KK. A shady walk up the steep steps behind central KK brings you to the Signal Hill Lookout Platform. White-bellied Sea Eagles and Brahminy Kites soar over the city. If the nearby fig tree is fruiting, look for feeding Green Imperial and Pink-necked Green Pigeons, Glossy Starlings and Koels.

7 **Tunku Abdul Rahman Park (TARP)** (5°59'N 116°00'E) 20min boat ride from KK. TARP consists of four small islands, Sulug, Manukan Mamutik and Sapi, and one large island, Gaya **Manukan** Overnight stays. Philippine Megapode Mangrove Whistler, Mangrove Blue Flycatcher **Gaya** Olive-winged Bulbul, Cream-vented Bulbul Hill Myna, Pied Hornbill, Grey-chested Jungle Flycatcher, Grey Imperial, Pied Imperial, Nicoba Pigeons occur. Green Imperial flies in to roost.

8 **Sutera Harbour Resort and marina** (5°57'N 116°03'E) on KK seafront facing Gaya Island Luxury resort backed by a golf course and edged by mudflats. Common here are Yellow-vented Bulbuls, Glossy Starlings, Paddyfield Pipits, Striated Grassbird, Cattle Egret, Common Iora. Also Great Little, Reef and Chinese Egrets, Whimbrels, Golden Plover on the mudflats to the south.

9 **Shangri-La Tanjung Aru Resort (STAR)** (5°57'N, 116°02'E) 10min by car south of KK Luxury coastal resort with extensive garden facing the islands of Tunku Abdul Rahman National Park. For the price of a drink see Yellow-vented Bulbul, Magpie Robin, Glossy Starling Chestnut and Dusky Munias, Brown-throated and Olive-backed Sunbirds, Zebra and Spotted-necked Doves, nesting Glossy Swiftlets and Green Imperial Pigeons. Blue-naped Parrots, Brown-capped Woodpecker all occur. Great, Chinese, Reef Egrets Striated Heron are regulars on the public beach.

10 **Tg Aru Beach and Prince Philip Park** (5°57'N 116°03'E) 10min by car south of KK. 4km o sandy beach, backed by a public park of shady *Casuarina* trees. Typical birds: Blue-naped Parrot Collared Kingfisher, Crested Myna, Chestnut Scaly-breasted and Dusky Munias. Collared Scops Owl at night. Occasional Peregrines Honey Buzzards. Many good restaurants. Highly recommended for an early morning or evening stroll. See Graphic Index for coastal birds.

11 **Crocker Range: Mt Alab, Rafflesia Centre** (5°40'N, 116°20'E) 2hr from KK by car. The Sinsuron road crosses the **Crocker Range** close to the peak of **Mount Alab** (1,964m), giving easy access to submontane and montane birdlife. Look for Ashy Drongo and Bornean Treepie. **Rafflesia Centre** on the far side of the range has pristine montane forest. Birds include Whitehead's Spiderhunter Mountain Barbet, Bornean Barbet, Long-tailed Broadbill, Bornean Leafbird, Bornean Bulbul. The Crocker Range can also be accessed via the Kimanis-Keningau Road along which the Crocker Range Park HQ is located. See map next page.

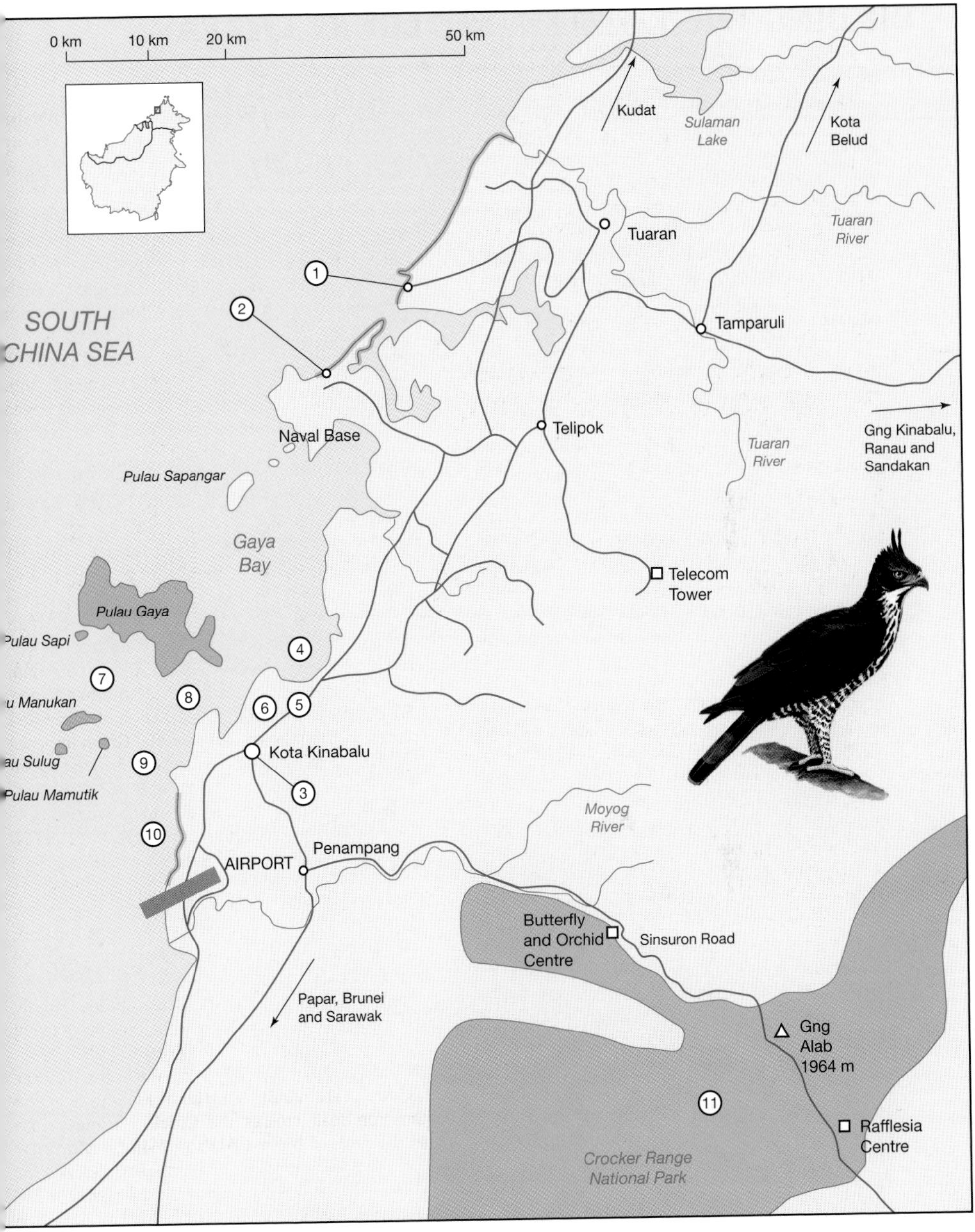

SOUTH CHINA SEA

Kudat

Sulaman Lake

Kota Belud

Tuaran

Tuaran River

① Tuaran

② Tamparuli

Naval Base

Telipok

Tuaran River

Gng Kinabalu, Ranau and Sandakan

Pulau Sapangar

Gaya Bay

Telecom Tower

Pulau Gaya

Pulau Sapi

④

⑦

⑧

⑥ ⑤

Pulau Manukan

Pulau Sulug

⑨

Kota Kinabalu

Pulau Mamutik

⑩

③

Moyog River

AIRPORT

Penampang

Butterfly and Orchid Centre

Sinsuron Road

Papar, Brunei and Sarawak

Gng Alab 1964 m

⑪

Rafflesia Centre

Crocker Range National Park

KEY to the Birdwatching Sites maps

- ○ town/village
- □ place of interest
- △ moutain peak
- ③ site mentioned in text
- — main road
- National Park
- sand
- political boundary

0 km   10 km   20 km   50 km

BIRDING WEST SABAH AND KINABALU PARK

1 Tip of Borneo (7°02'N, 116°44'E) 4hrs by car north of KK. 30min north of Kudat. Popular tourist spot on northernmost point of mainland Borneo. Pristine sandy beach, rocky headlands, mangroves and coconuts. During peak migration (late Oct. and March/April) look for migrant raptors on their flights to and from Palawan and NE Asia. Grey-faced Buzzard, Honey Buzzard, Peregrine, Osprey, Chinese Goshawk and Japanese Sparrowhawks expected.

2 Mantanani Islands (6°42'N, 116°22'E) 2hr drive from KK plus 1hr by boat from Kuala Abai. Three islands: Mantanani Besar, Mantanani Kechil and Lungisan. **Lungisan** has a nesting cave of German's (white nest) Swiftlets and is an important roost island for frigatebirds. **Mantanani Besar** is the sole Borneo location of Mantanani Scops Owl. Blue-naped Parrot is now locally extinct. Good location for rare island pigeons, Pied Imperial, Grey Imperial and Nicobar and Philippine Megapode. Rare migrants occur in October. Seabirds often seen on the sea crossing.

3 Tempasuk Plain (6°25'N, 116°26'E) 2hr by car north of KK. Transport essential. Swamps, padi fields and coastal grasslands. After passing Kota Belud, explore the side roads between the Kudat Road and the 20km beach. The best place in Borneo for migrant waterbirds and raptors from October to April. Raptors include Peregrine, Marsh Harrier, Black-winged Kite, Kestrel. Rare migrants include ducks, pratincoles, Hoopoe, Ruddy Kingfisher, Black Drongo. Look for Grass Owl and skulking warblers. No shade, can be very hot. See pages 6/7.

4 Pulau Tiga (5°43'N, 115°39'E) 2.5hr drive south of KK to Kuala Penyu plus a 30min boat trip. Three islands. **P Tiga:** Pristine beach and coastal forest. Pied Hornbill, Roller, Blue-throated Bee-eater, Phillipine Megapode, Nicobar Pigeon, Large-tailed Nightjar, Mangrove Blue Flycatcher, Chinese Egret in lagoon. **Kalampunian Besar:** Sand spit used by roosting seabirds. **Kalampunian Damit** (Snake Island)**:** Frigatebirds roost, nesting White-bellied Sea Eagles, Pied Imperial Pigeons. **Tg Nosong:** Rocky stacks on mainland have breeding terns April to June.

5 Klias Wetlands (5°21'N, 115°28'E) 3hr south of KK. Best visited on a Proboscis Monkey boat tour booked in KK. Large area of freshwater and mangrove swamp, drained by the Padas Damit river. Famous for fireflies at night and endemic Proboscis Monkeys. Large numbers of migrant egrets, herons, bitterns, ducks and other water birds during the winter months. See pages 6/7.

KINABALU NATIONAL PARK (KNP)
See Graphic Indexes pages 12–13 and 14–15. Als Zonation pages 32–33.

6 KNP Park HQ (6°00'35 N, 116°32'2 E) 1,563m, 2.5hr drive from KK. Good varied accommodation, surrounded by pristin mountain forest with an excellent trail system Best location for Borneo's magnificent endem montane birds including Whitehead's tri (Broadbill, Trogon and Spiderhunter). Als Bornean Treepie, Bornean Laughing-thrust Bornean Whistling Thrush, Chestnut-creste Yuhina, Everett's Thrush, Red-breasted Hi Partridge, Crimson-headed Partridge, Golder naped Barbet, Bornean Whistler. Weather coo often misty.

7 KNP Summit Trail (6°04'28 N, 116°33'4 E) 1,866m rising to summit at 4,095m. Startin above KNP HQ at Timpohon Gate (1,866m) strenuous climb of around 5hr takes you to th rest huts at Panar Laban (3,330m), and a furthe climb of 3hr will see you reach the summi (4,095m). Vegetation ranges from mossy forest t rhododendron scrub and bare rock higher up. Birds Island Thrush, Friendly Bush-warbler, Mountai Black-eye. Endemic squirrels and tree shrew common around rubbish bins. Weather often ver cold and wet.

8 KNP Mesilau Resort (5°59'55 N, 116°35'1 E) 2,000m, 45min drive from KNP HQ. O interest to botanists because of magnificen pitcher plant festooned cliffs, but little visite by birders because few good trails. Look fo Eye-browed Jungle Flycatcher, Bornean Flowe pecker, Bornean Whistling Thrush, Whitehead' Spiderhunter, Pale-faced Bulbul, Bornean Stubtai

9 KNP Poring (6°03'N, 116°42'E) 550m rising t 1,200m at the Langanan Waterfall. Excellent hi and submontane forest with a very long bird-list Often busy with noisy day trippers visiting th hot springs, splendid butterfly garden and canop walkway. Resident birds include Blue-bande Pitta, Banded Pitta, Chestnut-capped Thrush White-crowned and Chestnut-naped Forktail, Blue banded Kingfisher, Roulroul. Argus Pheasant call in the distance. Many frugivorous birds, e.g Hose's and Whitehead's Broadbill, bulbuls appea seasonally around main clearing. Hornbills scarce except Black. Langanan waterfall trail, whic rises to 1,200m, can be good for submontane an montane birds such as Orange-breasted Trogon Chestnut-crested Yuhina, Bornean Treepie. Th path passes a mini bat cave with Glossy Swiftle nests en route.

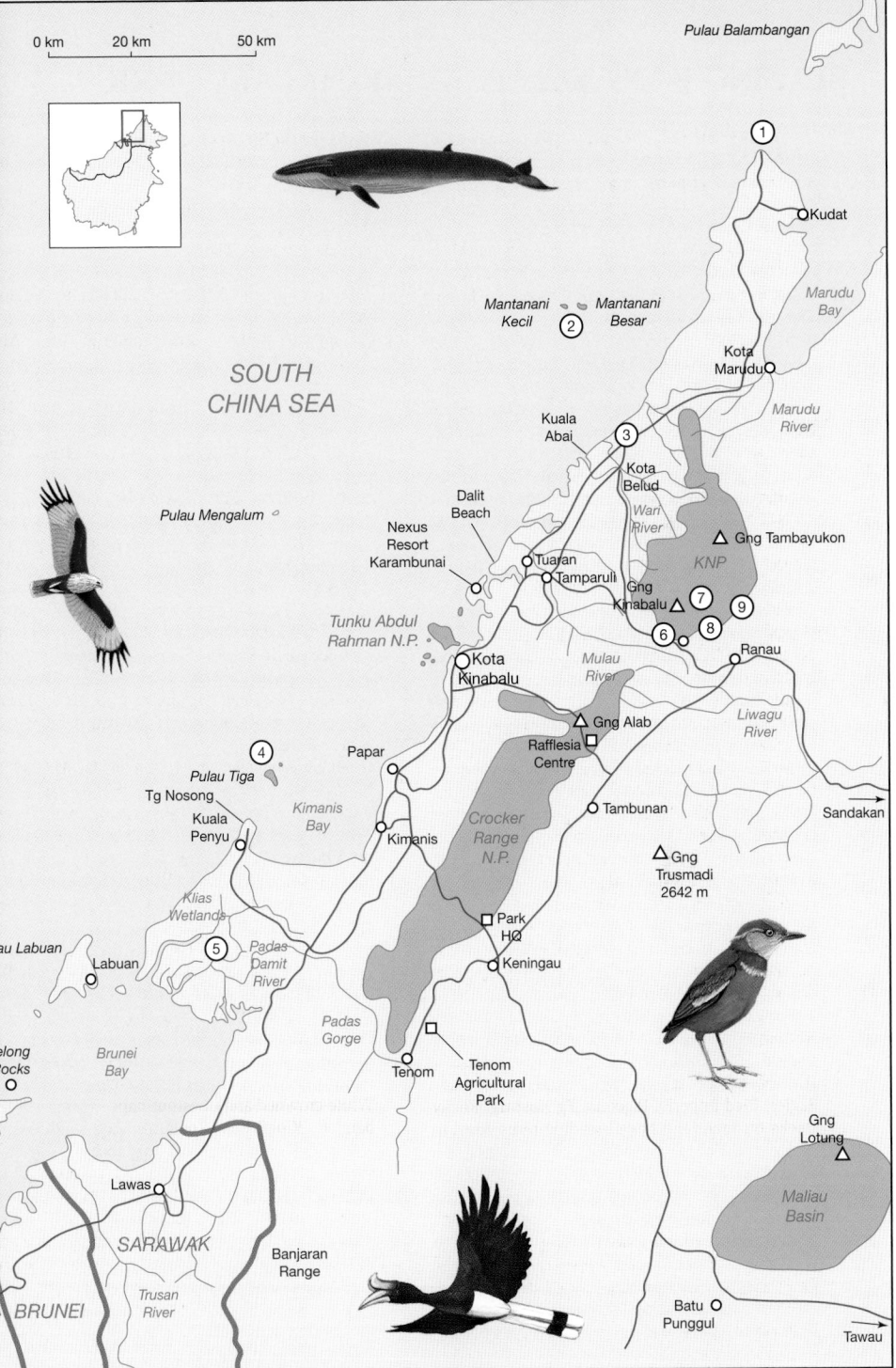

0 km   20 km   50 km

Pulau Balambangan

①

○Kudat

Marudu Bay

Mantanani Kecil   ②   *Mantanani Besar*

Kota Marudu○

Marudu River

SOUTH CHINA SEA

Kuala Abai

③

Kota Belud

Wari River

△ Gng Tambayukon

KNP

Pulau Mengalum

Dalit Beach

Nexus Resort Karambunai

○Tuaran
○Tamparuli

Gng Kinabalu △ ⑦ ⑨

⑥ ⑧

○Ranau

Tunku Abdul Rahman N.P.

○Kota Kinabalu

Mulau River

Liwagu River

④

Pulau Tiga

Papar○

△ Gng Alab
□ Rafflesia Centre

Kimanis Bay

○ Tambunan

Sandakan →

Tg Nosong

Kuala Penyu

○Kimanis

Crocker Range N.P.

△ Gng Trusmadi 2642 m

Klias Wetlands

lau Labuan

○Labuan

⑤

Padas Damit River

□ Park HQ

○ Keningau

elong Rocks ○

Brunei Bay

Padas Gorge

□

○Tenom

□ Tenom Agricultural Park

○Lawas

SARAWAK

Banjaran Range

Gng Lotung △

Maliau Basin

BRUNEI

Trusan River

Batu Punggul ○

Tawau →

331

BIRDING EAST SABAH

1 **Lankayan Island (Sugud Islands) (6°32'N, 117°55'E)** 3hr by boat from Sandakan. Remote dive island with some large trees. Look for turtles, whale sharks, rare island pigeons.

2 **Turtle Islands (6°10'21N, 118°3'37E)** 2hr by boat from Sandakan. Three islands: Selingan, Libaran and Gulisan. View turtles nesting at night. Stone Curlew, Reef Egret.

3 **Labuk Bay Proboscis Sanctuary (5°46'00N, 118°18'00E)** 1hr drive from Sandakan. Mangrove forest, surrounded by oil palm. Provides accommodation and opportunity to view the feeding of Proboscis Monkey, Silvered Langur and Pied Hornbill. Use boardwalk through the mangrove for Collared and Ruddy Kingfishers, Mangrove Whistler, Mangrove Blue Flycatcher.

4 **Sepilok Forest Reserve and Orangutan Centre (5°47'N, 117°55'E)** 45min drive from Sandakan. 60km² of primary lowland rainforest on Sandakan Bay. Good varied accommodation. Birding in local resort gardens, on canopy walkway at Rainforest Discovery Centre and along forest edge. A 2hr walk through forest to mangroves of Sandakan Bay allows birding for forest understorey birds. Pristine lowland rainforest is both the richest and now scarcest habitat in Borneo. Most Bornean lowland forest birds occur at Sepilok but are not easy to see. Look for Bristlehead, all eight hornbills, Giant Pitta, Great Slaty Woodpecker, trogons, kingfishers. Lots of flowerpeckers and spiderhunters in the mistletoe-infested, purple-flowered *Lagerstroemia* trees along the access road.

5 **Gomantong Caves (Forest Reserve) (5°33'N, 118°05'E)** 2hr drive from Sandakan. Vast complex of limestone caves, inhabited by echo-locating swiftlets with valuable, edible nests. Ideally visit at dawn or dusk to see changeover of bat and swiftlet populations. Good for birds of prey including Bat Hawk, Peregrine, Wallace's Hawk-eagle, Changeable Hawk-eagle, Rufous-bellied Hawk-eagle, Buffy Fish Owl. Surrounding logged forest often contains interesting birds.

6 **Kinabatangan River, Sukau, Bilit (5°30'N, 118°16'E)** 3hr drive from Sandakan. Magnificent riverside forest and oxbow lakes known for a large primate population of Orangutans, Proboscis, Hose's and Maroon Langurs, gibbons and macaques. Numerous popular basic lodges. Hornbills abundant, all eight species occur. Waterbirds include Stork-Billed and Blue-eared Kingfishers, Darter, Storm's Stork. Good location for Bornean Ground-cuckoo, Hooded Pitta, Black-and-yellow and Black-and-red Broadbills. Both Fish Eagles. See pages 14/15. www. worldlandtrust.org

7 **Tabin Wildlife Reserve (5°10'N, 118°45'E)** 2▮ drive from Lahad Datu. A core area of 86km² the last refuge of Sumatran Rhinoceros in Sabal Surrounded by 1,200km² of logged forest. Mu springs provide salts for elephants and dee Excellent birding along main roads, forest tra limited. Very good for eagles, hawks and owls whic live in the forest but feed on rats in the adjacent c palm. Hornbills can be viewed from mud volcar observation tower.

8 **Danum Valley Conservation Area (4°49'▮ 117°28'E)** 2.5hrs drive from Lahad Datu. core area of primary lowland and hill fore (438km²) surrounded by 2,400km² of logge forest (Ulu Segama and Malua Forest Reserve Highest point is Gng Danum at 1,093m. Luxur cabins at Borneo Rainforest Lodge (BRL) an hostel accommodation at DV Research Cente Both sites have similar birds but differer specialities and provide Asia's top forest birdin At BRL an excellent canopy walkway gives view of hornbills and gibbons. Look for Bristlehea all eight hornbills, Giant, Blue-headed, Bande Black-headed and Blue-banded Pittas. Creste Fireback and Argus Pheasants, Bornean Ground cuckoo, Orangutan, Clouded Leopard regular.

9 **Maliau Basin (4°50'N, 117°18'E)** 4hr driv from Tawau. Basic accommodation. 588km² o pristine hill forest in S Central Sabah. Altitud varies from 300m to 1,600m at summit of Gunun Lotung. Birds recorded include Bulwer's Pheasan Large Green Pigeon, Blue-headed Pitta, Bornea Blue Flycatcher and Large-billed Blue Flycatcher.

10 **Tawau Hills Park (4°22'33N, 117°59'02E)** 30mi drive from Tawau. 280km² of watershed hi forest ranging from lowland dipterocarp to moss mountain forest at the summit of Gng Magdalen (1,310 m). Extensive forest trails. Lodge and hoste accommodation. Avoid busy weekends. Good mix c forest birds. Specialty is the endemic Bornean Ibo common higher up on Gng Magdalena.

11 **Semporna Islands (4°34'44N, 118°56'57E** Extensive group of atolls and coral cays bes explored by boat from Semporna or the dive resor on Pulau Mataking. P Maiga is a frigatebird roos island. Si Amil has Blue-naped Parrots and White vented Whistler. Look for Pied and Grey Imperia Pigeons, Black-naped Fruit Doves, Metallic an Nicobar Pigeon, Beach Stone Curlew.

12 **Sipadan Island (4°07'N, 118°37'E)** 1hr by boa from Semporna or 20min from Mabul. Top oceani dive site, good for turtles, rays, sharks. Day trip only from nearby Mabul and Kapalai dive resorts Rare island pigeons and the major site in Borne for Philippine White-vented Whistler.

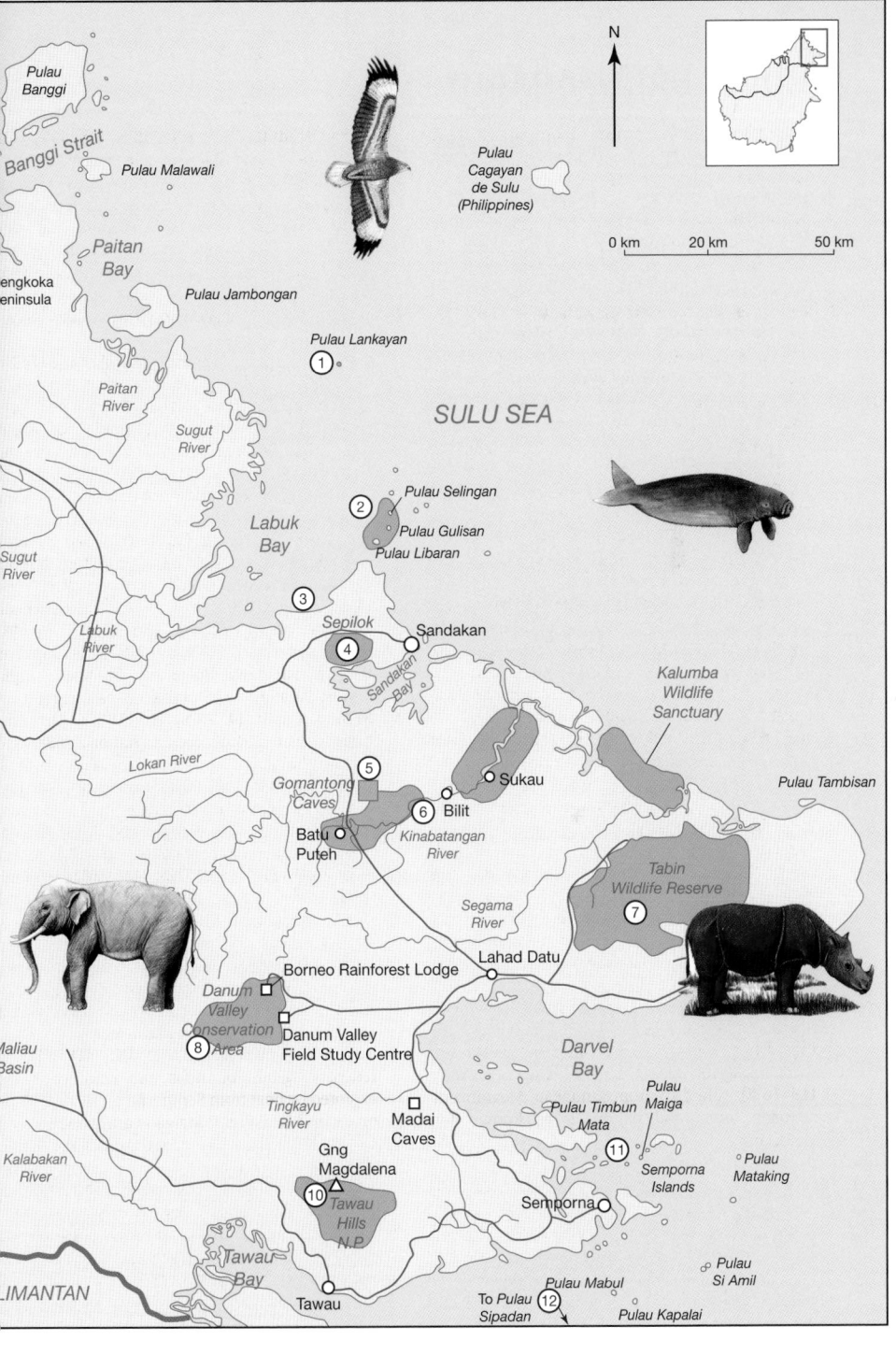

BIRDING BRUNEI DARUSSALAM   See Moore, J. (2009)

Temburong District   *45min by speedboat from BSB to Bangar in Temburong.*

1 **Peradayan Forest Reserve (4°45'N, 115°09'E)**   15min by car from Bangar. 1,070ha of forest including Bukit Peradayan (410m) and Bukit Patoi (310m). 1.6km forest trail and a 5km trail ascending Bukit Patoi, which takes 1hr each way. Hornbills often seen.

2 **Ulu Temburong National Park (4°28'N, 115°10'E)**   488km² of pristine primary forest, 7km of boardwalks. Canopy walkway and observation tower. Highest point is Gng Pagon 1850m. Stay at **Ulu Ulu Resort** accessible by boat up the Temburong River from Bangar. Book overnight tour from BSB. A chance to see most primary forest lowland birds. Seven hornbill species (not Pied), Gibbons, Hose's Langur and Pig-tailed Macaque are common. Hose's Civet occurs.

Bandar Seri Begawan (BSB) and SW Brunei

3 **Brunei Bay, Serasa Beach and sandspit (4°59'N, 115°04'E)**   25min by car from BSB. Lined with *Casuarina* trees, this sandspit juts out into Brunei bay from Muara. Migratory waders feed on the exposed mudflats during winter months.

4 **Pulau Selirong (Pulau Muara Besar) (4°53'N, 115°08'E)**   45min boat trip from Muara. 2,566ha mangrove island, nature reserve, with 2km walkway and observation tower.

5 **Kampung Ayer and the Brunei River (4°53'N, 114°56'E)**   Hire a water taxi from the jetty in BSB. Best time is early morning or late afternoon. Watch terns diving for food around K Ayer. The mangroves lining the river are home to kingfishers, macaques, Proboscis Monkeys, roosting herons and egrets. White-bellied Sea Eagles, Brahminy Kites often seen. Look for Storm's Stork.

6 **Tasek Lama Park (4°54'N, 114°56'E)**   10min walk from centre of BSB. Hilly secondary forest with various trails and a reservoir. Over 80 species of bird recorded including Straw-headed Bulbul, White-rumped Shama. Also watch for Proboscis Monkeys.

7 **Berakas Forest and Meragang Beach (4°59'N, 114°55'E)**   20min by car from BSB. Sandy beach backed by 348ha of kerangas forest. Macaques common, birds harder to spot.

8 **Jerudong Beach and Empire Golf and Country Club (4°58'N, 114°51'E)**   35min by car from BSB. Opulent sea front resort with golf course gardens and lakes. A wide variety of common birds.

9 **Wasan Rice Fields (4°47'N, 114°49'E)**   45min by car from BSB. 400ha of padi fields and swampland. Migrant waterbirds include duck, warblers, Green and Wood Sandpipers, Mars Harrier. Also Borneo residents Lesser Adjutant, Egrets, Straw-headed Bulbul, Blue-breasted Quail, Java Sparrow, Scaly-breasted Munia. Ma records of rare vagrants, e.g. Eurasian Bittern, Black-necked Stilt, Northern Lapwing, Gre headed Lapwing, Middendorff's Warbler.

10 **Tutong Beach and Kuala Tutong (4°48'), 114°38'E)**   10km of pristine sandy beach, line with *Casuarina* trees backed by the Tutong Riv Visit Tutong sewage farm for Darters and egrets

11 **Tasek Merimbun National Park (4°36') 114°41'E)**   1.5hr by car from BSB, 27km inla from Tutong. Brunei's largest freshwater lake with two islands, surrounded by 78km² pe swamp forest. Breeding Purple Herons, Darte and Night Herons. Also good for forest birds.

12 **Sungai Liang Forest Park Labi Rd (4°40') 114°28'E)**   1.5hr drive from BSB. Small fore arboretum. Nature trails, canopy walkway. Bu on public holidays.

13 **Sungai Seria and Kuala Seria (4°35') 114°20'E)**   Estuary and grasslands 2hr fro BSB. Very good for waders and waterbirds alor the coast, roosting inland at high tide. Al raptors Black-winged Kite, Peregrine Falcon. Lar colonies of roosting egrets during winter months

14 **Panaga, Seria (4°35'N, 114°15'E)**   Priva residential complex of 300ha for Shell employee including houses and gardens near the beac with large old trees. Large groups of breedi Oriental Pied Hornbills currently being studie Also Buffy Fish Owl, Collared Kingfisher, Whit bellied and Brown-capped Woodpeckers, Larg tailed Nightjar, Black-and-Red Broadbill.

15 **Badas Road (4°13'N, 114°25'E)**   Degrade peat swamp forest. Many birds include Falcone Bat Hawk, Crested Goshawk, Great Slaty ar Rufous Woodpeckers, Fairy Bluebird, Bristlehea

16 **Kuala Balai Road (4°27'N, 114°18'E)**   Fore along road is good for hornbills includir Wrinkled and Rhinoceros. Look for Malaysi Eared Nightjar at dusk. Road ends at Belait Rive

17 **Labi Road**   Follow road to Luagan Lalak Par 270ha of alluvial freshwater swamp within the La Hills FR. Follow road further south to Labi Hills ar Mulu View Ridge. Good selection of forest bir including Helmeted Hornbill and Bristlehead. 7k beyond Kg Labi a path off the road and a 2hr wa through primary forest leads to the summit of

18 **Bukit Teraja (4°30'N, 114°28'E)**   Good viev of the Baram river valley and Gng Mulu. Look fc Rhinoceros and Bushy-crested Hornbills.

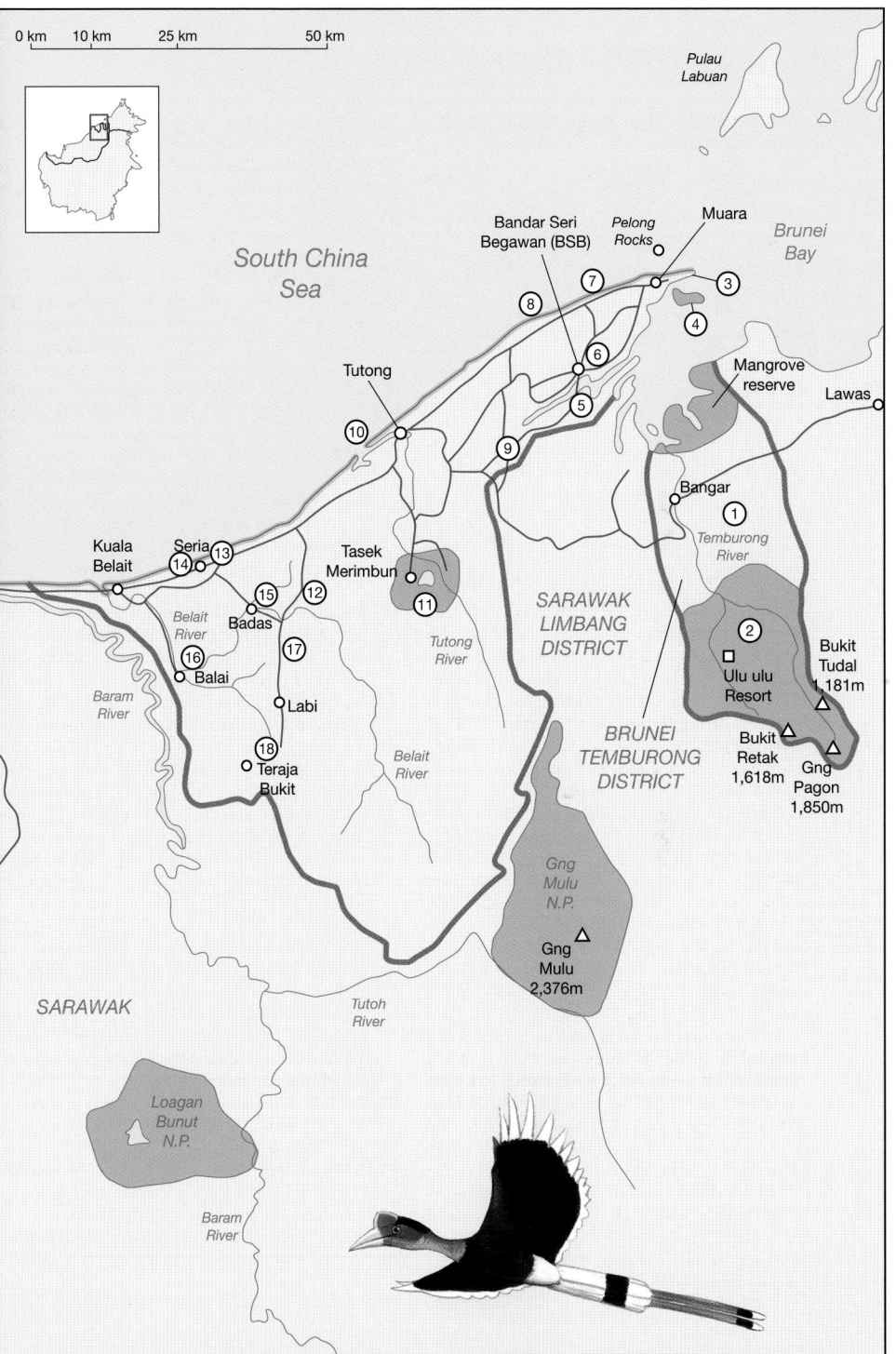

BIRDING THE KUCHING AREA

1 **Bako National Park (1°41'N, 110°17'E)** 27km², 45min drive from Kuching plus 25min boat ride. Sandstone cliffs, sandy beaches, mangroves, dipterocarp and kerangas (heath) forest. Accommodation: chalets, hostel and canteen. Excellent trails. Birds: Stork-billed and Collared Kingfishers, Mangrove Whistler, Mangrove Blue Flycatcher, Fairy Bluebird, Common Goldenback. House Swifts breed at Teluk Assam and German's Swiftlets at Pulau Lakei. Grey-capped Pygmy, White-bellied and Buff-necked Woodpeckers, Red-crowned and Brown Barbets, Chestnut-bellied and Chestnut-breasted Malkohas, Black and Pied Hornbills, Scarlet-rumped Trogon. Easy-to-see mammals include Proboscis Monkey, Silvered Langur, Long-tailed Macaque, Bearded Pig and Colugo.

2 **Buntal Bay (1°42'N, 110°21'E)** 45min drive from Kuching. Muddy bay with fishing village good for passage migrant waders, egrets, terns, gulls at low tide. Look for Chinese, Great, and Little Egret, plovers, whimbrel, curlews, godwits and dowitchers.

3 **Damai beach and Santubong National Park (1°42'N, 110°18'E)** 45min drive north of Kuching. A wide variety of habitats including sandy beach, mud flats, mangroves, golf courses and virgin primary forest. 5km offshore are the seabird breeding rocks Tukong Ara and Tukong Banun where Reef Egrets, Black-naped and Bridled Terns breed April to July (landing restricted). Several beach resorts provide luxury stays. At Damai hire boats to cruise the Kuching Mangroves NP to look for crocodiles at night and visit Pulau Satang Besar. Allow 5hr for the return birding walk to the summit of Gng Santubong (810m). Fine views, but good fitness essential. Commonest birds on Gng Santubong are White-chested Babbler and Cream-vented Bulbul.

4 **Central Kuching (1°33'N, 110°21'E)** Look for Brahminy Kite, Whiskered and White-winged Terns fishing along the river. Common Swallows roost in winter. A visit to the Sarawak Museum is highly recommended. Look for Palm Swifts and Javan Mynas in the gardens at rear.

5 **Semengoh Nature Reserve (1°24'N, 110°18'E)** 6.5km², 30min drive from Kuching. Orangutan Rehabilitation Centre set in lowland primary dipterocarp forest mixed with old secondary and some kerangas. Site of Sarawak Museum's long-term bird-ringing projects so an extensive bird list. Rehabilitated hornbills, gibbons and Orangutan. Resident birds include Black Partridge, Long-billed Partridge, Short-toed Coucal, Honeyguide, Bonaparte's Nightjar, Reddish Scops Owl. Check visiting hours, normal 8.00–1600hr. Nearby Semengoh Fisheries Cent is worth a visit for herons and waterbirds.

6 **Gunung Penrissen (1°08'N, 110°13'E)** Acce via the Borneo Highlands Resort 1.5hr drive SW Kuching. Highest point is Gng Penrissen (1,326m part of the range of low mountains which form th border with Kalimantan and include the extin volcano of Gng Niut (1,701m) in Kalimantar Birds recorded for this mountain range inclu Argus Pheasant, Long-billed Partridge, Wreathe Black and White-crested Hornbills, Bornea Barbet, Cinnamon-rumped Trogon, Blue-bande Pitta, Bornean Wren-babbler, Chestnut-creste Yuhina, Chestnut-hooded Laughing-thrush, Whit browed Shrike-babbler, Mountain Wren-babble Fruithunter, Pale Blue Flycatcher, Bornean Blu Flycatcher, Rufous-tailed Jungle Flycatcher, Everett White-eye, Bornean Ibon, Bornean and Yellow rumped Flowerpeckers, Temminck's Sunbird, Ash Drongo, Rail Babbler, Blythe's Hawk Eagle ar Black-thighed Falconet.

7 **Kubah National Park (Gunung Serap (1°35'N, 110°07'E)** 22km², 40min drive fro Kuching. Contains Matang Wildlife Centre (mii zoo of local rescued wildlife), chalets and hoste Mixed hilly primary forest rising to summit Gng Serapi (911m). Interesting forest with mai birds including Great Slaty Woodpecker an Argus Pheasant, Blue-banded Pitta, Blue-winge Leafbird and Bornean Blue Flycatcher. www organutanproject.com

8 **Gunung Gading National Park (1°43'N 109°50'E)** 54km², 2hr drive from Kuchin; or 10min from Lundu town. Highest point Gng Gading (900m). Famous for giant Raffles flowers. Good forest birding along steep hil trails. Hostel and chalets provide accommodatio

9 **Satang and Talang Islands Nation; Park** 45min drive from Kuching plus 30min b speedboat to Satang Besar. Four small foreste islands off the south west coast of Sarawa provide protection for nesting sea turtles. Loc for frigatebirds roosting on Satang Kecil and Pie Imperial Pigeons which feed on the mainlan but roost on the islands. Great Crested Tern an Reef Egret common. Also look for scarce islan pigeons: Grey Imperial and Nicobar and possib the extremely rare Silvery Pigeon. Pale rumpe German's Swiftlet nests in cracks in sea cliffs an House Swift under overhangs in sea cliffs. Landir allowed only on Satang Besar.

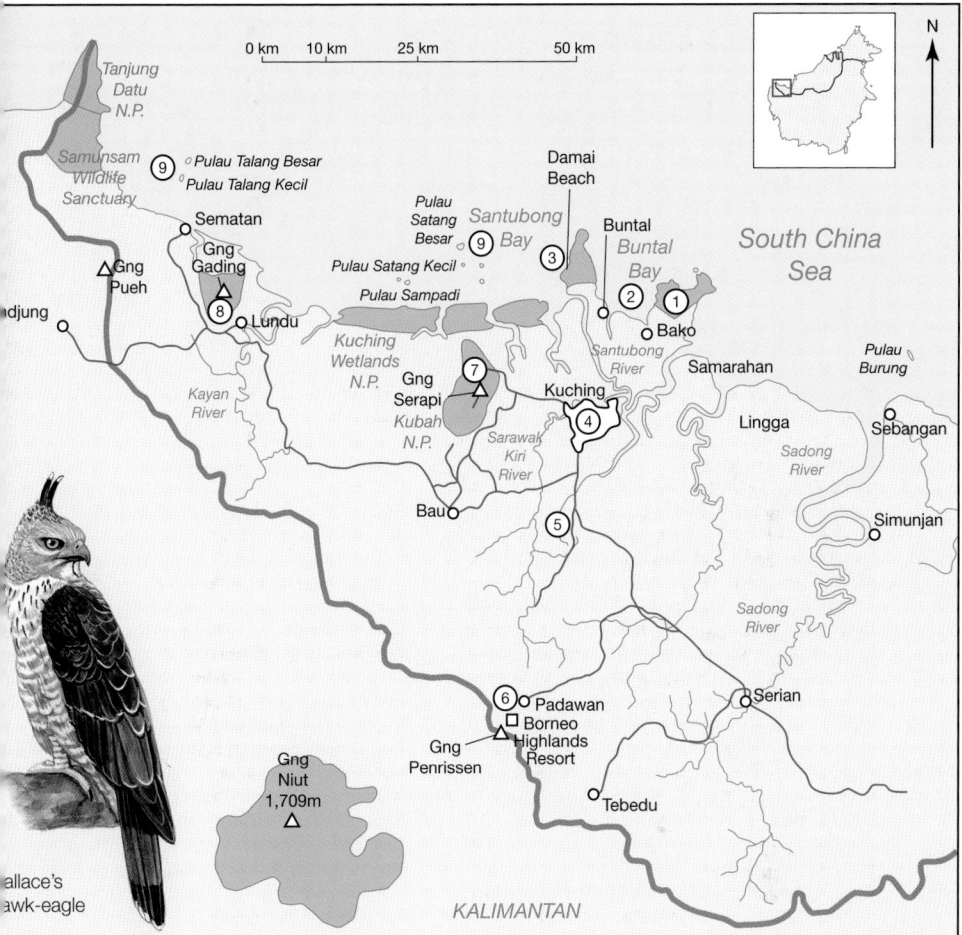

ALFRED RUSSEL WALLACE (1823–1913)

Wallace was one of the most influential naturalists of the 19th century. He is regarded as second in importance only to Darwin, with whom he co-operated in formulating the theory of evolution by natural selection. Unlike Darwin, who came from a wealthy family, Wallace earned his income from collecting and selling natural history specimens. Wallace spent 15 months in SW Sarawak between Nov. 1854 and Jan. 1856 as a guest of James Brooke the 'White Rajah', described in his book *The Malay Archipelago*. In appreciation he named Borneo's finest butterfly *Trogonoptera brookiana* (Raja Brooke's Birdwing) after his host. Wallace collected around Kuching, and also spent nine months in the forests near Simunjan, where he shot 17 Orangutans. A tiny relict population still exists in the area. One of the birds collected by Wallace was the Bornean Ground-cuckoo, but there are no Yellow-vented Bulbuls, Spotted-necked Doves, Little Spiderhunters or Yellow-bellied Prinias amongst his Sarawak bird skins at the British Museum (Cranbrook). This absence of evidence provides a clear indicator of the change in the birdlife and therefore the vegetation in S Sarawak in the last 150 years. Wallace's name is commemorated in Wallace's Hawk-eagle, see above, but he is best known for the concept of 'Wallace's Line', which highlights the very different wildlife between the Greater Sunda Islands (Borneo, Sumatra, Java and Bali) and Wallacea (Sulawesi, the Moluccas and the Lesser Sundas). Wallace wrote extensively about camouflage and mimicry in birds and was the first naturalist to point out the mimicry between Hawk-eagles and Honey Buzzards. See map page 23.

BIRDING SOUTHERN SARAWAK

1 **Similajau National Park (3°30'N, 113°15'E)** 71km², 20km N of Bintulu town. A 25km strip of sandy beaches, rivers and mangroves backed by coastal dipterocarp and kerangas forest. Varied accommodation: chalets, hostel and canteen at Park HQ. Good trails and boat trips available to view turtle hatchery and man-eating crocodiles. Listen for the calls of gibbons and Great Argus. Common birds: Brahminy Kite, White-bellied Sea Eagle, Black and Wrinkled Hornbills, Mangrove Blue Flycatcher, Copper–throated Sunbird, Whiskered Tree Swift, Chestnut-naped Forktail, White-rumped Shama, Fairy Bluebird. Useful site for kerangas specialists White-throated Babbler and Hook-billed Bulbul. Also recorded: Erpornis, Wallace's Hawk-eagle, Storm's Stork, Bristlehead, Bornean Wren-babbler, Black Partridge. Look for Red-banded Langur (*race P. m. cruciger* endemic to Sarawak) and Long-tailed Macaque.

2 **Lanjak Entimau Wildlife Sanctuary (1°37'N, 112°11'E)** 1688km². See Batang Ai below.

3 **Batang Ai National Park (1°20'N, 112°10'E)** 250km², 4hr drive from Kuching plus 1hr by boat to Park HQ and Hilton Resort. The best place to see most birds of lowland and hilly primary forest in Sarawak. Batang Ai is watershed protection forest for the 84km² lake and dam which supplies electricity to Kuching. Contiguous with Lanjak Entimau, which itself is contiguous with Betung Kerihun (8,000km²) in NW Kalimantan. Numerous trails and boat trips possible. Known for Orangutans, hornbills and gibbons. Seven out of eight hornbills occur (not Pied). Commonly seen and heard birds: Great Argus, Crested Partridge, Rufous and Maroon Woodpeckers, Blue-eared and Gold-whiskered Barbets, Bristlehead, Straw-headed Bulbul, White-rumped Shama, Spotted Fantail, Velvet-fronted Nuthatch, Asian Paradise Flycatcher, Little Spiderhunter. Other birds recorded: Bulwer's Pheasant, both Crested and Crestless Firebacks, Crimson-headed Partridge, Wallace's Hawk-eagle, Blue-banded, Blue-headed and Garnet Pittas, Yellow-crowned, Red-crowned and Red-throated Barbets, Bornean, Striped and Black-throated Wren-babblers, Brown-backed Flowerpecker, and Bornean, Pygmy and Large-billed Blue Flycatchers.

4 **Pulau Bruit National Park (Tanjong Sirik) (2°45'N, 111°13'E)** 18km² at the north tip of Pulau Bruit. This sandy spit is one of the best places in Borneo to see roosting migrant waders and seabirds during peak migration periods Sept.–Oct. and March–April each year. Access is by boat. Birds

seen here include Storm's Stork, Lesser Adjutant Chinese Egret, sand plovers, curlews, godwit Terek and Broad-billed Sandpipers, Dowitcher Gull-billed, Common, Little, Whiskered, an White-winged Terns, Black-headed Gull.

5 **Maludam NP** 431km². Access via boat fron the Malay fishing village at the mouth of th Maludam River which runs through the centr of the park. Largest area of peat swamp fore in Sarawak and Brunei. Birds include Black Pied and Rhinoceros Hornbills, Blue-eared an Stork-billed Kingfishers, Green Imperial Pigeor Slender-billed Crow, Greater Racket-tailed Drong and Storm's Stork. World's only surviving viabl population of Red-banded Langur. Proboscı Monkeys and Silvered Langur common.

6 **Gunung Pueh (Mt Poi) (1°46'N 109°40'E)** The summit (1,650m) is at the NV end of the low range of mountains stretching S to Gng Penrissen along the Sarawak–Kalimanta border. In Kalimantan known as Bukit Kany Approx 20km west of Lundu the only access via old logging tracks from Kg Sebako. Bird: Bornean Leafbird, Black-throated Wren-babble Mountain Wren-babbler, Blackeye, Bornean Ibon Everett's White-eye, Bornean Whistler, Chestnu hooded Laughing-thrush, Grey-chested an Eyebrowed Jungle Flycatcher, Snowy-browed an Little Pied Flycatchers, White-breasted Shrik babbler, and Mountain Tailorbird.

7 **Samunsam Wildlife Sanctuary (1°50'N 109°47'E)** 21km². Permit required. Mangrov and riverside forest which rises up to 1,200n behind the coast. Common birds includ Brahminy Kite, Green Imperial Pigeon, Blue crowned Hanging Parrot, Chestnut-breaste Malkoha, Lesser Coucal, Silver-rumped Spinetai Black Hornbill, Pacific Swallow, Fiery Minive Greater Racket-tailed Drongo, Velvet-fronte Nuthatch, Hill Myna, Copper-throated Sunbir Also recorded: Bristlehead, Storm's Stor Rufous-bellied Hawk-eagle and Ground-cucko Proboscis Monkeys a speciality.

8 **Tanjung Datu National Park** 13km², 40min b boat from Sematan when seas are calm (Apri Sept.). Small coastal park on western-most ti of Borneo adjacent to the Kalimantan borde Mixed virgin dipterocarp forest, pristine beache and coral reefs. Helmeted, Rhinoceros and Blac Hornbills recorded. Nesting turtles. Gibbons ar Long-tailed Macaques. Limited accommodatic at the park, otherwise stay at Sematan Beac Resort opposite the Talang Talang Islands 120k (2hr) drive from Kuching.

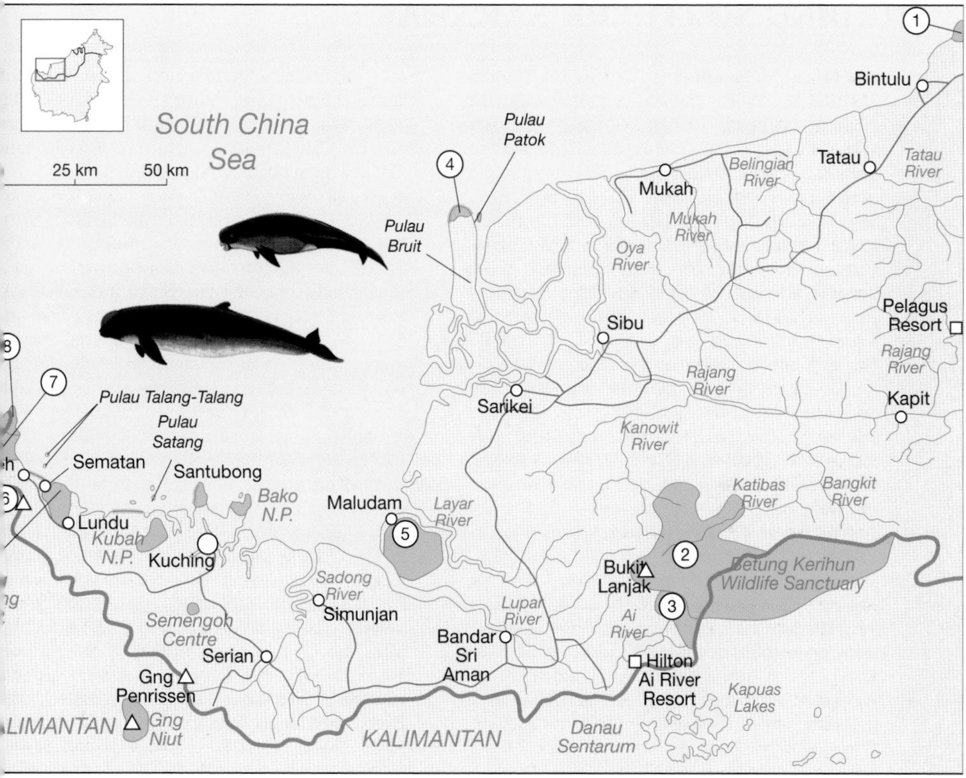

South China
Sea

25 km   50 km

Bintulu

Pulau
Patok

4

Mukah

Belingian
River

Tatau

Tatau
River

Pulau
Bruit

Mukah
River

Oya
River

Sibu

Pelagus
Resort

Rajang
River

Kapit

8

7

Pulau Talang-Talang

Pulau
Satang

Sematan

Santubong

Bako
N.P.

Maludam

Layar
River

Sarikei

Rajang
River

Kanowit
River

Katibas
River

Bangkit
River

h

Lundu

Kubah
N.P.

Kuching

5

Buki
Lanjak

2

Betung Kerihun
Wildlife Sanctuary

Sadong
River

Simunjan

Lupar
River

Ai
River

3

ng

Semengoh
Centre

Serian

Gng
Penrissen

Bandar
Sri
Aman

Hilton
Ai River
Resort

Kapuas
Lakes

LIMANTAN

Gng
Niut

KALIMANTAN

Danau
Sentarum

6

RTRAM E. (BILL) SMYTHIES (1912–1999) AND *THE BIRDS OF BORNEO*

The
BIRDS
of BORNEO

Fourth Edition
Revised by G. W. H. DAVISON

Natural History Publications (Borneo)
in association with The Sabah Society

iythies was a professional forester who authored three world-renowned natural history books. The first was *e Birds of Burma* completed in 1941. In 1949 Smythies joined the British Colonial Forest Service in Sarawak and Brunei where he worked until he retired as Director of Forests in 1964. *The Birds of Borneo* was first published in 1960 followed by a 2nd edition in 1968. A slimmed down 3rd edition updated by the Earl of Cranbrook appeared in 1981. An outstanding 4th edition, updated by Geoffrey Davison in inimitable Smythies style, was published in 1999 by C. L. Chan (NHPB, KK). The massive amount of research and work undertaken by Smythies, Cranbrook and Davison laid a very solid foundation for ornithology in Borneo, without which this Field Guide would not have been possible. By inclination Smythies was an early ecologist who was interested in how birds related to their environment as a whole, including plant life and local culture, and *The Birds of Borneo* has been widely and justifiably acclaimed as one of the world's finest bird books. In his final years Smythies was a joint author with Oleg Polunin of the well-regarded *Flowers of South-West Europe*. Smythies's name is permanently commemorated in a race of the White-bellied Munia, *Lonchura leucogastra smythiesi*, found only in SW Sarawak. On his death Smythies left a valuable legacy to the Oriental Bird Club to be administered for the benefit of Asian birds, but his magnificent books are his most valuable bequest to those who follow after.

BIRDING NORTHERN SARAWAK

1   **Lambir Hills National Park (Lambir Benut) (4°15'N, 114°00'E)** 70km². Located 30km south of Miri. Sandstone escarpment rising to 465m. Rich lowland primary dipterocarp forest with some kerangas. Surrounded by oil palms and shifting cultivation. Lambir has been the subject of much zoological and botanical research and has a long bird list. Attractions include numerous waterfalls, a tree tower for observations and numerous trails.

2   **Gunung Mulu and Gunung Buda National Park (4°02'N, 114°54'E)** 84km² of lowland to upper montane forest on the border with Brunei. Highest point is Gng Mulu (2,376m). Access: 45min flight or 1 day by boat from Miri. Good accommodation and extensive walkways and trails. One of the largest limestone cave systems in the world, host to millions of bats and thousands of Black-nest and Mossy-nest Swiftlets. For spectacular views of bats, swiftlets, owls and raptors visit Deer Cave (1hr walk from Park HQ) at dusk and dawn. Lowland birds include all eight hornbills, Crested and Crestless Firebacks, Argus and Bulwer's Pheasants, Black Partridge, Giant and Blue-headed Pittas, Bornean Ground-cuckoo, Bristlehead. The montane Whistling Thrush is found here at sea level. Most of Borneo's montane endemics occur at higher altitudes including Kinabalu Serpent Eagle, Whitehead's Broadbill, Trogon and Spiderhunter, but require a full 5-day trek to the summit and back as Park HQ is at sea level. Specialities are submontane birds scarce elsewhere: Blue-banded and Banded Pittas, Hose's and Long-tailed Broadbills, Bornean Oriole, Bornean Ibon, Bornean Bulbul, Bornean Leafbird, Hill Blue, Pale Blue and Bornean Blue Flycatchers.

3   **Niah National Park (3°50'N, 113°45'E)** 31km². 2hr drive from Miri to Park HQ where there is good accommodation, then cross the river by boat for a 4km board walk through tall riverside forest to the caves which riddle the impressive limestone hil of Gng Subis (494m). Good trails with spectacula views. Look for Pied Hornbills, Rail Babbler. Caves host large numbers of bats and Black and Mossy nest Swiftlets. Arrive at dusk or dawn to see active avian predators, Wallace's Hawk-eagle, Brahminy Kite, Bat Hawk, Eagle Owl and Buffy Fish Owl.

4   **Loagan Bunut Freshwater Lake (3°45'N, 114°16'E)** 107km². 650ha lake which acts as a seasonal flood reservoir for the Baram River. Water levels are lowest in May/June when the lake can dry out. The lake is surrounded by peat swamp and mixed dipterocarp forest. Common birds: Darters, egrets, herons, bitterns. Unusual record of Little Cormorants nesting on an island with Darters in 1968 (Sebastian). Listen for gibbons calling. Large roost of Long-tailed Parakeets.

5   **Kelabit Highlands (Bario) (3°43'N, 115°30'E) and Pulong Tau National Park** Access by plane from Marudi or Miri to Bario (45min). From Bario it is possible to trek to the summit of Mt Murud (2,423m) the highest mountain in Sarawak through the Tama Abo Range of steep hills in Pulong Tau NP, a 5-day hike. On the way check out the twin peaks of Batu Lawi (2,043 m) for the pair of resident *ernesti* race Peregrine Falcons. It is also possible to walk from Bario east over the border into the Apo Kayan plateau of the Kayan Mentarang NP in Kalimantan. This vast transnational area of hill and montane forest in the heart of Borneo is thinly settled by the Punan, Kenyah and Kayan tribes and, like Pulong Tau, contains most of Borneo's montane birds such as Whitehead's Trio. Only high mountain specialists, e.g. Island Thrush and Friendly Warbler, are absent. In particular look for submontane specialists and Short-tailed Green Magpie, Hose's Broadbill, Bornean Oriole, Dulit Frogmouth, Bulwer's Pheasant and Bornean Forktail.

THE FUTURE FOR OIL PALM: THE HAZARDS OF EXTENSIVE MONOCULTURES
Bornean lowland forests are known to be some of the richest in the world with 1,200 different tree species recorded in one 52ha plot (Ashton re Lambir Hills). Forest tree species are thinly scattered as the result of an evolutionary strategy to avoid plague attacks by insects, fungi and plant viruses. When the same species are adjacent, host-specific plant diseases spread easily and rapidly. As Ridley pointed out (see opposite), in West Africa where the Oil Palm *Elaeis guineensis* originates it cannot be grown as a plantation crop for this reason. In S America where a related species grows wild (*Elaeis oleifera*), oil palm plantations quickly become diseased. Millions of hectares of Borneo are now covered by monocultures of genetically similar oil palms. In an era of globalisation it is impossible to prevent plant diseases such as *Ganoderma* spreading internationally from their original native habitat. Disease can be spread both inadvertently by scientists or deliberately by commodity traders or bio-terrorists. Once cleared, diverse primary forest is impossible to replicate and restore. www.rspo.org and www.eia-international.org. See also *The Thief at the End of the World* (Jackson 2008) re rubber plantations in Brazil.

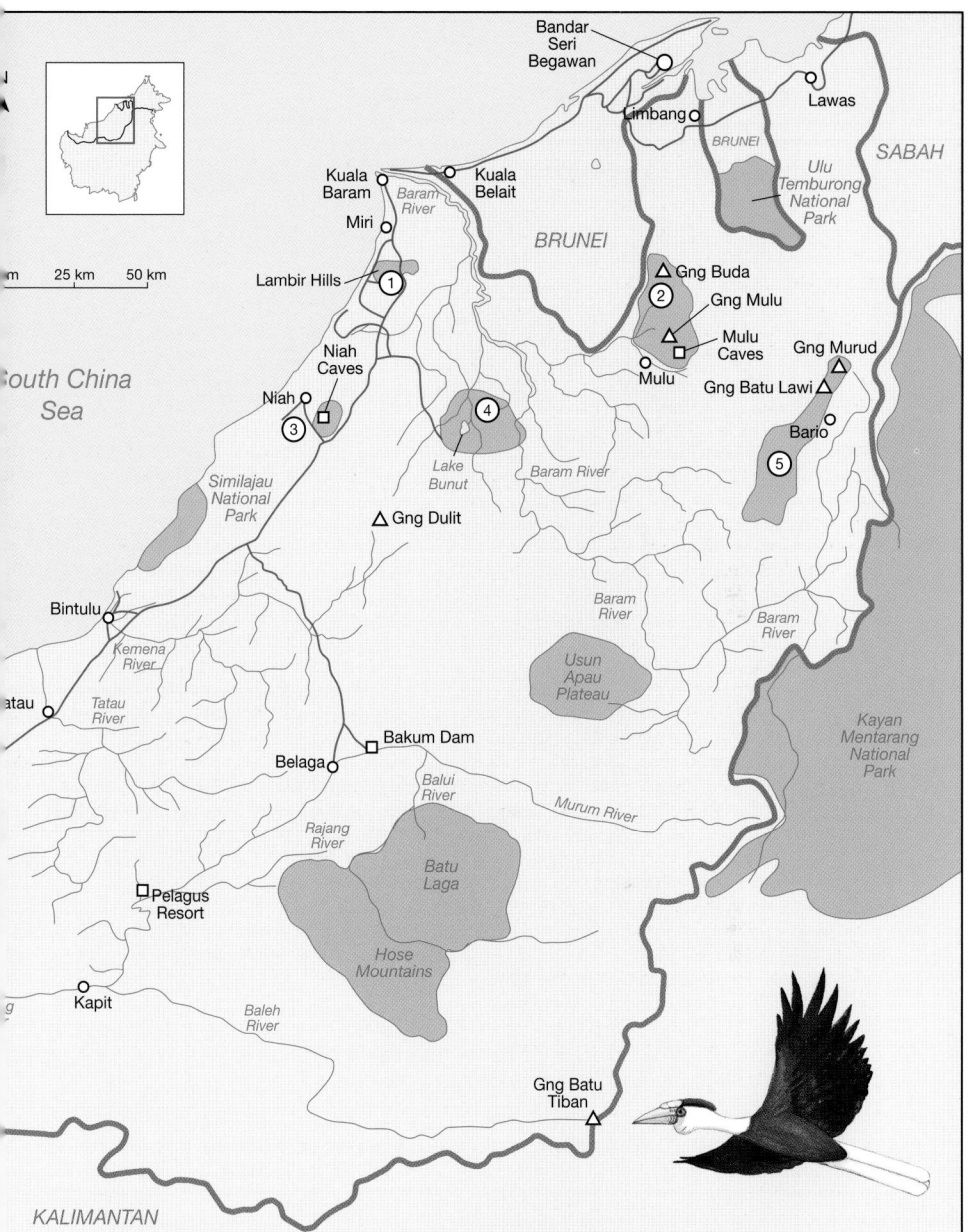

N. RIDLEY (1855–1956): THE 'FATHER' OF THE RUBBER INDUSTRY

enry Ridley was the first scientific director of the Singapore Botanic Gardens (1888–1911) and is most famous
r introducing and promoting rubber as a plantation crop in Malaya and Borneo. Ridley pointed out that tropical
antation crops grow best outside their area of origin. Rubber originates in the Amazon rainforest but grows best in
Asia. Bananas originate in SE Asia to New Guinea but grow best in Central America. Cocoa originates in Central
merica but grows best in Africa. Coffee originates in Africa but grows best in S America. Oil palm originates in
rica and S America but grows best in SE Asia. Ridley explained that plantation crops do not grow well in their
untry of origin if grown in extensive monocultures because these will be rapidly attacked and overwhelmed by
st-specific plant diseases and pests which have evolved for this purpose. See opposite re oil palm.

KALIMANTAN NATIONAL PARKS AND PROTECTED AREAS

The undeveloped Indonesian provinces of Kalimantan occupy 72.5% of Borneo, but facilities are generally only suitable for adventurous birders. Five accessible sites – Tg Puting, Sabangau, the Derawan Islands, Balikpapan and the Mahakam Lakes – are described in detail in the following pages. Listed here are most of the major national parks and some important bird sites for those lucky enough to get the opportunity to explore more widely.

1 **Betung Kerihun (0°40'-1°35'N, 112°15'-114°10'E)** 8,000km² of lowland, submontane and montane forest. Highest peak is Gng Kerihun (1,790m). The Kapuas River (1,143km) starts in the park. Undisturbed and little explored. Adjoins Lanjak Entimau (Sarawak). Proposed core component of the transnational Heart of Borneo Conservation Area.

2 **Danau Sentarum and Kapuas Lakes (0°53'N, 112°9'E)** 800km² of seasonal wetlands and lakes surrounded by swamp and dipterocarp forest. A *Ramsar* wetland site. Birds include Storm's Stork, Lesser Adjutant, Wallace's Hawk-eagle, Black Partridge, Bulwer's Pheasant, Bornean Peacock-pheasant, Bonaparte's Nightjar, Straw-headed Bulbul.

3 **Gunung Niut (0°57'N, 109°58'E)** 1,400km² of hill and montane forest. Highest point 1,709m. Remnant extinct volcano in same range of mountains as Gng Penrissen in Sarawak. Birds: Mountain Barbet, Fruithunter, Mountain Wren-babbler, Mountain Tailorbird.

4 **Bukit Baka and Bukit Raya (from Kapuas River) (0°44'S, 112°37'E)** Relatively inaccessible. 1,810km² of lowland dipterocarp up to montane forest. This area includes part of the Schwaner mountain range and the highest peak is Bukit Raya at 2,278m. Most hornbills and Bornean Peacock-pheasant recorded.

5 **Gunung Palung (1°14'S, 110°14'E)** Not very accessible. From Pontianak by boat to Ketapang and on to Sukadana, then by boat to the park. 900km² of mangrove, lowland and montane forest. Highest point is the horse-shoe-shaped Gunung Palung (1,116m). Long bird list from researchers studying Orangutans (est. population 2,500), gibbons and Sun Bear includes Bornean Ground-cuckoo. Large flocks of Long-tailed Parakeets near Sukadana.

6 **Karimata Islands**

7 **Natuna Islands and Anambas** (See page 315) There are numerous small islands in the S China Sea between Singapore and SW Borneo. The island birds are similar to those of Borneo with a number of distinctive races. The many interesting frigatebird roosting and seabird breeding islands are best explored by 'sleep on board' dive boat.

8 **Muara Kendawangan (Estuary) (2°42'S, 110°37'E)** 3,000km² of coastal and swamp forest.

9 **Tanjung Puting (3°4'S, 111°59'E)** 4,160km² of peat swamp forest. See following pages.

10 **Sabangau (2°34'S, 113°38'E)** 20km SW of Palangkaraya. 5,687km² of peat swamp forest, the subject of a Wetlands International forest restoration project. Birds include Crestless Fireback Pheasant and Bonaparte's Nightjar. Numerous Orangutan and gibbons. www.orangutantrop.com

11 **Barito Ulu Research Area (0°23'N, 114°08'W)** 1,950km² of remote hill forest in the headwaters of the Barito river. The subject of extensive research with a long bird list including Black Partridge, Crestless Fireback and Bulwer's Pheasants and Bristlehead.

12 **Negara Lakes (2°25'S, 115°01'E)** 2,500km² of swamps and lakes, in the heavily populated Negara river basin north of Bandjarmasin. Includes Bangkau Lake site of old nesting waterbird records for Dusky Moorhen, Comb-crested and Pheasant-tailed Jacanas.

13 **Muratus Mountains (2°27'S, 115°49'E)** 2,460km² of geographically isolated hilly and montane forest NE of Bandjarmasin. Highest point 1,907m. Speciality Bornean Frogmouth.

14 **Sungai Wain Protection Forest (1°00'S, 117°00'E)** 100km² water catchment forest north of Balikpapan. Small isolated populations of Bornean Ground-cuckoo and Bornean Peacock-pheasant recorded in a study of Sun Bears by Fredriksson and Nijman. Rehabilitation site for Orangutan from Wanariset/Samboja in Balikpapan. www.sambojalodge.com, www.orangutans.com.au

15 **Mahakam Lakes and Mahakam River (0°16'S, 116°23'E)** 4,000km². See following pages.

16 **Kutai (0°22'N, 117°16'E)** 2hr drive north of Samarinda to Bontang, then by boat from Sangatta to Mentoko. 2,000km² of beach, swamp and lowland primary forest much damaged by logging and forest fires. Highest point is Gng Tandung Mayang (397m). All eight hornbills occur.

17 **Derawan Islands, Sangkalaki, Maratua** See following pages.

18 **Kayan Mentarang (K Mentarang) (8°22'S, 123°57'E)** 13,650km². Borders Sabah to the north and Sarawak to the west. Research station at Long Alango. Fly from Samarinda or river boat from Tarakan. Long bird list includes Bulwer's and Peacock-pheasants and most montane endemics. Highest point 2,558m.

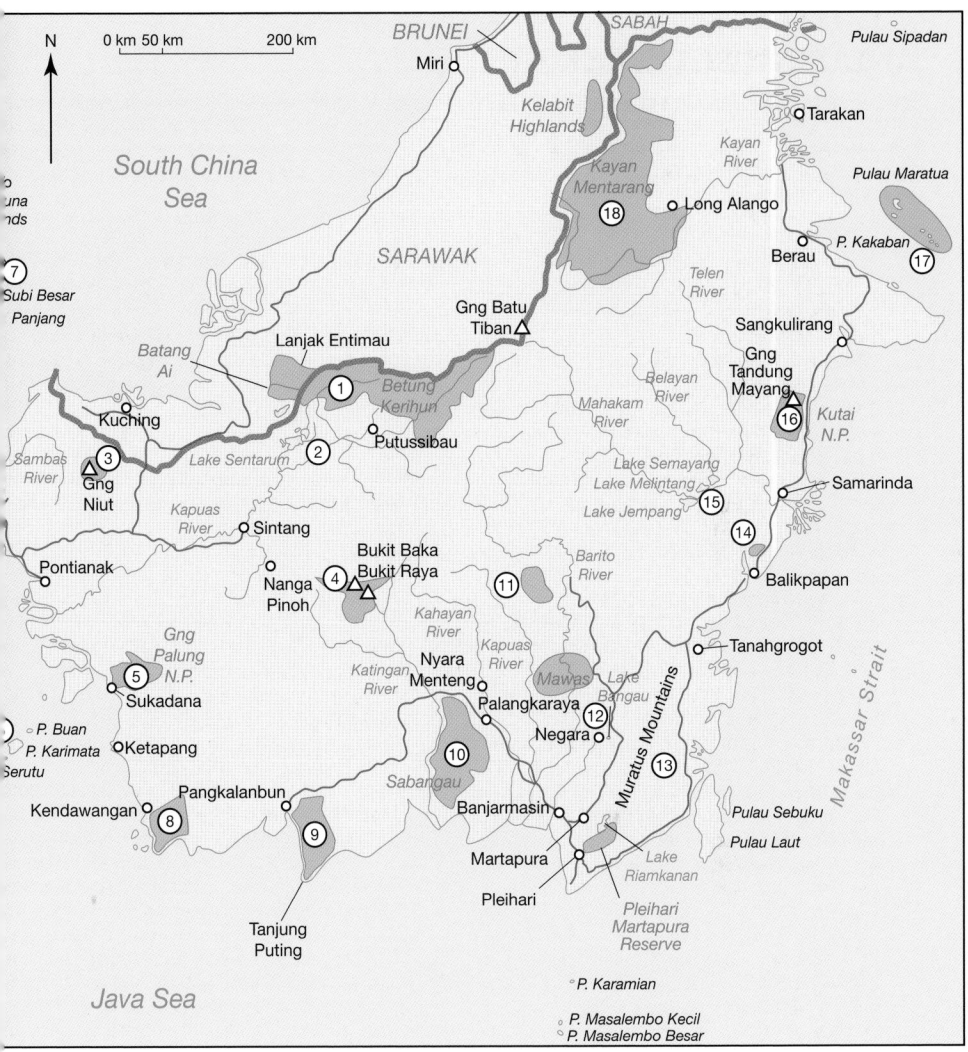

N

0 km 50 km   200 km

BRUNEI

SABAH

Pulau Sipadan

Miri

Kelabit Highlands

Kayan River

Kayan Mentarang

18

Long Alango

Tarakan

Pulau Maratua

South China Sea

una nds

7

Subi Besar Panjang

SARAWAK

Telen River

Berau

P. Kakaban

17

Gng Batu Tiban△

Sangkulirang

Lanjak Entimau

Batang Ai

1

Betung Kerihun

Belayan River

Gng Tandung Mayang△

16

Kutai N.P.

Kuching

Mahakam River

2

Putussibau

Sambas River

3

Gng Niut△

Lake Sentarum

Kapuas River

Sintang

Lake Semayang
Lake Melintang

Lake Jempang

15

Samarinda

14

Pontianak

Bukit Baka
Bukit Raya

4 △

Barito River

Gng Palung N.P.

Nanga Pinoh

11

Balikpapan

Kahayan River

Kapuas River

Tanahgrogot

5

Sukadana

Katingan River

Nyara Menteng

Palangkaraya

Mawas   *Lake Bangau*

Muratus Mountains

P. Buan

P. Karimata

Serutu

Ketapang

12

Negara

Makassar Strait

Kendawangan

8

9

Sabangau

10

Banjarmasin

13

Pulau Sebuku

Pulau Laut

Pangkalanbun

Martapura

Lake Riamkanan

Pleihari

Pleihari Martapura Reserve

Tanjung Puting

Java Sea

P. Karamian

P. Masalembo Kecil
P. Masalembo Besar

IRD CONSERVATION IN KALIMANTAN AND INDONESIA

here is a long tradition of keeping pet birds in Indonesia, the vast majority of which are taken from the wild. This ade had decimated wild populations of parrots, cockatoos and lories from the Moluccas. Despite some restrictions ere are very large bird markets in Jakarta and Medan.

e Ornithological Society of Indonesia (Pelestari Burung Indonesia), the local partner of BirdLife International, has a ogramme to encourage local breeding of preferred songbirds such as Straw-headed Bulbul, Orange-headed Ground rush, White-rumped Shama and Oriental Magpie Robin. The Society also publishes bird reports in English for the fferent provinces of Indonesia under the title *Kukila*. PO Box 310, Bogor 16003, West Java, Indonesia. www.burung.org

BIRDING TANJONG PUTING AND SABANGAU, CENTRAL KALIMANTAN

Peat swamp forest, which covers some 10% of lowland Borneo, is normally inaccessible to birders, but at these two Kalimantan sites it is dominant, enabling birders to see birds and other specialist wildlife rare elsewhere.

Birds of Peat Swamp Forest Hook-billed Bulbul, Grey-breasted Babbler, Cinnamon-headed Green Pigeon, Wrinkled Hornbill, Bristlehead, Black Partridge, Crestless Fireback, Fiery Minivet, Grey-chested Jungle Flycatcher and Copper-throated Sunbird

Specialist birds of S Borneo Savannah Nightjar, Sacred Kingfisher, Scarlet-headed Flowerpecker, Lesser Whistling Duck, Javan White-eye, Long-tailed Shrike. See also page 324.

Birds rare elsewhere in Borneo Storm's Stork, Lesser Adjutant, Dusky Heron, Large Green-Pigeon, Grey-headed and Lesser Fish Eagles, Bay Owl.

Climate Heaviest rains are Nov.–May with the driest period June–Oct. but very variable.

Mammals Both Tg Puting and Sabangau host 6,000 + orangutans the world's largest populations. Gibbons, Maroon Langur, Silvered Langur, Crab-eating Macaque, Pig-tailed Macaque are all common. Clouded Leopards, Marbled Cat, Flat-headed Cat and Sun Bears are rare residents.

Reptiles Monitor Lizards common. At Tg Putting there are large populations of man-eating Salt-water Crocodile and the fish eating False Gharial *Tomistoma schelegii*, rare elsewhere in Borneo.

Access See below for individual sites. Travel between Pangkalanbun (Tg Puting) and Palangka Raya (Sabangau) takes 8 to 10 hours by taxi or bus. There is also a rather erratic local flight between the two towns.

TG. PUTING (3°4' S, 111°59' E), 4,160 km². The most popular wildlife tourism destination in Kalimantan for viewing both 'tame' and truly wild orangutans as well as Proboscis Monkeys . Tg Puting was initially established by Birute Galidikas as a release site for rescued orangutans and publicised in her book *Reflections of Eden*. No orangutans are now released at Tg Puting to avoid problems with the wild population. Feeding stations attract the offspring of earlier releases. Silver Langurs, Proboscis Monkeys and Macaques are easy to see as they sleep in riverside trees at night to avoid predation by Clouded Leopards.

Common birds White-bellied Sea Eagle, Brahminy Kite, Black-and-Red Broadbill, Stork-billed, Blue-eared and Collared Kingfishers, Bushy-crested and Rhinoceros Hornbills. A large colony of herons breeds south of the Sungai Buluh Besar river (May to August).

Access By plane from Jakarta to Pangkalan Bun, then road to Kumai, then by speed boat (1.5 hrs) to Camp Leakey. Tours depart from Jakarta and attract many international tourists.

Accommodation Widely available just outside the park at Rimba Lodge or in the park itself at Tg Harapan. Many tourists rent 'sleep on board' klotoks (motor boats) moored in the river at night.

Contacts www.orangutan.org.uk and www.orangutan.org

SABANGAU (2°34' S, 113°38' E) 20km SW of Palangka Raya. 5,687 km². Originally established as a joint project of two UK Universities the core 50km² of Sabangau is now managed by CIMTROP (Centre for International Cooperation in Sustainable Management of Tropical Peatlands) based at the local University of Palangka Raya, as one of Borneo's most active Field Centres or Natural Laboratory with students from all over the world studying peat swamp ecology at Setia Alam Research Station.

Access By plane from Jakarta to Palangka Raya, where there is a variety of accommodation. Palangka Raya is also the location of the Kalaweit (Gibbon) Centre and Nyaru Menteng the largest orangutan rehabilitation centre in Borneo, and a focus for efforts to preserve Kalimantan's remaining lowland forests. Setia Alam is approximately one hour from Palangka Raya by bus, boat and rail. Setia Alam is surrounded by a grid of well marked trails used for studying the locally common Maroon Langur, Agile Gibbon and Orangutans. There are currently no facilities for casual tourists without research permits.

Common birds White-rumped and Rufous-tailed Shamas, Mangrove Whistler, Black-capped, White-chested, Short-tailed, Scaly-crowned, Rufous-crowned, Sooty-capped, Chestnut- rumped, Black-throated, Chestnut-winged and Fluffy-backed Babbler.

Specialist birds The best place in Borneo to see rare Bonaparte's Nightjar as well as most of the peat swamp specialists listed above.

Contacts: www.orangutantrop.com and www.outrop.blogspot.com

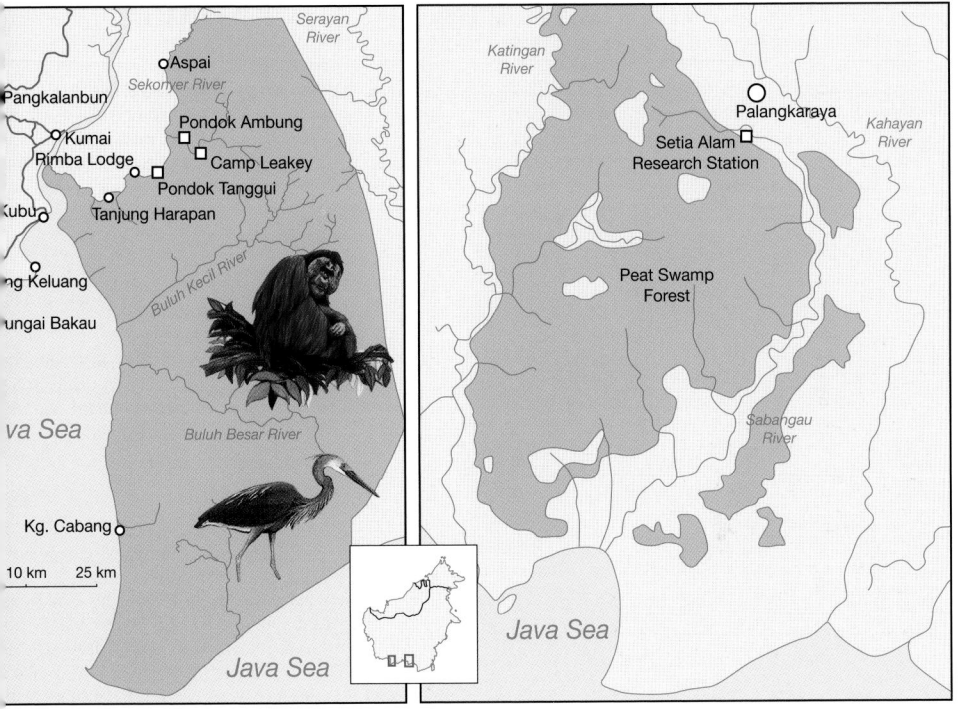

ORANGUTAN CONSERVATION IN THE PEAT SWAMP FORESTS OF KALIMANTAN

Before humans arrived in Borneo the orangutan population was likely in excess of 1 million. After 40,000 years of hunting and forest destruction less than 60,000 remain. These orangutans have only survived because Borneo's comparatively poor soils have made permanent plantation agriculture generally uneconomic – until the advent of oil palm. Peat swamp has both some of the least productive land and the highest remaining populations of Bornean orangutans at Tg Puting and Sabangau. Orangutans have evolved to be able to survive for long periods on a semi-starvation diet of tough leaves and bark, which gives them a comparative advantage over other primates in Borneo's unproductive forests when fruit is in short supply. The eventual fate of Bornean Orangutans and birds are truly entwined. Both groups need the same large areas of intact primary forest to thrive. Many international NGOs are now making sustained efforts to ensure the survival of the Bornean Orangutan by rescuing and 'rehabilitating' orangutans displaced by logging or oil palm plantations. These centres which are listed and mapped on the inside back cover of this book act as a focus for local and international forest conservation efforts, and their presence also deters illegal logging and squatting which eats away at the edge of protected forest. Without large areas of permanent protected forest neither orangutans nor birds can survive.

BIRDS FOLLOWING ARMY ANTS IN BORNEO
It is well documented that birds follow army ants in Latin America and Africa. They are attracted to abundant prey of invertebrates and small vertebrates which are flushed out of hiding to flee advancing dense swarms of voracious ants. This interesting phenomenon previously unrecorded in Asia has been discovered at Sabangau and other sites in Central Kalimantan for the first time with an un-named ant species of the genus *Leptogenys*. Terrestrial and understorey babblers, Hook-billed Bulbul, Grey-crested Jungle-flycatcher, Mangrove Whistler, Pied Fantail, Rufous-backed Kingfisher, skinks, and, tree-shrews have been documented attending, following, and taking prey at ant swarms.   marc.dragiewicz@gmail.com

BIRDING THE BALIKPAPAN AREA AND
THE MAHAKAM LAKES

Balikpapan (1°16'S, 116°51'E) Both a transport hub with E Kalimantan's only international airport and the focus of an oil and coal energy boom with new developments and luxury hotels springing up overnight. Balikpapan airfield has breeding Paddyfield Pipits. Look for interesting migrant waterbirds and waders in the rice fields along the coast N of Balikpapan Oct. and March.

Accommodation A large choice. Best place to stay is at Samboja Lodge, see below.

The best time to visit The heaviest rains are Dec. to May, with the driest period July to Sept. The best time to visit the Mahakam Lakes is July-August at the beginning of the dry season when water birds congregate around the reduced lakes and most birds are breeding. During droughts the lakes dry out and become covered in lush vegetation.

Sungai Wain 100km² of watershed protection forest c.1 hrs drive north of Balikpapan.

This rare fragment of lowland dipterocarp forest is the only accessible locality in Borneo where you may see the endemic Bornean Peacock Pheasant without extreme difficulty. Other resident birds include Bornean Ground Cuckoo, Bornean Bristlehead, Blue-headed Pitta, and Bornean Wren-babbler The normally very scarce White-throated Babbler (Grey-breasted Babbler) has been recorded. Sungai Wain was a release site for rehabilitated Orangtutan and Sunbears for many years so these mammals may be encountered. There is no visitor accommodation on site but it is possible to 'camp out' overnight at an abandoned research station in the middle of the reserve by prior arrangement with the park HQ. Tel: + 628125806329. Bring a mosquito net and food. Day tours can be arranged by any hotel in Balikpapan.

Samboja Lestari 20 km². A large Orangutan and Sunbear rescue and rehabilitation centre 45m drive from Balikpapan airport. A highly ambitious and successful project founded by the botanist/ecologist Willie Smits to restore agricultural land to native forest combined with the enrichment planting of wildlife friendly fruit trees is financed by donations from European supporters and an active volunteer programme. Good quality lodge accommodation needs advance booking. Day visits possible from Balikpapan (Saturdays only). www.sambojalodge.com

Mahakam Lakes (0°16'30'S, 116°32'E) From Samarinda upstream it is 135 km to Kota Bangun (90 km by road) where the river flows through the centre of a vast 4,000 km² area of seasonally flooded swam forest, marshes and freshwater lakes. The largest lak are Jempang (15,000 ha), Melintang (11,000 ha) ar Semayang (13,000 ha). The lakes attract both austr and northern winter visitors and passage migrants. you have time, travel upriver to Long Iram to find t very rare, relict White-shouldered Ibis.

Access to the lakes The large town of Samarin is 2 hrs by road from Balikpapan. At Samarinda hi a 'sleep on board' klotok (motor boat) to travel u the Mahakam River or drive to Tg Isuy where the is a Dayak longhouse tourist hostel and boat hire Lake Jempang.

Mammals Proboscis Monkeys, Crab eatin Macaque, Silvered Leaf Monkey, Smooth Otte Rare Irrawaddy dolphin *Orcaella brevirostris* a commonest at the entrance to the lakes.

Reptiles Three species of crocodile, False Gharia Siamese Crocodile (both rare elsewhere in Borne and Salt-water Crocodile occur. Monitor Lizards a also common.

Birds Abundant water birds including Storm Stork, Lesser Adjutant, Grey-headed and Lesser Fis Eagles, Cinnamon, Yellow and Black Bitterns, Java Pond Heron, Striated Heron, Black-crowned Nig Heron, Purple Heron, Great, Intermediate, Little an Cattle Egrets, Darter, Purple Swamphen, Commo Moorhen, White-browed Crake, White-breaste Waterhen,Wandering Whistling Duck, Comb-creste Jacana, Ruddy-breasted Crake.

Waders Large numbers of waders on passage i August–Sept. include Sandpipers, Stints, Plover Phalarope. Both Black-necked and White-necke Stilts occur and White-necked has bred.

Terns Little Terns breed on the dry lake shore i Aug–Sept. White-winged Terns are visitors from th north Aug–May. Whiskered Terns are seen in ver large numbers all year round, particularly in Augus Northern race *hybridus* winters Sept. to May. Austr race *javanicus* visits Feb.–Nov.

Kutai (0°19N,117°38'E) 2,000km². 4hrs driv north of Balikpapan. The site of the Leighton early studies of orangutans and hornbills. Despit problems this large reserve is well worth a visi Arrange overnight camping tours through the Par Office at Bontang for access to Mentoko for primar forest birds and wild Orangutans and to coastal Telu Kaba for Proboscis Monkeys and swamp birds.

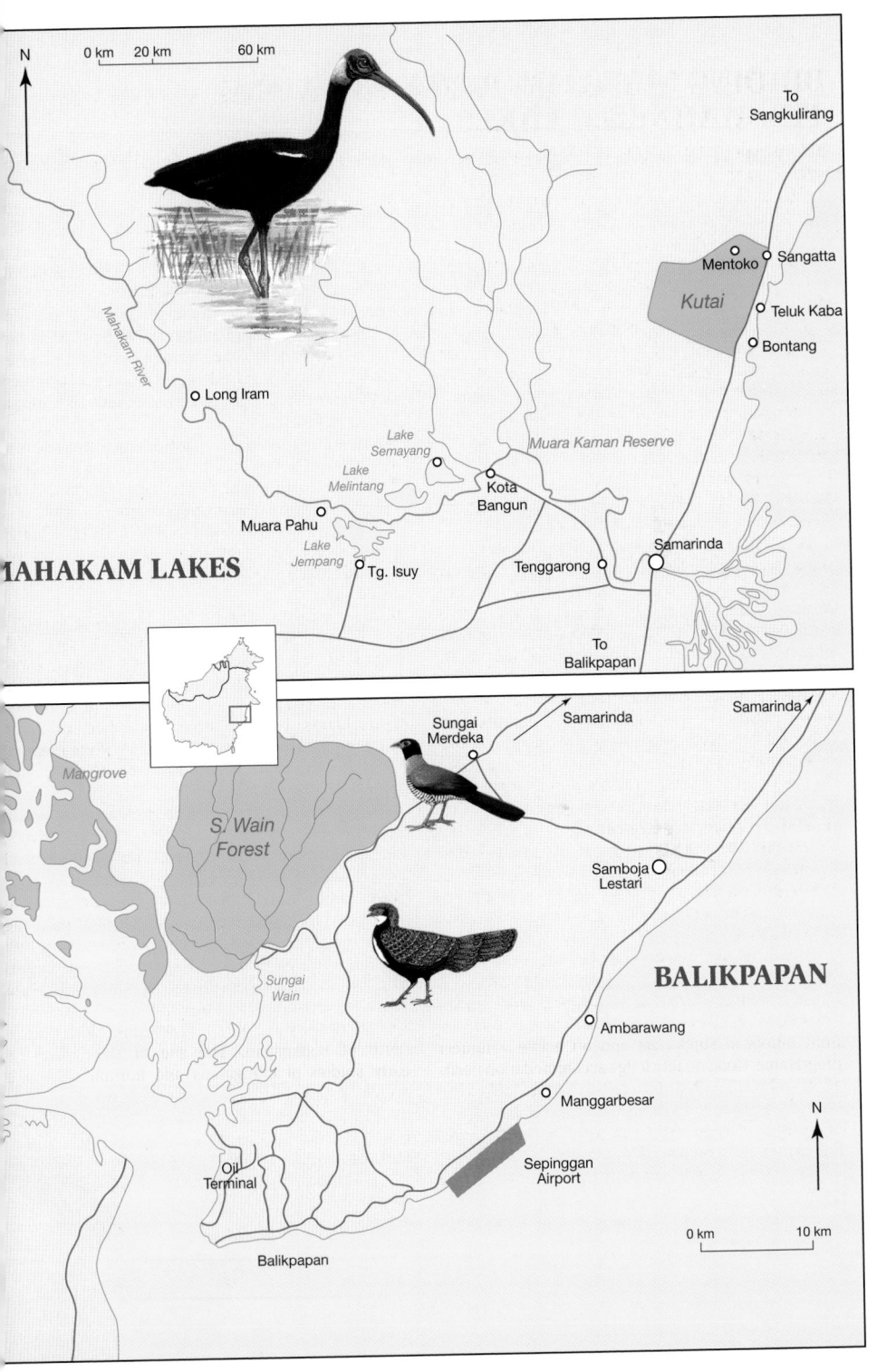

N

0 km   20 km   60 km

To
Sangkulirang

Mentoko ○ ○ Sangatta

Kutai

○ Teluk Kaba

○ Bontang

Mahakam River

○ Long Iram

*Lake
Semayang*

Muara Kaman Reserve

*Lake
Melintang*

Kota
Bangun

Muara Pahu

MAHAKAM LAKES

*Lake
Jempang* ○ Tg. Isuy

Tenggarong

Samarinda ○

To
Balikpapan

Mangrove

Sungai
Merdeka

Samarinda →

Samarinda ↗

*S. Wain
Forest*

Samboja ○
Lestari

BALIKPAPAN

*Sungai
Wain*

○ Ambarawang

N

Oil
Terminal

○ Manggarbesar

Sepinggan
Airport

0 km   10 km

Balikpapan

BIRDING MARATUA AND KAKABAN (DERAWAN ISLANDS) *(2.09' N, 118.20'E)*

The coast of Borneo is surrounded by many interesting small islands, but the 31 Derawan islands are exceptional. They have one of Indonesia's best collection of dive sites, with world class reef fish turtles and coral life. The two largest islands, Maratua and Kakaban, host two endemic birds found nowhere else in the world – the Maratua Bulbul and the Maratua Shama.

ACCESS Maratua (2 hrs by speedboat from Berau) has both a dive resort (Maratua Paradise Resort) and a cheap hotel in the largest village of Boheybukut. From Berau daily flights connect to Tarakan (with a daily ferry to Tawau in Sabah) and Balikpapan, which has daily flights to Singapore and weekly flights to Kota Kinabalu. There are also dive resorts on Nabucco and Nunukan islands.

DERAWAN (45 ha) A small heavily populated island with a dive resort and few birds.

SANGKALAKI (16 ha) is Borneo's top turtle nesting island. Four small cabins can be booked for overnight stays. Divers go to see the giant manta rays that feed offshore. In 2003 all the black rats on the island were poisoned to stop predation of young turtles. This is one of the best locations to look for rare island pigeons, but their presence is dependent on fruiting trees. Megapodes common.

KAKABAN (774 ha) A volcanic atoll with an isolated 400 ha saline lake in the centre of the island surrounded by a steep forested hill crossed by a wooden steps.

The lake contains large numbers of four species sting-less jellyfish. Caves in the rocky limestone clif surrounding the lake contain the valuable edible nes of German's Swiftlet. No overnight accommodation.

SEMAMA (91 ha) is a low lying uninhabited mangro covered island with one small beach. A one hecta isolated grove of ancient Sonneratia trees *c* 200 m offsho is one of Borneo's largest frigatebird roosting sites wi over 2,000 birds recorded. Gerygone has been reported

MARATUA (2,376 ha), the largest island, is a 'V'-shape atoll, approx. 26 km long by 1–2 km wide. Maratua is th remnant of a volcano which slowly sank into the sea coral grew up around the edge. Later uplifted by tecton movements, the coral is now a mass of sharp limesto covered in forest which has obstructed agriculture. Fi kampongs survive from growing coconuts, fishing, bo building and by harvesting the white nests of German Swiftlet from over 300 small caves.

BIRDS Normally rare island pigeons are commo including Grey Imperial, Pied Imperial, Nicoba Metallic Wood-pigeon and Black-naped Fruit Dov Maratua is the main refuge for Blue-naped Parrot Borneo. Sea Eagle, Brahminy Kite and Osprey ofte seen. Megapodes and the normally scarce Purpl throated Sunbird are common.

OTHER WILDLIFE Island Flying Foxes tame an common, Green Turtles abundant and dolphins ofte seen.

ENDEMIC BIRDS OF MARATUA

Maratua and Kakaban are 2 of only 4 Bornean islands which lie off the Sunda Shelf and have never been connected by land to Borneo itself. (The two others are Sipadan and Layang Layang, see map page 23). This means that, like the famed Galapagos Islands of S. America, the resident birds have arrived by chance event, and developed in isolation for many thousands of years adapting to local conditions. On Maratua are found two birds considered to be distinctive enough to be separate species, the Maratua Bulbul and the Maratua Shama, along with endemic races of the Black-naped Blue Monarch, Hair-crested Drongo, Brown-throated and Purple-throated Sunbird, Glossy Starling, Philippine Megapode and Blue-naped Parrot. When first described in 1927 by Bangs & Peters, the Maratua Bulbul and Shama were both listed as new species endemic to Maratua, however in his 1935 masterwork *A Handlist of Malaysian Birds* Chasen downgraded them to races of mainland Borneo birds, which was followed by succeeding authors. Recent DNA analysis by (Chua, Sheldon et al 2013) shows that the genetic divergence from the closest related mainland birds is sufficient for them to be regarded as separate endemic species.

MARATUA SHAMA *Copsychus barbouri* 30cm There are no babblers or pittas on Maratua, and as a result the Maratua Shama is unusually common throughout the forests of Maratua. Distinguished from the White-crowned Shama of NE Borneo by the lack of white feathers at the edge of the tail. Unfortunately locals are starting to trap this endemic shama for sale in Berau. Shamas are popular cage birds in Indonesia kept for their fine song and often entered into singing competitions. See pages 284 and 242.

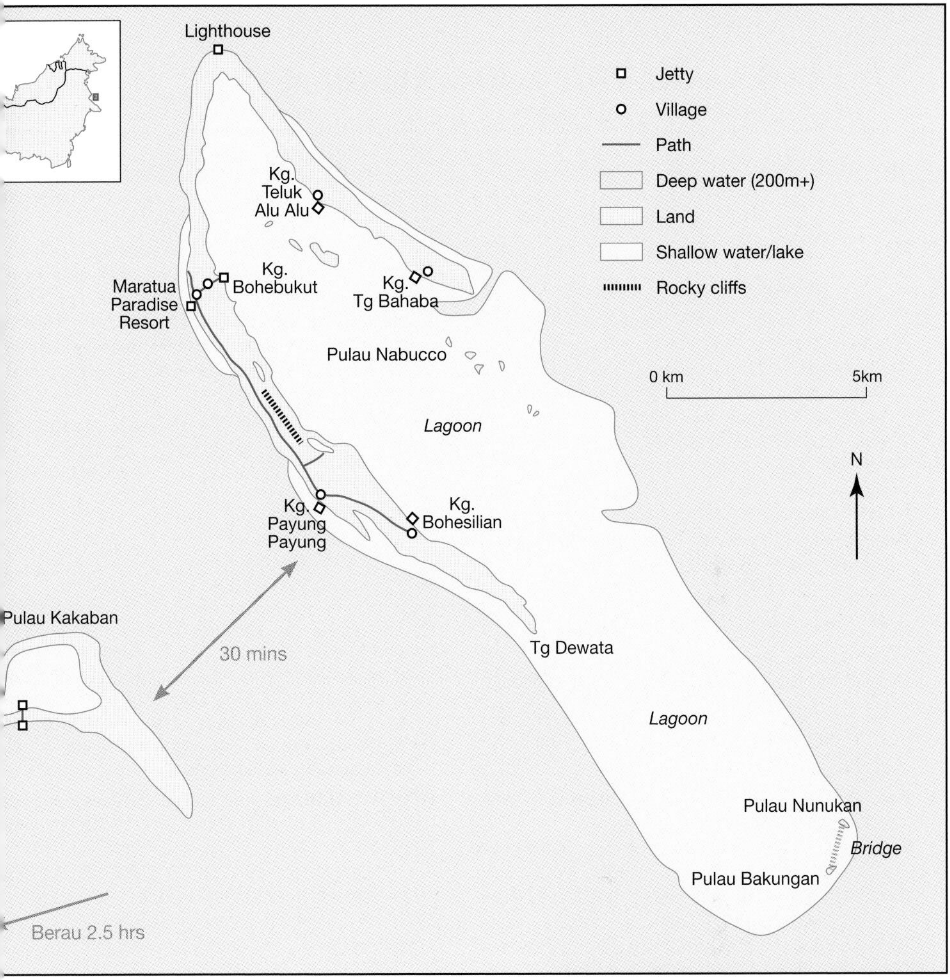

Map of Maratua island with labels:

Lighthouse

Legend:
- □ Jetty
- ○ Village
- — Path
- Deep water (200m+)
- Land
- Shallow water/lake
- ▥ Rocky cliffs

Kg. Teluk Alu Alu

Kg. Bohebukut

Maratua Paradise Resort

Kg. Tg Bahaba

Pulau Nabucco

Lagoon

0 km — 5km

N

Kg. Payung Payung

Kg. Bohesilian

Pulau Kakaban

30 mins

Tg Dewata

Lagoon

Pulau Nunukan

Bridge

Pulau Bakungan

Berau 2.5 hrs

...ARATUA BULBUL (BLACK-HEADED BULBUL)

...nonotus atriceps hodiernus 16.5cm

...s distinctive race of the Black-headed Bulbul is confined to ...ratua and Kakaban islands. **Description**: 5% larger than ... Black-headed Bulbul of the Borneo mainland. **Habits:** ... only bulbul on Maratua where it has occupied all the ...ant bulbul ecological niches. At night sleeps with greatly ...fed up back feathers (see photo) presumably to fool owls ...d snakes that it is too big for an easy meal. **Call:** A loud ...tallic contact call similar to the ***chank*** contact call of the ...ssy Starling. **Taxonomy:** The Black-headed Bulbul occurs ...m India to Palawan with 5 different races. On Bawean ...nd (Java Sea) a partially grey morph is common and on ...a and Bali the grey morph is rare. On Borneo the grey ...rph is unknown. See page 242.

SELECTED BIBLIOGRAPHY AND FURTHER READING

In addition to the works listed below local bird reports are published in the Sabah Society Journal, the Brun Museum Journal, the Sarawak Musuem Journal, Kukila (Indonesian Ornithological Society) and the Orient Bird Club publications Forktail and Birding Asia. Only the most significant of these reports are listed her Please note that where no date reference is given in a text citation e.g. (Lamb) this refers either to a person communication or an internet source.

A

Alstrom, P., Mild, K. and Zetterstrom, B. (2003) *Pipits and Wagtails of Europe, Asia and N America.* Helm, London.

Alstrom, P. et al (2011) The Arctic Warbler *Phylloscopus borealis*; three anciently separated cryptic species revealed.

Arlott, N. (2009) *Collins Field Guide. Birds of the Palearctic*, 2 vols. Collins, London.

Ahmad, A.H. (1999) The population status of Megapodes in Pulau Tiga. *Sabah Parks Journal.*

Argent, G., Lamb, A., and Phillipps, A. (2007) *The Rhododendrons of Sabah.*

B

Baker, K. (1997) *Warblers of Europe, Asia and N Africa.* Helm, London.

Bangs, O. and Peters, J.L. (1927) Birds from Maratua Island, off the east coast of Borneo. *Occas. Pap. Boston Soc. Nat. History*, 5: 235–242.

Banks, E. (1949) *A Naturalist in Sarawak*, pp. 1–125. Privately published in Kuching.

Batchelor, D.M. (1959) North Borneo bird notes. *Sarawak Mus. Journal*, 9: 263–266.

Beccari, O. (1904) *Wanderings in the Great Forests of Borneo.* Constable, London.

Becking, J.H. (1971) The breeding of *Collocalia gigas*. *Ibis*, 113: 330–334.

Beebe, W. (1921) *A Monograph of the Pheasants.*

Beebe, W. (1994) *Pheasant Jungles.* WPA.

Beintema, A. (2007) *Mijn Vogels.* Atlas, Amsterdam.

Berg, C.C. and E.J.H.Corner (2005). *Moraceae (Ficus) Flora Malesiana* Vol.17/Part 2. Page 20.

Bevis, W.W. (1995) *Borneo Log: the struggle for Sarawak's forests.* University of Washington Press.

Bildstein, K.L. (2006) *Migrating Raptors of the World, their Ecology and Conservation.* Cornell.

BirdLife International (2001) *Threatened Birds of Asia: The Birdlife International Red Data Book.*

BirdLife International (2004) *Important Bird Areas in Asia: key sites for conservation.*

Biun, A. (1999) *An Altitudinal Survey of the Birds of Mt Kinabalu, Sabah, Malaysia.* Sabah Parks.

Bloem, A. (2007) Asian Waterbird Census, Brunei Darussalam. Panaga Natural History Society.

Bock, C. (1881) *The Headhunters of Borneo.*

Bohap bin Jalan and Galdikas Birute (1987) Birds of Tg Putting NP. *Kukila*, 3.

Bransbury, J. (1993) *A Birdwatcher's Guide to Malaysia.* Waymark Publishing, Australia.

Brazil, M. (1991) *The Birds of Japan.* Helm.

Brazil, M. (2009) *Birds of East Asia.* Helm.

Bhushan, B., Fry, G., Hibi, A., Mundkur, 1 Prawiradilaga, D.M., Sonobe, K., Usui, S. an Taniguchi, T. (1993) *A Field Guide to the Waterbir of Asia.* Wild Bird Society of Japan.

Brickle, N., Eaton, J. and Rheindt, F. (2010). rapid bird survey of the Menyapa mountains 1 Kalimantan. FORKTAIL.

Buckton, S. (1992) *Sabah Trip Report.* OBC.

Byers, C., Curson J. and Olsson, U. (1995) *Sparrou and Buntings.* Houghton Miflin, Boston.

C

Cameron, M. (2007) *Cockatoos.* CSIRO Publishing.

Campbell, B. and Lack, E. (1985) *A Dictionary Birds.* T. & A.D. Poyser, UK.

Casement, M.B. (1979) Land birds reported at se Sea Swallow, 29.

Chang, J. (1980) *A Field Guide to the Birds of Taiwar*

Chantler, P. and Driessens, G. (1995) *Swifts: guide the swifts and treeswifts of the world.* Pica Press.

Chasen, F.N. (1935) *Handlist of Malaysian Bir* Bulletin Raffles Museum Singapore. No.11.

Cheke, R.A., Mann, C.F. and Allen, R. (2001) *Guide to the Sunbirds, Flowerpeckers, Spiderhunte and Sugarbirds of the World.* Helm.

Chua, V., Sheldon, F. et al (2014) *Maratua Bi Biogeography: Endemic bird species of Maratua Islan* Archives of the biogeographic history of Borneo.

Cleere, N. and Nurney, D. (1998) *A Guide t Nightjars and Related Nightbirds.* Pica Press.

Clement, P. and Hathaway, R. (2000) *Thrushes.* Helm

Coates, B.J. and Bishop, K.D. (1997) *A Guide to th Birds of Wallacea.* Dove Publications.

Collar, N.J. and Eames, J.C. (2008) Head colour an sex-size dimorphism in *Pseudibis papillosa* and *davisoni.* Birding Asia, 10.

Collar, N.J. and Long, A. (1996) Taxonomy an status of *Carpococcyx* cuckoos from the Greate Sundas. Forktail, 11.

Collins, N.M., Sayer, J.A. and Whitmore T.C. (eds) (1991) *The Conservation Atlas of Tropic Forests. Asia and the Pacific.*

Corlett, R.T. (2004) Flower visitors and pollinatio in the Oriental (Indomalayan) Region. *Biologica Reviews*, 73: 413–448.

Corner (1978) *The freshwater swamp forest of Sout Johore and Singapore.*

Corner, E.J.H. (1940) *Wayside Trees of Malaya.*

x, J.H., Frazier, R.S. and Maturbongs, R.A. (1993) Freshwater crocodiles of Kalimantan. *Copeia*, 2.

ranbrook, Earl of (2008) Alfred Wallace, Field Collector, in Smith, C.H. and Beccaloni, G. (eds) *Natural Selection and Beyond: the intellectual legacy of Alfred Russel Wallace*. OUP.

ranbrook, Lord. (1988) *The contribution of archaeology to the Zoogeography of Borneo*.

rane, E. (1999) *The World History of Beekeeping and Honey Hunting*. Duckworth.

ronin, E.W. and Sherman, P.W. (1977) A resource-based mating system: the Orange-rumped Honeyguide in Nepal. *Living Bird*, 15.

roxall, J.P. (1976) The composition and behaviour of some mixed species bird flocks in Sarawak. *Ibis*.

avison, G.W.H. (revised) (1999) *Smythies: the Birds of Borneo* (4th edn). Natural History Publications.

avison, G.W.H. and Chew Yen Fook (1996) *Photographic Guide to the Birds of Borneo*.

avison, G.W.H. and Gale, J. (1992) *Birds of Mount Kinabalu, Borneo*. Natural History Publications.

avison, G.W.H. and Yeap Chin Aik (2010) *A Naturalists Guide to the Birds of Malaysia and Singapore*.

e Korte, J. (1984) Status and conservation of seabird colonies in Indonesia, in *Status and Conservation of the World's Seabirds*, ICBP Technical Publication No. 2. Cambridge, pp. 527–545.

el Hoyo, J., Elliott, A. and Sargatal, J. (eds) *Handbook to the Birds of the World*, vols 1–13.

ecandido, R., Kasorndorkbua, C., Nualsri, C., Chinuparawat, C. and Allen, D. (2008) Raptor migration in Thailand. *Birding Asia*, 10.

elacour, J. (1951) *The Pheasants of the World*, 2nd edn. Spur Publications.

ickinson, E.C. (ed.) (2003) *The Howard and Moore Complete Checklist of Birds of the World*, 3rd edn. Helm.

uckworth, J.W. and Kelsh R. (1988) A bird inventory of Similajau NP. *Study Report*, 31. ICBP.

utson, G. (1990) Birds of Barito Ulu in Borneo. *OBC*.

utson, G., Wilkinson, R.J. and Sheldon B.C. (1991) Hook-billed Bulbul and Grey-breasted Babbler at Barito Ulu, Kalimantan. *Forktail*, 6.

ymond, N. (1999) Two records of Black-headed Bunting in Sabah. *Forktail*, 15.

dwards, D.P., (2009) The value of rehabilitating logged rainforest for birds. *Conserv. Biol.* 23.

dwards, D.P., et al (2010) *Degraded lands worth protecting: the biological importance of SE Asia's repeatedly logged forests*. Royal Society Proceedings.

lkin, J.A. (1993) Japanese Night-Heron, a species new to Borneo. *Forktail*, 8.

Ellis, D.H., Kepler, A.K. and Kepler, C.B. (1990) Evidence for a fall raptor migration pathway across the South China Sea. *Journal of Raptor Research*.

Emmons, L. (2000) *Tupai. A Field Study of Bornean Treeshrews*. University of California Press.

Erftemeijer, P.L.A. (1993) Seabird observations in the Spermonde Archipelago. *Kukila*, 6.

Erritzoe, J. and Erritzoe, H.B. (1998) *Pittas of the World*. Lutterworth Press, Cambridge.

Erritzoe, J., Mann, C., et al (2012) *Cuckoos of the World*.

F

Feare, C. and Craig, A. (1998) *Starlings and Mynas*. Helm.

Ferguson-Lees, J. and Christie, D. (2005) *Raptors of the World*. Helm.

Fogden, M.P.L. (1972) The seasonality and population dynamics of equatorial forest birds in Sarawak. *Ibis*, 114.

Fiala, B. and Maschwitz, U. (2008) *Food bodies and their significance for obligate ant-association in the tree genus Macaranga*. Botanical Journal of the Linnean Society.

Fogden, M.P.L. (1976) A census of a bird community in tropical rain forest in Sarawak. *Sarawak Museum Journal*, 24: 251–257.

Ford, H.A. (2000) Why does the distribution of the Honeyeaters (*Meliphagidae*) conform so well to Wallace's Line in Fauna and Floral Migrations and Evolution in SE Asia-Australia. Edited by Metcalf, Smith, Morwood and Davidson.

Francis, C.M. (1984) *A Checklist of the Birds of Sepilok*. Forest Dept., Sandakan, Sabah.

Francis, C.M. (1985) Recent immigration of the Striated Warbler *Megalurus palustris* to Borneo. *Bulletin British Ornithologists Club*, 105.

Francis, C.M. and Andau, P. (1997) White-vented Whistler of Sipadan Island. *Journal of Wildlife Management and Research, Sabah.*

Fredriksson, G.M. and Nijman, V. (2004) Habitat use and conservation status of two elusive ground birds (*Carpococcyx radiatus* and *Polyplectron schleiermacheri*) in the Sungai Wain Protection forest, East Kalimantan. *Oryx*, 38.

Fry, C.H., Fry, K. and Harris, A. (1992) *Kingfishers, Bee-eaters and Rollers*. Helm.

G

Galdikas, B. (1995) *Reflections of Eden. My Life with the Orangutans of Borneo*.

Galdikas, B., Shapiro, G. and Katz, F. (1985) Danau Burung, a bird lake in Kalimantan. *Ardea*, 73.

Galetti, M. and McConkey, K. (1998) *Black Hornbill following gibbons in Central Borneo*.

Gamauf, A. and Haring, E. (2004) Molecular phylogeny and biogeography of Honey-buzzards. *J. Zool. Syst. Evol. Res.*, 42: 145–153.

Gamauf, A., Gjershaug, J.-O., Rov, N., Kvaloy, K. and Haring, E. (2005) Species or subspecies? The dilemma of taxonomic ranking of some SE Asian hawk-eagles (genus Spizaetus). *Bird Conservation International*, 15: 99–117.

Galetti, M. and McConkey, K. (1998) Black Hornbill following Gibbons in C. Borneo. *Ibis*, 140.

Geering, A., Agnew, L. and Harding, S. (2007) *Shorebirds of Australia*. CSIRO.

Gibson-Hill, C.A. (1952) The apparent breeding seasons of land birds in North Borneo and Malaya. *Bulletin of the Raffles Museum of Singapore*, 24.

Glenister, A.G. (1951) *The Birds of the Malay Peninsula, Singapore and Penang*. OUP.

Goldenboth, F., Timotius, K.H., Milan, P.P. and Margraf, J. (2006) *Ecology of Insular SE Asia: the Indonesian Archipelago*. Elsevier.

Gönner, C. Birds of Lake Jempang and the Middle Mahakam area, East Kalimantan. *Kukila*, 11: 13–36.

Gooddie, C. (2010) *The Jewel Hunter*.

Goodwin, D. (1967) *Pigeons and Doves of the World*.

Gregory-Smith, R. (1998) Avian diversity of the Kelabit Highlands, in *A Scientific Journey Through Borneo: Bario: Kelabit Highlands*. Pelanduk Pubs.

H

Hall, R., and Holloway, (1998) J.D. Eds. *Biogeography and Geological Evolution of SE Asia*

Haile, N.S. (1964) Notes on birds on Spratly Island, Amboyna Bay and Swallow Reef, South China Sea. *Sabah Society Journal*, 2.

Haines, C.L. (2007) Comparative phylogeography of four montane bird species in Sabah, Malaysian Borneo. MSc thesis, Louisiana State University.

Hale, M. (1997) First record of Yellow-browed Warbler for Borneo. *Malayan Nature Journal*, 50.

Hanbury-Tenison, R. (1980) *Mulu The RainForest*.

Harrap, S. (1994) Little known oriental bird. Kinabalu Friendly Warbler. *Bulletin OBC 20*.

Harris, T. and Franklin, K. (2000) *Shrikes and Bush-Shrikes*. Helm, London.

Harrison, P. (1987) *Seabirds of the World: a photographic guide*. Helm, London.

Harrisson, T. (1952) Sea Birds of the Borneo coast and their scarcity. *Malayan Nature Journal*, 7.

Harrisson, T. (1959) *World Within: a Borneo story*.

Harrisson, T. (1960) Regularity of migrant dates in central Borneo. *Ibis*, 102.

Harrisson, T. (1963) Birds above the Borneo jungle canopy. *Ibis*, 105: 403–406.

Hazebroek, H.P. and Morshidi, A.K.b.A. (2000) *National Parks of Sarawak*. NHPB.

Hazebroek, H.P. and Morshidi, A.K.b.A. (2006) *A Guide to Bako National Park* NHPB.

Hessels, M. (2008) *Winging the Bornean Skies*. NHPB.

Higuchi, H., Shiui, H.-J., Nakamuta, H., Uematsu A., Kuno, K., Saeki, M., Hotta, M., Tokita, K.-J., Moriya, E. and Tamura, M. (2005) Migration Honey-buzzards *Pernis apivorous* based on satellite tracking. *Ornithological Science, Japan*.

Hoefferle, A. et al (2012) *Wintering Assemblage Arctic Warblers in the Philippines*.

Holmes, D. and Nash, S. (1990) *The Birds of Sumatra and Kalimantan*. OUP, Singapore.

Holmes, D.A. and Burton, K. (1987) Recent note on the avifauna of Kalimantan. *Kukila*, 3.

Holmes, D.A. and Phillipps, K. (1996) *The Birds of Sulawesi*. OUP, Singapore.

Hose, C. (1893) On the avifauna of Mt Dulit and the Baram District. *Ibis*, 5: 381–424.

Hose, C. (1929) *The Fieldbook of a Jungle-wallah Being a Description of Shore, River and Forest Life in Sarawak*

Holyoak, D.T. (1973) Significance of colour dimorphism in Polynesian populations of *Egretta sacra*. *Ibis*.

Holyoak, D.T. and Woodcock, M. (1973) *Nightjars and their Allies*. OUP, Oxford.

Hutton, W. (2008) *Tabin: Sabah's greatest wildlife sanctuary*. NHPB.

I

Iqbal, M. et al (2013) The occurrence of Common Myna and Javan Myna in Kalimantan, *Kukila*, 17.

Ismail, G. and Ali, L. (eds) (2001) *A scientific journey through Borneo, Crocker Range National Park*.

Itino, T., Kato, M. and Hotta, M. (1991) Pollination ecology of the two wild bananas, *Musa acuminata* subsp. *halabanensis* and *M. salaccensis*: chiropterophily and ornithophily. *Biotropica*, 23.

Itioka, T., Nomura, M.,Inui, Y., Itino, T., Inoue T. (2000) Difference in intensity of ant defence among three species of Macaranga myrmecophytes. Biotropica Vol.32.

J

James, D. (2004) Identification of Christmas Island Great and Lesser Frigatebirds. *BirdingAsia*, 1.

Jepson, P. (1997) *Birding Indonesia*. Periplus Editions

Jepson, P. (2008) Orange-headed Thrush *Zoothera citrina* and the avian X-factor. *Birding Asia*.

Jeyarajasingam, A. and Pearson, A. (1999) *A Field Guide to the Birds of West Malaysia and Singapore*

Johns, A.G. (1996) Bird population persistence in Sabahan Logging Concessions. *Biological Conservation 75*.

Johnsgard, P.A. (1997) *The Avian Brood Parasites*.

Johnsgard, P.A. (2000) *Trogons and Quetzals of the World*. Smithsonian Press.

Jones, D.N., Dekker, R.W. and Roselaar, C.S. (1995) *The Megapodes*. OUP, Oxford.

Juniper, T. and Parr, M. (1998) *A Guide to Parrots of the World*. Yale University Press.

anouchi, T., Abe, N. and Ueda, H. (1998) *Photographic Guide to Wild Birds of Japan.*

aplan, G. (2007) *Tawny Frogmouth.* CSIRO.

ato, M. (1996) Plant–pollinator interactions in the understorey of a lowland mixed dipterocarp forest in Sarawak. *American Journal of Botany.*

ato, M., Itino, T. and Nagamitsu, T. (1993) Melittophily and ornithophily of long tubed flowers in *Zingiberaceae* and *Gesneriaceae* in West Sumatra.

ear, J (ed.) (2005) *Ducks, Geese and Swans,* 2 vols.

ehoe, Chris (2007–2012) Naturetrek Tour Reports.

emp, A. and van Zyl, A. (1998) Co-operative breeding by Collared Falconets. *Forktail,* 13.

emp, A.C. (1995) *The Hornbills.* OUP, Oxford.

ennedy, R.S., Gonzales, P.C., Dickinson, E.C. Miranda, H.C. and Fisher, T.H. (2000) *A Guide to the Birds of the Philippines.* OUP, Oxford.

ennerley, P. R. Bakewell, D. N., Round, P. D. (2008) *Rediscovery of a long-lost Charadrius plover from South-East Asia.* Forktail 24: 63–79.

essler, P.J.A Ed. (2000) *Secondary forest trees of Kalimantan. A manual to 300 selected species* Tropenbos.

imura, K., Yumoto, T. and Kikuzawa, K. (2001) Fruiting phenology of fleshy-fruited plants and seasonal dynamics of frugivorous birds in four vegetation zones on Mt Kinabalu, Borneo. *Journal of Tropical Ecology,* 17: 833–858.

ing, B. (2002) Species limits in the Brown Boobook Owl *Ninox scutulata* complex. *Bulletin of the British Ornithologists Club,* 122.

ing, B., Woodcock, M. and Dickinson, E.C. (1975) *A Field Guide to the Birds of South-East Asia.* Collins.

innaird, M.F. and O'Brien, T.G. (2007) *The Ecology and Conservation of the Asian Hornbills: farmers of the forest.*

itayama, K. (1991) *Vegetation of Mount Kinabalu Park.* East-West Centre, Hawaii.

loss, C.B. (1930) The birds of Mangalum and Mantanani Islands, West coast of N Borneo. *Bulletin of the Raffles Museum, Singapore* 4.

oeniger, N. and Koeniger, G. (2009) *Honey Bees of Borneo.* NHPB.

onig, C., Weick, F. and Becking, J.H. (1999) *A Guide to the Owls of the World.*

ushlan, J.A. and Hancock J.A. (2005) *The Herons.*

aman, T.G. (1992) Comparison of mixed-species foraging flocks in a Bornean rain forest. *Malayan Nature Journal 46.*

aman, T.G. (1994) The ecology of strangler figs in the rainforest canopy of Borneo. PhD thesis.

Laman, T.G., Gaither, J.C. and Lukas, D.E. (1996) Rain forest bird diversity in Gunung Palung NP, West Kalimantan. *Tropical Biodiversity 3.*

Lambert, F.R. (1987) Fig eating and seed dispersal by birds in a Malaysian lowland rain forest. PhD thesis, University of Aberdeen.

Lambert, F.R. (1992) The consequences of selective logging for Bornean lowland forest birds. *Philosophical Transactions of the Royal Society London,* 335, 341–356.

Lambert F., and Collar, N. (2002) The future for Sundaic lowland forest birds: long-term effects of commercial logging and fragmentation. FORKTAIL 18.

Lambert, F.R. and Woodcock, M.W. (1996) *Pittas, Broadbills and Asities.*

Lammertink, M. (2004) A multiple site comparison of woodpecker communities in Bornean lowland and hill forests: effects of logging and conservation implications. *Conservation Biology,* 18: 746–757.

Lammertink, M. (2011) *Group roosting in the Grey-and-Buff Woodpecker involving large numbers of shallow cavities.*

Lee, M.T., Li, Y.D. and Pin, O.T. (2009) A photographic record of Silvery Pigeon. Bulletin BOC 129.

Lee, W.S., Koo, T.H. and Park, J.Y. (2000) *A Field Guide to the Birds of Korea.* LG Evergreen.

Lefranc, N. and Worfolk, T. (1997) *Shrikes. A Guide to the Shrikes of the World.*

Lei, C., Pang, Y.L. and Liu, N.F. (2004) Status of the Red-footed Booby on the Xisha Archipelago, South China Sea. *Waterbirds,* 28.

Leighton, M. (1982) Fruit resources and patterns of feeding spacing and grouping among sympatric Bornean Hornbills. Phd thesis.

Leighton, M. and Leighton, D. (1983) Vertebrate responses to fruiting seasonality within a Bornean rain forest, in *Tropical Rain Forest: ecology and management,* Blackwells, Oxford.

Lim, C.K. and Cranbrook, Earl of (2002) *Swiftlets of Borneo: builders of edible nests.* NHPB.

Lim, H.C., Sheldon, F.H., Moyle, R.G (2010). *Extensive color polymorphism in the southeast Asian Oriental Dwarf Kingfisher Ceyx erithaca.*

Lim, K.S. and Gardner, D. (1997) *Field Guide to the Birds of Singapore.* Sun Tree, Singapore.

Lumholz, C. (1921) *Through Central Borneo.*

M

Madge, S. and Burn, H. (1994) *Crows and Jays.* Helm.

Madge, S. and McGowan, P. (2002) *A Guide to the Pheasants, Partridges, Quails, Grouse, Buttonquails and Sandgrouse of the World.* Helm, London.

Madoc, G.C. (1947) *An Introduction to Malayan Birds.*

Mann, C.F. (1996) The avifauna of the Belalong forest, Brunei, Darussalam, in *Tropical Rainforest Research.*

Mann, C.F. (2008) *The Birds of Borneo*. BOU Checklist Series 23.

Marshall, J.T. (1978) *Systematics of Smaller Asian Night Birds Based on Voice*. Ornithological Monographs 25.

Mead, C. (2008) *The effects of logging on understorey birds in Borneo*, PhD thesis.

Mearns, B. and Mearns, R. (1998) *Biographies for Birdwatchers*. Academic Press, London.

McClure, H.E. (1967) The composition of mixed species flocks in lowland and submontane forests of Malaya. *Wilson Bulletin*, 79.

McClure, H.E. (1998) *Migration and Survival of the Birds of Asia*. White Lotus, Bangkok.

McKenzie, N.A. and Salter, R.E. (1986) Tern nesting and distribution along the coast of western Sarawak. *Malayan Nature Journal*, 39.

McKilligan, N. (2005) *Herons, Egrets and Bitterns: their biology and conservation in Australia*. CSIRO.

McKinnon, J. and Phillipps, K. (1993) *A Field Guide to the Birds of Borneo, Sumatra, Java and Bali*.

McKinnon, J. and Phillipps, K. (2000) *A Field Guide to the Birds of China*.

McKinnon, K., Hatta, G., Halim, H. and Mangalik, A. (1996) *The Ecology of Kalimantan*.

Medway, Lord and Wells, D.R. (1976) *The Birds of the Malay Peninsula*, vol. 5. *Conclusion and Survey of Every Species*.

Meijaard, E. (2006) *Life after Logging: reconciling wildlife conservation and production forestry in Indonesian Borneo.* (CIFOR).

Melville, D.S. (1997) Call of the Grey Imperial Pigeon. *Kukila*, 9.

Message, S. and Taylor, D. (2005) *Waders of Europe, Asia and North America*. Helm, London.

Mjoberg, E. (1930) *Forest Life and Adventures in the Malay Archipelago*.

Moore, J. (2009) Birdwatching and bird records in Brunei Aug.2005-Sept 2009. www.bsp.com.bn/Panaga Club/PNHS.

Morley, R.J. (2000) Origin and Evolution of Tropical Rain Forest.

Motley, J. and Dillwyn, L.L. (1855) *Contributions to the Natural History of Labuan and the Adjacent Coasts of Borneo*. London.

Motley, J. and Sclater, P.L. (1863) Observations on the birds of SE Borneo. *Proc. Zool. Soc. London*, 1863: 206–224.

Moulton, J.C. (1914) *Hand-list of the Birds of Borneo*.

Moyle, R.G., Hosner, P.A., Nais, J., Lakim, M. and Sheldon, F.H. (2008) Taxonomic status of the Kinabalu 'linchi' swiftlet. *Bulletin of the British Ornithologists' Club*, 128.

Moyle, R.G., Schilthuizen, M., Rahman, M.A. and Sheldon, F.H. (2005) Molecular phylogenetic analysis of the White-crowned Forktail in Borneo. *Journal of Avian Biology*, 36.

Moyle, R.G. and Sheldon, F.H. (2007) *List of bir recorded during the Grand Perfect Plantati trip* (Bintulu, Sarawak) January–February.

Moyle, R.G. and Wong, A. (2002) The low montane avifauna of Mt Trus Madi. *Raffles Bulle of Zoology*, 50.

Moyle, R.G. et al (2011) Diversification of Endemic Southeast Asian Genus: Phylogene Relationships of the Spiderhunters (*Nectariniid Arachnothera*). *The Auk*, **128** (4): 777–788.

Myers, S. (2009) *A Field Guide to the Birds of Borne*

N

Nakayasu, H., Asama, S. and Biun, A. (1996) *Photographic Guide to the Birds of Mt Kinaba Borneo*. Bun-ichi Sogoshuppan, Tokyo.

Nash, S.V. and Nash, A.D. (1988) An annotat checklist of the birds of Tanjong Puting Natio Park. *Kukila*, 3.

Nelson, B. (2005) *Pelicans, Cormorants and th Relatives*.

Newton, I. (2008) *The Migration Ecology of Birds*.

Nijman, V., Fredriksson, G., Usher, G.F.a Gonner, C. (2005) Little Black Shag in Ea Kalimantan. First confirmation of the presence Borneo in over 150 years. *Bioone Journals*.

Nijman, V., (2010) Variaiton in Great Argus pheasa densities. WPA Int. Newsletter.

Norman, M.N. (1964) Bird Notes from the Taw Area. *Sabah Society Journal II*.

Noske, R.A. (1991) Field Identification of the Grea Goldenback in Malaysia. *Forktail*, 6.

O

O'Brien, M., Crossley, R. and Karlson K. (20C *The Shorebird Guide*. Helm, London.

O'Brien, T.G., Winarni, N.L., Saanin, F. N Kinnaird, M.F. and Jepson, P. (1998) Distributi and conservation status of Bornean Peacoc Pheasant in Central Kalimantan. *Bird Conservati International*, 9.

Oberholser, H.C. (1932) *The Birds of the Natu Islands*. Smithsonian USNM Bulletin 159.

Olney, D. and Scofield, P. (2007) *Albatrosses, Petr and Shearwaters of the World*. OUP, Oxford.

Olsen, K.M. and Larsson, H. (1995) *Terns of Euro and North America*. Helm, London.

Olsen, K.M. and Larsson, H. (1997) *A Guide to t Skuas and Jaegers of the World*. Pica Press, Susse

Olsen, K.M. and Larsson, H. (2003) *Gulls of Euro Asia and North America*. Helm, London.

P

Parr, J.W.K., Benstead, P.J. and Tobias, J.A. (200 A first nest record for the Fruithunter. *OBC Forkta* 18.

Payne, R.B. and Klitz, K. (2005) *The Cuckoos*, OUF

etol, H., Petol, G. and Ong, R.C. (2013) *A photographic guide to the lowland birds of Sepilok.*

hillipps, Susan M. (1995) *Enchanted Gardens of Kinabalu: A Borneo Diary.*

ilcher, N., Oakley, S. and Ismail, G. (1999) *Layang Layang: a drop in the ocean.* NHPB.

izzey, G. and Knight, F. (2007) *The Field Guide to the Birds of Australia.* Harper Collins.

ponswad, Pilai.Ed. (1998) *The Asian Hornbills Ecology & Conservation.*

oulsen, A.D. (2006) *Etlingera of Borneo.* NHPB Kota Kinabalu.

rieme, A. and Heegard, M. (1988) A visit to Gunung Niut in West Kalimantan. *Kukila*, 3.

estall, R. (1996) Munias and Mannikins.

heindt, F. and Eaton, J. (2009). *Species limits in Pteruthius shrike babblers: a comparison between the Biological and Phylogenetic Species Concepts.* Zootaxa 2301.

heindt, F. and Eaton, J. (2010). *Biological species limits in the Banded Pitta Pitta guajana.* Forktail 26: 86–91.

iley, J.H. (1930) Birds from the small islands (Derawan Islands) off the NE coast of Dutch Borneo. *Proceedings of the United States National Museum*, 77.

obinson, H.C. and Chasen, F.N. (1926–36) *The Birds of the Malay Peninsula*, 4 vols. H.F. & G.

obson, C. (2000) *A Field Guide to the Birds of South-East Asia.* New Holland, London.

obson, C. (2002) *A Field Guide to the Birds of Thailand.* New Holland, London.

ohwer, S. (1990) Foraging differences between white and dark morphs of the Pacific Reef Heron. *Ibis*, 132.

angster, G (1998) *Purple Swamp-hen is a complex of species.* Dutch Birding 20: 13–22.

aitoh, T. et al (2010) Old divergences in an aboreal bird supports long-term survival through the ice ages.

akai, S. (2000) Reproductive phenology of gingers in a lowland mixed dipterocarp forest in Borneo. *Journal of Tropical Ecology*, 16.

akai, S., Kato, M. and Inoue, T. (1999) Three pollination guilds and variation in floral characteristics of Bornean gingers (*Zingiberaceae* and *Costaceae*). *American Journal of Botany*, 86.

hanahan, Mike and Compton, Stephen G. (2004) *Vertical stratification of figs and fig eaters in a Bornean lowland rainforest: how is the canopy different?* Plant Ecology on line.

harpe, R.B. and Whitehead, J. (1884) *Birds of Corsica, Birds of North Borneo.* Privately published.

heldon, F.H. (1983) The birds of the Mantanani Islands. *Sabah Society Journal*, 7: 165–174.

Sheldon, F.H. (1985) The taxonomy and biogeography of the Thick-billed Flowerpecker in Borneo. The Auk:102.

Sheldon, F.H. (2005) Report on a Survey and Collection of Birds Mt Trus Madi, Sabah.

Sheldon, F.H. and Brown, C.E. (2013) *Ornithology of the Kelabit Highlands of Sarawak.*

Sheldon, F.H. and Francis, C.M. (1985) The birds and mammals of Mount Trus Madi, Sabah. *Sabah Society Journal*, **8**: 77–88.

Sheldon, F.H., Moyle, R.G. (2009) Family Pityriaseidae (Bristlehead) in Handbook of the Birds of the World. Vol 14.

Sheldon, F.H., Moyle, R.G. and Kennard, J. (2001) *Ornithology of Sabah: history, gazeteer, annotated checklist and bibliography.* Ornithological Monographs No. 52. AOU, Washington.

Sheldon, F.H., Moyle, R.G. and Marks, B. (2004a) Report on a Survey and Collection of Birds Conducted at Klias Forest Reserve, Sabah.

Sheldon, F.H. Moyle, R.G. and Marks, B. (2004b) Report on a Survey and Collection of Birds Conducted at Serinsim, Kinabalu.

Sheldon, F.H. *et al.* (2009) *Observations on the Distribution, Ecology and Systematics of Forest Birds in Sabah, Malaysia.*

Sheldon F.H., Lohman, D.J., Lim, H.C., Zou, F. Goodman, S.M., Prawiradilaga, D.M., Winker, K., Braile, T.M. and Moyle, R.G. (2009) Phylogeography of the magpie-robin species complex. *Journal of Biogeography.*

Short, L. and Horne, J. (2001) *Toucans, Barbets and Honeyguides.* OUP, Oxford.

Sim, L.K. and Mizutani, A. (2005) First record of Aleutian Tern for Borneo. *BirdingAsia*, 4.

Simpson, D. (1982) Autumn migration of landbirds off N Borneo in 1981. *Sea Swallow*, 32.

Simpson, K. and Day, N. (1989) *Birds of Australia.* Helm.

Skertchly, S.B.J. (1891) On some Borneo traps. *Journal of the Royal Anthropological Institute.*

Slater, P., Slater, P. and Slater, R. (2003) *The Slater Field Guide to Australian Birds.* New Holland.

Smythies, B.E. (1960) *The Birds of Borneo* (1st edn).

Sodhi, N.S., Wilcove, D.S., Lee, T.M., Serercioglu, C.H., Subraj, R.,Bernard, H., Yong,D.L.,Lim, S.L.H., Styring, A.R. and bin Hussin, M.Z. (2004) *Foraging ecology of woodpeckers in lowland Malaysian rain forest.* Journal of Tropical Ecology.

Sozer, R. and van der Heijden, A.J.W.J. (1997) An overview of the distribution, status and behavioural ecology of the White-shouldered Ibis. *Kukila*, 9.

Stuebing, R. and Zazuli, J. (1986) The megapodes of Pulau Tiga. *Sabah Museum Journal*, 1: 16–49.

Styring, A.R. and bin Hussin, M.Z. (2003) *Effects of logging on woodpeckers in a Malaysian rain forest.*

Styring, A., Sheldon, F.H., Ragai, R. and Unggang, J. (2009) Determining the diversity of birds in Bornean tree plantations.

T

Taylor, B. and van Perlo, B. (1998) *A Guide to the Rails, Crakes, Gallinules and Coots of the World.*

Thiollay, J.M. (1989) Area Requirements for the Conservation of Rain Forest Raptors. Conservation Biology 3.

Thompson, M.C. (1966) *Birds from North Borneo*, vol. 17, No. 8. University of Kansas.

Tobias, J. et al (2010) *Quantitative criteria for species delimitation.*

Turner, A. and Rose, C. (1989) *Swallows and Martins of the World.* Helm, London.

U

Udin, J. and Al Qadri, A. (2012) First breeding record of Buff-banded Rail for Borneo. *Kukila* 16.

V

van Balen, S. (1998) A hybrid Munia. Bull. BOC 118.

van Balen, S. (1999) *Birds on Fragmented Islands. Persistence in the forests of Java and Bali.*

van Balen, S. (1999) Note on the distribution of the Kinabalu Serpent-Eagle with a first record for Kalimantan. *Kukila*, 10.

van Balen, S., Eaton, J. A. and Rheindt, F. E. (2011) Biology, taxonomy and conservation status of the Short-tailed Green Magpie *Cissa thalassina* from Java. Bird Conserv. Int.

van Balen, S. and Prentice, C. (1997) Birds of the Negara river basin, South Kalimantan. *Kukila*, 9.

van Balen, S., Sozer, R., Nijman, V., Meijaard, E., Dennis, R. and Jepson, P. (1999) Juvenile plumage of Javan crested honey buzzard with comments on mimicry in SE Asian *Pernis* and *Spizaetus*. *Dutch Birding*, 21.

Viney, C., Phillipps, K. and Lam, C.Y. (2005) *The Birds of Hong Kong and South China.*

Vowles, G.A. and Vowles, R.S. (1997) *An Annotated Checklist of the Birds of Brunei.*

W

Wallace, A.R. (1870) *The Malay Archipelago.*

Ward, P. (1969) The annual cycle of the Yellow-vented Bulbul in Singapore. *Journal of Zoology.*

Wells, D.R. (2007) *The Birds of the Thai-Malay Peninsula.* vols 1 and 2. Academic Press, London.

Wells, D.R., Hails, C.J. and Hails, A.J. (1979) A study of the birds of the Gunung Mulu National Park, Sarawak, with special emphasis on those of lowland forest. Report to the Royal Geographical Society, London.

Wheatley, N. (1996) *Where to Watch Birds in Asia.*

Whitehead, J. (1893) *Exploration of Mount Kina Balu, North Borneo.* Gurney and Jackson, London.

Whitmore, T.C. (1990) *An Introduction to Tropical Rainforests.* Clarendon Press, Oxford.

Whitten, T. *et al.* (1996) *The Ecology of Java and Bali.*

Wielstra, B., Boorsma, T. and Pieterse, S.N. (2012) An update on the avifauna of Gng Lumut Protection Forest. *Kukila* 16.

Wielstra, B. and Pieterse, S. (2009) *A Bird Survey of Gunung Lumut Protection Forest, E.Kalimantan and a Recommendation for its Designation as a IBA.* Kukila 14.

Wild Bird Society of Japan (1982) *A Field Guide to the Birds of Japan.* Wild Bird Society of Japan.

Wilkinson, R., Dutson, G., Sheldon, B., Darjono and Yus Rusila Noor (1990) The avifauna of Barito Ulu, Central Kalimantan. *Kukila*, 5: 99–116

Williams, R.S.R. (2002) The rediscovery and doubtful validity of the Blue-wattled Bulbul *Pycnonotus nieuwenhuisii.* Forktail, 18.

Wong, K.M. and Phillipps, A. (eds) (1995) *Kinabalu Summit of Borneo.* Sabah Society, Kota Kinabalu.

Wong, M. and Hj. Mohamed bin Hj Ibrahim (1966) *Birds of the Pelong Rocks.* Brunei Museum.

Wong, Tsu Shi (2012) *A Naturalists Guide to the Birds of Borneo.*

Worcester, D.C. (1911) Newly discovered breeding places of Philippine sea birds. *Philippine Journal of Science*, 6: 167–177.

Wycherley, P.R. (1990) A statistical analysis of the nesting seasons of birds in Western Malesia. *Sarawak Museum Journal*, Xli.

Y

Yahya, H.S.A. (2001) *Biology of Indian Barbets.*

Yamashina, Y. (1961) *A Field Guide. Birds in Japan.*

Yong, D., King, B. (2010) The song of the Dulit Frogmouth, *Batrachostomus harterti.* FORKTAIL 26.

Yong, Ding Li. (2009) Notes on the status and identification of the Silvery Pigeon. BirdingASIA 11

Yong, D.L. et al (2013) *A Naturalists guide to the Birds of Singapore.*

Yumoto, T. (2000) Bird-pollination of three Durio species (Bombacaceae) in a tropical rainforest in Sarawak, Malaysia. *American Journal of Botany.*

Yumoto, T., Itino, T. and Nagamasu, H. (1997) Pollination of hemiparasites (Loranthaceae) by spiderhunters in the canopy of a Bornean rainforest. *Selbyana*, 18: 51–60.

Z

Zalles, J.I. and Bildstein, K.L. (2000) *Raptor Watch: a global directory of raptor migration sites.* BLI.

USEFUL WEBSITES AND CONTACTS FOR BIRDING BORNEO

BORNEO
BORNEO PHOTOS AND BIRD CALLS:
www.borneobirdimages.com

REGIONAL BIRD PHOTOS AND ECOLOGY
www.orientalbirdimages.org
www.wildasia.org
www.nss.sg/
www.wwf.org.my
www.mns.my

SABAH
http://borneobirdclub.blogspot.com/
INS Sabah: Email:anna888@ums.edu.my.
www.sabahparks.org.my
www.sabahtourism.com
abah Society: Email: sabsoc@po.jaring.my
www.suterasanctuarylodges.com
www.pulau-tiga.com
www.borneosurvivor.co.my
www.brl.com.my
www.tabinwildlife.com.my
www.pompomisland.com
www.borneoecotourism.com
www.borneonaturetours.com
www.cedeprudente.com
www.wildlife-expeditions.com

SARAWAK
http://mnskuching.blogspot.com
http://mnsmiri.blogspot.com
www.sarawaktourism.com
www.kuching.net.my
www.sarawakforestry.com
www.arbec.com.my
www.ebario.com
www.orangutanproject.com
www.borneoadventure.com
www.catcityholidays.com
www.permairainforest.com

BRUNEI
www.bsp.com.bn/PanagaClub/pnhs
www.bruneinaturesociety.org
www.uluuluresort.com Temburong

DOWNLOAD BORNEO BIRD CALLS from
www.borneobirdimages.com
www.xeno-canto.org

REPORTING YOUR SIGHTINGS
. All rare birds in Borneo:
Email:Info@borneobirdimages.com

2. **Sabah and Sarawak** The Malaysian Nature Society-Bird Conservation Council Records Committee seeks to provide uniform standards of assessment for all claims of rare or previously unrecorded species in Malaysia, and to make up-to-date information available. Birders are requested to submit reports of rare or potentially new species for Malaysia to Email mnsrc.rc@gmail.com

3. **Bird watching records Sabah and Sarawak** Please submit to the Bird I Witness Malaysia database: http://www.worldbirds.org/malaysia

SOME BORNEO BIRDING BLOGS

Wong Tsu Shi: http://borneobirds.blogspot.com
Zaiton Yunus: mrsjordans.blogspot.com
Jordan Sitorus: http://amazingborneo.blogspot.com/
Susan Myers: http//birdtourleader.blogspot.com
Yeo Siew Teck: www.birderinborneo.blogspot.com
Cede Prudente: http://cedeprudente.blogspot.com
Ch'ien C Lee: www.wildborneo.com.my
David Bakewell: http://digdeep1962.blogspot.com
Denis Degullacion: www.degullacion.blogspot.com
Azahari Reyes@Jason: horukuru.blogspot.com
CK Leong: http://borneobirds.com
Andrew Siani:http://borneoavifauna.blogspot.com
Nazeri Abghani: http://miribirding.blogspot.com

TRIP REPORTS

www.birdtourasia.com
www.kingbirdtours.com
www.rockjumper.co.za
www.surfbirds.com
www.tropicalbirding.com
www.ventbird.com
www.birdtours.co.uk
www.birdquest.co.uk

Great care has been taken to maintain the accuracy of the information contained in this work. However, neither the publisher, the editors nor the authors can be held responsible for any consequences arising from the use of the information contained herein.

REPORTING UPDATES AND ERRORS

relating to the information contained in this Field Guide quentinphillipps@googlemail.com

Jika Anda ingin menulis dalam bahasa Indonesia yang akan menyambut

LIST OF ECOLOGICAL AND TEXT NOTES

© Karen Phillipps

Brown Wood Owl
Strix leptogrammica

Brown Wood Owl, *Strix leptogrammica*

INDEX OF COMMON NAMES

BUFF-RUMPED WOODPECKER *Meiglyptes tristis* feeding on an ant colony hosted by *Macaranga winklerii*. Macarangas are small (to 10 m), large-leaved, fast growing 'pioneer' trees of secondary forest abundant along roadsides. When ripe, the small yellow-green fruits attract hordes of bulbuls, leafbirds, Purple-naped Sunbirds and Yellow-eared Spiderhunters. Most macarangas have glands which produce either nectar or small 'food bodies' to attract ants. *M.winklerii* is one of a few which also have hollow stems designed to house ant colonies. The ants attack caterpillars which feed on the leaves (Fiala 2008). At Lambir Hills, Sarawak (Itioka 2000) found that *c.* 20% of *M. winklerii* plants were attacked by woodpeckers in search of ant colonies. Different macaranga species compete to occupy newly vacant land. *M.winkleri* grows fastest but has softer stems which are preferentially attacked by woodpeckers in search of ants. See page 371.

INDEX OF SCIENTIFIC NAMES

THE AUTHORS

Quentin Phillipps has been interested in the wildlife and natural history of Borneo all his life. Quentin was born in Sandakan Sabah in 1951 and grew up on Tuaran Rubber Estate. He was educated at Sabah College Kota Kinabalu; Bedales School, Hampshire, UK; and King's College Cambridge, where he studied Japanese and Economics. At age 17 he won the Wildlife Photographer of the Year competition (junior section) with the first ever photograph of a nesting Chestnut-capped Thrush taken at Poring. Currently he divides his time between London, where he owns a property business, and Tg Aru, Kota Kinabalu.

Karen Phillipps was also born in Sandakan and educated at Bedales School, Hampshire, UK and Camberwell College of Arts and Technology, London, UK, where she studied graphic design. Karen has illustrated numerous books on Asian wildlife including *A Field Guide to the Birds of Borneo, Sumatra, Java and Bali*; *Mammals of Borneo*; *A Colour Guide to Hong Kong Animals*; *Chim Vietnam*; *A Field Guide to the Birds of China*; *The Birds of Hong Kong and South China*; and the *Birds of Sulawesi*. Karen spent many years living in Hong Kong and travelling in Borneo and the Far East, and is currently resident in the Algarve, Portugal.

BLACKEYE *Chlorocharis emiliae* on **LOW'S PITCHER PLANT** *Nepenthes lowii*
Low's Pitcher Plant is a common Bornean endemic growing above 3,000 m on Borneo's highest mountains. The majority of pitcher plants live in areas of poor soils, and trap insects which drown in the pitcher fluid and are then digested to provide extra nutrients for the plant. Unusually, Low's Pitcher plant also produces round waxy pellets or 'Beccarian food bodies' on the underneath of the pitcher lid. Both the Blackeye and Mountain Treeshrews feed on these food bodies. The pitcher itself is shaped like a toilet bowl and birds and mammals have to sit on the rim of this bowl to access the food bodies. It is believed that the plant benefits from the faeces deposited into the pitcher by their visitors.

A large number of Bornean plants produce either nectar or food bodies from glands on the leaves and stalks. The primary purpose is to attract ants which then defend the plant by overpowering and eating leaf eating insects. Birds benefit because unlike fruit and flowers which arrive in short bursts, food bodies are produced steadily year round. The small, rare, endemic Red-bellied Sculptor Squirrel (see opposite) is also believed to be a specialist feeder on the food bodies produced by a species of strangling fig on the underside of its leaves. See page 365 and Payne 2010.

ORANGUTAN WATCHING SITES IN BORNEO

(MAP OPPOSITE)

1. **SEPILOK** Rehabilitation centre. Tourist site. *www.orangutan-appeal.org.uk*
2. **KINBATANGAN RIVER** Wild population. *www.redapeencounters.com*
3. **DANUM VALLEY** Wild population. *www.borneonaturetours.com* and *www.searrp.org*
4. **TABIN** Wild population. *www.tabinwildlife.com*
5. **KUTAI** Wild population. *www.borneotourgigant.com*
6. **SUNGAI WAIN** Wild population. *www.borneotourgigant.com*
7. **SAMBOJA LESTARI** Rehabilitation centre. *www.sambojalodge.com*
8. **SABANGAU** Wild orangutan research. *www.orangutantrop.com*
9. **NYARU MENTENG** Rehabilitation centre. *www.savetheorangutan.co.uk*
10. **TG PUTING** Tourist site. Feeding wild orangutans. *www.orangutan.org.uk*
11. **LAMANDAU** Rehabilitation and release site. *www.orangutan.org.uk*
12. **GUNUNG PALUNG** Wild orangutan research. *http://people.bu.edu/orang/*
13. **SINTANG** Rehabilitation centre. *www.orangutanprotection.com*
14. **SEMENGOH** Rehabilitation and release. *www.forestry.sarawak.gov.my*
15. **MATANG** Rehabilitation and release. *www.orangutanproject.com*
16. **RASA RIA RESORT** Tame orangutans wander grounds.

REGIONAL MAP SHOWING THE LOCATION OF BORNEO

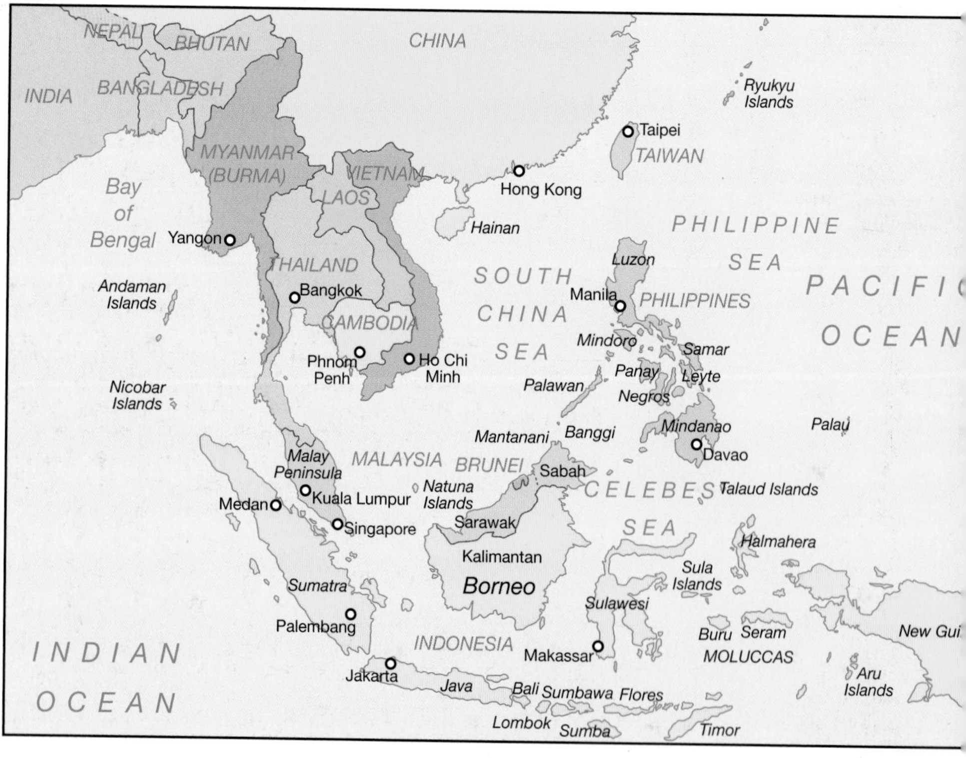

NEPAL BHUTAN CHINA

INDIA BANGLADESH

Ryukyu Islands

MYANMAR (BURMA)

Bay of Bengal Yangon

VIETNAM LAOS

Taipei
TAIWAN

Hong Kong

Hainan

PHILIPPINE SEA

Andaman Islands

THAILAND Bangkok

CAMBODIA

SOUTH CHINA SEA

Luzon

Manila PHILIPPINES

PACIFIC OCEAN

Nicobar Islands

Phnom Penh Ho Chi Minh

Mindoro

Palawan

Samar
Panay Leyte
Negros

Malay Peninsula Medan Kuala Lumpur

MALAYSIA BRUNEI Sabah
Natuna Islands
Sarawak

Mantanani Banggi

Mindanao Davao

Palau

CELEBES SEA

Talaud Islands

Singapore

Kalimantan

Halmahera

Sumatra Borneo

Sula Islands

Palembang

INDONESIA Makassar

Sulawesi

Buru Seram
MOLUCCAS

New Gui

Jakarta Java Bali Sumbawa Flores

Aru Islands

INDIAN OCEAN

Lombok Sumba Timor